MATTHEW SARDON

Theosis

Becoming What You Were Made For

Copyright © 2025 by Matthew Sardon

All rights reserved. No part of this publication may be reproduced, stored or transmitted in any form or by any means, electronic, mechanical, photocopying, recording, scanning, or otherwise without written permission from the publisher. It is illegal to copy this book, post it to a website, or distribute it by any other means without permission.

Matthew Sardon asserts the moral right to be identified as the author of this work.

First edition

This book was professionally typeset on Reedsy.
Find out more at reedsy.com

To my children,
Valentino and Rafael,
who remind me daily that the call to glory begins in the smallest acts of love.
And to the Church — East and West —
that keeps alive the fire of deification,
so that every soul may remember it was made for God.

"God became man so that man might become god."
— St. Athanasius, On the Incarnation

"He has granted to us His precious and very great promises, that through them you may become partakers of the divine nature."
— 2 Peter 1:4 (RSV-CE)

"The Son of God became man so that we might become God."
— Catechism of the Catholic Church, §460

Contents

Preface   iii
Introduction   1

I   The Call to Glory: Recovering the Purpose of Human Nature

1   Why You Exist: The Divine Image and Likeness   7
2   More Than Forgiven: Deification as the True Goal of...   42
3   What Is Theosis? A Historical and Dogmatic Overview   98

II   The Way of Ascent: Means of Divinization in Christ

4   The Incarnation: The Descent That Raises Humanity   165
5   The Sacraments: The Mysteries of Participation   187
6   The Interior Life: Prayer, Stillness, and the Illumined...   219
7   The Divine Liturgy as Mystical Theophany   256
8   The Liturgy: Participation in the Heavenly Worship   287

III   Becoming Flame: The Lived Experience of Deification

9   The Saints: Testimonies of Transfigured Humanity   333
10   The Cross and Resurrection in the Life of the Believer   359
11   Union without Absorption: Theological Boundaries of...   395

12 You Shall Be All Fire: Living the Theotic Life in the World   442

APPENDIX A - Key Catechism Passages on Participation in the...   480
APPENDIX B - Select Patristic Texts on Theosis (Greek and...   483
APPENDIX C — Magisterial & Conciliar Witness   489
APPENDIX D - Glossary   493
APPENDIX E - Sources and References by Chapter   506
About the Author   520

Preface

This book was born out of a tension I have lived with for years.

On one hand, I grew up with a faith that was rich, sacramental, and demanding — a faith that asked me to pray, confess, receive, and obey. I knew about sin and forgiveness, grace and salvation. And yet, for all its depth, something in that vision felt incomplete. It explained the "what" of Christianity, but not the "why."

On the other hand, as I encountered the Fathers of the Church, the mystics, the saints, and even the official Catechism itself, I kept running into a startling claim: that the whole purpose of the Christian life is not merely to be forgiven, but to be *divinized*. That God became man not simply to pardon us, but to raise us into His own life.

This claim — called *theosis* in the East, or deification — was everywhere in the tradition, and yet almost nowhere in modern catechesis. It was bold, dazzling, and at first unsettling. But it made sense of everything else: the sacraments, prayer, suffering, holiness, mission. Without it, the pieces of the Christian life sat disconnected. With it, they suddenly formed a radiant whole.

That discovery became a kind of conversion within my conversion.

Theosis reshaped the way I read Scripture, the way I approached liturgy, the way I understood grace. It turned the saints from distant moral heroes into living icons of what I too was called to become. It gave meaning to suffering and hope to struggle. And it opened my eyes to the deep unity of East and West, whose different vocabularies and emphases converge on the same astonishing mystery: that man was created for communion with God.

This book is my attempt to share that vision. It is not an academic monograph, though it draws on history, theology, and magisterial texts. It is not a devotional manual, though I hope it will inflame devotion. It is, rather, a work of retrieval: a re-presentation of what the Church has always taught, but what many of us have forgotten.

The chapters that follow move in three movements:

- **Part I** lays the theological foundations, showing how theosis emerges from Scripture, the Fathers, the scholastics, and the Magisterium.
- **Part II** turns to the concrete means: the sacraments, prayer, fasting, asceticism, and liturgy — the practices through which divine life is communicated to us.
- **Part III** explores the fulfillment: the saints as witnesses, the Cross and Resurrection as our pattern, the boundaries that safeguard true participation, and the mission of living theosis in the world.

My hope is that this book will awaken both memory and desire: memory of a truth too long obscured, and desire for the glory it promises. Theosis is not for the few. It is the normal Christian life. It is not a metaphor. It is our destiny.

If anything in these pages strikes you as strange, excessive, or even frightening, I invite you to linger with it rather than dismiss it. For the language of fire and glory has always been the language of the Church at her boldest and truest.

I offer this work with gratitude to the teachers, pastors, and traditions that have preserved this vision across centuries, and with hope that it may play a small part in helping us recover the truth that changes everything: that God became man so that man might become God.

Introduction

For many people today, Christianity has been reduced to a moral code. Go to Mass when you can. Be kind to others. Try to avoid serious sin. Say a few prayers. If you succeed often enough, perhaps God will weigh the scales in your favor at the end.

This "gospel of moralism" is well-intentioned, and not entirely false. Goodness does matter. Sin is real. Grace is necessary. But this thin version of Christianity misses the heart of the faith. It shrinks the Gospel down to sin management, to religious duty, to moral self-improvement. And when that happens, Christianity becomes boring, burdensome, and lifeless. It leaves many restless — sensing that they were made for something more, but unable to name what it is.

That restlessness is not a mistake. It is a clue. It is the human heart's protest against a truncated gospel.

Because the true Gospel is not primarily about avoiding hell or securing pardon. It is about transformation. It is about communion. It is about glory.

The Fathers of the Church never hesitated to say this with stunning boldness. St. Athanasius declared: *"God became man so that man might become god."* St. Irenaeus proclaimed: *"The glory of God is man fully alive."* St. Augustine dared to say: *"If we have been made sons of God, we have also been made gods."* To modern ears, these words can sound shocking, even heretical. But for the early Church they were the very proclamation of salvation: the Son of God took on our humanity so that humanity could be lifted into His divinity.

This mystery is called *theosis*, or deification. It is not metaphor. It is not poetic exaggeration. It is the bold, ancient teaching that the Christian life is nothing less than participation in the very life of God.

The Catechism of the Catholic Church does not hide this truth. In paragraph 460, it cites 2 Peter 1:4 directly: *"The Word became flesh to make us 'partakers of the divine nature.'"* It then repeats the chorus of the Fathers: *"The Son of God became man so that we might become God."* Yet, despite being enshrined in magisterial teaching, this vision has all but disappeared from the imagination of many Catholics. It is buried under moralism, obscured by centuries of polemic, and eclipsed in a culture that prizes comfort over glory.

And yet, this vision is the reason you exist. You were not created merely to survive, or to obey, or to pass divine judgment unscathed. You were created to become radiant. You were made to burn with the light of the Trinity.

Theosis is not an exotic Eastern specialty. It is not reserved for monks or mystics. It is not postponed until heaven. It is the universal vocation of every baptized person. Every sacrament, every prayer, every act of love is ordered toward this single destiny: that Christ may live in you, that His Spirit may dwell in you, that you may become "all flame," as the desert Fathers described the saints.

This book is about recovering that forgotten destiny.

We will begin by looking backward. **Part I** explores the deep foundations of theosis. We will turn to Scripture, where Genesis names man as the image and likeness of God and where Peter speaks of participation in the divine nature. We will hear the voices of the Fathers — Irenaeus, Athanasius, Augustine, Gregory — who thundered that salvation is nothing less than divinization. We will examine the scholastic framework of Thomas Aquinas, who articulated grace as a *created participation* in God's life. And we will hear the Magisterium itself, which, from the Councils to Vatican II to the Catechism, safeguards this vision as Catholic doctrine. Part I is the theological map: it shows that deification is not an optional spirituality, but the golden thread woven through the whole of tradition.

Then we will turn from vision to practice. **Part II** unfolds the concrete means by which deification takes place. We will descend into the mystery of the Incarnation, where Christ's assumption of human nature becomes the bridge of our ascent. We will walk through the sacraments, not as rituals of maintenance but as the very Mysteries by which the divine life enters us: Baptism as ontological rebirth, Chrismation as Pentecost sealed, the Eucharist as the flesh of God given for our transformation. We will step into the interior life — prayer, stillness, silence — and discover how the heart itself is transfigured. We will recover the discipline of fasting and asceticism as training in love, not punishment. And we will ascend into the liturgy, where heaven breaks into earth and the faithful join the angels in worship before the throne. Part II is the path: the sacramental, ascetical, and mystical means by which theosis becomes a lived reality.

Finally, we will look at fulfillment. **Part III** considers what it means to become flame. Here we will study the saints, whose lives are luminous testimonies of transfiguration. We will explore how the Cross and Resurrection shape the daily pattern of the Christian life, teaching us that glory is found through death and rising. We will guard the boundaries of true theosis, clarifying how union with God differs from pantheism, absorption, or New Age illusions. And we will end with the call to live deification in the world: in prayer and mission, in witness and love, in the restoration of all creation through Christ. Part III is the horizon: the vision of theosis lived out in history and consummated in glory.

Theosis is not a theory. It is not a metaphor. It is the axis of Christian existence. Without it, the Gospel shrinks into a moral system. With it, the Gospel becomes fire — fire that purifies, illumines, and glorifies.

This path will not be easy. It will cost you your ego, your comfort, your false self. It will burn away what is not love. But it will give you everything. For in dying to self, you will be raised to share in the life of the Triune God.

You were made for this. You were made not simply to be forgiven, but to be glorified. Not simply to serve, but to shine. Not simply to pray, but to burn.

This is not metaphor. This is your future.

Let us begin.

I

The Call to Glory: Recovering the Purpose of Human Nature

PART I

Why You Exist: The Divine Image and Likeness
More Than Forgiven: Deification as the True Goal of Redemption
What Is Theosis? A Historical and Dogmatic Overview

1

Why You Exist: The Divine Image and Likeness

"Let us make man in our image, after our likeness..."
— Genesis 1:26

The Imago Dei in Scripture and Tradition

The doctrine of the *imago Dei* does not arise from speculative philosophy but from the inspired utterance of Genesis 1:26-27. The creation of man is marked by a solemn intimacy: unlike the impersonal commands that precede it—"Let there be light," "Let the waters bring forth..."—this act begins with divine deliberation: "Let us make man in our image, after our likeness." The plural form has stirred centuries of theological reflection. While some have interpreted it as a royal or angelic plural, the Church has long understood it in a Christological and Trinitarian sense: the Father, speaking within the eternal communion of the Trinity, initiates the creation of a being capable of participating in that very communion.

The Hebrew terms *tselem* ("image") and *demuth* ("likeness") are paired intentionally, inviting not only poetic resonance but profound theological distinction. In the ancient Near Eastern world—particularly in Mesopotamian, Egyptian, and Ugaritic sources—*tselem* (or its cognates) referred to carved representations of deities or kings: statues installed in temples as visible extensions of divine authority. The pharaoh was hailed as "the image of Ra," the living mediator of divine rule. Kings were regarded as "sons" or "images" of the gods, bearing their dominion but not their nature.

Genesis radically subverts this cultural backdrop. It declares that every human being—not merely kings or elites—is made in the image of God. The dignity of divine representation is democratized. Man is not a mute idol in the cosmic temple, but a living icon: a creature in whom the invisible God is mysteriously made present within the visible order. The hierarchical pagan vision collapses; in its place stands a theology of universal vocation and ontological worth.

This revolutionary anthropology echoes throughout Jewish interpretive traditions. The *Targum Onkelos*, an early Aramaic paraphrase of the Torah, renders Genesis 1:26 to emphasize man's spiritual faculties over corporeal form. In Second Temple literature, the *imago Dei* was understood not merely as reason, but as priestly and royal commission: man was charged with representing God's dominion (cf. Wisdom 2:23; Sirach 17:3–4). This interpretation aligns seamlessly with Genesis 1:28, in which dominion over creation follows directly from man's image-bearing nature.

The *imago Dei*, then, is not a static resemblance but a dynamic vocation. Man is appointed to represent God, to mediate His presence, and to cultivate creation as a sacred offering. Formed from the dust (Gen 2:7), yet animated by divine breath, he is a being suspended between worlds—material and spiritual, temporal and eternal. In him, heaven and earth converge.

The second term, *demuth* ("likeness"), deepens the mystery. While *tselem* denotes man's ontological grounding in God, *demuth* points to his moral and spiritual trajectory. It speaks not only of what man is, but of what he is called to become: a growing resemblance, a dynamic participation in divine life.

Importantly, Genesis affirms that this image and likeness are bestowed equally upon male and female:

"So God created man in his own image, in the image of God he created him; male and female he created them." (Gen 1:27)

This verse resists all reductionist attempts to confine the divine image to traits of strength, rationality, or masculinity. The *imago Dei* transcends biological sex while finding expression within sexual differentiation. Male and female together reveal a relational icon of the divine.

This insight has profound implications for both anthropology and ecclesiology. Man and woman are not interchangeable, but complementary. Their union reflects something of the inner life of God Himself (cf. Eph 5:32; 1 Pet 3:7; CCC §252). As St. John Paul II expressed:

"Man becomes the image of God not so much in the moment of solitude as in the moment of communion."

(General Audience, November 14, 1979)

The *imago Dei* is thus most fully revealed not in isolated faculties like intellect or will, but in the capacity for communion. Just as God is a Trinity of Persons—Father, Son, and Spirit—so too is man created as a relational being: from another, for another, with another. This Trinitarian anthropology finds its most articulate expression in the writings of the Cappadocian Fathers.

St. Basil the Great and St. Gregory of Nazianzus taught that personhood itself is constituted by relation. Just as the Father is never without the Son and the Spirit, so too is human identity never complete in isolation. To be a person in the image of God is to be inherently open to the other. The self is not erased in this openness but fulfilled in love. This structure of being in-relation forms the foundation of charity, family, society, and the Church—not as human inventions, but as the flowering of our deepest nature.

This vision corrects the distortions introduced by later philosophical systems. The Enlightenment exalted autonomy and rational independence as the apex of human dignity. Scripture and tradition offer a radically different vision: the human person finds his true greatness not in self-sufficiency, but in vulnerability to love—in the capacity to give and receive communion. The *imago Dei* is filial. It is the mark of a creature called not merely to exist, but to be a child of God (cf. Rom 8:14–17).

The foundational declaration in Genesis 1:26–27 is not an isolated anthropological claim. It initiates a canonical trajectory, a theological thread woven throughout the Old and New Testaments, in which the reality of man as image is reiterated, expanded, and ultimately fulfilled in Christ. This is seen already in Genesis 5:1–3, where the language of image and likeness reappears in a genealogical context:

"When God created man, he made him in the likeness of God. Male and female he created them… When Adam had lived 130 years, he became the father of a son in his own likeness, after his image, and named him Seth."
(Gen 5:1–3, RSV-CE)

This passage is remarkable for its structure. It both reaffirms the divine image in humanity and mirrors it in the generative act of human fatherhood. Seth is described as being in the likeness and image of Adam, just as Adam was in the image and likeness of God. The implication is theological: to be made in God's image is to be made in sonship. Man is not merely a rational animal, but a child of the Creator, called into a relationship of filial dependence and growth.

This filial dimension is developed explicitly in Luke 3:38, where the genealogy of Jesus concludes with the phrase:

"…the son of Enos, the son of Seth, the son of Adam, the son of God."

Here, Scripture affirms what Genesis had already implied: Adam was not merely a creature, but a son. This designation becomes crucial for understanding the Christian vision of baptism and deification, as will be explored in later chapters. Even after the Fall, the image persists. In Genesis 9:6, God reaffirms this image in a postlapsarian, covenantal context:

"Whoever sheds the blood of man, by man shall his blood be shed, for God made man in his own image."

Despite a world now marked by violence and death, the divine image endures. Its persistence forms the basis for justice, the sanctity of life, and the inviolable dignity of the human person. As the Catechism of the Catholic Church teaches:

"Man is the only creature on earth that God has willed for its own sake, and he alone is called to share, by knowledge and love, in God's own life. It was for this end that he was created, and this is the fundamental reason for his dignity."

(CCC §356)

The sapiential texts of the Old Testament add further depth to the doctrine of the image. In Wisdom 2:23, we find this striking affirmation:

"God created man for incorruption, and made him in the image of his own eternity."

Here, the image is not static. It is associated with incorruption and eternal participation. The *telos* of the image is underscored: it is not merely a mark of origin but a pointer toward eschatological destiny.

Sirach 17:1–4 develops this further:

"The Lord created man out of earth, and turned him back to it again… He endowed them with strength like his own, and made them in his own image. He gave them few days, a limited time, but granted them authority over the things upon the earth."

In this vision, the divine image is connected not only to human dignity but also to human vocation. Man is entrusted with dominion, not as an autonomous sovereign, but as a steward who represents the divine. The phrase "strength like his own" subtly evokes the divine attributes: rationality, relationality, and moral authority, all embedded within the human constitution.

This rich Old Testament imagery prepares the way for its Christological fulfillment. The pattern is both typological and liturgical. The image given in creation, reaffirmed in covenant, and deepened through Israel's wisdom tradition reaches its culmination in Christ, in whom the image is made radiant and complete. The longing for incorruption, the vocation of divine likeness, and the priestly stewardship over creation all converge in the one who is Himself the perfect image of the invisible God.

St. Paul writes:

"He is the image of the invisible God, the firstborn of all creation."

(*Colossians 1:15*)

Christ is not merely made in the image of God. He is the image. He is the archetype after whom humanity was formed. The Logos, through whom all things were made (John 1:3), is the divine blueprint of man. In Christ, the image becomes radiance, and the archetype becomes fulfillment.

This insight is deepened in Romans 8:29:

"For those whom He foreknew He also predestined to be conformed to the image of His Son…"

Here, conformity to Christ is the goal of salvation. The *imago Dei* given in creation finds its perfection not in autonomous self-realization, but in union with the Son. The Greek phrase *symmorphous tēs eikonos* ("to be conformed to the image") implies a real transformation of being, not mere imitation. It is a participation in Christ's form, a reshaping of the soul in divine likeness.

St. Paul echoes this in 2 Corinthians 3:18:

"We all, with unveiled face, beholding the glory of the Lord, are being changed into His likeness from one degree of glory to another."

This is the logic of *theosis*. Grace does not simply repair what sin has broken. It elevates. It draws man into divine glory. The image is not a fixed attribute. It is an eschatological vocation. To be conformed to Christ is to be drawn into the Trinitarian life, to become by adoption what Christ is by nature.

This transformative participation finds its summit in 2 Peter 1:4, where believers are said to become "partakers of the divine nature" (*theias koinōnoi physeōs*). This phrase is extraordinary. It proclaims that, through the promises of Christ—particularly through the sacraments and the moral life of grace—the human person is not merely a distant imitator of God but a participant in His very life. This is not a collapse of Creator and creature, nor a confusion of essences, but a mystical communion grounded in divine love. The image, obscured by sin, becomes luminous again through divine initiative that heals, elevates, and glorifies.

This is *theosis* in its most unadulterated sense: transformation not by nature, but by gift. It is achieved in and through Christ, the true Image. As the Eastern Catholic Catechism *Christ Our Pascha* affirms:

"Theosis is the goal of human life, for the human person is created in the image of God in order to attain the likeness of God."

(Christ Our Pascha, §202)

This vision is not a mystical novelty. Already in the fourth century, St. Athanasius declared:

"The Son of God became man so that we might become god."

This is not poetic exaggeration, but the logic of salvation itself.

What began in Adam is consummated in Christ, the new Adam (cf. 1 Corinthians 15:45–49). The image and likeness language of Genesis is not an isolated cosmological reflection. It is the opening of a redemptive arc that stretches from Eden to Golgotha, from the breath in Adam's nostrils to the fire of Pentecost. The image remains. The likeness is restored. Humanity's destiny is not a return to paradise, but an ascent beyond it, into full participation in divine life through the grace of Christ.

St. Paul makes this trajectory explicit in 1 Corinthians 15:45–49. He contrasts Adam, "the man of dust," with Christ, "the man of heaven," and states:

"Just as we have borne the image of the man of dust, we shall also bear the image of the man of heaven."

This movement from the earthly to the heavenly is not incidental. It is essential. It reveals that the *imago Dei* is not fully actualized in Adam, but in Christ, the prototype of redeemed humanity. In Him, the image becomes likeness, and the likeness becomes glory.

The Church Fathers did not receive this truth as abstract theory. They embraced it as a mystery to be lived. In Scripture, they saw not only doctrine, but a summons echoing through the soul of man: become what you were made for.

Justin Martyr, writing in the crucible of second-century apologetics, described the human soul as bearing the *logikon*—the rational imprint of the divine *Logos*. This was not merely a capacity for thought, but a calling. Man bears within himself the Word, and is therefore bound to truth, to justice, to worship.

"Those who lived according to reason," he wrote, "are Christians, even if they were called atheists."

(First Apology, 46)

Theophilus of Antioch echoed this vision, affirming that man was made in God's image so that he might imitate God. The image was not passive, but active. It was a summons to *mimesis*, to live in such a way that the invisible God would become visible through a righteous life (To Autolycus II.27).

Against the Gnostics, who derided the body as a prison and matter as evil, the Church proclaimed something revolutionary: that the human person, body and soul together, is a sacramental icon of the Creator. The image is embodied. It is visible in flesh and spirit, in reason and desire, in liturgy and love.

Yet the image, though real, is fragile. Like a mirror in a storm, it can be cracked or obscured. Some, then and now, reduce the *imago Dei* to a poetic metaphor, a symbol with no ontological weight. Others err in the opposite direction, imagining man as a kind of junior deity, blurring the boundary between Creator and creature. Both extremes lead to ruin.

The Church walks the narrow way. The image is real, but it is created. It reflects, but it does not originate. Man does not possess divinity by nature; he participates in it by grace. The Catechism states with clarity:

"The divine image is present in every man. It shines forth in the communion of persons, in the likeness of the unity of the divine persons among themselves."

(CCC §1702)

And again:

"Endowed with a spiritual and immortal soul, the human person is 'the only creature on earth that God has willed for its own sake.'"

(CCC §1703, citing Gaudium et Spes §24)

This "for its own sake" has nothing to do with modern individualism or self-invention. It means that man exists for communion. He is not self-explanatory, nor self-contained. His intellect, memory, and will are not tools of self-glorification, but windows through which divine light may shine. His soul yearns for God. His very structure is ordered toward liturgy.

That is why the Church, from the beginning, has viewed the *imago Dei* not only as an anthropological fact, but as the foundation of worship. Man alone among earthly creatures can lift creation back to its Source in thanksgiving. He alone is capable of priesthood.

The image, then, is not a possession. It is a vocation. Man is made to worship. He is called to offer. He is created for glory. And it is precisely because he has lost the likeness, while retaining the image, that the Incarnation was not optional but necessary.

The great Fathers of the Church—Irenaeus, Gregory of Nyssa, Basil the Great, and others—did not treat the image of God as a decorative doctrine. They saw in it the key to human destiny and divine purpose.

St. Irenaeus, writing in the second century amidst heresies and persecutions, spoke of man as a child formed by God's hands, bearing the image but not yet the likeness. The image was bestowed in creation. The likeness was to be attained through growth, obedience, and union with God. In his words:

"Man received the breath of life, that he might know Him who made him... And he was made in the image of God, possessing the divine imprint from the beginning; the likeness, however, was not yet complete, but was to be attained by his own moral effort under the guidance of God."

(*Against Heresies* 5.6.1)

Here, the Fall is not the rebellion of a perfected being, but the stumble of a child still maturing. Redemption, then, is not only the restoration of what was lost, but the completion of what was left unfinished. Salvation is not a return to Eden. It is a journey beyond it.

St. Gregory of Nyssa would bring this vision to greater heights. For him, the human person is not a static image, but a being in motion, created for unending ascent. God is infinite, and man, called to participate in that infinity, never ceases rising. Even in eternity, Gregory writes, the soul continues to ascend—ever drawn by divine beauty, never exhausted by the One who is inexhaustible.

"The true vision of God is never being satisfied in the desire to see Him."

(*Life of Moses II.239*)

In this vision, likeness is not a fixed state, but a path. The image is the foundation. The likeness is the journey. And the journey is eternal.

This sets Christian anthropology apart from the philosophical systems of the ancient world. In the Hellenistic mind, perfection meant stasis. The soul's goal was to dissolve into the impersonal One, extinguishing all desire. But in the Christian vision, desire is not an enemy to be suppressed. It is to be sanctified. It is the engine of theosis. Desire is not silenced. It is fulfilled.

Man is not called to be absorbed into God, but to become like Him—not in essence, but in love, in light, in holiness. Always becoming. Always alive. This is the sacred rhythm of human existence: made in the image, moving toward the likeness, destined for glory.

St. Basil the Great, one of the towering minds of the fourth century, understood that to speak of man as image was not merely to confer nobility, but to declare responsibility. Man's very being is stamped with capacity for God, not by merit, but by divine generosity. To be made in the image is to be capable of communion, of transformation, of receiving what no creature could ever deserve.

"This is the goal of our hope: to become like God, to be called children of God, to be His heirs, to reign with Christ."

(*On the Holy Spirit 9.23*)

Basil is not engaging in poetic theology. He is articulating the end for which man was created. And in his vision, there is no divide between theology and worship, no gap between anthropology and liturgy. Man is not simply a rational being. He is a liturgical being. His voice was made for blessing. His hands were made for offering.

The Greek Scriptures call man a *leitourgos*—not merely a thinker, but a celebrant, a servant of mystery. That is why the Church has never viewed the image of God as a private truth, hidden in the soul like a secret. It is revealed in worship, in offering, in self-gift. Man discovers himself not by turning inward, but by turning upward. He lifts his eyes, his hands, his heart.

The image is revealed in sacrifice. And sacrifice, in the Christian sense, is not destruction. It is transformation. It is the soul becoming what it was always meant to be: a priest of creation, standing between heaven and earth, offering the world back to its Maker in love.

St. Maximus the Confessor would later bring this vision to breathtaking clarity. For Maximus, the entire cosmos is in motion toward union. Man, made in the image, is both participant in and mediator of this cosmic liturgy. Through Christ, the true Image, all creation is being drawn into communion. And man, through Christ, becomes the place where heaven and earth are joined.

Maximus identified five great divisions within creation: between male and female, paradise and the world, heaven and earth, intelligible and sensible, uncreated and created. In Christ, each of these divisions is not only reconciled but reordered. More profoundly, Maximus taught that these reconciliations begin in man himself. Man is a microcosm, a living icon, the place where opposites converge. He unites the visible and invisible, the temporal and eternal, the bodily and spiritual—not by force, but through love.

The image of God is not a static imprint. It is a living capacity. Man, in Christ, can bridge every chasm, heal every division, and ascend every height. Likeness is not an accessory to human nature; it is the very reason the image was given.

In the theology of Maximus, theosis is not a spiritual excess. It is spiritual normalcy. The goal of human life is not to become something foreign to our nature, but to become what we were always meant to be. Christ, the Image of the invisible God, makes this possible.

The Fathers are united on this point. To be made in the image of God does not mean that man possesses divinity by nature. It means he is capable of receiving it by grace. This grace is a gift, but it is not passive. It demands surrender, it awakens desire, it draws man into worship. The image is not inert; it longs for illumination.

This longing, planted in the soul from the beginning, is the source of man's restlessness. It explains his hunger for truth, his ache for beauty, his search for love that does not fade. Man was made for God, created for glory, destined for transfiguration.

From her earliest centuries, the Church never lost sight of this truth. In every age, through persecution and heresy, through synods and councils, she has proclaimed the same mystery: man is made in the image of God that he might grow into His likeness. Theosis is not a marginal idea. It is the inner logic of the Christian life.

In the final analysis, the doctrine of the image and likeness is not a philosophical concept. It is a divine vocation. It explains the purpose of creation, the necessity of redemption, and the aim of every sacrament. Man is a creature, but one called to become a son. He is dust, but dust infused with the breath of God. He is mortal, yet invited into uncreated light.

To be made in the image is to carry within oneself the possibility of divine transformation. To be called to the likeness is to begin the journey of love, holiness, and union. And the path has a name: it is Christ. In Him, the image finds its origin, its renewal, and its fulfillment.

This is why you exist.

Man as Microcosm and Priest of Creation

From the beginning, Christian theology has affirmed that man is not merely one creature among many, nor simply the crown of creation in terms of authority or intelligence. He is something far more mysterious and profound: a microcosm, a "little cosmos," in whom all the strata of created reality converge. This idea, inherited in part from Hellenistic philosophy, was transformed by the Church Fathers into a deeply theological vision, one that reveals the human person as both a cosmic bridge and a liturgical mediator.

St. Gregory the Theologian declares with awe that man is "a great miracle," a composite being who reflects both the visible and invisible realms. He writes:

"God sets up man as another world within the world, a microcosm, a new angel, a worshipper, a spectator of creation, a light amidst the world, a being midway between nothingness and divinity."

— *Oration 45, On Holy Pascha*

In this vision, man is not an isolated individual but a synthesis of all created reality. His body links him to the earth, the animals, and the rhythms of time. His soul unites him to the angelic and the divine. In one person, clay and spirit are joined, temporality and immortality coexist, and the entire mystery of creation finds its point of convergence. This is not accidental; it is the very architecture of his being.

St. Maximus the Confessor brings this theme to its highest articulation. According to Maximus, all of creation is marked by a set of polarities: intelligible and sensible, heaven and earth, male and female, paradise and the world, Creator and creature. These opposites are not contradictions but distances, chasms waiting to be bridged. Man, uniquely among creatures, is created with the vocation to reconcile them. He is, in Maximus's language, the "natural mediator" of the cosmos.

"The human person is a laboratory that contains everything: body and spirit, the created and the uncreated, the material and the immaterial… He is the bond of the cosmos."

— *Ambigua to John, 41*

In this framework, the concept of the microcosm is not merely descriptive. It is vocational. Man's very constitution bears within it a divine purpose: to reconcile opposites, to heal divisions, and to gather the many into unity. He is not a passive observer within creation. He is the one through whom creation is to be sanctified and offered.

St. Gregory of Nyssa echoes this insight with profound theological clarity. In *On the Making of Man*, he portrays the human person as the meeting point of the entire cosmos. Man possesses the properties of mineral, plant, animal, and rational being, and yet he is not reducible to any of them. He is something else entirely: a living synthesis, an icon of creation elevated by grace toward the divine.

This synthesis is not arbitrary. It prepares man to offer creation back to its Source. Just as the priest lifts up bread and wine—the fruits of the earth and the work of human hands—and offers them to God, so too does man, in his very being, lift the material world through worship, thanksgiving, and a transfigured life.

To be human, therefore, is not merely to exist within the world. It is to gather the world within oneself, not as a hoarder but as a celebrant. The rivers, the trees, the stars, and the animals all find their voice in man's hymn of praise. His consciousness gives them meaning. His gratitude lifts them into liturgy.

This is what it means to be a microcosm: not simply a biological marvel, but a mystical center, the heart of creation, made to unite all things in Christ. For it is in Christ, the perfect man, that this vocation reaches its fulfillment. In him, heaven and earth are fully reconciled. In him, matter becomes the dwelling place of God. And in him, we begin to see that our microcosmic nature is not a curiosity but a calling.

"For in him all things were created, in heaven and on earth, visible and invisible… all things were created through him and for him. He is before all things, and in him all things hold together."

— *Colossians 1:16–17*

To be human, then, is to be created for communion—not only with God, but with all creation. To live truly as a human being is to live this mystery: to be priest of creation, bearer of its meaning, and celebrant of its return to the Creator. To be made in the image of God is not merely to resemble him. It is to represent him. And to represent God in creation is to serve as priest.

The Scriptures are not content with giving us a biography of man. They give us a liturgy. Genesis is not merely the story of human origins. It is the unveiling of a cosmic sanctuary and the ordination of its first priest. Before Israel had a tabernacle, before there were Levites or sacrifices, there was Eden. And in Eden, there was a man, clothed in innocence and glory, whose task was not merely to survive, but to sanctify.

When the sacred author writes, "The Lord God took the man and put him in the garden of Eden to till it and keep it" (Genesis 2:15), it is easy to skim past this line as though it were a footnote about gardening. But Scripture does not waste words. The Hebrew terms used, *'ābad* ("to serve") and *šāmar* ("to guard"), are the same terms later used in the Torah to describe the liturgical ministry of the priests and Levites in the tabernacle (cf. Numbers 3:7–8; 18:5–6). Adam's role, therefore, is not merely agricultural. It is sacerdotal.

Eden is not a park. It is a holy place—a sanctuary in which God walks "in the cool of the day" (Genesis 3:8) and communes with man face-to-face. And the man, formed from dust yet breathing with divine breath, stands not merely as a creature within the garden, but as its mediator. He is to serve the divine presence and guard the boundaries of holiness—not from weeds or predators, but from anything profane, from anything that would rupture the communion between heaven and earth.

This is why man is made in the image of God: not merely to reflect divine glory, but to stand in God's stead within creation. He is the appointed icon, through whom the created world is invited into praise. The early Church Fathers understood this from the beginning. Man's vocation was not to tame the wilderness for his own purposes, but to offer it back to its Creator. His life was not utilitarian. It was sacrificial. It was liturgical.

Accordingly, the faculties that make us human—reason, imagination, memory, desire, and creativity—are not arbitrary evolutionary byproducts. They are instruments of consecration. They constitute the interior architecture of a being designed to turn the world into worship. When man invents, he glorifies. When he sings, he praises. When he kneels, he returns all things to the Source.

St. Ephrem the Syrian captures this vision with poetic intensity. For him, paradise was not merely a geographical location, but the first holy of holies—a temple not made by hands—and Adam its ordained celebrant:

"The Garden of Eden is the Holy of Holies, and the entire world is its sanctuary. Adam, clothed in glory, entered like a priest to worship, to bless, and to give thanks."

— *Hymns on Paradise*, 15:3

To be clothed in glory is not a metaphor. It is the natural state of a man rightly ordered toward God. Before he was naked and ashamed, Adam was robed in light. The Psalms speak of God as one "clothed with honor and majesty, wrapped in light as with a garment" (Psalm 104:1–2). In the same way, man, bearing the divine image, was meant to be a vessel of light, not merely reflecting it, but transmitting it.

In this light, we perceive the radical truth of human origin: man is not his own. He is priest before he is king. He is steward before he is master. His dominion over the earth is not a license for exploitation. It is a commission to consecrate.

This priesthood is not solitary. Genesis is clear: "Male and female he created them" (Genesis 1:27). The image of God is not fully expressed in isolated individuality but in communion. This mirrors the Trinity, where perfect unity and perfect distinction subsist eternally in love. Man and woman together constitute the full icon of divine relationality. Just as the Persons of the Trinity eternally give themselves to one another in love, so too is humanity called to self-gift.

Marriage, family, and community are not peripheral to human identity. They are expressions of the original liturgical vocation. When a husband loves his wife sacrificially, he acts as a priest. When a mother prays over her child, she fulfills her priestly calling. When work is performed with integrity, when food is shared with gratitude, when creation is received with reverence, these acts become liturgy. This is the image of God at work in the world.

Even after sin entered the world and Adam was cast from the garden, the echo of priesthood lingered in the human soul. The heart still longs to worship. Every altar built, every temple raised, every incense offering in the ancient world—even among the pagans—testifies to a shared hunger: to return, to reconcile, to behold the divine.

But it is Christ who fulfills that ache. He is not only the perfect image of the Father (Colossians 1:15), but also the true High Priest (Hebrews 4:14). In him, Eden is not merely restored, it is transfigured. The veil is not merely repaired, it is opened forever.

"You are a chosen race, a royal priesthood, a holy nation."
— *1 Peter 2:9*

This is not a poetic flourish. It is a revelation of what humanity was always meant to be. In baptism, the image of God is sealed anew. The likeness begins to be restored. The Church becomes the new Eden, the living temple of the world. In the Eucharist, the supreme act of thanksgiving, man finally fulfills his original calling: to take the fruit of the earth and offer it to God in praise.

This sacred drama does not end at the altar. Every Christian is called to become a liturgy in motion. The single mother who prays through exhaustion. The elderly man who forgives quietly. The young father who rises early to bless his children. The worker who endures hardship with dignity. The monk who chants in the silence of his cell. These are the priests of the Kingdom. Their altars are scattered throughout the world. Their incense is the gift of self poured out in love.

This is the mystery: the image of God is not a static quality. It is a living flame. And the only way to bear it rightly is to offer it back.

The tragedy of Genesis 3 is not merely that man disobeyed. It is that man ceased to believe the truth about who he was. In the beginning, Adam and Eve walked with God. They stood unclothed and unashamed, clothed not in garments but in glory. The uncreated light of divine friendship surrounded them. They bore the image of God and were advancing toward his likeness. Their every breath was an act of thanksgiving. Their vocation was not a burden. It was a joy: to till and keep the garden, to reflect the Creator in body and soul, and to grow into ever-deepening union with him.

But a lie entered the garden.

"You will not die… you will be like God."

— *Genesis 3:4–5*

The serpent's temptation was not a call to overt rebellion. It was a distortion of desire. It took the very goal for which man was created—to become like God—and proposed a counterfeit path. It suggested that the likeness of God could be seized, rather than received as a gift through obedience and communion. Adam reached for what he already possessed in seed. He grasped for divinity on his own terms.

He who had been formed "according to God" reached as though

something essential were lacking. He who had been made a priest attempted to become his own god. He took what had not been offered. The hands that were meant to lift creation in thanksgiving closed around it in grasping. In that moment, the light dimmed.

This is the nature of the Fall: not merely a moral infraction, but an ontological rupture. Not simply sin, but separation. Not only a legal transgression, but a metaphysical wound. The image of God remained—man did not cease to be rational, moral, and relational—but the likeness was fractured. The clarity of man's spiritual vision faded. The garment of grace fell. Shame rushed in like a tide.

The Church Fathers interpreted this moment not only as the origin of death and suffering, but as the beginning of spiritual amnesia. Man forgot who he was. And in forgetting, he fell further. He who had been made for communion now hid from the face of God. He who once walked with the Creator now feared his voice in the garden. The mirror of the image cracked, and what stared back was unfamiliar.

St. Athanasius writes:

"Man, having rejected the contemplation of God, turned to the things of corruption… and so the image of God in man was no longer preserved."

— *On the Incarnation*, 4

Yet Athanasius, like all the Fathers, is careful not to say that the image was destroyed. No sin, however grave, can erase the divine imprint. The image is indelible. What is lost is its clarity, its orientation, its radiance. Man becomes like a compass still magnetized, but no longer pointing north. He remains an image-bearer, but a fallen one. A broken icon. Sacred, but shadowed.

St. Gregory Nazianzen describes fallen man as "God's own work defiled," a temple profaned, a priest in exile. Yet even this is not the final word. For if the image had truly been obliterated, there would be nothing left to redeem. But man remains man. God sees his own image in the dust and is moved not to wrath, but to rescue.

When Adam turned away from the face of God, the whole world shuddered. The harmony that once bound heaven and earth together—the seamless communion of Creator, creature, and creation—was torn. From that tear spilled death. Not merely biological death, though that too, but a deeper death: separation, disintegration, the collapse of what had once stood whole.

Man, who had been fashioned to live, now bore within himself the certainty of decay. The body, once radiant with divine glory, became vulnerable to disease, violence, and age. The soul, once ordered toward the light, now turned inward, fragmented, and confused. The rupture reached into the very structure of the human person. What was created to be whole became divided against itself.

This unraveling was not isolated. It was cosmic. As man fell, so did his dominion. The creation that had once rejoiced in his praise now groaned under the weight of his sin (Romans 8:22). The soil turned against him. Thorns sprang from the ground. Pain entered into birth. Sweat entered into labor. Distance entered into love. The rupture ran in every direction.

Within the human heart, desires became disordered. The will, created to move effortlessly toward the good, now faltered. Reason grew clouded. Memory dimmed. The passions surged out of place. Man became at war with himself, pulled between glory and dust. He desired what would destroy him. He feared what could save him. The likeness of God, once unfolding through grace, became buried under layers of self-will and confusion.

Within human relationships, trust gave way to blame. "The woman you gave me..." Adam said, severing communion with a single phrase. What had once been one flesh now bristled with accusation. The first exile was not merely from Eden. It was from each other. And then, from God.

The expulsion from Eden is not merely geographical. It is liturgical. Man is cast out from the sanctuary. The gateway is sealed. A flaming sword now guards the path to the tree of life (Genesis 3:24). The priest of creation is defrocked. The liturgy of paradise ceases. Sacrifice continues, but it is marked by distance, blood, and longing. Cain and Abel will offer outside the garden what Adam was once invited to offer within. The altar remains, but the glory is veiled.

And yet, something persists.

The image is not erased. Even in exile, man builds altars. He weeps. He hopes. He remembers, however faintly, a garden, a voice, a light. This memory becomes ache. And the ache becomes a question: can what was lost ever be found again?

God does not abandon his image-bearer. Even when man hides in shame, the Lord walks toward him.

In the very moment of judgment, a promise is spoken. It is veiled and cryptic, yet luminous with hope: "I will put enmity between you and the woman... he shall bruise your head, and you shall bruise his heel" (Genesis 3:15). This is the protoevangelium—the first Gospel. The serpent who deceived will be crushed by the fruit of the very womb he tried to corrupt. The woman, through whom death entered, will become, in the fullness of time, the gateway of life.

God clothes Adam and Eve with garments of skin, a gesture both tender and terrible. Tender, because it is an act of care. Terrible, because it foreshadows death. Something innocent must now die to cover man's shame. And so begins the long liturgy of history: a procession of altars, sacrifices, covenants, prophets, and kings—all gesturing toward a healing that no man can achieve alone.

The likeness has been lost. But the image remains—wounded, clouded, diminished, but not destroyed. And that changes everything. For if the image remains, then God can speak. Man can still respond. The ache for transcendence still stirs in the soul. The longing for communion still burns. The heart still dreams of glory, even in exile.

The Fathers of the Church saw this persistence of the image as the great mercy of God. St. Irenaeus teaches that man retains the image even in disobedience, though the likeness is forfeited. Athanasius adds that if the image had been obliterated, man would have slipped into non-being. But because the image remains, the Logos himself can enter. He can descend into the broken icon. He can restore what was shattered. He can lift dust into fire.

Christ comes not merely to forgive sin, but to restore the likeness. To renew the image in its fullness. To deify what was defiled. And here, the story begins again, but on a new and greater axis. Eden was not the end. It was the beginning. A seed. And now, through Christ, the tree will grow again—deeper, higher, brighter than before. The image will not merely be preserved. It will be glorified.

The path from Adam to Christ is not a circle. It is a spiral. Redemption does not merely rewind history. It elevates it. In Christ, man is not simply returned to the garden. He is brought beyond it.

The Fathers were not content with a theology that only solved the problem of guilt. They spoke instead of transformation. Man is not merely forgiven. He is transfigured. The image, wounded by sin, becomes the place where divine light breaks through again. The likeness, once lost, becomes the goal of grace.

St. Gregory Nazianzen expresses this mystery in a single breathtaking phrase: "God became man so that man might become god." Not by essence—for God remains God alone—but by grace, by participation, and by love. This is not poetic exaggeration. It is the heart of the Christian Gospel. In Christ, the image becomes radiance. The archetype becomes fulfillment. The clay that once bore shame is now illumined. Man, restored in Christ, becomes again what he was always meant to be: a being of communion, of light, of sacrificial joy.

This is the mystery the Church calls theosis. It is not a metaphor. It is real participation in the life of God, begun in baptism, nourished in the Eucharist, purified through struggle, and crowned in glory.

We began with Genesis. But the true destination is Revelation: "They shall see His face, and His name shall be on their foreheads… and they shall reign for ever and ever" (Revelation 22:4–5). In this final vision, the likeness is not merely restored. It is transformed into light. The image becomes communion. The human person becomes flame. This is what it means to be human. This is why we exist.

The world was never meant to be ordinary. From the beginning, creation bore the fingerprints of a divine Artist. The cosmos was shaped not merely for function, but for worship. The stars were not flung into the heavens only to burn, nor the mountains raised merely to tower. Every element was measured and ordered for glory. The earth was not a machine, but a temple. And into this living temple, God placed his image.

When God formed man from the dust, breathing into him the breath of life, it was not merely to populate the earth. It was to crown it. The human person was created to be the living bridge between heaven and earth, a creature who could hold the soil in his hands while lifting his eyes to the divine. In him, all things could be gathered, and all things could be offered back. He was, from the beginning, a priest.

Scripture tells this story with liturgical patience. The six days of creation unfold like the architecture of a temple. Light, sky, land and sea, sun and moon, living creatures—all are formed in rising order. Then, on the sixth day, man is created. But the true crescendo is the Sabbath. Genesis is not recounting chronology alone. It is shaping a sanctuary. The Sabbath is not a day of rest in the modern sense, but the veil through which God dwells within his creation.

Adam belongs not outside this temple, but within it. His very being is designed for it. He is not simply a part of creation. He is its voice. No other creature names the animals, tends the garden, blesses the gifts, or enters into covenant. He alone walks with God in the cool of the day. He alone is made to worship. And in this sacred role, he carries creation with him. The mountains cannot speak, but Adam can. The rivers cannot sing, but Adam can. The beasts and the trees cannot offer thanks. But man, fashioned in the divine image, can lift the beauty of the world as an offering.

He is a microcosm, certainly. But more than that, he is a mediator.

Man is made of dust, but he is not merely dust. In his body, he bears the humility of the earth. But in his spirit, he bears the glory of divine breath. This union is not accidental. It is vocation. He is earth and heaven in a single being. The beasts roam the ground. The angels behold God. But man walks both terrains. He bleeds, and he prays. He hungers, and he worships. In him, matter and spirit are joined—not in confusion, but in harmony. He is, as the Fathers declared, the microcosm, the "little cosmos" in whom all things converge and from whom all things are to be lifted back to their Source.

To be a microcosm is not an honorific. It is a task. What is gathered in man must be consecrated. His hands are made to shape the world, but also to lift it in blessing. His voice is not merely to name, but to praise. His mind is not merely to reason, but to adore. All of creation awaits its transformation through the praise of man.

St. Maximus the Confessor articulates this with unmatched theological clarity. He describes the human vocation as fivefold mediation—between male and female, paradise and the world, heaven and earth, the intelligible and the sensible, and finally, between God and creation. Man is created to unify, to reconcile, to offer. He is the cosmic priest, the one in whom the scattered elements of reality find their voice, and through whom the world is returned to God.

Maximus writes:

"Man stands in the middle between created and uncreated things, called by grace to make both one."

— *Ambigua*, 41

This is not abstraction. It is reality as concrete as bread and blood. When a mother prays through her tears, she offers her pain to God. When a farmer blesses the harvest, he consecrates the labor of the earth. When a monk chants in the silence of night, he gives voice to the stars. These are not private devotions. They are priestly acts. They are liturgy lived in time and space.

But to fulfill this vocation, man must live with open hands. He cannot clutch the world as possession. He must lift it as offering. He cannot hoard the gifts. He must consecrate them. And in that offering, he himself is changed. For as he lifts creation to God, God lifts man from dust to glory. From creature to icon. From image to likeness.

Creation is not a backdrop. It is not scenery. It is not inert matter. The rivers and fields, the animals and atoms—all of it exists not for utility alone, but for liturgical elevation. Everything God made, he made good. But good in the biblical sense means charged with purpose, made for a destiny beyond itself. Every oak leaf, every comet, every cell is capable of being gathered into man's worship and lifted into God's light.

This is why the Church, from the beginning, has never ceased to bless the material world. In every liturgy, bread and wine—the simplest fruits of earth and human labor—are brought to the altar. They are not presented as trophies of effort, but as offerings of thanksgiving. And in that act of offering, they are transfigured. Bread becomes Body. Wine becomes Blood. Earth becomes heaven. And man, in the act of worship, becomes again what he was created to be: a living altar.

This mystery is not confined to the sanctuary. All of life is meant to be liturgical. Every act of love, every moment of sacrifice, every breath of beauty can become an act of worship. The priesthood of man is not a ritual. It is an existence. The mother's lullaby, the father's labor, the martyr's silence—all of these are echoes of Eden and foreshadowings of glory.

This is what Alexander Schmemann meant when he said that man is what he offers. Not in a materialist sense, but in a theological one. What we offer reveals who we are. If we offer in thanksgiving, we become vessels of grace. If we live liturgically, we become divine. Man becomes what he loves. He becomes what he blesses. He becomes, by grace, what Christ is by nature.

The early Christians lived this reality. They gathered on the first day of the week not to escape the world, but to sanctify it. They brought the cosmos to the altar—in jars of oil, in baskets of bread, in hymns and psalms, in water and flame. The Liturgy was not a retreat from the world. It was its restoration.

This liturgical worldview changes everything. It means the world is not closed. It is open. It has not been given to us for exploitation, but for praise. When man receives creation rightly, when he gives thanks and lifts it up, Eden is restored. The flame that once guarded paradise becomes the flame of Pentecost. The veil is lifted. The sanctuary reopens.

This is why saints radiate peace. Why monks kiss the ground. Why icons shimmer not just with color, but with presence. Because the world is holy. It has always been holy. And the vocation of man is not to escape the world, but to transfigure it.

The Fall was not merely a moral failure. It was a liturgical collapse. Eden was desecrated. The offering ceased. In place of thanksgiving came grasping, hiding, and blame. Man, who was made to lift creation, now clutched it in fear. He no longer blessed. He consumed. The voice of God, once a comfort in the garden, now resounded as judgment.

Yet God did not forsake his priest.

Even in exile, the memory of Eden remained. It lingered in sacrifices and psalms, in temples and tears, in longing and love. The priesthood was wounded, but it was not lost. From the beginning, God prepared its healing. That healing came not in shadow, but in flesh. Not in symbol, but in a man. Christ, the new Adam, the true High Priest, enters not to abolish sacrifice, but to fulfill it. Not to end worship, but to restore it.

He does not act alone. He gathers around himself a people, a royal priesthood. In baptism, the image is washed clean. In chrismation, the Spirit re-anoints the soul. In the Eucharist, the offering of the world is renewed. Earth is lifted. Heaven descends. Man becomes flame. This is not metaphor. This is liturgy. This is the Church.

The Church is not merely a society. She is the new Eden, the altar of the world. In her worship, the cosmos is healed. In her sacraments, the image is restored. In her saints, the likeness shines. This is the final word of the mystery: that the priesthood of man is not a metaphor. It is the logic of creation fulfilled in Christ.

To be human is to receive the world as gift, to offer it in thanksgiving, and to become, by grace, what Christ is by nature—a priest, a son, a bridge between earth and heaven.

The Likeness Lost: Consequences of the Fall

The Fall of man, as depicted in Genesis 3, is not a simplistic origin myth nor a fable designed to explain moral failure. Nor can it be reduced to a violation of divine law, as though its gravity lay chiefly in juridical terms. Rather, the Fall is a mystery of tragic inversion—of ontological distortion and metaphysical rupture. It represents the fragmentation of man's very being, the sundering of the soul from its Creator, the darkening of the divine image, and the forfeiture of the likeness for which man was destined. This primordial event marks not only a catastrophic shift in the trajectory of human history but also a collapse in the inner constitution of human nature itself. It is nothing less than a theological anthropology in disintegration.

The narrative of Eden reveals that man was created not simply to dwell near God but to grow into deeper communion with Him through a gradual ascent of love. Man stood as the mediating bridge between the visible and invisible realms, possessing a unity of body and soul that symbolically wove together heaven and earth. His task was eucharistic: to offer creation back to the Creator in thanksgiving, to exercise dominion not as exploitation but as sacramental stewardship. The sacred writer affirms that man was placed in the Garden "to till it and keep it" (Genesis 2:15). These verbs, 'ābad and shāmar, are not incidental. They reappear in later passages of the Pentateuch exclusively to describe the liturgical duties of priests and Levites within the sanctuary (cf. Numbers 3:7–8; 8:26; 18:5–6). The Garden, therefore, was not merely an idyllic pasture but a cosmic temple, and Adam its consecrated hierophant. Eden was the protological sanctuary, the place of divine indwelling, and the very soil upon which Adam walked was altar-ground, set apart for doxology.

Within this sacred context, God establishes a single prohibition: not to eat from the tree of the knowledge of good and evil (Genesis 2:17). This command is not arbitrary or authoritarian, nor is it a trap designed to induce failure. The Church Fathers unanimously interpret it as a sacramental boundary—a visible token of invisible mystery. It was meant to safeguard the asymmetry between the Giver and the recipient, to cultivate humility and self-emptying, and to orient man toward receptivity rather than grasping. As St. Gregory of Nyssa observes, the command is like the instruction of a loving father, guiding his child not to reach prematurely for what he cannot yet bear. St. Basil likewise affirms that the purpose of the command was pedagogical, given not to restrict man but to perfect him through obedient love. "Obedience," he writes, "is the first step toward the likeness of God."

God gave the command not to prevent man from becoming like Him, but to teach him how to do so rightly—through humility and love, not through pride.

— St. Gregory the Theologian, *Oration* 38.12

Man, however, chose otherwise. Tempted by the serpent and inwardly seduced by the desire to possess divinity apart from communion, he grasped at what was meant to be received. He attempted to become like God not by participation but by self-determination, not through grace but through appropriation. Here lies the essence of sin: not merely a transgression of law but the disintegration of the relational order between Creator and creature. The Fall represents the collapse of trust, the inward turn of the self, and the refusal to remain in a posture of receptivity. Man, created to offer himself in thanksgiving, seized that which was not his to claim. He no longer lifted creation to God; he consumed it for himself.

This rupture did not annihilate man's faculties, but it did disfigure their integration. The intellect, or nous, which once moved effortlessly toward divine contemplation, became scattered and distracted. Desire, which had been lifted in yearning toward the divine, now bent toward the earth, enslaved to sense and appetite. Memory, which once preserved the imprint of paradise, now broods on absence, sorrow, and confusion. The passions, which had formerly been governed by reason and grace, now revolted and usurped control of the soul. Man, still bearing the image, became fragmented from within—a creature haunted by his former glory, yet lost in the labyrinth of disordered longing.

If you are a theologian, you will pray truly; and if you pray truly, you are a theologian.

— Evagrius Ponticus, *Chapters on Prayer* 60

The consequences of the Fall were both immediate and total. The divine image, stamped upon man by the Logos in the act of creation, remained ontologically intact. It cannot be erased, for it is not something acquired, but something constitutive of what it means to be human. Yet the likeness—understood by the Fathers as the dynamic progression into divine resemblance through grace—was tragically lost. What had been illuminated by divine participation became darkened by self-will and self-reliance. The intellect (νοῦς), formerly clear and ordered toward contemplation of God, was now clouded and divided. The passions, which had once been shaped and elevated by love and reason, now turned against the soul, seeking to dominate and enslave it. Man, once clothed in glory and crowned with honor (Psalm 8:5), now covered himself in shame and hid in fear before the face of his Creator.

By transgressing the commandment, man fell from grace and became clothed in the garments of mortality. His soul, once radiant with divine light, was covered in the shadow of corruption.

— St. Ephrem the Syrian, *Hymns on Paradise*

The personal disintegration of man was only the beginning. The Fall issued in a cosmic fracture. Man, appointed to bring harmony between creation and Creator, forfeited his priestly role. The result was not only internal chaos but also external disarray. The bond between body and soul, between man and woman, and between man and the created world was shattered. What had been a cosmic liturgy became a desecrated temple. The altar was left in ruins, and the hymns of praise turned into the lament of exile.

St. Maximus the Confessor identifies five ontological ruptures introduced by the Fall: the separation of man from God, the division of mind from sense perception, the disjunction between soul and body, the alienation of human beings from one another, and the estrangement between man and creation. These ruptures are not simply relational or emotional; they are structural. They reveal an alteration at the very level of being. The Fall, therefore, is not to be relegated to a mythic past but must be understood as an enduring condition—one passed down generationally, not as juridical guilt, but as corruption, mortality, and the darkening of the noetic faculty.

St. Gregory Palamas articulates this with striking clarity. Adam's sin, he teaches, "turned the eye of the heart away from God." In that turning, man became blind to divine things and fixated upon the merely visible. The nous, which is the organ of spiritual perception, became disabled, incapable of discernment without illumination from above.

The signs of this rupture appear immediately in the Genesis narrative. The man and the woman, once naked and unashamed, now clothe themselves. Shame emerges—not as a superficial emotion, but as a spiritual condition, a symptom of a consciousness severed from divine communion. When God draws near, they hide. Fear replaces intimacy. Guilt supplants trust. Man no longer walks with God in the garden but flees from His presence. Even Adam's naming of the woman shifts in tone—from joy and recognition to subtle blame. "The woman whom You gave to be with me, she gave me fruit of the tree" (Genesis 3:12). What was once a bond of communion is now tinged with rivalry and alienation.

The expulsion from Eden is not a punitive sentence in the modern sense. It is revelatory. It exposes what man has become by turning from the Source of life. Mortality is not merely an imposed punishment; it is the inevitable outcome of separation from the One who alone is immortal. St. Athanasius writes:

Man, having turned away from the eternal, began to return to the nothingness from which he was made.

— *On the Incarnation*, 4

This drift toward non-being is the deepest tragedy of the Fall. Man, created for immortality and communion, now moves toward dissolution.

Yet even here, divine mercy remains. God's barring of the Tree of Life is not vengeance but preservation. To live forever in a fallen state would be to immortalize corruption. Death, paradoxically, becomes a form of medicine—a temporal limit placed upon the reign of sin, and the veil through which Christ will one day pass in order to destroy death by death (cf. Genesis 3:22).

Creation itself bears the imprint of man's dislocation. The earth, once docile under Adam's hand, now resists him. It brings forth thorns and thistles. The harmony between the steward and his domain has been broken. Work, which had once been an act of liturgical participation in divine creativity, now becomes burden and toil. The womb, once a sanctuary of fruitful joy, is now visited by anguish. Fertility, dominion, labor, and love—all dimensions of human life suffer disorder. The creature who was meant to unite heaven and earth now finds both realms veiled in conflict. The curse upon the ground is not an arbitrary sentence but the natural consequence of man's loss of grace. The world becomes hostile not because God turns it against man, but because man has fallen out of right relation to it.

The creature was subjected to futility, not of its own will but by the will of Him who subjected it in hope.

— Romans 8:20

Yet within the words of exile, the divine promise is already present. The protoevangelion, the first Gospel, is spoken not to man but to the serpent: "I will put enmity between you and the woman, between your seed and her seed. He shall crush your head, and you shall bruise His heel" (Genesis 3:15). Even as man hides in shame, the promise of a Redeemer is announced. The likeness may be lost, but it is not irrecoverable. The way of ascent, once forsaken, will be walked again—by One who will not fail.

The Fathers often use medical imagery to describe the Fall and its consequences. Sin is a sickness that begins in the heart and spreads outward. It affects the whole person, then society, and ultimately the world itself. St. Cyril of Alexandria describes this condition with sobering clarity: "Our nature became diseased by sin, having been corrupted at the root." The Fall is not only a personal misfortune but a universal infection. And the cure, correspondingly, must be cosmic. It must address the very substance of human nature. Only one who is fully divine and fully human—united without confusion—can reach into this abyss and bring healing without contamination. As Christ Himself declares, "Those who are well have no need of a physician, but those who are sick. I have not come to call the righteous, but sinners to repentance" (Luke 5:31–32).

Although the likeness of God in man was lost through the Fall, the image remains. It is not extinguished, only obscured. The Church Fathers are united in this affirmation. The image is essential to human identity and cannot be undone, for it is implanted in the very act of divine creation. But the image no longer shines with its intended clarity. It is tarnished, weathered, worn. St. Cyril of Jerusalem offers a poignant metaphor: the soul is like a coin that still bears the King's face, yet one dulled and defaced by misuse.

The image calls out to its Archetype, even beneath the sediment of sin. It is like a flame buried under ash, awaiting the breath of the Spirit to stir it again into brilliance.

The soul, though darkened, retains the form of its beauty; and through virtue it can be made to shine again.

— St. Gregory of Nyssa

This Eastern distinction between image and likeness provides deep theological insight into the paradox of human dignity amid fallenness. The image is what man is by nature. The likeness is what he was meant to become by grace. To lose the likeness is not to lose one's humanity, but to lose the path to its fulfillment. The journey of theosis is interrupted, but not erased. The destination grows dim, but the road is not closed.

The Genesis account, even in its most sorrowful moments, bears witness to divine mercy. God does not annihilate Adam and Eve. He does not revoke their existence or destroy their dignity. Instead, He seeks them out. "Adam, where are you?" (Genesis 3:9). This is not the interrogation of a wrathful judge. It is the lament of a grieving Father. God does not ask because He lacks knowledge, but because man no longer knows himself. The question pierces the silence of shame and reveals that relationship, though wounded, still remains.

Even in exile, God clothes Adam and Eve. The garments of skin (Genesis 3:21) are not tokens of divine rejection but symbols of divine mercy. They reveal a God who continues to care for His fallen creatures—not as a concession, but as a preparation. These garments foreshadow the Incarnation itself: the eternal Word will one day clothe Himself in the same mortality Adam now wears. He will enter the exile, not from without but from within, that man may be led back to paradise clothed in light.

The early Fathers recognized this typology with astonishing clarity. St. Irenaeus writes:

He recapitulated in Himself the long history of mankind and furnished us, in a brief, comprehensive manner, with salvation.

— *Against Heresies*, 3.18.1

Likewise, St. Melito of Sardis, in his Paschal Homily, declares:

He put on the suffering of the one who had suffered, and the flesh of the one who had fallen.

This divine condescension—God clothing Himself in the flesh of the fallen—is the beginning of the ascent. The movement of God toward man never ceases. Even when man turns away, God draws near. The Fall does not halt the divine initiative. It becomes the occasion for its most profound expression.

The entire narrative of salvation, typologically, is already embedded in the Genesis account. The Tree of Life, once barred, becomes the Cross upon which the New Adam redeems the old. The cherubim who guarded the entrance to Eden with flaming swords reappear at Christ's tomb, not with weapons, but as angelic witnesses to resurrection. The curse upon the ground finds its reversal in the earth that opens to receive the slain Lamb. The woman, whose sorrow in childbirth was multiplied, becomes the Theotokos—the God-bearer—who brings forth the Life of the world. Every detail of the expulsion becomes, in Christ, a moment of recapitulation.

I said, "You are gods, sons of the Most High, all of you."

— Psalm 82:6

St. Gregory Nazianzen affirms the cosmic dimension of Christ's obedience. He is the second Adam who bears the image of the first yet reverses the trajectory of human history by the manner of His surrender. The path of theosis, once blocked by pride, is reopened through humility. The likeness, once forfeited, is now raised in Christ, not by human merit, but by divine mercy.

The Lord did not assume a humanity untainted by the Fall. He did not come in the innocence of prelapsarian Adam, but in the weakness of postlapsarian flesh. As St. Paul writes:

> Though He was in the form of God, He did not count equality with God a thing to be grasped, but emptied Himself, taking the form of a servant, being born in the likeness of men… becoming obedient unto death, even death on a cross.
> — Philippians 2:6–8

This is the scandal and glory of the Gospel. The one who knew no sin became sin—not in essence, but in solidarity—so that man, imprisoned by corruption, might be raised in incorruption. The healing of man begins not in law but in love. Not in condemnation, but in communion. The Logos assumes not only our nature, but our condition. In assuming it without stain, He raises fallen nature to glory.

Yet the effects of the Fall persist. The human heart remains wounded by Adam's rebellion. Each soul enters the world with a nature inclined toward fragmentation: the intellect darkened, the will weakened, the passions disordered. The struggle to recover what was lost is the great labor of the spiritual life. What Adam squandered in a single moment must now be regained over a lifetime. This labor is not moralistic striving but ascetical restoration—a synergy of divine grace and human repentance.

St. Isaac the Syrian speaks with quiet urgency: "This life was given to you for repentance; do not waste it in vain pursuits." The journey of deification begins again wherever the soul turns in contrition to its origin. The likeness of God is not regained through external reform or moral performance, but through inward transfiguration. Man must be remade from the inside out. This is possible only because the Image Himself—the uncreated Logos, the eternal Archetype—entered into the condition of the fallen image. He took flesh, suffered death, and rose again. Through this divine solidarity, the path of ascent has been cleared and illumined.

Yet even the Fall, with all its ruin, is not the end. It is the threshold through which divine love breaks forth, and the descent that gives rise to ascent. It is the descent that makes the ascent possible. It is the rupture that necessitates the Incarnation. The likeness may be lost, but the desire of God for man's union remains. Eden's tragedy is overcome by the mystery of Christ. The breath that once animated dust in the beginning returns, not as mere animation but as deifying indwelling. The Holy Spirit comes not only to revive but to divinize.

I have darkened the image of Thy countenance, O Savior, and broken Thy commandment.

— *Great Canon of St. Andrew of Crete*

This lament, chanted in the Church's great penitential hymn, is not a cry of despair but of awakening. It confesses the truth of human failure while also affirming the possibility of restoration. For the image remains. The likeness can be regained. The path of theosis, though wounded, is not destroyed.

Every turning of the soul toward God, every act of repentance, every embrace of grace is a step back into the likeness. Through baptism, the image is cleansed. Through the Eucharist, it is nourished. Through the ascetical life, it is refined in fire. Through prayer and sacrament, through struggle and love, the human person is reconfigured from within. All of this is possible because the Word who formed man in the beginning has come to reform him at the end.

The image that had been blurred by sin is once more etched with clarity. The likeness that had been lost is rediscovered, not in Adam's strength but in Christ's humility. The glory that had been forsaken is now offered anew, as gift.

This is the Christian story: not merely the forgiveness of guilt, but the restoration of being; not simply moral improvement, but ontological transformation. The goal is not to escape the world but to sanctify it. Not to return to Eden, but to surpass it. In Christ, the first things become new things. The exile becomes pilgrimage. The dust becomes light. The image, once obscured by sin, now shines anew with uncreated light.

Man was created for glory—not the fleeting glory of earthly triumph, but the uncreated radiance of union with God. The divine image he bears is not a symbol, but a seed: a mark of origin and a summons to destiny. Though the likeness was lost through sin, the image endures: dimmed but not erased, wounded but not destroyed.

In Christ, the image is not merely repaired; it is glorified. The Word who formed man in His image has Himself taken on that image so that man might be raised into His likeness. The dust was not cast off. It was assumed, transfigured, and enthroned. Theosis is not poetic aspiration; it is the very purpose of our creation.

The story of the image and likeness thus prepares the ground for the mystery that follows. Creation discloses man's divine vocation; the Fall exposes his inability to achieve it apart from grace. Between these two stands the turning point of all history—the descent of God into what He made. The same Word who called man into being now enters his broken condition, not as a stranger to heal from without, but as the very Image made flesh. In Him, the drama of the image reaches its climax: what was wounded will be restored, what was finite will be filled, and what was earthly will be lifted into uncreated light.

We now turn to the way of ascent. The Son of God has descended so that man might rise. Through His Incarnation, His sacraments, His Cross, and His resurrection, He opens the path by which the image is fulfilled and the likeness restored. And so, the image calls us home, and the likeness, once lost leads us there, until at last we are transfigured in His light and partakers of the divine nature.

2

More Than Forgiven: Deification as the True Goal of Redemption

"The Word of God became man so that man might no longer live for himself according to the flesh, but might live in the Spirit for God who made him."
— St. Maximus the Confessor

The Inadequacy of Moralism and Legalism

The juridical model of salvation—where guilt is balanced by punishment, and justice is satisfied through substitution—emerged early in the Latin theological tradition and gained dominance in the Western Christian imagination. While containing elements of truth, this legal paradigm is ultimately partial and inadequate to express the depth and mystery of salvation as presented in the Scriptures and the early Fathers.

The roots of this model can be traced to the influence of Roman legal culture upon Latin theologians. Tertullian, trained in law, began framing sin as debt and punishment as juridical satisfaction. His understanding of divine justice mirrored Roman contract law: violation incurred liability, and restoration demanded compensatory action. Augustine, in responding to Pelagianism, further developed this framework by emphasizing original guilt and inherited corruption, necessitating divine justice as the only possible response to humanity's fallen state. While his soteriology also included deep insights into divine love and grace, his legal vocabulary laid the groundwork for later Western developments that would prioritize retributive justice.

By the time of Anselm's *Cur Deus Homo*, the courtroom metaphor had become dominant. Anselm framed the atonement in terms of feudal honor: man had offended God's infinite dignity and could not repay the debt. Only a God-man could offer satisfaction proportionate to the offense. Though intellectually rigorous, Anselm's approach reduced the incarnation and crucifixion to a mechanistic exchange—an infinite transaction to balance an infinite offense. This framework internalized a conception of God as offended ruler rather than healing Father.

The Eastern Fathers never saw the Cross as a transaction of wrath appeasement, but as the victorious descent of divine love into the realm of death. St. Basil the Great affirms that Christ "voluntarily accepted death in order to destroy death itself." His crucifixion was not the payment of debt, but the conquest of corruption. St. Irenaeus, long before Anselm, taught that Christ "recapitulated" human life in Himself, including death, so that all of it might be healed and made new (*Against Heresies*, V.23.2). The Cross, then, is not the balancing of scales, but the medicine that heals the corruption of nature. As St. Gregory the Theologian writes, "That which He has not assumed He has not healed; but that which is united to God is also being saved." (Ep. 101). The Passion is salvific not because it satisfies divine demand, but because it is the divine cure.

"Sin is not giving God what is due to Him. The honor taken away must be repaid, and none but God can make the satisfaction." — St. Anselm, *Cur Deus Homo*, Book 1

Thomas Aquinas, while building on Anselm, nuances this view. In *Summa Theologiae* III, q.48, he explores multiple dimensions of Christ's passion—as merit, satisfaction, sacrifice, and efficient cause of salvation. He introduces the concept of infused grace, whereby the believer is interiorly changed. Still, Aquinas's system retains the juridical scaffolding. Yet while scholastic theology in the West built itself within juridical categories, the Fathers of the East consistently spoke another language altogether. Their metaphors were not legal but medicinal, not transactional but participatory. Where the West spoke of satisfaction, the East spoke of healing; where the West sought acquittal, the East proclaimed union.

The dominance of Roman legal imagery shaped the very imagination of Western Christianity. God became associated first with courtroom robes rather than priestly vestments, and salvation became a matter of acquittal more than healing. This influence filtered down through catechesis, liturgy, and devotional life, leading many to conceive of sin primarily as law-breaking, and grace as the suspension of penalty rather than participation in divine life.

Yet when one turns to Scripture, the legal metaphor is never the dominant frame. The Old and New Testaments speak frequently of salvation as healing (Ps 103:3), washing (Isa 1:18), rebirth (John 3:3), renewal (Titus 3:5), and union (John 17:21–23). The Pauline epistles, often cited for forensic justification, speak also of being "in Christ," of the old man dying and the new man rising (Rom 6:3–5), of being "a new creation" (2 Cor 5:17). The imagery is not merely legal, but ontological and participatory. Salvation is a reconstitution of human nature in and through Christ.

In Eastern Christian tradition, this participatory vision remained central. St. Athanasius declares, "God became man so that man might become god" (*On the Incarnation*, 54). St. Gregory of Nazianzus insists that "what is not assumed is not healed" (Epistle 101), underscoring that salvation is not a mere legal transfer, but a real healing of the totality of human nature. Sin is not merely guilt—it is disease. And redemption is not simply pardon—it is resurrection.

Thus, the legal model, while containing aspects of truth, is too narrow to account for the vast sweep of salvation history. It fails to express the drama of deification, the healing of the image, and the restoration of the likeness. Theosis demands more than a verdict; it demands a transformation. The image of God in man is not merely acquitted—it is reformed, refashioned, and glorified. It is lifted up, not into the courtroom, but into the bridal chamber, the temple, and the divine dance of Trinitarian life.

If the juridical model of salvation reduces redemption to external acquittal, the moralistic model collapses it into self-help. It is one of the most persistent and subtle heresies in both antiquity and modernity: the notion that man, by his own will, discipline, or virtue, can ascend to God. It is the triumph of the Pelagian impulse, dressed in theological language and often concealed beneath religious fervor. Moralism is not merely a theological error; it is an anthropological lie. It does not underestimate man's greatness—it misunderstands his wound.

The ancient heresy of Pelagianism, articulated most forcefully by the British monk Pelagius in the early fifth century, held that man could fulfill the moral law by nature alone. Grace was helpful, but not essential. Sin was an act, not a state. Adam's fall was not inherited but imitated. For Pelagius, Christ's role was to offer a perfect example to follow, not to redeem a nature enslaved by death. This optimistic anthropology was condemned at the Council of Ephesus in 431, and again at Carthage and Orange, not only for its error in doctrine but for its catastrophic implications: if man is not broken, Christ need not be a Savior. He becomes instead a moral instructor—a divine Socrates, rather than the incarnate Logos.

Even Semi-Pelagianism, the more moderate position that man takes the first steps toward God and grace completes the work, was formally rejected by the Church. The Eastern Fathers, while maintaining the synergy of human freedom and divine grace, insist that even the first movement of repentance is itself a work of the Spirit. St. Gregory of Nyssa writes that "the soul cannot even begin to desire the good unless the divine impulse precedes it." St. John Damascene affirms, "We could not even form a thought toward God without His enabling."

The disease of moralism, however, is not confined to ancient heresy. It remains deeply embedded in modern religious consciousness, both East and West. It often masquerades as holiness. It infiltrates ascetical life, preaching, and even sacramental theology. It equates holiness with rigor, salvation with behavior, repentance with technique. It subtly converts the Gospel into a program. This moralism is not always doctrinal—it is cultural and psychological. It manifests in perfectionism, scrupulosity, prideful self-reliance, and despair masked as discipline. It has destroyed countless souls under the guise of virtue.

The Church Fathers diagnose sin not primarily as legal guilt but as ontological corruption. St. Maximus the Confessor insists that "the human person, apart from divine energy, is unable to will the good in the manner that leads to union with God." St. Basil the Great writes, "Without the Spirit, man cannot even know the depths of his illness, let alone be healed from it." St. Gregory Palamas warns that any virtue apart from grace is a "glittering vice," a demonic mimicry of holiness that reinforces the ego rather than dissolving it.

The moralistic worldview collapses Christianity into anthropology. It replaces mystery with method. In the secularized world, this becomes evident in the therapeutic reinterpretation of religion. The Gospel is no longer the proclamation of death and resurrection, but of balance, peace, and personal growth. Christ becomes a wellness coach. Grace is redefined as psychological insight. And the Church becomes an institution for self-betterment. But this is not the Cross. This is not the empty tomb. This is not Pentecost.

Moralism fails because it misidentifies both the problem and the solution. It presumes that sin is merely behavioral and that the cure lies in effort. But sin is death. Sin is estrangement from divine life. Sin is the disintegration of the image and the paralysis of the likeness. As such, no ethical program, no matter how rigorous, can raise the dead. No ascetical rule, no matter how exacting, can restore communion. Moralism is the attempt to build a ladder to heaven from dust. It is Babel in ecclesial clothing.

This is why the New Testament speaks of salvation not as ethical success but as ontological rebirth: "Unless one is born from above, he cannot enter the Kingdom of God" (John 3:3). St. Paul does not urge men to improve, but to die: "I have been crucified with Christ. It is no longer I who live, but Christ who lives in me" (Gal 2:20). He declares that those in Christ are "a new creation" (2 Cor 5:17), not a better version of the old man, but the emergence of something ontologically new.

The saints are the Church's answer to moralism. They are not ethical superheroes. They are transfigured beings, icons of deified flesh. Their holiness is not the fruit of rigorous rule-keeping, but of surrender to grace. St. Symeon the New Theologian writes that the saint is not one who merely fulfills commandments, but one who is "illumined by uncreated light and made one with the Spirit." The Desert Fathers, in their relentless struggle, were not moralists. They were lovers—wounded by grace, broken open to receive divine fire. Their tears were not legal repentance but bridal longing.

The moralist either succeeds and becomes proud, or fails and despairs. But the man of grace neither exalts in his virtue nor wallows in his sin. He lives in the tension of already and not yet, upheld by mercy. The Gospel is not the triumph of willpower—it is the victory of the Crucified. And the Church is not a factory of virtue but the Bride of Christ, whose holiness is received, not achieved.

Thus, the failure of moralism is not simply doctrinal. It is existential. It does not merely err in theology—it suffocates the soul. It builds systems but obscures the Face. It organizes behavior but forgets the Bridegroom. Theosis cannot be attained by moralism because moralism operates on the wrong plane. It seeks to heal the soul without communion, to polish the image while ignoring the flame.

The Church does not call man to become good. She calls him to become gods by grace. She does not invite him to improved performance but to divine participation. For this reason, the Fathers speak not of rules, but of fire; not of balance, but of transfiguration; not of management, but of union. Moralism is a counterfeit Gospel. Theosis is the truth of man.

The doctrine of justification, as it developed in post-Augustinian Western theology and crystallized during the Reformation, has too often been framed in juridical terms: a change in legal status rather than in nature, a courtroom verdict rather than a metaphysical re-creation. In this model, man is declared righteous by a forensic decree, his sins imputed to Christ and Christ's righteousness imputed to him. Yet however scripturally grounded this may seem when extracted from isolated Pauline texts, it does not reflect the consensus patrum nor the deeper soteriological vision of the Church. The tradition of the undivided Church, East and West, consistently presents justification not as a legal fiction but as ontological participation in the divine life.

The problem with the juridical model is not that it is entirely false, but that it is abstract and incomplete. It treats sin as a legal debt rather than a metaphysical disease. It locates salvation in the mind of God—how He regards the sinner—rather than in the actual being of the person. It severs the act of justification from regeneration, as if God could declare a man righteous without making him righteous. This conception is foreign to the biblical worldview, which understands righteousness (δικαιοσύνη) not merely as a judicial standing but as a state of being in right relationship with God, rooted in covenant, fidelity, and interior transformation.

The Scriptures speak with a different accent. In Romans 5–8, St. Paul situates justification not within a courtroom, but within a drama of new creation: "As sin reigned in death, grace also might reign through righteousness to eternal life through Jesus Christ our Lord" (Rom 5:21). In Romans 6, justification is inseparable from baptismal death and resurrection. The believer is not merely acquitted; he is buried and raised. Baptism is not symbolic cleansing but mystical death, a real participation in the death and resurrection of Christ. In 2 Corinthians 5:17, Paul declares, "If anyone is in Christ, he is a new creation." This is not imputation—it is infusion, reconstitution, recreation. The old man does not simply receive a new label; he dies and is remade.

The Greek word δικαιόω, traditionally rendered "justify," carries a much broader semantic field than its Latin counterpart *iustificare*. In Greek usage, particularly in the Septuagint and New Testament, δικαιοσύνη (righteousness) is relational and dynamic. It is the condition of fidelity, right worship, and harmony with the divine will. In Psalm 1 and throughout the Psalter, the "righteous man" is not merely acquitted but is one whose entire being is aligned with God's law. St. John Chrysostom, commenting on Romans, repeatedly insists that justification is not a mere verdict but a transformation wrought by grace. "He does not merely deliver from punishment," Chrysostom writes, "but also makes righteous and gives the power to live righteously." (*Homilies on Romans*, 11).

Patristic theology is unambiguous on this point. St. Athanasius is even more explicit. In *On the Incarnation*, he asserts that the Word took on flesh not only to cancel guilt, but to restore the divine image in man: "He became man that we might become gods." This is justification as deification. Likewise, St. Cyril of Alexandria, in his *Commentary on John*, teaches that Christ unites human nature to His own divine life, not merely externally but hypostatically, so that we may participate in the life He shares with the Father. Justification, for Cyril, is incorporation into Christ's life, not exemption from wrath. The Logos assumed human nature not merely to erase a record of wrongs, but to reconstitute the human essence from within, healing it by grace through union.

For St. Gregory of Nazianzus, justification is not external arrangement but internal transfiguration: "What is not assumed is not healed." The Logos heals the very nature He assumes, and thus the justification of man is inseparable from the ontological mystery of the Incarnation. St. Gregory of Nyssa, in his *Great Catechism*, likewise insists that the divine economy is therapeutic in nature—God, like a skilled physician, applies the remedy not to the courtroom but to the soul itself. Thus, justification cannot be viewed as external arrangement but as inner healing: the restoration of the likeness by participation in divine life.

This vision was safeguarded in the East, where justification was never severed from the larger mystery of theosis. To be justified is to be made righteous; to be made righteous is to be healed, illumined, and glorified. The Cappadocians, St. Maximus the Confessor, and St. Symeon the New Theologian all speak of salvation as the gradual transformation of the entire human person by the divine energies. For Maximus, the passions are not merely behavioral flaws but disordered movements of the soul that require divinization. The righteousness of the believer is not a cloak that hides his sin, but a fire that purifies his being. In this light, the Pauline term "in Christ" becomes the very heart of justification. It is not a metaphor. It is a mystical ontology.

This Eastern insistence on ontological transformation stands in stark contrast to the Reformation-era division of justification and sanctification. Martin Luther's *simul iustus et peccator*—"simultaneously righteous and a sinner"—captures a forensic tension: the believer remains ontologically sinful while being declared righteous by divine fiat. But this model, however pastoral in intention, introduces a deep dualism into the spiritual life. It treats righteousness as an external status, not an interior renewal. It offers comfort but not cure, assurance but not transfiguration. This soteriology breeds a form of spiritual passivity, where man is left unchanged beneath the legal verdict.

The Catholic tradition, particularly in the Council of Trent, partially resists this bifurcation by affirming that justification involves the infusion of sanctifying grace. Yet even here, juridical metaphors continue to shape catechetical understanding. Eastern theology, less burdened by medieval categories, preserved the older patristic vision: salvation as healing, justification as transformation, and grace as the very energy of God. As St. Gregory Palamas writes, "The grace of justification is nothing less than the uncreated energies of God dwelling in man." This is not legal pardon but divine indwelling. While Catholic theology does not formally adopt the metaphysical distinction between God's essence and His energies, it affirms with Palamas the experiential reality of divine life communicated to the soul. Grace is not a created intermediary, but the very life of God truly present and active in the believer.

And yet, the Catholic Magisterium has never severed grace from participation. The Catechism of the Catholic Church affirms that "the grace of Christ is the gratuitous gift that God makes to us of his own life" and that it "introduces us into the intimacy of Trinitarian life" (CCC §1997). Vatican II likewise proclaims that "all the faithful... are called to the fullness of the Christian life and to the perfection of charity" (*Lumen Gentium*, §40), a perfection which is not moral performance, but divinized communion. St. John Paul II, echoing the Eastern Fathers, declared that "man is called to a full sharing in the life of God" (*Orientale Lumen*, §6).

These voices show that theosis is not a theological option—it is the very heart of Catholic soteriology.

The ontological model also clarifies the role of the sacraments. Baptism is not merely the removal of legal guilt but the infusion of divine life. Chrismation seals the believer with the uncreated energy of the Spirit. The Eucharist is not merely commemorative—it is participatory. In receiving Christ's Body and Blood, the believer is made righteous not by decree but by communion. The entire sacramental economy presupposes a soteriology of participation, not substitution.

Ultimately, justification cannot be divorced from the Incarnation. Christ does not simply take our place—He takes our nature. He does not merely obey on our behalf—He recreates from within. In Him, the human and divine are united, and through Him, we are drawn into that union. To be justified, then, is to be reconstituted in Christ: to become, in the words of St. Peter, "partakers of the divine nature" (2 Pet 1:4).

Therefore, the language of courtroom must give way to the language of communion. The legal metaphor, while useful in limited scope, cannot bear the weight of theosis. The Gospel is not a transaction—it is a transformation. The cross is not merely a substitution—it is a marriage. And justification is not the pronouncement of a judge—it is the embrace of the Bridegroom. It is not the cold dismissal of guilt, but the warm infusion of divine light. It is not acquittal—it is union.

Just as a wild branch is grafted into a cultivated vine, so the human soul is joined to the divine life in a union that is both real and regenerative. This is no external alliance—it is an ontological merger. The graft takes on the sap of the Vine; the branch lives because the life of Another now flows through it. "Abide in me, and I in you," says the Lord (John 15:4). This is not metaphorical sentiment—it is mystical reality. In the sacraments, in prayer, in the synergy of grace and will, the divine life courses through mortal flesh. Salvation is not a legal adoption—it is a grafting into God

Theology must become flesh. If the Gospel we proclaim cannot be embodied, it cannot be believed. For the Church, the definitive proof of the truth of theosis is not found in syllogisms, dogmatic decrees, or theological treatises, but in the radiant lives of her saints. The saints are not exceptions to the Christian life; they are its full flowering. They are not anomalies but icons—living demonstrations of what man is called to become when united to divine grace.

In a world shaped by legalism and moralism, the saints stand as eschatological signs that something more is possible. Their lives reveal that salvation is not merely about being declared righteous or behaving righteously—it is about becoming light. "You are the light of the world," says the Lord (Matt 5:14). This is not hyperbole. The saints radiate uncreated light because they have been united to the Light. They are not models of perfection in a moralistic sense, but living theophanies—sacramental presences of Christ's victory in time.

The lives of the Desert Fathers illustrate this most clearly. St. Anthony the Great, after decades in solitude, emerged from the wilderness not as a broken ascetic, but as a being of peace, whose presence alone healed the tormented and silenced the demons. St. Macarius the Great was said to be so transfigured by grace that wild beasts approached him without fear, as though recognizing Eden restored. Their sanctity was not the result of behavioral refinement—it was the manifestation of a nature deified.

St. Symeon the New Theologian is explicit: true Christian life is participation in divine light, not simply adherence to law. He insists that the saint is one who "sees the divine light with the eyes of the soul," not metaphorically but mystically. "Those who have been baptized in truth," he writes, "have received the fire of the Spirit, and this fire illumines them from within." This is not private ecstasy—it is the norm of life in Christ. Those who are in Him become by grace what He is by nature.

St. Seraphim of Sarov affirms this when he declares: "Acquire the Spirit of Peace, and thousands around you will be saved." His life, marked by radiant gentleness and miraculous insight, bore witness to the reality that union with God is not confined to heaven but begins in the present. When asked why his face shone like the sun, he responded, "I am filled with the joy of the Holy Spirit." Justification, for Seraphim, was not a doctrine—it was luminosity. He was no moralist. He was a burning bush.

The saints, then, confront both moralism and legalism with their very existence. They do not fit into these categories because they have transcended them. They do not simply do what is right—they become what is divine. Their freedom is not autonomous but relational. Their obedience is not submission to external law, but inner harmony with divine love. Their holiness is not the triumph of effort, but the overflow of grace.

The Church honors saints not to elevate them as untouchable paragons, but to show what every Christian is called to become. The liturgical calendar, the iconostasis, and the troparia are not nostalgic ornaments—they are testimonies to the future made present. When we gaze at the icon of a saint, we do not merely see their history—we see our destiny. The transfigured saint is the unveiled prophecy of human nature fulfilled.

Their witness also provides the clearest criterion for theological truth. Any gospel that cannot produce saints is not the Gospel of Jesus Christ. The measure of a doctrine is not its elegance but its capacity to sanctify. "By their fruits you shall know them," said the Lord (Matt 7:16). If a theology leads to fear, pride, or despair, it is false. If it leads to love, humility, and radiant joy, it bears the marks of the Spirit.

Thus, the saints are the Church's answer to every distortion of salvation. Against legalism, they manifest intimate union. Against moralism, they reveal grace-driven transformation. Against rationalism, they shine with mystery. Against secularism, they walk in resurrection. They are not artifacts of a bygone age—they are icons of the age to come. They are the theological proof that theosis is not poetry, but reality.

In the saints, we see the Church's dogma incarnate. They are the logos of doctrine made visible. Their silence often speaks louder than sermons, their tears more eloquent than treatises. They show us that salvation is not information—it is fire. They do not merely affirm truths—they become truth, because they are one with Him who is the Truth.

Therefore, if one wishes to understand justification, sanctification, and deification, one must look not first to books, but to saints. The saint is the final argument of Christianity. He is the vindication of dogma in living form. He is what Christ looks like when He is lived, not just believed.

Indeed, the saints do not merely follow Christ—they are assimilated into Him. St. Paul's cry, "It is no longer I who live, but Christ who lives in me" (Gal 2:20), is not the privilege of the apostle alone. It is the measure of every life transformed by grace. Their lives no longer belong to them. They have been swallowed into the mystery of divine life. They have become "partakers of the divine nature" (2 Pet 1:4) in actuality, not metaphor. And this is not spiritual elitism—it is normative Christianity.

St. Gregory Palamas emphasizes that the saints are radiant not because they have earned merit, but because they have opened themselves to the uncreated energies of God. This divine light is not a created symbol—it is God Himself in His activity. The saints do not simply contemplate this light—they shine with it. Palamas writes, "They have become light, not by nature but by participation… they are truly gods by grace." In this framework, theosis is not a reward for good conduct, but the organic outgrowth of union.

Their relics exude myrrh, their words pierce consciences, their memory alters lives. Why? Because they are vessels of the One who alone is holy. In the saints, we touch the eschaton. The boundary between heaven and earth becomes porous. Miracles cluster around them not as spectacle but as a natural overflow of sanctity. And even in death, their bodies—sometimes incorrupt, sometimes fragrant—testify to the resurrection breaking into time.

The witness of the saints also carries immense pastoral relevance. In an age of confusion and contradiction, they offer clarity. In a culture of despair, they radiate joy. In a Church tempted to reduce sanctity to policy or performance, they show us that holiness is not managed—it is unleashed. Their lives cry out, not for compromise, but for burning love. And they demand from us not admiration, but imitation.

For this reason, the saints are not merely devotional accessories—they are ecclesiological foundations. The Church is not a club for the morally improving; it is the body of those being transfigured. The goal of Christian life is not respectability but radiance. The saints show us what this looks like, not as theory but as flesh and blood. And in beholding them, we remember who we are. Or rather, who we are meant to become. For they are the ultimate commentary on the Gospel. They are what man looks like when grace is allowed to complete its work. They are what it means to be justified—not merely forgiven, but glorified.

Legalism is not simply a misreading of Scripture—it is a misdiagnosis of the human condition. It takes the wound of fallen man and prescribes a bandage of behavior. It mistakes the disease of ontological estrangement for a mere lapse in moral effort. In doing so, it reduces the Gospel to a transaction, salvation to acquittal, and God to a distant judge whose approval must be earned. The tragedy of legalism lies not only in its theological distortion, but in the existential toll it inflicts on the soul: shame masked as humility, fear mistaken for reverence, despair hidden behind piety.

In the legalistic framework, the Christian life becomes a courtroom drama. God is cast as judge, man as defendant, Christ as substitute, and the moral law as the standard of divine justice. While there is truth in the juridical metaphor—Scripture itself uses such language—it becomes tragic when abstracted from the broader mystery of divine communion. For in this model, salvation is no longer about becoming one with God; it is about escaping punishment. Theosis is eclipsed by appeasement.

This has profound anthropological consequences. The person no longer sees himself as a son called to grow in divine likeness, but as a criminal perpetually on parole. The spiritual life devolves into anxiety: Have I done enough? Have I confessed well enough? Have I prayed enough? Grace becomes not divine power transforming the soul, but a loophole in the divine courtroom. Christ is no longer the Bridegroom of the soul, but the scapegoat of man's guilt. And God, far from being "Abba," becomes a cosmic auditor.

This mindset breeds several distortions: scrupulosity in the sensitive, pride in the disciplined, despair in the weary. It turns the commandments into burdens rather than invitations. It weaponizes theology into a tool of self-measurement rather than self-offering. The result is a Christianity without joy, without intimacy, without light. A Christianity that no longer resembles Christ.

St. Gregory the Theologian warns against this in his *Orations*, reminding his hearers that "It is not the Law that saves, but Grace—not the letter, but the Spirit." St. Isaac the Syrian likewise rebukes the legal spirit: "Do not call God just, for His justice is not as man's... If God rewarded the righteous as they deserve, paradise would be empty." The Fathers understood that justice and mercy are not opposites in God—they are identical, because both flow from divine love. Legalism splits them apart. It cannot see that the judgment of God is His mercy revealed in truth.

The pastoral consequences are severe. Legalistic preaching produces anxious Christians. Moralistic exhortation breeds performative faith. Over time, such souls either burn out or become hardened. Some give up entirely, convinced they will never measure up. Others grow cold, trading love for law, tenderness for technique. The sacramental life becomes mechanical. The Scriptures, once living and active, are reduced to rules. And the Gospel, the "power of God unto salvation" (Rom 1:16), becomes a burden too heavy to bear.

Yet into this darkness, the voice of Christ still speaks: "Come to me, all who labor and are heavy laden, and I will give you rest" (Matt 11:28). This is not rest from effort, but rest from striving to earn what can only be received. It is the rest of sonship, the peace of those who know they are loved not for what they do, but because they are His. The tragedy of legalism is that it deafens the soul to this voice. The call to divine union is not erased—it is drowned out by the clamor of performance.

To recover the truth of the Gospel, we must return to its Trinitarian center. For salvation to be theosis, it must be Trinitarian. The Father is not a distant lawgiver, but the origin and goal of all things, who calls His children back into His bosom. The Son, as the eternal Image, descends to restore the image in man by assuming it in Himself. And the Spirit, proceeding from the Father and resting upon the Son, is poured into the hearts of the redeemed—not merely to guide, but to divinize. As St. Basil the Great writes, "Through the Spirit we become partakers of God" (*On the Holy Spirit*, 9.23). Theosis, then, is not union with a divine essence in the abstract, but entry into the mutual indwelling life of the Three. This is why St. Gregory Nazianzus could say, "The goal of the Spirit is the Son, and the goal of the Son is the Father," for it is into this eternal movement of love that man is drawn.

God is not primarily Creator or Judge—He is Father. The Son does not come to fulfill legal obligations, but to restore filial union. The Spirit is not an administrator of divine decrees, but the Giver of life and communion. The Christian life is not about passing a test, but entering into a mystery. Salvation is not forensic; it is nuptial. It is not a verdict declared—it is a marriage consummated.

This is why the Eastern Fathers speak of deification as the goal of human life. For them, grace is not a created aid, but uncreated participation in divine energy. Justification is not external acquittal, but inner illumination. And obedience is not legal compliance, but harmonious synergy with divine love. The human person is not a subject in a courtroom, but a son in a house, a bride in a chamber, a temple being filled with glory.

The call, then, is not merely to reject legalism as an error—but to weep for what it has stolen. It has replaced communion with calculation. It has turned the luminous face of Christ into the cold mask of abstraction. But the Gospel still burns with light. The invitation remains: to become one with the One who made us. To return to the likeness that was lost. To ascend, not by merit, but by mercy.

As St. Gregory of Nyssa writes, "The goal of a virtuous life is to become like God." Not to satisfy a law, but to enter into love. This is the Gospel: not that God tolerates us, but that He desires us. Not that He relieves our guilt, but that He shares His glory. Not that He justifies us from afar, but that He makes His home within us.

This is the path we now begin to rediscover. For if moralism has diminished the grandeur of salvation to a system of merit and shame, and if legalism has obscured the light of divine intimacy beneath the shadow of obligation, then Christ comes not simply to pardon—but to restore. Theosis is not poetic exaggeration. It is the very grammar of salvation.

Man was made not to be acquitted, but to be transfigured. He was not created for compliance, but for communion. And this communion is made possible only in the One who is both the eternal Image and the merciful Restorer: Jesus Christ. In Him, the veil is torn, the distance abolished, and the divine life once more opened to man. For salvation, in its truest sense, is not transaction—it is union.

Salvation as Union, not Transaction

Too often, the question of salvation is framed in terms of rescue from punishment—God as judge, man as criminal, Christ as substitute. This conception, while containing partial truths, rests upon a juridical metaphor that has over time hardened into a reduction. Salvation becomes a contract ratified by faith, a transactional acquittal wherein God's justice is satisfied and the soul escapes eternal penalty. Yet the Church Fathers never spoke in such terms. For them, salvation was not an external pardon granted by a distant deity but the inward transformation of man through union with the living God. The Gospel is not a divine loophole—it is the healing of the chasm that sin had opened between Creator and creature. It is not courtroom procedure, but nuptial mystery; not a ledger wiped clean, but a heart made new.

This misunderstanding is not merely academic—it is existential. If salvation is imagined as a legal arrangement, then Christ is cast primarily as a mediator of wrath, and the Christian life becomes the maintenance of good standing. But if salvation is union, then Christ is the Bridegroom who draws the soul into communion, and the Christian life becomes the unfolding of that union in love. St. Gregory of Nazianzus captured this vision with luminous brevity: "It was not by compulsion, but by persuasion, that God saved us. He did not use violence, but love." The saving work of Christ is not an act of coercive justice but a divine wooing, an invitation to return to the intimacy for which man was created.

To reframe salvation as union is to return to the very language of Scripture. When Christ lifts His eyes to the Father on the night of His

Passion and prays, "that they may be one, even as we are one... I in them and Thou in me, that they may become perfectly one" (John 17:21–23), He is not describing mere reconciliation. He is describing participation—indwelling—oneness that reflects the eternal life of the Trinity. The Apostle Peter echoes the same in his epistle: we are made "partakers of the divine nature" (2 Peter 1:4). Paul speaks not of external membership but of mystical incorporation: "It is no longer I who live, but Christ who lives in me" (Gal 2:20). And again: "He who is joined to the Lord becomes one spirit with Him" (1 Cor 6:17). These are not metaphors. They are theological descriptions of a mystery that transcends the categories of contract and debt.

The early Fathers saw clearly that this union was not a reward but the goal. St. Athanasius declared that "the Son of God became man so that we might become god"—not in essence, but by grace; not by nature, but by adoption and participation. For Athanasius and those who followed, the Incarnation was not a stepping stone to crucifixion, but the very beginning of man's elevation. God does not merely rescue man from wrath; He unites Himself to man in order to draw him into the divine life. To be saved, then, is not simply to be forgiven—it is to be grafted into the very body of the Son, to be drawn up into communion with the Father, through the Spirit.

This understanding demands a shift—not only in soteriology, but in the very way we approach the Christian mystery. No longer is the Gospel a divine transaction executed for the benefit of an otherwise passive soul. It is the story of a Lover descending into the depths of His beloved's ruin in order to lift her into His own glory. It is the drama of divine-human union, enacted not in legal courts, but in womb and manger, in Jordan and Tabor, in chalice and tomb. The whole arc of salvation bends toward communion.

This communion is not an abstract ideal but a concrete reality enacted through the very life of Christ and perpetuated through the sacramental life of the Church. In the Eucharist, the believer does not merely remember Christ—he receives Him. The chalice is not a symbol of reconciliation—it is the vessel of divine life. "He who eats My flesh and drinks My blood abides in Me, and I in him" (John 6:56). Here, union is not inferred, it is enacted. The Incarnate Word, who once tabernacled among men, now dwells within them, not as a metaphor but as an ontological reality. St. Cyril of Alexandria writes, "He mingles Himself with us, as if to transform us into Himself." The Eucharistic mystery is thus not an addendum to salvation—it is its sacramental enactment. In this holy exchange, the believer does not merely receive grace—he is joined to the very body of the Crucified and Risen Lord.

Nor is this union confined to isolated sacramental moments. It is the entire orientation of the Christian life. Baptism is not merely a rite of initiation, but the mystical death and rebirth into Christ: "Do you not know that all of us who were baptized into Christ Jesus were baptized into His death?" (Rom 6:3). Confirmation seals this life with the Spirit, who does not hover externally but indwells, animates, and transforms. Confession restores this union when it is wounded, not through juridical absolution alone but through the healing power of repentance, in which the soul is re-knit to its source. And the ascetical life—prayer, fasting, almsgiving—is not spiritual self-discipline for its own sake, but the path of deeper assimilation to Christ. As St. Maximus the Confessor teaches, "The Word of God, by becoming man, enabled man to become god by grace. The practice of the virtues leads to union with Him."

In this light, every movement of the Christian journey is participation in the life of the Trinity. The believer is not a client of divine justice, but a living member of Christ's body, being conformed—through suffering, virtue, and sacrament—into His very likeness. Theosis is not the destiny of a spiritual elite; it is the call addressed to all who have been baptized into Christ. And this call, far from being a future hope only, is a present reality. As St. Paul writes, "We all, with unveiled face, beholding the glory of the Lord, are being transformed into the same image from glory to glory" (2 Cor 3:18). This transformation is the signature of true salvation—not mere pardon, but participation; not a moral upgrade, but mystical union.

Yet such language can sound foreign to ears trained in contractual religion. The modern Christian, formed more by forensic categories than mystical vision, may struggle to see salvation as anything more than a debt paid. But the tradition of the Church, East and West, has always contained deeper currents. The Catechism of the Catholic Church affirms this without hesitation: "The Word became flesh to make us partakers of the divine nature" (§460). This is not metaphor—it is magisterial. Pope St. Leo the Great preached it boldly: "Christian, recognize your dignity... You have been made a partaker in the divine nature." Vatican II echoed the same: "The human person... is called to communion with God... this invitation to converse with God is addressed to man as soon as he comes into being" (*Gaudium et Spes* §19).

Therefore, the Catechism teaches not merely that we are pardoned, but that we are brought into divine intimacy: "Grace is a participation in the life of God" and "introduces us into the intimacy of Trinitarian life" (CCC §1997). *Lumen Gentium* declares that the faithful, "united with Christ and anointed by the Holy Spirit, are consecrated into a spiritual house and a holy priesthood" (§10), not by external status, but by inner transformation. And Pope Benedict XVI, echoing the Fathers, affirmed that "being in communion with God is the fulfillment of every human desire" (*Spe Salvi*, §12). In this light, theosis is not theological ornament—it is the revealed structure of salvation, upheld from Scripture through the Fathers, and enshrined in the Magisterium itself.

This is the beating heart of the Gospel—not a contract to be signed, but a mystery to be entered. The prodigal does not return to find a courtroom, but a feast. The lost sheep is not scolded, but carried home. The Father does not negotiate—He embraces. For union, not transaction, is the final word of salvation.

But how is this union made possible? How does the soul, darkened by sin and subject to death, come to share in the very life of God? It is here that we must turn to the mystery of the Cross—not as a juridical payment to divine wrath, but as the supreme act of restorative love, the reconstitution of fallen humanity in the person of Christ. The tradition does not deny that sin ruptures justice, nor that Christ satisfies what man could not repay. But it insists that the satisfaction is not forensic—it is filial. Christ does not offer a substitute punishment to placate divine anger; He offers Himself as the New Adam, reuniting mankind to God by becoming what we are and returning it, transfigured, to the Father.

St. Irenaeus describes this as *recapitulation* (*anakephalaiosis*): the Son gathers all things into Himself, retracing the steps of Adam in obedience and healing what was broken at every level of human life. He does not merely *cover* sin—He undoes it. He does not stand apart from humanity as a scapegoat—He enters into the depths of our condition to elevate it from within. "What was not assumed was not healed," says St. Gregory Nazianzus, and so Christ assumes the totality of fallen human nature—yet without sin—to heal it at its roots. The Cross, then, is not the point at which God's justice overwhelms His mercy, but the moment where mercy becomes justice: God gives man what he does not deserve—Himself.

The Fathers did not interpret Christ's death in legal isolation from His life or His resurrection. Rather, the Paschal Mystery was always one integrated act of divine-human reconciliation. St. Athanasius speaks of Christ entering into death not as a victim, but as a conqueror: "By offering His body to death in place of all, He destroyed death for all." This victory is not abstract—it is ontological. In dying, Christ does not merely endure suffering; He swallows death itself. He takes the curse into Himself—not to appease a wrathful Father, but to drain the poison at its source. He allows sin to exhaust itself upon Him, and in doing so, disarms it.

But the healing is not automatic. It must be entered into freely. The grace of union is offered—but it must be participated in. The Cross is not a commercial transaction completed behind the veil of divine mystery—it is a nuptial offering made in public, to which each soul is invited. In the words of St. Ambrose: "He suffered that He might conquer; He conquered that He might call; He calls that He might justify; He justifies that He might glorify." Atonement, therefore, is not a divine arrangement over our heads; it is a divine summons into the very heart of the Son's offering. Christ is not a shield who takes the blow in our place. He is the Bridegroom who draws us into Himself, so that His offering becomes ours. His cry—"Father, into Thy hands I commend My spirit"—becomes the cry of every soul joined to Him in the liturgy of redemption.

This is why the Apostle Paul never speaks of the Cross without speaking also of incorporation: "We have been united with Him in a death like His… we shall certainly be united with Him in a resurrection like His" (Rom 6:5). The Cross is not where Christ suffers *instead* of us—it is where He suffers *with* us and *in* us, that we might rise with Him. The sacraments are the means by which this union is effected: baptism plunges us into His death; the Eucharist feeds us with His risen life; penance rebinds us to His wounds; confirmation seals us in His Spirit. Atonement, in this light, is not merely satisfaction—it is sanctification.

And here, the ancient liturgy provides language more potent than any legal metaphor. When the celebrant lifts the chalice and prays, "This is My Blood… poured out for you and for many for the forgiveness of sins," it is not a symbolic statement of debt-payment. It is the mystical proclamation that the New Covenant has been written not on stone but in blood—that man is not merely absolved but united. Christ's death is not the end of a sentence; it is the beginning of a marriage. The altar is not a courtroom—it is the bridal chamber.

This bridal imagery is not poetic flourish—it is biblical theology. St. Paul writes that "Christ loved the Church and gave Himself up for her… that He might present her to Himself in splendor" (Eph 5:25–27). The Cross is not simply the site of substitution—it is the wedding of God and man, where the Bridegroom offers His very body and blood to the Bride. The early Fathers understood this mystery with bold intimacy. St. John Chrysostom preached that "the Cross is the marriage bed of the King," and St. Ambrose declared, "He gave Himself, not merely His riches, to His Bride." The Eucharist, then, is the nuptial banquet, where the covenant is not just remembered but consumed. The soul does not approach a courtroom for pardon—it is drawn into the embrace of the Bridegroom, whose body is broken not to appease, but to unite.

St. Maximus the Confessor writes that Christ, by His Passion, "transformed the whole of human nature into Himself, making it wholly divine by grace." This is not imagery. It is metaphysics. It is the core of Christian soteriology: that God did not save us from a distance. He entered our dust, bore our wounds, endured our death—and in doing so, opened the path to our deification. He restores not just what was lost, but grants what was never possessed: full communion with the triune life of God.

This, then, is the mystery of the Atonement—not a transaction, but a transformation. Not an exchange of penalties, but an exchange of persons. He takes what is ours, and gives what is His. He dies our death, that we may live His life. And in that exchange, salvation is no longer a verdict rendered—but a mystery entered, a life begun, a union fulfilled.

This is why the Church Fathers did not speak of salvation as an external declaration or juridical pardon, but as participation in divine life—an ontological transformation made possible through the Incarnation. St. Athanasius of Alexandria, writing in the fourth century and standing as one of the most influential theological voices of the early Church, famously articulated this mystery in his treatise *On the Incarnation*: "God became man so that man might become god." This is not rhetorical flourish. It is the heart of patristic soteriology. For Athanasius, the Incarnation was not merely a precursor to penal substitution or a prelude to crucifixion—it was the very beginning of man's elevation, the first movement of theosis. In uniting human nature to Himself, the Logos began restoring what sin had fractured: the capacity of man to be in communion with God, to be filled with divine life.

This logic of participation is echoed in the thought of St. Irenaeus of Lyons, writing more than a century earlier. Irenaeus saw the entirety of Christ's work as a "recapitulation" (*anakephalaiosis*), in which the Son gathers up all things into Himself in order to heal, reorder, and glorify them. The Fall, in Irenaeus's vision, was not primarily a legal offense but a rupture in communion—a distortion of man's orientation toward God. Thus, salvation required not a juridical settlement, but a cosmic reordering. Christ re-enacts and reverses Adam's disobedience at every stage of human life: "He became what we are, that He might bring us to be even what He is Himself" (*Against Heresies*, V. Preface). The goal was never mere pardon, but restoration—restoration to union, to divine intimacy, to the likeness of God.

St. Cyril of Alexandria deepens this theme in his commentary on John's Gospel. For Cyril, the salvific work of Christ consists in making us "members of His body, of His flesh, and of His bones" (cf. Eph 5:30). Salvation is not the reception of a distant benefit—it is incorporation into the very Person of the Word. "He is in us through the Spirit," Cyril writes, "and we are in Him through our communion in the Holy Spirit" (*Commentary on John*, Book 11). Here the language is not legal but mystical; not transactional, but nuptial and organic. Salvation is not Christ doing something *for* us apart from us—it is Christ drawing us *into* Himself, that His life may become ours. The whole mystery of redemption, for Cyril, is Eucharistic and Trinitarian: God gives Himself to man so that man may dwell in God.

This patristic consensus was not a fringe speculation. It formed the living heart of the Church's understanding of Christ's mission. St. Gregory of Nazianzus writes, "What is not assumed is not healed." Therefore, "He assumes the whole man"—not merely to represent him juridically, but to transfigure him ontologically. Salvation is not Christ standing in for us like a legal proxy; it is Christ taking us into Himself, healing every part of our nature, and raising it to share in His own glory. As St. Basil the Great taught, "The Spirit joins us to God—not by mere similarity of will, but by a real participation in His very being" (*On the Holy Spirit*, 26.61). The very language of the Fathers presses beyond mere metaphor. They speak not of analogies, but of actual union—ontological participation, not symbolic reconciliation.

The Fathers were deeply sensitive to the difference between Creator and creature, and never confused essence with participation. Yet they were just as insistent that divine grace does not merely forgive—it transforms. Man is not merely declared righteous; he is made new, made luminous, made capable of bearing the divine. The great Cappadocian theologians—Basil, Gregory of Nazianzus, and Gregory of Nyssa—insisted again and again that salvation is nothing less than the reconstitution of man in the divine likeness, the restoration of the image marred by sin. Gregory of Nyssa, in his *Life of Moses*, casts the entire Christian journey as one of ascending into union: "The soul that looks to God is being changed into the same image from glory to glory, as by the Spirit of the Lord" (cf. 2 Cor 3:18). This ascent is not a reward—it is the telos. It is what salvation *is*.

To summarize the Fathers is to be confronted by a single unbroken intuition: that salvation is nothing less than the restoration of man to communion with God, and that this communion is effected not through external acquittal, but through internal participation. Christ does not remain outside the sinner, offering a legal solution from above. He enters into the very condition of man—uniting Himself to flesh, enduring death, rising in glory—that we might be raised with Him. As St. Maximus the Confessor would later write, "God made Himself man so that man might become God—not by nature, but by grace." This is not poetry. It is dogma. It is the beating heart of the Christian faith. Theosis is not a mystical add-on—it is the grammar of salvation itself.

This mystery of divine-human communion, so clearly articulated by the Fathers, is not an abstraction reserved for theologians, nor a future gift deferred until heaven. It is a present, embodied reality—lived and enacted within the sacramental life of the Church. The very structure of Christian worship, from the font to the chalice, is shaped by this vision of salvation. The sacraments are not external signs pointing to a legal pardon—they are the very means by which participation is made real, by which the believer is mystically joined to Christ and drawn into the divine life. In baptism, the old man is buried with Christ and raised in Him (Rom 6:3–4); the waters do not merely symbolize cleansing, but effect a real death and resurrection—a transformation that joins man to the Paschal mystery. In the Eucharist, the believer does not merely remember a sacrifice; he receives into himself the Body and Blood of the God-Man. He is fed with divinity, not metaphorically but mystically. As St. Cyril of Jerusalem proclaimed, "By partaking of the Body and Blood of Christ, we become Christ-bearers, his body and blood being distributed through our members."

The language of the liturgy itself testifies to this reality. The Church does not say, "This represents my body," but "This is my Body." Nor does she pray merely to be counted worthy of acquittal, but to be made worthy to partake of the divine mysteries "for the remission of sins and life everlasting." The sacraments are not symbolic tokens of a distant redemption—they are the very touchpoints of divine-human union. The altar is not a stage upon which a drama is re-enacted, but the place where heaven and earth converge, where the eternal enters time and the finite is drawn into the infinite.

Eastern liturgical theology makes this explicit. In the Divine Liturgy of St. John Chrysostom, the celebrant proclaims: "Thou it was who didst bring us from non-existence into being, and when we had fallen, didst raise us up again, and didst not cease to do all things until Thou hadst brought us up to heaven, and endowed us with Thy Kingdom to come." This is not a statement of legal exchange, but of ontological ascent—a narration of theosis in liturgical form. And when the faithful approach the chalice, they do not do so as criminals seeking reprieve, but as sons and daughters hungering for communion, praying, "Of Thy Mystical Supper, O Son of God, receive me today as a communicant."

This sacramental vision saturates the theology of the Fathers. For St. Irenaeus, the Eucharist is the pledge of resurrection, because it is the very Body of the risen Christ that we consume: "Our bodies, nourished by it, are no longer corruptible, but possess the hope of resurrection." For St. Gregory of Nyssa, baptism is the beginning of divinization, "the birth of the divine image within us." For St. Cyril of Alexandria, it is through the Eucharist that Christ "transforms us into His own likeness and makes us partakers of the divine nature." These are not devotional exaggerations. They are the consistent witness of the Church that salvation is union—and the sacraments are its means.

To lose this vision is to reduce Christianity to ritual and ethics. But in the liturgical and sacramental life, the mystical telos is preserved. The sacraments are not ends in themselves—they are the nuptial veils behind which Christ comes to the soul. They are the "earnest of the Spirit" (2 Cor 1:22), the divine pledge of what shall be, even as they already make present the glory to come. The Church is not merely a society of the forgiven—it is the temple of the transfigured, the Body of the deified, the living extension of Christ into the world. She does not merely point to theosis—she enacts it. Through her sacraments, Christ's Incarnation continues, not in idea but in flesh; not in theory, but in bread and wine, in water and oil, in voice and silence.

And in this enactment, every reductionist account of salvation collapses. The courtroom metaphor cannot hold here. For how shall one reduce to legal categories the mystery by which God places His own life within the soul, by which the finite is drawn up into the infinite, and the dust of the earth becomes the dwelling place of glory?

If the sacraments bear witness to the intimate and transformative union that is salvation, then any framework that reduces the Gospel to a transactional model must be found wanting—not because it is entirely false, but because it is tragically incomplete. The juridical metaphor, rooted in images of law courts, contracts, and debt satisfaction, has at times served a limited pedagogical purpose. But when elevated to the dominant or exclusive paradigm, it distorts the very character of divine love and obscures the mystical telos of human existence. It mistakes a means for the end and risks portraying God not as Father, but as creditor; not as Bridegroom, but as judge; not as the Lover of mankind, but as the custodian of an abstract justice.

Such frameworks—especially as developed in post-Reformation theology—tend to conceive of salvation as a legal transaction wherein Christ "pays" the penalty owed by sinners, satisfying divine wrath and allowing the Father to forgive without compromising His justice. Man's problem, under this view, is not alienation or corruption, but legal guilt; and the solution is not union, but acquittal. Faith, then, is reduced to assent to this transaction, and the sacraments become mere reminders or signs of a justification accomplished entirely outside the believer.

But this picture is deeply foreign to the mind of the early Church. The

Apostolic Fathers, the great bishops of the Councils, and the spiritual theologians of East and West all speak with one voice: the heart of salvation is participation, not substitution; communion, not contract. St. Irenaeus does not speak of Christ as satisfying divine wrath, but as recapitulating Adam, healing the human nature by assuming it. St. Athanasius does not describe the Cross in terms of forensic satisfaction, but as the climax of the Incarnate Word's work to deify man. For him, and for the tradition that followed, the problem of sin is not debt but death—not judicial guilt, but the ontological rupture of communion with God. The solution, therefore, is not penal substitution, but resurrectional union. Christ conquers sin not by absorbing its punishment, but by entering its domain and defeating it from within.

This is why the Fathers speak so often of the Cross not merely as sacrifice, but as victory—as healing, as illumination, as exaltation. St. Gregory of Nazianzus resists the idea of God demanding the blood of His Son in exchange for human acquittal: "To whom was the blood offered, and for what cause? If to the Father, then how? ... Was He not pleased by the sacrifice of His only Son, whom He would not receive without recompense? Away with such barbarity!" For Gregory and others, the death of Christ is not a divine transaction but a divine embrace—the descent of love into the depths of human ruin to transfigure it from within.

This is not to deny that there is judgment in the Christian life. But judgment in Scripture is not a forensic sentence delivered in a courtroom—it is the encounter with truth. Christ says in John's Gospel that "this is the judgment: the light has come into the world, and men loved darkness rather than light" (John 3:19). The judgment is the revelation of the heart before the light of God's presence. In the face of Christ, the soul is either drawn into glory or recoils in shame. But this encounter is ontological, not juridical. The judgment of God is the unveiling of reality, not the imposition of penalty.

The same applies to the doctrine of justification. When Paul speaks of being "justified by faith," he is not referring to a legal declaration enacted in heaven's court. He is referring to the realignment of the soul with God through trustful surrender—the opening of the heart to divine life. The Greek word *dikaiosyne*, often rendered "justification," does not denote merely forensic innocence, but righteousness as participation in divine order. Justification is not the imputation of alien merit; it is the infusion of divine grace that renders man righteous by transforming his being.

The early Church spoke not in the Latin idioms of contract and acquittal, but in the living language of participation. They used words like *koinōnia* (κοινωνία), meaning communion or shared life; *methexis* (μέθεξις), denoting a real share in being; *theōsis* (θέωσις), the transformation of man into god by grace; and *oikonomia* (οἰκονομία), the divine economy of salvation. These were not rhetorical flourishes but ontological claims. Salvation was never conceived as a divine accounting exercise, but as a metaphysical event—a real participation in the being and life of God. To be justified was not merely to be pronounced innocent—it was to be grafted into the divine mystery and conformed to the image of the Son.

The danger of the transactional paradigm is that it severs salvation from relationship. It isolates the Cross from the Incarnation, and the Atonement from theosis. It turns the drama of divine love into a mechanistic exchange—where Christ's role is to endure wrath so the Father may forgive, and man's role is to mentally assent to the terms of that arrangement. In this schema, the Gospel loses its nuptial character, and the Church loses her mystical identity. She becomes a distribution center for benefits already secured, rather than the living Body through which Christ continues to unite heaven and earth.

Modern Western soteriology has often fallen into this reduction—not because of malice, but through abstraction. The Reformation, reacting against late medieval distortions, sought assurance in the legal categories familiar to its age. But in doing so, it often exchanged the vibrant mystery of communion for a system of compensatory exchange. The tragic result is a conception of Christianity in which salvation is no longer the journey of the soul into divine life, but the recalculation of spiritual accounts. Grace becomes an accounting term, the sacraments become signs of reassurance, and holiness becomes optional. The infinite becomes contractual.

But the Gospel will not be contained in such frameworks. Its horizon is not legal pardon, but beatific participation. The Son did not become man to alter God's attitude toward humanity; He became man to unite humanity to God. The problem of sin is not that God is angry, but that man is dead. And the solution is not a satisfied wrath, but a resurrected life. The Cross is not a payment—it is a bridge. The Eucharist is not a symbol—it is union. The Church is not a courtroom—it is a temple. The Christian is not acquitted—he is deified.

And it is precisely this truth which leads us to the final affirmation: that the whole economy of salvation, from Incarnation to Cross to Resurrection, is not a series of disconnected interventions, but a single, continuous movement of divine love restoring communion. The answer to sin is not transaction—but participation.

If salvation is not transaction but union, not legal acquittal but ontological transformation, then the entire logic of redemption must be reinterpreted through the lens of participation. The Fathers did not merely add theosis as a poetic flourish atop a juridical scaffold; they began and ended with it. It was not the mystical fringe of Christian doctrine—it was the heart. The early Church did not ask, "What must we do to escape wrath?" but rather, "What must we become to enter glory?" The difference is not semantic. It is seismic. For the latter assumes that God's desire is not to balance books but to raise sons.

This is why the mystery of salvation was always spoken of in sacramental and nuptial terms, not contractual ones. The Church is the Bride, not the defendant; the altar is the marriage bed, not the bench of judgment; the Eucharist is the consummation of union, not a ceremonial receipt of pardon. In the baptismal font, man dies to the old Adam and is grafted into the Body of Christ—not symbolically, but really. In chrismation and confirmation, he is sealed with the Spirit—not as a badge of belonging, but as the indwelling fire of divine life. In the Eucharist, he consumes Christ not as a memorial, but as the real food of immortality. All of these are signs—but signs that *do what they signify*, because they arise from the incarnational logic of union, not the representational logic of transaction.

To recover the mystical core is to rediscover the ontological nature of grace. Grace is not divine favor abstractly applied; it is the very life of God infused into the soul. It is not a "thing" granted as a reward—it is God Himself given as Gift. As such, salvation is not a verdict rendered, but a transformation enacted. It is not external to the person—it is the rebirth of the person. The New Testament does not speak of Christians as merely "declared righteous," but as new creations (2 Cor 5:17), temples of the Holy Spirit (1 Cor 6:19), branches of the Vine (John 15:5), members of Christ's Body (1 Cor 12:27), sharers in the divine nature (2 Peter 1:4). These are not metaphors. They are ontological claims. They describe a reality more real than any forensic fiction.

It is here that the image of Christ as Vine becomes especially poignant. He does not stand outside the sinner offering acquittal—He draws the sinner into Himself. "Abide in me," He says, "and I in you." This is the mystery of salvation: not exchange, but incorporation; not appeasement, but indwelling. We are not merely declared forgiven—we are made one with Him. In becoming one with Him, we are drawn into the very life of the Trinity. For the Son is always in the bosom of the Father, and the Spirit always rests upon the Son. To be united to Christ is, therefore, to be brought into the eternal movement of divine love.

This union with Christ cannot be reduced to a Christocentric metaphor. It is, at its core, Trinitarian. The believer is not simply joined to the Son in isolation, but drawn into the very circulation of divine life, Word became flesh to make us partakers of the divine naturthe eternal exchange of love between Father, Son, and Spirit. As Christ abides in the bosom of the Father and is anointed by the Spirit, so too the Christian, through grace, enters this dynamic of divine indwelling. "We will come to him and make our home with him," says the Lord (John 14:23). St. Basil the Great teaches, "Through the Spirit we become conformed to the Son, who leads us to the Father" (*On the Holy Spirit*, 15.35). This is not poetic excess—it is the metaphysical reality of salvation. Grace is not a static possession; it is the indwelling presence of the triune God.

This is why the Church Fathers never spoke of salvation without speaking of transformation. For them, justification was never abstracted from sanctification. To be justified was to be made just—because the Just One now lived within. St. Augustine, wrestling with the Pauline language of justification, concluded that it must mean not a legal fiction, but a real infusion of righteousness. The soul, touched by grace, is changed—lifted, illumined, made luminous with the presence of God. St. Gregory of Nyssa describes this process not as a momentary event, but as an infinite ascent: the soul rising ever more deeply into God, forever growing in capacity, forever becoming more divine by participation.

This ascent is not reserved for the elite. It is the vocation of every Christian. It is what baptism begins, what Eucharist sustains, what prayer cultivates, what suffering purifies. Yet this transformation does not end in this life. Theosis stretches into eternity. As St. Gregory of Nyssa teaches, the soul ascends "from glory to glory," ever deepening in its capacity to receive God, yet never exhausting the Infinite. This is the mystery of *epektasis*—endless movement into the divine life. The Beatific Vision is not static contemplation but dynamic participation. "They shall see His face," says the Apocalypse (Rev 22:4), and this vision will not satisfy by completion but by continual inflaming. Heaven is not the cessation of desire—it is the perfection of desire in endless union. In this light, salvation is not simply rescue—it is glorification without limit. It is what the Church exists to enact. And it is what Christ came to make possible. To be saved, then, is not merely to be spared—it is to be reborn. Not merely to avoid hell—but to become heaven.

The mysticism of the Fathers is not a private spirituality—it is the air that the New Testament breathes. It is the logic of the Incarnation, the grammar of the sacraments, the soul of the liturgy, the horizon of eschatology. Without it, Christianity collapses into moralism, or sentimentality, or legalism—into all the things it was sent to overcome. The Gospel is not an instruction manual. It is an invitation into fire.

This fire is not destructive. It is purifying. It is the radiant love of the Trinity, poured out into creation, drawing all things back to the Source. And to enter into that fire—to be drawn into the perichoresis of divine life—is the end for which man was made. Theosis is not optional. It is not a theological addendum. It is the very reason Christ came. "I came," He said, "that they may have life, and have it abundantly" (John 10:10). That abundance is not material comfort. It is participation in God.

The Christian, then, is not a pardoned criminal standing acquitted in a divine courtroom—but an adopted son, a divinized image, a co-heir of the Kingdom drawn into the eternal Sonship of Christ. Salvation is not the end of guilt; it is the beginning of glory. The Cross is not merely the payment of a debt; it is the wedding of earth and heaven. In Christ, justice and mercy meet—not in the balancing of accounts, but in the communion of persons. He descends, not to satisfy a juridical calculus, but to bring man home. The sinner is not merely absolved; he is embraced, cleansed, illumined, and elevated. In Him, we are no longer merely creatures—we are temples of the Spirit, members of Christ's body, participants in the divine life.

Thus, we return to the mystery that has guided us from the beginning: that the end for which man was made is not mere forgiveness, but union. Theosis is not a mystical excess—it is the grammar of salvation itself. The Fathers speak with one voice: God became man that man might become god—not in essence, but by grace; not as rivals to divinity, but as sons restored to the Father through the Son, by the Spirit. This is no metaphor. It is the reality for which the Incarnation was undertaken, for which the Cross was endured, and for which the Church lives and prays. In this light, we are now prepared to examine more deeply how this mystery is made possible—how Christ, in His Passion, Death, and Resurrection, has opened once more the path of participation

Atonement and the Restoration of Participation

Too often, the word "atonement" conjures an image foreign to the patristic mind: a courtroom, a wrathful deity, and a penal transaction by which guilt is offset through the suffering of another. In this model, reconciliation between God and man is achieved not by the healing of man's nature, but by the satisfaction of a juridical demand. Yet such a notion is alien to the early Church, whose vocabulary of salvation was not forensic but filial, not contractual but ontological. Atonement (*at-one-ment*) is not a legal fiction but a metaphysical reality—the reintegration of fallen man into divine communion through the incarnate God-Man. For Athanasius, the Logos assumed humanity not to appease wrath, but to restore participation: "He became man that we might become god" (*On the Incarnation*, 54). The Cross is not the satisfaction of vengeance, but the marriage-bed of the Bridegroom and the Bride—the place where divine love descends into death and reclaims creation from estrangement. As St. Gregory the Theologian declares, "It was not demanded, but it was accepted… not because the Father required it, but because humanity needed it" (*Oration 45*, On Holy Pascha). In this light, atonement is not the appeasement of the Father, but the descent of the Son into our mortality to heal it from within. Sin exiled man from the Garden of participation; the Cross becomes the Tree of life planted anew in Golgotha's soil, by which the gates of Paradise are reopened. In the Christian East, the atonement is not the mechanism by which we escape punishment, but the mystery by which we are made partakers of the divine nature (2 Peter 1:4). It is not about God changing His mind toward man, but about man being recreated through union with God.

The conceptual drift of atonement from mystical union to juridical transaction constitutes one of the most consequential misdirections in the history of Christian theology. Whereas the early Fathers articulated salvation in terms of transformation, healing, and union with divine life, later Western developments increasingly reframed the redemptive act through the lens of legal obligation and forensic satisfaction. This reconfiguration, which took centuries to crystallize, marked a profound departure from the patristic vision of Christ as the divine Physician and Bridegroom, who enters into human nature to heal and unite it to Himself. In the shift toward a legal paradigm, the Cross is no longer primarily the nuptial bed of divine-human union, but a courtroom scaffold on which a penalty must be exacted and justice appeased. What had once been the mystery of communion became, in the emerging scholastic imagination, the fulfillment of juridical necessity.

This trajectory reached its systematic form in the theology of Anselm of Canterbury, whose *Cur Deus Homo* (c. 1098) stands as the pivotal moment in the rise of satisfaction theory. In a feudal world structured by honour, hierarchy, and debt, Anselm proposed that sin was not simply a wound or corruption of the soul, but an offence against the infinite dignity of God—one that created an immeasurable debt humanity could not repay. Divine mercy, in his schema, could not override divine justice without violating the rational order of the universe. Thus, only a God-man—fully divine to render infinite satisfaction, fully human to represent the guilty race—could repay the honour due. While Anselm sought to preserve the majesty of God's justice and the gravity of sin, he did so by introducing a transactional logic that was foreign to the ontological soteriology of the Fathers. Salvation became, in effect, a divine compensation rather than a divine assumption. Reconciliation was not the fruit of restored participation, but the legal resolution of debt.

Yet even within the Latin tradition, there were important correctives. Thomas Aquinas, while adopting Anselm's framework of satisfaction, reframed it in terms of merit, sacrifice, and charity. For him, Christ's Passion satisfied divine justice precisely because it was the supreme act of love, freely offered; its efficacy lay not in punishment, but in the superabundant charity of the God-Man (Summa Theologiae III, q.48). Likewise, the Council of Trent resisted purely forensic readings by insisting that justification is not imputed but infused — the sinner is interiorly renewed by sanctifying grace (Session VI, Decree on Justification). Later, Vatican II and the Catechism of the Catholic Church confirmed this participatory thrust, teaching that grace is nothing less than "a participation in the life of God" (CCC §1997). These developments show that even in the West, juridical imagery was never the whole story, and the ontological horizon of the Fathers endured within Catholic dogma.

Yet it is important to recognize that even in Anselm there remained residues of the older patristic vision. He explicitly denied that the Father demanded blood out of wrath, and instead framed Christ's death as a voluntary act of love offered to the Father. This nuance is often forgotten in later caricatures, but it demonstrates that the penal element was not yet fully entrenched. The decisive move toward a wrath-bearing Christ occurs later, especially in Reformation-era Protestantism.

This model was not merely a scholastic formulation—it reoriented the Western imagination. Sin became primarily guilt; justice became retribution; atonement became appeasement. The metaphysical vision of the Cappadocians and Athanasius—who saw salvation as the healing of human nature through the indwelling of the Logos—was displaced by the courtroom metaphor. Yet, significantly, even Anselm stopped short of portraying the Cross as an act of divine wrath. He rejected the idea that God required blood in order to forgive, and emphasized that Christ's offering was a free gift of love offered to the Father, not demanded by Him.

It was John Calvin, writing four centuries later, who radicalized the juridical logic into the fully penal model now commonly associated with Western atonement theory. Departing from Anselm's honour-based framework, Calvin framed atonement in terms of divine retribution. Humanity, standing condemned under the law, faced the full wrath of God. In order for the demands of justice to be satisfied, that wrath had to be executed—not withdrawn. Christ, then, became the sin-bearer, upon whom God's anger was poured out. "God, by transferring the guilt of the sinner to Him, punished Him for our offences," Calvin writes (*Institutes*, II.16.10). In this vision, Christ is not primarily the healer of our nature or the restorer of communion, but the substitute who absorbs the penalty due to us.

Here the soteriological imagination shifts decisively: no longer Christus Victor, Physician, or Bridegroom, but penal surrogate. The Reformation thus hardens into a double polarity foreign to the patristic synthesis: on the one hand, divine wrath requiring execution; on the other, an extrinsic imputation of righteousness rather than intrinsic transformation. The effect is a diminished anthropology and a truncated eschatology—man is acquitted, but not healed; forgiven, but not deified.

By attempting to defend divine justice, the penal framework in fact distorts the very unity of the Trinity and fractures the character of salvation. The Cross becomes a site of divine violence, not divine condescension; a place where justice is executed, not where love descends. The penal model reduces atonement to a transactional mechanism of debt transfer, in which guilt is imputed to Christ and righteousness imputed to the believer in an external legal exchange. But such a schema, while rhetorically powerful, is metaphysically hollow. It presupposes a model of salvation that bypasses the very healing of human nature which the Incarnation came to effect.

The consequences of this distortion are not only theological but existential. When salvation is imagined as a legal acquittal rather than a healing union, the Christian life easily collapses into scrupulosity, fear, and despair. The soul becomes anxious about satisfying a Judge, rather than confident in the embrace of a Father. Pastoral experience confirms what theology predicts: legalism breeds servile fear, pride in the strong, and paralysis in the weak. The patristic vision, by contrast, liberates man for filial boldness, for "perfect love casts out fear" (1 John 4:18).

This shift also risks collapsing the rich biblical typology into a narrow framework. The Exodus becomes not liberation into covenant but repayment of a debt; the Paschal Lamb becomes not the feast of deliverance but a victim appeasing wrath; the Temple becomes not the locus of divine presence but a slaughterhouse for divine anger. In short, the juridical model strips salvation of its sacramental depth, reimagining it as transaction rather than transfiguration.

This is not how the Fathers spoke of atonement. For them, the drama of redemption was not a legal fiction but a cosmic healing. Christ did not come to shield us from the wrath of the Father, but to unite us to the Father in Himself. The fundamental problem was not divine wrath but human death; not God's disposition, but our condition. "It was unworthy of the goodness of God that those created by Him should perish through the deceit of the devil," writes St. Athanasius (*On the Incarnation*, 6). The remedy, then, was not punishment but participation. The Logos assumed our mortal nature not to bear a sentence in our stead, but to penetrate our estrangement and transfigure it from within.

For the Fathers, the Cross was never a stage of retribution but the place of nuptial union, where death itself was wedded to life. The imagery of *Christus Victor* dominates the early liturgies and writings—not the appeased judge, but the triumphant King who descends into the realm of death and shatters its dominion. As St. Irenaeus proclaims, "The Lord has redeemed us through His own blood, giving His soul for our souls, and His flesh for our flesh" (*Against Heresies*, 5.1.1). Redemption, in this light, is not a balancing of accounts but the transfiguring assumption of our condition. It is Christ becoming what we are, that we might become what He is.

The early liturgical tradition confirms this: Byzantine Holy Week hymns extol Christ as the Bridegroom who comes at midnight, not the condemned criminal; as the physician who binds up wounds, not the scapegoat appeasing fury. The prayers of Basil and Chrysostom consistently frame the Passion as philanthrōpia—"the love for mankind" of God—rather than as satisfaction of a demand. The Church's worship itself is thus a hermeneutic: it interprets the Cross not in juridical terms, but in nuptial and therapeutic ones.

The Cross is thus the apex of the Incarnation, not its interruption. "That which He has not assumed, He has not healed," declares St. Gregory the Theologian (Epistle 101). The Cross is the moment in which Christ assumes the totality of human alienation, including death itself, and fills it with divine life. It is the nuptial act of the Bridegroom who weds Himself to fallen humanity—not to pay a debt, but to restore communion. As Maximus the Confessor affirms, "God and man are wholly interpenetrated in Christ, without confusion, division, or change" (*Ambigua*, 5.11). This union is not the aftermath of atonement—it is the very meaning of atonement. Here the Christological dogma of Chalcedon provides the indispensable foundation: in confessing Christ as one person in two natures "without confusion, change, division, or separation," the Council safeguarded the logic that underwrites all patristic soteriology. Only if the humanity of Christ is fully united to His divinity can human nature itself be healed, elevated, and restored. In other words, Chalcedon secures in doctrine what the Fathers proclaimed in doxology: what is not united is not saved.

Here Maximus offers a metaphysical key: the Passion is not external to the Incarnation, but its fullest extension. The same union of natures that defines Christ's person is enacted soteriologically in His suffering. Death itself, the ultimate separation, is drawn into hypostatic union and thereby disarmed. This is why Maximus can describe the Passion as a cosmic liturgy: creation itself is offered back to God through the obedient love of the incarnate Word.

To reduce the mystery of redemption to a forensic arrangement is to mistake metaphor for metaphysics—to exchange the symbolic vocabulary of guilt for the ontological reality of healing. In the Eastern tradition, this distortion was never canonized. The Byzantine liturgy exalts Christ not as the appeased victim, but as "the Physician of souls and bodies," "the Sun of righteousness," and "the Lover of mankind." Theosis is not the result of atonement; it is its consummation. Atonement, rightly understood, is not the appeasement of divine anger but the restoration of divine intimacy—the return of man to God through the humanity of Christ, and the return of God to man through His indwelling Spirit.

This is why the Fathers continually intertwine atonement with sacrament: Baptism is death and resurrection with Christ, Eucharist is participation in His flesh and blood, Chrismation is the seal of the Spirit's indwelling. Each sacrament is not a reminder of forgiveness but a real entry into restored participation. The atonement, therefore, is not a single event "behind us" but a living mystery we enter liturgically and existentially.

In contrast to the juridical metaphors that dominated later Western theology, the earliest Christian models of atonement were grounded in motifs of Christus Victor, recapitulation, and ontological healing. The Christus Victor framework, evident throughout the New Testament and universally attested in the pre-Scholastic Fathers, presents the Passion as Christ's decisive conquest over the dominion of sin, death, and the devil. St. Irenaeus, writing in the second century, declares: "The Lord has redeemed us through His own blood, giving His soul for our souls, and His flesh for our flesh, and has poured out the Spirit of the Father to bring about the union and communion of God and man" (*Against Heresies* 5.1.1). This is not a juridical substitution, but a mystical exchange—whereby the Word assumes the entirety of our condition, that He might overcome it from within and unite it to God.

Recapitulation (*anakephalaiōsis*), a doctrine most explicitly articulated by St. Irenaeus and later expanded by St. Athanasius and St. Maximus the Confessor, offers a sweeping vision of redemption. Christ, as the New Adam, "sums up" all things in Himself (Ephesians 1:10), reliving and reversing the history of Adam. Through His obedience, He undoes disobedience; through His death, He destroys death. This is not a substitutionary payment, but a participatory union: the Logos assumes the full arc of human existence in order to redeem it from within. "That which He has not assumed He has not healed," writes St. Gregory the Theologian (Epistle 101). The end is not satisfaction, but transformation—not appeasement of wrath, but the renewal of human nature in the life of God

The contrast between these two visions—the legal and the ontological—is not a superficial divergence of emphasis but a fundamental difference in theological ontology. The juridical model externalizes salvation: man is declared righteous without inward change. The ontological model, by contrast, understands atonement as the healing and transfiguration of man's being through union with the divine. In the forensic schema, the sinner is pardoned; in the participatory vision, he is recreated. The former offers legal acquittal; the latter, ontological renewal—"a new creation" (2 Corinthians 5:17).

Moreover, the juridical framework tends to obscure the nuptial, sacramental, and relational language that saturates both Scripture and liturgy. In the Byzantine tradition, the Cross is not presented as a legal scaffold, but as the bridal chamber of the Bridegroom and His beloved. Christ descends into death not to receive punishment, but to seek His bride. The Resurrection is the explosion of divine eros—the love that is stronger than death (cf. Song of Songs 8:6). As the Paschal Homily of St. John Chrysostom proclaims: "Christ is risen, and not one dead remains in the tomb."

To retrieve the true meaning of atonement, we must move beyond the cold calculus of debt and penalty and return to the burning mystery of divine-human communion. We must recover salvation not as courtroom verdict but as nuptial union; not as penal satisfaction but as ontological restoration. It is not justice that is transacted, but love that is poured out—not wrath that is appeased, but man who is deified. And to recover this vision, we must return to the Scriptures themselves—not through imposed lenses, but by entering their native theological lexicon, where terms like *katallassō*, *hilastērion*, and *koinōnia* speak not of legal mechanisms, but of restored presence, healing communion, and the participation of man in God.

The conceptual clarity of the Fathers finds its deepest consonance not in abstract speculation, but in the very words of Holy Scripture. The biblical language of redemption—far from lending itself to the juridical scaffolding later imposed upon it—speaks in tones of healing, reconciliation, and communion. To recover the true heart of atonement, one must enter the semantic structure of the New Testament, where key terms such as *katallassō* (καταλλάσσω), *hilastērion* (ἱλαστήριον), and *koinōnia* (κοινωνία) reveal not the cold machinery of legal compensation, but the warmth of restored intimacy and the mystery of participatory transformation.

St. Paul's vocabulary of reconciliation, particularly the term *katallassō*, offers the first key to this grammar of union. The Apostle writes in 2 Corinthians 5:18–19: "All this is from God, who through Christ reconciled us to Himself... that is, in Christ God was reconciling the world to Himself, not counting their trespasses against them." The use of *katallassō* and its noun form *katallagē* (reconciliation) presupposes not a legal imbalance but a broken relationship—estrangement that must be healed. Reconciliation in Paul's context is not a matter of legal adjustment but of restored communion. The emphasis is decisively on divine initiative: it is not we who appease God, but God who, in Christ, crosses the chasm to reconcile us. This directionality utterly reverses the penal substitution model. The Father is not the reconciled party, but the Reconciler. There is no trace of divine wrath needing satisfaction; rather, there is divine love overcoming estrangement.

Romans 5:10 further confirms this: "While we were enemies, we were reconciled to God by the death of His Son." The "enmity" is not God's hostility toward us, but our alienation from Him. The death of Christ is not a transaction that placates wrath, but the act by which the barriers of separation—sin, death, and corruption—are broken down. Here, the relational and ontological dimensions of reconciliation converge: we are not merely declared forgiven but are reoriented toward the One in whom life consists. Atonement, then, is the realignment of being, the reintegration of man into divine communion through the humanity of the Son.

The second pillar of the biblical lexicon—*hilastērion*—has often suffered from mistranslation and theological distortion. Found in Romans 3:25, "God put [Christ] forward as a *hilastērion* by His blood, to be received by faith," this term has been frequently rendered as "propitiation," thereby importing notions of appeasement into the text. But the Septuagint and the broader Second Temple Jewish context clarify its true meaning. *Hilastērion* refers specifically to the "mercy seat" (cf. Exodus 25:17–22; Leviticus 16:14–15)—the golden cover of the Ark of the Covenant, situated in the Holy of Holies, where the high priest would sprinkle the blood of atonement on Yom Kippur.

This context is decisive. The *hilastērion* was not a place of punishment but of presence. It was the site of divine indwelling, the meeting place of heaven and earth, where the glory-cloud of the Shekinah rested between the cherubim. To call Christ the *hilastērion* is to say that He has become the new Holy of Holies—the embodied locus of God's presence, the place where reconciliation occurs, not by penal discharge, but by sacramental union. The Cross, in this view, is not the instrument of divine wrath, but the liturgical fulfillment of the mercy seat. Christ's blood is not a payment—it is an offering of love, poured out to unveil the face of the Father and make possible the indwelling of the Spirit.

This theme of indwelling and union finds its culmination in the New Testament's repeated use of *koinōnia*—a term which transcends its usual rendering as "fellowship" and bears the weight of metaphysical participation. In 1 Corinthians 1:9, Paul declares that "God is faithful, by whom you were called into the *koinōnia* of His Son, Jesus Christ our Lord." This is no mere social belonging or institutional affiliation; it is a sharing in the very life of the Son. Likewise, in 2 Peter 1:4, believers are said to become "partakers [*koinōnoi*] of the divine nature"—a phrase which shatters the categories of legal religion and enters into the mystery of deification. The goal of Christ's atoning work is not that we would be excused, but that we would be transfigured—drawn into the life of God Himself.

It is in the Gospel of John, however, that the fullest expression of this participatory theology is unveiled. In the high priestly prayer of John 17, Christ reveals the ultimate purpose of His mission: "that they may all be one; even as You, Father, are in Me, and I in You, that they also may be in Us" (John 17:21). This is the language of indwelling mutuality, not judicial reconciliation. "The glory which You have given Me I have given to them," Christ says, "that they may be one, even as We are one: I in them and You in Me, that they may become perfectly one" (vv. 22–23). Here, salvation is nothing less than entry into the Trinitarian communion. Atonement is not the settling of accounts but the restoration of Trinitarian likeness—humanity caught up into the perichoresis of divine life.

The Johannine emphasis on indwelling love finds liturgical embodiment in the Eucharist, where Christ offers His flesh and blood not merely as a memorial, but as real participation. "He who eats My flesh and drinks My blood abides in Me, and I in him" (John 6:56). This is not metaphor, but ontology. The blood that was poured out on Calvary is the same blood that courses through the veins of the mystical body. The atonement is not simply something Christ accomplished; it is something into which we are drawn—sacramentally, existentially, and mystically.

Taken together, the biblical lexicon renders the penal paradigm both linguistically and theologically untenable. *Katallassō* speaks of relationship healed, not debt paid. *Hilastērion* speaks of divine presence revealed, not wrath diverted. *Koinōnia* speaks of participation in the divine, not legal status conferred. Scripture does not know a salvation external to the person of Christ; it knows only the in-breaking of divine life into the heart of fallen man. The Bible, when heard with the ears of the Fathers, proclaims not a courtroom verdict, but a nuptial call; not a divine ledger balanced, but a divine heart opened. The God who in the beginning said "Let us make man in our image" now says, through the pierced side of His Son, "Let him return to Me, that I may dwell in him, and he in Me."

This biblical language—rooted in participation, reconciliation, and indwelling—is not only consistent with but foundational to the patristic vision of atonement. For the Fathers, salvation was not the removal of a legal barrier, but the healing of a metaphysical wound; not the appeasement of an angry deity, but the reconstitution of a shattered image. Their theological grammar was never dominated by law, retribution, or forensic substitution. It was grounded in the Incarnation as the definitive act of ontological restoration—the descent of the Logos into the totality of our condition, not to endure wrath in our place, but to unite us to Himself, that we might be raised into His life. The Cross, in this schema, is not the satisfaction of justice, but the apex of assumption: the moment when death is swallowed up by the presence of Him who is Life.

St. Athanasius stands as the clearest witness to this ontology of atonement. Writing in the fourth century amidst the Arian crisis, Athanasius situates the redemptive work of Christ not in penal imagery but in the metaphysical decay of human nature caused by sin. "Man, who was made in the image and likeness of God, was disappearing," he writes. "The rational creature was being undone, and death reigned." The divine response to this dissolution is not judicial punishment, but merciful intervention: "It was unworthy of the goodness of God that those created by Him should perish... and it was supremely unfitting that the work of God in mankind should come to nothing" (*On the Incarnation*, 6). Thus, the Logos takes flesh—not to bear wrath, but to restore being. In Athanasius' soteriology, sin is not first an offense against God's honour, but a rupture in human ontology—a turning away from the Source of life, resulting in corruption, death, and decay. The remedy is participation in the incorruptible One: "The Word became flesh that He might make man capable of incorruptibility" (*On the Incarnation*, 44).

The famous phrase of Athanasius—"God became man that man might become god" (*De Incarnatione*, 54)—is not rhetorical flourish, but a summary of the entire patristic doctrine of atonement. Theosis is not a reward granted post-forgiveness; it is the very essence of salvation. The Incarnation is not a prelude to punishment—it is the actualization of reconciliation. The Son enters into our death so that we might enter into His life.

This is equally true in the theology of St. Irenaeus, whose doctrine of recapitulation (*anakephalaiōsis*) presents Christ not as a penal substitute, but as the One who retraces and heals every aspect of the human condition. "He came to save all by Himself becoming all," Irenaeus declares, "summing up in Himself the long history of humanity and furnishing us, in a brief, comprehensive manner, with salvation" (*Against Heresies*, 3.18.1). Through His obedience, Christ undoes the disobedience of Adam; through His birth, life, death, and resurrection, He restores each stage of human life to its original vocation. The Fall is not juridical guilt inherited but the distortion of human orientation; the Cross, therefore, is not penal satisfaction but the final act in the divine recapitulation of human nature. In Irenaeus, as in all the Fathers, the focus is not what Christ suffers in our place, but what He accomplishes *in us and for us by assuming us*.

The same vision animates the soteriology of St. Gregory the Theologian, particularly in his famous *Oration 45* on Holy Pascha. There, Gregory confronts and rejects the idea that the Father demands the death of the Son: "To whom was that blood offered that was shed for us, and why was it shed? If to the Evil One... then it is an outrage. If to the Father, then first, how? And secondly, why?" He declares clearly: "It was not demanded, but it was accepted. Not because the Father required it, but because man needed it." This is a profound rebuke to juridical logic. The Cross is not the price God demanded, but the gift God gave. In Gregory's vision, the Father is not reconciled through wrath, but reveals His love by permitting the Son to descend into our death and raise us through it.

It is Gregory who gives us the clearest articulation of the metaphysical logic of redemption: *"That which He has not assumed He has not healed."* These words, directed against the Apollinarians, establish the theological foundation for understanding atonement as ontological healing. The Incarnation is not a symbolic gesture; it is a real and total assumption of human nature—mind, soul, body, and even death itself. Only by entering the totality of our condition can Christ heal it from within. The Cross is not God turning away from the Son, but the Son descending into the lowest depths of the human condition, bearing it all in order to transfigure it all.

This same metaphysical logic is advanced with extraordinary precision by St. Maximus the Confessor, whose synthesis of patristic soteriology clarifies the nature of participation. For Maximus, salvation is the reconciliation of opposites: Creator and creature, time and eternity, death and life, united without confusion in the Person of Christ. The Passion is not punishment, but purification. It is not an act of violence required by justice, but of love offered in freedom. "The Word of God, becoming incarnate, reconciled all creation to Himself, restoring it to its natural motion toward God" (*Ambigua* 7). In Maximus, atonement is cosmic: Christ does not simply satisfy a moral requirement; He reconfigures the structure of being itself, bringing back into harmony what had become disordered.

Through the hypostatic union, the Son becomes the bridge between God and man—not a legal bridge spanning a chasm of guilt, but an ontological bridge uniting two natures in one Person. The Cross is the moment when this union is made complete by the descent of divine life into death. Christ dies not to satisfy the Father's wrath, but to bring life to the realm of death.

As Maximus teaches, "He did not die because death had power over Him, but to destroy death's power by His own death" (*Questions to Thalassius* 61).

In this entire patristic vision, the fundamental dynamic of salvation is union, not substitution; healing, not penal exchange. The Fathers knew nothing of a God who needed to be reconciled. Rather, they spoke of a God who in Christ reconciles the world to Himself (2 Cor 5:19). They knew nothing of a wrath that had to be quenched through punishment, but everything of a love that had to descend into corruption and lift it up. Atonement is not an event that happens *to* Christ on our behalf; it is an act that happens *in* Christ and through Christ, into which we are drawn, that we might become what He is.

Thus, the entire logic of patristic soteriology flows from this one principle: only what is united to God is saved. And Christ has united not just our legal guilt, but our entire nature, to Himself. The Cross is not the place where justice overcomes sin; it is where love overcomes death. It is not an execution—it is a marriage. In the words of the Byzantine liturgy, "The Bridegroom of the Church has stretched out His hands upon the Cross, that He might draw all to Himself." And in that drawing, He does not merely cleanse our record—He restores our being.

If the Incarnation initiates the healing of human nature by uniting it to the divine, then the Cross is the moment in which that healing is brought to its most radical depth—the point where the full extent of human estrangement is entered, embraced, and transfigured. It is not the beginning of divine wrath, but the fulfillment of divine love. The Cross is not the point at which the Father turns away from the Son, but the moment in which the Son, bearing all the weight of fallen existence, penetrates the final frontier of death and opens it from within. Here, the Logos does not merely suffer for humanity; He suffers *in* humanity and with humanity, so that death itself may be filled with divine presence. This is not penal substitution—it is ontological participation.

This truth is expressed in the liturgy and hymnography of the Christian East with profound clarity. The Cross is described not as a place of punishment, but as the Tree of Life re-planted in the world: "Today the Tree of Life blossoms with salvation for the world," proclaims the *Exapostilarion* of Holy Friday. The body of Christ becomes the new Paradise, and the Cross becomes the gate through which man re-enters divine communion. It is the axis mundi, the center of all things, because upon it the God-Man stretched out His arms to embrace all creation.

In this moment of total self-offering, Christ accomplishes not only a moral act of obedience, but a metaphysical reversal. The disorder introduced by Adam—his disobedience, pride, self-will, and separation from the divine life—is reversed through the total, free, and loving obedience of the New Adam. As St. Irenaeus writes, "Just as through a tree we were made debtors to God, so through a tree we receive the remission of that debt" (*Against Heresies*, 5.17.1). But the tree here is not an instrument of wrath—it is the sign of nuptial fidelity, the marriage bed upon which Christ unites Himself to fallen humanity in its most broken form.

This nuptial imagery, often overlooked in Western juridical models, lies at the very heart of the Church's mystical theology. The Cross is the moment of union between the Bridegroom and the Bride. In the Byzantine tradition, Christ is hymned during Holy Week as "the Bridegroom of the Church," and the Cross is depicted as the consummation of His spousal love. This is not mere metaphor, but metaphysics: the divine Word unites Himself to humanity with such totality that even death, the final consequence of sin, is embraced and overcome. "He who is lifted up on the Cross draws all things to Himself" (cf. John 12:32). The Cross, therefore, is not merely the site of suffering; it is the bridal chamber where human nature is rejoined to God in a bond stronger than death.

This theme is echoed by the Fathers. St. John Chrysostom, in his *Catechetical Homily* for Pascha, declares: "The Cross has become the Cross of light. The sting of death is broken. The gates of Hades are smashed. Christ is risen, and not one dead remains in the tomb." Chrysostom does not describe the Cross as the satisfaction of justice, but as the triumphant act of divine invasion into the realm of death. For him, the Passion is not retribution, but restoration; not wrath satisfied, but communion renewed. The image of Christ's body upon the Cross is not that of a condemned substitute, but of the true High Priest offering Himself as both victim and temple—a self-offering not demanded, but freely given in love.

St. Maximus the Confessor articulates this even more deeply in his cosmic soteriology. In his view, the Passion of Christ is the moment in which the created and uncreated are most intimately joined. "Through His suffering," Maximus writes, "He willingly accepts the division introduced by sin, and by His divine power reunites what had been separated" (*Ambigua* 5.11). The Cross is thus not only the forgiveness of sins, but the ontological healing of the human will—Christ, as the New Adam, conforms human will to the divine without coercion, restoring the natural harmony that was lost through the Fall. The obedience of Christ, then, is not simply moral compliance, but the transfiguration of the human mode of existence: from self-will and autonomy to the ecstatic self-giving proper to divine love.

This notion is grounded in the synergy of Christ's two wills, as affirmed at the Sixth Ecumenical Council (Constantinople III, 681 AD). Christ, in His humanity, freely offers Himself in obedience to the Father—not as one appeasing wrath, but as one restoring the proper orientation of human desire toward the divine. "Not My will, but Yours be done" (Luke 22:42) becomes the axis upon which all of fallen creation is redirected back toward God. His obedience is not a mere act of submission, but the recentering of the human will in divine love. It is through this obedience, unto death, that humanity is restored to its telos—not acquittal, but union.

Thus, the Cross is the axis of restored participation. It is the place where death is transfigured, where sin is consumed in divine mercy, and where man is re-ordered toward God. It is not a mechanical necessity in a system of justice, but the overflowing superabundance of divine compassion. In the words of St. Ephrem the Syrian: "Death killed the natural body, but itself was killed by the divine body. Death snatched up the body which it saw, but met God and fell" (*Hymns on the Resurrection*, 1.8). Atonement, therefore, is not merely about forgiveness—it is about the reconstitution of human nature through its union with the crucified and risen Christ.

Participation is restored because the Cross is not the end, but the beginning: it is the place where the mortal is touched by the immortal, and where the human is re-opened to the divine. The Bridegroom has lifted His Bride from the ashes of sin and carried her into the chamber of eternal life. What Adam shattered, Christ has restored—not by bypassing our nature, but by assuming it, enduring it, and exalting it.

If the Cross is the nuptial act that restores humanity's participation in divine life, then the Eucharist is the ongoing consummation of that union—the sacramental perpetuation of the atonement, not as juridical memory, but as mystical reality. In the logic of divine economy, Christ did not merely die once to accomplish a past reconciliation; He offers Himself perpetually to unite His Body, the Church, to Himself in a communion that transcends time. The Eucharist is thus not the memorial of a legal transaction, but the extension of the Incarnation and Passion into the present: a re-presentation, not a repetition, of the Paschal Mystery.

This distinction is vital. Atonement, in the biblical and patristic vision, is not a historical moment confined to Calvary, but a mystical event that unfolds within the Church through the sacramental life. The New Testament itself frames the sacrifice of Christ in liturgical terms. St. Paul writes: "Our paschal lamb, Christ, has been sacrificed. Let us therefore keep the feast" (1 Corinthians 5:7–8). The grammar of this passage is not judicial but liturgical. The Cross is the fulfillment of the Paschal typology—the Lamb slain not to absorb wrath, but to liberate from bondage and lead into covenantal communion.

This same logic animates the institution narrative of the Last Supper. "This is My body, which is given for you... This is My blood of the covenant, which is poured out for many for the forgiveness of sins" (Luke 22:19–20; Matthew 26:28). These words are not legal pronouncements but covenantal and Eucharistic. The language echoes Exodus 24:8—"Behold the blood of the covenant which the Lord has made with you"—linking the Passion not to penal substitution, but to the ratification of a new and eternal bond. Christ, as the true High Priest, offers Himself not to appease divine anger, but to inaugurate the New Covenant by joining His flesh to ours.

St. Cyril of Jerusalem expresses this sacramental logic with crystalline clarity: "Since Christ Himself has declared the bread to be His Body, who shall dare to doubt it? And since He has affirmed and said, 'This is My Blood,' who shall ever hesitate, saying that it is not His Blood?" (*Mystagogical Catecheses*, 4.1). The realism of this statement is not philosophical literalism, but theological conviction: the Eucharist is the means by which the atoning work of Christ becomes personal, participatory, and transformative. It is the sacrament not of substitution, but of union.

The Fathers consistently affirm this vision. St. Ignatius of Antioch, writing in the early second century, calls the Eucharist "the medicine of immortality, the antidote against death" (*Letter to the Ephesians*, 20). Such a description only makes sense within the context of a soteriology grounded in participation. If Christ's death is the destruction of death, then the Eucharist is the means by which that victory is communicated to the faithful. The Eucharist is not a ritualized reminder of a judicial act, but the very Body and Blood of the God-man, offered so that humanity may partake of divine life.

St. Irenaeus, too, emphasizes the transformational nature of this sacrament. In *Against Heresies* (5.2.3), he writes: "Our opinion is in accordance with the Eucharist, and the Eucharist confirms our opinion. For we offer to Him His own, announcing consistently the fellowship and union of the flesh and Spirit. For as the bread from the earth, receiving the invocation of God, is no longer common bread, but Eucharist… so also our bodies, receiving the Eucharist, are no longer corruptible, having the hope of resurrection." This is no mere symbolic meal—it is the sacramental interface of atonement. The same flesh that destroyed death on the Cross is now offered to the faithful as the seed of immortality.

St. John Chrysostom reinforces this theology in his *Homilies on the Gospel of Matthew*, noting that "we partake of the very same body that was nailed to the Cross." He does not isolate the Cross from the altar, nor the Passion from the Eucharist. For Chrysostom, the altar of the Church is the continuation of Golgotha—the place where Christ offers Himself, and where man is drawn into His life. "The offering is the same," he says, "He who then offered Himself is the same who now offers by the ministry of priests."

In this way, the Eucharist is not merely the result of atonement; it is the mode through which atonement is continually enacted and consummated. It is the liturgical manifestation of theosis—Christ entering into man, not by analogy or legal decree, but by literal, substantial, and sanctifying communion. The juridical model of salvation cannot account for this: it renders the Cross a completed external payment, and the Eucharist a commemorative rite. But in the patristic mind, the Eucharist is the Cross sacramentally unveiled—the Paschal Mystery extended into time, transforming the faithful into living members of Christ.

Herein lies the final contradiction to any atonement theory that views the Cross as an isolated act of penal exchange. For if the Eucharist is truly the Body and Blood of the crucified and risen Lord—offered that we may "abide in Him and He in us" (John 6:56)—then atonement must be understood as union. The gift of the Eucharist is not the legal benefit of a past death; it is the ongoing communion with the living Christ who, having destroyed death, now nourishes His Bride with His very self. Theosis is not a subsequent blessing—it *is* the atonement in its fullness. The goal of the Cross is not that man would be forgiven from afar, but that he would eat the flesh of the Son of Man and live forever.

Thus, the Eucharist reveals the true shape of redemption: not transaction, but transformation; not appeasement, but participation; not mere forgiveness, but union. The altar is not the shadow of the Cross, but its radiant fulfillment. And those who approach it do not receive a verdict—they receive a Person. The same Person who hung upon the Cross now gives Himself to be consumed, that in consuming, we may be consumed by Him.

The Cross, as the summit of divine self-offering, reaches its fulfillment not in the cessation of breath, but in the descent into the realm of the dead. The Passion does not terminate with the cry of "It is finished" (John

19:30), but continues into the unseen depths, where the victory of love is completed. For the early Church, the descent of Christ into Hades was not a theological appendix—it was the dramatic climax of redemption. Just as the Cross restores communion on earth, so too the descent into death reopens participation for the dead, ransoming those bound in the darkness of Sheol and orienting the entire cosmos back toward its Creator.

In Western theology, this doctrine has often been marginalized, treated as a doctrinal curiosity rather than a central pillar of soteriology. Yet in the Christian East, and in the earliest strata of the Church's liturgical and theological tradition, Christ's descent into Hades (*katabasis*) is inseparable from His victory. It is the moment when divine life enters death, not to be vanquished by it, but to dissolve its tyranny from within. In the language of St. Peter: "He went and preached to the spirits in prison" (1 Peter 3:19), and again, "the Gospel was preached even to the dead" (1 Peter 4:6). This is not metaphor. It is the cosmic dimension of atonement—the descent of the immortal into the place of dissolution, so that even those who died in darkness might be brought into light.

The patristic consensus is unwavering on this point. St. Ephrem the Syrian, in his *Hymns on the Resurrection*, speaks with lyrical power of Christ's triumph over death:

"Death slew [Christ] by means of the body which He had assumed; but that same body proved to be the weapon with which He conquered death. Concealed beneath the cloak of His manhood, His Godhead engaged death in combat. But in slaying our Lord, death itself was slain." (*Hymn I*, 8)

This paradox—death swallowed by life, corruption undone by incorruption—is at the heart of the harrowing of hell. Christ does not descend as a captive, but as a conqueror. He is not dragged into death; He enters it willingly, filling it with the light of His divinity. The icon of Holy Saturday depicts Him standing atop the shattered gates of Hades, grasping Adam and Eve by the wrists, pulling them from the tomb. This is not imagery—it is theology in color: the restoration of participation begins from the very foundations of the grave.

St. John Chrysostom, in his *Paschal Homily*, proclaims this victory with exultant finality:

"Let no one fear death, for the death of our Savior has set us free. He has destroyed it by enduring it... Hell took a body, and discovered God. It took earth, and encountered heaven. It took what it saw, and was overcome by what it did not see... Christ is risen, and the tomb is emptied of its dead."

This is not rhetoric—it is dogma. The atonement is not exhausted by the Cross; it is unveiled in the descent. There, in the silence of the tomb and the darkness of Hades, the Word of God speaks once more: not to condemn, but to summon forth life from death. Participation is restored from below. Christ does not merely open the heavens—He opens the grave.

The theological implications of this descent are profound. If the Cross is the healing of man in history, then the descent into Hades is the healing of man in death. The Incarnation reaches its extremity here: not only does the Logos assume our life and suffering, He assumes our death—entering it not as a victim, but as the One who cannot be held. Death, which entered through Adam (Romans 5:12), is now expelled by the New Adam. St. Gregory of Nyssa writes, "As the darkness vanishes when light appears, so death, where the Life appears, is swallowed up and disappears" (*Great Catechism*, 32).

Moreover, the descent into hell affirms the ontological solidarity of Christ with all of humanity—even those who lived and died before the Cross. In descending to the dead, Christ embraces all time and all history. The harrowing of hell is the universal dimension of atonement: no one is excluded from His reach. The descent is not an aside—it is the revelation of divine love without remainder. "For as in Adam all die, so in Christ shall all be made alive" (1 Corinthians 15:22). This is no abstraction. It is a historical, cosmic, and personal act: Christ goes to where man is most forsaken and most powerless, and from there, He raises him up.

The liturgy echoes this mystery with profound theological density. On Holy Saturday, the Church sings: "Today Hades groans and cries aloud: 'It had been better for me had I not received the One born of Mary; for when He came upon me, He broke my dominion, and the souls I had held captive He set free.'" The tomb becomes the bridal chamber, and death becomes the threshold of resurrection. Atonement, in this light, is not a mechanism of substitution—it is the movement of God into the depths of our estrangement, in order to make even those depths a place of communion.

Participation, then, is restored not only from above, but from below. The Son descends into the earth, not only to raise us with Him, but to ensure that there is no condition of human existence—no grief, no loss, no death—untouched by His redeeming presence. Christ is the One who fills all things (Ephesians 4:10), including the abyss. The atonement reaches its fullness when even the gates of Sheol are lifted, and the dead, who once dwelt in shadow, behold the light of His face.

In every movement of the divine economy—from the Incarnation to the Cross, from the tomb to the chalice, from the descent into Hades to the ascension into glory—the pattern is the same: not appeasement, but union; not transaction, but transformation. The God who once walked with man in the garden comes now to dwell in man through the humanity of Christ, healing the rupture that sin introduced and restoring the communion for which man was made. The question is no longer how divine wrath is satisfied, but how divine love overcomes every boundary that separates Creator and creature.

What was lost in Adam was not merely innocence, but intimacy. The image was not erased, but obscured; the likeness was not revoked, but veiled. Man, made for participation in the divine life, became turned inward, fractured, dying. Atonement, therefore, is not a legal solution to a moral problem, but a sacramental answer to an ontological crisis. It is the reconstitution of man through the union of his nature with the divine—first in the Person of Christ, then in the mystical Body of His Church, and finally in each soul that comes to abide in Him through the Spirit.

In this light, the Cross is no longer a scene of retribution, but the nuptial axis of a restored cosmos. It is where the Word-made-flesh binds Himself irrevocably to the human condition—even unto death—so that death itself might become a passage to life. The descent into Hades is not the defeat of the Son, but the extension of His love to the very limits of human forsakenness. And the Eucharist is not a memory of this victory, but its present realization—the communion by which those once estranged are now made partakers of the divine nature.

The fullness of the atonement, then, is theosis. It is not merely that man is forgiven, but that man is refashioned, refilled, reoriented toward his original destiny. Forgiveness is the threshold, but communion is the goal. As St. Maximus teaches, the Word became man "in order that man might become God by grace—not merely by sharing in divine blessings, but by actual participation in the very life of God Himself" (*Ambigua* 7). This is the true meaning of reconciliation: not the ceasing of hostility, but the indwelling of God in man and man in God.

Thus, the question of atonement is ultimately a question of love—not love as sentiment, but love as union. And the God who is love (1 John 4:8) has shown that love not by punishing another in our place, but by taking our place Himself, so that our place may become His. The distance is bridged, not by decree, but by descent. And the rift is healed, not by the weight of divine justice, but by the weightlessness of divine mercy—mercy that enters into estrangement, drinks its bitter cup, and transforms it into joy.

The path to participation is open once more. The veil is torn, the tomb is emptied, and the gates of Paradise swing wide. The atonement is not a divine transaction—it is a divine embrace. And in that embrace, man is not merely acquitted—he is made new.

3

What Is Theosis? A Historical and Dogmatic Overview

"The tradition of the Eastern Churches is clear: the purpose of human life is the divinization of the human being through the grace of the incarnate Word."
—Pope St. John Paul II, Orientale Lumen, §6

Defining Theosis: Participation vs. Transformation

The mystery of theosis—man's participation in the divine life—cannot be approached without first clarifying the foundational language through which the Church has historically spoken of this mystery. The early Christian tradition, rooted in both Scripture and Hellenistic intellectual culture, developed a precise theological vocabulary to articulate the transformation that takes place in the soul united to God. Among these terms, five stand at the center of the Church's conceptual grammar: *theosis* (θέωσις), *metamorphosis* (μεταμόρφωσις), *koinōnia* (κοινωνία), *methexis* (μέθεξις), and *homoiosis* (ὁμοίωσις). Each is distinct, yet all converge on a single vision: that man, created in the image of God, is called to ascend into full likeness through grace.

Theosis—literally "divinization" or "deification"—designates the end for which man was created: not to become God by nature, but to share in His life by grace. This concept is not an extrinsic theological speculation but the unifying goal of Christian anthropology, soteriology, and eschatology. St. Athanasius's celebrated formulation—"God became man that man might become god" (On the Incarnation, 54)—was not a poetic flourish but a theological axiom rooted in Scripture and universally affirmed by the early Fathers. It expresses the paradox of divine condescension: the Creator stoops into creation not merely to rescue it, but to elevate it into union with Himself. In 2 Peter 1:4, believers are said to "become partakers [κοινωνοί] of the divine nature," a verse that was treated by the patristic tradition not metaphorically, but ontologically. This *participation* (*koinōnia, methexis*) in God's very life is the essence of salvation, not its aftereffect.

Yet to speak of theosis without qualification is to risk misunderstanding. The Church has always guarded against pantheistic or monistic distortions by insisting upon the unbridgeable ontological divide between Creator and creature. Theosis is not an absorption of human essence into divine essence—*ousia* (οὐσία)—but a real participation in the divine life through grace, in a manner that preserves the distinction of natures. This distinction is vital, not as an abstract metaphysical safeguard, but because the integrity of both God's transcendence and man's creaturely identity depends upon it. As St. Basil the Great affirms, "We do not call ourselves gods by nature, but gods by participation" (On the Spirit, 9.23). In this framework, participation (*methexis*) does not collapse the divine into the human but renders the human luminous with divine glory. Here the Christological dogma of Chalcedon provides indispensable grounding: only because Christ is one person in two natures "without confusion, change, division, or separation" can human nature itself be united to divinity without being destroyed. As the Fathers summarized, "what is not united is not saved."

It is this participation which effects transformation. *Metamorphosis*, the Greek word translated as "transformation" or "transfiguration," is found in Romans 12:2 ("Be transformed by the renewal of your mind") and in 2 Corinthians 3:18, where Paul writes that "we all... are being transformed [μεταμορφούμεθα] into the same image from glory to glory." Yet even here, the transformation is not self-generated or merely moral. It is the visible fruit of participation. Man is changed because he is united; he becomes luminous because he stands in the light. As Gregory of Nyssa writes, "The goal of a virtuous life is to become like God" (*Life of Moses*, II.225)—but this *likeness* (*homoiosis*) is neither achieved through ethical striving alone, nor gifted as an external reward. It arises from communion.

Historically, the Western theological tradition struggled to retain this ontological vision of theosis. While certain Latin Fathers—such as St. Augustine, who spoke of *deificatio* in *City of God* (22.30)—maintained an awareness of man's end in God, the post-Scholastic West increasingly subordinated the mystery of theosis to categories of merit, imputation, and reward. The very idea of divinization was gradually displaced by a juridical framework that stressed justification as an external declaration rather than an ontological renewal. As a result, the original patristic synthesis—rooted in both biblical realism and Greek metaphysics—was eclipsed by a moralized and individualized soteriology. That said, it is important not to flatten the tradition: Augustine's *deificatio*, Bonaventure's affective theology, and even Aquinas's teaching on *participatio divinae naturae* (ST I–II q.112, a.1) all preserve elements of the participatory vision. In the twentieth century, ressourcement theologians such as Henri de Lubac explicitly retrieved this language, reminding the West that nature itself was made for grace. The Eastern tradition, by contrast, retained the full theological weight of participation as the very ground of salvation.

To fully recover the meaning of theosis, one must therefore return to the semantic richness of the biblical and patristic lexicon. Each term is a window into the Church's vision of salvation not as legal pardon, but as the transformation of human nature through union with God. The language of participation (*koinōnia*), sharing (*methexis*), transformation (*metamorphosis*), and assimilation to God (*homoiosis*) all converge in the great mystery of deification. These are not poetic ornaments or mystical metaphors—they are theological realities which define the Christian life from baptism to glorification. Here, the teaching of St. Gregory

Palamas becomes crucial: by distinguishing between God's inaccessible essence and His communicable energies, Palamas showed how deification is possible without collapsing the Creator–creature distinction. This essence–energies framework secures the very possibility of theosis.

Indeed, even the most exalted moral transformation remains insufficient unless it is rooted in participation. For in the Christian vision, sanctity is not the result of moral self-improvement, but the fruit of divine indwelling. This is why theosis begins with grace, continues in sacramental communion, and ends in glory. It is not a ladder climbed by effort alone, but a gift received and deepened through life in Christ. As we now turn to explore the biblical ground of this participation, we will see how Scripture itself affirms—again and again—not merely an ethic to imitate, but a life to be entered, a nature to be conformed, and a God to be shared.

This participatory vision is not the invention of later theological synthesis but is inscribed in the very fabric of divine revelation. The New Testament speaks not in abstract propositions, but in relational and ontological terms—terms that presuppose a union more intimate than imitation and more profound than pardon. In 2 Peter 1:4, the apostle proclaims that believers are destined to "become partakers [κοινωνοί] of the divine nature, having escaped the corruption that is in the world because of lust." This statement, unparalleled in its clarity, provides the cornerstone of the doctrine of theosis. The language of "partaking" (*koinōnia*, κοινωνία) suggests more than moral agreement or legal association; it implies a real sharing, a communion, a metaphysical participation in that which is uncreated.

The early Church did not interpret this verse symbolically, nor did it shy away from its ontological implications. The Cappadocian Fathers, steeped in both Scripture and Hellenic precision, taught that the human soul is capable of entering into real participation with God—not by essence, which remains inaccessible, but by grace, which is God Himself given to man. St. Gregory of Nazianzus, in his *Oration 45*, declares, "Man has been commanded to become God." This is not rhetorical flourish; it is the doctrinal horizon within which all Christian life is to be understood.

Participation in the divine nature is the very telos of the Incarnation, as St. Athanasius so clearly articulates: "The Word was made man so that we might be made divine" (*On the Incarnation*, 54).

This participation is, at its core, Trinitarian. It is not a generic elevation of man to an abstract divinity, but an incorporation into the very perichoresis of Father, Son, and Holy Spirit. In the high priestly prayer of John 17, Christ does not merely ask that His followers be preserved or forgiven. He prays "that they may all be one; even as You, Father, are in Me, and I in You, that they also may be in Us" (John 17:21). The goal is not moral alignment with divine values, but existential inclusion in the intra-Trinitarian communion. This is the deepest context in which theosis must be understood: not the deification of isolated individuals, but the entry of the redeemed into the divine communion that is God Himself.

This same logic permeates the Pauline epistles. In Galatians 2:20, Paul can say with unveiled boldness, "It is no longer I who live, but Christ who lives in me." The life of the believer is not merely shaped by Christ—it is indwelt by Christ. The apostle's entire identity is reconstituted by a new metaphysical reality: union with the Son. Similarly, in 2 Corinthians 13:5, he exhorts the faithful: "Do you not realize that Jesus Christ is in you?" These are not metaphorical slogans, but ontological declarations. Salvation is the indwelling of God in man, and of man in God—a mutual inhabitation that constitutes true life.

The patristic tradition received and developed this vision with reverent precision. St. Cyril of Alexandria, interpreting John 1:12 ("To all who received him... he gave power to become children of God"), affirms that the Word grants to those who believe "a share in His own nature, and a transformation into what He is by nature, so far as is possible for man" (*Commentary on John*, I.12). Here, participation is not abstract union but a concrete assimilation—a becoming by grace what Christ is by nature. Cyril, like the Fathers before and after him, held that salvation means ontological elevation, not forensic acquittal.

Maximus the Confessor brings this theology to its metaphysical zenith. For Maximus, theosis is not a spiritual metaphor but the end for which creation itself exists. "God and man are wholly interpenetrated in Christ, without confusion, division, or change" (*Ambigua*, 5.11). This perichoretic union—the complete interpenetration of the divine and the human in Christ—becomes the pattern and principle of all deified life. The believer, through participation in the mysteries, is drawn into that same union, becoming "by grace all that God is by nature, except identity of essence" (*Ambigua*, 7). The crucial qualifier—"except identity of essence"—safeguards divine transcendence, even as it affirms the shocking intimacy of divine-human union.

At no point does this participation collapse the distinction between Creator and creature. Rather, it is precisely in the preservation of that distinction that communion becomes possible. God remains utterly transcendent in essence, yet freely communicates His life to creation through grace. The human soul, remaining finite, is nonetheless capacitated by God to receive what is infinite—not in its totality, but truly and intimately. As St. Basil affirms, "Through the Holy Spirit we are restored to paradise, ascend to the Kingdom of Heaven, and are called children of God, through whom we cry 'Abba, Father.' We become partakers of divine grace, we are called children of light and sons of God" (*On the Holy Spirit*, 15.35). Grace, in this framework, is not merely the favor of God but the very divine life poured into the soul.

This is the beating heart of the Christian life. The commandments are not moral hurdles, but invitations into divine likeness. The sacraments are not symbols, but means of participation. The life of prayer is not psychological therapy, but the soul's ascent into uncreated Light. And the Church herself is not a social body, but the locus of divine-human communion—"the fullness of him who fills all in all" (Ephesians 1:23). Salvation, in this light, is not escape from punishment, but entry into participation. It is not moralism or legal pardon, but the indwelling of the divine life in the body, soul, and spirit of man.

Having now seen the biblical and patristic foundations for participation in the divine life, we must turn to the visible consequences of that union: the transformation of the believer in mind, body, and heart. For theosis, while rooted in participation, blossoms in transformation. It is not enough to be united to Christ in mystery; one must also be transfigured by His grace in life.

What emerged in the post-Scholastic West was a conceptual shift of immense consequence—one in which the dynamic language of participation gave way to the forensic categories of merit, punishment, and reward. As Latin theology became increasingly systematized, especially in the wake of the 12th century, the mystery of theosis was eclipsed by a juridical framework that reimagined grace as a created habitus, salvation as a legal justification, and sanctification as primarily moral progress. The transformation of the soul became less a question of ontological union and more a matter of ethical conformity.

This shift was not accidental. It was fueled by a deeper metaphysical realignment. Influenced by the rediscovery of Aristotle in the 13th century, particularly through the thought of St. Thomas Aquinas, the West increasingly defined grace as an *accident* inhering in the soul—created, measurable, and elevated in proportion to merit. While Aquinas affirmed participation in God (*participatio divinae naturae*, cf. *ST* I-II, q. 112, a. 1), the metaphysical scaffolding around his system tended toward abstraction. Grace was interior but quantified. The believer was made just not through transformative union with uncreated energies, but through a created gift that elevated nature toward its supernatural end. Thus, deification became implicit, subordinated to a teleological moral framework.

Even more significantly, the distinction between nature and grace hardened into opposition. While the Fathers spoke of grace as the fulfillment of nature—the realization of its deepest structure—the scholastic tradition increasingly conceived nature as a self-contained order, capable of functioning apart from grace. The result was a semi-Pelagian anthropological model, in which grace assists nature rather than transfigures it. The human person became a moral agent striving toward beatitude, aided by divine power but not fundamentally restructured by divine indwelling.

This logic was further codified at the First Vatican Council (1870), which affirmed the distinction between the natural and supernatural orders.

While intended to preserve the gratuity of grace, the unintended effect was to obscure the patristic insight that nature itself was created for grace. Deification was reduced to the external reward of the beatific vision—a static contemplation of God's essence rather than a participatory union with divine life. The mystical realism of the Fathers—Athanasius, Gregory, Maximus—was supplanted by an intellectualist vision of salvation that leaned heavily on abstraction.

Such distortions were only exacerbated in the post-Reformation debates. Protestant theology, particularly in its Lutheran and Reformed forms, reacted against the medieval system by collapsing justification into imputed righteousness—an extrinsic declaration of innocence without interior renewal. Salvation became a legal fiction: the sinner declared just while remaining unchanged. In this schema, there is no theosis because there is no ontological union. Christ's righteousness is "credited" to the believer, but the soul remains fragmented, wounded, unhealed. Grace is not transformative—it is transactional.

Yet even within Catholicism, theosis became marginalized. Manuals of theology, catechetical texts, and scholastic treatises rarely spoke of deification. The mystical vocabulary of participation and transformation was replaced by juridical and merit-based systems. The East, by contrast, preserved the language of communion, the vision of grace as uncreated light, and the sacramental economy as a real participation in divine energies. The Byzantine tradition, drawing from the Cappadocians, Dionysius, and Maximus, retained a cosmology and anthropology capacious enough to hold the mystery of theosis without reduction. But in the West, especially from the high Middle Ages onward, theosis became an esoteric doctrine—relegated to mystical theology, rarely integrated into the central dogmatic framework of redemption.

This divergence is not merely a matter of emphasis. It reflects two fundamentally different theological instincts: one views salvation as internal healing and participation in divine life; the other views it as legal acquittal and moral progression toward a vision of God abstracted from communion. The former sees grace as union, the latter as aid. The former sees transformation as the fruit of participation, the latter as the product of virtue. And while elements of theosis can be found even in the Western scholastics—Aquinas himself occasionally uses the term—what is lacking is the ontological density, the participatory realism, the Trinitarian framework that defines the Eastern vision.

To reclaim theosis in its full depth, therefore, requires more than recovering patristic vocabulary. It demands a reconfiguration of metaphysics, a retrieval of the sacramental imagination, and a renewed understanding of man as one who is not merely called to obey God, but to become godlike through grace. This vision does not cancel the moral life, but grounds it. It does not reject justification but places it within the deeper telos of communion. Theosis is not a marginal theme—it is the inner logic of all Christian doctrine, the end for which man was made, and the path by which the divine condescends to raise man into His own life.

To speak of theosis, then, is not to propose a mystical addendum to the Christian life, nor to reserve a higher spiritual path for the few. It is to articulate the very heart of the Gospel. The Incarnation was not a means to an end—it was the end for which creation was made. From before the foundation of the world, the divine intention was that man should not merely know God by analogy or obey Him by command but enter into the very life of God by grace. This is not poetry, but doctrine; not aspiration, but revelation. "God became man so that man might become god," wrote St. Athanasius (On the Incarnation, 54). In this seemingly paradoxical formula lies the entire logic of salvation.

Theosis is thus both participation and transformation, simultaneously metaphysical and moral. It begins with incorporation into Christ through Baptism, is nourished by the Eucharist, deepened through ascetical struggle, and crowned in the vision of God—not as abstract essence, but as personal communion. It is neither fusion nor confusion, neither absorption nor annihilation. Rather, it is the restoration of the image into likeness, the elevation of created persons into eternal intimacy with the uncreated Trinity.

This participation is not metaphorical. The divine life is not merely imitated; it is communicated. As St. Cyril of Alexandria writes, "We are all united to Christ through His flesh… receiving Him, we become partakers not only in the flesh, but also in the divine nature" (*In Ioannis Evangelium*, 11.2). Here, theosis is not a reward for moral performance, but the very mode by which Christ saves—by uniting to Himself what He came to heal. The Eucharist, in this light, is not symbolic memorial but ontological grafting: "He who eats My flesh and drinks My blood abides in Me, and I in him" (John 6:56). It is in this abiding that the transformation unfolds.

Yet this transformation, so central to the patristic vision, is not a secondary result of grace—it is the visible flowering of participation. St. Gregory of Nyssa describes it as an "ever-increasing ascent into the divine," a metamorphosis by which the soul becomes increasingly transparent to the God who dwells within. "The soul that draws near to God," he writes, "is changed into the image it beholds" (*Life of Moses*, II.231). Here, participation is the fountainhead, and transformation its radiant stream. The more the believer enters into communion with the divine, the more he becomes radiant with divine likeness—clothed not in borrowed righteousness, but transfigured by indwelling glory.

To reduce the Christian life to mere moral effort or external conformity is to miss this mystery. The Church is not merely a society of the justified, but the body of those being divinized. Her sacraments are not rituals of legal grace, but means of ontological communion. Her liturgy is not performance, but participation in heavenly reality. Her saints are not exemplary rule-keepers, but icons of transformed humanity—proofs that man, by grace, can become fire.

This is why theosis is not a doctrine to be tolerated at the edges of theology, but the light by which all theology must be read. Christology, ecclesiology, sacramentology, eschatology—all find their telos in this one truth: that the Word became flesh to draw all flesh into divine life. It is this mystery that animates the creed, fulfills the commandments, and transfigures the soul. Theosis is not one theme among many; it is the crown. For it is only when man becomes god by grace that he becomes what he was always meant to be.

Key Patristic Witnesses

Among the earliest and most forceful articulators of theosis in the Christian tradition is St. Athanasius of Alexandria (c. 296–373), whose bold declaration—"God became man so that man might become god" (De Incarnatione, 54.3)—has echoed through the centuries as the quintessential patristic summary of the divine economy. For Athanasius, the Incarnation is not merely the precondition for salvation but the very mechanism by which the divine image is restored, human corruption reversed, and participation in divine life actualized. His theology operates within an ontological framework in which sin is less a juridical offense and more a metaphysical rupture—a descent into non-being, disorder, and dissolution. Redemption, then, is not the removal of guilt but the reconstitution of being; not a verdict declared, but a nature healed.

The foundation of Athanasius's soteriology lies in his robust doctrine of creation. In *Contra Gentes* and *De Incarnatione*, he presents a vision of man as created ex nihilo, fashioned in the divine image (cf. Gen 1:26), and sustained in existence through participation in the Logos. The human person is thus not autonomous but contingent—dependent upon the indwelling Word for both rational integrity and ontological stability. Sin, in this context, is not merely moral transgression, but the severing of that participatory bond. As Athanasius writes, "Men, having turned from the contemplation of God to evil of their own devising, have come inevitably under the law of death" (*De Incarnatione*, 4.5). The fall is not first a forensic event but a metaphysical collapse, whereby the soul inclines toward non-being and the body toward corruption.

It is for this reason that Athanasius emphasizes the Incarnation as a redemptive act that begins not on the Cross, but in the womb of the Virgin. The Word takes on human nature precisely to arrest its dissolution and re-anchor it in the divine. "The Word of God came in His own person," he writes, "because it was He alone, the image of the Father, who could recreate man made after the image" (*De Incarnatione*, 13.7). This language of recreation, of *palingenesia*, is central: Christ does not merely repair but reconstitutes; He does not merely pardon but transfigures. In assuming human flesh, the Logos establishes a new mode of existence for mankind—one in which humanity is reconfigured by its union with divinity, not in essence but in participation. Here Athanasius anticipates the later Cappadocian distinction between essence (οὐσία) and energies (ἐνέργειαι): while God remains transcendent in essence, His life is truly communicated to man through participation.

Crucially, Athanasius's understanding of theosis is grounded in the communication of life and incorruptibility. In Adam, humanity inherited the power of death; in Christ, that power is undone. "He surrendered His body to death in place of all," he writes, "and offered it to the Father... in order that in Him all might die, and the law of death thereby be abolished" (*De Incarnatione*, 8.2). Yet the abolition of death is not merely the cessation of mortality—it is the restoration of life in communion with God. For Athanasius, life is not biological animation but ontological participation. Christ conquers death not by escaping it, but by entering it and filling it with the divine presence, thereby "making death to disappear utterly, as straw from fire" (*De Incarnatione*, 27.2).

What distinguishes Athanasius's theology is its insistence that deification is not a future reward, but a present reality inaugurated by Christ's assumption of our nature. The Logos, in uniting Himself to our humanity, causes a kind of ontological overflow—His incorruptibility becomes communicable through sacramental participation. Baptism, in this vision, is not symbolic cleansing but ontological rebirth; the Eucharist not memorial but actual union with the life-giving body of the risen Christ. This sacramental logic shows that Athanasius' thought is liturgical as well as metaphysical: the Eucharist is not only the remembrance of Christ's death, but the means by which incorruption is communicated to the faithful. The deified man, then, is not one who is simply pardoned or instructed, but one who becomes, in the words of 2 Peter 1:4, "a partaker of the divine nature"—not by essence, but by grace.

This participation is not static but dynamic. It demands ascetical cooperation, the cultivation of virtue, the purification of the passions.

Yet even this synergy is grounded in grace, for Athanasius never permits an anthropology that would reduce deification to moral achievement. The transformation of man into god is not the apotheosis of nature but the elevation of nature by grace. "Being by nature Word of the Father," he writes, "He dwelt in all men, and in His own creation" (*De Incarnatione*, 43.1), indicating that the divine initiative is primary and sustaining. It is the Word who acts, who unites, who sustains, who deifies.

Furthermore, Athanasius avoids any suggestion of pantheistic fusion. His doctrine of theosis always preserves the distinction between Creator and creature. The human person is "made god" not by becoming consubstantial with the divine essence (*ousia*), but by sharing in the uncreated life of God through the indwelling Logos. Here, one sees the patristic insistence on participation without confusion—a distinction later sharpened in the debates of the Cappadocians, but already implicit in Athanasius. Grace, for him, is not a created intermediary but the self-communication of the uncreated Logos.

In sum, Athanasius stands as the axial figure in the early Church's vision of theosis. He rejects the juridical metaphors that would later dominate Western soteriology, offering instead a metaphysical and ontological account of redemption. The Cross, for him, is not a payment but the final descent of the Logos into the depths of our condition; the Resurrection, not the cancellation of punishment, but the bursting forth of incorruptible life into human nature. In Athanasius, deification is not a metaphor—it is the meaning of salvation. God became man not to change His disposition toward us, but to change our condition in Him.

If Athanasius provides the metaphysical foundation of deification through the Incarnate Word, then St. Augustine of Hippo (354–430) offers a psychological and interiorized vision of the same mystery—one shaped by the West's deepening emphasis on grace, will, and the soul's ascent to God. While the explicit terminology of "theosis" is rare in Augustine, the reality it expresses permeates his theology: the transformation of the human person through participation in divine life, effected by grace and fulfilled in glory. What distinguishes Augustine is his focus on interior renewal and beatitude, in which the soul, created imago Dei, is re-formed through grace into the full likeness of God.

For Augustine, the foundation of deification lies in the imago Dei itself. In *De Trinitate*, he describes man as created "in the image of God" not in his body or even in his rational nature alone, but in the trinitarian structure of memory, understanding, and will (*memoria, intelligentia, voluntas*)—a triadic vestige of the divine life implanted within the soul (De Trin., XIV.7.9). Yet this image, though indelible, is obscured by sin, which Augustine views primarily as a disordered will—an interior turning from God to the self. In this framework, the restoration of the image involves not only the healing of human nature but the reorientation of the soul's interior faculties toward God as final end.

The transformation that Augustine envisions is both ontological and moral. It is not simply a juridical acquittal but an inner re-creation. "You were made in the image of God," he writes, "but that image was corrupted by sin. You are being remade in the likeness of your Creator" (Sermon 95.7). Here, *imago* becomes *similitudo*—not a return to a neutral state, but an ascent into glory. This movement is not achieved by human effort but by divine grace, which Augustine defends with singular fervor against Pelagian distortions. Grace, for him, is not assistance but transformation: "It is not by your strength that you are made sons of God, but by His grace" (In Jo. Ev. Tract., 12.13). The believer is not merely forgiven, but renewed; not declared righteous from without, but made righteous from within.

At the heart of this renewal lies participation in Christ, the *Mediator Dei et hominum*. For Augustine, it is through union with Christ's humanity that man is raised into communion with divinity. "He became what we are, that we might become what He is," he writes—echoing Athanasius, yet recasting the formula in terms of relational transformation (Sermon 23.2). Christ is the Head in whom the members are mystically joined; through His humanity, the soul is grafted into the divine life. The *totus Christus*—the whole Christ, Head and body—is the locus of deification. In Him, man is not only reconciled but transfigured.

Augustine's vision reaches its apex in his eschatology. In *City of God*, he portrays the final beatitude not merely as the enjoyment of created goods, but as the soul's participation in God Himself: "Then we shall be made gods, not by nature, but by participation in Him who is God by nature" (De Civ. Dei, XXII.30). Here Augustine employs the Latin formula *participes Dei*, mirroring Athanasius's θεοποίησις. This lexical parallel demonstrates that the Eastern and Western Fathers shared a common grammar of deification, even if expressed through different conceptual frameworks. This participation does not entail ontological fusion but communion. As he insists, "We are not turned into the nature of God, but we are made partakers of God" (*participes Dei*), receiving in grace what the Son possesses by nature. In this way, Augustine safeguards the Creator-creature distinction while affirming the unimaginable intimacy of redeemed union.

The sacramental life, especially the Eucharist, plays a vital role in Augustine's theology of deification. For him, the Eucharist is not merely a sign but a vehicle of transformation. "If you receive worthily, you are what you receive," he proclaims (Sermon 272). The body of Christ, received in faith, conforms the believer to Christ, forging the mystical unity of the Church as His body. In this liturgical context, deification is not a private ascent but an ecclesial incorporation—a communal ascent into the divine life through the sacraments of the Church, which is both the bride of Christ and the site of His ongoing presence.

In Augustine, then, we find a vision of theosis that is deeply personal, psychologically profound, and spiritually rigorous. While lacking the metaphysical terminology of the Greek Fathers, his soteriology shares the same heart: the healing of human nature, the restoration of the divine image, and the soul's elevation into communion with the Triune God. For Augustine, grace is not simply the means to an end—it is the very presence of God reordering the will, enlightening the intellect, and drawing the soul into eternal rest. Theosis, in this Augustinian key, is the fulfillment of the deepest longing of the human heart: "You have made us for Yourself, O Lord, and our hearts are restless until they rest in You" (*Conf.*, I.1).

If Athanasius grounds theosis in the ontology of the Incarnate Logos and Augustine interiorizes it through grace and the reordering of the soul, then St. Maximus the Confessor (c. 580–662) magnifies the doctrine into a cosmic key, revealing the deification of man as the very axis of creation's restoration. His thought is at once deeply metaphysical and profoundly liturgical—an integrated vision in which Christ, as the incarnate Logos, reconfigures the entire cosmos and gathers all created realities into union with God. In Maximus, theosis ceases to be merely anthropological and becomes cosmic: the purpose not only of human salvation, but of the created order itself.

At the heart of Maximus's theology is the affirmation that creation is not an accident, nor merely a platform for redemption, but a theophanic act of divine love—a dynamic revelation of the Logos in whom all things were made and to whom all things are drawn. The created world exists *in* the Logos and is *for* the Logos. The human being, made in the image of God, is the microcosm and mediator within this order, bridging the sensible and intelligible realms. The Fall, in this light, is not only moral disobedience but a rupture of cosmic harmony—a fragmentation of the unity intended by God. Thus, redemption must be cosmic reintegration. "The Logos of God, who is God," Maximus writes, "willed through His ineffable love to effect the mystery of His embodiment, thereby uniting the fragments of the universe in Himself" (*Ambigua*, 41). The Christological foundation for this is Chalcedon (451 AD) and later Constantinople III (681 AD): only if Christ is confessed as one person in two natures, with two wills and two energies, can His human obedience and suffering truly be salvific for us. Maximus's defense of dyothelitism is therefore not a narrow controversy, but the dogmatic underpinning of theosis itself.

This universal unification is made possible through the Incarnation, which Maximus describes as the *recapitulation* of all things in Christ (cf. Eph 1:10). But unlike a mere reversal of the Fall, recapitulation is also an elevation: it not only restores nature to its original condition, but transfigures it beyond what was first given. This is why, for Maximus, the Incarnation is not a response to sin alone—it is the eternal purpose of God for the world. Christ is not a divine contingency plan, but the telos of all creation, the one in whom human nature is fully realized and divinized.

Deification, therefore, is the realization of the cosmos' deepest logic. It is the movement of all things toward God through Christ, by the Spirit. Man, as the nexus of creation, is the key participant in this drama. Through ascetic purification, sacramental union, and the contemplation of divine truths, the human being not only regains paradise but ascends toward God in an unending movement of love. "The deified person is one who by grace has become all that God is, without ceasing to be fully human," Maximus writes (*Ambigua*, 7). There is no confusion of natures, no absorption of the finite into the infinite, but a profound participation in divine life through grace—a movement eternally sustained by God's initiative.

In Maximus's mystical anthropology, the human person possesses five great divisions within himself—intelligible and sensible, heaven and earth, male and female, paradise and world, divine and human—and it is the vocation of man to unite them all, both in himself and in liturgical offering. This interior synthesis is not achieved merely through speculation but through *praxis*—a spiritual and sacramental life ordered toward union. The liturgy, in particular, is the site of this integration. It is not merely symbolic, but participatory: the Eucharist is the real presence of the Logos through whom the faithful are conformed to Christ and drawn into the mystery of the divine-human communion.

For Maximus, then, theosis is inseparable from liturgy. The Church, in her sacramental life, becomes the arena in which creation is reordered, time is sanctified, and man is transfigured. The divine liturgy is both a foretaste of the eschaton and its very enactment. As the faithful ascend in heart and mind to the heavenly altar, they are progressively reshaped into the image of the glorified Christ, participating already now in the divine life that will be fully unveiled in the age to come. It is here that the synthesis of Athanasius's ontological realism and Augustine's interior ascent is gathered into Maximus's cosmic and liturgical vision—a single, unbroken movement from fragmentation to fullness, from division to divine communion.

Thus, in the witness of Maximus, theosis emerges not only as man's destiny but as the consummation of all creation. In Christ, the Logos through whom all things were made and for whom all things exist, every boundary is overcome: God and man, heaven and earth, time and eternity converge. The human vocation is lifted to its highest dignity: to be, in Christ, the reconciler and celebrant of the cosmos, offering the world back to God in the liturgy of love. In this priestly act of participation, deification becomes not a private ascent but a cosmic hymn—where all that is, in its own mode, is drawn into the luminous mystery of divine union.

Among the later patristic witnesses to the mystery of theosis, few have contributed so profoundly to its experiential articulation as St. Gregory Palamas (1296–1359). A monk of Mount Athos and later Archbishop of Thessalonica, Palamas emerged not as a metaphysical innovator but as a spiritual physician, defending the lived experience of contemplative union with God as witnessed in the hesychast tradition. His importance lies not in speculative formulations about divine ontology, but in his unwavering insistence—rooted in Scripture, the liturgy, and the Fathers—that man is truly deified through intimate communion with the living God.

Palamas wrote at a time when the spiritual heritage of the East, particularly the tradition of stillness (hesychia), was under intense scrutiny. The hesychasts of Mount Athos practiced a disciplined form of contemplative prayer centered on the invocation of the name of Jesus—the so-called "prayer of the heart"—which was believed to lead, by grace, to the vision of divine light. This light, they maintained, was not a symbolic or created phenomenon, but the very radiance that shone from Christ at His Transfiguration on Mount Tabor. Their claim to behold the uncreated light provoked the objections of Barlaam of Calabria, a Western-trained theologian who rejected such experiences as irrational and heretical.

In his Triads in Defense of the Holy Hesychasts, Palamas upheld the legitimacy of these ascetical experiences, grounding them in the biblical witness of divine manifestation. When Moses descended from Sinai, his face shone with the glory of the Lord (Exodus 34:29–35). When Christ was transfigured, "His face shone like the sun, and His clothes became white as light" (Matthew 17:2). For Palamas, these moments were not mere historical events, but revelations of the divine presence that the saints continue to participate in through purification, illumination, and union. He affirmed that God, though utterly transcendent in His essence, makes Himself communicable in His divine life and presence—experienced not abstractly, but tangibly through grace, prayer, and communion.

It is important to underscore that Palamas's contribution does not lie in erecting a metaphysical dualism between God's essence and energies—as later interpretations have sometimes caricatured—but in safeguarding the possibility of real, transformative union with God while preserving divine transcendence. He follows the spiritual grammar of the Cappadocians and St. Maximus the Confessor, insisting that the ineffable God remains beyond all comprehension and yet truly indwells the soul of the saint. This is no abstract theology: for Palamas, the theosis of man is enacted and confirmed through the life of prayer, ascetic struggle, and the reception of divine grace in the sacraments. It is Christ Himself who, through the Spirit, dwells in the purified heart and transforms it with uncreated light.

Palamas's theology of deification is thus inseparable from the monastic tradition. For him, the whole structure of Christian life is ordered toward communion with God. This is not reserved for the intellect or for the elite, but for the whole human person, body and soul, who through humility, repentance, and love is drawn into the life of God. As he writes, "The kingdom of God is not the enjoyment of food and drink, but the ineffable and incomprehensible light of God. And the saints, through their union with God, become themselves light" (Triads I.3.22).

The importance of Palamas for a Catholic theology of theosis lies in this experiential clarity: he gives voice to the profound truth that salvation is not simply the rectification of man's status, but the radiant transfiguration of his being. When understood as a mystical and pastoral teacher—rather than a metaphysical polemicist—Palamas offers a vital testimony to the enduring reality of theosis. His writings remind the Church that deification is not merely a doctrine to be affirmed, but a life to be lived; not an idea to be debated, but a union to be entered.

What emerges from these diverse patristic voices—Athanasius, Augustine, Maximus, and Palamas—is a unified and unyielding affirmation: that the end of man is not merely moral rehabilitation, but real participation in divine life. Later Western voices, such as Gregory the Great, who speaks of man as *particeps divinitatis* (Moralia in Iob, 23.24), and Thomas Aquinas, who defines grace as a *participatio divinae naturae* (ST I–II, q.112, a.1), show that the logic of theosis is not absent in the Latin tradition, even if it took different emphases. Whether expressed in the language of incarnation, interior renewal, cosmic recapitulation, or luminous communion, the Fathers converge upon the same telos—man's transformation through union with God. Yet this vision, though forged in the crucible of early Christian theology and monastic experience, did not remain confined to the first centuries or the eastern cloisters. In the unfolding life of the Church, and especially within the Magisterium of the Catholic tradition, theosis has continued to surface—sometimes subtly, sometimes explicitly—as the horizon of redemption. It is to this living witness, articulated in conciliar documents, papal teaching, and the sacramental economy, that we now turn.

Theosis in the Magisterium

Though the term "theosis" is rarely found in post-Scholastic Latin magisterial texts, the substance of deification is unmistakably present in the official teaching of the Catholic Church. Nowhere is this clearer than in the Catechism of the Catholic Church, which synthesizes the deposit of faith through the lens of Scripture, patristic tradition, conciliar declarations, and the living Magisterium. Far from being a marginal mystical concept, theosis is embedded within the very grammar of Catholic doctrine. It is not a metaphorical flourish, but the ontological core of redemption.

The Catechism opens its Christological and soteriological treatment with a striking statement in paragraph §460, a direct citation from 2 Peter 1:4: "The Word became flesh to make us 'partakers of the divine nature.'" Then, drawing from three great witnesses: St. Irenaeus and St. Athanasius,

Fathers of the Church, and St. Thomas Aquinas, Doctor of the Church.

"For this is why the Word became man, and the Son of God became the Son of man: so that man, by entering into communion with the Word and thus receiving divine sonship, might become a son of God" (St. Irenaeus).

"For the Son of God became man so that we might become God" (St. Athanasius).

"The only-begotten Son of God, wanting to make us sharers in his divinity, assumed our nature, so that he, made man, might make men gods" (St. Thomas Aquinas).

Here, the Catechism affirms the classical patristic formula of deification, placing it at the very heart of the Incarnation. The Christological movement of condescension is not merely instrumental to moral reformation, nor reducible to juridical justification—it is ontological and participatory: a descent into human nature in order to elevate it into divine communion. The authority of these three witnesses—Eastern, Alexandrian, and Western—demonstrates that theosis is not an isolated strand but the golden thread binding together the Catholic vision of salvation.

The same synthesis is evident in the teaching of Vatican II, which can be read as a deliberate *ressourcement* retrieval of the theotic vision of the Fathers. *Lumen Gentium* §2 states unambiguously that man was created "to be made a sharer in the divine life." *Gaudium et Spes* §22 affirms that Christ "fully reveals man to himself" by restoring the divine likeness. These are not Eastern imports but Catholic retrievals. And in the East, this grammar was never lost: the Byzantine tradition, through its liturgy and mysticism, preserved what the Latin Magisterium later re-expressed doctrinally. Together they form a single Catholic symphony.

This theological trajectory continues with the Church's teaching on the sacraments, particularly Baptism and the Eucharist. Paragraphs §1265–1267 of the Catechism describe Baptism as the ontological beginning of divine life in the soul. The baptized are "incorporated into Christ," "become a new creature," and are "made partakers of the divine nature." This is not symbolic language, nor a legal declaration; it is a metaphysical transformation. The Catechism goes further: "Baptism makes us members of the Body of Christ: 'Therefore... we are members one of another'" (Eph 4:25). To be a member of Christ is not simply to belong to a collective, but to be ontologically united to the divine-human organism that is Christ's glorified Body. As such, Baptism is not merely a rite of initiation—it is the entry into the divine life of the Trinity through union with the incarnate Son.

Likewise, in the treatment of the Eucharist (CCC §1391–1405), the language of divine participation intensifies. The Eucharist is described not only as the memorial of Christ's sacrifice, but as "communion in the divine life and a foretaste of the heavenly banquet." Paragraph §1391 states: "Holy Communion augments our union with Christ." This union is not a psychological sentiment or ethical imitation, but a substantial participation. The Eucharist effects what it signifies: "The principal fruit of receiving the Eucharist in Holy Communion is an intimate union with Christ Jesus." The sacramental realism embedded in this teaching is unambiguous: the believer receives the true Body and Blood, Soul and Divinity of Christ—not as a symbol, but as the living means of theosis.

St. John Paul II made this unity explicit in *Orientale Lumen* (1995), insisting that the Church must "breathe with her two lungs" and that the mystical theology of the Christian East—rooted in theosis—is "a treasure for the whole Church." He did not treat the East as a curiosity, but as an indispensable dimension of Catholic identity. Benedict XVI continued the same trajectory, framing salvation in *Spe Salvi* as a transformative participation in divine love, while Francis in *Lumen Fidei* describes faith itself as "participation in God's way of seeing." Thus, from Trent to Vatican II, from *Orientale Lumen* to the *Catechism*, the Catholic Magisterium consistently safeguards the same truth: salvation is deification, even if expressed with varying accents.

In §1405, the Catechism declares: "There is no surer pledge or clearer sign of this great hope in the new heavens and new earth in which righteousness dwells, than the Eucharist." This eschatological dimension is central: the Eucharist not only unites the communicant with Christ in the present, but configures the soul for eternal participation in the divine life. The believer is drawn, even now, into the life of the Trinity through sacramental communion. In other words, the Eucharist is both the means and the pledge of theosis.

The Catechism's language of divine filiation also testifies to this vision. Paragraph §1997 defines sanctifying grace as "a participation in the life of God," and further clarifies: "It introduces us into the intimacy of Trinitarian life." This is not merely metaphorical intimacy but metaphysical indwelling. It continues: "Through the Holy Spirit, we are made sharers in the divine nature... This vocation to eternal life is supernatural." Here, the structure of Catholic soteriology is unmistakably participatory. Grace is not merely the aid to obey moral law—it is the divine life itself, given and received in the soul, transforming the believer by uncreated light and love.

Moreover, §1996 declares that "grace is favor, the free and undeserved help that God gives us to respond to his call to become children of God." But this divine sonship is not merely forensic or adoptive in the human legal sense; it is, in patristic terms, a "divinizing" sonship—a real conformity to the Son. Thus, the entire life of grace is oriented toward deification, even if the terminology is rarely made explicit.

The Catechism also integrates this vision into ecclesiology. In §795, we read: "Christ and his Church thus together make up the 'whole Christ' (Christus totus). The Church is one with Christ." This mystical identification is not simply institutional—it is sacramental and mystical: the members of the Church, united to Christ the Head, share in His divine life. To belong to the Church is to dwell in Christ's Body, and thus to partake of the divinity into which the humanity of Christ has been lifted.

One must also note how the Catechism situates this theotic vision within the anthropology of freedom and moral transformation. Paragraph §1988 states: "Through the power of the Holy Spirit we take part in Christ's Passion by dying to sin, and in his Resurrection by being born to a new life; we are members of his Body, which is the Church, branches grafted onto the vine which is himself." This dynamic of death and resurrection, of being grafted into Christ, evokes precisely the participatory logic of the Fathers: not mere imitation, but mystical union.

The Catechism thus reflects, through its integral synthesis of Scripture, liturgy, patristic theology, and magisterial doctrine, the perennial truth that salvation is nothing less than participation in the divine life. Though the term theosis may not appear frequently, its doctrinal substance pervades the Catechism from beginning to end. It is the deep grammar of Catholic soteriology—the logic by which all the mysteries of the faith cohere: Incarnation, sacrament, grace, Church, and eschaton.

This vision of theosis is neither speculative mysticism nor Eastern idiosyncrasy. It is, as the Catechism affirms, the very reason for the Incarnation, the heart of the sacramental economy, and the eschatological destiny of the human creature. As such, it prepares the ground for a fuller exploration of how the Second Vatican Council recovered and deepened this patristic vision of participation, and how the Eastern Catholic Churches have preserved it as a living spiritual heritage.

If the Catechism of the Catholic Church offers a doctrinal summary of theosis grounded in Scripture and patristic tradition, the Second Vatican Council provides the ecclesial and theological vision within which that doctrine is reanimated for the modern age. Vatican II was not a doctrinal rupture, but a retrieval—a ressourcement that sought to re-anchor the Church's mission in the Trinitarian and Christological foundations of divine revelation. It is in this context that the language of participation, communion, and divinization reemerges—not as novelty, but as a return to the spiritual grammar of the early Church.

Foremost among the conciliar texts that articulate theosis implicitly and explicitly is *Lumen Gentium*, the Dogmatic Constitution on the Church. In its very opening lines, the Council speaks of the Church as "in Christ like a sacrament or as a sign and instrument both of a very closely knit union with God and of the unity of the whole human race" (*LG* §1). The ecclesial reality is here defined not juridically or institutionally, but ontologically: the Church is the sacrament of divine-human union. This is not merely a metaphorical or functional designation. Rather, it reflects the patristic insight that the Church is the extension of the Incarnation—the place where Christ's own life continues in history, drawing the members of His Body into the very communion of the Trinity.

This Trinitarian orientation becomes explicit in *Lumen Gentium* §2, where the Council affirms that the eternal Father "in His exceedingly great and gratuitous mercy and kindness" freely created man so that "he might make him a sharer in His own divine life." The purpose of creation, then, is not simply moral obedience or natural flourishing, but the ontological elevation of the creature into divine communion. The Council grounds this movement in the Son's Incarnation and the Spirit's indwelling: "He determined to call all together in a holy Church, which, foreshadowed from the beginning of the world, prepared in marvelous fashion in the history of the people of Israel and in the old Alliance, established in these last times, was made manifest by the outpouring of the Spirit" (*LG* §2). Theosis is thus not an accidental or peripheral grace, but the very telos of divine economy—a Christocentric and pneumatological ascent into God.

The pneumatological depth of this vision is more fully developed in *Lumen Gentium* §4, which describes the Spirit as "the principle of the Church's unity" and "the Spirit of life, a fountain of water springing up to life eternal" (cf. John 4:14). The Spirit's work is not limited to animation or governance, but participation: "He dwells in the Church and in the hearts of the faithful, as in a temple" (*LG* §4; cf. 1 Cor 3:16). Here, the Council retrieves the ancient image of the believer as the naos of God—an image long associated with deification. St. Basil the Great had declared, "Through the Spirit, we are restored to paradise, ascend to the kingdom of heaven, and are called children of God, to whom we cry, 'Abba, Father'" (*On the Holy Spirit*, 15.36). Vatican II, while not employing the term *theosis*, mirrors this theology in substance and scope.

This same participatory language pervades *Gaudium et Spes*, the Pastoral Constitution on the Church in the Modern World. In one of its most frequently cited passages, the Council affirms the mystery of the Incarnation as the revelation of man's own destiny: "Christ... by the revelation of the mystery of the Father and His love, fully reveals man to himself and makes his supreme calling clear" (*GS* §22). But this is not a revelation of mere ethical example; it is an ontological unveiling. Christ's assumption of human nature discloses the potential of that nature—to be raised into the very life of God. "He who is the 'image of the invisible God' (Col. 1:15) is Himself the perfect man who has restored in the children of Adam that likeness to God which had been disfigured ever since the first sin" (*GS* §22). The purpose of redemption is restoration of likeness—a return to the divine image in the mode of participation, echoing Genesis 1:26 and 2 Peter 1:4 alike.

Indeed, *Gaudium et Spes* places this ascent within the broader eschatological vision of divinization: "The Lord left behind a pledge of this hope and strength for life's journey in that sacrament of faith, in which natural elements refined by man are changed into His glorified Body and Blood, providing a meal of brotherly solidarity and a foretaste of the heavenly banquet" (*GS* §38). The Eucharist, in this context, is the sacramental expression of theosis—it is not merely memorial or nourishment, but anagogical participation. As Pope Benedict XVI would later affirm, "The eucharistic transformation of the gifts of the earth is meant to transform us, to make us partakers of the divine nature" (*Sacramentum Caritatis*, §70).

The liturgical constitution *Sacrosanctum Concilium* similarly places theosis at the center of the Church's worship. In its foundational definition of the liturgy, it declares: "In the liturgy the sanctification of man is signified by signs perceptible to the senses and is effected in a way which corresponds with each of these signs; in the liturgy, full public worship is performed by the Mystical Body of Jesus Christ... from the Head flows all sanctification" (*SC* §7). Here, sanctification is not mere moral instruction or ritual decorum, but real participation in divine life. The liturgy is the locus where deification is enacted—where the faithful are united to the Son through word, sacrament, and Spirit, and are thereby rendered partakers of what they receive.

This principle is made even more explicit in *Presbyterorum Ordinis*, the decree on the ministry of priests, where the Council affirms that the priest's primary task is to mediate sacramental union with the divine life:

"In the Holy Spirit, Christ continually gives life to the members of His Body... He communicates to them His Spirit of sanctification, through whom the faithful become capable of offering themselves, their works, and all creation, in union with Christ" (*PO* §2). The priesthood is not administrative, but sacramental—the priest is a steward of deification, a minister of theosis through the mysteries of grace.

Finally, in *Dei Verbum*, the Dogmatic Constitution on Divine Revelation, the Council affirms that revelation itself is divinizing: "It pleased God, in His goodness and wisdom, to reveal Himself and to make known the mystery of His will... that men through Christ, the Word made flesh, in the Holy Spirit, may have access to the Father and come to share in the divine nature" (*DV* §2). This is no mere communication of data or moral law, but a communion of being—a movement from hearing to becoming, from reception to participation. Revelation, in this context, is the unveiling of divine intimacy and the invitation into ontological transformation.

Vatican II, therefore, stands as a monumental witness to the Catholic doctrine of theosis—not by way of new definition, but by retrieval of the deepest currents of the tradition. Through its Christocentric, pneumatological, and sacramental vision, the Council re-centers the Church's life around the mystery of divine-human communion. Though the term *theosis* may be rare in its documents, the substance of the doctrine pervades every articulation of grace, Church, liturgy, and sacrament. The Council does not invent theosis—it presupposes it. And in doing so, it calls the modern Church to recover what the Fathers always knew: that salvation is not mere acquittal, but participation; not abstraction, but union; not law, but life.

If one were to ask how the early Church understood salvation, the answer would not have been framed in the juridical or moral categories so common to post-Scholastic theology. Rather, the answer would have been saturated with liturgical, mystical, and participatory language. Salvation was not merely being saved from sin—it was being united to God. This ancient understanding, passed down through the living Tradition of both East and West, finds one of its most robust and uninterrupted expressions in the Eastern Catholic Churches, particularly within the Byzantine tradition. These Churches, in communion with the See of Rome and fully embracing the Catholic faith, have nevertheless preserved a theological and liturgical worldview that remains strikingly close to the patristic roots from which Christianity first blossomed. In their prayers, hymns, icons, sacraments, and catechisms, theosis—deification—does not merely survive. It sings.

While the Latin West has often favored a more systematic, analytical, and juridical articulation of doctrine—one not without its own legitimate metaphysical depth—the East has always preferred a more holistic and doxological mode of theology. In the Eastern mind, truth is not merely to be defined; it is to be contemplated, entered into, and lived. As Vladimir Lossky famously remarked, "In the Eastern tradition, theology is never a purely intellectual discipline, but always a matter of experience, of union with God." Although Lossky himself was Orthodox, his insight is especially apt when applied to the Eastern Catholic Churches, who, in their fidelity to both the patristic vision and the Magisterium of the Catholic Church, offer a privileged window into the continuity between ancient deifying theology and contemporary Catholic dogma.

It is in this context that one must approach the question of how theosis is understood in the Eastern Catholic tradition. This is not a question of novelty or innovation, nor is it a matter of retrieving some esoteric tradition hidden away in distant monasteries. Rather, it is an examination of how the foundational truth of Christian salvation—participation in the divine life—has been faithfully preserved, practiced, and proclaimed in the heart of the Church's life. The Eastern Catholic tradition, far from being a romanticized otherness within Catholicism, is a living expression of Catholic wholeness, manifesting in liturgical and theological form what the universal Catechism declares doctrinally: "The Word became flesh to make us partakers of the divine nature" (CCC §460, cf. 2 Peter 1:4).

Among the most striking witnesses to this integration is the *Catechism of the Ukrainian Catholic Church*, titled *Christ Our Pascha*, which systematically presents the entire Catholic faith through the lens of

Eastern theological heritage. Promulgated by the Synod of Bishops of the Ukrainian Greek Catholic Church and approved by the Holy See, *Christ Our Pascha* does not merely echo Roman formulations—it develops them liturgically and mystically in the language of the Eastern Fathers. Theosis is not treated as a marginal note in the economy of salvation; it is its very heart. From its early chapters on anthropology and Christology to its later treatment of sacramental life and liturgical theology, *Christ Our Pascha* articulates a vision of man not merely as a moral agent in need of forgiveness, but as a liturgical being called to communion. In its pages, we encounter a Church that has never forgotten that the goal of creation is not escape from corruption, but elevation into uncreated life.

This is not a new development. Rather, the Eastern Catholic preservation of theosis stands in deep continuity with the early Church's understanding of salvation. The writings of St. Athanasius, St. Gregory Nazianzen, St. Cyril of Alexandria, St. Maximus the Confessor, and St. John Damascene, among others, are not relics of a bygone age—they are the living voice of Eastern Catholic theology today. Their vision of salvation as a real participation in the divine life has never been lost in the East. The Byzantine liturgy, for example, does not pray that the faithful be excused or legally acquitted; it prays that they may be made partakers of the Holy Spirit, inheritors of the Kingdom, and sanctified by divine grace. The sacraments are not symbolic acts, nor are they mechanisms of grace dispensed from afar. They are epiphanies of the divine presence, moments when heaven kisses earth, and man is drawn upward into God.

Moreover, the Eastern Catholic Churches offer a necessary corrective to tendencies in Western theology that, over time, have reduced salvation to categories of merit, justice, and satisfaction. Without rejecting the truth contained in these categories, the Eastern tradition reminds the Church that salvation is not fundamentally about moral improvement or legal pardon, but about communion. The image of man before God is not that of a guilty defendant seeking acquittal, but of a wounded lover returning to his beloved; a prodigal son being embraced by the Father; a created being being drawn into the fire of uncreated light. The language is not forensic—it is nuptial, Eucharistic, and transfigurative.

In the pages that follow, this section will demonstrate precisely how the Eastern Catholic Churches have preserved and proclaimed this vision. Drawing heavily on *Christ Our Pascha*—particularly §§202–205—we will explore how deification is presented as the telos of salvation, the fruit of sacramental life, and the fulfillment of Christ's work. We will examine how the Divine Liturgy itself proclaims, enacts, and embodies the process of theosis, making the Church not merely a community of believers, but a communion of divinized persons. And we will show how this vision is not only liturgical but magisterial—affirmed by synods, bishops, and catechisms in continuity with Catholic dogma.

This is the vision that will now unfold. Drawing directly from *Christ Our Pascha*, the catechism of the Ukrainian Catholic Church, we will see how theosis is not a marginal theme but the very heartbeat of salvation. We will step into the rhythm of the Divine Liturgy, where the prayers, hymns, and sacraments draw the faithful into real participation in divine life. And we will hear the voice of Eastern Catholic bishops and synods who have never ceased to proclaim that to be saved is not merely to be forgiven—it is to be transfigured. In all this, what emerges is not an alternative theology, but the Church's original vision still radiant in the East: that man was created to become God by grace, and that every movement of liturgy, sacrament, and soul exists for this end.

To step into the world of Eastern Catholic theology is to step into a tradition where the goal of human life is not explained merely in terms of morality or doctrinal assent, but in terms of transformation—where the entire story of salvation, from the breathing of Adam's lungs to the descent of the Spirit at Pentecost, is oriented toward one end: the deification of man. This is not an innovation of mystical piety or the invention of poetic liturgy; it is the inheritance of the Fathers, confessed by the ancient Churches, and made luminous again in the teachings of the Eastern Catholic Churches today.

Few modern catechisms express this vision with the clarity and authority of *Christ Our Pascha*, the official catechism of the Ukrainian Greek Catholic

Church. And yet, though Ukrainian in origin, its voice speaks for more than one particular Church. It draws deeply from the well of the Byzantine tradition shared by Melkite, Romanian, Slovak, and other Greek Catholic Churches, and resonates with the liturgical and theological pulse that beats across all Eastern Catholic traditions—Alexandrian, Syriac, Armenian, Chaldean, and beyond. In these Churches, the truth confessed in the Creed is not simply recited—it is lived through sacraments, sung in liturgy, and breathed in prayer.

Christ Our Pascha wastes no time in naming the destiny of the human person. In paragraph 202, it declares with luminous simplicity: "Theosis is the final goal of human life. It consists in attaining eternal life, which is possible only through unity with God." There is no hesitation in this claim, no qualification that this is merely one school of thought within a broader system. It is, rather, the theological horizon in which everything else is situated. Theosis is not a spiritual bonus added to the essentials of salvation—it is the very shape of salvation. And unity with God is not a metaphor for spiritual closeness; it is a real participation in divine life, made possible by grace, and given form through the Church.

This participation, however, is not reserved for the afterlife. It begins here. In paragraph 203, the catechism makes this astonishing affirmation: "In the sacraments of Christian initiation—Baptism, Chrismation, and Eucharist—we are divinized by the grace of the Holy Spirit." Not symbolically, not aspirationally—divinized. In the mystery of Baptism, the old man dies and the new man is born. In the oil of Chrismation, the Spirit seals the body as temple. In the Eucharist, Christ's own deified flesh becomes the nourishment of the soul. And this is not rhetoric. This is what the sacraments *do*. What the early Church sang in its hymns, what the Fathers proclaimed from the cathedrae of Antioch and Alexandria, the Eastern Catholic Churches still proclaim today: that salvation is not the remission of guilt alone, but the sharing in divine being.

Paragraph 204 deepens this claim, placing theosis within the entire arc of salvation history. "God created man for participation in his divine life," it states. "This participation was lost through sin, but in Christ it has been restored, and in the Holy Spirit it is offered to each person in the Church." Here we are given the shape of the whole narrative: creation, fall, restoration, deification. The story is not one of legal satisfaction or punishment averted, but of a communion broken and healed. The tragedy of sin is not merely that it incurs penalty—it is that it severs man from the divine presence. And the glory of redemption is not only that sin is forgiven, but that the relationship is restored and exceeded. For what Adam lost in paradise, Christ restores in the Church. And not only restores—He perfects it. For the first Adam was made in the image; the New Adam is the image, and draws us into likeness.

This is why, as paragraph 205 emphasizes, "theosis is not something external or added to human nature, but its fulfillment." Here the Eastern vision becomes clear. Grace is not a supplement to nature—it is its fulfillment. The human person was made not for autonomy, but for communion. To live apart from God is not to be free—it is to be dead. To live in God is not to lose oneself—it is to become fully what one was created to be. This is why the Fathers could speak with such boldness, not only about the redemption of man but about his glorification. As St. Basil the Great proclaimed: "Man is a creature who has received the command to become God."

The truth expressed in these catechetical paragraphs is not confined to Ukrainian Catholicism. The same vision is found in the catechetical and liturgical texts of the Melkite Greek Catholic Church, which draws deeply from the Antiochene tradition. In the Melkite understanding of the sacraments, for example, Baptism is the entry not only into the Church, but into the divine life itself. Chrismation is the Spirit's descent not as token, but as fire. The Eucharist is not a means to an end—it *is* the end: communion with God through the flesh and blood of the Incarnate Word. In the Synaxarion readings, the saints are not remembered as moral exemplars—they are praised as those "divinized by grace." In the anaphoras prayed at every Liturgy, the faithful ask not merely for mercy, but for "communion in the Holy Spirit, the inheritance of the Kingdom, and boldness before the dread judgment seat of Christ." These are not ornamental phrases. They are expressions of the Church's confidence that Christ has not only come to save sinners, but to make them sons—to raise them to where He is.

Across the Chaldean, Syro-Malabar, Ethiopian, and Armenian Catholic traditions, this same anthropology emerges in different accents. The Syriac tradition, for instance, speaks of the Church as the bridal chamber in which humanity is united to divinity. The Ethiopian liturgy sings of the "God who makes His dwelling in man," and the Armenian Divine Liturgy proclaims that through communion "our bodies are sanctified, our souls made bright, and we become temples of Your divinity." In each rite, the same heartbeat echoes: that the grace of Christ does not stop at forgiveness—it transforms.

What the Catechism of the Catholic Church affirms with doctrinal precision in paragraph 460—"so that we might become partakers of the divine nature"—the Eastern Catholic Churches render with liturgical and mystical power. There is no contradiction between East and West, but a difference in tone and emphasis. Where the West has tended toward clarity of concept, the East has preserved clarity of vision. And in *Christ Our Pascha*, this vision is given a modern voice without losing its ancient fire.

Theosis, then, is not a marginal interest of Eastern Catholic theology. It is the lens through which the entire Christian mystery is perceived. It is the reason Christ took flesh, the purpose of the sacraments, the energy of ascetic struggle, and the destiny of every soul. And in the Eastern Catholic Churches, it remains not a theory to be explained, but a reality to be entered. One does not study deification from afar. One steps into it, like Moses into the burning bush—not to analyze, but to be consumed.

If theosis is the goal, then the sacraments are the path—not merely rites of passage or visible signs, but living encounters with the God who transforms. In the Eastern Catholic tradition, the sacraments—called *mysteria*—are not spoken of as static means of grace but as living moments of communion, encounters in which the divine and human interpenetrate without confusion. They are not empty forms waiting to be filled with meaning; they are the very places where meaning takes on flesh. The God who became man to unite Himself with us does not leave us a system—He gives us Himself. And He gives Himself *in* the Mysteries.

It is here that the Eastern Catholic Churches offer something indispensable to the broader Catholic world. While all Catholics affirm the objective efficacy of the sacraments, the Eastern tradition speaks of them in a way that emphasizes their dynamic, transformative power. Grace is not conceived as a substance or a thing imparted from heaven like a divine commodity. It is the very life of God—His energy, His presence, His operation—freely given and personally received. It is not an external assistance; it is the divine fire that enters the soul and makes it luminous. In the words of *Christ Our Pascha* §203, "we are divinized by the grace of the Holy Spirit." This statement bears no hesitation. The sacraments do not merely sanctify—they *divinize*.

The Mysteries of Christian initiation—Baptism, Chrismation, and the Eucharist—are treated in the Eastern tradition not as separate stages, but as one unified movement of transformation. From the moment the child or adult is immersed in water, the Church understands that something ontological has occurred. The old man has died. The image has been washed clean, and the likeness has begun to re-emerge. The newly baptized is not merely forgiven—he is clothed in Christ, as St. Paul declared and as the Church sings: "As many as have been baptized into Christ have put on Christ. Alleluia." This is not an abstract metaphor. The East takes these words with the seriousness of one who knows that clothing oneself in Christ is not a legal status, but a new mode of being.

Immediately following Baptism, the neophyte is anointed with holy Chrism in the Mystery of Chrismation. Here the theology of theosis is enacted with unmistakable clarity. The priest touches the forehead, the eyes, the nostrils, the lips, the ears, the chest, the hands, and the feet with the myron, proclaiming each time, "The seal of the gift of the Holy Spirit." These are not simply blessings—they are consecrations. The body itself is rendered a temple. The senses, through which man once fell, are now anointed for glory. The one who once used his eyes to sin is now given the capacity to see the uncreated light. The ears are no longer tuned to the world, but to the whisper of divine wisdom. The lips are sealed not for silence, but to praise. The feet are made ready for the path of peace. This is sacramental anthropology in action: the human person is not bypassed in salvation; he is transfigured.

In the Eastern Catholic understanding, Chrismation is not an add-on to Baptism. It is Pentecost made present. Just as the Spirit descended as fire upon the Apostles, so now the Spirit descends in the oil and seals the soul with divine energy. The person becomes a bearer of the Spirit—not figuratively, but really. And this reality flows naturally into the reception of the Holy Eucharist. Unlike some Western practices where First Communion is delayed until the age of reason, Eastern Catholic Churches—especially those of the Byzantine and Syriac traditions—administer all three Mysteries at once, even to infants. This is not a gesture of accommodation—it is a theological statement. Theosis does not wait for intellectual comprehension. It is a gift given, a fire lit, a communion begun.

And what communion it is. In the East, the Eucharist is not spoken of as a symbol or a memorial, even in the most reverent sense. It is the Body and Blood of the risen and glorified Christ, given for the life of the world. The liturgy prepares the faithful not simply to receive something holy, but to receive *holiness itself*, hypostatically united to the divine Word. When the priest raises the Holy Gifts and declares, "The holy things are for the holy," the people respond not with a claim of worthiness, but with a confession of transformation: "One is holy, one is Lord, Jesus Christ, to the glory of God the Father. Amen." It is as if to say: *we are made holy only because we receive the Holy One Himself.*

The prayers of the anaphora confirm this vision again and again. In the Liturgy of St. Basil, the celebrant prays that those who partake of the Eucharist may receive it "for the communion of Your Holy Spirit, the fulfillment of the Kingdom of Heaven, and boldness before You—not for judgment or condemnation." Here, the goal is not spiritual benefit in some general sense. It is participation—communion with the Spirit, the coming of the Kingdom into the soul, and the transformation of the fearful creature into one who stands with confidence before the Face of God. This is the language of deification made liturgical. And it is prayed not as poetry but as fact.

This Eucharistic understanding is echoed in the Syriac and Coptic Catholic rites as well, where the altar is understood not as table alone but as throne and tomb, place of offering and place of descent. In the Qurbana of the Syro-Malabar Church, the priest prays: "Let this sacrifice be for us a pledge of life and salvation, for the forgiveness of our debts, the remission of our sins, and for the great hope of resurrection from the dead." But this "pledge" is not merely legal assurance—it is a mystical reality, for the Body offered is the Body that conquered death. And the one who receives it receives that same victory, not in promise only, but in real participation.

The sacramental life in Eastern Catholicism, then, is not a ladder of grace distributed at intervals. It is a single living movement of deification, begun in water, sealed in oil, and consummated in fire. And all of it is the work of the Spirit—not in the abstract, but poured into the body, spoken through the priest, tasted on the tongue, and felt in the soul. Grace is not a token. It is a Person—the Holy Spirit Himself—who makes His dwelling in the soul and begins the slow and glorious work of making man like God.

It is this vision that makes sense of fasting, of preparation, of the seriousness with which the sacraments are approached. For if these are the places where God enters the soul, then they cannot be casual. The one who receives the Eucharist in the Eastern tradition is called to prepare with prayer, confession, and fasting—not out of legalism, but out of awe. The house must be clean if the King is to enter. And when He does, the walls are not merely blessed—they are remade.

In the Mysteries, then, the Church gives not only what Christ commanded, but what He *is*. The sacraments are not the means to another end—they are the end already breaking into time. In Baptism, man dies and rises. In Chrismation, he is sealed with divine fire. In the Eucharist, he eats the flesh of the deified Christ and becomes what he receives. And in all of it, grace is not from afar. It is within. It burns. It heals. It makes new.

To speak of theosis in the Eastern Catholic tradition is to speak, inevitably, of the Divine Liturgy—not as a topic or a doctrine, but as the very breath of the Church. The Liturgy is not a reflection *on* theosis—it is the *enactment* of theosis. It is the place where the Church not only proclaims that man is made for divine life, but actually enters into it. Every word, gesture, and movement is charged with this purpose. The chants and prayers do not merely describe divine things—they invite the soul into them. The sanctuary is not a stage for ritual—it is heaven opened on earth. And at the center of it all stands the sacrificial banquet where the Son of God gives His Body and Blood—not only that sins may be forgiven, but that the faithful may become sons in the Son.

This reality begins even before the liturgy proper, in the *Prothesis* or Proskomide—the rite of preparation in which the bread and wine are mystically set apart to become the Body and Blood of Christ. As the priest carefully cuts the Lamb from the prosphora and places it on the diskos, he silently reads words drawn from Isaiah: "He was led as a sheep to the slaughter." This is not mere remembrance. It is anamnesis in its deepest sense—a making-present of the Paschal mystery. The priest adds particles for the Theotokos, the saints, and the living and departed members of the Church, arranging them around the Lamb. And already, before the public liturgy has begun, the altar has become a microcosm of the heavenly banquet, where all creation is gathered around Christ, the slain and risen Lord. Even here, the logic of theosis is visible: man is not saved alone, but drawn into the divine life together with the whole Body.

As the Liturgy begins, the very opening words—"Blessed is the Kingdom of the Father and of the Son and of the Holy Spirit"—place the entire celebration within the eschatological horizon. This is not a gathering of like-minded believers. It is an irruption of the Kingdom into the world. Time is suspended. Earth is elevated. The faithful do not merely recall what God has done—they are lifted into what He is doing now. In this space, theosis is not explained. It is lived.

The structure of the Liturgy itself is an ascent. The Liturgy of the Word prepares the heart; the Liturgy of the Faithful leads it to union. Each hymn, each litany, each response draws the soul deeper into the mystery. In the Trisagion—"Holy God, Holy Mighty, Holy Immortal, have mercy on us"—the Church joins the angels in the eternal hymn of heaven, echoing Isaiah's vision of the seraphim. This is not ornamentation. It is the beginning of transformation. The human voice is taught to sing with the voice of the angels, and in doing so, begins to take on their likeness.

The readings from Scripture are not lessons to be studied—they are divine words spoken anew, piercing the heart. The Gospel is carried in solemn procession, not as a book to be admired but as the living Word going forth into His people. The incense that rises as it is proclaimed is not perfumed air—it is the cloud of divine presence, the sign that heaven is descending. The entire assembly stands not as spectators, but as a priestly people being prepared to offer themselves.

It is in the Anaphora—the Eucharistic prayer—that the vision of theosis becomes most explicit. In the Liturgy of St. Basil the Great, used during Great Lent and on major feasts, the priest proclaims to the Father:

"When we had fallen away, You raised us up again, and did not cease to do everything until You had led us to heaven and granted us Your Kingdom that is to come."

Here, the entire history of salvation is summed up not in terms of guilt and reparation, but in terms of healing and elevation. God does not merely forgive—He lifts. He does not merely restore—He glorifies. The goal of redemption is not return to Eden, but entrance into heaven. This is the telos of the Incarnation, and the Liturgy names it without hesitation.

Then, at the Epiclesis, the priest calls down the Holy Spirit—not only on the gifts, but "upon us and upon these gifts here offered." The bread and wine are transformed, yes—but so too are the people. The descent of the Spirit is not a one-time event. It happens at every liturgy. And it happens not to confirm a rite, but to change the world. The faithful, in partaking of the deified Body and Blood of Christ, are themselves drawn into His divinity. The Anaphora goes on to ask that communion may be "for vigilance of soul, forgiveness of sins, communion of Your Holy Spirit, fulfillment of the Kingdom of Heaven, and boldness before You." These are not merely hopes—they are effects. And they are not delayed until the next life. They begin now.

This theology of transformation is not unique to the Liturgy of St. Basil. In the Liturgy of St. John Chrysostom—prayed most Sundays throughout the liturgical year—the language is equally rich. The priest prays that God would make the Holy Gifts "unto sanctification of soul and body, unto the fulfillment of the Kingdom of Heaven," and that the faithful may be made "partakers of Thy heavenly and awesome Mysteries, of this sacred and spiritual Table, with a pure conscience, unto remission of sins, unto forgiveness of transgressions, unto the communion of the Holy Spirit." Every clause is a declaration that deification is real, now, in this moment, for those who receive in faith and love.

Even the hymns echo this vision with luminous beauty. In the Cherubic Hymn, the faithful sing: "Let us who mystically represent the Cherubim… lay aside all earthly care." Why? Because they are about to enter the presence of the King. The hymn does not merely call for reverence—it calls for transformation. The faithful become icons of the Cherubim. They cease being merely natural beings and begin to act as heavenly ones. This is theosis, sung by the Church in every liturgy, week after week.

And at the end of the Liturgy, when the faithful come forward to receive the Mystical Supper, the priest places the Holy Gifts on the tongue and declares, "The servant of God [Name] receives the precious and all-holy Body and Blood of our Lord and God and Savior Jesus Christ, for the remission of sins and for life everlasting." There is no doubt in these words, no hesitation. The one who receives does not merely make an act of devotion. He receives Christ. And in receiving Christ, he receives all that Christ is.

Throughout the Eastern Catholic liturgies—whether Byzantine, Syriac, Armenian, or Alexandrian—this pattern holds. The liturgy is not a reenactment. It is an encounter. It is not a symbolic memorial. It is a divine eruption. And it is in this liturgical space that theosis ceases to be a theory and becomes a fact. The faithful, assembled in faith, are lifted into the presence of the living God. They hear His Word, they eat His Body, they drink His Blood, and they are changed. Not superficially. Not metaphorically. Really. Ontologically. Eternally.

In the Liturgy, then, we find the most comprehensive theological statement of the Eastern Catholic vision of salvation. It is not written in textbooks—it is prayed. It is sung. It is received. And in receiving it, the soul is drawn toward the very purpose for which it was made: union with God. Theosis is not appended to the liturgy as an afterthought. It is the Liturgy's secret heart.

One of the most remarkable aspects of the Eastern Catholic witness to theosis is that it has never been confined to liturgical poetry or monastic reflection. It has been consistently and consciously affirmed by the shepherds of these Churches—bishops, patriarchs, and synods—who have not only preserved the patristic vision of salvation but proclaimed it as the normative shape of Christian life. In their catechisms, synodal documents, pastoral letters, and theological declarations, we find a striking continuity: deification is not a poetic flourish. It is the heart of the Gospel. And it is the Church's task, in every age, to say so clearly.

The *Catechism of the Ukrainian Catholic Church*, *Christ Our Pascha*, stands as the most formal and comprehensive articulation of this vision in recent memory. But it is not alone. From the Antiochene theology of the Melkite Greek Catholic Church to the Armenian Catholic emphasis on Christ as the true Light who divinizes, to the Syro-Maronite and Coptic Catholic understandings of salvation as mystical union, the same truth is echoed again and again in different accents: man was created for communion, wounded by sin, healed by Christ, and glorified by the Spirit. This is not regional doctrine. This is Catholic doctrine, spoken with Eastern clarity.

The Melkite Church in particular, rooted in the patristic soil of Antioch, has preserved a vibrant theological tradition that refuses to reduce salvation to moralism or mere pardon. In its liturgy and theological reflection alike, the emphasis remains not only on the forgiveness of sins but on the full transfiguration of the person. Patriarchal letters and synodal reflections have regularly affirmed that the sacraments do not merely cleanse—they elevate. In a pastoral letter from the Patriarchate of Antioch issued to mark the Great Jubilee of the Incarnation, the hierarchy declared that "God has not come simply to repair what was broken, but to divinize what was human—to lift it beyond the reach of corruption, into glory." This is not speculative theology—it is the faith received, preserved, and passed on.

Such affirmations are not limited to grand theological statements. They are embedded in the catechetical and pastoral life of these Churches. Eastern Catholic seminaries teach the doctrine of theosis not as a chapter in mystical theology but as the central thread running through Scripture, liturgy, patristics, and spirituality. Children preparing for First Communion are told not merely that Jesus is present in the Eucharist, but that by receiving Him, they are made holy, changed, filled with light. In the confessional, the priest prays not only for absolution but for healing and restoration. In homilies, bishops and priests speak not only of duty, but of destiny—that every soul, however small, is called to become radiant with divine light.

The connection between liturgical life and magisterial teaching is not incidental—it is deliberate. The Eastern Catholic Churches have never seen a divide between theology and worship. The truths confessed at the altar are the same truths taught in the classroom and preached from the ambo. This integration is a hallmark of the Eastern mind: that dogma must be doxological, and doxology must be dogmatic. One cannot worship rightly if one believes wrongly. And one cannot believe rightly if one does not see that the end of all things is not obedience, but communion.

This ecclesial commitment to theosis is also expressed through synodal texts that align Eastern theology with the broader Magisterium of the Catholic Church. There is no contradiction—only complementary emphasis. The Eastern Churches, in full communion with Rome, do not need to suppress their heritage or translate it into Western categories. On the contrary, they are encouraged to live and teach according to their own theological expressions, so long as they remain within the bounds of orthodoxy. And in this context, theosis has not only been permitted—it has been celebrated.

Pope St. John Paul II, whose love for the Eastern Catholic Churches was well known, affirmed this in his apostolic letter *Orientale Lumen*: "The words of the West and the words of the East may have different resonances, but in the one Church they join in a single harmonious symphony." And what are the words of the East if not the echo of deification sung by Basil, Gregory, Maximus, and continued by the liturgies of today? John Paul went further, insisting that the Church must "breathe with both lungs," and that the East brings to the West "that great mystical tradition which has its origins in the works of the Cappadocian Fathers and the spirituality of the Desert Fathers." This is not sentimental rhetoric. It is an ecclesiological mandate.

The Eastern Catholic bishops, recognizing this, have not treated their theological vision as a private treasure but as a gift to be offered to the whole Church. In regional and patriarchal synods—from the Ukrainian Greek Catholic Synod to the Melkite and Maronite synods—documents have reaffirmed that theosis must be taught explicitly in catechesis, integrated into homiletics, and reflected in pastoral practice. Where juridical categories have narrowed the imagination of the faithful, Eastern bishops have urged a return to the biblical and patristic language of union. Where moralism has replaced mystery, they have called for liturgical catechesis that reawakens the soul to wonder. The task is not innovation—it is restoration.

Even beyond formal statements, the continuity of this vision is seen in the lives of modern Eastern Catholic saints and spiritual elders. Figures like Josaphata Hordashevska, Klymentiy Sheptytsky, and Bishop Martyr Theodore Romzha bore witness to deification not through theological treatises, but through lives transfigured by grace. Their suffering under persecution did not dim the light within them—it revealed it. In their martyrdoms, their bodies became living icons of theosis: broken by men, but already radiant with the glory of God.

This is the context in which *Christ Our Pascha* must be read—not as a stand-alone catechism, but as the distilled voice of a living Church, rooted in the Fathers and faithful to the Catholic communion. Its clear declarations about theosis—beginning in §202 and developed in the pages that follow—are not isolated assertions. They are the doctrinal flowering of a liturgical and ecclesial tradition that has never stopped believing what St. Athanasius once dared to say: "God became man so that man might become God."

And the Eastern Catholic Churches, in all their diversity—in Byzantine, Syriac, Alexandrian, Armenian, and Chaldean form—have never stopped saying it. In their synods, they teach it. In their liturgies, they enact it. In their saints, they embody it. And in their communion with the universal Church, they offer it back as a gift—not to replace the West's theological heritage, but to deepen it, to complete it, to remind it that salvation is not less than pardon—but far, far more.

There is a quiet radiance that emanates from the Eastern Catholic Churches. It is not loud. It does not demand attention. But it is persistent and unmistakable—the steady glow of a tradition that has never lost sight of the goal. In a world that often forgets why it was made, the Eastern Churches continue to sing, fast, anoint, bless, and break bread with one unshakable conviction: that man was created to share in the life of God. That the purpose of Christ's coming is not merely that we might be saved from death, but that we might be filled with divine life. That the Gospel is not just pardon—it is transfiguration.

This witness is not a theological novelty, nor a cultural flourish. It is the living expression of the Church's deepest inheritance, preserved with fidelity and offered again to the whole Body of Christ. In the Eastern Catholic Churches, theosis is not argued—it is breathed. It is not a theme to be explored—it is the horizon against which all theology is understood. Whether in the golden chant of the Cherubic Hymn, the shimmering icon of the Transfiguration, the whispered repetition of the Jesus Prayer, or the solemn invocation of the Holy Spirit in the anaphora, everything speaks of ascent. Everything points to union.

And this is what makes the Eastern Catholic tradition not merely relevant, but indispensable to the universal Church. At a time when so many voices reduce Christianity to a moral code or a system of belonging, the Eastern tradition dares to proclaim that God's desire is nothing less than to make man a sharer in His own life. That salvation is not completed when the ledger is cleared, but when the image is restored and glorified. That the sacraments are not symbolic confirmations of interior grace, but living flames that burn away corruption and make the soul luminous. That the Church is not only the place where God is worshipped—but the place where God dwells.

In this, the Eastern Catholic Churches offer not a correction to the West, but a complement. They do not ask the Latin tradition to abandon its clarity, its depth, or its theological precision. They offer instead a remembrance—a re-centering—on what those precise doctrines ultimately serve. For what is justification, if not the beginning of participation? What is sanctification, if not the unfolding of divine likeness in the soul? What is the Eucharist, if not the marriage feast of the Lamb, where the creature is joined to the Creator in unbreakable communion? What is the Church, if not the new temple, filled not with smoke and shadow but with the uncreated light of God?

The Eastern Catholic voice does not compete. It completes. It sings with a different timbre, but in the same harmony. And its melody calls the universal Church to remember that salvation is not a concept. It is a person—Jesus Christ. And to be united to Him is not to be managed, tolerated, or reformed. It is to be raised, glorified, divinized. Theosis is not the exception. It is the normal Christian life, seen clearly, prayed deeply, and lived liturgically.

This is why the liturgy matters. Why fasting matters. Why the icons matter. It is not nostalgia or exoticism. It is because in these signs, the form of glory is already present. The golden dome does not simply reflect sunlight—it reflects heaven. The incense does not merely please the senses—it reveals the unseen. The icons are not portraits—they are presences. Every detail, every gesture, every syllable is oriented to communion. The entire ecosystem of Eastern Catholic spirituality exists to lift man beyond the veil, into the very life of the Trinity. It is not a style. It is a destiny.

And the greatest gift the Eastern Catholic Churches give is not their history or their liturgy or their music, as precious as these are. It is their unwavering fidelity to the truth that St. Peter confessed, that the Fathers defended, and that the martyrs died for: that the Son of God took on human nature not to condemn it, but to heal it—not to manage it, but to glorify it. And that this glorification is not a future prize but a present mystery, enacted at every liturgy, received at every altar, planted in every soul that dares to believe that Christ truly meant it when He said, "That they may be one, as You, Father, are in Me, and I in You."

In the East, that mystery is not forgotten. It is alive. And it is offered back to the Church in full Catholic communion—as light, as leaven, as reminder, as prophecy.

It is offered in the hope that the whole Church, breathing fully with both lungs, may once again speak with one voice the great truth she was always meant to proclaim: that God became man so that man might become God—not in essence, not in nature, but in grace and glory, by the power of the Spirit, through the Body of Christ.

And that this is not a metaphor. It is our calling.

Theosis and the Magisterium: Bridging East and West

There are moments in the life of the Church when the language of theology evolves not by abandoning what came before, but by unveiling what was always there. Such is the case with the doctrine of theosis in the Latin West. While the terminology of *divinization*—*theosis* in Greek—finds its most immediate home in the Eastern Christian tradition, the reality it expresses was never foreign to the Latin Church. From her earliest fathers to her scholastic theologians, the Western tradition has always carried within it the logic, language, and metaphysical depth of deification, even if that doctrine was not always rendered in the same mystical tones or poetic forms. The difference was not one of content, but of expression. Beneath the West's emphasis on justification, sanctifying grace, moral perfection, and the beatific vision lies the same mystery: that man is destined not merely for forgiveness, but for participation in the divine life. That he is to be made, by grace, what God is by nature—not by essence, but by communion.

Already in the formative centuries of the Western Church, we find this vision articulated in unmistakable terms. St. Augustine, though sometimes perceived through the lens of later juridical interpretations, must be understood as a deeply metaphysical thinker whose doctrine of grace points directly to deification. In his *De Trinitate*, he writes of man being created in the image of God not merely as a static imprint, but as a dynamic capacity for communion. The image is not a possession; it is a calling. It demands a return to its source, a movement from likeness to union. For Augustine, grace is not a mere forensic pardon—it is the very presence of God dwelling in the soul, transforming it from within. "God," he writes, "by making us gods, is not born in us as He is in the Only-Begotten, but is made in us by His own gift" (*De Trin.*, XV.27). Here, the gift is not an external help, but the very life of God infused into the soul by the Holy Spirit. The human person, drawn into divine charity, becomes what he was always meant to be: a sharer in God's own being.

Augustine's doctrine of *participatio Dei* runs throughout his works. In Sermon 192, he declares with characteristic directness: "Factus est Deus homo, ut homo fieret Deus"—"God became man so that man might become God." Though the phrase is more often associated with St. Athanasius, Augustine too dares to use it in his own Latin idiom, showing the shared patristic conviction that salvation means participation in God's life. Deification, for Augustine, is not ontological absorption or confusion, but a true elevation of nature by the presence of the Creator. It is, to use later language, *gratia elevans*—grace that lifts man beyond the limits of his own created being, not by erasing his nature, but by perfecting it.

This perfection is understood most clearly in the context of love. For Augustine, it is love that binds man to God, not sentimentally but metaphysically. Charity, as infused by the Spirit, is not simply man's response to God—it is God Himself dwelling in man. "The love of God is poured into our hearts by the Holy Spirit who has been given to us" (Rom 5:5), he repeats again and again. But this pouring is not symbolic; it is efficacious. It causes man to become capable of divine action. "By loving," Augustine says, "we become like Him whom we love." This is the transformation at the heart of his soteriology. Grace does not merely assist the will—it divinizes it, infusing it with divine energy so that man may not only obey, but become holy.

St. Leo the Great, writing in the fifth century, continues this vision in a Christological key. In his Christmas homilies, still read in the Roman Breviary, he declares: *"Agnosce, o Christiane, dignitatem tuam!"*—"Recognize, O Christian, your dignity!" That dignity is grounded in the Incarnation. For Leo, the mystery of salvation lies in the assumption of human nature by the Word, and in the elevation of that nature in the resurrection. "Partakers of the divine nature," he writes, "we are not to return to the old baseness of our former condition." The assumption of human nature by Christ is not merely a redemptive act—it is a transformative one. In Him, our humanity is not only healed, but glorified. And the faithful, through baptism and the Eucharist, are drawn into that glorified humanity, sharing in what Christ is by nature through what He gives by grace.

In the West's early Trinitarian theology, we also find deep roots for the doctrine of theosis. St. Hilary of Poitiers, in his *De Trinitate*, writes: "Through the sacrament of regeneration man is made like unto God... by the communication of the divine nature." He is careful to uphold the Creator–creature distinction, but affirms that in Christ, the creature is made to share in the very life of the Trinity. This sharing is not poetic—it is real. It is accomplished by the sacraments, especially Baptism and Eucharist, and sustained by the presence of the Holy Spirit. Hilary, whose theology is shaped by the Nicene faith, insists that the goal of salvation is not simply pardon but participation. As he writes elsewhere: "We are not adopted into a metaphor; we are adopted into divinity."

St. Ambrose of Milan, likewise, speaks in sacramental terms that evoke the mystery of deification. In his catechetical lectures, he reflects on Baptism as a rebirth not into moral effort alone, but into divine sonship.

"You went down into the water," he tells the neophytes, "and you rose a new man—divinized by the Spirit, clothed in immortality, made heir with Christ." The mystagogical tone of his theology is grounded in liturgical reality: in the sacrament, what is spoken becomes true. The soul is not merely declared righteous—it is remade.

As the Latin theological tradition matured in the Middle Ages, this vision was taken up and systematized by the Scholastics. St. Thomas Aquinas, while rarely using the language of *theosis*, offers a metaphysical framework that affirms it in substance. For Aquinas, the soul is made for God, not merely as its end in a moral or intellectual sense, but as its final cause—its telos. The soul's perfection lies in its elevation to the *visio beatifica*, the beatific vision, by a supernatural light—*lumen gloriae*—infused by God alone. In *Summa Theologiae* I-II, q. 112-113, he explains that sanctifying grace is not simply the favor of God, but a created participation in His nature: *gratia gratum faciens*.

Participation (*participatio*) is a crucial concept in Aquinas. In the metaphysical tradition of Aristotle and the Neoplatonists, to participate means to share in the being or activity of another without becoming that thing in essence. For Aquinas, grace enables precisely this: it allows the soul to participate in the divine life, to be elevated to acts proper to God—knowledge of the divine essence, love of the divine will, and union with the divine Person. "By grace," he writes, "the rational creature is admitted to a participation of the divine nature" (STh I-II, q. 110, a. 1). For Aquinas this participation is created, not uncreated: the soul remains finite, but is raised by grace to share in divine operations without collapsing the Creator–creature distinction. It is nonetheless real and transformative. The creature does not become divine in substance, but becomes capable of divine operations through infused light and charity. In this sense, the beatific vision is not merely the reward of the just—it is the culmination of theosis.

What is more, Aquinas understands this participation as nuptial. Drawing on the Song of Songs and the theology of Ephesians 5, he likens the soul's union with God to a spiritual marriage—a union not only of will, but of life. This marriage is consummated in glory, but begins even now, in grace. The sacraments, especially the Eucharist, are for Aquinas the "cause of grace," because they unite the soul to Christ not only as a teacher or judge, but as its very life. In receiving Christ's Body, the faithful are not merely nourished—they are divinized. They are made, in the words of the early Fathers, "flesh of His flesh, bone of His bone."

The Western tradition, then, does not reject theosis. It reframes it. It speaks of sanctification, glorification, divine adoption, infused charity, supernatural beatitude. But all of these point to the same reality: man's transformation through grace into a living participant in God's own inner life. While the vocabulary differs from the East, the mystery does not. Grace in the West is not a tool—it is an elevation. The sacraments are not reminders—they are encounters. And salvation is not escape—it is communion.

Even in its most juridical moments, Western theology has never lost this horizon. Though post-Reformation debates often emphasized the forensic dimension of justification, the deeper metaphysical and mystical traditions continued to affirm the call to divine participation. In the Carmelite mystics—St. Teresa of Avila, St. John of the Cross—this language returns with renewed power. The soul, purified by suffering and illuminated by grace, is drawn into the transforming union. The prayer of quiet becomes the prayer of union, and in that union, the creature becomes radiant with the presence of God. "The soul," writes John of the Cross, "becomes what it loves."

Thus the Latin tradition, even when not always naming theosis, has never ceased to proclaim it. It is there—in the Fathers, in the liturgy, in the saints, in the sacraments, in the very structure of grace itself. It is the quiet truth beneath the Western language of holiness, merit, glory, and reward: that God desires not simply to forgive, but to transform—not simply to save, but to share His own divine life. And in this, East and West meet—not in contradiction, but in the convergence of love.

If there is one concept that has come to define the Latin Catholic vision of salvation in its eschatological fullness, it is the *visio beatifica*—the beatific vision. This doctrine, often cited as the crowning dogma of Western soteriology, proclaims that the ultimate destiny of the redeemed is to behold God face to face, not in figure or shadow, but in the fullness of unveiled glory. From Augustine through Aquinas and into the magisterial definitions of the Second Council of Lyons, the Council of Florence, and the Constitution *Benedictus Deus* (1336), the beatific vision has stood as the West's clearest articulation of what it means to be saved. And yet, beneath the scholastic precision and metaphysical sophistication of this doctrine lies something deeply consonant with the theology of theosis. For the beatific vision is not merely a reward—it is a participation. It is not simply a vision granted to the intellect, but a communion that transfigures the entire soul. To behold God is to be made like Him. To see Him is to be drawn into His very life.

St. Thomas Aquinas, in his treatment of the beatific vision in the *Summa Theologiae* (I q.12), lays out the framework with exquisite care. He begins by acknowledging the fundamental asymmetry between Creator and creature. No created intellect, left to itself, can comprehend God as He is in Himself. The divine essence, being infinite, is not proportionate to any finite power of knowing. Yet—and this is the crucial development—the soul is elevated by a special light, *lumen gloriae*, infused directly by God, which enables it to see God "sub ratione essendi"—as He is in His essence, not merely through His effects. This elevation is not natural. It is entirely gratuitous. And it is utterly transformative.

For Aquinas, this vision is the perfection of the rational creature. It is the end for which man was made—not to know truths about God, but to know God Himself, directly and intuitively, in a way otherwise reserved to the divine Persons alone. In that act of vision, the soul is not absorbed into the divine essence—Aquinas is careful to preserve the ontological distinction—but it is so united to God in knowledge and love that nothing further can be desired. The soul is beatified. It is, in effect, divinized—not by becoming God, but by seeing and loving God with the very light and love of God Himself.

This vision, then, is not an optical metaphor. It is a mystical ontology.

To "see" God is to be raised into His own mode of knowing, to think with His own light, to be conformed to His truth in such a way that the soul's faculties are no longer merely human, but elevated beyond their created proportion. Aquinas writes in *STh* I, q.12, a.5, *"In the beatific vision the created intellect sees the Divine Essence not by its own natural power, but by a light that proceeds from God, elevating it to a supernatural mode of vision."* That light is not a veil—it is the very presence of God dwelling within, enabling the soul to act in a way that exceeds nature. This is not simply reward for merit. It is deification, articulated through the metaphysics of grace.

Moreover, this transformation is not limited to the intellect. The will is also perfected in love. For Aquinas, knowledge and love are not parallel acts—they are integrated movements of the soul. The intellect beholds; the will delights. The act of vision causes the soul to cleave to God in perfect charity, which in turn causes it to rest in Him with unshakable joy. This rest is not stasis—it is fulfillment. The soul is no longer journeying. It is home. And in being home, it is glorified.

This twofold perfection—knowing and loving—leads to what Aquinas calls *complacentia* in God, a resting of the whole being in the divine. This is not merely the satisfaction of desire; it is the transformation of desire. The soul no longer loves with its own finite energy, but with the divine charity infused by the Holy Spirit. "The Holy Spirit," Aquinas writes in *De Veritate* q.10 a.10, "makes the soul love God with the very love by which He loves Himself." This is perhaps the most profound statement of Western theosis: that the soul is not merely drawn toward God, but made to love with the very love that is God. For if God is charity (*Deus caritas est*), then to love with divine charity is to be united with God in His own interior life.

In this light, the beatific vision is not simply the intellectual consummation of salvation—it is the full flowering of deification. It is the soul becoming, by grace, capable of receiving God as He is. And not only receiving—but being shaped by that reception into a creature who shines with divine glory. The Fathers of the Latin tradition understood this implicitly. St. Gregory the Great, in his *Moralia in Job*, writes: "When God is seen, the soul is filled with Him, and being filled, it is transformed into His likeness." This likeness is not external. It is participatory. The soul becomes what it beholds, not by nature, but by gift.

This is why Aquinas insists that the beatific vision is possible only for those in the state of grace. Grace is not merely the ticket to heaven—it is the beginning of theosis. It is the seed of glory planted in the soul, the *habitus gloriae*, which matures into vision. The life of grace, cultivated through the virtues and sacraments, is the slow preparation for that moment when faith gives way to sight and hope yields to possession. In that moment, the soul sees God and is satisfied, not in a way that ends desire, but in a way that fills it completely.

The Council of Florence (1439), reaffirming the theology of the *visio Dei*, declared that "the souls of the just… see the divine essence with an intuitive vision and face to face, so that the divine essence is made manifest to them immediately, plainly, and clearly." The language is juridical and concise—but what it describes is nothing less than theosis. The vision is not symbolic. It is immediate. And the one who beholds it is changed.

What the Eastern tradition calls *theosis*, the Latin calls *glorificatio* or *deificatio*, terms that appear in medieval and patristic texts, though with less frequency and without systematic development. But the theology is there. To be glorified is to be filled with the light of God. To be deified is to be perfected in divine love. The soul, once wounded by sin, is now crowned with grace. And in that crown is not merely mercy, but majesty.

This vision of salvation does not stand in opposition to the Eastern emphasis on participation. It is participation, rendered in metaphysical terms appropriate to the Latin tradition. The elevation of the intellect by the *lumen gloriae* is not far from the Eastern notion of the uncreated light illuminating the soul. While the Orthodox tradition often explains this through St. Gregory Palamas' distinction between essence and energies, the Catholic Magisterium has not defined that terminology as binding; instead it affirms the same participatory reality in the language of sanctifying grace and the beatific vision. The difference is not of essence, but of language. The West speaks in the idiom of cause, proportion, and finality; the East in the idiom of fire, glory, and transformation. Both speak truly. Both describe the soul's entry into God.

In this way, the doctrine of the beatific vision stands not as a rival to theosis, but as its articulation in Western form. It is the affirmation that the final end of man is not moral improvement or juridical pardon, but divine union. That the soul was made not merely to obey God, but to see Him. And in seeing, to be changed. And in being changed, to dwell forever in the love that is God Himself.

By the close of the second millennium, the theological vocabulary of theosis—once robust in the patristic era and then largely subdued in the Latin West—began to resurface not merely in scholarly studies or liturgical rediscoveries, but in the highest levels of Catholic magisterial teaching. The moment was more than symbolic. It was the Church, through the voice of Peter's successor, reclaiming what had long remained implicit within her doctrinal life: that the destiny of man is not mere salvation from sin, but communion with God; that the Gospel is not simply about pardon, but about participation; and that the mystery of deification—so vibrantly preserved in the East—belongs to the whole Body of Christ.

This voice was that of Pope St. John Paul II. His writings, particularly *Orientale Lumen* (1995) and *Novo Millennio Ineunte* (2001), mark a decisive magisterial moment in the modern Catholic articulation of theosis. These are not theological opinions or ecumenical pleasantries. They are authoritative affirmations—issued by the Pope himself—recognizing that the theology of divinization is not an exotic addition to the deposit of faith, but a luminous dimension of it. And more than this, they acknowledge that the Church cannot be fully herself unless this vision is recovered and made central once again.

In *Orientale Lumen*, John Paul II writes not as a distant observer of Eastern Christianity, but as a man steeped in its spiritual atmosphere. Drawing upon the Fathers of the East and his own familiarity with the Byzantine tradition, he affirms with clarity: "The Church must breathe with her two lungs! In the first millennium, the Church was undivided and truly 'Catholic' in that she embraced both East and West. The legitimate diversity of traditions is not opposed to the Church's unity, and is, in fact, a precious source of enrichment" (*Orientale Lumen*, §5). The theological traditions of East and West are not rivals to be reconciled—they are symphonic expressions of the same truth. And chief among those truths, for the East, is the doctrine of deification.

John Paul does not merely affirm this passively. He declares it vital for the renewal of the entire Church. In §6, he writes: "The Christian East has known how to express the mystery of salvation through a particularly intense emphasis on divinization, which is the ultimate destiny of man: called through grace to participate in the divine nature by union with the only-begotten Son, made man." The language is unmistakable. Theosis is not optional. It is not a stylistic feature of Eastern piety. It is the *telos* of salvation. And it must once again shape the imagination of the universal Church.

What is striking in this magisterial text is not only what is said, but how it is said. John Paul does not attempt to reframe theosis in purely Latin categories. He does not reduce it to moral improvement or juridical adoption. He allows it to speak with its own voice—with the voice of the Fathers. He recognizes that the Eastern tradition, by its very nature, safeguards a mystical anthropology that is essential to the Church's full understanding of the Gospel. And he invites the West not to domesticate this theology, but to let it challenge, deepen, and complete its own vision.

This invitation is repeated with even greater urgency in *Novo Millennio Ineunte*, issued at the close of the Great Jubilee Year 2000. In this Apostolic Letter, addressed to the whole Church, John Paul sets forth a bold call: "The time has come to re-propose wholeheartedly to everyone this high standard of ordinary Christian living: the call to holiness must be placed in the context of the great mystical tradition of the Church, East and West." (§31) But this is not a generic exhortation. It is immediately followed by an explicit reference to divinization: "This training in holiness calls for a Christian life distinguished above all in the art of prayer... It is prayer that develops that conversation with Christ which makes us his intimate friends: 'Abide in me and I in you' (Jn 15:4). This reciprocity is the very substance and soul of the Christian life, and the condition of all true pastoral life. It is a mystery of 'divinization' lived out daily by so many men and women."

This passage is the theological summit of *Novo Millennio Ineunte*. Here, the pope declares that the heart of holiness—the heart of the Christian life—is divinization. Not as a theory. Not as a doctrine to be filed away. But as a daily mystery, lived in the hidden fidelity of the saints. The Church is not a community of moral achievers. She is a communion of those being divinized by grace. The priest, the mother, the monk, the child—all are called to this same end. And for this reason, the pope insists, "the great mystical tradition" of the Church must be reclaimed, not in fragments, but as a living source of pastoral renewal.

What is remarkable here is the way in which John Paul links the mystical with the magisterial. He does not isolate deification to the realm of monasticism or advanced spirituality. He brings it into the center of ecclesial life. Theosis is not for the few. It is for the baptized. It is not a hidden treasure. It is the very shape of salvation. And the Church, if she is to be herself, must recover this shape—not abstractly, but in the lived reality of grace.

Elsewhere in *Novo Millennio Ineunte*, John Paul roots this vision in the Eucharist. "We must rediscover the Eucharist as the source and summit of Christian life," he writes (§34), echoing *Lumen Gentium* §11. But for him, the Eucharist is not simply the "summit" in a hierarchical sense—it is the place where theosis is made present. In the act of communion, the faithful receive not merely Christ's presence, but His deified humanity. They are joined to Him not only spiritually, but ontologically. They become, as the Eastern liturgies say, "partakers of the divine nature." And the Eucharist, rightly understood, is the foretaste of the beatific vision—not in symbol, but in sacrament.

These papal texts, then, are not simply gestures of appreciation toward the East. They are bold magisterial affirmations that theosis belongs to the whole Church. They do not collapse the legitimate distinctions between

East and West, nor do they erase theological diversity. But they recognize that without the language, theology, and reality of divinization, the Catholic understanding of salvation remains incomplete. The Christian life, John Paul insists, must be seen not only as a path of obedience, but as a journey into glory.

This recovery is not accidental. It is providential. For the Church, in the modern age, faces not only intellectual skepticism and moral confusion, but also spiritual exhaustion. Too often, the faith has been reduced to ethics, catechesis to information, salvation to status. But the vision of theosis restores the soul's imagination. It reminds the faithful that they were not created to be good citizens of a moral order, but sons and daughters of God—called to partake in His life, to shine with His light, to be filled with His Spirit.

John Paul knew this. He preached it, taught it, and wrote it into the fabric of the Church's post-conciliar renewal. His call to holiness was not a return to rigorism, but a rediscovery of radiance. And his appeal to the East was not a nostalgia for lost unity—it was an ecclesiological conviction that without the theology of divinization, the Church cannot breathe fully.

In him, the doctrine of theosis found not just a defender, but a pastor. Not just a philosopher, but a father. And through him, the universal Church began to remember what it had always known: that to be saved is not merely to be forgiven, but to be made new. That to live in Christ is to become like Him. And that the goal of the Christian life is nothing less than to "become partakers of the divine nature" (2 Pet 1:4)—not as metaphor, but as mystery.

The Church has always spoken in many voices. She is a communion, not a monolith—a symphony of theological traditions, liturgical rites, philosophical schools, and pastoral expressions, each seeking to unveil the same inexhaustible mystery of Christ. This diversity is not a problem to be resolved, but a gift to be received. And nowhere is that diversity more evident—and more fruitful—than in the different ways East and West have spoken of salvation. One emphasizes theosis, the other justification; one speaks of uncreated light, the other of sanctifying grace; one of participation, the other of adoption. Yet beneath these distinct vocabularies and theological frameworks lies a shared confession: that man was made not simply to be forgiven, but to be transfigured. That the final end of the human person is not merely moral conformity or legal acquittal, but communion with God.

This Catholic plurality of theological expression has been affirmed again and again by the Church's Magisterium. The First Vatican Council, even in its most dogmatic definitions, carefully acknowledged that divine mysteries can be expressed in diverse modes of thought, provided that the underlying truth remains intact. The Second Vatican Council deepened this affirmation, especially in *Unitatis Redintegratio* (§17), where it recognized that "the various theological expressions of doctrine, formulated in different cultures and times, need to be seen as complementary rather than opposed." This recognition is not a capitulation to relativism. It is a reaffirmation of the Church's catholicity—a truth capable of being spoken in many tongues without losing its unity.

In this light, the theology of theosis is not a competitor to Latin soteriology. It is its complement, its clarification, even its deepening. When the Eastern tradition speaks of man being divinized by grace, and the Western tradition speaks of sanctification through infused virtues, they are not describing two different realities. They are naming the same transformation from two different angles. For what is sanctifying grace if not a participation in the divine nature? And what is the indwelling of the Holy Spirit if not the beginning of deification?

St. Thomas Aquinas, who rarely if ever used the term *theosis*, nevertheless taught its reality with full metaphysical force. For him, grace is not a mere divine favor, but a created participation in the uncreated life of God. The rational soul, elevated by grace, is rendered *capax Dei*—capable of receiving God Himself. The soul is transformed not only in its moral capacity but in its ontological orientation. In the language of the West, this is called *gratia gratum faciens*—the grace that makes one pleasing to God. But it is, in effect, the very same mystery that the East names as theosis.

The difference is in the conceptual framework, not in the substance.

Similarly, the Western doctrine of the *visio beatifica* is not an alternative to deification—it is its consummation. As we have seen, in the moment of beatific vision, the soul is elevated by the *lumen gloriae*, enabling it to see God in His essence and to rest in that vision with perfect charity. This is not a merely intellectual experience. It is transformative. It is union—not absorption, but communion of the highest order. It is, in fact, the same mystery of participation that Eastern mystics describe when they speak of the uncreated light flooding the soul. Again, the difference is not in what is received, but in how it is named and understood.

The same dynamic is evident in the various spiritual theologies of the Church. The Carmelite tradition, so prominent in Western mysticism, speaks of the *transforming union*—a stage of spiritual maturity in which the soul becomes inflamed with divine love and begins to live no longer by its own power, but by the life of God. St. John of the Cross describes this state as "the soul becoming God by participation." St. Teresa of Avila likens it to the marriage of the soul with the Word, a union so intimate that the soul no longer acts independently, but is moved by the Spirit from within. These are not exaggerations. They are the Western expression of theosis.

Even the language of *adoptio filiorum*—adoption as sons—which features so prominently in Latin theology, is a form of divinization. In being adopted by the Father through the Son, the Christian does not merely receive a new legal standing; he receives a new life. He becomes, in the words of Romans 8:17, "an heir of God and fellow heir with Christ." He shares not only in Christ's righteousness, but in His sonship. And to share in the sonship of the Eternal Word is to share in His communion with the Father. It is, by definition, a movement into divine life.

The Eastern language of "participation in the divine energies" and the Western insistence on "created grace" are often treated as oppositional, but this is a false dichotomy. In truth, both traditions affirm that the soul is elevated by God to share in what is proper to God alone. The East may emphasize uncreated operations; the West may emphasize the ontological elevation of the rational creature. But both speak of a real union—one that does not collapse the Creator-creature distinction, but fulfills the creature's capacity to become luminous with the presence of God.

This is why the language of multiple theological "schools" has always been used carefully within Catholic theology. The Dominican, Franciscan, Augustinian, and Eastern patristic traditions are not divergent paths leading to different destinations. They are distinct vantage points from which to contemplate the same mystery. As the Church has always taught, theological pluralism is not division—it is depth. It is the richness of truth refracted through the prism of human language, culture, and insight. And when those voices are brought together—not in confusion, but in harmony—the fullness of the mystery begins to shine.

The theology of theosis, then, must not be confined to the East as a stylistic preference or mystical ornament. It belongs to the entire Church. It is the grammar of the Gospel, the telos of the sacraments, the secret beneath every dogma, every liturgy, every saint. Whether it is spoken in the language of Maximus or of Bonaventure, of Palamas or of Aquinas, of the Cappadocians or of Leo the Great, it remains the same: that Christ came not only to forgive sinners, but to divinize them. That grace does not merely cleanse—it transforms. That salvation is not merely legal—it is luminous.

And when the Church learns to speak again with both lungs—with the mystical boldness of the East and the metaphysical precision of the West—she does not lose her unity. She discovers it. She does not flatten her traditions into uniformity. She allows them to sing in harmony. And in that harmony, the voice of Christ is heard anew: not only calling His people to faithfulness, but to glory. Not only to repentance, but to radiance. To become what they were always meant to be—not merely good, but godlike. Not merely restored, but transfigured.

The Church is not a system. She is a body. And like every living body, she breathes. Her breath is not drawn from theory or ideology, but from the Spirit who animates her, the Spirit who speaks in many tongues and gathers all into one communion. Pope St. John Paul II gave this mystery a name when he wrote that the Church must "breathe with both lungs"—East and West. He did not mean this metaphorically. He meant it ontologically. The Church, if she is to be whole, must inhale the mystical, sacramental air of the Christian East and the doctrinal, juridical clarity of the Christian West. Not one or the other. Both. Together. Each vital. Each corrective. Each incomplete without the other.

In the theology of theosis, this need becomes unmistakably clear. The East has preserved the vocabulary, the imagery, the spiritual grammar of deification. In her liturgies, hymns, icons, and mysticism, the entire life of the Church is oriented toward transformation—toward the radiant truth that man is made to partake of the divine nature. It is a vision that shatters mediocrity. It lifts the soul beyond moralism and into mystery. And yet, when untethered from the West's insistence on moral clarity, doctrinal exactitude, and sin's devastating gravity, even this luminous theology can become distorted. A theology of deification without discipline risks romanticism. A mysticism of light without the ascetic struggle against darkness becomes sentiment, not sanctity.

There is a temptation, even within Eastern Christian circles, to interpret deification as a kind of automatic process—as though receiving the sacraments, praying the Jesus Prayer, or beholding the icon were sufficient in themselves to transfigure the soul. But the Fathers never spoke in such passive terms. For St. Maximus the Confessor, theosis demanded the crucifixion of the passions. For St. Gregory of Nyssa, it required unending ascent. For St. Basil the Great, it was inseparable from ascetic training. And yet, in some modern expressions of Eastern theology, this synergy has been obscured. The mystical vocabulary remains, but the moral edge is dulled. Sin is spoken of in terms of illness rather than rebellion, disorder rather than guilt. This has its place—but when the legal dimension of sin is entirely eclipsed, the urgency of repentance, the necessity of penance, and the fear of judgment can fade from view.

Here, the West has something essential to offer. Its tradition, forged through centuries of moral theology, canon law, and confessional spirituality, has never forgotten the seriousness of sin. From Augustine's doctrine of concupiscence to Aquinas's meticulous taxonomy of vice and virtue, from the rigors of medieval monastic penance to the clarity of Tridentine sacramental theology, the West has insisted that salvation is not magic. That grace demands response. That freedom must be purified. That holiness is not a mystical glow—it is a moral fight. Without this emphasis, theosis risks becoming aesthetic. But when the Western sense of judgment is united to the Eastern vision of glory, the result is not tension—it is balance. Not dilution—but fulfillment.

The West, too, stands in need of the East. For all its strengths—the intellectual precision, the dogmatic development, the moral seriousness—it has at times forgotten the end for which it strives. In defending the integrity of doctrine, it has sometimes reduced mystery to syllogism. In articulating the necessity of grace, it has sometimes spoken as if the Christian life were merely the management of guilt. But grace is not merely pardon—it is power. And the goal of grace is not simply to forgive, but to transform. The Eastern tradition remembers this. It sings it. It lives it. And the West must learn again to see salvation not as acquittal, but as ascent.

John Paul II knew this well. His appeal to "breathe with both lungs" was not a call for cultural exchange or ecumenical politeness. It was a theological necessity. The Church, he insisted, is impoverished when she forgets half her soul. She is weakened when her mysticism is divorced from her morality, and when her morality is detached from her mysticism. What is needed is not synthesis in the modern sense—not a homogenized theology—but communion. A mutual exchange. A deep listening. So that each lung may purify, stretch, and heal the other.

Theosis, then, becomes the place where this mutual need is most apparent. In the East, it is sung and shown and enacted. In the West, it is safeguarded, interrogated, and clarified. The East gives the language of light and fire; the West gives the grammar of judgment and grace. The East reminds the soul that it is made for glory; the West reminds the will that it must be trained. Together, they offer the fullness of the Gospel. Together, they say what neither can say alone: that man is not only broken—he is destined. That sin must be confessed, but that more than sin must be conquered. That Christ came not only to restore the image, but to realize the likeness.

This is the vision the Church must recover. Not a competition of traditions, but a mutual enrichment. Not a triumph of one lung over the other, but a drawing of breath that fills the Body with life. For in that breath, the Spirit moves. And where the Spirit moves, deification begins.

It is not enough, then, to affirm that theosis is present in the West. It must be awakened. And it is not enough for the East to preserve its mystical vision. It must be sharpened. Each must become more fully itself in order to become more fully Catholic. For theosis is not the preserve of one tradition. It is the inheritance of the whole Church. And the time has come to speak of it not as the language of the few, but as the calling of all.

The soul was made to shine. But it must be purified. It was made to ascend. But it must be crucified. It was made to live in God. But it must first die in Christ. These are the paradoxes that both East and West have known, prayed, and suffered. And together—only together—they give voice to the one mystery that explains all others: that God became man so that man might become God.

From the first stirrings of Genesis to the solemn declarations of the Church's Magisterium, a single, incandescent truth rises to the surface: man was made for God—not simply to serve Him, but to become one with Him. This is the staggering claim at the heart of the Christian proclamation: not only that man bears the image of his Creator, but that he is destined to share in His very life. The drama of salvation is not, at root, a rescue from punishment or a balancing of accounts—it is the restoration of glory, the transfiguration of the created into the uncreated by grace. Part I of this work has traced that vision, seeking to unveil the deeper currents beneath the dogmas and devotions of Catholic life. What emerges is a call—not a call to mere obedience, but to glory. Not simply to be saved from sin, but to be made radiant with the divine.

This call is inscribed in the very act of creation. In the first movement, we beheld man formed in the divine image, a living icon of the invisible

God. We saw that the language of Genesis is not poetic flourish, but ontological claim. Man is not merely another creature among creatures—he is a microcosm of the cosmos and a priest of creation, uniquely poised to unite heaven and earth. This vocation was not accidental, but essential to human nature. To bear the image was to be oriented toward likeness; to be created was to be called into communion. And when this image was marred by sin—when likeness was lost—it was not the end of man's story, but the beginning of God's descent.

In the second movement, we challenged truncated soteriologies. We rejected the notion that salvation is a mere legal pardon, a forensic fiction that leaves man untouched in his depths. The Gospel, we argued, is not a transaction—it is a transformation. The Cross is not a loophole in divine justice, but the wedding bed where God unites Himself irrevocably to our broken nature. In Christ, God does not merely act on behalf of man—He becomes man, so that man may become God. The goal of salvation is not escape, but participation. It is not freedom from punishment alone, but entrance into the divine life.

Then, in the third movement, we turned to the tradition—to the Fathers, the Doctors, and the Magisterium of the Church—to recover the language that once thundered from every altar and echoed through every hymn: theosis. We discovered that this language was never absent from Catholic thought, only obscured by the drift of time and the narrowing of theological vision. The Catechism, Vatican II, and the Eastern Catholic Churches all bear witness: theosis is not an Eastern innovation, but the inheritance of all. It is the golden thread that unites Athanasius to Augustine, Basil to Bernard, Palamas to the Pontiffs.

But this vision, radiant though it is, would remain a phantom were it not made concrete. A doctrine must become a destiny. A promise must become a path. Having beheld the call, we now turn to the way. Part II of this work opens the gates to the ascent—the concrete means by which man is divinized in Christ. For theosis is not a wishful metaphor, but a sacramental reality. It is not an abstract ideal, but a liturgical and ascetical process rooted in the Incarnation and enacted in the flesh of the Church.

WHAT IS THEOSIS? A HISTORICAL AND DOGMATIC OVERVIEW

We begin with the great condescension—God's becoming man—not merely as a rescue mission, but as the ontological bridge by which created nature is united to the divine. We will see how the Hypostatic Union is not a static fact, but a dynamic wellspring that reshapes what it means to be human. In Christ, man finds not only redemption, but his archetype. He is no longer adrift in the cosmos—he is anchored in the Theanthropos.

From this descent flows the life of the sacraments. Baptism, Chrismation, and Eucharist will be revealed not as rituals of initiation, but as mysteries of participation. In them, the believer is not merely welcomed into the Church—he is reborn, sealed, and consumed into the divine. Confession and Anointing will appear not as acts of repair, but as the healing of the image, the restoring of the likeness, the lifting of the veil.

We will then descend into the inner chamber of the soul, where the ascent continues in silence and fire. Prayer, especially in the Jesus Prayer, will be shown as the continual breathing of the divine Name into the heart. Watchfulness, stillness, and the purification of the nous will emerge not as esoteric practices, but as the daily work of becoming transparent to God.

Nor will the body be forgotten. Fasting and asceticism—so often misunderstood as punitive or external—will be recovered as the training of the passions and the liberation of the soul. Here, both Eastern and Western traditions will offer their riches, and we will see how suffering, rightly embraced, becomes not a curse but a ladder.

At last, we will arrive at the summit—the Divine Liturgy, the heavenly worship into which every Christian is invited. There, icon and chant, incense and light, Scripture and Sacrament will converge as signs of the age to come already breaking into time. In the Liturgy, man does not remember a distant God—he participates in the self-offering of the Son to the Father in the Spirit. It is here, above all, that theosis is no longer spoken, but enacted.

Thus, we pass from the vision to the means, from the call to the ascent. Theosis is not a chapter in theology—it is the reason for theology. It is not a peripheral doctrine—it is the axis around which all dogma turns. The glory glimpsed in Eden, lost in the fall, unveiled in Christ, and proclaimed by the Church is now offered to each soul as destiny. Part I has shown that we were made for glory. Part II now shows how glory is made in us.

II

The Way of Ascent: Means of Divinization in Christ

PART II

The Incarnation: The Descent That Raises Humanity
The Sacraments: The Mysteries of Participation
The Interior Life: Prayer, Stillness, and the Illumined Heart
Asceticism: Purification unto Illumination
The Liturgy: Participation in the Heavenly Worship

4

The Incarnation: The Descent That Raises Humanity

"Heaven and earth are united today, for Christ is born! God has come down to earth, and man has been raised to heaven."
— Kontakion of the Nativity, Byzantine Liturgy

Hypostatic Union and Its Implications for Human Nature

The Incarnation unites uncreated and created without confusion or division, so that human nature—assumed, healed, and glorified in Christ—becomes the pathway and pledge of our theosis.

The mystery of the Incarnation is the ground upon which all Christian theology stands and the key that unlocks the doctrine of theosis. If God had not united Himself to man, man could never have been united to God. The hypostatic union—the eternal Word assuming a complete human nature into His own divine person—lies at the heart of this drama. It is not a theological ornament, nor merely one point in the creed to be recited and set aside. It is the permanent center of salvation history, the decisive act in which the Creator crossed the infinite divide between uncreated and created being, so that what is human might be healed, exalted, and divinized in Him. The Church names this mystery with

Chalcedonian precision: one and the same Son, perfect in divinity and perfect in humanity, consubstantial with the Father as to His Godhead and with us as to His manhood—two natures, without confusion, change, division, or separation, united in one person and hypostasis.

The Council of Chalcedon in 451 gave classical voice to this confession: Christ is "one and the same Son, perfect in divinity and perfect in humanity, truly God and truly man, of a rational soul and body, consubstantial with the Father according to the divinity, consubstantial with us according to the humanity, like us in all things but sin." Here the Church preserved the paradox: one Person in two natures, "without confusion, change, division, or separation" (Chalcedon, AD 451). This is not an abstract puzzle; it is the ground of salvation. Because the one subject is the divine Son, the humanity He assumes is capable of healing, elevating, and glorifying ours (cf. CCC 464–469). If He is truly man, our nature is truly assumed; if He is truly God, that assumption truly saves.

The Fathers understood this with piercing clarity. St. Gregory of Nazianzus gave the principle that has shaped all subsequent Christology: "That which He has not assumed He has not healed; but that which is united to His Godhead is also saved." Christ did not take fragments of human nature but the whole—body, mind, soul, and will—so that nothing in us might be left outside redemption. Even the weakness of mortality, the capacity to suffer, the struggle of freedom, were embraced in order to be sanctified. The divine Son thirsted, wept, hungered, and died. And in every one of those acts, it was God Himself who was present in human experience. Hence the axiom: *quod non est assumptum, non est sanatum*—what is not assumed is not healed (cf. CCC 470). The assumption is total, so the healing can be total.

St. Cyril of Alexandria opposed any mere moral partnership: "The Word Himself, united to flesh endowed with a rational soul, in an ineffable manner, became man." This is why the Fathers speak of Christ's deeds as theandric—divine acts performed humanly, human acts suffused with divinity (John Damascene, *Expos.* III.19). The *communicatio idiomatum* (communication of properties) expresses the grammar of this union:

because the acting subject is the one divine Son, predicates of either nature can be truly affirmed of the Person (CCC 468–469). Thus the Church does not hesitate to speak of the "blood of God" (Acts 20:28), or of a man who calms the sea—without confusing the natures or splitting the subject.

The Passion atones with infinite dignity precisely because the sufferer is a divine Person. The value of the satisfaction flows from the worth of the subject (CCC 616; 468–469). Hence Aquinas: Christ's Passion is "superabundant satisfaction" (STh III, q.48, a.2–6). The communicatio idiomatum is not rhetoric; it is the logic of redemption.

The Western tradition drew from the same well, even if it expressed the mystery in different accents. St. Augustine, ever the metaphysician of grace, described the Incarnation as the foundation of divine participation. In his *Tractates on John*, he wrote: "God became partaker of our mortality so that we might become partakers of His divinity." Augustine knew the danger of confusion and therefore insisted on the permanence of the distinction between Creator and creature. But precisely in maintaining that distinction, he saw the wonder of the hypostatic union: God does not need to blur boundaries in order to lift the creature; He respects the creature's integrity even as He elevates it beyond its natural capacity.

St. Leo the Great offered a pastoral application of the same doctrine. Preaching on Christmas, he exhorted: "Our Savior, dearly beloved, was born today: let us rejoice. For it is not fitting to be sad on the birthday of Life. He who took away the fear of death and brought us the joy of eternity is none other than the Son of God made Son of Man." For Leo, the hypostatic union is a summons to recognize one's dignity and live accordingly. The Christian cannot return to a life of sin and degradation without betraying the exalted nature that Christ has raised. To live beneath one's dignity is not merely moral failure; it is ontological amnesia.

The Magisterium of the Church has consistently underscored this Christological foundation. The Catechism, echoing the Council of Constantinople III, insists that Christ possessed not only a human nature but also a human will. "Christ possesses two wills and two natural operations, divine and human. They are not opposed but cooperate, in such a way that the Word made flesh willed humanly in obedience to His Father all that He had decided divinely with the Father and the Holy Spirit for our salvation" (§475). The significance is immense: if Christ did not have a true human will, then our freedom would remain untouched by redemption. But because His human will was fully assumed and perfectly obedient, our own wills can be healed, purified, and conformed to God without loss of freedom. The hypostatic union safeguards the possibility of sanctified liberty.

This truth also illumines the sacramental economy. The sacraments are efficacious precisely because of the hypostatic union. In them, Christ's humanity—inseparably united to His divinity—becomes the conduit of divine life. The water of Baptism regenerates not by natural property but because it is Christ who baptizes. The bread and wine become the Body and Blood of Christ because His humanity, united to His divinity, is the living source of sacramental grace. St. Thomas Aquinas articulated this with precision: the sacraments are "instruments" of Christ's humanity, and His humanity is the instrument of His divinity. Grace flows through signs because divinity has flowed through humanity. The sacramental order is nothing other than the prolongation of the Incarnation.

Nor should we neglect the mystical and ascetical dimensions of this doctrine. For the saints, the hypostatic union was not a topic of speculation but the living source of their transformation. St. Symeon the New Theologian, in the East, could describe his mystical union with Christ in terms of sharing the very light of the Incarnate Word. St. Catherine of Siena, in the West, spoke of Christ as the bridge between heaven and earth, the one in whom our human weakness is borne and transfigured. St. John of the Cross saw the soul's union with God as an extension of the Incarnation, in which the divine Bridegroom unites Himself to human poverty in order to clothe it with glory. These testimonies remind us that Chalcedon is not a dead council but the pulse of Christian mysticism.

Anthropologically, the hypostatic union demands a rethinking of what it means to be human. If Christ reveals man to himself, as Vatican II affirms, then humanity is essentially the capacity for God. Our rationality, freedom, embodiment, and relationality are not ends in themselves but orientations toward communion. This does not diminish their natural value; it reveals their supernatural telos. To think is ultimately to be capable of knowing God; to love is to be capable of sharing God's charity; to be free is to be capable of offering oneself to God in obedience. The Incarnation shows that human faculties reach their perfection not in self-assertion but in self-giving, not in autonomy but in communion.

Finally, the hypostatic union confronts us with the paradox of suffering and glory. Christ's assumption of human weakness means that suffering is no longer merely a deficit to be endured but a participation in the mystery of salvation. When the Son of God hungered, suffered fatigue, wept over Lazarus, and agonized in Gethsemane, He sanctified the very experiences that often seem most alien to divinity. And when He rose, those experiences were not erased but transfigured. For the Christian, this means that nothing in human life is wasted. Every sorrow, every act of obedience, every hidden suffering can become a site of communion with God. Theosis is not triumphal escape but cruciform ascent.

Thus the hypostatic union is not only a dogma to be professed but the logic of Christian existence. It secures the mystery of salvation against distortion, but more than that, it opens the horizon of glory. In Christ we see what humanity is: finite yet capacious of the infinite, weak yet destined for incorruption, created yet made to partake of the uncreated. The union of natures in the one hypostasis of the Word is the axis around which all theology turns, the fountain from which all grace flows, and the pledge that our humanity, united to His, will one day shine with uncreated light.

The final word on the hypostatic union, then, is not abstraction but adoration. Before this mystery, the theologian must become a worshipper. Chalcedon is not a syllogism to be solved but a doxology to be sung. The union of God and man in the one Person of Christ is the sanctuary where heaven and earth meet, and to confess it rightly is already to step into its light. For when the Church bows before the crib, the cross, and the altar, she is not venerating a theory but encountering the God-Man Himself, in whom our humanity has been forever enthroned in glory.

This is why the Fathers spoke with such daring of our destiny. If Christ is the new Adam, then in Him we see not only what God has done but what man is called to become. His human body, glorified beyond decay, is the seed of our own transfiguration. His human will, perfectly conformed, is the pledge of our freedom made whole. His human love, crucified and risen, is the pattern by which our hearts are enlarged beyond measure. The hypostatic union is not simply the condition of theosis; it is the first fruits of it. In Christ, man has already been divinized, and the Church waits in hope to share fully in what He already is.

Thus, to contemplate the Incarnation is to contemplate our own future. The hypostatic union declares that the chasm has been crossed, that flesh can bear divinity, that history itself can become eternity's dwelling. It is the miracle of miracles, the mystery of mysteries, the ground of every sacrament and the horizon of every hope. And it whispers to every soul the staggering truth: you were made for nothing less than to share the life of the God-Man, whose humanity is your own and whose glory will one day be your crown.

Christ as Archetype of Deified Humanity

The Incarnation is not a static miracle but the living pattern of restored humanity. What begins as union in Christ becomes participation in us. The hypostatic union is not only the foundation of salvation; it is also the unveiling of what humanity was always meant to become. In Christ, theosis ceases to be a hidden possibility and becomes a visible reality. He is not merely the instrument of our redemption but the archetype of redeemed humanity itself. To behold the incarnate Son is to see simultaneously the fullness of divinity and the fullness of humanity transfigured in God. The Fathers never tired of proclaiming that Christ is both the revealer of the Father and the revelation of man's true destiny. "The Word of God, Jesus Christ, through His boundless love, became what we are, that He might make us what He Himself is" (St. Irenaeus, *Adv. Haer.*

V, Preface).

This archetypal role is embedded in Scripture. St. Paul declares that God's eternal plan is that we should be "conformed to the image of His Son, that He might be the firstborn among many brethren" (Rom 8:29). Christ is not simply the agent of grace but the pattern into which grace molds us. He is the "firstfruits of those who have fallen asleep" (1 Cor 15:20), the one whose resurrection is the pledge and prototype of our own. To the Corinthians Paul insists: "Just as we have borne the image of the man of dust, we shall also bear the image of the man of heaven" (1 Cor 15:49). The contrast between Adam and Christ is not only juridical but ontological. In Adam we inherit corruption and death; in Christ we inherit incorruption and glory. He is therefore both Redeemer and exemplar: the one who saves us, and the one whose glorified humanity shows what salvation truly is.

The Fathers expand on this biblical witness with luminous clarity. St. Athanasius insists in *De Incarnatione* §54 that Christ "was made man that we might be made God." But Athanasius means by this not a blurring of essence but a true conformity: the humanity of Jesus, inseparably united to the Word, becomes the exemplar of what humanity in grace is destined to be. St. Augustine echoes the same theme: "God became man that man might become God" (*Sermon* 192). Augustine stresses that this participation never abolishes the Creator–creature distinction, but rather perfects it. In Christ we see that humanity is not fulfilled by autonomy but by participation in God.

The New Testament offers a privileged glimpse of this archetypal humanity in the mystery of the Transfiguration. On Mount Tabor, Christ's face shines like the sun and His garments become white as light (Matt 17:2). This is not a theatrical miracle but the unveiling of what His humanity already is: suffused with divine glory. St. Peter, recalling the event, insists: "We were eyewitnesses of His majesty" (2 Pet 1:16). The Catechism interprets the Transfiguration as a foretaste of the Resurrection and a revelation of the destiny of humanity: "Christ's Transfiguration aims at strengthening the apostles' faith in anticipation of His Passion... but it also gives us a foretaste of Christ's glorious coming, when He 'will change our lowly body to be like His glorious body'" (§556; cf. Phil 3:21). In the Transfiguration, then, Christ's humanity becomes the visible icon of theosis: what He already is, we shall become.

The Resurrection makes this even more explicit. Christ rises not as a soul liberated from flesh but as man restored in body and soul, now incorruptible. St. Paul insists: "Christ being raised from the dead will never die again; death no longer has dominion over Him" (Rom 6:9). His risen body, bearing the marks of the Passion yet radiant with divine life, is the pledge of our own. The Catechism states: "Christ's Resurrection is the principle and source of our future resurrection: 'Christ has been raised from the dead, the first fruits of those who have fallen asleep'" (§655). The risen humanity of Christ is thus not only the victory of God but the prototype of glorified man. What has been accomplished in Him is promised to all who are joined to Him.

The Ascension crowns this archetypal role. Christ does not shed His humanity when He returns to the Father but carries it into the very life of the Trinity. The eternal Son who is consubstantial with the Father now bears a human nature enthroned at the right hand of God. St. Leo the Great, preaching on the Ascension, exclaims: "The exaltation of Christ is our exaltation; and whither the Head has gone in glory, thither the Body is called in hope" (*Sermon* 73). In Christ, our humanity is already in heaven, interceding before the Father, radiant with divine glory. The archetype is not abstract. It is living, present, and active in the glorified Christ.

Patristic voices consistently highlight Christ's humanity as the pattern for ours. St. Cyril of Alexandria teaches that in Christ's glorified flesh we see the restoration of the image: "He transformed our nature into His own glory" (*In Joannis Evangelium*, XI). St. Hilary of Poitiers, in *De Trinitate*, insists that through regeneration "man is made like unto God by communion with the divine nature." St. Ambrose, instructing the newly baptized, could say: "You were washed, you were sanctified, you were justified... and in rising from the font you were clothed with Christ" (*De Mysteriis* 7). These Fathers saw that incorporation into Christ means

THE INCARNATION: THE DESCENT THAT RAISES HUMANITY

incorporation into His humanity, which is itself the humanity of God. Thus, to belong to Him is already to begin to share in His divinized life.

The scholastic tradition sharpened this intuition. St. Thomas Aquinas describes Christ as the "exemplar cause" of our sanctification (*STh* III, q.1, a.2). Because His humanity is united to the Word, it becomes the standard according to which ours is elevated. Aquinas explains that sanctifying grace is a participation in the divine nature, and this participation is mediated through Christ's humanity. His beatific vision is the cause of ours, His charity the source of ours, His glory the pledge of ours. In Him, deified humanity is already realized; in us, it is being realized by grace.

The Magisterium affirms this Christological archetype with clarity. Vatican II declares: "Christ, the final Adam, by the revelation of the mystery of the Father and His love, fully reveals man to man himself and makes his supreme calling clear" (*Gaudium et Spes* §22). The "supreme calling" is nothing less than deification, and Christ's humanity shows what this means. The Catechism likewise insists: "The Son of God... assumed our nature, so that He, made man, might make men gods" (§460, citing Aquinas). Moreover, §521 states: "Christ enables us to live in Him all that He Himself lived, and He lives it in us." His poverty, obedience, suffering, death, and resurrection are not only salvific events but archetypal patterns. The Christian life is the slow conformity to His form, the gradual unveiling of His archetypal humanity in us.

This truth explains the vocation of the saints. They are not moral examples in the ordinary sense but icons of Christ, whose lives have been conformed to the archetype. St. Paul himself understood this when he could say: "It is no longer I who live, but Christ who lives in me" (Gal 2:20). The saints, from Anthony of Egypt to Thérèse of Lisieux, from Augustine to Seraphim of Sarov, are luminous precisely because Christ's life has been impressed upon theirs. Their holiness is nothing other than His humanity shining through them.

Thus, to confess Christ as archetype of deified humanity is to recognize that theosis is already embodied in Him and already operative in His Body, the Church. The sacraments are the means by which His archetypal life is communicated to us. Baptism unites us to His death and Resurrection (Rom 6:3–4). The Eucharist makes us "one Body in Christ" (1 Cor 10:17), feeding us with the humanity that is inseparably united to divinity. Confession restores the likeness lost by sin. Anointing configures suffering to His Passion. In each sacrament, the archetype is imprinted upon us, and our humanity is shaped into His.

In Christ we therefore see both the image of God and the image of man. He is the revelation of divinity to humanity, but also the revelation of humanity to itself. His glorified humanity is the prototype of our destiny, the visible expression of theosis accomplished. To be Christian is not to imitate Him from afar but to participate in Him from within. Our lives are hidden with Christ in God (Col 3:3), and when He appears, we too shall appear with Him in glory (Col 3:4).

The archetype is already given; the pattern is already set. The task of the Christian life is to be conformed to it, until the day when, as St. John promises, "we shall be like Him, for we shall see Him as He is" (1 Jn 3:2).

The recognition of Christ as the archetype of deified humanity also demands a careful consideration of His earthly life in its fullness. The Church does not isolate His miracles or His Resurrection as moments of divine disclosure; rather, she proclaims that the entire life of Christ is archetypal. The Catechism underscores this when it teaches: "Christ's whole life is a mystery of recapitulation. All Jesus did, said and suffered had for its aim restoring fallen man to his original vocation" (§518). His hidden years in Nazareth, His baptism in the Jordan, His ministry of teaching and healing—all of these are not only events in history but moments that reveal what deified humanity looks like when lived out in obedience to the Father and filled with the Spirit.

St. Gregory of Nyssa expressed this with clarity in his *Great Catechism*: "He becomes the model of all virtues for us, in His birth, in His upbringing, in His growth, in His teaching, in His miracles, in His sufferings, and in His rising from the dead." For Gregory, Christ is not merely the giver of commandments but the living embodiment of their fulfillment. His life is the mirror in which we see what human life conformed to God truly is.

In Him, virtues are no longer abstract qualities but divine realities lived in human form.

This is why the Church confesses that every aspect of Christ's life has salvific value. As Vatican II affirms: "The Son of God worked with human hands, He thought with a human mind, acted with a human will, and loved with a human heart. Born of the Virgin Mary, He has truly been made one of us, like us in all things but sin" (*Gaudium et Spes* §22; cf. *CCC* §470). Each of these human realities—labor, thought, freedom, affection—becomes in Him not only sanctified but transfigured. To say Christ is the archetype is to say that His humanity demonstrates the full flourishing of what it means to be human.

The saints repeatedly testify to this archetypal pattern. St. Bernard of Clairvaux described Christ's life as the "ladder" by which we ascend to God: "The humility of Christ is the stair by which we may climb to the heights of divinity." St. Catherine of Siena similarly spoke of Christ as the "bridge" uniting earth to heaven: His humanity is the path across which we must walk to reach the Father. In both cases, Christ is not only the one who opens the way but the very way itself. His humanity is the bridge because it is the humanity of God.

Christ's archetypal role also casts light on the human body and its destiny. In a culture tempted to reduce the body either to a tool or to an obstacle, the Incarnation reveals the body's true vocation: to be the dwelling place of God. St. John Damascene defended the veneration of icons precisely on this principle: "In former times God, who is without form or body, could never be depicted. But now, when God is seen in the flesh conversing with men, I make an image of the God whom I see" (*On the Divine Images* I.16). Because Christ's humanity is visible, depictable, and venerable, our humanity too—body and soul—is revealed as capable of divine glory. The glorified body of Christ is not an appendage to salvation but the revelation of our eschatological future.

This truth is not only eschatological but also sacramental. In the Eucharist, the archetypal humanity of Christ is given to us as food. St. Augustine insists: "Behold what you are; become what you receive"

(*Sermon* 272). The body and blood of Christ, already deified by union with the Word, are communicated to us so that our bodies and souls may be conformed to His. The Eucharist is therefore not simply a memorial of redemption but the active impressing of the archetype upon the communicant. St. Cyril of Alexandria goes so far as to say: "When we receive the Eucharist, we receive the Word Himself, who makes us sharers of His own immortality" (*In Joannis Evangelium* IV). Here the sacrament becomes the means by which the archetype is replicated in us.

Christ's archetypal humanity also grounds the moral and ascetical life of the believer. The call to chastity, humility, obedience, and charity is not an arbitrary burden but a participation in His own life. St. Maximus the Confessor explains this synergy: "The Word of God, by becoming man, has made human the divine manner of living, and He has deified the human manner of living." For Maximus, to live virtuously is already to live divinely, because virtue is nothing other than Christ's own life reproduced in us. The ascetical struggle, therefore, is not an external discipline but the process by which the archetype is impressed upon our passions, thoughts, and desires.

Moreover, Christ's archetypal humanity provides the measure for true freedom. Modernity often defines freedom as self-determination or the absence of constraint. But in Gethsemane, Christ reveals that true freedom is perfect obedience to the Father: "Not my will, but yours be done" (Luke 22:42). His human will, fully assumed, is not suppressed but perfected in this act of filial surrender. The Council of Constantinople III declared: "His human will, moved and guided by His divine and almighty will, was not abolished but was rather made divine" (DH 556). Thus, Christ becomes the archetype of redeemed freedom: not autonomy against God, but freedom fulfilled in communion with God.

This archetypal reality also illumines suffering and death. In Christ, even the darkest aspects of human life become luminous. His Passion shows that suffering endured in love can become salvific. His death shows that mortality itself can be transfigured into the gateway of life. St. Gregory of Nazianzus described the paradox: "He is baptized as man, but He remits sins as God; He is tempted as man, but He conquers as God; He is weak, but He is mighty; He dies, but He gives life" (*Oration 29*). Each aspect of His humanity, even in its weakness, becomes a site where divinity shines through. The Christian, conformed to Him, can therefore say with Paul: "I rejoice in my sufferings for your sake... in my flesh I complete what is lacking in Christ's afflictions" (Col 1:24). The archetype embraces even suffering and death, transfiguring them into means of communion.

The eschatological horizon brings this to its fulfillment. The Book of Revelation describes Christ as "the firstborn of the dead" (Rev 1:5) and the "Lamb standing as though slain" (Rev 5:6). His glorified humanity, bearing the wounds of the Passion, is the definitive archetype of the new creation. The Catechism declares: "What the Son of God did and suffered for all men participates in the divine eternity, and so transcends all times while being made present in them all" (§1085). In this sense, Christ's archetypal humanity is not a past reality but an abiding one, present in every liturgy and sacrament, shining as the destiny of the faithful.

Finally, the ecclesial dimension must be noted. If Christ is the archetype, the Church is the icon of the archetype in history. St. Paul calls the Church "the Body of Christ" (1 Cor 12:27). To belong to the Church is to belong already to the humanity that is united to the Word. St. Augustine could therefore say: "Let us rejoice and give thanks that we have become not only Christians, but Christ Himself" (*In Jo. Evang.* 21.8). This bold statement is only intelligible if Christ's humanity is truly the archetype: the Church is not an external society but the extension of His humanity across time and space, drawing believers into conformity with Him.

In sum, Christ as archetype of deified humanity means that in Him we see both the goal and the means of salvation. His life, death, resurrection, and glorification are not only events of redemption but patterns of divinization. To be Christian is to be gradually reshaped into His image, until the archetype is perfectly reproduced in each soul. The saints are the visible proof, the sacraments the means, the Spirit the artisan, and Christ Himself the living model. In this way, theosis is not speculative but practical, not distant but present, for the archetype Himself is alive and active, reigning in heaven and dwelling in His Church.

Christ, then, is not a distant exemplar but the living archetype in whom all humanity finds its true form. To contemplate Him is not merely to admire, but to be summoned. To receive Him is not only to be forgiven, but to be transformed. In His face we behold what we were created to become; in His body we see our own destiny already glorified.

This is why the Fathers could speak with such daring clarity. "In Him," writes St. Irenaeus, "the invisible becomes visible, the incomprehensible comprehensible, the impassible passible, the Word man, so that man, by entering into communion with the Word, might become a son of God" (*Adv. Haer.* III.20.2). For Irenaeus, the Incarnate Word does not merely save—He shapes, molds, and elevates. Humanity is not repaired as one restores a broken tool, but re-fashioned as one crafts an icon, burnished to reflect the uncreated light.

To see Christ as the archetype is to accept that Christianity cannot be reduced to moral improvement or cultural inheritance. It is an ontological claim: that in Christ we glimpse not only who He is, but who we are called to be. He is the measure of man, the new Adam, the blueprint of the redeemed.

This truth is not reserved for the few. It is for every baptized soul, for every life drawn into His. In the Eucharist, in the liturgy, in prayer and in silence, His archetypal humanity is pressed into ours. The more we surrender, the more we resemble. The more we resemble, the more we live.

Thus, the Incarnation is not simply the descent of God into man—it is the unveiling of man's ascent into God. Christ is both the beginning and the end, the archetype and the fulfillment, the mirror in which every face may one day see itself ablaze with glory.

The Theanthropic Person as Ontological Bridge

The mystery of the Incarnation finds its apex in the *Theanthropos*—the God-Man, the single divine Hypostasis in whom divinity and humanity meet without confusion or division. In this one Person, the infinite enters the finite not as a passing symbol but as an enduring reality: the very being of man is joined to the very being of God. The Word did not dwell *near* human nature; He *assumed* it, taking it wholly into His personal existence so that what belongs to God could truly act through what belongs to man. In the union of natures, heaven and earth are reconciled, and the gulf opened by the Fall is bridged not by decree but by *being itself*.

The result is not a mythic hybrid but a perfect communion: the divine nature remains what it is—uncreated, impassible, infinite—while the human remains fully human, passible, and temporal; yet both are united in the one Person of the Logos. This personal union allows the divine life to be lived humanly and the human life to be filled divinely. In Christ, all opposition between Creator and creature is overcome, not by erasure but by participation. He is therefore the living bridge, the ontological axis through whom every grace flows, the meeting-place where God's eternity enters history and history is opened to eternity.

This is the mystery the Council Fathers of Vatican II echoed when they declared that "the Son of God… worked with human hands, He thought with a human mind, acted with a human will, and loved with a human heart" (*Gaudium et Spes* §22). The total humanity of Christ is not an incidental medium but the very means of revelation. Every human act of Jesus is theandric—an act of the divine Person operating through a human nature. In this sense, Christ's words, gestures, and even His silence communicate the very being of God. The hypostatic union therefore becomes the grammar of revelation itself: God makes Himself known by living a human life.

The hypostatic union is not a metaphor for divine intimacy but a metaphysical fact: in the single Person of Christ, the divine and human natures subsist without mixture, without separation, each retaining its full integrity. What occurs in the Incarnation, therefore, is not an act of imagination or sentiment, but the creation of a real ontological bridge between God and creation. Through the humanity of Christ, the divine life truly touches the created world; through His divinity, humanity is drawn into the very life of God.

The Letter to the Hebrews describes Him as the "mediator of a new covenant" (Heb 9:15)—not a negotiator between equal parties, but the living contact point between holiness and corruption, immortality and mortality. The mediation is not conceptual but ontological: in His very being He unites the two orders. St John Damascene summarized it with precision: "He deified that which He assumed, and thus He became the cause of our deification." (*De Fide Orthodoxa* III.17). What is assumed is healed; what is healed is sanctified; and what is sanctified becomes a conduit of divine life.

The Fathers saw in this union the end for which creation itself was made. The Logos, through whom all things were spoken into being, now becomes part of His own creation so that the created order might, through Him, return to the Father. St. Thomas Aquinas writes that "Christ's humanity is the instrument of His divinity" (*ST* III, q.2, a.6). This means that the flesh of the Word—His human body and soul—are not mere vessels or disguises but the living instrument of divine action. Everything Christ does as man, God does through Him: when He touches, God heals; when He speaks, God reveals; when He dies, God conquers death. The instrumentality of the humanity does not imply inferiority, but participation—it is the means by which the eternal enters the temporal.

Here lies the theological foundation for every sacrament and every act of grace: the humanity of Christ is the perpetual instrument of the divinity. The scholastic term *instrumentum coniunctum*—an instrument joined to its principal cause—describes it exactly. The hammer in a craftsman's hand acts only when moved, but Christ's humanity acts always with the divine will itself. Therefore the gestures of Jesus—touching lepers, raising the dead, breaking bread—are not mere examples of compassion but the very operations of God in human form. In them, creation first experienced the touch of its Creator through matter, preparing the way for sacramental life.

This divine-human mediation is utterly unique. There are many prophets, yet only one Mediator; many saints, yet only one Savior.

All priesthoods and sacrifices before Him were figures awaiting their fulfilment. In Christ, the Mediator and the mediation are one. He stands between God and man, not as a messenger crossing a distance, but as the place where distance itself is abolished.

St Paul names this mystery: "There is one mediator between God and men, the man Christ Jesus" (1 Tim 2:5). His mediation does not diminish the transcendence of God; it manifests it. Divine condescension is not weakness but omnipotence expressed in humility—God's power revealed through flesh and suffering.

Pope Leo the Great saw this with luminous clarity: *"What was visible in our Redeemer has passed into His mysteries."* The acts of Christ in the flesh disclose the invisible God and continue sacramentally within the Church. Through the humanity of Christ, God's self-communication has taken a permanent form: His saving action in history is henceforth human-shaped, and humanity's return to God is Christ-shaped.

Thus, the Incarnation is not a transient contact between heaven and earth but an enduring covenantal structure within reality itself. As the Council of Chalcedon defined, *"One and the same Son is to be acknowledged in two natures, without confusion or division, concurring in one person and one subsistence."* In that concurring—the perfect unity of divine and human—the bridge is established.

Because the hypostatic union is permanent, its effects are everlasting. The Word did not simply *put on flesh* to remove it after His work was done; He remains forever incarnate. The glorified body of Christ is the eternal sign that matter, history, and personhood have been taken up into the life of God. In Him, the boundaries between uncreated and created are crossed, not by collapse, but by communion. The chasm that no creature could bridge has been spanned by God Himself from the divine side. The bridge stands, and through it passes the whole river of grace that irrigates the Church and the world.

The Incarnation is not an isolated marvel completed in Bethlehem and Calvary; it endures as a living reality in the Church. The same humanity that united heaven and earth in the womb of the Virgin now unites them in the sacraments. What Christ once accomplished in His historical body, He continues to accomplish in His mystical body. Every sacramental action is, in essence, the divine life operating through His glorified humanity.

In baptism, His death and resurrection are communicated to the soul, cleansing it from sin and configuring it to His risen life. In the Eucharist, His deified flesh and blood become the nourishment of immortality, joining creaturely matter to the uncreated Word. In every sacrament, Christ's humanity remains the living instrument of divinity—the bridge through which the infinite Love of God descends and through which human beings ascend to that Love in return. The Church is therefore not an external institution but the continuation of the Incarnation extended through time.

This is why the Fathers spoke of the Church as the "body of Christ" not only metaphorically but ontologically. St. Augustine declared, *"The whole Christ is Head and Body."* The hypostatic bridge is widened: what was joined in the Person of Christ now expands to embrace the members of His body. Grace, therefore, is not an impersonal force or a legal favor, but the communication of the divine life through the humanity of Christ—a transmission that remains fully personal and ecclesial.

St. Leo the Great captured this truth in one crystalline sentence: *"What was visible in our Savior has passed into His mysteries."* The sacraments are the continuation of the Word's touch, voice, and power in the world. They are the points where the bridge between God and man is encountered in concrete form: water that cleanses, oil that consecrates, bread that becomes God. Each is the divine-human synergy made visible. The Incarnation thus becomes the ongoing grammar of salvation; what was once localized in Nazareth, Cana, and Calvary is now present wherever the Church lifts her hands in blessing.

The consequence is staggering: every act of the Church is potentially an event of theosis. When the priest absolves, it is Christ who forgives; when the faithful receive, it is Christ who divinizes. The humanity of the Word is the enduring medium through which God reaches us and through which we are lifted to Him. The bridge holds, and we walk upon it in sacramental light.

From the earliest centuries, the Church Fathers perceived the mystery of Christ as the cosmic hinge of existence—the living bridge upon which creation crosses into divinity. They did not treat the title *Theanthropos* ("God-Man") as a poetic flourish but as the key to reality itself. St. Gregory Nazianzen, in his *Oration on the Holy Pascha*, called Christ "the great bridge-builder," the one who "joins what was divided and heals what was rent asunder." In Him, the Creator stands on the creature's side, and the creature stands within the Creator's embrace. Every opposition—spirit and matter, heaven and earth, God and man—is gathered and reconciled in His single Person.

St. Maximus the Confessor expanded this vision with metaphysical grandeur. For Maximus, the entire cosmos is a vast movement of ascent and descent, divided by five great chasms—between uncreated and created, intelligible and sensible, heaven and earth, paradise and the world, male and female. Humanity was created to bridge these divisions but failed. In the God-Man, Maximus saw that vocation fulfilled. "Christ," he writes, "has accomplished the unification of the divided, making the extremes one through Himself." (*Ambigua* 41). The Incarnation, therefore, is not simply the repair of sin but the consummation of creation. It brings to completion the purpose for which the universe was made—to participate in God through the humanity of His Son.

St. Irenaeus glimpsed the same truth when he described Christ as the *recapitulation* of all things. What had fallen in Adam is summed up and renewed in Christ; the human story, scattered by disobedience, is retold in the Word made flesh. St. Athanasius, with the simplicity of a seer, gave it its immortal formula: "The Son of God became man so that man might become god." The Fathers were unanimous that this theosis is not metaphorical or moral but ontological: a real participation in divine life, made possible by the bridge of the Incarnation.

This is why the Cross, far from negating the Incarnation, is its fullest expression. On Calvary the bridge is completed: the arms of the Crucified stretch from heaven to earth, from eternity into time, reconciling all things in Himself. "I, when I am lifted up from the earth," He said, "will draw all men to myself" (John 12:32). In that lifting, divinity and humanity converge in a single act of self-giving love. The bridge is not made of stone or doctrine but of flesh offered and glorified.

The mystics of the Church have always understood this intuitively. St. Catherine of Siena saw Christ as the "bridge stretching from heaven to earth, built upon the wood of the Cross." St. Symeon the New Theologian described the soul's union with Christ as a "single flame born of two lights." Though separated by language and culture, East and West converge in this vision: Christ is the mediator who is also the mediation, the priest who is also the sacrifice, the bridge who is also the traveler.

To contemplate Him, therefore, is to stand at the meeting point of all reality. The Incarnation is not one event among others; it is the axis around which creation turns and redemption unfolds. The bridge that spans heaven and earth runs not through geography but through the heart of Christ—and, by grace, through the hearts of all who are joined to Him.

In the *Theanthropos*, divinity and humanity are not parallel lines but a single living harmony. The divine Word does not annihilate human nature; He transfigures it. His humanity remains the eternal instrument through which the divine acts and through which creation responds. The bridge between heaven and earth is not an abstraction but a Body—a human heart beating with uncreated life. From that heart flows the Spirit who renews the face of the earth.

When the spear pierced His side, the bridge was opened forever. From His wounded humanity poured blood and water, the visible signs of the invisible life of God: the sacraments of the Church. What was once the path of descent—God entering flesh—becomes now the path of ascent: flesh entering God. In Christ's glorified body, our nature stands radiant at the right hand of the Father, not as a symbol but as a fact. Matter has touched eternity, and eternity has touched matter; both remain distinct, yet both are united in love.

St Augustine marvels, "God became man that man might know he is nothing without God, yet that in God he is made divine." (*Sermon*

128). This paradox defines Christian dignity: humility is the pathway to glory. The Eastern tradition expressed the same mystery with the term *theosis*, a reality not foreign to the West but implicit in the doctrine of sanctifying grace. Participation in divine life does not divide God's essence but communicates His action. Grace is not a symbol of friendship; it is the created share in uncreated Love. Thus, when the saints radiate holiness, it is not metaphor—they truly partake of the divine light that shines in Christ's humanity. The bridge between God and man becomes visible in their transfigured lives.

The whole cosmos leans upon this bridge. Every prayer whispered by the saints, every absolution pronounced by the priest, every drop of chrism and every morsel of consecrated bread flows from the living humanity of the Word. The Church does not merely speak of Christ; she speaks *from* Him. Her worship is the echo of His own divine-human act of offering, resounding through time.

Here lies the heart of Christian mystery: the descent of God becomes the ascent of man. The bridge built in the womb of Mary stretches into the heavens, and upon it the human race is carried home. Christ is the living axis of the universe—the eternal Ladder seen by Jacob, the new Temple not made by hands, the Word through whom all things were made and in whom all things are made divine.

And so the Incarnation does not end—it continues. It continues in the Church, in the sacraments, and in every soul that opens itself to grace. The God-Man remains forever the meeting place of Creator and creature, the portal through which the divine passes into the world and the world ascends into God.

The hypostatic union is not a relic of history but the eternal bridge of salvation—through which the divine humanity of Christ communicates grace to every age, until at last all creation stands deified in the light of His glory. In Him, time and eternity are forever joined; His glorified body is the meeting place of God and creation, the living altar upon which heaven and earth are reconciled.

The Fathers saw this mystery not only as a doctrine to be defined but as a vision to be adored. In the Divine Liturgy of St John Chrysostom, the priest proclaims, "You have united heaven and earth." Every Eucharist is the re-enactment of that union: the same Christ who sits at the right hand of the Father descends upon the altar. Here theology yields to worship, and contemplation becomes communion. To understand the bridge is not merely to analyze it, but to walk upon it—to enter the liturgy where the eternal Word continues His exchange of life with the world.

The mystery of the Incarnation, therefore, does not remain abstract or distant. It becomes tangible in the sacramental life of the Church, where the same divine-human exchange continues to unfold. In baptism, chrismation, and the Eucharist, the humanity of Christ—once the instrument of divine action in history—remains the channel of grace in time. The Incarnation extends itself through these holy mysteries: what was united in His Person is now communicated to His members. Having contemplated the *Theanthropos*, we now turn to the means by which His life is shared—the sacraments, through which the Word made flesh continues to divinize creation.

5

The Sacraments: The Mysteries of Participation

"From the side of Christ sleeping on the Cross there came forth the wondrous sacrament of the whole Church."
— *St Augustine, Tractate on John 120.2*

The Sacramental Continuation of the Incarnation

The mystery of the Incarnation did not end when the stone was rolled away from the tomb. The Word made flesh did not withdraw His humanity once the work of redemption was "accomplished." Rather, that humanity became the abiding instrument through which the divine life continues to touch the world. What was once confined to a single body in Nazareth and Jerusalem is now diffused through the Body of the Church. The Incarnation, in other words, *continues*—not by repetition, but by extension.

The sacraments are the form this continuation takes. They are not memorials of a distant event but living operations of the same Christ who walked the earth. In them, His glorified humanity acts in history. "The sacraments," teaches the Catechism, "are powers that come forth from the Body of Christ" (§1116). Through water, oil, bread, and word, the one divine life that united heaven and earth in the God-Man now flows outward, vivifying creation.

Every sacrament bears the mark of the Incarnation: matter is assumed, consecrated, and made a vehicle of grace. In baptism, the most common element of the world—water—becomes the womb of new creation. In chrismation, fragrant oil becomes fire. In the Eucharist, bread and wine become God Himself. Even in confession and anointing, words and touch, so ordinary to human interaction, become the gestures of divine forgiveness and healing. The same humility of God that once stooped to wash feet now stoops to cleanse souls.

This is why the Church calls the sacraments *mysteria*—not because they are obscure, but because they disclose the inexhaustible presence of the Word. They are the visible shapes of invisible realities, the outward form of the divine descent. The Incarnation established the pattern; the sacraments perpetuate it. In each, the human and divine cooperate: a minister performs the rite, but Christ acts through him; material elements are used, but grace is their content. The Council of Trent expressed it with juridical precision: *ex opere operato*—it is Christ Himself who works in the work.

The sacramental economy is therefore nothing less than the continuation of the hypostatic union's energy in time. Just as the divine nature operated through the humanity of Jesus, so it now operates through the material and ecclesial body joined to Him. The difference is only in mode: what was once visible in the Redeemer is now visible in His mysteries. As Pope Leo the Great said, "What was apparent in our Savior has passed into His sacraments." The Christ who once healed by touch now heals through water and oil; the Christ who spoke forgiveness to the paralytic now speaks through the priest; the Christ who offered Himself on Calvary now offers Himself on the altar.

The Holy Spirit is the living bond that makes this continuity possible. At Pentecost the Spirit descended not merely to inspire the apostles but to inhabit the Church as the soul of Christ's Body. It is the Spirit who transforms material signs into means of divine communication, who makes the Church's acts the acts of Christ Himself. Where the Spirit breathes, the Incarnation expands. The bridge built in the flesh of the Word becomes a living network of grace spanning the centuries.

The sacraments, then, are not seven isolated rituals but one coherent mystery manifest in seven modes. Each sacrament unfolds a particular aspect of Christ's saving work—birth, growth, nourishment, healing, mission, union—until the whole of human existence is penetrated by divine life. They recapitulate salvation history in miniature: creation's matter, the water of the Flood, the oil of kings, the bread of the Exodus, all find their fulfilment in the mysteries of the Church.

In them the believer is not simply reminded of God's promises; he is inserted into the very movement of divine life. Grace is not an external favor but an interior participation in the Trinitarian exchange revealed in the Incarnate Word. The sacraments make theosis possible because they communicate the deified humanity of Christ—His life, His Spirit, His virtues—into the depths of human being. They are, as St Irenaeus foresaw, "our communion with God" (*Adv. Haer.* IV.18.5).

To speak of the sacramental life, therefore, is to speak of the continuing Incarnation. The Church's liturgy is the breathing of Christ's humanity through the centuries; her ministers are the hands of the God-Man extended in time. Each mystery is a fresh manifestation of the same descent that began in Mary's womb: the divine life entering creation so that creation might enter the divine life.

Thus the path of theosis now passes through the font, the oil, the altar, and the word of absolution. The believer who touches these mysteries touches Christ Himself. The Incarnation, having united heaven and earth, now unites the soul with God.

Through the sacraments, the descent of God becomes the daily ascent of man.

Baptism as Ontological Rebirth

The first entrance into divine life comes not through speculation or moral effort but through water. Baptism is not a rite of passage or the formal beginning of religious identity; it is the moment when the human being is ontologically re-created. What began in the descent of the Word into flesh continues in the descent of grace into the human soul. In the baptismal font, the old creation dies and the new creation is born. The water that once covered the face of the deep now becomes the matrix of resurrection. It is there that human nature, cleansed of corruption and infused with divine life, begins its ascent toward deification.

When Christ spoke to Nicodemus of being "born of water and the Spirit" (John 3:5), He revealed the very architecture of salvation. The first birth draws life from flesh; the second draws it from God. In that moment the Spirit, who brooded over the primordial waters at the dawn of creation, now broods over the baptismal waters to bring forth a new creation within the creature. Saint Paul would later unfold the same mystery in cosmic terms: "All of us who have been baptized into Christ Jesus were baptized into His death ... so that, just as Christ was raised from the dead by the glory of the Father, we too might walk in newness of life" (Rom 6:3–4).

Pope Benedict XVI notes that baptism's sign—the descent into water—is not accidental but divinely chosen to express the full drama of redemption. Water, in Scripture, is always ambivalent: it is both life-giving and destructive, cleansing and engulfing. The flood, the Red Sea, and the Jordan all bear witness to its double meaning. To enter the water is therefore to enter the realm of death, to go down into the chaos from which only God can call forth new creation. "Being immersed in the water," Benedict writes, "is the symbol of death, which means that our old self is buried in the water so that a new life can rise" (*Jesus of Nazareth*, I:18). The act is not mere washing but participation in Christ's own burial: as He descended into the waters of the Jordan, prefiguring His descent into the tomb, so the baptized descend into the waters to share His dying. Rising from the water, they share His resurrection. The symbolism, therefore, is not decorative; it is the sacramental expression of ontological reality. The sign reveals what it effects: death to sin, burial of the old Adam, and the birth of the new man from the waters of chaos into the light of divine life.

Baptism therefore is not merely a symbol of cleansing or belonging; it is the soul's participation in Christ's death and resurrection.

The one who descends into the water descends with Adam into the grave; the one who emerges rises with Christ into divine light. The act is historical, but the transformation is ontological: being itself is refashioned.

The early Fathers understood this with a literalness we have largely forgotten. Saint Cyril of Jerusalem, instructing the newly illumined, told them: "You were led to the holy pool as Christ was led to the tomb; each of you was asked, 'Do you believe in the Father, and the Son, and the Holy Spirit?' and you made the saving confession. Then you were plunged three times beneath the water and raised again. That descent and ascent prefigured the three days of Christ." For Cyril, baptism was both tomb and womb—death to sin, birth to divine sonship. Saint Ambrose of Milan declared that "the water does not cleanse the body but the soul; the flesh is washed that the spirit may be made stainless." The rite may seem simple, but in its depths the cosmos is reordered. The font becomes the Jordan, the Jordan becomes the tomb, and the tomb becomes the threshold of heaven.

In the language of the East, baptism is *photismos*—illumination. The newly baptized were called "the enlightened" because the uncreated light now dwelt within them. Saint Gregory Nazianzen called it "the most beautiful and magnificent of the gifts of God ... a new birth, a restoration of the image." The image that had been darkened by sin is re-polished until it again reflects the divine light. Through baptism, humanity is returned to its original clarity, but now with a greater glory, for the Spirit does not merely restore but inhabits. Grace is not external favour but divine indwelling; the creature becomes a temple.

The Church's teaching expresses this transformation with the sobriety of metaphysics. Saint Thomas Aquinas writes that baptism imprints upon the soul an *indelible character*, a spiritual seal that configures the person to Christ Himself. It is not a psychological memory but an ontological mark— an invisible form that enables participation in divine worship. "Grace," he says, "is nothing other than a certain participation in the divine nature" (*ST* I-II, q.110, a.2). In baptism this participation begins: the created subject is grafted onto the uncreated Vine, and a supernatural mode of being takes root.

The Fathers spoke of this as the "second creation." Just as the Spirit hovered over the waters of chaos to bring forth the world, so He now hovers over baptismal waters to bring forth the new man. The font is the Spirit's workshop, where He reshapes the clay of Adam into the likeness of Christ. Through this act the human being becomes not only reconciled but re-made, drawn into the Trinitarian life. The baptized are adopted not by legal decree but by ontological communion: the Father beholds in them the image of His Son and, through the Spirit, calls them His own.

This is why the early Church surrounded baptism with such awe. It was administered by immersion, by night, in the Paschal vigil, amid the blaze of lamps and the chanting of psalms. The catechumen descended into the waters naked as Adam, renouncing Satan and his works; he emerged clothed in a white garment, sign of the restored image and the wedding robe of the Lamb. Over him was anointed the oil of gladness, sealing him as a member of the royal priesthood. In that moment the Church saw fulfilled what Ezekiel had foretold: "I will sprinkle clean water upon you, and you shall be clean ... and I will put my Spirit within you" (Ezek 36:25–27). Baptism is thus the first personal Pentecost; the dove that descended upon the Jordan now rests upon the soul.

In the Catholic understanding, this grace is not a mere promise but an operative power. The Council of Trent teaches that through baptism "the guilt of original sin is remitted, all that is truly sin is taken away, and nothing remains that would impede entrance into heaven." Yet beyond remission lies regeneration: the new life of God is infused, not just credited. The Catechism captures it succinctly: "Baptism not only purifies from all sins, but also makes the neophyte 'a new creature,' an adopted son of God, who has become a 'partaker of the divine nature'" (§1265). Here the theology of theosis finds its first sacramental form—the creature truly shares in the Creator's life.

All of this happens through matter sanctified by the Word. Water, that primal element over which the Spirit first moved, becomes the chosen instrument of rebirth. It cleanses, cools, and gives life, mirroring the Trinity's action: the Father as the fountainhead, the Son as the living water, the Spirit as the flowing current. The immersion into water signifies not only purification but penetration; grace seeps into the depths of being, not resting on the surface but renewing nature from within. When the minister speaks the Trinitarian name, he does not merely describe God—he invokes Him. The same Word who said "Let there be light" now says, through His priest, "I baptize you," and a new light begins to burn within the soul.

Through baptism we do not merely begin a moral journey; we begin an ontological ascent. The divine life implanted in the soul is the seed of deification, destined to blossom in glory. The waters do not simply cleanse—they divinize, for in them the creature is joined to the Creator's own resurrection.

Baptism, then, is the first tangible step in the restoration of the image and the beginning of likeness. The image is the structure of being made for God; the likeness is the dynamic movement toward union with Him. In the font the image is re-polished and the likeness rekindled. The divine life, planted as seed, begins its slow unfolding toward glory. This is why the Fathers called baptism the "seed of immortality." What has begun invisibly will one day blossom visibly in resurrection.

To be baptized is to enter the Body of Christ, but also to be conformed to His pattern of descent and ascent. The baptized person lives in the rhythm of Paschal transformation: dying daily to sin, rising daily to grace. The event of baptism inaugurates a lifelong process of participation—an ever-deeper assimilation to the divine life that was implanted in the font. Every subsequent sacrament unfolds what baptism contained in germ.

For this reason the Church never separates baptism from its fulfillment in the other mysteries. The water that gives birth must be followed by the oil that gives strength, the fire that illumines, and the bread that divinizes. The Spirit who conceives new life in the waters now seeks to inflame it in chrismation and nourish it in the Eucharist. Baptism is thus the portal through which the entire sacramental economy opens. Without it, no other mystery can be received, for no unbaptized nature can bear the weight of divine indwelling.

And yet baptism is not the end of conversion but its beginning. The font is a gate, not a resting place. The neophyte emerges into the light not as one perfected but as one destined for transformation. The image has been restored, but the likeness must grow. Divine life, once planted, must be tended by faith, prayer, and sacramental nourishment. What baptism gives potentially must be realized actually, until the entire person—mind, heart, body—becomes transparent to the presence of God.

In this sense baptism is the first act of divinization, but also the perpetual call to divinization. It inserts man into the movement of Christ's own life: the descent into death, the ascent into glory, the abiding in love. To recall one's baptism is not nostalgia; it is to renew the covenant of being. Every drop of holy water, every sign of the cross, every confession of the Creed echoes that primal immersion into the Trinity.

Thus the waters of baptism are the starting point of the cosmic restoration. In them creation begins again, and humanity recovers its vocation as mediator of the world. The Church, born from the pierced side of Christ, continues to bring forth children by the same mingled water and blood. To step into that water is to step onto the bridge built by the God-Man; to rise from it is to find oneself standing in the dawn of the new creation.

Chrismation and the Sealing of the Divine Fire

If baptism is birth, chrismation is breath. The newly created soul, drawn from the waters of rebirth, must now receive the living Spirit who animates and perfects it. Just as the risen Christ breathed on His disciples and said, "Receive the Holy Spirit" (John 20:22), so the Church breathes upon her children, sealing them with the same divine Breath. Baptism restores the image; chrismation ignites the likeness. It is the personal Pentecost of every believer—the descent of divine fire into human clay.

From the first days of the Church, the two mysteries were joined. In the

Acts of the Apostles, those baptized in the name of Jesus are immediately confirmed by the laying on of hands: "Then they laid their hands on them, and they received the Holy Spirit" (Acts 8:17). The gift that descended in tongues of fire at Pentecost now descends sacramentally through the anointing of holy chrism. What the apostles experienced in the upper room, the faithful now experience through the hands of the bishop or priest. The Spirit, who overshadowed Mary at the Incarnation and the Church at Pentecost, now overshadows each soul, making it fertile with divine life.

The Church has always understood this anointing as more than blessing or dedication; it is consecration—the sealing of the human person as a living temple of God. Saint Paul writes, "It is God who establishes us with you in Christ and has anointed us, by putting his seal upon us and giving us his Spirit in our hearts as a guarantee" (2 Cor 1:21–22). The anointing, therefore, is both mark and pledge: a visible sign that the Holy Spirit has entered and a promise that divine life will reach its fulfillment in glory. The East calls this moment the "seal of the gift of the Holy Spirit." The West names it "confirmation," because it confirms and strengthens baptismal grace. Both speak of the same mystery: the Spirit's abiding indwelling that transforms what was merely alive with grace into what is ablaze with it.

The Fathers loved to speak of oil and fire together. Saint Cyril of Jerusalem told his neophytes, "Beware of supposing this to be plain ointment ... it is not so; as the bread of the Eucharist, after the invocation of the Holy Spirit, is no longer ordinary bread, so also this holy ointment is no longer simple ointment, but the gift of Christ and of the Holy Spirit." (*Mystagogical Catecheses* 3.3) The oil, fragrant and penetrating, becomes a visible expression of the invisible flame. Saint John Damascene compared the Spirit to fire that burns without consuming, making the anointed one luminous without destroying his humanity. In this sacrament, the believer is not merely touched by grace but saturated with it; the Spirit seeps into the very pores of being, consecrating intellect, will, and body as instruments of divine energy.

The symbolism of oil itself carries the weight of revelation. In Scripture it anoints kings, priests, and prophets, marking them as bearers of divine authority. The same Spirit who empowered David to sing and Isaiah to speak now empowers every Christian to live a royal, prophetic, and priestly life. Saint Ambrose told his newly confirmed: "You are anointed because you have become a member of Christ, and Christ means anointed; therefore you share in His anointing and His kingship." (*De Sacramentis* 3.2) Chrismation, then, is not the privilege of the few but the vocation of the baptized: to reign by self-gift, to prophesy by truth, to offer the world to God in thanksgiving. The oil of gladness poured upon the Head runs down upon the body, until the whole Church shines with one fragrance.

In the Catholic tradition, chrismation is inseparable from the action of the bishop, the successor of the apostles, for it is through apostolic hands that the fire of Pentecost is handed on. The minister's touch is not his own but Christ's; the perfumed oil he uses is not mere substance but sacramental matter infused with the Spirit's power. The prayer of consecration of the chrism at Holy Week reveals the Church's faith: "May this oil be the sign of life and salvation to those anointed with it; may it make them sharers in eternal life and partakers of heavenly glory." The Spirit's descent upon the oil during this prayer is the mirror of His descent upon the bread and wine at the Eucharist. Both are acts of sanctification through matter; both prolong the Incarnation in visible form.

The effect of chrismation is not fleeting emotion but ontological change. The Spirit who once hovered above creation now dwells within the creature as in His temple. He strengthens what baptism has begun, bestows His gifts, and roots the soul in the divine likeness. The scholastics spoke of this as a "character" imprinted upon the soul—an indelible capacity for divine operation. In this seal the human person becomes permanently configured to Christ the Anointed One. Grace does not sit upon the surface; it pervades the depths, transforming the faculties from within so that divine life may flow outward through them. The Spirit becomes the new rhythm of existence, the pulse of the deified heart.

This anointing also signifies mission. The Spirit who descended on

Christ at the Jordan immediately drove Him into ministry; so too, the Spirit given in chrismation propels the faithful into witness. The fire received must spread. "You shall receive power when the Holy Spirit has come upon you," Christ promised, "and you shall be my witnesses" (Acts 1:8). Confirmation is thus not a private enrichment but an ecclesial empowerment. The Christian, sealed with the Spirit, becomes an extension of Pentecost in the world. The same tongues of fire that once hovered above the apostles now rest invisibly upon every believer who bears the seal. To live confirmed is to live aflame.

The Fathers saw in this sacrament the restoration of what Adam lost. The first man was formed from dust and given the breath of life; the new man, formed in baptism, receives the breath of the Spirit. The oil that now anoints him restores the radiance that once clothed humanity in Eden. The seal of the Spirit is the garment of glory regained. Saint Ephrem sang of this mystery: "The Spirit came down and clothed the baptized as a robe of glory; He made them children of light and gave them a new name." (*Hymns on the Epiphany* 6.17) Through the chrism the baptized become not merely cleansed but clothed, not merely forgiven but crowned.

The anointing also establishes the soul's eschatological destiny. Saint Paul calls the Spirit "the guarantee of our inheritance" (Eph 1:14). The seal placed upon the believer is a pledge that what has begun in time will be consummated in eternity. The Spirit's presence is both first-fruit and foretaste, the down-payment of deification. What we experience sacramentally now we shall experience in fullness when God is all in all. The oil that glistens on the forehead is the shadow of that future glory which will shine from every part of the transfigured body.

In this light, chrismation is the hinge between baptismal birth and eucharistic union. It completes the process of initiation and opens the way to communion. The Spirit who breathes within now hungers for the flesh of the Word; the fire seeks its fuel. The divine life poured into the soul now desires nourishment in the sacrament of the altar. The mysteries form one ascending movement: the water gives life, the oil gives fire, and the bread gives God. Together they make the human person a living liturgy, an altar of the Spirit's indwelling.

The seal of the Spirit also bestows discernment. Where the Spirit dwells, there the mind is illumined; truth becomes not information but participation. "You have an anointing from the Holy One," writes Saint John, "and you all know the truth" (1 John 2:20). The chrism opens the interior senses; the believer begins to perceive reality sacramentally, to see creation as charged with divine meaning. The same Spirit who inspired Scripture now interprets it within the heart. The Christian no longer reads with the eyes of the flesh but with the gaze of the Spirit, in whom all things are made new.

Ultimately, chrismation is the moment when the divine and human spirits meet and coinhere. It is the Spirit of God resting upon the spirit of man until their movements are one. Theosis begins to take on fire: the creature becomes translucent to the Creator. In the words of Saint Seraphim of Sarov, "The true aim of Christian life is the acquisition of the Holy Spirit." To be confirmed is to begin that acquisition; to live confirmed is to become what one has received.

The Church, in her wisdom, completes every baptism with this anointing because the Christian vocation is not only to live but to burn. The Spirit who sealed the humanity of Jesus at the Jordan now seals every member of His Body, that the world may behold divine fire blazing through human hearts. When the priest or bishop traces the sign of the cross with chrism on the forehead and proclaims, "The seal of the gift of the Holy Spirit," heaven and earth meet again. The same breath that stirred the chaos in Genesis, the same wind that filled the upper room, the same fire that consumed the bush without burning—it is that very Spirit who now claims the human soul as His dwelling.

The mystery of chrismation is, in essence, the sacrament of *energeia*—of divine activity communicated to the creature. If baptism gives being, chrismation gives movement; it enables the new creation to act with God. The Holy Spirit, poured forth upon the anointed, does not simply sanctify the soul as an object of grace; He makes it a participant in divine operation. Grace ceases to be passive gift and becomes living energy.

What the Fathers called *synergeia*—cooperation between divine and human freedom—is born in this anointing. Here theosis becomes dynamic: the believer begins to think with the mind of Christ, to love with the love of God, to will with the will of the Spirit. The very faculties of the soul are drawn into the current of divine life, not overwhelmed but illumined, so that human actions begin to bear divine radiance.

Thus, chrismation marks the transition from image restored to likeness inflamed. The Spirit, received as seal, is also received as fire, and that fire is nothing other than the uncreated life of the Trinity dwelling within the creature. The deified life is now no longer future promise but present reality: "We all, with unveiled face, beholding the glory of the Lord, are being changed into His likeness from glory to glory" (2 Cor 3:18). The seal of the Spirit is the imprint of that glory; it is the inner shape of divinization impressed upon the soul. To be confirmed is not only to belong to Christ but to begin living His very mode of existence—to become, in miniature, what He is by nature: the human image of divine fire.

Through chrismation, the descent of God becomes flame. The Spirit who overshadowed the Virgin now overshadows the baptized; the fire that descended on the apostles now descends on the neophyte. The human person, once cold and inert, becomes incandescent with divine energy. What was potential in baptism becomes power in confirmation. The image restored now begins to shine; the likeness begins to move. In the seal of the Spirit, humanity rediscovers its vocation to be light for the world and warmth for creation. The bridge between God and man blazes with glory, and the journey of deification continues.

Eucharist as the Metabole of Man into God

If baptism is birth and chrismation is breath, the Eucharist is life itself—the pulse of divinized existence. It is the sacrament in which the descent of God reaches its most intimate depth and the ascent of man reaches its highest point. Every mystery of the faith converges here, for in this meal of fire the humanity of Christ, glorified and deified, becomes our food.

What began in the womb of Mary and was consummated on the Cross is now placed into our hands. The Incarnation does not merely touch the world through the Eucharist; it enters it again, continually.

The Word who took flesh now gives that flesh; the blood poured out on Calvary now flows into the chalice. In this mystery, the whole economy of salvation becomes edible. "My flesh is true food and my blood is true drink," Christ declared (John 6:55). These are not metaphors but metaphysics: through the Eucharist, the Logos continues His own theandric act—divine life communicated through human matter. The same Person who once said, "Let there be light," now says through the priest, "This is My Body," and creation trembles under the weight of those words.

The Fathers never tired of this mystery. Saint Ignatius of Antioch called the Eucharist "the medicine of immortality, the antidote that we should not die but live forever in Jesus Christ." Saint Irenaeus saw in it the final proof of deification: "When the mingled cup and the broken bread receive the Word of God, the Eucharist becomes the Body and Blood of Christ, and from them our flesh is nourished and grows; how, then, can they deny that the flesh is capable of receiving God's gift of eternal life?" (*Against Heresies* IV.18.5). The bread of angels has become the bread of men; and men, by consuming it, become citizens of heaven.

The Eucharist is the sacrament of *metabole*—of transformation. The first change is that of the elements: bread and wine are transubstantiated into the deified Body and Blood of the Lord. But the deeper change, the one for which the first exists, is the *metabole of man into God*. Saint John Chrysostom spoke of this audacious mystery: "He gives Himself to those who desire Him, not only to see Him but to touch and eat Him; He unites Himself to them so closely that they are one body." (*Homily on Matthew* 82.5) What occurs in the gifts occurs also in the communicant: what was once bread becomes God, and what was once merely human becomes divine by participation.

This participation is not poetic but ontological. The same hypostatic union that joined divinity and humanity in Christ now extends to those who commune with Him. In receiving the Eucharist, we are inserted into His personal life; His deified humanity becomes ours. Saint Thomas Aquinas writes, "The effect of this sacrament is the transformation of man into Christ, so that he can say, 'I live, now not I, but Christ lives in me.'" (*ST* III, q.73, a.3) The communicant is not absorbed or annihilated but perfected; individuality is not lost but glorified, for grace never destroys nature—it fulfills it. Theosis through the Eucharist is the supreme expression of that principle: the finite taken up into the infinite without ceasing to be itself.

The Eucharist is therefore the living continuation of the Incarnation. As Christ assumed human nature once for all in the Virgin's womb, He now assumes human persons one by one in this sacrament. The liturgy becomes a new Bethlehem where the Word takes flesh anew in those who receive Him. Saint Augustine described this mystery with startling clarity: "If you receive well, you are what you receive." (*Sermon* 272) The communicant becomes the Body he consumes; the many are gathered into one in Christ. The Eucharist thus accomplishes what the Cross made possible and what baptism and chrismation began: full incorporation into the divine life.

It is for this reason that the Eucharist stands at the centre of the Church's existence. Without it, Christianity becomes moralism; with it, the moral becomes mystical. Every other sacrament tends toward it. Baptism makes one capable of receiving it; chrismation ignites the Spirit that recognizes it; confession restores the capacity for it; anointing strengthens the soul for its final reception. The Eucharist is the heart of the theotic organism. In it the blood of God circulates through the veins of the Church, making every member alive with divine vitality.

The transformation effected by this mystery is twofold: *the change of the elements* and *the change of the communicant*. Both are wrought by the same Spirit who overshadowed the Virgin and descended at Pentecost. During the Epiclesis, the priest prays that the Holy Spirit may "make this bread the precious Body of Christ ... and this cup the precious Blood of Christ ... changing them by His Holy Spirit." Yet immediately the prayer continues, asking that "those who partake ... may be filled with the Holy Spirit and become one body and one spirit." The Spirit who changes the bread also changes the believer. The material becomes divine so that the human may become divine. Here the bridge between God and man is not only traversed—it is crossed in both directions at once.

The Eucharist also reveals the paradox of divine humility and human exaltation. The infinite hides Himself in a fragment of bread so that finite creatures may receive infinity without fear. This is the logic of love: the greater lowering Himself so that the lesser may be raised. Saint Maximus the Confessor saw in this mystery the fulfilment of the cosmic purpose: "The Word of God, wishing to accomplish the mystery of His love for men, unites Himself through flesh to the whole of human nature, and so unites it to God Himself." (*Ambigua* 5) In the Eucharist that uniting becomes immediate; divinity and humanity converge in the act of communion.

The realism of this union has always been the scandal of unbelief and the glory of faith. The Eucharist defies reduction to symbol or memorial; it is event. It is the same theandric action that occurred in Nazareth, on Golgotha, and in the empty tomb, now made present under the veil of the elements. When the communicant receives the Body and Blood of Christ, he receives the whole Person—divinity and humanity inseparable. Theosis here becomes physical: the flesh of man is mingled with the flesh of God, not by confusion but by communion. The divine life is not imagined; it is eaten.

This eating, however, is not a carnal act but a spiritual assimilation. Saint Gregory of Nyssa explains, "Since our nature is joined to the divine by the participation in this holy body, we are no longer corruptible, having the hope of resurrection through the body which is immortal." (*Oratio Catechetica* 37) The Eucharist infuses immortality into mortality; it is the antidote to death, the seed of resurrection planted in every cell of the body. What was once dust destined for decay becomes the vessel of uncreated light.

The mystery also bears an ecclesial dimension. In partaking of one bread, the many become one body. "Because there is one bread," writes

THE SACRAMENTS: THE MYSTERIES OF PARTICIPATION

Saint Paul, "we who are many are one body, for we all partake of the one bread" (1 Cor 10:17). Deification is therefore never solitary; it is communal. To be divinized is to be incorporated—to live in the Trinitarian pattern of communion. The Eucharist fashions not isolated saints but the mystical organism of Christ, the Church, radiant with divine unity. It is the sacrament of ontological communion, making the many one without erasing difference, reflecting in time the unity-in-distinction of the Trinity itself.

The Eucharist also has an eschatological dimension. It is not only remembrance of the past but anticipation of the future. Every Mass is a glimpse of the wedding feast of the Lamb; every altar is a threshold of the Kingdom. The deification begun in baptism and inflamed in chrismation will be completed when what is now sacrament becomes vision. "The Eucharist," wrote Pope Benedict XVI, "draws us into Jesus' act of self-oblation. More than just statically receiving the incarnate Logos, we enter into the very dynamic of His self-giving." (*Sacramentum Caritatis* §11) Participation in the Eucharist is therefore participation in the Trinitarian life itself—the Son's eternal offering of love to the Father in the Spirit. In this offering, humanity finds its ultimate transformation: no longer spectator, it becomes participant in the inner life of God.

In the liturgy, this mystery unfolds not as abstract doctrine but as enacted theosis. The procession of the gifts, the epiclesis, the communion—all reveal the same rhythm of descent and ascent, of divine self-giving and human participation. When the faithful approach the chalice, they do not merely approach a symbol; they approach the uncreated fire veiled in the created. "See," says Chrysostom, "He gives Himself to you; He sets before you His body, not to gaze upon only, but to touch and eat and receive within." The communicant stands at the intersection of heaven and earth, participating in the perpetual exchange of love that is the life of God Himself.

The effect of this communion cannot be contained in words. It transforms not only the soul but the body; not only individuals but the cosmos. For as the communicant is divinized, so too creation begins to be transfigured. The elements offered on the altar represent the whole material world; when they are consecrated and consumed, all matter symbolically passes through death into resurrection. The Eucharist thus accomplishes what creation was made for: to become praise, thanksgiving, offering. It is the fulfilment of the cosmic liturgy begun in Genesis and consummated in the New Jerusalem.

The Eucharist is also the daily rhythm of deification, the steady pulse that keeps the divine life alive within the soul. The grace received in baptism and enflamed in chrismation is nourished here, lest it wither. Divine life, like all life, must be fed; and the food that sustains immortality can only be God Himself. The believer who hungers for the Eucharist hungers for deification, for the assimilation of every part of his being to the divine Word. To receive often is to consent repeatedly to the transformation of one's nature, allowing grace to seep into the smallest fibres of existence until even thought and gesture begin to carry a Eucharistic fragrance.

This mystery also shapes the soul's interior life. Each communion extends the Incarnation deeper into the human person. The Word becomes flesh again—not in Bethlehem, but in the heart. The communicant's memory, imagination, and will become new spaces of incarnation where divine presence takes root. The more the soul is interiorly conformed to Christ, the more it becomes Eucharistic—offered, broken, poured out for others. Theosis here becomes charity: divine love manifested in human form. The Body received becomes the Body lived.

In this way the Eucharist unites contemplation and action, worship and mission. The divine life received at the altar must radiate into the world. The communicant leaves the temple bearing within himself what the world most longs for—God made present in humanity. Thus, through the Eucharist, the Church becomes what she celebrates: a living icon of the Word made flesh, a humanity filled with God.

In this sacrament, then, the bridge between God and man is no longer merely contemplated—it is crossed. The believer who receives the deified flesh of Christ becomes himself a living Eucharist, a being offered and transfigured. What was created to eat now becomes capable of being food for God's delight, as Augustine dared to imagine: "You will not change Me into yourself, as food for your body, but you will be changed into Me." (*Confessions* VII.10) This is the final word of theosis: transformation into Christ through communion with His deified humanity. The Eucharist is not only the summit of the Church's worship but the horizon of human destiny. Through it, the flesh of man becomes the dwelling place of God, and the love that moved the Word to descend now lifts the creature into the fire of the divine.

Confession

The mystery of confession must be understood not merely as a juridical pardon but as an interior theophany—a meeting of light and darkness within the soul. In every sincere confession, the same voice that called Adam in the garden—"Where are you?"—calls again. The question is not accusation but invitation. God seeks the hidden heart, not to condemn it but to draw it back into communion. *Metanoia*—repentance—is therefore not self-loathing but the turning of the intellect toward its proper horizon, the vision of God. When the sinner turns, he discovers that grace has already gone out to meet him. The Father runs to embrace the prodigal before a word is spoken.

Christ Himself entrusted this ministry to the Church: "Receive the Holy Spirit. Whose sins you forgive are forgiven them" (John 20:22–23). The keys given to Peter (Matt 16:19) are here placed in the hands of the apostles, and through them in the hands of their successors. According to the Church's constant teaching, this sacrament acts *ex opere operato*: the absolving word of Christ, spoken through His priest, truly effects what it signifies. Its human "matter" is the acts of the penitent—contrition, confession, and satisfaction—while its "form" is the priestly absolution. None of this is merely juridical mechanism; it is the very economy of deification at work: the Word heals by speaking, the Spirit restores by indwelling, and the Father receives the returning child into communion.

In this way confession is itself an act of theosis, for it is the moment when divine love and human freedom coincide in truth. The sinner, by naming the fracture within himself, aligns his word with the Word; speech becomes participation in Logos. The priest, hearing the confession, stands sacramentally as the ear of Christ—listening not to record but to redeem. When absolution is spoken, creation hears again its original blessing: "Let there be light." The light that dawns in the soul at that instant is not borrowed illumination but the returning radiance of the divine image.

Through this sacrament, the believer is restored not only to grace but to the vocation of likeness itself. Saint Irenaeus taught that "the glory of God is man fully alive, and the life of man is the vision of God." Sin dims that vision; confession restores it. The human person, recreated in the light of forgiveness, begins again to mirror the filial life of the Son. The Father does not merely remove guilt—He restores communion so that His image-bearer may once more share in His likeness. This is why absolution is more than declaration: it is a creative act, a new breathing of the Spirit into the clay.

The Fathers often described sin as the darkening of the *nous*—the spiritual intellect. Confession is therefore illumination. Saint Maximus the Confessor wrote that "the one who confesses truthfully already begins to see." The very act of bringing hidden things into the open restores sight. Just as the blind man in the Gospel washed in the pool of Siloam and saw, so the penitent, washing his conscience in confession, begins to behold reality again. In this moment the heart's mirror, once clouded, is polished by humility until it can reflect the divine light without distortion. Yet illumination is not the end of confession; it is its beginning. When light enters, it does not merely reveal but transforms. The intellect, once purified, is conformed to the divine likeness; vision becomes communion.

There is also an ascetical dimension: confession renews the synergy between divine grace and human effort. It is not a mechanical reset but a cooperation in transformation. The Spirit does not simply erase guilt; He heals the will, strengthening it for divine action. Saint John Climacus called repentance "the renewal of baptism and the commerce of humility with God." Each confession is a trade between divine mercy and human honesty: man offers his truth, and God bestows His life. The humility that confesses becomes the vessel of divinity, for the proud cannot be deified—only the contrite can receive fire without being consumed. As the Catechism teaches, it is called *the sacrament of conversion* because it makes present Jesus' call to return to the Father and restores the life of grace (cf. CCC 1423–1424).

The traditional "acts of the penitent" are themselves remedies that divinize. Contrition is the will turned back toward God—a first participation in divine love. Confession conforms human speech to Truth; the tongue becomes priestly. Satisfaction is not payment but medicine: the will freely cooperating with grace to repair what love has wounded. Through these acts the soul is not merely pardoned but trained to love as God loves. Justice is restored and charity rekindled; the human person learns again to act with divine rhythm.

Moreover, confession deepens the image beyond its original innocence. The saints often said that Adam before the Fall was good, but the forgiven sinner is glorious. For innocence knows love only as gift; repentance knows it as mercy. When divine life returns to the heart that has known its own poverty, it burns hotter and brighter. The forgiven soul participates in Christ's own descent and rising, tasting the Paschal rhythm from within. This is why the penitent emerges not merely restored but transfigured: his wounds, touched by grace, become sources of compassion; his weakness becomes a conduit of divine strength. "The greater the sinner, the greater the right he has to My mercy," Christ told Saint Faustina—a statement that is not sentiment but metaphysics: mercy is divinity entering human misery to make it luminous.

Confession, then, is a mystery of divine pedagogy. Each return teaches the soul anew how to receive love. The perfection of theosis does not consist in never falling but in never ceasing to rise. Holiness matures through the rhythm of being forgiven. The penitent who has tasted mercy becomes wise in a way innocence never could: he learns what it means that God is patient, that divine holiness bends down to touch clay. In this lowering, God reveals Himself as He truly is—humble love. The human soul, humbled in response, becomes more God-like, for humility is the visible form of divine glory. The road of repentance, therefore, is not detour but direct path; it passes through the heart's own Golgotha to the light of resurrection.

Confession also initiates an ongoing rhythm within the deified life. Theosis is not a single ascent but a spiral: approach, fall, and deeper approach. The more one grows in grace, the more subtle the awareness of distance becomes, and the more eagerly the soul returns to the confessional as to a spring. In this way repentance becomes not exceptional but habitual—a perpetual *metanoia* that keeps the soul supple to the Spirit. Saint Isaac the Syrian wrote, "This life has been given to you for repentance; do not waste it in vain pursuits." The saint does not cease confessing; he confesses more deeply, not out of fear but out of longing for ever greater purity of communion.

There is, in the silence of the confessional, a profound sacramental anthropology at work. Human beings need to speak to be healed, for the wound of sin is communicative—it distorts relationship. God heals relationally, through hearing and speaking. The sacrament restores dialogue: between man and God, between the self and its own depths. The word of confession is therefore creative; it reforms what sin deformed. The absolving word, in turn, is re-creative; it breathes new being into what was dying. Together they enact in miniature the creative exchange of the Incarnation: the human word offered, the divine Word responding.

Reconciliation is never private. Sin fractures communion; absolution repairs it. The forgiven member strengthens the whole Body (1 Cor 12:26). Each healed soul adds warmth to the Church's life—prayer brightens, charity deepens, worship becomes more radiant. Every confession is therefore a hidden liturgical act, enlarging the Church's share in divine holiness.

Here the confessional reveals itself as an incarnational extension: the eternal Word taking up our poor human words and filling them with His power. In this encounter, language—fallen and fragmentary since Babel—is redeemed. Human speech, once used to hide from God, becomes again the medium of communion. The tongue that confessed sin now praises mercy; the lips that spoke death now speak life. The Incarnation thus reaches us through sound: God's Word fills human words, transforming them into instruments of grace. In this exchange, the creature regains its priestly vocation—to speak creation back to its Creator in truth and thanksgiving.

Confession also renews the Eucharistic vocation of the believer. One cannot approach the altar without first being reconciled. The sacrament re-opens the path to communion, ensuring that participation in the deified Body is real, not hypocritical. The purified conscience becomes once more a fitting altar upon which divine fire may rest. The soul that confesses prepares itself for new Eucharistic transformation, and thus the cycle of deification continues: repentance leading to communion, communion calling forth deeper repentance, until humility and glory become indistinguishable.

The same grace that first deified in baptism and is enkindled in chrismation is nourished in the Eucharist and rekindled here. Penance is, as the Fathers loved to say, a second baptism—not because it repeats the first, but because it reopens the floodgates of divine life when sin has dammed them. The fire received in the anointing and the light consumed at the altar blaze again in this sacrament of mercy. Thus the whole rhythm of deification remains unbroken: birth in the font, breath in the anointing, nourishment at the altar, healing in confession—until, as the Apostle says, "Christ is formed in you" (Gal 4:19).

For this reason, the saints called tears of repentance "baptism in miniature." The heart that weeps for love of God experiences a kind of interior anointing—the Spirit moving within as gentle rain. These tears, wrote Saint Symeon the New Theologian, "wash the soul more perfectly than baptismal water." He speaks with holy hyperbole: sacramental baptism is unique and unrepeatable in its efficacy; tears do not rival the sacrament—they prolong its grace in daily life. Thus devotion serves sacrament, and sacrament sustains devotion. The penitent who learns to weep in love has entered the rhythm of divine compassion itself.

Thus the sacrament of confession is not an appendix to Christian life but its pulse of renewal. It is the place where divinization proves itself stronger than sin, where grace shows that it can re-create as easily as it can create. Every absolution is a new beginning of theosis, for the soul once again reflects the image of the Son in whom it was made. The prodigal returns not to servitude but to sonship; he is clothed again in the robe of glory and feasted upon the Lamb. Confession, then, is not the end of the road but its rediscovery—the door through which the lost find their way home to divine light.

This rediscovery is never solitary. Each confession heals not only the individual but the Body of Christ. Sin isolates; repentance restores communion. When the soul is reconciled, the Church herself becomes more radiant, for every forgiven member reflects more clearly the face of the Bridegroom. Theosis, then, is ecclesial as well as personal—it is the beautifying of the entire Body through the renewal of each part. The absolution whispered in one corner of the world reverberates through the whole Mystical Body, strengthening the bonds of divine charity that hold creation together. Even the angels, says Saint John Climacus, "rejoice when they see the soul rise from its fall, shining more brightly than before." As the Lord Himself teaches, "there will be more joy in heaven over one sinner who repents" (Luke 15:7).

Confession therefore stands as the Church's perpetual Easter. In every absolution, Christ descends once more into the tomb of the human heart and rises there, radiant and victorious. The soul walks out clothed in divine light, bearing in itself the proof that divine love can re-create what sin has destroyed. The image is not only restored—it glows with the beauty of one who has been found. For in the Church's ceaseless confession, the world itself is quietly renewed. Each absolution pushes back the night; each act of repentance clears a window through which divine light enters creation. The confessional is thus not only the healing room of the soul but a workshop of cosmic restoration. In the trembling voice of the penitent and the steady word of forgiveness, creation rehearses the final reconciliation when God will be "all in all" (1 Cor 15:28).

In that final vision, every act of repentance will be seen as a spark within the great conflagration of divine mercy—the countless forgiven hearts forming together the radiant Body of the glorified Christ. Through Him, the universe itself is transfigured and led into the freedom of divine glory.

Anointing and the Healing of the Image

If confession restores the image within the soul, anointing restores it within the body. The mystery of the Anointing of the Sick is the Church's declaration that divine life seeks to penetrate every dimension of human existence—even pain, weakness, and mortality. Grace does not recoil from decay; it descends into it. The same Word who touched lepers and raised the dead continues to touch the afflicted through oil and prayer, revealing that suffering itself can become translucent to glory.

This sacrament is no late addition to Christian piety but a direct continuation of the Incarnation's healing touch. Saint James commands: "Is any among you sick? Let him call for the presbyters of the Church, and let them pray over him, anointing him with oil in the name of the Lord" (Jas 5:14). The Church has obeyed this injunction from the beginning, understanding the anointing not as magic nor as mere consolation, but as a genuine participation in the redemptive power of Christ's Passion. As the Catechism teaches, "the special grace of the sacrament of the Anointing of the Sick has as its effects the uniting of the sick person to the passion of Christ, the strengthening, peace, and courage to endure, and the forgiveness of sins" (§1520–1523). In this union of weakness and divinity, theosis reaches into the final shadows of the Fall.

The Incarnation ensures that no part of human nature lies beyond the scope of sanctification. Christ did not assume an abstract humanity; He took flesh subject to hunger, weariness, and death. By entering the full measure of human limitation, He made it possible for limitation itself to become the meeting point of grace. In the Anointing, this truth is made sacramental: the divine power that once healed by physical contact now touches through consecrated oil, communicating both healing and hope.

The priest who anoints does not merely bless; he extends the hand of the Incarnate Word into the world once more.

The anointing therefore unites the believer to Christ not merely in consolation but in cruciform participation. Saint John Chrysostom called suffering "the gold of the crucible," for the soul is refined by fire until it reflects the divine image. In the prayer of anointing—"May the Lord who frees you from sin save you and raise you up"—the Church does not deny the Cross; she enters it. Every drop of oil becomes a sharing in Gethsemane's sweat and Calvary's blood, revealing that redemption is not evasion of pain but its transfiguration from within. To be anointed is to be drawn into the Son's own oblation, where love and suffering become indistinguishable, and where the wound itself becomes the window of divine energy.

The grace communicated in anointing is therefore not merely remedial but configurative. It conforms the sick to the Son's filial posture before the Father—"Abba... not my will, but yours be done"—and this filiality is the very atmosphere of deification. Theosis is not a technique of ascent but a sharing in the Son's obedient love. When the Spirit strengthens the infirm to consent in faith, the creature's will is gently braided into Christ's own "yes," and that consent is participation in the Trinitarian life. Here the human person becomes most God-like, not by seizing power, but by receiving and returning love in weakness.

The oil used in this rite, consecrated by the bishop on Holy Thursday, is more than medicinal—it is metaphysical. In Scripture, oil marks kings, prophets, and priests, sealing them for divine service. Here it seals the suffering body as a royal temple of the Spirit. Saint Irenaeus saw in the anointing of the flesh the continuation of baptismal grace, writing that "as dry wheat cannot become a single loaf without moisture, so we who are many cannot become one in Christ Jesus without the oil of God" (Adv. Haer. IV.33.2). The body, threatened by dissolution, is moistened once more by the oil of divine compassion, made supple again to the Spirit's touch.

The Council of Trent described Anointing as truly sacramental in both sign and effect, teaching that it confers grace, remits sins, and sometimes restores bodily health when conducive to salvation (Session XIV). The old fear that this rite signals surrender is thus inverted: it is an infusion of power—not worldly vigor, but Paschal strength, the courage to suffer without despair and to hope without illusion. The grace does not anesthetize; it transfigures. "Strengthening, peace, and courage" (CCC 1520) name not three sentiments but one movement: the Spirit drawing the believer into the Son's victorious endurance.

Theologically, Anointing guards two borders that keep theosis Catholic. First, it refuses dualism: the body is not a prison to be discarded; it is the form of the person destined for glory. Second, it refuses quietism: grace does not cancel the human; it heals, elevates, and co-opts our freedom into love. The sacrament enacts both truths at once: matter is ministered to and meaning is made, while the person consents to God's work—not by achievement but by availability. This is the grammar of participation the whole book is teaching.

This sacrament also proclaims the inseparability of body and soul in the divine economy. Modern thought too easily divides the two, yet the Creator fashioned them as one reality, destined together for glory. Sin ruptured this unity, introducing sickness and death as foreign intrusions; grace restores it, not by abolishing mortality but by filling it with meaning. Saint John Paul II, in *Salvifici Doloris*, taught that "in suffering there is concealed a particular power that draws a person interiorly close to Christ." The anointing reveals this power: suffering, when united to divine love, becomes participation in the redeeming energy of the Cross. Pain, accepted in faith, ceases to be mere loss and becomes liturgy.

In the Roman tradition, Anointing often stands beside Viaticum, the Eucharist given as "food for the journey." Together they crown the sacramental life: the body is anointed for glory, and the soul is fed with Immortality. Theosis reaches a luminous concentration here: the Bread of God enters the anointed temple, and mortal flesh is sealed with the oil of resurrection. What began at the font as adoption is finalized as arrival: the baptized, confirmed, absolved, and fed are now set like a seal upon the heart of Christ for passage through death.

Here the movement of divine descent and human ascent reaches its most comprehensive form. The oil taken from the fruit of the earth, blessed by the bishop's hand, and placed upon the suffering body, mirrors the Eucharistic pattern of offering and transformation. Creation itself enters the liturgy of healing: the earth offers its element, the Church consecrates it, and the Spirit fills it with uncreated life. The human body thus stands as the meeting-place of cosmos and Creator. The material world, once subject to futility, begins to taste its liberation in the touch of this oil. Through the anointing, the Church enacts in miniature what she awaits in glory—the renewal of all things when matter itself will shine with Spirit.

The Fathers therefore spoke of the sickbed as an altar and the sufferer as priest. Saint Gregory Nazianzen called the sick "those who offer themselves as a living sacrifice, joining their wounds to Christ's." The anointed person becomes a visible icon of kenosis—the divine humility that bends down to the dust. His weakness, sealed by the Spirit, becomes proclamation: "My grace is sufficient for you, for my power is made perfect in weakness" (2 Cor 12:9). The sacrament thus completes the process of divinization begun in baptism: what was purified in the font and illumined in chrism now glows through fragility. The human person, stripped of all self-sufficiency, becomes transparent to divine strength.

Anointing also reaffirms the eschatological dignity of the body. Saint Paul calls it "the temple of the Holy Spirit" (1 Cor 6:19), destined not for abandonment but resurrection. The oil that touches the forehead and hands is a pledge that this body, though wasting away, will be raised in power. The prayer of the Church for the sick—"raise up your servant"—speaks not only of temporal healing but of the resurrection to come. As Saint Ambrose wrote, "The flesh is anointed that the soul may be strengthened; the body receives the oil that the spirit may be renewed." The sacrament therefore points beyond itself, situating the believer within the Paschal horizon where sickness and death are already transfigured into life.

The Eastern Churches have long grasped this cosmic breadth. The communal celebration of Holy Unction in Holy Week manifests that the whole Body suffers and the whole Body is healed. The anointed faithful stand as icons of the world's groaning and its future transfiguration (Rom 8:22–23). Oil, that ancient gift of the earth, is lifted into liturgy and returned as mercy; the materials of creation are enlisted into the final ascent. The sacrament is thus both personal and planetary: it heals the believer and hints at creation's own anointing when "God will be all in all" (1 Cor 15:28).

The grace of anointing also reaches outward into communion. The sufferer, united to Christ's Passion, becomes intercessor for the world. His offering of weakness, silently accepted, contributes to the redemption of others. The Church venerates such hidden co-workers of grace, for they embody the deepest law of theosis: that divine love is revealed most perfectly in self-emptying. The anointed believer participates in that divine compassion which bears the pain of creation until it is made whole. In this sense, the sacrament transforms private suffering into ecclesial sacrifice. The sickbed becomes a place where heaven and earth meet, and where the world is secretly healed through the endurance of the saints.

The saints offer concrete exegesis of this mystery. Saint Thérèse of Lisieux, anointed in her last illness, did not escape suffering; she learned its language. Her "little way" was not the glorification of pain but the consecration of littleness—a eucharistic offering of weakness. Saint John Paul II, himself publicly anointed, wrote that suffering becomes a place where love is proved and shared (*Salvifici Doloris*). And in countless ordinary believers—unknown to history—the sacrament has wrought a quiet heroism: a patience that is not resignation but radiance, a tenderness for others that flows precisely from one's own frailty transfigured.

The Anointing of the Sick is also the consummation of the sacramental rhythm of life. Baptism gave birth; chrismation breathed fire; the Eucharist nourished; confession restored; now anointing prepares for glory. Each mystery builds upon the last, until even death becomes a door of communion. The body that was once washed, sealed, and fed is now anointed for its final journey—the last theophany before resurrection.

The same Spirit who once brooded over the waters now hovers over the frail flesh of the dying, preparing it to be raised incorruptible.

Ultimately, the Anointing of the Sick unveils the paradox at the heart of the Christian mystery: that death itself becomes the passage into divine life. "For me to live is Christ, and to die is gain" (Phil 1:21). The body, consecrated by oil, becomes the seed of resurrection, its mortality a veil for hidden glory. In the hands of the priest, the oil glistens like dawn on the horizon of eternity. What began as frailty ends as promise. The creature, once marked by corruption, is sealed with immortality.

Thus the healing of the image is complete. The soul restored in confession and the body consecrated in anointing together bear witness that no fragment of human existence lies outside the reach of divinizing grace. The Spirit who hovered over the waters and overshadowed the Virgin now descends upon mortal weakness, making even suffering luminous with participation. The image is purified, the likeness illumined, and the person drawn toward union. What began as washing in baptism and feeding in Eucharist now culminates in the anointed stillness of surrender, preparing the creature for vision. For when the wounds of sin are healed and the body sealed with glory, the heart is freed to enter the interior temple where God dwells in silence. The bridge between sacrament and contemplation is now crossed: the outward mysteries yield to the inward life, and the soul, cleansed and consecrated, is ready to learn the language of stillness—the prayer of union that is the life of the deified heart.

The Sacramental Life and the Journey Within

The sacraments are not seven isolated channels of grace but one continuous current of divine descent. From the waters of baptism to the oil of anointing, the same Christ acts, the same Spirit breathes, and the same Father receives. The mysteries are the prolongation of the Incarnation across time: the eternal Word still touching matter, still healing flesh, still drawing creation into His fire. Through them, the human story is folded into the divine. What was once external to God becomes the very space of His self-manifestation. Grace is not a supplement added to nature; it is nature's transfiguration through participation in the life of the Word made flesh.

Each sacrament discloses a facet of this one mystery of theosis. In baptism, the creature is re-created; in chrismation, it breathes divine fire; in the Eucharist, it is nourished with immortality; in confession, it is restored to truth; in anointing, it is sealed for glory. The same divine life that once dwelt bodily in Christ now dwells sacramentally in the Church. The believer who receives these mysteries is not merely touched by grace but indwelt by God. Participation replaces symbolism; encounter replaces recollection. The economy of salvation is not a metaphor but a metabolism—the continuous exchange of divine and human energies within the Body of Christ.

In this way the sacramental life forms the grammar of theosis. It teaches the soul to live by the rhythm of descent and ascent: God stoops, man rises; God gives, man offers; the Word speaks, creation answers. Liturgy is this rhythm made audible. Every gesture of the Church—water poured, hands laid, bread broken—is a syllable in the conversation of God with His world. And as the believer consents to that rhythm, the external rites begin to shape the interior life. What was first enacted in symbol becomes habit of being; what was once received becomes lived.

The goal, however, is not to remain forever at the level of signs, but to pass through them into the mystery they contain. The outer liturgy exists to awaken the inner. The Spirit who descends upon the bread and wine in the Eucharist seeks also to descend upon the heart, transforming it into a living altar. The same fire that sanctifies matter longs to ignite the will. The Christian who has been washed, sealed, nourished, forgiven, and anointed is invited to carry the liturgy inward—to become himself a sanctuary where heaven and earth meet.

This movement from sacrament to contemplation is not a flight from the Church but its deepest fulfillment. The Spirit who animates the liturgy is the Spirit of prayer. What begins in the communal celebration must echo in the silence of the heart, where words fall away and only presence remains. The Fathers called this the *anaphora* of the soul—the continual lifting up of the heart into God. There, beyond ritual yet born from it, the believer learns that worship is not only something done but something become. The Eucharist received at the altar must become the Eucharist lived in the interior life: the offering of thought, breath, and desire in unceasing thanksgiving.

The journey of theosis thus moves from the font to the heart, from visible sign to invisible union. The same Spirit who once hovered over the waters now hovers over the soul, bringing order to its chaos and light to its darkness. Every sacrament leaves within the believer a trace of that creative Breath—a seal that urges the creature toward likeness. The more the soul cooperates with this grace, the more it discovers that the mysteries were never external ceremonies but divine energies working within, shaping the person into the image of the Son.

In the end, the sacramental life and the contemplative life are not two paths but one continuous ascent. The former initiates, the latter interiorizes; the one gives grace through matter, the other allows that grace to become consciousness. The Christian who prays is the same one who was baptized and anointed; the hands that fold in stillness are the same that were marked with oil and blessed with peace. When the sacraments have done their work, the soul begins to mirror their action spontaneously: it washes itself in contrition, anoints itself with mercy, breaks itself in love, and offers itself in praise. The liturgy of the Church becomes the liturgy of the heart.

Through these mysteries the soul learns the rhythm of divine life, until worship itself becomes interior, and the liturgy of the Church becomes the liturgy of the heart.

6

The Interior Life: Prayer, Stillness, and the Illumined Heart

"Make peace with yourself, and heaven and earth will make peace with you."
— St Isaac the Syrian, *Ascetical Homilies*

From the Sacramental to the Interior Temple

The sacraments do not end at the church door. They press inward. What was celebrated in water, oil, bread, and wine must be realized in flesh and spirit. The mysteries are not theatrical displays of grace; they are the gradual interiorization of divine life until the whole human person becomes Eucharist. The Incarnation, prolonged in the sacramental life, seeks now to incarnate itself in the secret chambers of the soul. The temple has moved within.

The same Christ who touched the leper through human hands, who breathed peace upon His apostles, who feeds His people with His own Body and Blood—this same Christ descends invisibly into the heart. The sacraments are His footsteps; the heart is His dwelling. Every baptismal font points toward an inner Jordan, every anointing toward the soul's hidden fragrance, every Eucharist toward the mystery of divine indwelling. "Do you not know," asks St Paul, "that your body is a temple of the

Holy Spirit within you?" (1 Cor 6:19). The revelation of Pentecost was not merely tongues of fire descending upon a gathering—it was the inauguration of the interior sanctuary, the confirmation that God no longer visits from without but abides from within.

The early Fathers never separated liturgy from interiority. They saw the sacraments as the outer manifestation of an inward deification. Baptism is rebirth, Chrismation the sealing of divine energy, the Eucharist the continual nourishment of that life. Yet the goal of these mysteries is not only reception but transformation. The water and the fire, the oil and the bread, all conspire toward a single end: that man himself become the living temple of God. St Macarius of Egypt writes, "The heart itself is a small vessel, yet there are dragons and lions within it, and there also is God and the angels." The cosmic drama narrows to the interior stage. Heaven and hell meet in the heart; grace and passion wrestle there. And when grace prevails, the heart becomes a cosmos renewed.

This is not inwardness as isolation. The Christian does not withdraw from the world into a private spirituality; he enters the world's depth through his own heart. For the heart is the meeting-place of creation and Creator, the point at which the entire cosmos is gathered and offered back to God. The movement from sacrament to interiority is not a retreat from the communal to the personal, but the flowering of the communal within the personal. The liturgy of the Church is meant to become the liturgy of the soul. The incense that once rose in the sanctuary now rises from within the breast; the altar of stone becomes the altar of flesh.

The Scriptures already trace this transition. The temple of Jerusalem, with its concentric courts leading to the Holy of Holies, prefigures the human person. Beyond the senses, beyond reason, beyond imagination lies the sanctuary of the heart where God waits to dwell. The tearing of the temple veil at Christ's death is not only a historical event but a revelation of anthropology: the veil that separated God from man, spirit from flesh, has been rent. Access to the divine presence is now immediate, interior, continuous. "If anyone loves Me," says Christ, "he will keep My word, and My Father will love him, and We will come to him and make Our home with him" (John 14:23). The promise is domestic as well as cosmic—the Trinity seeks an address in the human heart.

This interior temple, however, is not built of sentiment. It is constructed of obedience, humility, and continual remembrance. Just as the outer Church has its architecture and its rites, so too the soul has its liturgy. There is the narthex of repentance, the nave of mindfulness, the altar of pure prayer. The priest is the mind purified of distraction; the sacrifice is the will offered in love; the incense is the sigh of the Spirit interceding within. When these converge, the heart becomes a miniature Divine Liturgy. The psalmist's words find new resonance: "Let my prayer be counted as incense before Thee, and the lifting up of my hands as an evening sacrifice" (Ps 141:2).

The saints teach that the descent into the heart is not achieved by imagination but by grace. St Gregory Palamas describes it as the continuation of the Incarnation within the believer: the divine light that once shone on Mount Tabor now illuminates the interior Mount of every baptized soul. Yet this light is gentle, for it waits upon consent. God does not invade; He indwells. The work of prayer is to clear the inner space, to still the turbulence that obscures the Presence already given. Hence the watchword of the hesychasts: *hesychia*, stillness—not inert quiet, but vibrant receptivity, the silence in which divine speech resounds.

The transition from outer rite to inner stillness mirrors the movement of salvation history itself: from the visible theophanies of the Old Covenant to the invisible indwelling of the Spirit. Just as the tabernacle yielded to the temple, and the temple to the Body of Christ, so now the Body of Christ yields to the mystical body of each believer united to Him. The Church does not vanish in this inward turn; she becomes personal. The Spirit who overshadowed Mary now overshadows the soul that listens. The Word again becomes flesh—this time, within.

In this interiorization lies both gift and peril. For the same inward chamber that can become a temple may also become a tomb. The grace received sacramentally must be guarded or it will dissipate. The sacraments are seeds; the interior life is their cultivation. If the soul does not till the soil through prayer, vigilance, and repentance, the divine life remains latent. The mysteries are not magic. They demand cooperation, synergy—the continuous yes of faith working through love. Without interior response, sacramental participation risks becoming mere ritualism. Without sacramental grounding, interior prayer risks disembodiment. The two must interpenetrate like soul and body, word and breath.

The Fathers therefore insist that the spiritual life is a continuation of baptismal grace, not its replacement. The Christian must become consciously what he already is mystically. To "pray without ceasing" (1 Thess 5:17) is to allow the baptismal waters to flow perpetually within. The believer carries the font in his chest. The Eucharist he receives on Sunday is to be digested through remembrance throughout the week, until the boundary between liturgy and life dissolves. Every heartbeat becomes Kyrie eleison; every breath, communion.

This is the path of interior theosis—the progressive transformation of the soul into the dwelling place of God. It is not achieved by withdrawal from the world, but by descent into its spiritual center. The world is transfigured when the heart is illumined. The Church's sacraments sow divinity into human substance; the interior life cultivates it until it shines. Thus the movement of the Christian is both outward and inward, ecclesial and personal, sacramental and contemplative. The temple without and the temple within are one continuous mystery.

Through the sacraments, the temple has been built in water and Spirit. Now the fire descends upon the altar within.

The Heart as Temple : Anthropology of the Interior Man

To speak of the "interior life" in Christian theology is not to retreat into abstraction or mere emotional introspection. It is to enter the geography of revelation. Scripture speaks constantly of the *heart*—not as metaphor, but as the center of the person, the deep core where body, mind, and spirit converge. The heart (*kardia*) is not sentiment; it is ontology. It is the living sanctuary in which creation meets Creator, the inner Mount Zion where the divine presence dwells.

"Keep your heart with all vigilance," says Proverbs, "for from it flow the springs of life" (Prov 4:23). Christ echoes this in His Beatitude: "Blessed are the pure in heart, for they shall see God" (Matt 5:8). In these two verses lies an entire anthropology. The heart is both fountain and window—the source of vitality and the organ of vision. To guard the heart is to preserve one's very being; to purify it is to recover the lost capacity for theophany.

In biblical consciousness, the heart names that dimension of the person that thinks, feels, chooses, and prays all at once. It is the throne of conscience, the workshop of desire, the seat of wisdom, and the hidden chamber where God and man commune. "Man looks on the outward appearance," says the Lord, "but the Lord looks on the heart" (1 Sam 16:7). The divine gaze does not survey human externals; it pierces the veil of personality to the core of personhood. There, beneath words and masks, He seeks His image.

The Hebrew Scriptures treat the heart not as a poetic flourish but as the locus of covenant. When God promises through Ezekiel, "I will give you a new heart, and a new spirit I will put within you" (Ezek 36:26), He is speaking of the restoration of human nature itself. The new covenant is not written on stone tablets but upon "tablets of human hearts" (2 Cor 3:3). The shift is profound: the divine law becomes interior, not imposed from without but inscribed from within by the Spirit. Grace relocates revelation from the sky to the soul.

The Fathers of the Church inherited this biblical anthropology and developed it with luminous depth. They were not content with psychological speculation; they saw in the human constitution a sacramental mirror of divine realities. The soul is not a ghost in a body; it is the body's form and life. And at the soul's center—the point where intellect, will, and desire meet—stands the heart.

Evagrius Ponticus, the great desert theologian of the fourth century, defines the heart as "the deep self where thoughts arise and where God speaks." For him, the spiritual struggle is not waged in the intellect alone but in the heart, where the logismoi—the streams of thought and passion—either darken or illumine the soul. Purity of heart is therefore not mere moral blamelessness; it is the clarity of inner vision, the restoration of the heart's natural transparency to God. "The goal of the monk," Evagrius writes, "is apatheia of the heart, which makes possible the knowledge of God."

St Macarius of Egypt, whose homilies stand among the earliest systematic treatments of interior life, goes further. He describes the heart as the microcosm of the universe: "Within the heart are the angels and the demons, life and death, light and darkness, the kingdom of heaven and the depths of hell." The heart, for Macarius, is not merely a psychological center—it is the ontological axis of the human being, the meeting place of all cosmic realities. When grace descends, it descends there; when sin takes root, it takes root there. Every human soul is a potential liturgy: the heart its altar, the intellect its priest, the will its offering.

Macarius's imagery captures the paradox of the Christian condition. The heart, created for glory, has become battlefield. It is both holy of holies and field of war, a space where the divine and demonic contest for dominion. Hence the urgency of asceticism. The Fathers insist that to be human is to be liturgical—yet the liturgy must be purified before it can be true. When the passions reign, the heart becomes idol temple; when grace reigns, it becomes the dwelling of the Trinity.

Here enters the great distinction of Eastern Christian anthropology: between the *nous* and the *dianoia*—between the spiritual intellect and discursive reason. Western modernity often collapses these into one, equating knowledge with rational analysis. The Fathers, however, see them as profoundly different. The *dianoia* is the reasoning faculty, the capacity to analyze, compare, and infer. The *nous* is the eye of the heart, the organ of contemplation. It does not reason about God; it beholds Him. In the Fall, this eye was darkened. The mind, once turned Godward, became scattered among created things. The task of the spiritual life is the return of the *nous* to the heart—the reintegration of the person around divine awareness.

St Gregory Palamas would later formalize this anthropology in his defense of the hesychasts. He teaches that the human person possesses not only rational consciousness but a deeper center of awareness, capable of direct communion with God's uncreated energies. When the *nous* descends into the heart through prayer, the whole person is united; thought and desire, reason and emotion, body and soul are harmonized in grace. The scattered fragments of existence coalesce around divine presence. "The heart," he writes, "governs the whole body; and when grace occupies the heart, it rules over all the members and thoughts." To bring the mind into the heart is thus to heal the human being at its root.

This descent is not metaphorical. The Fathers describe it as a real movement of attention, a turning inward and downward from the surface of cognition into the depth of being. The outer man, dispersed among sensations and distractions, must become recollected. The inner man awakens when the noise of the senses subsides and the *nous* begins to rest in the heart. There, beneath language, the soul encounters God not as concept but as communion. This is not the annihilation of thought but its transfiguration: reason illuminated by love.

The heart, then, is not merely emotional center but theological organ. It is the *place* of theosis. St Diadochos of Photiki writes in the *Philokalia*: "When the grace of the Holy Spirit enters the depths of the soul, it reigns over the heart and over all the members." The divine presence does not hover above the believer; it indwells, sanctifying the very faculties of perception and desire. The eyes see differently, the thoughts move differently, the world itself begins to shimmer with sacramental transparency. The illumined heart perceives creation as it truly is: suffused with divine energy.

For this reason, the Fathers identify three primary movements of the interior life—purification, illumination, and union—each corresponding to a transformation of the heart. Purification (*katharsis*) cleanses the heart of disordered passions, restoring its capacity for spiritual perception. Illumination (*photismos*) fills it with divine light, allowing the mind to behold God within. Union (*henosis*) consummates the process: the heart becomes flame, no longer reflecting light but radiating it. These are not stages in time but deepening dimensions of participation. In each, the heart moves closer to becoming what it was created to be—a living icon of divine beauty.

The integration of intellect, will, and desire within the heart reveals the profound unity of human nature. Modern psychology, dividing the person into compartments of cognition, emotion, and volition, cannot grasp this wholeness. The patristic vision sees man as symphonic. Thought, feeling, and action are distinct yet harmonized when grace governs. Sin is dissonance—the intellect knowing one thing, the desire craving another, the will vacillating between the two. Grace is harmony—the intellect illumined by truth, the desire aflame with love, the will moving in freedom. The heart is the conductor of this symphony; when it is tuned to God, the whole person resounds with peace.

This integrated anthropology also guards against the reductionism that haunts modern spirituality. To speak of the "heart" is not to discard the body or intellect, but to gather them. The body participates in the heart's prayer through posture, breath, and sensation; the intellect serves it through understanding; the emotions through holy affection. Nothing in man is excluded from deification. The same Spirit who overshadowed the Virgin now overshadows the whole human person, transfiguring dust into dwelling place.

St Symeon the New Theologian describes this transformation with luminous daring. He speaks of the heart as a lamp in which the divine light burns without consuming. "When the Spirit illumines the soul, He transforms the heart into the very throne of God. There the Lord sits, and the whole body becomes radiant with light." For Symeon, this is not allegory but experience. The uncreated light that shone at the Transfiguration may be perceived, in measure, within the purified heart. The human being becomes a living Tabor. What once occurred in Christ's body upon the mountain becomes, by grace, the destiny of every soul united to Him.

Yet such radiance presupposes struggle. The temple must be cleansed before it can be filled with glory. Just as the priests of old purified themselves before entering the sanctuary, so the Christian must cleanse the heart through repentance and ascetic watchfulness. Every confession, every tear, every act of mercy sweeps dust from the inner altar. The heart, said St Isaac the Syrian, is "a furnace of fire; and the more you throw yourself into it, the more it burns away the thorns." To enter one's heart is to consent to this purification. It is to allow the Spirit to burn away everything incompatible with divine indwelling.

This process is not morbid self-scrutiny but joyful restoration. The heart was made for light. When freed from passion, it becomes translucent, like a window cleaned of soot. Then, in the words of St Gregory of Nyssa, "the soul becomes mirror of divine beauty." Theosis is not the acquisition of new faculties but the unveiling of what was hidden. The image of God, long obscured, begins to shine again from within.

The heart as temple thus encapsulates the entire mystery of human vocation. In creation, God formed man as microcosm; in redemption, He reforms man as micro-temple. The Spirit who filled Solomon's temple with cloud now fills the soul with uncreated light. The *Shekinah* no longer rests between cherubim but within the baptized heart. When man prays, it is not he who begins the conversation but God who already prays within him. The interior life is therefore not self-generated contemplation but response to indwelling Presence. "It is God who works in you," writes St Paul, "both to will and to work for His good pleasure" (Phil 2:13).

To recognize this is to recover wonder. The Christian is not merely a moral creature striving to behave; he is a temple being filled. The ethical life flows from liturgical being. Every virtue is an ornament of the sanctuary; every sin a defilement of its purity. Holiness is not external conformity but internal luminosity. "Be transformed by the renewal of your mind," says the Apostle (Rom 12:2)—but that renewal begins when the mind is restored to its proper throne in the heart.

When the heart is illumined, perception itself changes. The world ceases to appear as inert matter and becomes sacrament. The heart beholds the divine energies radiating through creation—the "light of the knowledge of the glory of God in the face of Jesus Christ" (2 Cor 4:6). This is why the saints love the world with such serenity: they see it in God. The inner temple becomes the lens through which the outer world is redeemed. The cosmos is re-sanctified through the heart that perceives it rightly.

Yet, as the Fathers remind us, this vision is fragile. The heart, if left unguarded, can be overrun. Thoughts multiply, passions rise, the temple grows noisy with merchants once more. Prayer and watchfulness must be continuous. The same fire that illumines can also consume if untended. Thus the next step of the interior path is vigilance—the ceaseless guarding of the heart so that the divine Presence remains undisturbed.

For the temple has been revealed; the altar has been built.

Yet the heart cannot become temple without the prayer that calls down its Priest.

Contemplative Prayer and the Invocation of the Holy Name

Prayer is the breath of the soul and the continuation of the Incarnation within the heart. The Word who once prayed among us now prays within us; the Spirit who descended at Pentecost makes every sigh, every silence, a participation in the divine dialogue between the Son and the Father. In prayer the Christian does not merely address God; he enters the movement of divine life itself. To pray is to breathe in rhythm with the Trinity.

Prayer, says St Thomas Aquinas, is "the expression of desire for God." Desire, when purified, becomes the very medium through which grace works. In prayer, the intellect stretches toward truth and the will toward goodness, and in that stretching, the divine likeness is slowly impressed upon the soul. The human person learns to love what God loves, to will what He wills. Every genuine act of prayer therefore reshapes the faculties, conforming them to divine proportions. The one who prays rightly begins to *feel* with God, to *see* as God sees.

This is why the Fathers describe prayer not merely as an obligation but as an *ontological necessity*. As the lungs require air, the soul requires communion. "To be deprived of prayer," writes St John Chrysostom, "is to die spiritually." The soul that ceases to pray begins to decay, for it turns in upon itself and cuts off the circulation of grace. The converse is equally true: the more one prays, the more one becomes capable of divine life. Prayer is not one activity among others; it is existence according to its proper form—creature turned toward Creator, image reflecting Archetype.

All authentic Christian prayer flows from this mystery: that the eternal Son, made man, has united human speech and longing to His own eternal communion with the Father. The disciples did not ask Jesus for eloquence, but for participation: "Lord, teach us to pray" (Luke 11:1). He responded not with technique, but with revelation—"Our Father." In those two words, the whole chasm between Creator and creature is bridged. Prayer begins when man dares to speak the language of the Son. It is not a monologue ascending from earth, but a conversation already begun in heaven.

To pray, then, is to awaken the baptismal grace that already abides in us. The Spirit, St Paul writes, "intercedes for us with sighs too deep for words" (Rom 8:26). Even our stammering is caught up into His eloquence. Every Christian, whether in choir stall or marketplace, carries within him the capacity for ceaseless prayer, for the indwelling Spirit never ceases His own. The task is not to begin prayer but to become conscious of it—to attune the heart to the current of divine life that already flows through it.

The Church has always recognized that this life of prayer deepens through stages: from the lips, to the mind, to the heart. The early Fathers spoke of prayer as a ladder whose rungs are made of attention and love.

Each degree of prayer corresponds to a degree of participation in divine life (grace). In vocal prayer, grace touches the body and sanctifies the senses; in meditation, grace illumines the intellect; in contemplation, grace simplicifies and gathers the whole person into the stillness of divine simplicity. The progression is not linear but circular—each movement returns to the others transfigured. The saints who live in contemplation still pray the rosary and chant the psalms, but now every syllable vibrates with interior fire. As matter becomes transparent to spirit, the once external words become vehicles of glory.

At the base lies vocal prayer, the sacred words that shape and form the soul. The Psalms, the Our Father, the Hail Mary—these are the Church's breath. To pray them faithfully is to allow Scripture itself to think and feel within us. "The Word of God," says St Ambrose, "is the food of the soul; whoever reads it with love becomes what he reads." The voice begins the ascent, because the Word first descended in sound and flesh.

From vocal prayer, the soul is led naturally to meditation. Here the mind engages divine truth, turning it over as one turns a precious stone in the hand. The intellect reflects on Christ's mysteries; memory draws them close; desire begins to burn. Meditation is not analysis but attentiveness—*lectio divina* in which reading becomes hearing and hearing becomes encounter. The mind, illumined by faith, becomes transparent to revelation. "When you read," says St Augustine, "God speaks to you; when you pray, you speak to God." The dialogue of salvation history becomes interior, the Scriptures transforming from text into voice.

But beyond both word and reflection lies a third movement: contemplation. Here the faculties fall silent before the immediacy of God's presence. The intellect ceases to reason and begins to behold; love no longer seeks but rests. This is the prayer of simplicity, of pure gaze, the "one thing necessary" of which Christ spoke to Martha and Mary. St Teresa of Avila calls it "a loving awareness of God," a quiet where thought becomes affection and affection becomes union. St John of the Cross describes it as "the inflowing of God Himself into the soul," not achieved by effort but granted by grace. Contemplation is not a technique; it is a visitation. It is God praying Himself in the soul.

Prayer thus mirrors the entire sacramental economy: the Word becomes flesh so that flesh might become word. What the sacraments confer externally, prayer interiorizes. Baptism planted divine life; prayer breathes it. The Eucharist unites; prayer prolongs that union. Confession heals; prayer guards the restored purity. Through prayer the mysteries of grace become rhythms of consciousness. The sacraments open the door; prayer walks through.

The Church, faithful to Scripture and tradition, teaches that such contemplation is not the preserve of mystics but the flowering of baptismal life itself. "Contemplative prayer," says the *Catechism of the Catholic Church*, "is a gaze of faith, fixed on Jesus, an attentiveness to the Word of God, a silent love" (§2715). It is the maturation of charity within the heart, the fulfillment of Christ's promise: "If anyone loves me, we will come to him and make our home with him" (John 14:23). To live in a state of prayer is therefore to live Trinitarianly—to allow the Father's gaze to meet the Son's within the soul.

Within this universal movement of prayer, the invocation of the Holy Name holds a special place. To speak the Name of Jesus is not superstition but sacrament. The Name is not a mere label; it is presence. "There is no other name under heaven given among men by which we must be saved" (Acts 4:12). The Church has always venerated this Name with profound reverence. From the earliest centuries Christians traced it upon themselves as protection; by the Middle Ages entire confraternities arose dedicated to its honor. St Bernard of Clairvaux wrote that "the Name of Jesus is honey in the mouth, music in the ear, joy in the heart." St Francis of Assisi wept whenever he pronounced it; St Catherine of Siena called it "a blazing furnace of love." The invocation of Jesus' Name became, in both East and West, the purest expression of the soul's faith and love.

In this sense, the Eastern "Jesus Prayer" belongs to the Church universal, not as a distinctive method but as an embodiment of the Christian instinct to make prayer unceasing. "Lord Jesus Christ, Son of God, have mercy on me, a sinner." In those few words the Gospel is condensed: the confession of divinity, the acknowledgment of sin, the cry for mercy, and the trust that redemption is present. It is a miniature *Kyrie eleison* echoing the Church's liturgy in every breath. The Catechism itself recommends this form, affirming that "the invocation of the holy name of Jesus is the simplest way of praying always" (§2668). Whether spoken by monks in solitude or by the faithful in daily labor, the Name becomes the pulse of the heart.

This invocation, when joined to faith and humility, leads naturally toward contemplation. For to repeat the Name is to invite the presence of the One who bears it. Each utterance is a small *epiclesis*, a calling down of grace. Gradually the mind grows still, the will softens, and the heart begins to burn quietly with love. The repetition does not hypnotize; it harmonizes. It gathers the scattered faculties into a single flame. The lips speak, the mind listens, the heart responds, and the whole person becomes prayer. Thus what begins as petition matures into communion.

What occurs within the soul during true prayer is nothing less than a gradual assimilation to divine life. The intellect, purified of error, begins to mirror the divine Wisdom; the will, detached from lesser loves, begins to move in harmony with divine Love. Grace does not merely assist these faculties—it *inhabits* them. The soul learns the grammar of heaven, where thought and love are one act. In this way, prayer becomes the school of divinization: the human faculties are not destroyed but deified, their capacities stretched until they can contain God.

This transformation is never abstract. It leaves traces even in the body: the eyes softened by mercy, the voice gentled by peace, the countenance illumined by interior light. The saints speak of "prayer of fire," when the presence of God so fills the heart that the senses seem to participate in the soul's brightness. This is not mysticism as spectacle; it is theology incarnate. The body, too, is drawn into theosis, for grace seeks to transfigure the whole person.

Yet the invocation of the Name must never be detached from the life of the Church. It is not a private mantra but a continuation of the liturgy. The same Name invoked over the bread and wine at the altar resounds now in the believer's heart. The Eucharist, received sacramentally, overflows into interior adoration. The word whispered in solitude is the echo of the Church's "Amen." Every heart that calls on the Name prolongs the mystery of the Mass; the worship of the sanctuary continues invisibly in the temple of the soul. In this way, prayer becomes the inner liturgy of daily life.

The theology of the Holy Name, then, is profoundly Christological. In uttering "Jesus," the soul enters into His mediatorship. His humanity becomes the door of divine access; His divinity the source of transforming grace. The Christian prays not merely *to* Christ but *in* Christ. "Through

Him, with Him, and in Him," as the Eucharistic doxology proclaims, the whole Church offers her praise to the Father in the unity of the Holy Spirit. Contemplative prayer is this doxology internalized: the self offered as silent hymn.

At its summit, prayer becomes simple presence. The heart no longer speaks but abides. The intellect, purified by faith, rests in the mystery it cannot grasp; the will, purified by love, delights in surrender. The silence of contemplation is not emptiness but plenitude—the stillness of a flame that burns without consuming. It is the soul's participation, by grace, in the eternal contemplation of God by God. Here begins the deifying transformation longed for by every saint: the creature seeing with God's sight, loving with God's love. "He who is joined to the Lord becomes one spirit with Him" (1 Cor 6:17).

In contemplation, the human spirit is introduced into the divine mode of knowing. Faith becomes sight, not by natural light but by participation in God's own self-knowledge. St John of the Cross calls this *infused contemplation*—an inbreaking of divine light so delicate that the soul perceives it as darkness only because its intensity surpasses comprehension. The faculties, long accustomed to labor, are now suspended in love. The soul experiences what the theologians call *connaturality* with God: it begins to know divine things not by reasoning but by sympathy, by being made like what it loves.

This is why contemplation is not escape from theology but its crown. What the intellect once pondered as doctrine it now perceives as presence. The Trinity ceases to be a formula and becomes relationship felt within the heart. Theosis is precisely this: participation in the Son's own contemplation of the Father. The Christian begins to share the interior life of Christ Himself, loving the Father with the same Spirit of filial joy. In that gaze, creature and Creator meet without confusion—the finite soul taken up into the infinite act of divine self-giving.

The saints testify that such contemplation can be given even amid activity. St Elizabeth of the Trinity spoke of "being a praise of glory" wherever she went, her soul interiorly recollected even in outward duties.

St Francis de Sales called it the "spirit of gentle recollection," a habitual turning of the heart toward God. This is the Catholic form of unceasing prayer: not withdrawal from the world but its sanctification through continual awareness of divine indwelling. The mother at her work, the priest at his altar, the laborer at his craft—all may keep the flame of prayer alive within. "Whether you eat or drink, or whatever you do," says St Paul, "do all to the glory of God" (1 Cor 10:31).

Such prayer transforms perception itself. The one who abides in continual prayer gradually becomes transparent to God. Words, gestures, even silences begin to communicate something not of this world. The Spirit, who first hovered over the waters of creation, now hovers over the depths of the human heart, bringing forth a new creation. The eyes become chastened, the tongue restrained, the heart pacified. Every encounter becomes sacramental. The world no longer appears as neutral matter but as the theater of grace. The soul that once prayed from afar now prays from within the very light of God.

Here the moral and mystical converge. Charity is no longer an external command but the spontaneous outflow of divinized being. The one who prays ceaselessly cannot but forgive, bless, and heal, for the heart itself has become the dwelling of Mercy. "If you truly wish to love your neighbour," said St John Vianney, "pray much; for prayer draws down the love of God, and where that love reigns, the impossible becomes easy." Prayer, then, is not merely the path to theosis; it is its very expression. In prayer the divine nature becomes operative in man—the Spirit loving through human hearts, speaking through human tongues, sanctifying the ordinary through hidden fire.

And yet, the path of contemplation requires purification. The Name can be spoken in vain if the heart remains divided. Humility, repentance, and charity are the soil in which prayer takes root. Without them, invocation becomes self-enclosure rather than communion. The saints therefore insist that interior prayer must always issue in mercy. To repeat "have mercy on me" is to be formed in mercy toward others. The contemplative gaze that sees God in all things must also see all things in God. The fruit of true prayer is not ecstasy but compassion.

The Church's masters of the interior life never tire of reminding that contemplation is pure gift. No method can produce it; it descends like dew. One prepares by fidelity to the sacraments, by silence, by love of Scripture, by acts of charity—but the moment of union is always grace. The soul learns to wait, to consent, to be still. "In quietness and trust shall be your strength" (Isa 30:15). When God comes, He comes not in storm or earthquake, but in the "still small voice." The entire spiritual life is the training of the ear to recognize that voice within the heart.

Thus prayer, in its fullest sense, is not an activity but a state of being—a dwelling in God. It is the interior Eucharist of the soul, where every thought becomes thanksgiving and every breath becomes doxology. To live in this way is to fulfill the command of Christ to "abide in Me" (John 15:4). The sacraments sow divine life; prayer cultivates it until the whole person becomes luminous. The heart, once restless and divided, becomes unified in the simplicity of love. The temple stands silent; within it, God speaks Himself.

To pray, then, is to enter the rhythm of deification. Each "Our Father," each silent remembrance of Jesus' Name, deepens the soul's likeness to the Son. Prayer reshapes the faculties until they operate according to divine rhythm: knowing as God knows, loving as God loves, resting as God rests. The creature, without ceasing to be creature, begins to live the life of God. Such is the mystery of Christian contemplation: the human heart made word, the word made silence, the silence filled with God.

The progress of prayer is the gradual unveiling of glory. What begins as scattered desire ends as union; what begins as faith ends as sight. In this sense, the life of prayer is the temporal unfolding of the beatific vision. Heaven is not interruption but consummation. The contemplative who prays in this life already breathes the air of the next. His silence anticipates the stillness of eternal worship, when every distinction between liturgy and life, time and eternity, will dissolve in love.

This is why the saints call prayer the foretaste of paradise. It is the soul rehearsing eternity, learning the rhythm of divine being. When the heart beats in harmony with the Word, the creature has reached its telos. Theosis is nothing other than this consummate prayer—the mutual indwelling of God and man, each delighting in the other without end.

To invoke the Name is to summon light; but to bear the light one must first guard the flame.

Watchfulness and the Guarding of the Heart

The spiritual life, like a lamp, burns only when guarded from the wind. Prayer kindles the flame of divine life within, but vigilance keeps it alight. Without watchfulness, grace disperses as smoke, and the heart once illumined grows dim again beneath the weight of distraction and desire. To guard the heart is not a secondary discipline; it is the very art of remaining in God.

Scripture speaks of this interior vigilance with the gravity of a commandment. "Keep your heart with all vigilance, for from it flow the springs of life" (Prov 4:23). The heart is the fountain of every thought, word, and deed; if the source is pure, the stream is pure. If the source is poisoned, the whole landscape of the soul grows sick. Hence St Peter's counsel: "Be sober, be watchful. Your adversary the devil prowls around like a roaring lion, seeking someone to devour" (1 Pet 5:8). Watchfulness—*nepsis* in the Greek—is this sobriety of spirit, the alertness of love that perceives where grace is at work and where it is being opposed. It is the posture of the sentry who refuses to sleep while the King dwells within his walls.

The Fathers of the desert made this vigilance the cornerstone of their ascetical life. They discovered that the battlefield of the Christian is not first in the world but in the heart, and that the enemy wages his war through thoughts—*logismoi*. "Sit in your cell," said Abba Moses, "and your cell will teach you all things." The monk's "cell" is not only the stone chamber but the inner chamber of the soul. To remain there in awareness is to stand guard at the gate where thoughts enter and leave. Evagrius of Pontus, that subtle psychologist of the desert, taught that every sin begins as a suggestion, a whispering image that seeks consent. "Cut off the thought at its first appearance," he wrote, "for if it lingers, it will take root, and when it has rooted, it bears fruit in action."

This wisdom is not reserved for monks. Every Christian, living in the world's noise, must learn the same interior discipline. For even in modernity's ceaseless motion, the demons of distraction remain ancient. They no longer speak from desert caves but from screens, anxieties, and inner noise. The same vigilance is required: the steady attention that discerns what comes from grace and what from self-love. To be watchful is to live awake—to refuse the dullness that mistakes habit for holiness.

St John Cassian, who carried the desert tradition to the West, describes this watchfulness as the *custodia cordis*, the custody of the heart. He compares the soul to a walled city: its gates are the senses, its watchmen the thoughts. "We must keep continual guard over our hearts," he says, "for when the guard sleeps, the enemy enters without warning." The battle is not between equal forces: grace is stronger, but it requires cooperation. The ascetic watches not to achieve perfection by effort, but to prevent negligence from dissipating the gift. Grace is the treasure; vigilance is the lock.

This inner warfare is not paranoid suspicion but luminous awareness. The Fathers distinguish between vigilance born of fear and that born of love. The first is anxious and narrow; the second is spacious and bright. True *nepsis* is the attentiveness of the lover who cannot bear to lose sight of the beloved even for a moment. St Hesychios the Priest writes, "Watchfulness is a continual fixing of the mind upon the heart and an unbroken gentleness of thought." It is gentleness, not strain, that characterizes the truly watchful soul. The ascetic is not a soldier grimly pacing the walls, but a lover keeping lamps lit for the return of the Bridegroom.

At the heart of this vigilance lies the discernment of thoughts. The *logismoi*, according to Evagrius, arise from three sources: God, the angels, and the demons. Those inspired by God bring peace and humility; those whispered by the demons breed agitation, pride, and despair. The soul must learn to test the spirits, to ask of each thought: does this lead me toward love or away from it? Cassian insists that such discernment is impossible without humility, for pride blinds the heart to its own movements. The humble man sees clearly because he no longer defends himself. He can observe his thoughts without fear, confessing those that wound him and dismissing those that flatter. Thus humility is the sentinel of the virtues, for without it no guard can stand long.

Watchfulness therefore requires silence—not the muteness of repression, but the calm of attention. The soul must be quiet enough to hear its own interior motion. This is why the desert Fathers spoke so often of *hesychia*, stillness. The still heart is a polished mirror; it reflects the light of God without distortion. When noise reigns within, the light shatters into fragments, and perception becomes confused. Hence St Isaac the Syrian counsels, "Love silence above all things, for it brings you near to fruit without labor." Silence is not the absence of words but the fullness of presence. It gathers scattered energies and focuses them upon God. In that stillness, one sees temptation coming from afar and grace approaching like dawn.

This vigilance is a form of participation in divine awareness itself. The watchful soul shares in the all-seeing gaze of God—not omniscience, but purity of perception. "Be perfect as your heavenly Father is perfect" (Matt 5:48) is not a demand for flawlessness but an invitation to unclouded vision. God's perfection is His undivided love; to watch in love is to begin to see as He sees. The purified heart perceives the world through the lens of mercy. What once provoked envy now awakens gratitude; what once aroused judgment now summons prayer. In this sense vigilance is not merely defensive; it is creative. It guards the wellspring of compassion.

In the theology of theosis, such vigilance is the cooperation of human awareness with divine illumination. Grace does not obliterate freedom; it transforms it into attentiveness. The Spirit becomes the soul's watchman, whispering at the edge of thought, "Stay awake." The Christian who guards his heart learns gradually to see his own interior life as Christ sees it. Each movement of desire is weighed before the cross; each impulse is judged by love. This is what St Paul calls "the renewal of the mind" (Rom

12:2)—not the replacement of intellect but its conversion. The mind becomes luminous, translucent to grace. It no longer serves the passions; it becomes their physician.

But vigilance, like prayer, must embrace the body. The ascetic tradition never divorced the spiritual from the physical. The eyes must learn modesty; the tongue, restraint; the hands, gentleness. Every member becomes a watchpost. When the body obeys the soul, the soul can attend to God without distraction. When the body rebels through excess, the senses become gateways of temptation. This is why fasting and self-discipline accompany prayer: they quiet the flesh so that the spirit may listen. The aim is not hostility toward the body but its transfiguration—the body becoming instrument rather than obstacle.

To live in this state of awareness is to live in continual discernment. Not every movement of zeal comes from the Spirit, nor every silence from peace. The watchful person tests each impulse in the light of Christ's meekness. St Dorotheos of Gaza advises: "Everything you do, do with discernment; it is discernment that preserves the virtues." Without discernment, even good intentions turn destructive. Vigilance therefore is not suspicion of the world but sobriety toward oneself. The watchful soul learns that the true enemy is not external but internal—the ego that insists on autonomy. When this false self is unmasked, freedom dawns.

Yet such attentiveness cannot be constant without grace. No one can keep watch indefinitely by willpower. The vigilance demanded by the Gospel—"Watch and pray that you may not enter into temptation" (Matt 26:41)—is sustained only by the Spirit, who Himself is vigilance in us. As prayer is God praying within, so watchfulness is God watching within. The soul cooperates, remaining open, consenting, alert to grace's whisper. When the mind grows weary, it returns to the Name; when memory falters, it recalls gratitude. Thus vigilance and prayer intertwine like inhalation and exhalation: one receives, the other preserves.

In the language of the Fathers, the passions—anger, lust, pride, acedia—are disordered energies of the soul. They are not evil in themselves but misdirected forces. Watchfulness reorders them by restoring consciousness of God at their center. When anger becomes zeal for justice, lust becomes longing for union with God, pride becomes the dignity of divine sonship, and acedia becomes the restful joy of surrender. The passions transfigured become powers of love. The vigilant soul, then, is not passionless but rightly passionate—its fire purified, its energy radiant with peace.

This transformation has cosmic reverberations. When a single heart is purified, creation feels the difference. The saint's serenity extends outward like warmth. In the desert tradition, the one who has attained pure prayer reconciles even the wild beasts; interior peace restores the harmony of Eden. Such is the mysterious social dimension of watchfulness: the guarded heart becomes a sanctuary not only for itself but for the world. The man or woman who lives in nepsis becomes, as the ancients said, "the peace of creation."

Yet the work remains humble and hidden. The watchman is often unnoticed, his labor carried out in silence. Much of vigilance is simply beginning again after failure. The heart drifts, the thoughts scatter, the will weakens—but awareness, once regained, is already victory. For even the fall becomes grace when it leads to renewed humility. "A monk," said the elders, "is one who falls and rises again." The Christian who keeps watch does not expect perfection but perseverance. God asks not that the eyes never close, but that they open again in repentance.

Watchfulness, then, is love's persistence. It is the soul refusing to lose sight of its Beloved. The same vigilance that guards against sin also guards joy, wonder, and gratitude. The one who watches rightly is the one who notices grace: the sunlight on a wall, the mercy in a word, the forgiveness already offered before confession is made. This attentiveness transforms existence into thanksgiving. The vigilant heart lives eucharistically; every moment becomes a liturgy of awareness.

In the end, to guard the heart is to share in the Father's eternal vigilance over His creation. "He who keeps Israel neither slumbers nor sleeps" (Ps 121:4). The watchful Christian mirrors that divine sleeplessness not through restlessness but through love that never forgets. When this grace ripens, the soul enters a peace that is not passivity but alert repose—

the Sabbath rest of those who labor in love. The passions are stilled, the thoughts clarified, the will pacified. The city within stands quiet, illumined by an unsetting sun.

When the watchman no longer sleeps, the city within becomes filled with peace; and peace matures into silence.

The Role of Silence in Interior Transfiguration

If prayer is the breath of the soul and watchfulness its heartbeat, then silence is the atmosphere in which both can live. It is the element of divine communion, the hidden air of the kingdom. Words lead the soul to the threshold of mystery, but silence opens the door. The end of speech is not muteness but fullness—the point where human language yields to divine presence. As the psalmist commands: *"Be still, and know that I am God"* (Ps 46:10). Stillness (*hesychia*) is not the absence of sound, but the interior condition that allows truth to be heard.

From the first pages of Scripture, silence is woven into revelation. Creation begins not in noise but in a Word spoken into stillness: "And God said, 'Let there be light.'" The command presupposes the listening void that receives it. So too, when Elijah fled into the wilderness, the Lord was not in the wind, or the earthquake, or the fire, but in "the sound of sheer silence" (1 Kings 19:11–13). The prophet, stripped of every external sign, found God in a whisper that was barely a sound—silence speaking to silence. It is there, in the quiet beyond event, that divine intimacy begins.

The spiritual life unfolds along this same path: from noise to word, from word to silence. In the beginning, we must speak to God; later, we listen; at last, we are silent together. St John of the Cross describes this progression as the soul's transformation from discursive meditation to *silent music*. "The Father spoke one Word, which was His Son, and He speaks it in an everlasting silence," he writes, "and in silence the soul must hear it." The more the soul is purified, the more it resonates with this Wordless Word, until its silence becomes participation in the eternal speech of the Trinity.

Silence, then, is not mere quiet but a mode of knowledge. It is the intellect's consent to be illumined rather than to control. In ordinary knowing, we grasp; in contemplative knowing, we are grasped. The intellect purified by love becomes receptive, like a clear pool mirroring the sky. The Fathers called this the "simple gaze"—a seeing that is also loving, an awareness that no longer divides object from subject. St Gregory the Great called contemplation *"the rest of the mind in God."* When understanding ceases to dissect, it becomes whole. The mind does not lose its light; it enters a brighter one.

The Greek Fathers described this transformation through the theology of *apophasis*, the way of negation. Words can describe only what is below us; to approach what is above us, we must unsay. St Gregory of Nyssa called this movement the "luminous darkness" where the soul enters into God beyond the limits of concept. "Moses," he writes, "left behind all things seen and heard and went into the darkness where God was." It is not that God is absence, but that His presence exceeds the reach of speech. The intellect, purged of images, discovers that unknowing is the true knowledge of the Infinite.

St Isaac the Syrian says it more simply: "Silence is the mystery of the age to come." In silence, the saints taste the life of heaven while still on earth. Heaven is not a realm of endless chatter but of mutual indwelling—each soul resting in God and God resting in each soul. The one who learns silence here already breathes the air of eternity. Theosis, seen from this angle, is the expansion of being into this infinite quiet. God does not enter the soul by storm but by stillness; and when the soul has become silent, He speaks Himself within it.

This is why the masters of prayer, East and West, insist that silence is not passive. It is a labor, sometimes the most demanding of all. To be silent outwardly is easy; to be silent inwardly is crucifixion. The tongue can be still while the mind storms with noise. True silence is an inner stilling of the passions, the calming of imagination and thought until the soul is unified around love. This is what the desert Fathers meant by *hesychia*. The term implies peace, balance, and attentiveness—not inertia but collectedness. It is the soul become simple, gathered into itself as a harp tuned to one note.

To enter this silence requires purification of both body and mind. The body must cease from restless activity; the mind from compulsive judgment. Fasting, restraint of speech, moderation of sleep—all are means to a single end: the restoration of interior quiet. For grace does not shout. As St Francis de Sales said, "God's voice is one of love and sweetness; He speaks to the heart in peace." The Christian discipline of silence is not rejection of the world but the preparation of hearing. It is the ear cleaning itself to catch the whisper of the Beloved.

At first, this quiet may feel like emptiness, even absence. The mind accustomed to sound panics in the stillness. It interprets silence as abandonment. Yet precisely in this seeming void, faith matures. "In silence and hope shall be your strength" (Isa 30:15). God uses silence as His most searching pedagogy; He allows the soul to feel its own poverty so that it might learn receptivity. When words no longer suffice, the believer discovers that love alone remains—and love, stripped of speech, becomes pure. This is the night that leads to dawn.

St Gregory Palamas, commenting on the mystery of divine stillness, teaches that the soul's quiet is a reflection of the divine life itself. God, being all-sufficient, is eternally at rest in His own goodness. The peace of the Trinity is not motionless, but perfectly harmonious activity. When the soul becomes silent, it begins to share that rest. Its silence is not emptiness but participation in the eternal Sabbath of God. "The silence of God," Palamas says, "is His love which cannot be expressed in words." Thus the silence of the saint is not the muteness of ignorance but the overflowing of knowledge too great to speak.

The Catholic mystics of the West echo this same mystery of divine stillness in their own language. St Teresa of Avila calls the highest form of prayer *oración de quietud*—the prayer of quiet—when the soul, drawn by grace, rests in loving awareness of God's presence without words or effort. "It is as though the soul were asleep," she writes, "but not with a sleep that causes forgetfulness; rather, she is fully awake to God, yet unaware of anything else." For Teresa, this silence is not an escape from action but its purification: once the soul has learned to rest in God, every movement of daily life becomes an extension of that stillness.

St John of the Cross describes the same reality in the language of the "dark night." When the intellect, memory, and will are emptied of all images and attachments, they are not destroyed but transformed. God Himself becomes their light and object. "The quieter the soul," he writes, "the more God acts within it." This night of silence is the womb of illumination; the very absence of sensation becomes participation in God's own immaterial clarity. The darkness is divine light too bright for the eye. Here contemplation and silence merge: the soul enters into the silent music of the Trinity.

Other saints speak with the same breath. St Francis de Sales counsels that prayer should "dwell more in affection than in thought," and that the goal is a gentle repose of the heart in God. St Thérèse of Lisieux, living in hidden silence, discovered within her "little way" that love itself can be a wordless gaze: "For me, prayer is a surge of the heart; it is a simple look turned toward Heaven." In each, we find the same theology: silence is the flowering of charity, the place where faith matures into vision.

The convergence of these witnesses—Carmelite, Franciscan, Dominican, Eastern—reveals the catholicity of stillness. Whether called *hesychia*, *quiet*, or *silent love*, the mystery is one: the human spirit, purified of noise, entering the rhythm of divine rest. What Palamas calls participation in God's uncreated peace, Teresa calls union of wills; what John of the Cross calls transformation of the faculties, the Eastern Fathers call deification. The language differs, but the truth is shared: silence is the atmosphere of glory.

In this silence, prayer and knowledge become one. The mind no longer frames petitions but abides in adoration. The will no longer strains but yields. The heart becomes temple and altar simultaneously: temple, because it receives; altar, because it offers. This is the stage where prayer becomes Eucharist of existence—where every breath, every thought, becomes an act of worship. The one who has entered this quiet carries within him the peace of the age to come. "My peace I give to you," said

Christ; this peace is silence made luminous.

The path to such stillness is gradual. First, silence of the tongue; then of the imagination; finally of the heart. The first teaches restraint; the second teaches detachment; the third opens the abyss of love. Many souls never pass beyond the first two, yet even there grace works. Each act of withholding unnecessary speech is a small participation in divine simplicity. The more one practices silence out of charity—listening instead of asserting—the more one is conformed to the Word who emptied Himself. Humility is the root of silence, as pride is the root of noise. The proud man must speak; the humble can rest.

This silence has apostolic fruit. It does not turn the soul inward in sterile isolation, but outward in compassion. The one who has learned to listen to God hears also the unspoken cry of others. Silence makes the heart porous to suffering. In a noisy world, the silent man becomes an oasis. His presence heals without speech because peace radiates from him like fragrance. The saints rarely argue; they embody truth. Their quiet is not withdrawal but transmission. The world's conversion begins in hearts that have stopped shouting.

In the light of theosis, silence is the medium through which the divine likeness is perfected. For God's knowing is wordless and His love soundless. When the soul's faculties are purified into this wordless knowing and soundless loving, it participates in God's own way of being. The intellect becomes transparent to Wisdom, the will to Love. Here, deification is not an ascent into abstract infinity but a descent into interior simplicity. The more the soul is emptied of noise, the more space there is for God. Silence is therefore not the suspension of life but its transfiguration. It is creation returning to its first Sabbath, when all was "very good" and nothing more needed to be said.

To live in this silence is to live in continual adoration. The saints describe it as an unceasing Amen. When speech is no longer needed to affirm truth, the whole being becomes assent. This is what the author of the *Cloud of Unknowing* calls "naked intent toward God." The soul, stripped of images and thoughts, loves God for His own sake alone. It no longer measures experience by consolation or dryness; silence itself is enough. The soul has become music—soundless, yet vibrating with the uncreated Word.

Such silence cannot be forced. It arrives as gift, like dusk descending upon the fields. One can prepare by stillness, solitude, and prayer, but the final quiet is bestowed, not achieved. It is the Spirit who hushes the interior storm. "Peace I leave with you," Christ promises (John 14:27). That peace is not merely moral calm; it is the entry of divine order into the human heart. The Spirit who brooded over the waters now broods over the depths of the soul, and the same command is uttered again: "Let there be light."

When this silence matures, it overflows into song—not the song of sound, but of being. The soul that has ceased to speak begins to listen; and in that listening, it becomes praise. Every created thing finds its voice in such a soul. The wind and the trees, the laughter of children, the ache of the poor—all resound within the quiet heart as one great hymn. The silence of union is not negation of the world but its consecration. The soul has become the world's ear, hearing God everywhere.

In the end, the measure of prayer is not how much we say but how much we can bear to be silent. Silence is the language of the kingdom. Those who have learned it will recognize one another beyond words, for heaven's communion is wordless understanding. The saints do not converse; they behold. To taste that stillness, even for a moment, is to know what it means to be truly alive. For in silence God gives Himself entirely—and the soul, emptied of every other sound, receives Him whole.

When the soul ceases to speak, it begins to listen; and in that listening it becomes song.

The Journey from Image to Likeness

Human life is a pilgrimage toward likeness. In creation, God stamped His image upon the soul; in redemption, He calls that image to become likeness. The Fathers spoke of this as the movement from *imago Dei* to *similitudo Dei*—from potential resemblance to actual participation in divine life. The

Catholic mystical tradition expresses this transformation as a journey through three ways: purgative, illuminative, and unitive. These are not separate stages so much as deepening dimensions of a single grace—the soul's progressive assimilation to the life of God.

The path begins in purification, passes through light, and finds rest in love. Yet the ascent is not linear, nor does it lead the soul away from creation. It is a spiral inward and upward, where each movement deepens intimacy with the indwelling Trinity. "The path of the righteous," says Proverbs, "is like the light of dawn, which shines brighter and brighter until full day" (Prov 4:18). This is the story of every saint: the image of God cleansed, illumined, and finally set ablaze with charity.

The threefold path is not the invention of mystics but the logic of grace itself. The soul must be emptied to be filled, enlightened to love, united to rest. The ascent of the spirit is, in truth, the descent of God: the more the soul descends in humility, the higher it rises in glory. Purgation, illumination, and union are the stages of that one miracle— grace transforming dust into light.

The Purgative Way: The Fire That Cleanses

The journey of divine likeness begins not in ecstasy but in repentance. The first movement of grace is the turning of the soul away from sin and toward God—the reordering of love. The purgative way is that beginning: the painful yet beautiful cleansing of all that obscures the image of God within. It is the soul's conversion from self-love to divine love, from darkness to light.

Scripture speaks of this purgation as fire. "The Lord will sit as a refiner and purifier of silver" (Mal 3:3); "the tested genuineness of your faith— more precious than gold—though tested by fire" (1 Pet 1:7). This fire is not punitive but purifying; it burns to heal, not to destroy. In this stage, the Spirit acts as divine physician, cauterizing the wounds of the soul so that love may flow freely again. The first grace is always painful because it awakens conscience. One begins to see the contrast between what is and what should be. Yet even this sorrow is the beginning of joy, for to recognize sin is already to glimpse holiness.

St Catherine of Siena describes the purgative path as the "cell of self-knowledge." There the soul discovers its misery and God's mercy side by side. The light that reveals one's poverty simultaneously reveals the inexhaustible tenderness of God. "Knowledge of self and knowledge of God," she says, "are the two wings by which the soul flies to heaven." The first lessons of sanctity are humility and trust. When one ceases to defend the false self, grace can begin to rebuild the true.

St Teresa of Avila calls this beginning the "First Mansions" of the interior castle—a place of awakening where the soul becomes aware that it has a soul. Many reptiles, she says, still dwell there: distractions, vanity, fear. Yet the draw of God has begun, and the soul starts to desire purity. St John of the Cross speaks of the "active night of the senses," wherein the attachments of appetite and pride are stripped away. The soul learns detachment not by contempt for the world but by ordering its loves according to God. "Love of the creature," he writes, "diminishes love of the Creator; love of the Creator expels love of the creature."

This purgation is already a participation in the holiness of God. The divine fire that cleanses is nothing other than the love that sanctifies. To enter it willingly is to begin to share God's own life, for God's purity is His charity. The purgative way, therefore, is not a punishment for sin but the first stage of theosis—the transformation of desire. The soul enters the furnace not to be consumed but to become transparent, that the divine light may shine through without obstruction.

Once the soul is cleansed, the divine light can begin to illumine.

The Illuminative Way: The Dawn of Divine Light

When the fires of purification have tempered the soul, light begins to dawn. The purgative way clears the window; the illuminative way opens the view. The mind, cleansed of illusion, grows transparent to divine truth. The will, steadied by grace, learns constancy in virtue. This is the stage of interior growth, of maturity in prayer, of deepening intimacy with God's presence.

Scripture describes this passage with luminous imagery: "In Your light we see light" (Ps 36:9). The divine light does not dazzle or overwhelm; it clarifies. The soul now perceives God not only as Judge and Physician but as Teacher and Friend. The Christian who has passed through repentance discovers that grace is not merely for healing but for enlightenment. Faith, once held as an assent to truths, becomes an interior illumination—a participation in divine knowing. The intellect, once scattered by curiosity, begins to see all things in unity under the gaze of God.

St Bonaventure, in his *Itinerarium Mentis in Deum*, calls this ascent of the mind the journey "through Christ the Mediator into the light of the Trinity." The soul moves from the contemplation of creation to the contemplation of God in creation, and finally to God beyond creation. Yet this movement is not escape but transfiguration: the world, once opaque, becomes transparent to the Creator's glory. Knowledge becomes thanksgiving. Every truth becomes a spark of the eternal Light.

St Teresa of Avila situates this illuminative stage in the middle mansions of the soul. Here prayer becomes more interior, less about words and more about attention. The faculties no longer strive but begin to cooperate. The mind receives inspirations, the will tastes quiet joy, and virtue blossoms almost effortlessly. The soul is learning the rhythm of grace. "It is as though the sun had risen," she writes, "and all things are seen in their proper color." Yet Teresa warns that such illumination can bring new temptations: the pride of spiritual comfort and the subtle self-satisfaction of progress. True light humbles; false light flatters. Hence even illumination must be purified by humility.

St Catherine of Siena compares the illuminative path to walking upon the Bridge who is Christ. The soul passes over the river of sin, sustained by His wounds. "He is the way and the door," she says; "by His light we come to see the Father." The light that fills the soul is Christ Himself, the "Sun of Justice" whose rays pierce the intellect with love. As understanding deepens, love expands. The intellect and will, those twin powers of the soul, begin to move together as one—knowledge becoming affection, affection becoming praise.

This illumination is participation in divine Wisdom. The Holy Spirit, the "Spirit of truth," guides the soul into all truth not by dictation but by indwelling. The virtues mature, the gifts of the Spirit awaken, and the believer perceives that holiness is not effort but cooperation. The soul begins to see with what the tradition calls the "mind of Christ" (1 Cor 2:16). Vision and love converge. As the light grows, even prayer becomes radiant simplicity—a loving gaze more than a striving.

Yet illumination is not the summit. Light, if it is true, always leads beyond itself into love's silence. For the closer one approaches to the source of light, the less one sees by natural sight. "Faith," says St John of the Cross, "is like a ray of darkness." The divine brilliance blinds the intellect so that love alone may perceive. The dawn gives way to noonday, and noonday to a brightness that dissolves all distinctions. Thus illumination prepares the way for union: the light that once shone upon the soul now burns within it.

Yet even illumination is not the summit; light leads beyond itself into love's silence.

The Unitive Way: The Marriage of the Soul with God

When illumination ripens into love, the soul passes into its final transformation—the unitive way. Here the light that once shone upon the soul now burns from within it. The will is united to God's will, the mind to His truth, the heart to His love. The soul no longer seeks God as object but rests in Him as presence. "It is no longer I who live," says St Paul, "but Christ who lives in me" (Gal 2:20). This is the perfection of charity, the summit of contemplation, the beginning of heaven within the heart.

In the unitive state, the distinction between the lover and the Beloved remains, yet the distance is gone. Love has bridged what nature could never cross. The human will, once divided, becomes simple; every desire is gathered into the single act of loving God for His own sake. The soul lives in continual consent. What was once duty becomes delight; what was effort becomes ease. The law is fulfilled not by command but by communion. As the fire consumes the wood and makes it flame, so divine love transforms the soul into itself without confusion of substance. "Love transforms the lover into the beloved," says St John of the Cross; "and since God is all love, the soul becomes love itself."

The mystics of the Church describe this mystery with the language of nuptial union. St Teresa of Avila calls it "spiritual marriage," the soul's espousal to its Creator. "Now the two natures," she writes, "are so joined that they cannot be separated; it is as if rain fell from the sky into a river, becoming one with its waters." In this marriage, the soul loses nothing of its individuality but gains everything of God's life. The human faculties—memory, intellect, and will—no longer act apart from grace but in harmony with it. The soul's silence becomes a perpetual *fiat*: "Be it done unto me according to Thy word."

St Catherine of Genoa, consumed by divine charity, described this state as "a soul living in God and God living in the soul." In her *Treatise on Purgatory*, she writes that when love has purified everything unworthy, "the soul remains in God without intermediary." It is a condition of perpetual adoration, the soul's whole being turned toward the divine beauty that holds it. This union is not static: it breathes, it burns, it overflows. From it arises the charity that saves the world, for the soul united to God becomes instrument of His mercy.

In this final stage theosis is complete, though never finished. The soul lives the Trinitarian life by participation. The Father's love begets, the Son's obedience redeems, the Spirit's indwelling sanctifies—all within the heart now made divine by grace. The unitive way is the soul's Sabbath, the rest of God shared with His creature. The once-wayfaring heart has found its homeland. Love, which began as purification and grew as light, has now become identity: "God is love, and he who abides in love abides in God, and God in him" (1 John 4:16).

Union, however, does not end in isolation. The soul united to God becomes more open, not less; more human, not less human. It sees every creature as beloved because it now shares the gaze of Love Himself. The unitive life is missionary not by command but by overflow. The saint becomes a living transparency of divine charity. Wherever he walks, heaven leaves footprints. Theosis has flowered into fruit.

When the soul has reached this union, it no longer ascends but abides; love has found its rest.

The Circle of Grace

The spiritual ascent, traced through purgation, illumination, and union, is not a ladder to be climbed and left behind. It is a rhythm of grace, a continual deepening of divine life within. The purgative way never ceases, for love forever burns away new impurities; the illuminative way never ends, for light always increases; the unitive way never grows old, for charity eternally renews itself. These are not stages but dimensions of one mystery: the soul's gradual transfiguration into the likeness of Christ.

In this vision, the threefold path and the Eastern theology of theosis meet as two languages describing the same reality. Both proclaim that salvation is not only forgiveness but participation—the creature becoming radiant with the Creator's life. The image of God, once blurred by sin, is restored, illumined, and glorified until the soul becomes itself a living sacrament of divine presence. Grace does not abolish nature but perfects it, and in that perfection nature finds its rest.

The soul that has passed through purification and light into love has become what it was always meant to be: prayer made flesh, silence made praise, creature made godlike.

The Heart as Liturgy of the Spirit

The soul's journey, traced from the sacraments to the interior life, from prayer to silence, from vigilance to union, reveals a single movement: the descent of God into man and the ascent of man into God. The outer rites of the Church have become inward realities; the liturgy that once surrounded the believer now unfolds within the depths of his being. The heart has become the sanctuary, the altar, the choir. The Spirit who brooded over the waters of creation now broods over the inner abyss, fashioning a new world where divine life breathes through human faculties.

In this interior liturgy, the sequence of worship is reversed: it is no longer man who offers praise to God, but God who prays within man. "The Spirit Himself intercedes for us with sighs too deep for words" (Rom 8:26). Theosis, seen in this light, is not a possession to be attained but a life to be lived—the life of God moving through the creature as breath through lungs. The sacraments are its fountain; prayer is its current; silence is its ocean. The divine initiative sustains every moment: grace invites, transforms, and then sings within the one who consents.

The purgative way taught the soul to surrender its idols; the illuminative way taught it to see through divine light; the unitive way taught it to rest in love. These are not stages left behind but notes in a single harmony. Purgation remains the humility that keeps the soul open; illumination the clarity that perceives grace; union the charity that gives itself back to the world. The heart, purified, illumined, and deified, becomes the living sanctuary where heaven and earth meet. "Do you not know that you are God's temple and that the Spirit of God dwells in you?" (1 Cor 3:16). In the interior temple, every act, however small, becomes liturgical. The washing of dishes, the greeting of a neighbor, the tending of wounds—all can become priestly gestures when offered in the awareness of divine indwelling.

Thus the journey of contemplation turns outward again. The silence of the heart is not withdrawal but readiness. The Spirit who once descended as fire upon the apostles now ignites within each believer the same apostolic flame. Action becomes an extension of contemplation, movement the overflow of stillness. The Christian who has learned to dwell in God carries that presence into the world; he becomes, in the words of St Elizabeth of the Trinity, "a praise of glory." His being is prayer, his silence proclamation, his labor worship. The liturgy of the Church continues in his heart, radiating through his words and deeds the hidden light of the Kingdom.

Prayer, in this mature sense, is theosis in motion—the soul's participation in divine consciousness. It is God seeing the world through human eyes, loving creation through human hearts, redeeming through human hands. The Christian life ceases to be divided between sacred and secular; it becomes a continuous epiclesis, an invocation of the Spirit over every moment. The Eucharistic rhythm of offering and receiving extends beyond the altar into every breath. The believer who lives this way is not merely imitating Christ but participating in Him. The mind begins to think with His wisdom, the heart to love with His charity, the will to act with His freedom. The creature moves as instrument of divine energy, transparent to the glory that sustains it.

In the mystery of such transformation, the Trinity is no longer a doctrine but an experience. The Father's creative will, the Son's self-offering, and the Spirit's indwelling joy are enacted within the soul as continuous liturgy. The illumined heart becomes an icon of this eternal exchange—a living reflection of the triune life. The believer who abides in this state no longer prays *to* God so much as *with* God. The divine life circulates through him as through a living organ in the Body of Christ. The heart becomes a chalice of uncreated light, and the soul's silence a hymn that never ceases.

This is the consummation toward which all sacraments and all prayer are ordered: that the creature may become the dwelling place of the Creator. The liturgy celebrated in stone sanctuaries finds its completion in the sanctuary of flesh. The Gospel moves from parchment to pulse. The divine mysteries once encountered in symbol are now tasted as life. The Spirit who consecrated bread and wine consecrates now the whole person—mind, heart, and body—as offering and temple. The Christian becomes the Eucharist he receives: blessed, broken, and given for the life of the world.

In this state of interior worship, time itself is redeemed. The hours no longer divide but disclose eternity. Every moment becomes *kairos*, God's appointed time. The heart, united with the eternal Word, beats with the rhythm of heaven. Stillness is no longer a pause between acts but the medium of all action; silence no longer absence but fullness; the soul no longer petitioner but participant. This is the divine liturgy of the

heart—the unending celebration of God's presence within His creation.
When the heart becomes still, it prays without ceasing;
when it prays without ceasing, it burns with uncreated light;
and in that light, man becomes what he was made to be—
the dwelling place of God.

7

The Divine Liturgy as Mystical Theophany

"The man who has found humility is like one who has found the light; by that light he sees his own soul, and through that vision he beholds God."
— St Isaac the Syrian, Homily 34

The Body as Arena of Theosis

The drama of salvation unfolds not in abstraction but in flesh. The Word did not redeem ideas, but bodies; not disembodied souls, but men and women of dust and breath. From the beginning, the body has been the theatre of divine intention—the place where the invisible God desired to become visible. In Christ, this desire was fulfilled: divinity clothed itself in our material weakness, and the human body became once again what it was always meant to be, a living icon of God. To speak of theosis without the body is to forget the Incarnation. The divine life that deifies the soul also sanctifies the senses; grace must become tangible or it has not yet reached its goal.

The early Fathers, from Irenaeus to Athanasius, were adamant that salvation is not an escape from matter but its transfiguration. "The glory of God," writes Irenaeus, "is man fully alive; and the life of man consists in the vision of God." To be fully alive is to be integrated—to let spirit, soul, and body resound in harmony under the music of grace. Sin fractured that harmony; the Fall was not the body's rebellion against the soul, but the soul's forgetfulness of its own embodiment. The passions became tyrants not because the flesh was evil, but because the soul ceased to govern with love. Redemption, therefore, is not the spirit's victory over the body but the reconciliation of both in the Spirit.

The Christian ascetical life begins here, with the restoration of friendship between flesh and spirit. Asceticism is not a flight from the body but its education. The disciplines of fasting, chastity, and moderation are not contempt for matter but reverence for its true purpose. The body is not an obstacle to holiness; it is the vessel through which holiness is made visible. As Clement of Alexandria called it, the body is "the soul's humble brother"—stubborn, needy, yet faithful when loved rightly. Grace never despises the physical; it dignifies it. The body that once carried sin must now become the companion of grace.

The Incarnation gives this transformation its pattern and its power. The Word became flesh so that flesh might again become word. In Christ, matter speaks God's language. His fasting, His wounds, His resurrection—all proclaim that the body is the instrument through which divine life enters history. The forty days in the wilderness were not a theatrical display of endurance but the renewal of Adam's lost obedience. Where the first man grasped at fruit, the Second restrained His hunger. In the desert, the body of Christ learned again to listen; appetite was restored to worship. The ascetic, following the Lord, disciplines the body not to silence it but to teach it to sing in tune with the soul. Fasting is the body's prayer—a confession that man lives not by bread alone.

The ascetical struggle therefore belongs to every Christian vocation. It is not a specialty of monastics, but the common language of discipleship. Christ's command to deny oneself and take up the cross (Matt 16:24) was not metaphorical advice for zealots but the grammar of baptismal life. To be baptized is to enter a death that leads to life; to fast is to allow that pattern to penetrate even the body's rhythms. In a world enslaved to consumption, fasting is a prophetic memory of paradise and a rehearsal of resurrection. It teaches the flesh to hunger rightly—to desire the Bread that came down from heaven.

In the theology of theosis, the body becomes an active participant in divinization. The Eastern Fathers spoke of *praxis*—ascetical practice—as the foundation of *theoria*, contemplation. The body's obedience prepares the soul's vision. St Maximus the Confessor writes that "the Word of God, by becoming flesh, united the sensible and the intelligible, so that through the body we might ascend to the Spirit." Matter is the ladder, not the barrier. When the body is trained in temperance, the passions that once enslaved it become powers of love. Appetite becomes gratitude, desire becomes prayer, weakness becomes compassion. Grace does not annihilate natural impulses; it tunes them to divine harmony.

Western theology, though sometimes accused of neglecting the body, teaches the same mystery. St Paul insists that salvation is not complete until "our mortal bodies are made alive by His Spirit" (Rom 8:11). St Thomas Aquinas calls the body "the instrument of the soul's virtue," and fasting a work of *latria*—worship. The Catholic ascetical tradition, from Benedict to Francis, from Catherine of Siena to Thérèse of Lisieux, never treats mortification as contempt but as cooperation. The body is disciplined not to earn grace, but to respond to it. The flesh that was once the servant of sin becomes the servant of sanctity.

Modern thought often separates interior devotion from physical discipline, as though spiritual life could flourish without bodily form. Yet even psychology acknowledges that the rhythms of fasting, rest, and self-restraint shape consciousness. The Church knew this long before science rediscovered it. Human beings are not angels housed in flesh but embodied spirits whose salvation must be felt in muscle and bone. The saints shine not only in their minds but in their very countenances—the transfigured faces of those who have learned to live Eucharistically.

Fasting and ascetic practice thus reclaim the unity of human nature. They remind the believer that grace penetrates all the way down—that the salvation of the soul implies the sanctification of the body. To kneel, to fast, to watch in prayer is to confess faith with one's limbs. Each act becomes sacramental: an outward sign of inward grace, a gesture of the body's "yes" to God. The Christian disciplines not out of disdain but out of desire—to make space for the divine within the finite.

This restoration of bodily harmony has cosmic reach. The human being, microcosm of creation, bears within his body the material world. When he sanctifies his flesh, he offers creation back to its Maker. The fasting of one heart becomes the purification of the earth. The groaning of creation that St Paul speaks of (Rom 8:22) finds its answer in ascetic holiness: matter offered through the body becomes prayer. The body thus stands at the threshold between nature and grace, priestly in its vocation—to unite heaven and earth within its obedient form.

In the end, asceticism is not about what is renounced but what is recovered. It is the reclaiming of the body as friend, temple, and instrument of praise. The ascetic does not flee from the world but restores its proper order. Through the discipline of the flesh, he learns the freedom of the Spirit. Through hunger, he remembers the banquet; through fatigue, he learns rest; through limitation, he touches infinity. In the words of St Paul, "You were bought with a price; therefore glorify God in your body" (1 Cor 6:20).

The Word became flesh so that flesh might again become word; fasting is the body's way of remembering this truth.

Bodily Discipline and the Reclamation of the Passions

Human salvation does not bypass the passions; it redeems them. In the Catholic tradition, the passions are not sinful by nature but part of the soul's created goodness—movements of love, anger, sorrow, and desire that express our capacity to respond to truth and goodness. Sin did not invent the passions; it disoriented them. The Fall turned the harmony between reason and appetite into conflict. The work of grace, therefore, is not to destroy passion but to heal and elevate it—to restore in the human person that moral and spiritual integration which reflects the image of

God.

The disorder began with appetite wrongly directed. In Eden, Adam's sin was not hunger but self-assertion—the refusal to receive life as gift. Appetite became rebellion, and pleasure ceased to serve communion. Redemption, therefore, must begin in the same arena. Christ's forty days in the desert are the great reversal: the Word made flesh reorders human desire from within. His fasting is not mere deprivation but the sanctification of bodily hunger. "Man shall not live by bread alone" (Matt 4:4) is the manifesto of all Christian asceticism: the human person lives by participation in God, and fasting is the body's confession of that truth.

The Catholic ascetical tradition—shared with the ancient monastic wisdom of East and West—recognizes the passions as the field where the moral and mystical life take root. St John Cassian, synthesizing the desert wisdom of Egypt for the Latin world, describes fasting and bodily discipline as the *praeparatoria gratiae*—the preparations of grace. They dispose the soul to receive divine illumination. "Through fasting," he writes, "the body is tamed, the mind becomes clear, and the heart is made vigilant." The body's restraint becomes the soul's freedom; hunger teaches the will to govern itself according to reason enlightened by faith.

The Fathers of the Church consistently teach that grace perfects, not suppresses, nature. St Gregory the Great defines virtue as *ordo amoris*—the right ordering of love. The passions, when disciplined by temperance and fortitude, become instruments of sanctity. Anger, purified, becomes zeal for justice; desire, purified, becomes longing for God; fear, purified, becomes reverence; joy, purified, becomes thanksgiving. The ascetical life is not a campaign against the body but the education of the passions, their elevation by grace until they become movements of charity.

Aquinas explains the mechanics of this healing: reason, elevated by faith, directs the will; the will, inflamed by charity, gently commands the passions; the passions, steadied by infused temperance and fortitude, become docile to love. Even sorrow and fear find baptism: hope purifies sorrow into patient endurance, and holy fear purifies fear into reverence that guards love from presumption. Above the virtues stand the gifts of the

Holy Spirit, which render the soul pliable to divine motion—*piety* softens harsh zeal into filial tenderness; *fortitude* carries ascetic effort beyond calculation; *fear of the Lord* keeps the heart lowly and therefore luminous. In this way, fasting is not stoicism but cooperation with supernatural habits that let grace "think," "will," and even "feel" within us.

Scripture confirms that the path of holiness runs through the education of desire. St Paul speaks of "putting to death the deeds of the body by the Spirit" (Rom 8:13)—a phrase that does not mean mutilation but mastery. The Spirit does not annihilate appetite but brings it under divine order. Likewise, the Beatitudes reveal this transformation of emotion: those who mourn are comforted, the meek inherit, the pure see. The Gospel calls not for apathy but transfigured feeling—the passions harmonized with the will of God. The fasting Christ stands as the archetype: fully human in desire, yet perfectly obedient in love.

St Paul's language of *flesh* and *spirit* clarifies the point: he does not pit body against soul, but fallen orientation against redeemed life. The "body of sin" (Rom 6:6) becomes, by baptism and obedience, "a temple of the Holy Spirit" (1 Cor 6:19). Thus bodily discipline is not dualism; it is baptism made practical. Nor is Christian fasting a novelty: Moses fasted on Sinai (Ex 34:28), Elijah on Horeb (1 Kgs 19:8), Daniel abstained to seek wisdom (Dan 10:3), Esther called a fast for deliverance (Esth 4:16), and even Nineveh humbled itself with fasting (Jon 3:5). In each case, bodily restraint opened room for divine action. The Church's ascetic life simply gathers these threads into the Christic pattern: the body learns the grammar of covenant so that charity may become its native speech.

The Catholic ascetic therefore stands with the Son in the desert, not as one rejecting creation but as one re-learning its purpose. The wilderness becomes a classroom of dependence. There, stripped of luxury, the Christian discovers that every satisfaction is provisional until it ends in God. Fasting is this pedagogy of dependence made visible. The body remembers through hunger that it is not self-sufficient. When the stomach kneels, the soul rises.

The Church's discipline of fasting and abstinence thus continues Christ's pedagogy. Wednesdays and Fridays, Lent and Ember days—these rhythms inscribe the Gospel into time and flesh. The pattern of the liturgical year becomes the body's school of virtue. Each fast is an embodied homily on grace: the soul does not grow by indulgence but by receptivity. The Catholic understanding of asceticism is therefore profoundly sacramental. Matter becomes the means of interior conversion. Bread withheld becomes a confession of faith in the Eucharist; thirst endured becomes anticipation of the chalice of salvation. The flesh participates in the soul's repentance, and the whole person is reconciled to God.

The liturgical year binds this pedagogy to time: Advent's sober longing, Lent's forty-day desert, Ember days' quarterly repentance—all tutor the body to hope. Every fast bends toward the altar. We abstain so as to desire, and we desire so as to receive: the Eucharist is the feast for which hunger trains the heart. Fasting, then, is Eucharistic in aim; it clears the palate for the Bread of angels. In our age, the Church also encourages prudent "ascetics of attention"—digital fasts, curfews for screens, quiet hours without noise—so that the senses, no longer saturated, can hear God again. These are not concessions to modernity but applications of perennial wisdom: asceticism must touch the concrete distractions that dissipate love.

The masters of the interior life speak of this bodily discipline as the beginning of illumination. Cassian calls it *discretio*, discernment—the moderation that keeps zeal from turning to pride. Evagrius, the great psychologist of the monastic soul, catalogued the *logismoi*, the eight tempting thoughts that corrupt the heart: gluttony, lust, avarice, sadness, anger, acedia, vainglory, and pride. For each passion he proposed not repression but conversion: the energy of the vice redirected toward God. The Catholic tradition adopts the same insight while embedding it within the framework of virtue. The seven deadly sins are healed not by negation but by opposite habits—temperance, chastity, charity, humility. Each vice, when turned Godward, becomes its own antidote.

Cassian links fasting explicitly to the goal of *puritas cordis*—purity of heart—without which contemplation cannot flower. In his *Conferences*, he weds restraint of food to restraint of thought, and pairs both with simple manual labour so that the body, occupied in humility, may quiet the roving mind. The hands at work keep the heart at prayer. Western Fathers echo the same realism: Augustine diagnoses sin as disordered love (*amor sui* curved in on itself) healed by *amor Dei*, love set right; Gregory the Great's *Moralia* turns that diagnosis into pastoral wisdom, urging concrete disciplines that train feeling for charity. Nothing here is frenzy or show; it is the steady school of holiness where body, mind, and will learn one lesson: to love in measure—and then beyond measure, by grace.

Thus the Western and Eastern Fathers converge: the body's labour, rightly ordered, becomes a ladder of contemplation. Ascetic realism is the grammar of theology; before one speaks of God, one learns to breathe with Him

St Maximus the Confessor, read within Catholic theology as a luminous witness of integrated anthropology, teaches that the human person is a microcosm of creation, uniting matter and spirit. The passions, in his view, are the very energies by which the soul moves outward toward communion. Sin dislocates these energies from their end; asceticism relocates them within grace. This is precisely how Catholic theology understands sanctifying grace: as the created share in God's own life that heals and elevates nature. When the soul lives in grace, even its most bodily desires become movements toward charity. The human person becomes, as St Paul says, "a living sacrifice, holy and acceptable to God" (Rom 12:1).

From this theology flows a clear praxis. Fasting, vigils, chastity, and moderation are not isolated devotions but facets of one art: the reclamation of the passions. Fasting disciplines appetite; vigils discipline time; chastity disciplines desire; moderation disciplines possession. Together they restore the faculties to their true harmony. Each is an ascetical exercise in freedom—the training of the flesh to cooperate with the Spirit. "The athlete is not crowned," writes Paul, "unless he competes according to the rules" (2 Tim 2:5). The ascetic trains not for earthly crowns but for incorruptible ones. Every renunciation is a rehearsal of resurrection.

The Catholic approach to chastity, in particular, reveals this pedagogy of integration. The Church does not praise virginity because it denies the body, but because it orders love wholly to God. Nor does it despise marriage; rather, it sanctifies it as the sacrament where flesh becomes the language of grace. In both vocations, chastity signifies the same mystery: self-mastery that enables self-gift. The body, when governed by charity, becomes icon of divine fidelity. "The chaste person," wrote St John Paul II, "is the guardian of the mystery of another's person." Thus the virtue most maligned by the world is in fact love made wise.

So too with vigils—those long hours of nocturnal prayer in which body and soul share the same longing. To stand before God in darkness is to train the body for faith. The drowsy limbs that resist prayer become witnesses of perseverance; the heaviness of flesh becomes participation in Christ's agony. In the silent watches of the night, the believer learns that weariness can itself be worship. The eyes that refuse to close become the soul's declaration that God is worth losing sleep for. This is why the Church treasures Eucharistic adoration, the perpetual vigil of love: the body keeping faith before the mystery of Presence.

Moderation binds all these disciplines together. Without it, zeal becomes vanity and austerity self-destruction. The Catholic ascetic follows the wisdom of St Benedict: "Let all things be done with measure." The body must be guided like a faithful servant, neither indulged nor crushed. Balance is the secret of endurance; joy is the sign of true discipline. The one who practices moderation walks the royal road between excess and laxity, the narrow path where freedom grows. The rule of life becomes the liturgy of temperance—the steady heartbeat of grace within time.

True asceticism flowers in joy, not in severity. Its quiet fruits are patience, gentleness, and cheer—the outward signs of an interior harmony already tasting heaven. The disciplined Christian becomes a source of peace for others; his self-mastery is not withdrawal but availability. The world's noise meets a soul that does not echo it. This, too, is charity: the peace won in struggle offered back to the Church.

THE DIVINE LITURGY AS MYSTICAL THEOPHANY

The theology behind these practices is simple yet profound: the human being is a unity of matter and spirit destined for glory. Grace does not bypass the body; it passes through it. The passions are not to be silenced but sanctified. In this transformation the body becomes, as the Fathers loved to say, "docile to the Spirit." It moves as instrument of divine love, luminous in obedience. The more the flesh yields, the more it shines. This is the Catholic meaning of theosis—the created share in divine life manifest in a redeemed humanity. In the saints, this radiance becomes visible: the serenity of Francis, the transparency of Thérèse, the incorruptible gentleness of countless hidden souls whose very gestures revealed God's peace.

All of this strains forward to glory. Asceticism is ordered to resurrection: the body disciplined in love now will be raised in love then. "It is sown in weakness, it is raised in power" (1 Cor 15:43). The Eucharist seals that promise within our flesh— "He who eats me will live because of me" (John 6:57)—so that every fast anticipates the day when appetite will be perfectly obedient to charity and the senses perfectly luminous with God. Saints witness to this paschal logic even here: in Catherine of Genoa, suffering became transparency; in Elizabeth of the Trinity, silence became radiance. Their bodies did not vanish from holiness; they shone with it. The more the Spirit indwells, the more creation itself begins to gleam through the obedient flesh of the redeemed.

Bodily discipline, then, is not moralism but mysticism. The fast, the vigil, the mortification—all are sacraments of longing. They remind the soul of its destiny: to hunger for God as the deer pants for running streams. When the body consents to this hunger, it becomes what it was created to be—a vessel of praise. Through fasting, creation itself begins to heal, for the human being, priest of the material world, offers his own flesh as first fruits of redemption. The body becomes the Church's liturgy in miniature: sacrifice, offering, and communion in one living act.

When the body learns silence, the soul begins to hear; discipline gives birth to contemplation.

Redemptive Suffering and Voluntary Mortification

The Cross is the central paradox of Christianity: the place where defeat becomes victory, suffering becomes glory, and death becomes the womb of life. Every religion wrestles with pain, but only Christianity dares to claim that God Himself entered into it. The Cross does not simply explain suffering; it transforms it. In its shadow, human pain ceases to be meaningless. It becomes sacramental—a visible participation in invisible love.

When Jesus first uttered the words, "If anyone would come after Me, let him deny himself and take up his cross and follow Me" (Matt 16:24), He spoke them immediately after rebuking Peter's protest against the Passion. Peter, scandalized by the idea of a suffering Messiah, had said, "This shall never happen to You." Jesus' response—"Get behind Me, Satan"—was not anger but revelation: Peter was trying to have Christ without the Cross. The Lord's next words were addressed not only to Peter but to all disciples for all ages. The Cross is not an optional accessory to Christian life; it is the pattern of that life.

The call begins with a single imperative: "deny himself." In Greek, *aparnesastho heauton*, it literally means "to renounce one's claim to oneself." It does not signify self-hatred or psychological repression, but a radical reorientation of ownership. The human will, wounded by sin, continually seeks autonomy—to be a god unto itself. Self-denial is the reversal of that primordial lie. It is the renunciation of the illusion that life belongs to me. To deny the self is to return it to its Maker; to say with Mary, "Be it done unto me according to thy word." In this act, man ceases to be a tyrant over himself and becomes again a steward of grace.

This interior renunciation is the soil of all true discipleship. It requires surrender not only of external pleasures but of inward claims: the demand to be understood, to be vindicated, to be in control. In this sense, the ascetic's fast, the monk's silence, the mother's hidden patience, all express the same logic of the Gospel. Self-denial is not an erasure of identity but its purification. By stripping away the false self—formed by pride, fear, and desire for mastery—the true person emerges, transparent to God. The paradox of Christianity is that the more one surrenders the self, the more one becomes fully personal. Freedom is not self-assertion but self-gift.

Christ then adds the second clause: "take up his cross." In the first century, this phrase would have sounded like a death sentence. To "take up the cross" was to carry the beam on which one would soon be executed. It was not an image of moral discipline but of total surrender. Yet Jesus transforms the symbol of shame into the emblem of divine intimacy. To bear the cross is to walk the road He walked; it is the concrete shape love takes in a fallen world. The believer does not seek suffering for its own sake but receives it when fidelity demands it. Every cross is unique, tailored by Providence to conform the soul to Christ's own obedience.

To "take up" the cross means acceptance, not passivity. It is an act of cooperation with grace. The will consents to what nature recoils from, not because pain is good in itself, but because love is greater than pain. When Christ shouldered the Cross, He sanctified every human burden that would follow. The disciple who carries it after Him participates in that same redemption—not adding to it, but entering its power. The cross carried willingly becomes, in time, a throne; the instrument of death becomes the ladder of ascent.

Finally, the Lord commands, "follow Me." The Cross is not an abstract symbol but a path, and this following is continual. The Greek verb *akoloutheito* means to walk behind, to stay close enough to trace the Master's footprints. It implies imitation, yes, but more: communion of destiny. To follow Christ is to conform one's steps to His—through joy and humiliation, through work and prayer, through rejection and resurrection. It is to allow His itinerary to overwrite our own. The Christian does not chart his course; he learns to walk within the rhythm of divine providence.

The three imperatives—deny, take up, follow—form a single movement: death, acceptance, and rebirth. "He who loses his life for My sake will find it" (Matt 16:25). In dying to the false self, the believer discovers the true self, hidden with Christ in God. Self-denial leads not to emptiness but to fullness. The soul stripped of its idols becomes a vessel large enough for divine indwelling. This dying to self is not once-for-all but lifelong: every resentment relinquished, every ambition surrendered, every comfort sacrificed becomes another grain of wheat falling into the ground. And as the Lord promised, "unless a grain of wheat dies, it remains alone; but if it dies, it bears much fruit" (John 12:24).

To die to self, then, is to imitate the pattern of the Paschal Mystery in miniature. Baptism already initiates this death—"Do you not know that all of us who were baptized into Christ Jesus were baptized into His death?" (Rom 6:3)—but the sacramental seed must grow through daily consent. Each mortification, each patient endurance, renews that baptismal vow. The old man dies so that the new man, renewed in grace, may rise. This is not stoic endurance but Eucharistic transformation. As bread is broken to become Body, so the believer is broken that he might become love.

Christian tradition distinguishes between the crosses *permitted by Providence*—sickness, injustice, loss—and the crosses *freely chosen* by the believer, such as voluntary penance, fasting, and restraint. God never positively wills evil, yet in His providence He permits it so that grace may draw good from it. Both the passive sufferings accepted in faith and the active sacrifices freely embraced cooperate in the same divine pedagogy: to teach the heart to love as God loves. Grace does not erase suffering but anoints it; it consecrates what would otherwise destroy.

Yet Christ's command is never given in isolation. The One who says "follow Me" also says "My yoke is easy, and My burden light" (Matt 11:30). The apparent contradiction resolves only in love: the Cross crushes what must die and frees what must live. What makes it light is not its weight but its companionship. The disciple does not carry the Cross alone; he carries it *with* Christ. The wood of His Passion becomes a shared burden, a mutual embrace. The saints knew this paradox well: that the heaviest cross, borne in union with Jesus, becomes sweet.

Thus, in the command of Matthew 16:24 lies the whole grammar of sanctity. Self-denial uproots pride; the cross purifies desire; following Christ perfects charity. This is not a call to ascetic despair but to divine participation. It is the blueprint of deification—the process by which human nature is drawn into the life of the Crucified and Risen One. Every Christian vocation, whether cloistered or public, domestic or apostolic, passes through this same doorway. To follow Christ without the Cross is to follow an illusion; to embrace the Cross with Christ is to touch resurrection already.

In this mystery, suffering becomes not punishment but participation, not curse but communion. The soul that has died to itself begins to breathe with the heart of God. Its sorrows no longer isolate; they intercede. Its wounds no longer fester; they shine. Here the paradox is complete: in losing life, one finds it; in dying, one lives; in the Cross, love triumphs. This is the secret of Christian asceticism—the acceptance of divine wisdom that makes foolish the wisdom of the world.

When Christ calls the disciple to self-denial, He is not asking for less of humanity but for its restoration. The human person, fractured by sin, becomes whole only when surrendered. To deny oneself is to be healed; to take up the cross is to be ennobled; to follow Christ is to be transfigured. And so the Christian life begins, as it ends, at the foot of the Cross—where the wisdom of God is revealed not in power but in love.

The Cross is not an isolated event; it is the axis around which all Scripture turns. From the first shedding of blood in Eden's exile to the cry of victory on Calvary, divine revelation unfolds as the history of redemptive suffering. The Bible does not romanticize pain—its pages groan with lament—but it reveals that through the mystery of the Cross, suffering is no longer merely endured but transformed. The story of salvation is the story of a God who enters our affliction to fill it with His presence.

The Gospels make the invitation explicit (Matt 16:24). As already seen, Christ sets the pattern of discipleship: renunciation, participation, imitation.

The Old Testament foreshadows this mystery with astonishing precision. Abraham's willingness to sacrifice Isaac on Mount Moriah prefigures the Father's self-offering of the Son. The ram caught in the thicket is the symbol of substitution—the first whisper of the Lamb of God who takes away the sin of the world. The Exodus continues the theme: liberation comes through the blood of the Passover lamb, suffering becomes the price of freedom. Israel learns, in the desert, that dependence is not humiliation but holiness. The prophets, too, read suffering in the key of redemption. Isaiah's Servant Songs reach their climax in the portrait of the Suffering Servant—"by His wounds we are healed" (Isa 53:5). The Servant's pain is not only exemplary but vicarious: he suffers *for* others, turning affliction into intercession.

The Psalms form the inner dialogue of this revelation. In their pages, anguish and adoration interweave. "My God, my God, why hast Thou forsaken me?" (Ps 22:1) becomes the very prayer Christ breathes on the Cross. The psalmist's cry of desolation becomes the Son's voice of perfect obedience. Even the psalms of lament, when read through Calvary, become hymns of hope: the honest expression of pain that refuses to let go of faith. "Though He slay me, yet will I trust in Him" (Job 13:15)—Job's defiance of despair—becomes the confession of every saint who endures darkness without bitterness.

In the New Testament, this scattered music resolves into harmony. The Cross, which seemed a scandal and folly, is proclaimed by St Paul as the wisdom and power of God (1 Cor 1:23–24). Paul's theology of suffering is not abstract but experiential: he writes as one marked by beatings, shipwrecks, and imprisonments. Yet he can say, without contradiction, "I rejoice in my sufferings for your sake, and in my flesh I complete what is lacking in Christ's afflictions for the sake of His Body, the Church" (Col 1:24). This is one of Scripture's most startling claims: that the redeemed are drawn into the very redemptive act of the Redeemer. Nothing is *lacking* in Christ's Passion in itself, but God, in His generosity, wills that the members participate in the Head's saving work. The sufferings of the saints are not substitutes but echoes of His once-for-all Sacrifice. The Church's pain is the Church's glory, because it makes visible the love that continues Christ's mission in time.

For Paul, this participation is not morbid fascination with pain but the deepest expression of love. "I have been crucified with Christ; it is no longer I who live, but Christ who lives in me" (Gal 2:20). The Cross becomes the grammar of a new existence. To "take up the cross" is to enter a living exchange—the "marvelous commerce" in which Christ takes our wounds and gives us His life. Paul's phrase "carrying in the body the death of Jesus" (2 Cor 4:10) describes not simply persecution but interior conformity: the soul learns to die to selfishness and live in charity. The pattern of death and resurrection repeats daily in the believer, until grace becomes habit and love becomes nature.

The First Letter of Peter continues this line: "Rejoice insofar as you share Christ's sufferings, that you may also rejoice and be glad when His glory is revealed" (1 Pet 4:13). The joy of suffering is not masochism but foresight—the awareness that pain endured in faith will be transfigured into glory. This is the same paradox Christ revealed in the Beatitudes: "Blessed are you when men revile you and persecute you... for your reward is great in heaven" (Matt 5:11–12). In the logic of the Kingdom, humiliation becomes blessedness because it unites us with the Humble One. The Cross reverses all human calculations of worth. What the world discards, God crowns.

No apostolic writer develops this mystery more tenderly than John. For him, the Cross is not tragedy but enthronement. Jesus speaks of His Passion as His glorification: "Now is the Son of Man glorified, and God is glorified in Him" (John 13:31). At Calvary, love reigns. The piercing of the side is not only the wound of death but the birth of the Church—the water and blood, symbols of Baptism and Eucharist, flowing from the open Heart of the Redeemer. In John's Gospel, the Cross is not where God abandons humanity but where He weds it. The wood of shame becomes the bridal bed of divine-human communion.

At the foot of that Cross stood Mary, sharing not in His divinity but in His compassion. Simeon's prophecy—"a sword will pierce your soul also" (Luke 2:35)—is fulfilled as she unites her maternal sorrow to the Redeemer's offering. In her, the Church contemplates the perfect model of redemptive participation: suffering transformed into intercession, love consenting to stand beneath the world's sin without bitterness. She is the first disciple of the Crucified and the icon of all who suffer in faith.

This is the "logic of the Cross"—a logic foreign to the world, yet radiant with coherence to faith. Sin entered through the misuse of freedom; redemption enters through its right use. Where Adam grasped, Christ relinquished. Where man asserted, God emptied Himself. "Though He was in the form of God, He did not count equality with God a thing to be grasped, but emptied Himself, taking the form of a servant" (Phil 2:6–7). The Greek term *kenosis*—"self-emptying"—captures the inner motion of divine love: power humbled into mercy, omnipotence choosing vulnerability. Yet this descent must be understood rightly. The Son of God emptied Himself not by losing divinity but by assuming our humanity. In the Incarnate Word, obedience is learned in His truly human life (Heb 5:8), while His divinity remains impassible and undiminished. What is new is not God's love, but its human experience: the eternal Word now suffers in the flesh He assumed. The Cross is divine humility made visible.

Within this kenotic pattern lies the blueprint of Christian life. The believer is called to live this same descent and ascent: "If we suffer with Him, we shall also be glorified with Him" (Rom 8:17). The Cross is therefore not an exception to divine love but its supreme revelation. To love in a fallen world is to suffer, for love always gives and suffers loss. Yet that suffering, offered in union with the Crucified, becomes participation in His creative power. Pain united to love becomes redemptive. The saints understood this not as theology alone but as lived reality. Their joy amid trial is the surest sign of the Gospel's truth.

Thus, the Scriptures trace one luminous arc: from the first tears of Eden to the final promise of Revelation—"He will wipe away every tear from their eyes" (Rev 21:4). Between those two moments stretches the Cross, standing at the center of history and of every soul's journey. To read Scripture without the Cross is to read without its heart. In every covenant, sacrifice, and prophecy, the shadow of Calvary already falls; in every sacrament and act of charity, its light already dawns.

The logic of the Cross, then, is not absurdity but wisdom hidden for ages in God. It reveals that divine omnipotence is not domination but love poured out to the end. Through it, the Scriptures are not merely read—

they are fulfilled in the flesh of the believer. The disciple who suffers in faith becomes a living exegesis of the Word made flesh.

The early Church did not treat the Cross as a philosophical problem to be solved but as a mystery to be entered. For the first Christians, the Crucified was not an abstract image of pain but a living presence. To gaze upon the Cross was to learn the mind of Christ—to see love made visible in suffering. The Fathers called this the *schola crucis*, the "school of the Cross," because it was here that the believer learned what it meant to love as God loves.

From the dawn of Christian history, the martyrs bore witness to this paradox. St Ignatius of Antioch, writing on his way to execution in Rome around the year 107, described his coming death not with fear but with Eucharistic longing: "I am God's wheat, and I am to be ground by the teeth of beasts, that I may be found the pure bread of Christ." For Ignatius, martyrdom was not destruction but transformation; his suffering became liturgy, his death a participation in the sacrifice of the altar. The blood of the martyrs, he wrote, was "seed for the Church"—not because of its violence but because of its love. They were not consumed by pain; they were transfigured by charity.

This same logic shaped the spiritual life of the patristic era. When open persecution ceased, the Fathers taught that the same martyrdom must continue inwardly. The arena became interior. St Anthony and the desert monks withdrew into solitude not to escape suffering but to confront its deepest cause: the rebellion of the self. "Without battle," said St Evagrius, "there is no crown." Their fasts, vigils, and renunciations were interior crucifixions—voluntary sufferings embraced as training in divine love. For them, asceticism was not a competition for holiness but the imitation of the Lamb: to conquer evil by bearing it.

St Augustine would later call the Cross *cathedra amoris*—the chair of love. In his sermons on the Passion, he speaks of Christ as both teacher and lesson: "The tree upon which the Master hung is the school in which He teaches us." For Augustine, the Cross revealed the grammar of divine charity: humility, obedience, forgiveness. "See how He loved you," he writes; "He hung upon the Cross, He endured the insults, He sought you when you fled, He followed you even to death." To contemplate the Crucified was to hear the Word made silent, to study love not in theory but in blood.

For Augustine, suffering is not in itself good, but love transforms its meaning. Evil twists suffering into resentment; grace transforms it into offering. When the will consents to God's will, pain becomes prayer. This is why Augustine insists that the Christian does not seek suffering but accepts it when fidelity demands it. "He who loves the Cross," he writes, "loves Christ." Yet that love never despises life; it sanctifies it. The saint's endurance is not stoic indifference but participation in Christ's compassion.

Other Fathers deepened this vision. St Gregory the Great described the Cross as a ladder between heaven and earth—"the ladder of humility by which we ascend to glory." Gregory's commentary on Job interprets human suffering as divine pedagogy: God, by permitting affliction, teaches the soul detachment and humility. "The fire of tribulation," he writes, "tests the gold of virtue." The believer who bears the cross patiently learns the truth of charity: that love is strongest when it costs. Suffering is thus the crucible of divine likeness. It does not make the saint heroic; it makes him merciful.

In the same spirit, St Irenaeus of Lyons had already written that "the glory of God is man fully alive." Yet this life is revealed most perfectly in death freely embraced. For Irenaeus, the Passion is the supreme manifestation of divine pedagogy: Christ, the new Adam, re-traces every step of the old. Where Adam disobeyed by grasping pleasure, Christ obeyed through pain. The Cross, then, is not arbitrary suffering but the perfect reversal of the Fall. Through obedience in affliction, Christ heals the disobedience of comfort. "As by a tree we fell," writes Irenaeus, "so by a tree we are raised."

The Fathers understood suffering through this logic of reversal: the very instruments of death become instruments of salvation. St John Chrysostom, preaching on Good Friday, exclaims, "I call Him King because

I see Him crucified. The Cross is His throne." For Chrysostom, the paradox of the Cross reveals the true nature of power: not domination but self-emptying love. To reign is to serve; to triumph is to forgive. In the wounds of Christ, he sees not shame but radiance: "The Cross is brighter than the sun, because it illumines the whole world."

Even the ascetical writers—those who taught self-denial and mortification—never viewed suffering in isolation from love. For them, mortification was love's discipline. St John Cassian speaks of voluntary suffering as a way to reclaim freedom: "The body is subdued not for its destruction but for the soul's peace." Pain, accepted in humility, breaks the tyranny of the passions and restores harmony between flesh and spirit. In this way, asceticism becomes an extension of the Cross—the application of redemption to one's own nature. The monk's cell, Cassian says, is "the anvil on which the heart is forged."

The same theology echoes in the writings of St Maximus the Confessor. For him, every suffering endured in faith becomes a microcosm of Christ's redemptive act. Maximus describes love as "the crucifixion of the will"—not the annihilation of freedom, but its purification. True love, he teaches, always contains a cross, because it demands the surrender of self-centered desire. The believer, then, imitates Christ not only by suffering externally but by letting his will be crucified internally—accepting contradiction, patience, and humiliation as the slow birth of divine charity.

The Fathers did not idealize pain; they baptized it. Their insight was profoundly incarnational: since the Word became flesh, even suffering can be sanctified. The Cross reveals that the material and the spiritual are not opposed but interwoven in redemption. The nails that pierce flesh open heaven; the wounds that bleed become windows of glory. When the believer unites his trials with Christ's Passion, he does not merely endure them—he consecrates them. The world's curse becomes the Christian's crown.

For the early Church, then, the Cross was not simply the price of salvation but the pattern of sanctity. The saints learned that to love God is to love as He loves—to bear with others, to forgive the unworthy, to rejoice in hiddenness, to accept weakness as the place of encounter. The "school of the Cross" taught them to see suffering not as proof of absence but as proof of presence. The God who suffers with us is the God who dwells within us.

To meditate on the Cross, the Fathers insisted, is to discover that love and suffering are two names for the same mystery. The soul that resists the Cross resists transformation; the soul that embraces it becomes luminous. As St Ignatius wrote before his martyrdom, "Now I begin to be a disciple." It was in the arena, not the classroom, that theology became life.

In the Catholic tradition, mortification is among the most misunderstood of all spiritual disciplines. To modern ears it sounds harsh, even pathological—a relic of medieval rigor. Yet rightly understood, mortification is not a rejection of life but the path to its transfiguration. The Latin *mortificatio* means "to make dead," but in Christian theology, what dies is not the self but the ego—everything in us that resists divine love. It is not annihilation but purification: the pruning of the soul so that it may bear fruit. "Unless a grain of wheat falls into the ground and dies, it remains alone; but if it dies, it bears much fruit" (John 12:24).

At its heart, mortification is the practical outworking of Christ's call to "deny yourself." It is love learning to say no to what diminishes it so that it may say yes to what enlarges it. The goal is never pain for pain's sake, but love purified of self-seeking. This is the paradox of Christian asceticism: to lose life is to find it; to die is to live. As the Cross reveals, suffering freely embraced in love becomes participation in the life of God Himself.

The theology of mortification begins with Christ's own obedience. "He humbled Himself and became obedient unto death, even death on a cross" (Phil 2:8). In this single verse lies the foundation of all Christian penance. The Son of God, who had no need of purification, entered human suffering so completely that even His death became an act of love. Obedience, not compulsion, sanctified His Passion. In His submission, pain was transfigured into prayer. Mortification, then, is not self-imposed punishment but the imitation of that obedience. It is the human will's agreement to be reshaped by the Cross until it becomes transparent to divine charity.

The saints consistently teach that the aim of mortification is freedom. St John of the Cross, in his *Ascent of Mount Carmel*, warns that "the soul attached to anything, however small, will not reach the freedom of divine union." Detachment is not disdain for created goods but refusal to let them enslave the heart. Mortification, in this sense, is the education of freedom—the painful yet liberating process by which the soul learns to love God above all things. St Francis de Sales captures this beautifully: "The mortified heart is the free heart; and to be free is to possess all." True mortification does not narrow the soul; it expands it to the measure of divine love.

In the Catholic theology of grace, mortification operates as cooperation rather than competition with God. Grace initiates, empowers, and completes; mortification consents, responds, and cooperates. As St Augustine put it, "He who created you without you will not save you without you." Grace heals the will, but the healed will must act. Mortification is that action: the will's participation in its own sanctification. In this sense, it is profoundly Eucharistic—the offering of one's own small sufferings to be united with the great Sacrifice of Christ. Every penance offered in charity becomes an extension of the Mass: suffering turned into worship.

St Thomas Aquinas gives mortification its theological precision. He distinguishes between *penance*—sorrow for sin—and *satisfaction*—acts that repair its consequences. Mortification participates in both. It expresses sorrow for disorder and cooperation in reordering love. For Aquinas, the body and soul share one moral life; therefore, discipline imposed on the body can heal the soul. Fasting, abstinence, and voluntary renunciations are "medicines of the spirit." They reestablish the right relation between sense and reason, desire and charity. Thus, the penitent does not destroy nature but restores it to health. Such satisfaction, for Aquinas, is medicinal rather than meritorious apart from Christ; its whole efficacy flows from union with His once-for-all Sacrifice. The penitent's cooperation does not compete with grace but becomes its instrument of healing.

But the deepest mystery of mortification lies not in self-control but in love's solidarity with Christ's redeeming Passion. To mortify the flesh is to share in the Cross of the Beloved. The Catechism echoes this truth: "By uniting ourselves with Christ's sacrifice, we can become a living sacrifice to God" (§2100). When suffering is offered in love, it ceases to be sterile. It becomes redemptive—not because it adds to Calvary, but because it applies Calvary's grace within us. St Paul's bold words—"I complete what is lacking in Christ's afflictions" (Col 1:24)—express this mystery perfectly: the Body of Christ participates in the suffering of its Head so that the grace of salvation may reach every member.

The saints embody this theology in luminous paradox. St Francis of Assisi called his frail body "Brother Ass"—a stubborn servant to be guided, not destroyed. His fasting, vigils, and tears were not self-contempt but gratitude, a way of participating in the poverty of the Crucified. St Catherine of Siena begged Christ to share His thirst: "Let me suffer for love of You, as You suffered for love of me." For her, suffering was not an end but a language—the speech of love between Creator and creature. In her *Dialogue*, she writes that the soul united to Christ desires to "suffer pain for the honor of God and the salvation of souls." The wound of compassion becomes the seal of divine intimacy.

This interior logic—love revealed in suffering—shapes the entire Christian moral vision. Mortification detaches us from lesser loves so that charity may reign without rival. Each voluntary sacrifice, from fasting to forgiving, is a small crucifixion of pride and a resurrection of humility. In this sense, mortification is continuous conversion: not a single act but a disposition of surrender renewed daily. St Paul's exhortation, "I die daily" (1 Cor 15:31), describes the rhythm of sanctity—the continual relinquishing of self-will in exchange for divine love.

Catholic theology distinguishes sharply between mortification and self-harm. The former is motivated by love and sustained by grace; the latter by despair and self-hatred. The penitent does not wound himself; he allows grace to wound pride. Mortification that forgets love ceases to be Christian—it becomes cruelty. "Penance without charity," warns St Francis de Sales, "is the body's martyrdom without the soul's." True mortification bears joy as its fruit, for it restores the heart to simplicity. The saint's austerity is always gentle, radiant, free of bitterness. The Cross, when embraced with Christ, flowers in peace.

This understanding allows even involuntary suffering—illness, loss, humiliation—to become mortification in grace. When accepted in union with Christ, these passive sufferings accomplish more than any self-chosen austerity. They train the heart in abandonment, the purest form of love. St Alphonsus Liguori advises: "He who suffers in patience suffers less and saves more." The measure of holiness is not the quantity of pain but the depth of consent. The soul that can say with Christ, "Not my will but Yours be done," has reached the summit of mortification.

Ultimately, mortification is the Cross written into daily life. It sanctifies the small, unnoticed renunciations that compose the fabric of love: holding one's tongue, bearing delay without irritation, forgiving the ungrateful, praying when weary, serving when unseen. These are the modern asceticisms, the daily crucifixions that prepare the soul for resurrection. Even the smallest acts—offering daily work, enduring irritation patiently, keeping the Morning Offering—extend the Cross into ordinary time. The believer's day thus becomes a liturgy of hidden mortifications, the quiet heroism of love in detail. The Cross does not stand only on Golgotha; it rises in every human heart that says yes to love amid pain.

Mortification, then, is the art of transfigured suffering. It does not exalt pain but baptizes it. It takes what would destroy and turns it into offering. Pain, when united with charity, becomes luminous—it reveals rather than conceals God. Every thorn, every deprivation, every sigh can become a spark of participation in the divine life. The saints do not flee from the cross because they have found the secret inscribed upon it: *Amor vincit omnia*—Love conquers all.

In the spiritual tradition of the Church, the saints and mystics reveal what theology can only point toward: that suffering, when united to divine love, becomes the very fire by which the soul is purified and united to

God. The mystics do not glorify pain for its own sake—they uncover its transfiguration. What the intellect calls "the problem of suffering," the saints call *the mystery of love's purification*. They teach that the Cross, once accepted, becomes not a wound but a furnace.

St John of the Cross stands as the supreme doctor of this mystery. His *Dark Night of the Soul* is not a poetic exaggeration but a theological map of sanctification through suffering. The "night," he says, is twofold: the night of sense, when the soul is stripped of earthly attachments, and the night of spirit, when it is deprived even of spiritual consolations. In both, God purifies the soul of possessiveness—first in the realm of pleasure, then in the realm of pride. The soul, unable to see or feel God, is led by pure faith. It is a descent into seeming absence that leads to union. "O guiding night," he writes, "more lovely than the dawn!" For in that darkness, divine light burns unseen.

This paradox—darkness as illumination, pain as purification—expresses the mystic's deepest insight: God is not found by clinging but by letting go. The soul must be emptied so that it may be filled. "To reach satisfaction in all," writes John, "desire satisfaction in nothing." The purification of the senses through fasting and the purification of the soul through mortification prepare for this final stripping: the purification of the spirit itself. In that night, even good things—spiritual sweetness, holy success, consoling images—must be surrendered. The soul learns to love God for His own sake, not for His gifts. Such love cannot coexist with self-possession; it is pure receptivity.

St Thérèse of Lisieux, though writing centuries later, lived this doctrine in simplicity and fire. Her "little way" was the transposition of the Carmelite night into the key of childlike trust. In her hidden sufferings—physical pain, misunderstanding, spiritual dryness—she found intimacy with the Crucified. "I will seek out a means of getting to Heaven by a little way," she wrote, "very short and very straight, a little way that is wholly new." That way was surrender through love in the midst of suffering. To be a "little victim of love" was not for her a morbid desire for pain but a readiness to let God's love consume every obstacle in her soul. Her "victimhood" was not tragedy but offering—the heart's consent to be a living holocaust of charity.

The saints agree that this fire of suffering, though painful, is not destructive. It is the creative action of divine love within the soul. St Catherine of Genoa describes purgation as "the soul's fire of love that burns away all rust." In her *Treatise on Purgatory*, she insists that the pain of purification and the joy of divine presence coexist: "The more the rust is consumed, the more the soul sees God." This is the pattern of the "purgatory on earth" lived by the saints. They endure suffering not as punishment but as participation in divine purification. Pain and love become one flame—the burning of everything that is not love.

In this sense, mystical suffering is not confined to saints in cloisters; it is the hidden vocation of every Christian soul. The *night of faith*—when God seems silent or absent—is the crucible in which trust becomes pure. Many experience this in loneliness, failure, or illness. Yet, as John of the Cross assures, the apparent loss of light is not a sign of abandonment but of divine proximity: "For the soul, though it walks in darkness, is not forsaken; it is being secretly guided by God's love." The disappearance of consolation is the proof that God desires intimacy, not sentiment. He draws near in ways that strip away illusion.

The mystics teach that this process mirrors Christ's own Passion. In Gethsemane, Jesus experiences the utter solitude of obedience. On the Cross, He cries, "My God, my God, why have You forsaken me?" (Matt 27:46). Yet even this desolation is an act of communion: the Son enters the farthest reaches of human alienation so that no suffering may be outside redemption. Every soul that endures the night in faith is joined to that cry. In the apparent silence of God, the believer shares in the Son's own intimacy with the Father. "Into Your hands I commend My spirit" (Luke 23:46) becomes the prayer of every purified heart.

This theology of suffering as union reveals the inner meaning of mortification and penance. They are not ends in themselves but preludes to transformation. In the mystics, the Cross ceases to be merely external— it becomes interiorized. The believer discovers that Christ crucified lives within him, carrying him into the depths of divine compassion. St Elizabeth of the Trinity expressed this with crystalline clarity: "Everything that happens to me is a sacrament of communion with Him." For her, suffering was not interruption but participation—the continuation of Calvary in the soul. The interior crucifixion becomes the meeting place of divine and human love.

Catholic mysticism thus unites ascetic realism with mystical joy. It does not promise the absence of pain but the transfiguration of pain into love. The soul that consents to purification begins to experience suffering as a sacrament of divine intimacy. This is why the saints could speak of joy in affliction—not because they denied its agony, but because they saw in it the touch of the Crucified. "Love," wrote Thérèse, "is repaid by love alone." To suffer in love is to let God's love speak in our silence.

This mystical transformation has cosmic dimensions. The suffering of the saints is not isolated; it contributes to the redemption of the world. United with the Passion, their pain becomes intercession. The "communion of saints" is also a communion of suffering: the mystical Body of Christ distributing His grace through the wounds of its members. Every hidden sacrifice, every act of patience, ripples outward through the Church like unseen light. The mystic's darkness illumines others. In this way, the suffering of one becomes the healing of many.

The Cross, then, is not only an event to be remembered but a state to be lived. It is the form of divine life as it enters creation. In the crucible of suffering freely embraced, the soul is conformed to the Lamb who takes away the sin of the world. The night becomes radiant with meaning; the wounds of love become doors of light. The mystic, purified of self, sees that pain and glory are not opposites but stages of the same ascent.

In the end, this is the summit of Christian mysticism: not flight from the world, but transformation of it. The soul united to Christ through suffering becomes a living conduit of divine compassion. It can pray with St Paul, "It is no longer I who live, but Christ who lives in me" (Gal 2:20). Such a soul has entered the very rhythm of the Trinity: love poured out, received, and returned. Suffering, far from being a curse, becomes communion—the passage through which divine fire renews the world.

The mystery of redemptive suffering reaches its summit in the doctrine of *theosis*: that the human being, through participation in Christ's Passion, is drawn into the very life of God. The Cross, then, is not only a historical event or a moral example—it is the form of divine glory entering creation. The God who is Love reveals Himself most perfectly not in power but in woundedness, not in domination but in self-giving. Thus, the one who suffers in Christ does not simply imitate Him; he is conformed to His image until his very suffering becomes luminous with divine life.

Theosis through suffering does not mean that pain is divine; it means that love is stronger than pain. Grace does not erase agony—it penetrates it, transfiguring its interior meaning. The wounds of the Crucified do not vanish after the Resurrection; they shine. This is the icon of redeemed suffering: what once was a mark of death becomes the seal of glory. The risen Christ shows His wounds not as scars of defeat but as windows of light through which the world sees the mercy of God. Every Christian who bears the cross in faith begins to share in that radiance. "If we suffer with Him, we shall also be glorified with Him" (Rom 8:17).

This is not metaphor. Grace truly divinizes—not by nature but by participation. As St Peter writes, 'You have become partakers of the divine nature' (2 Pet 1:4). The path by which that participation unfolds, however, is cruciform. The uncreated holiness of God does not bypass the wounds of creation but enters through them. Suffering becomes the narrow door through which divine life passes into the world. The mystics call this transformation *the luminous exchange*—Christ takes our afflictions into Himself, and we receive His peace. It is not that pain disappears, but that its interior logic changes: what was chaos becomes communion.

St Paul's letters echo this mystery in every line. "I rejoice in my sufferings for your sake," he writes to the Colossians, "and in my flesh I complete what is lacking in Christ's afflictions for the sake of His Body, the Church" (Col 1:24). The apostle does not suggest deficiency in the Redemption; rather, he reveals participation. The sufferings of Christ are inexhaustible, and the Body of Christ extends them through time. The Church becomes the living continuation of the Passion. When the faithful endure trial in faith, they become conduits of redemptive grace—vessels through which the charity of Calvary reaches new souls.

St Augustine's commentary on the Psalms beautifully unfolds this mystery. In his exposition of Psalm 60, he writes, "The whole Christ prays—Head and Body together." For Augustine, Christ's cry on the Cross, "My God, my God, why have You forsaken me?", continues in His members. The saints' groaning, he says, is the ongoing prayer of the suffering Christ within history. Thus, Christian suffering is not isolated; it is liturgical. The wounds of believers are joined to the eternal intercession of the Son before the Father. This is why the Church venerates martyrs and penitents: their pain is the prayer of Christ prolonged in time.

In the light of this mystery, suffering ceases to be meaningless. It becomes a language of divine communication. God does not will suffering as punishment; He permits it as participation. The believer, by uniting his pain to Christ, turns it into praise. This is the meaning of redemptive suffering: not that pain in itself saves, but that love borne through pain becomes salvific. St Thomas Aquinas teaches that "the Passion of Christ is sufficient for all, but its fruits are applied to each through participation." Our sufferings, offered in union with His, become channels of that fruitfulness. In this way, the Cross is extended not in time but in depth—its grace unfolding in each human life that consents to love through pain.

For the saints, this participation often becomes visible as a mysterious joy. St Teresa of Avila, tormented by illness and contradiction, could write, "Pain is never unbearable when one loves." St Paul of the Cross called suffering "the most certain mark of divine love." Even Thérèse, dying in physical agony and spiritual desolation, exclaimed, "I am not suffering; I am rejoicing." Such paradoxical joy is not denial—it is the fruit of divine indwelling. When the Spirit fills the soul, sorrow becomes song. "As sorrowful, yet always rejoicing" (2 Cor 6:10): this is the music of sanctity.

Theosis through suffering also illuminates the relationship between the Church militant and the Church suffering. Purgatory, as the mystics describe it, is not punishment but final purification—the completion of the same transformation begun on earth. The souls in purgatory are already holy, already saved; their suffering is love's fire refining the last dross of self. St Catherine of Genoa's insight returns here: "The souls in purgatory enjoy the greatest happiness and the greatest pain; the one does not hinder the other." On earth, voluntary mortification and patient endurance of trial accomplish in time what purgatory completes in eternity—the total transparency of love. Thus, even purgation is theosis in process: suffering consumed by glory.

In this vision, every human sorrow, however small, acquires cosmic meaning. The mother's sleepless night, the worker's hidden fatigue, the sickbed's prayer—when offered in faith—become acts of divine participation. The Cross, extended across history, gathers them all. The saints' union with Christ does not remove their humanity; it perfects it. Their sufferings, far from isolating them, make them profoundly compassionate. The more they share in His pain, the more they share in His mercy. This is why true holiness always carries the mark of tenderness: the divinized soul, having suffered, can no longer wound.

Ultimately, theosis through suffering reveals that the Cross is not the end of the story but the beginning of transfiguration. The Resurrection does not cancel the Crucifixion; it interprets it. The wounds remain, but they shine. So too in the Christian life: when the soul consents to love through pain, its very wounds become radiant. The body, chastened by grace, becomes the vessel of divine compassion. The mind, purified by trial, becomes mirror of divine wisdom. The heart, pierced by sorrow, becomes the throne of mercy. The divine image, once marred by sin, now gleams again with its original splendor.

The Eastern Fathers often spoke of the *resplendence* of the saints—their bodies, faces, and even gestures irradiated by inner light. Catholic theology reads this not as poetic flourish but as eschatological truth. The risen body of Christ, bearing luminous wounds, is the pattern of our glorification. The saints' peace amid suffering prefigures that same transfigured state. What grace begins in the crucible of pain, glory completes in the vision of God. The soul purified by the Cross becomes what it beholds: light within Light, love within Love.

To embrace the Cross, then, is to embrace deification. It is to allow the fire of divine charity to pass through one's life until every trace of darkness becomes translucent. The path of suffering freely accepted is not tragic but sacramental. It is the liturgy of redemption unfolding within the flesh. As Christ entered glory through His wounds, so must His Body, the Church, pass through the same door.

The Eucharist is the summit of this mystery. In every Mass the Church gathers all human sorrow into Christ's perfect oblation. There the believer's small sufferings—illness, failure, heartbreak—are placed upon the altar and made fruitful in love. The same Body once crucified now feeds the members who share His Passion, so that the Cross offered becomes the Cross lived.

When the wounds of Christ are welcomed into the flesh, they become doors of light. Through them the soul passes from imitation to communion, from endurance to illumination. The fire that once burned as pain becomes radiance. The Cross, once a symbol of death, becomes the very form of divine life—and man, remade in that image, shines with the glory for which he was created.

8

The Liturgy: Participation in the Heavenly Worship

"The purpose of every hierarchy is to lift those below it into the likeness of the divine;

   the sacred rites exist to make the human godlike by participation in the heavenly."

— Pseudo-Dionysius the Areopagite, Celestial Hierarchy III. 1

The Divine Liturgy as Mystical Theophany

"He took, blessed, broke, gave—and their eyes were opened" (Lk 24:30–35). The Church never forgot the Emmaus pattern. That fourfold action is not stagecraft but revelation. In the breaking of the bread, the Risen Lord discloses Himself and gathers wanderers back into the fire of communion. From that evening forward, the Eucharist has been the place where Christ makes Himself known—not by removing veils but by taking them up into His presence, so that through them He may be seen, touched, adored, and received.

The great theophanies of Scripture converge here. Sinai's radiance and covenant sacrifice (Ex 24), Isaiah's vision of the seraphim crying "Holy, Holy, Holy" (Is 6), the mountain of the Transfiguration where the Son shines with the Father's glory (Mt 17), the Emmaus table where sorrow turns to joy (Lk 24), and the heavenly worship of Revelation where "a Lamb standing as though slain" is enthroned amid elders and living creatures (Rev 4–5): all find their fulfilment in the Eucharist. The sanctuary is a threshold—heaven's court opens, the Church sings with the angels, and the Lamb reigns by His wounds.

The Eucharist is Christ's own priestly act. "We have such a High Priest," says Hebrews, "a minister in the sanctuary and the true tent" (Heb 8:1–2). His sacrifice—offered "once for all" (Heb 10:10)—is not repeated in time but made sacramentally present through His command: "Do this in memory of me" (Lk 22:19–20). In biblical memory (*anamnesis*), the saving deed is not recalled at a distance; it is brought before the Father and applied to the faithful in the Spirit The Mass is not another sacrifice but the very Sacrifice present in sacramental mode; we are admitted into it. "For as often as you eat this bread and drink the cup, you proclaim the Lord's death until He comes" (1 Cor 11:26): the past accomplished, the future anticipated, the present transformed.

The Church expresses this truth with luminous precision. Christ is truly present in the minister who offers, in the proclaimed Word, in the assembled faithful, and "most especially under the Eucharistic species" (*Sacrosanctum Concilium* 7–8). The Eucharist is "the source and summit of the Christian life" (CCC 1324–1327); in it "the sacrifice of the Cross is made present" (CCC 1367). Because, in virtue of Christ's promise and power, the sacraments *effect what they signify* (*ex opere operato*), the liturgy is a genuine theophany. Its fruitfulness in us, however, still asks for living faith and proper disposition (*ex opere operantis*)—precisely what the rite itself trains. Within it, the Son's filial offering is presented to the Father, and the Spirit makes that offering ours. In this exchange the Church is divinized—not by nature, but by sanctifying grace, a created participation in the divine life.

The Fathers of the Church give this mystery concrete voice. St Cyril of Jerusalem, catechizing neophytes, insists: "Under the appearance of bread you receive the Body of Christ; in the chalice, His Blood"—and because it is truly He, heaven touches earth. St Ambrose, in a Western register, links the change to the Spirit's invocation: the same Spirit who overshadowed Mary now overshadows the gifts, effecting a real conversion for the sake of communion. St Augustine widens the horizon: in the Eucharist, the "whole Christ"—Head and members—offers one sacrifice of praise (*City of God* X). The altar is both table and throne; chalice and cross are one mystery present under veils.

Revelation is therefore not described so much as enacted. "The hour is coming, and is now here," says Jesus, "when true worshipers will worship the Father in spirit and truth" (Jn 4:23–24). His "hour"—the Pasch of the Cross and Resurrection—becomes accessible in the liturgy; those who enter it stand within His self-offering. The faithful "have come to Mount Zion and to the city of the living God, the heavenly Jerusalem… and to Jesus, the mediator of a new covenant" (Heb 12:22–24). That verse is no metaphor; it names the Church's actual address during the Mass. When the *Sanctus* rises, the faithful do not pretend to join the angels; they genuinely take up their hymn. When the priest pronounces the words of the Lord, it is Christ who speaks through him; when he offers, it is Christ who offers in him; when he breaks, it is Christ who feeds; when the faithful receive, it is Christ who divinizes.

Since the liturgy is God's work before it is ours (*opus Dei*), it forms a people who belong to God's order. The divine is not summoned by us; rather, we are drawn into His action. Hence the reverence of rubrics, the sacramental hierarchy, and the *ars celebrandi* that serves rather than eclipses the Mystery. Sacred order does not constrain worship; it protects the primacy of God's action from our improvisations and keeps the Church inside Christ's priestly form. The priest's fidelity, the deacon's service, the lector's proclamation, the cantor's chant, and the assembly's response are all coordinated ministries within a single priestly act. Disorder would distort what is not ours to shape; form allows grace to shine through.

This priestly act stretches as widely as creation and as deeply as sin. Malachi foretold a pure offering "from the rising of the sun to its setting" (Mal 1:11); the Church recognizes that prophecy fulfilled each day at the

Eucharistic altar. The psalmist's summons, "Sing to the Lord a new song" (Ps 96), becomes the Church's *cantus novus*—the new song that only the Lamb can teach. In the Roman Canon's contemplative stillness, in the majestic *anamnesis* of St Basil, and in the radiant thanksgiving of St John Chrysostom, the same Paschal mystery shines in varied light. Distinct tongues utter one Word; diverse melodies resound with one Sacrifice.

The liturgy's theophany is wholly Trinitarian. The Father is the fountain of blessing and the end of all praise; the Son is both Priest and Victim; the Holy Spirit consecrates gifts and people alike. The Eucharistic Prayer is a river of divine life: it thanks the Father, remembers the Son, invokes the Spirit, intercedes for the living and the dead, and returns all glory "through Him, and with Him, and in Him… in the unity of the Holy Spirit." To be present at this prayer is already to be drawn into the Son's own filial worship. Theosis, in Catholic theology, is this filial participation: the Spirit shapes us into "sons in the Son," so that our "Amen" becomes a share in Christ's eternal "Yes" to the Father.

Every sign within the rite serves that communion. Bread—humble, daily, shared—and wine—festive, poured, gladdening—retain their natural meanings yet are transfigured. Reading and homily open the heart to truth; offerings bear the labour of human hands; the exchange of peace enacts reconciliation before communion (cf. Mt 5:23–24); kneeling confesses adoration; standing proclaims resurrectional readiness; the procession enacts pilgrimage toward God. Nothing is arbitrary, for nothing is merely human. The liturgy educates desire until love learns the rhythm of divine charity.

To say the Mass is a theophany is to confess that God both reveals and gives Himself. Revelation here is presence that communicates; communion is a real increase of sanctifying grace and charity. Through sanctifying grace—infused, stable, elevating—the Father makes us capable of worship "in Spirit and truth." The faithful do not attend a sacred pageant; they enter a holy exchange. Offered with the oblations, consecrated with the gifts, raised with the praise, and sent forth with the blessing, the Church becomes what she receives: one Bread, one Body (1 Cor 10:16–17).

The sanctuary is therefore not a stage but a doorway. "Behold, I stand at the door and knock" (Rev 3:20); in the liturgy Christ opens from within. A Lamb stands, His wounds radiant; angels veil their faces; the poor are fed with God. Here the Bride learns her name and speaks it back in thanksgiving. Here time thins, heaven stoops, and earth is lifted. Here the Father hears again the Son He loves and, hearing Him, receives us.

Liturgical Time and the Eschatological In-Breaking

Since this worship is truly Christ's, it bends time and draws the Church into His "hour." Liturgical time becomes the soul's apprenticeship to eternity.

Time is the first creature that the liturgy redeems. It gathers the scattered hours, heals the fractures of chronology, and bends history toward its fulfillment. When the Church enters the Eucharist, she does not travel backward to recall an event long past, nor forward to await a promise still remote. She steps into the "hour" of Christ—the eternal moment in which all moments are embraced. The Cross, the Resurrection, and the Coming Glory converge, not as memories or hopes, but as a single mystery made sacramentally present.

In the language of Scripture this mystery is called *anamnesis*. When Christ commanded, "Do this in memory of Me," He did not entrust His disciples with an act of recollection, but with the power to make present what was once accomplished. The memorial is not human nostalgia but divine action. The Lamb "standing as though slain" (Rev 5:6) is not remembered upon the altar; He stands there. The same sacrifice, once offered in blood, is now offered sacramentally, so that every generation may touch the one event in which all salvation is contained. The liturgy, says the Catechism, is the place where "the events of salvation become in a certain way present and real" (CCC 1363). In the chalice of the Church, Golgotha is not revisited—it is *here*.

In the Church's anamnesis, the temporal distance between Calvary and today collapses under the weight of eternity. The Mass does not multiply sacrifices; it renders the one Sacrifice present by divine power. "The sacrifice of Christ and the sacrifice of the Eucharist are one single sacrifice," teaches the Catechism (CCC 1367). The priest does not offer anew what Christ completed, but makes that completion accessible in time. The same Victim, once immolated, now reigns upon the altar under sacramental signs. This is the deep paradox of Catholic worship: history remains history, yet eternity penetrates it. The faithful kneel before what the angels see everlastingly—the Son offering Himself to the Father in the unity of the Spirit.

But anamnesis alone does not suffice to name the wonder. The Eucharist also carries the future within it. It is *prolepsis*—anticipation, a foretaste of the final transfiguration. "We proclaim the Lord's death until He comes" (1 Cor 11:26). That "until" is the horizon of the Mass. In every Eucharist the Church stands on the thin edge between history and its completion. The bread we break is the pledge of the banquet that has no end; the cup we share is the wine of the Kingdom, already flowing through mortal veins. The altar is both Cross and throne, the site of offering and of feast. Past and future meet and embrace, and the present is made translucent to eternity.

For this reason the Church names the Eucharist *pledge of future glory* (CCC 1402–1405). The bread of pilgrims is also the food of the blessed. Every communion is a prophecy of vision, every altar a promise of the New Jerusalem. The heavenly liturgy of Hebrews 12 is not postponed; it presses into the earthly celebration. "You have come," says the Apostle—not "you will come"—"to the city of the living God, to innumerable angels in festal gathering." The Eucharist is that approach made visible. It is the moment in which the Church already stands among the choirs of heaven, praising the Lamb who was slain and lives forever. Thus every liturgy, even the humblest weekday Mass, is the mountain of God in miniature, the threshold where history trembles beneath glory.

The Fathers perceived this double movement as the rhythm of salvation itself. Justin Martyr, describing the Sunday gathering, saw already the heavenly liturgy breaking into the assemblies of the faithful. Augustine called the Eucharist the "alleluia of pilgrims" that prepares for the "alleluia of citizens." For him, every Mass is rehearsal for the vision of God: faith stretching toward sight, hope ripening into possession, charity beginning its endless song. In this tension of remembrance and anticipation, the soul learns how to dwell in the eternal now of God.

The Church expresses this mystery not only in the Eucharistic moment but in the sanctification of time itself. The calendar is not a wheel that turns, but a spiral that ascends. Through Advent she learns to ache for the Bridegroom; at Christmas she kneels before the nearness of the Infinite; in Lent she follows the narrow path of purification that ends in light; at Easter she bursts into the joy of creation reborn; at Pentecost she receives the fire that makes all things new. Even the long stretch of Ordinary Time—is not ordinary at all; it is the slow schooling of charity in daily life. Each return of the feast does not repeat but deepens. History is educated into holiness.

The liturgical year is therefore the Church's school of divine memory. It teaches time to speak theology. Advent opens the heart to yearning; it cultivates the ache that only God can satisfy. Christmas answers that ache with the revelation that the Infinite can dwell in swaddling clothes. Lent disciplines the flesh and purifies the will, teaching us to be co-offerers with the Crucified. Easter shatters every horizon of despair, making joy the Church's natural climate. Pentecost scatters the fire of charity into the common day, and the long green stretch of Ordinary Time unfolds that charity in the soil of the mundane. Each cycle engraves Christ's mysteries more deeply in the soul, until the entire year becomes a single doxology stretched across time.

So too the Church consecrates the hours of the day. "Seven times a day I praise You," sings the Psalmist, and the monastic office has become the heartbeat of the world. Morning recalls creation's first light and the rising of the Sun of Justice; noon remembers the Crucified suspended between earth and heaven; evening gathers the labours of the day into thanksgiving; night keeps vigil for the coming dawn. Through this rhythm, chronos—the measured time of human toil—is pierced again and again by *kairos*, the God-filled moment. Time is taught to worship.

The sanctification of hours is not a monastic privilege but the hidden architecture of Christian existence. When the Church keeps vigil, she does so not merely for herself but on behalf of the world. Every psalm prayed in the night steadies a cosmos adrift in darkness. The bells that mark the canonical hours are the heartbeat of creation being re-tuned. Morning and evening prayer are not private devotions but public acts by which the Bride keeps step with the Bridegroom. In the Liturgy of the Hours the whole Body of Christ sings with one voice, "Through Him, and with Him, and in Him," joining earth's frail rhythm to heaven's unbroken hymn.

To live liturgically, then, is to perceive the world within this transformed horizon. The believer no longer moves through a series of vanishing instants but through sacraments of presence. Every hour bears a hidden invitation; every season is charged with meaning. The Eucharist becomes the measure of all time: what has been is offered, what will be is promised, what is now is sanctified. Time itself learns to breathe the divine life.

This bending of time is not metaphor but Christological fact. When the Word entered flesh, eternity entered duration and did not depart. The Incarnation is not an episode within history but the transfiguration of history's fabric. The Son who reigns at the right hand of the Father continues to offer Himself in the Church's worship, and through that offering time is drawn into His eternal priesthood. The liturgy is the intersection where God's timelessness touches the world's temporality—not to annul it, but to deify it.

Thus the Christian learns to live from the altar outward. The rhythm of the year and of the day becomes a participation in the great procession of salvation: creation, fall, redemption, consummation—all enfolded in the single act of divine love made present here and now. The heart that beats in this rhythm becomes eschatological; it begins to desire as heaven desires. The Eucharist plants within the soul the habits of the Kingdom—hope that waits with serenity, charity that loves with eternity's patience. Grace sows within time the seeds of vision; the future already germinates in the present.

The Eucharist thus forms within the soul the very habits that will blossom in the Kingdom. Hope becomes not mere expectation but familiarity with what is to come; charity becomes the native language of eternity spoken in the accent of time. St. Maximus the Confessor calls this the *sabbath rest of creation*: the whole cosmos labouring toward the stillness of divine communion. When the Christian participates in the liturgy with a purified heart, he already begins to breathe that sabbath air. The grace received now is the seed of vision then; what will one day blaze as glory begins as quiet conformity to the Son's offering. The liturgy is both the path and the arrival, both journey and foretaste, both apprenticeship and homecoming.

The liturgy therefore is not a flight from history but its transfiguration. It does not abolish waiting; it sanctifies it. It does not end the world; it reveals its true direction. In the Eucharist, history itself learns its purpose: to become thanksgiving. "Behold, I make all things new" (Rev 21:5)—not at the world's conclusion only, but each time bread becomes Body and wine becomes Blood. In that moment, the Church stands where time and eternity meet, and learns to live from that meeting.

This divine hour reaches us through human signs—image, sound, fragrance, movement—the senses themselves are invited into transfiguration. What is heavenly is tasted on earth, that by what we see and hear and touch, the soul may be raised to what no eye has seen.

Iconography, Chant, and the Senses as Vehicles of Theosis

The Word who became flesh sanctified the entire field of sense. The eyes, the ears, the tongue, the hands—all that once served appetite now stand ready for adoration. Through the Incarnation, the material world ceases to be a neutral stage on which grace performs and becomes instead the very instrument of grace's song. In the liturgy, matter is not accessory but ally. The same clay from which man was formed is again employed by the Spirit to reveal glory. Through water, bread, oil, and word, creation itself becomes the vesture of divinity. The Christian, therefore, approaches the altar not to escape the physical but to see it transfigured. Every sense becomes a doorway through which the soul may enter the splendour of God.

The senses are not silenced by holiness; they are educated by it. Sin dulled perception until beauty became an object of consumption rather than communion. Worship heals this distortion by returning the senses to their priestly vocation: to offer and to receive. The body that once absorbed the world now learns to lift it. The liturgy re-teaches sight to adore, hearing to attend, taste to discern, touch to revere, and scent to remember. Through such sanctification, the creature made of dust is prepared again to breathe the air of paradise.

Among all visible forms, the sacred image stands first as teacher of this redeemed vision. The icon is theology written in colour, the Word translated into line and light. It does not pretend to reproduce the natural world but to reveal the world transfigured. The flattened perspective and luminous stillness confess the new creation where shadow is no more. As the Second Council of Nicaea declared, the honour shown to the image passes to the prototype; to bow before the painted face of Christ is to acknowledge the Incarnate Word Himself. In that reverent gaze, vision becomes prayer. What the eye contemplates, the soul begins to resemble. Thus the icon is not ornament but participation—an epiphany that draws the beholder into the radiance it portrays. To look rightly is already to be converted.

In the East the iconostasis stands as the membrane between heaven and earth: barrier and bridge, veil and revelation. Through its ranks of saints, the Church on earth beholds the Church in glory; through its open doors, the mysteries unfold like the descent of light through cloud. To venerate the icon is to confess that the invisible has entered the visible without ceasing to be divine. In such contemplation the mind is purified of fantasy, the heart of self-projection. The image does not feed imagination; it disciplines it, teaching the soul to see only what God has shown.

The West proclaims the same mystery in the idiom of stone and glass.

Stained windows pour coloured fire across the nave; light, once indifferent, becomes Scripture made luminous. The crucifix, standing at the heart of every altar, is the *summa* of sacred art: revelation compressed into gesture. The twisted body of the God-Man is not aesthetic shock but theology of love; the wood of suffering becomes the throne of mercy. Statues, frescoes, and mosaics join this chorus of forms—each translating doctrine into beauty. As the Catechism teaches, "The Christian image is to be honoured because the Word of God became visible" (CCC 1159). In a civilisation that worships its own reflections, these holy images rescue sight from narcissism. They restore to the eye the lost art of reverence.

Hearing too must be healed. The music of the liturgy is not entertainment but theology in sound. Chant does not seek applause but adoration. It is the breath of Scripture stretched into melody, the Word dwelling in the lungs of the Church. Gregorian plainsong, born of psalmody and purified by silence, bends language toward eternity; its single unbroken line mirrors the simplicity of divine being. Polyphony, when chaste, accomplishes the same by harmony: many voices finding unity without erasing difference, an audible image of the Body of Christ. In both, beauty serves truth, not vanity. "He who sings prays twice," said Augustine, not because sound multiplies merit but because it draws the whole person—mind and flesh—into worship. Sacred music converts breath into prayer and teaches the heart to keep time with heaven.

Breath itself is the primal liturgical act. In Genesis, God breathes into the dust and man becomes a living soul; in the Upper Room, the risen Christ breathes on His disciples and says, "Receive the Holy Spirit." Every sung note extends that double breathing. In chant, human respiration becomes participation in divine inspiration. The Spirit who gives life also gives rhythm; He draws sound from lungs as once He drew being from nothing. The singer thus learns what it means to live eucharistically—to receive breath as gift and return it as praise.

Chant orders passion without extinguishing it. Its measured contour is not restraint but peace—the taming of turbulence into offering. Melisma replaces outcry with adoration; intensity becomes patience. Through melody, the heart learns divine proportion. St Basil called psalmody "the tranquillity of the soul, the author of concord," for it unites emotion to reason and reason to grace. When words are sung, they enter memory like warmth into blood; doctrine becomes devotion.

This is why sacred music stands at the border between theology and mysticism. It teaches the faith to the mind while carrying the mind beyond speech. St Augustine confessed that tears rose when he heard the Church sing: "Truth poured into my heart, and the affection of devotion overflowed." In such moments, the passions are not suppressed but transfigured; love itself becomes intelligible sound. Theosis here is not concept but experience: the creature, filled with divine breath, gives voice to God's own joy.

Even silence belongs to this same pneumatology. The pauses of chant are not absences but inhalations of the Spirit, the soul's preparation to sound again. Silence and song alternate like systole and diastole—the beating of the Church's heart. The faithful who enter that rhythm begin to live, quite literally, by the breath of God.

The other senses are drawn into the same consecration. Incense renders the invisible tangible; it rises like prayer and returns like blessing. Its fragrance, older than words, carries the memory of temple and sacrifice, Sinai and Revelation. The smoke that veils the altar unveils the truth: mystery is not grasped but inhaled. Candles burn beside it, their small flames participating in the Paschal Fire that conquered darkness. To watch wax consume itself in light is to behold love's own parable—glory born of offering. Vestments continue this liturgy of signs: linen recalling baptismal purity, stole signifying service, chasuble enfolding charity. The minister's individuality disappears; what remains is office, sacrament, presence. Even the smallest gesture becomes hieroglyph of grace.

Incense is the visible parable of intercession. Rising from burning coal, it images the soul set aflame by charity and lifted by the Spirit into the Son's own offering to the Father. "Let my prayer rise before Thee like incense" (Ps 141:2): the psalmist's plea becomes literal in the sanctuary. The sweet smoke consecrates the air itself, reminding creation that nothing is too

THE LITURGY: PARTICIPATION IN THE HEAVENLY WORSHIP

material to become praise.

Light is the element of resurrection. Every candle repeats the Paschal flame that shattered the tomb's darkness. Its brightness is not utilitarian but sacramental; it is a share in that uncreated light which illumines the saints. To gaze on flickering fire is to see matter fulfilling its vocation—to burn without consuming, to reveal without wounding. The believer who carries the baptismal candle is already practicing the art of deification: to become luminous by surrender.

Vesture translates sanctity into texture. The alb clothes the minister in baptismal whiteness, the stole in the yoke of charity, the chasuble in mercy's embrace. The priest does not adorn himself; he disappears into sign. In him, the Church beholds the Second Adam clothed again in glory. Even the simplest surplice whispers of Eden restored.

The body itself speaks this language. Posture confesses creed. Standing proclaims resurrectional dignity; kneeling declares adoration; the bowed head remembers humility; the folded hands gather wandering thought into unity. When the faithful process toward the altar, they enact the entire history of salvation—the long pilgrimage of creation returning to its source. Every movement becomes a miniature of the cosmic dance: the material world ordered again toward its Maker. The disciplined body forms the attentive soul; through ritual gesture, desire learns order and delight learns reverence.

Sacred architecture gathers these arts into one vast doxology of space. The church building is not a shelter for devotion but the world remade in stone. Its very proportions are theological: vertical lines drawing the mind upward, horizontal breadth embracing humanity. Orientation to the East is confession made brick—the hope that all history rises with the Sun of Justice. The nave gathers the pilgrim people; the sanctuary, raised and veiled, reveals the Holy of Holies where heaven stoops to kiss the earth. Font, ambo, and altar trace the soul's ascent from cleansing through illumination to communion. The dome, crowning the whole, signifies creation gathered beneath the gaze of God. In such space, theology becomes habitable; the believer prays not in concept but within revelation's architecture.

Yet the architecture of stone mirrors an architecture of soul. The visible sanctuary trains the invisible one. As the faithful pass from narthex to nave to altar, they re-enact the soul's journey from worldliness through purification into communion. The church building is thus not only symbol but pedagogy; it teaches interiority through exterior order. The holy space outside becomes the form of the holy space within, until conscience itself acquires the shape of a temple.

The Fathers often spoke of man as microcosm—a small world uniting matter and spirit. In sacred space that microcosm finds its echo: the dome like the intellect illuminated, the nave like the heart expanded, the altar like the will offered. When the faithful cross the church's threshold, they enter their own redeemed humanity. To stand beneath that dome is to remember that the cosmos and the soul were made for the same end—to become dwelling places of God.

Even acoustics are grace's ally. In the great basilicas, the lingering echo of chant suggests that time itself refuses to end the praise. Sound, like incense, hangs in the air as testimony that what is offered is not lost. The building does not contain worship; it prolongs it. Every stone and arch becomes articulate; the structure breathes doxology.

This harmony of arts is not ornamentation but ontology. It springs from the Church's sacramental understanding of reality: that matter, touched by the Incarnation, can bear the weight of glory. Beauty is not accessory to truth but its radiance. When worship loses beauty, doctrine itself grows opaque; when beauty serves truth, the soul perceives God even before it comprehends Him. Banality, therefore, is not merely poor taste but theological amnesia. The flattening of worship de-forms desire, for it teaches the heart to expect little from grace.

Beauty is not an accessory to truth but its radiance. St Thomas calls the beautiful *splendor veritatis*, the splendour of truth; the Fathers would say it is the form of divine goodness made visible. Where truth convinces and goodness compels, beauty invites. It draws without coercion; it persuades by delight. In the liturgy, this splendour becomes pedagogy: the soul learns to love what it first admires. Such beauty is not luxury but revelation—it discloses God as the harmony of truth and love. Hans Urs von Balthasar, reading this same tradition, warned that when theology forgets beauty, it forgets joy. Without splendour, truth appears cold and goodness harsh. Beauty reconciles them in glory. In the liturgy, this harmony becomes sacramental: form, colour, and sound manifest what words proclaim. The creature beholding such beauty does not merely approve it; he participates in it. For to delight in divine splendour is already to share its light. In that joy, theosis is quietly accomplished: the soul becomes radiant with what it beholds.

True beauty, by contrast, awakens longing for sanctity; it is moral as well as aesthetic. It purifies affection by directing it toward the infinite. This is why the Church's tradition guards beauty with such zeal. It is not luxury but necessity—the very language by which faith becomes tangible. The poorest mission chapel, if shaped by reverence, can reveal more splendour than a cathedral built for display. Fidelity to the rite, modesty of form, clarity of symbol: these are the conditions of beauty because they are the conditions of truth. Where art obeys mystery, splendour follows; where it seeks to eclipse the mystery, even brilliance becomes empty. Liturgy does not borrow art; it begets it. Icon and hymn, vesture and architecture, are not embellishments added to faith but the natural flowering of a faith that believes the Word truly became flesh.

The divinization of the senses thus becomes the tangible sign of sanctifying grace. What grace accomplishes invisibly in the soul, the liturgy enacts visibly through the body. The believer learns to perceive sacramentally: every created thing hints at its Creator, every beauty recalls the Beauty from which it flows. The senses, once doors of temptation, become channels of communion. The Christian who has seen the icon and sung the chant carries their resonance into the world; his gaze softens, his speech gentles, his work becomes offering. The liturgy does not end with the dismissal; it continues in the sanctified senses of those who depart to make the world transparent to God.

Such is the goal of sacred aesthetics: not art for its own sake but creation's return to its priestly role. The cosmos, through man, praises its Maker; matter, through sacrament, becomes grace's ally. The Church's beauty is therefore not escape but prophecy. It reveals what creation was meant to be and what, by Christ's redemption, it shall become. In the shining of the chalice, the chant of the psalm, the sweetness of incense, the harmony of light upon stone, the faithful glimpse the first dawn of the transfigured world.

In this harmony of sense and spirit the mystery of theosis reaches its tactile form. Man, priest of creation, gathers all that is material into offering and all that is spiritual into love. The eye, purified by beauty, begins to see as God sees; the ear, trained by chant, begins to hear the Word resonating in all things; the body, disciplined by ritual, becomes transparent to grace. The whole human being—spirit, soul, and flesh—enters the rhythm of divine life. What was once divided by sin is unified in worship; what was fallen into dust is lifted into light. Here the created world finds again its original vocation: to be the place where God is pleased to dwell.

When the senses are taught to adore, the heart learns to see. The worshipper, transfigured by what he beholds, becomes himself an icon—the visible mercy of the invisible God. Beauty becomes the ladder by which charity climbs, each rung fashioned from matter made obedient to grace. And when the Church worships thus, earth learns heaven's rhythm; from this rhythm the Christian lives and serves, radiant with a beauty that is charity made visible.

The Beauty and Tradition of the Divine Liturgy: The History of Heaven on Earth

The liturgy did not appear as a later ornament upon the Gospel; it was born with the Gospel itself. When the Spirit descended at Pentecost, the first fruit of that fire was communal praise. "They devoted themselves," writes Luke, "to the apostles' teaching and fellowship, to the breaking of bread and the prayers" (Acts 2:42). In that single verse the Church already possesses her form: doctrine proclaimed, communion shared, Eucharist celebrated, prayer rising. The liturgy is Pentecost's echo—the Spirit shaping a people whose very gathering becomes revelation.

From the beginning, the Church's worship was both intimate and cosmic. The upper room in Jerusalem was a fragment of the new creation: wood, bread, and human breath enlisted into divine use. The apostolic community did not invent ritual; it received one already implicit in the Lord's command, "Do this in memory of Me." Each celebration of the breaking of bread was an anamnesis of that first Supper and the Cross it prefigured. The structure—reading of Scripture, homily, intercession, offering, thanksgiving, fraction, communion—emerged organically from obedience to that word. No council decreed it, because grace had already inscribed it in the Church's heart.

The Didache, likely compiled before the close of the first century, lets us overhear that living rhythm. Its brief Eucharistic prayers bless the Father for "the life and knowledge" made known through Jesus His servant and beg that the scattered grains be gathered into one bread. Already unity and thanksgiving, the twin pulses of the Eucharist, are beating. What theology would later articulate in treatises is here sung by ordinary believers: redemption as communion, salvation as participation. In these simple thanksgivings the Church confesses her destiny—to be the Body of Christ offered for the world.

By the mid-second century, St Justin Martyr's *First Apology* describes Sunday worship with the clarity of daylight. The faithful assemble; readings from the prophets and apostles are proclaimed; the president exhorts imitation of the things heard; bread, wine, and water are brought forward; prayer and thanksgiving follow; the people respond *Amen*; and the consecrated gifts are distributed and carried to the absent. The outline is recognisable today. Justin calls this act the "Eucharist," for nothing less than thanksgiving defines Christian existence. What is striking is his insistence that the elements are not received as common food but as the Body and Blood of the Incarnate Word. The Church, scarcely a century removed from Calvary, already speaks the language of transubstantiation in seed form: what faith perceives, matter conveys. Here is Catholic realism before scholastic vocabulary, the mystery of theosis rendered edible.

A generation later, Hippolytus of Rome gives the earliest complete Eucharistic prayer in his *Apostolic Tradition* (early third century). It begins with thanksgiving for creation, redemption, and sanctification, then invokes the Spirit upon the gifts: "Send Your Holy Spirit upon the offering of Your holy Church." The entire prayer moves like the Incarnation itself—Word descending, Spirit overshadowing, flesh glorified. The structure of Christian history and the structure of Christian worship are one. What began as Christ's own act now continues as His Body's act, the same sacrifice made present under sacramental form. In Hippolytus the Trinitarian shape of liturgy stands revealed: to the Father, through the Son, in the Holy Spirit. The liturgy has found its grammar.

The fourth century saw that grammar flower into poetry. When persecution ceased and basilicas replaced catacombs, worship acquired architectural voice: space itself became theology. Yet the essence remained what it had been in the upper room—a people gathered into the offering of their Lord. St Cyril of Jerusalem, in his *Mystagogical Catecheses*, unfolds the Eucharist line by line for the newly baptised. His tone is both didactic and awed. "Under the appearance of bread you receive the Body of Christ," he tells them; "in the chalice, His Blood." The realism of faith has not dimmed; it has deepened. But Cyril also sees in the Eucharist the restoration of Adam: "Through this Body and Blood the elements of our nature are united to the divine." In receiving, the faithful become what they consume—the Body of Christ. Theosis has passed from the language of vision to the language of sacrament.

St Ambrose in the West voices the same conviction with Roman clarity. In *De Mysteriis* he instructs the neophytes that the words of Christ, spoken by the priest, effect what they signify: "The word of Christ which was able to make out of nothing that which was not, can it not change what is into what it was not before?" For Ambrose, the creative fiat continues at the altar; consecration is a new Genesis. The Spirit who hovered over primordial waters now descends upon wine and bread, forming within them the new Adam. And the communicant, receiving that Adam, is drawn into His risen life. The miracle of conversion—bread to Body, sinner to saint—unfolds by the same creative Word.

In North Africa, St Augustine contemplates the same mystery from another angle: the unity of the Body. "You are the Body of Christ and His members," he tells his people. "On the table lies your mystery; you receive what you are." For him, the Eucharist is ecclesial theosis—the transformation of the many into the One. The bread, made from countless grains, becomes one loaf; so the faithful, scattered across the world, become one body in Christ. Participation in the sacrament creates the Church itself. Thus the liturgy is not a devotional act within the Church; the Church is the living form of the liturgy. To exist as Christian is to be Eucharistic.

Through these Fathers the line from the upper room stretches unbroken. No revolution separates apostolic worship from patristic splendour; development is organic, like a tree growing from seed. The same sap—the Spirit—courses through each age. Diversity of language and culture appears, yet the form remains one: thanksgiving to the Father, memorial of the Son, invocation of the Spirit, communion of the faithful. The earliest generations already live the pattern that later theology will call Trinitarian, sacramental, and eschatological. History is not dilution but revelation—the deepening of what was whole from the start.

By the time of the great councils, the Church had woven her worship into the texture of civilisation. The Nicene Creed entered the liturgy as sung confession; the kiss of peace became the social grammar of charity; the calendar began to shape time itself. The rhythm of days and seasons echoed salvation's rhythm—Advent's longing, Easter's exultation, Pentecost's fire. What began in the hidden room now filled the world's architecture and calendar. The Word who became flesh had also become rite, and through that rite the world was learning again how to breathe in God.

Thus the apostolic and patristic centuries stand as the liturgy's adolescence: faithful to its birth, radiant with growth. Every prayer and gesture, every architectural form and hymn, proclaimed the same conviction—that the Incarnate Word continues His saving presence through the Church's worship. Heaven and earth were no longer parallel realms but interpenetrating spheres. The liturgy was the seam where they met. And in that meeting theosis began its historical career: the transfiguration of time itself into thanksgiving.

By the fourth century the Church's prayer had found mature voice in the great anaphoras, those rivers of thanksgiving that still irrigate her worship. Among them two shine as twin constellations in the Catholic sky—the Anaphora of St Basil the Great and the Divine Liturgy of St John Chrysostom. Both arose in the East, yet their radiance illumines the whole communion of Christendom. In them theology becomes poetry, and the Church's doctrine is not merely spoken but sung into being.

Basil's Liturgy bears the grandeur of his theology—vast, cosmic, Trinitarian. It opens with a roll call of divine perfections: "O existing One, Lord God, Father Almighty, adorable, all-powerful, eternal King, ineffable, incomprehensible, invisible, infinite…" The words themselves stretch language until it trembles before mystery. Basil's vision is not abstraction; it is adoration articulated. Every attribute confessed is an act of love naming its Beloved. The prayer moves through creation, fall, covenant, incarnation, and redemption, gathering the whole history of salvation into one sweep of praise. Nothing is excluded—angels, patriarchs, prophets, apostles, martyrs, even the elements of creation—each offered back to the Father through the Son in the Holy Spirit. The world is re-created by thanksgiving.

At the heart of Basil's anaphora lies the epiclesis, the invocation of the Spirit upon the gifts and upon the faithful: "Send down Your Holy Spirit upon us and upon these gifts here offered, and make this bread the precious Body of Your Christ, and that which is in this cup the precious Blood of Your Christ, changing them by Your Holy Spirit." Here theology and mysticism converge. The Spirit who once descended upon Mary now descends upon the altar; the same creative Breath that formed the flesh of the Word now forms the sacrament of His Body. The invocation embraces not only the elements but those who receive them—"that they may be to all who partake for the cleansing of soul, for communion of the Holy Spirit, for fulfillment of the kingdom of heaven." Grace thus moves outward in widening circles: gifts transfigured, worshippers divinized, creation sanctified. Theosis is not implied but enacted.

Basil's invocation of the Spirit is more than a consecratory moment; it is a revelation of divine pedagogy. The Father creates through the Word; the Word redeems through the Spirit; the Spirit perfects by returning all things to the Father. In that downward and upward motion lies the entire economy of salvation. The Spirit does not only change the gifts—He changes the worshippers. The hands that lift the paten are anointed extensions of Pentecost; the breath that utters the words becomes instrument of divine speech. Thus the Eucharist is not merely pneumatic but pneumatic in the most literal sense: the Church breathes with the breath of God.

Basil's Eucharistic vision is cosmic without ceasing to be personal. The prayer names Abraham, Isaac, Jacob, Moses, Aaron, Samuel, and all who have pleased God, then turns tenderly to the living: "Remember, O Lord, those who bring offerings and do good works in Your holy churches; remember those who are in deserts and mountains, and in caverns and pits of the earth." The Church's geography extends into eternity; intercession becomes the cartography of communion. Each remembered soul is gathered into the same sacrifice. Heaven and earth are reconciled in the memory of God.

Basil's cosmic horizon is no rhetorical flourish. For him, the Eucharist is the true interpretation of the universe. The same wisdom that ordered the stars now orders the liturgy; the altar is the microcosm of creation restored. Every creature finds its meaning at this table: wheat fulfils its purpose in becoming Bread of Life, grapes in becoming the Blood of the Covenant, man in becoming priest of the cosmos. In Basil's Eucharistic worldview, creation itself is not a background but a participant—it groans toward transfiguration. The world's materiality, far from opposing the divine, is its appointed medium. In this sense, Basil anticipates the theology of sacramentality later perfected in Aquinas: *gratia non tollit naturam, sed perficit*—grace does not destroy nature but perfects it. What the philosopher calls participation, Basil calls thanksgiving.

If Basil's liturgy is the hymn of divine majesty, Chrysostom's is the hymn of divine mercy. Shorter in form yet equal in depth, it carries the music of the golden preacher's heart—ardent, pastoral, radiant with compassion. Its very rhythm is more intimate: where Basil's sentences march like psalms of creation, Chrysostom's flow like a prayer whispered from the heart of the Church to her Bridegroom. "You brought us from non-existence into being, and when we had fallen away, You raised us up again." In that single line the whole Gospel is compressed: creation, fall, redemption, all in one breath. His God is the Physician bending over the wounded soul, the Shepherd searching for the lost, the Friend who "has done all things for our salvation." The language has no ornament apart from its sincerity. The liturgy is the heart of a pastor teaching his people to love mercy.

Yet Chrysostom's tenderness never abandons awe. The dialogue before the anaphora—"Lift up your hearts… We lift them up unto the Lord"—is like a key turning in the lock of heaven. What follows is an ascent: "It is meet and right to hymn You, to bless You, to praise You, to thank You, and to worship You in every place of Your dominion." The worshipper climbs by words into the company of angels. The *Sanctus* bursts forth, joining Isaiah's vision to John's: "Holy, holy, holy, Lord of Sabaoth, heaven and earth are full of Your glory." At that moment heaven leans down. The priest's quiet recitation continues the angelic hymn without pause, as though earth and heaven were one choir antiphonally singing across a thin veil. The curtain between worlds becomes porous; what was symbol becomes event.

Chrysostom's epiclesis repeats Basil's theology in a key of tenderness. The priest prays, "Make this bread the precious Body of Your Christ… that which is in this cup the precious Blood of Your Christ, changing them by Your Holy Spirit." But where Basil's invocation stretches toward cosmic amplitude, Chrysostom's feels almost domestic—an intimacy at the altar where divine condescension stoops to human need. The Spirit's descent is not thunder but breath, entering quietly into the common elements so that the common may share the divine. The priest adds, "That those who partake may be filled with the Holy Spirit, may be confirmed in faith, and may find healing of soul and body." The Eucharist thus becomes medicine as well as mystery—Christ's own life applied to the wounds of His members. Theosis takes the form of healing.

Chrysostom's Eucharistic theology continues Ignatius of Antioch's phrase *pharmakon athanasias*—"the medicine of immortality." The healing is not metaphorical. In receiving the Body of Christ, the faithful receive the divine life that conquers death from within. The altar is both hospital and heaven, and the priest acts as physician, applying the remedy of charity to the wounds of sin. Where Basil sees the Spirit descending as Creator, Chrysostom sees Him descending as Healer. The two visions together reveal the full breadth of redemption: the world renewed and the heart restored, the cosmos sanctified and the sinner reconciled. Theosis here takes on tenderness—it is not only ascent into divine life but the slow healing by which human nature becomes transparent to that life.

Both anaphoras are built on the same Trinitarian architecture: thanksgiving to the Father, memorial of the Son, invocation of the Spirit, communion of the faithful. But their characters differ as sunlight differs from moonlight—one majestic, the other tender, both illumining the same landscape of grace. The Church, in her wisdom, has never forced a choice between them. She lets both breathe, because together they reveal the fullness of Christ's priesthood: the divine majesty that stoops, the divine mercy that exalts. Where Basil teaches the grandeur of God's economy, Chrysostom teaches its familiarity. Each corrects the other's potential distortion—Basil saving worship from sentimentality, Chrysostom saving it from distance. Their harmony is itself a sign of catholicity: diversity held in truth.

The Western tradition, though distinct in cadence, mirrors the same theology. The Roman Canon—older even than Basil's—breathes the same awareness that creation is drawn into one eternal sacrifice. Its Latin sobriety conceals fire; its measured clauses lead to the same climactic petition that the angel may bear the offering "to Your altar on high." Here too is the union of heaven and earth, of visible and invisible, of time and eternity. The canon's silence is not absence but reverence—the Western mode of Basil's awe and Chrysostom's intimacy fused into contemplative stillness. East and West thus form not parallel but concentric circles around the same Mystery. The Church's heart beats with two rhythms yet one pulse.

The anaphoras also demonstrate how language itself participates in revelation. Words are not mere vehicles of ideas; they are icons of the mysteries they proclaim. Basil's rolling cadences and Chrysostom's intimate appeals are not stylistic differences but theological modes: one teaches transcendence through magnitude, the other immanence through mercy. Both protect the faith from reduction—Basil from the domestication of the divine, Chrysostom from its remoteness. Their language is not ornamental but sacramental: meaning and melody converge so that doctrine may become doxology. This is why the Fathers were poets before they were systematists. The anaphora is theology kneeling; it speaks what cannot be said by making language itself an act of worship. In this transformation of word into praise, human speech participates in the eternal Word. Logos draws language into Himself, and through that consecration even grammar becomes grace.

In these anaphoras, theology achieves its most concrete expression. Doctrines that elsewhere appear as propositions—Trinity, Incarnation, Redemption, Theosis—here become gestures of prayer. The Church does not merely profess them; she performs them. When the priest extends his hands over bread and cup, he embodies the Son's own mediating act. When the people answer *Amen*, they ratify the covenant with their own flesh. When the Spirit descends, the community becomes the very thing it celebrates—the Body of Christ offered to the Father. Liturgy is not commentary upon salvation; it is salvation enacted.

This is why the Fathers call the Eucharist *mysterion*—not puzzle but participation. To hear Basil's or Chrysostom's anaphora is to stand within

THE LITURGY: PARTICIPATION IN THE HEAVENLY WORSHIP

the self-communication of God. The words do not describe grace; they deliver it. Each syllable is steeped in the conviction that the divine life once poured into flesh continues to pour through sign and sound. The faithful who attend not as spectators but as participants are caught into that descent and ascent; they breathe with the Spirit who descends and rise with the Son who ascends. Theosis is the liturgy's inner logic: man becoming prayer because God first became flesh.

Thus the two rivers, though flowing in different channels, meet in the same sea—the eternal Eucharist of the Lamb. Their waters mingle in the Church's heart, forming one tide of thanksgiving that carries creation back to its source. Whenever the deacon proclaims, "Let us lift up our hearts," the entire history of worship answers. From the upper room to Basil's Cappadocia, from Chrysostom's golden pulpit to the modern altar, the same Breath moves, the same Fire burns, the same God gives Himself. The liturgy remembers forward and backward at once; it is the memory of heaven upon earth. In these prayers humanity finds its own voice again, and that voice is the voice of the Son. Through them the Church learns not merely to speak to God but to speak with Him, until every *Amen* becomes an echo of the eternal Word.

The liturgy's history is not the history of human taste but the unfolding of divine pedagogy. What seems to the historian a series of rubrical adjustments and artistic fashions is, to the eyes of faith, the Incarnation extended through centuries. The same Word who assumed human flesh continues to assume the flesh of culture, language, and art. Tradition is therefore not a fossil record of piety but a living Christology: divine form continually taking historical flesh without ceasing to be divine. The Church's worship changes as bodies grow — by organic maturation, not mutation. When the liturgy acquires new expression, it is the growth of the same life in fresh tissue; when it sheds accretions, it is the pruning of love seeking clarity of gaze.

From the apostolic assemblies in private homes to basilicas resounding with antiphons, the movement of liturgical history has always been toward visibility. The hidden mystery presses outward until it shapes sound, gesture, and space. What began as words whispered in fear beneath persecution becomes cathedral chant rolling like thunder through marble domes. Yet through all these outward transfigurations, the inward essence remains constant: the one sacrifice, the one thanksgiving, the one fire. History does not obscure revelation; it makes it audible.

The councils that codified rites were therefore not acts of bureaucratic consolidation but epiphanies of fidelity. Nicaea, Constantinople, Chalcedon, Trent, and Vatican II each served as mirrors reflecting the same light in different ages. Their decrees on worship are not legal intrusions into prayer but the Church's attempt to guard the integrity of revelation within the flux of culture. When Trent confirmed the Roman Canon, or when the East preserved the ancient anaphoras of Basil and Chrysostom, they were doing what the Council of Chalcedon did for Christology: affirming that change must never alter substance. The divine form may clothe itself in new languages, but its identity — the self-offering of the Son to the Father in the Spirit — remains inviolable. To guard the rite is to guard the mystery it enacts.

Thus the liturgy's development mirrors the logic of the Incarnation itself. Just as the Word did not abolish humanity but fulfilled it, the Church's worship does not escape history but divinizes it. Every council, reform, or codification is a new mode of divine accommodation — God stooping to meet His creatures in their changing circumstances while drawing them into His unchanging life. The rubrics, vestments, and melodies of successive centuries are not mere accessories; they are the fingerprints of God upon time. The variety of rites — Roman, Byzantine, Alexandrian, Armenian, Syro-Malabar — is not a symptom of division but of plenitude. The same mystery, refracted through different peoples, yields a spectrum of praise as rich as creation itself. The Holy Spirit does not produce uniformity but harmony; unity is symphonic, not monochrome.

The early Fathers sensed this harmony long before theology named it. St Irenaeus likened the Church's preaching and worship to a living symphony — many instruments sounding one melody. Origen described Scripture, doctrine, and liturgy as three strings of a single lyre: together they make the Word resound in the world. When the great basilicas rose under Constantine, architecture itself joined that music. Space became theology in stone. The dome mirrored heaven's vault, the apse enthroned the Pantocrator, and the altar, fixed at the heart, became the still point around which the cosmos turned. Each generation of artisans and monks continued this same translation of faith into matter — not inventing beauty but discovering the shapes by which grace could be seen.

The councils and reformers who pruned or enriched the rites understood that to deform beauty is to distort truth. The lex orandi is the lex credendi: the rule of prayer is the rule of belief. Whenever doctrine was threatened, worship itself became the first battleground, because beauty is where truth first becomes visible. Iconoclasm in the eighth century was not an aesthetic debate but a Christological crisis. To deny the image was to deny that the Word truly became flesh. The Seventh Ecumenical Council at Nicaea therefore defended iconography as the logical extension of the Incarnation: "The honour paid to the image passes to the prototype." In that single decree, theology and aesthetics were wedded forever. The Church's visual continuity became a theological confession.

This understanding underlies all later reforms. When the Western Church codified the Gregorian chant repertory, it was not indulging in antiquarian neatness but in the same defense of truth. The plainchant's purity of line embodied theological proportion: melody subordinated to text, text subordinated to meaning, meaning surrendered to God. The sound itself became an icon of humility. In Byzantium, the modal system accomplished the same end through different intervals: the tension between drone and melody mirrored the tension between transcendence and immanence. In both, music was not decoration but participation in divine order. Each tone was an act of theology — an audible claim that beauty, rightly ordered, evangelizes.

The evolution of vesture tells the same story. The simple tunic of the early presider became the alb, the chasuble, the dalmatic — each garment layered with centuries of symbolic refinement. Yet these are not costumes; they are the theology of mediation stitched into cloth. The stole, once a servant's towel, became the yoke of Christ's service; the chasuble, originally the travel cloak of the poor, became the sign of charity covering all. To codify such vesture is not to institutionalize aesthetics but to sanctify the body's role in worship. What the Word once clothed in flesh, the Church now clothes in fabric, so that even colour and texture may confess the glory of the Incarnation.

Incense too developed from practical origin to theological statement. In the pagan world, it masked odour; in the temple it symbolized sacrifice. In Christian hands it became a sacrament of ascent: the visible image of invisible prayer, matter converted into praise through fire. Its curling smoke is history itself rising through purification. When councils prescribed its use, they were not legislating perfume but teaching metaphysics — that creation's destiny is to become fragrance before God. Thus every later rubric, from the wave of the thurible to the kiss of the altar, carries the same conviction: matter is not backdrop but participant in redemption.

Seen through this lens, the Church's aesthetic unity is not an artistic accident but the gradual manifestation of divine order within time. The Romanesque arch, the Byzantine dome, the Gothic spire, the Baroque reredos — each era reveals another facet of the same splendour. The continuity of art across centuries testifies that the Spirit has not ceased to brood over chaos, drawing form from formlessness. The Church's beauty is therefore a historical proof of theosis: material culture slowly conformed to divine proportion. What began in the upper room as bread and word has become a universe of symbols — and yet the substance remains one.

In this light, every period of liturgical development becomes an icon of the Incarnation's own paradox. God reveals Himself not by negating history but by inhabiting it. The liturgy's outward mutations are the footprints of that indwelling. When a new language enters the Mass, when fresh music arises, or when architecture changes scale, what we witness is not departure but deepening: revelation stretching to embrace new flesh. Just as Christ's divinity did not eclipse His humanity but made it radiant, so divine worship, clothed in human art, shines with greater glory. The Church's continuity is thus the form of her sanctity — an unbroken chain of beauty through which the light of heaven continues to take shape in time.

If revelation took flesh in Christ, it continues to take form in the Church's art. The aesthetic coherence of Christian worship—its architecture, music, vesture, fragrance, and light—is not an accumulation of devotions but the incarnation of doctrine. These are not accessories to belief; they are belief become sensible. The cathedrals and chants, icons and incense, are the body language of faith, articulating through matter what dogma articulates through words. The liturgy's splendour is therefore not opposed to its humility; splendour is humility made articulate. Matter bows before its Maker by becoming transparent to His light.

Every visible element of the liturgy carries a theology. The church building itself is the first catechism, its geometry the grammar of heaven. The dome, curved like the firmament, proclaims creation's order restored; beneath it the apse enthrones Christ the Pantocrator, whose gaze gathers all time into mercy. The iconostasis in the East—too often mistaken by outsiders for a barrier—is in truth a veil of revelation: the visible threshold of the invisible kingdom. Its doors open not to expose the sacred but to invite the world inside the mystery. In the West, the rood screen once served the same function, guarding the altar's secrecy until the faithful were mature enough to behold what was unveiled. Architecture thus embodies pedagogy: it teaches approach, patience, and awe. The faithful, by passing from narthex to nave to sanctuary, learn the stages of the soul—purification, illumination, and union. Space becomes mystagogy.

Within that sacred architecture, sound performs the same ministry. Gregorian chant, rising and falling like the breath of the Church, is theology sung before it is spoken. Its melodic restraint is not poverty but purity; it holds the word as a chalice holds wine. The single melodic line refuses theatrical display so that the Word may dominate the emotion it arouses. Here humility becomes melody; adoration learns to breathe in time. The chant's modal structure, neither major nor minor, preserves the otherness of divine harmony—music unpossessed by ego, free from sentimentality yet full of tenderness. It teaches the heart to desire without grasping.

The Byzantine modes extend this theology of humility in another idiom. Their strange intervals, hovering between lament and jubilation, remind the soul that true joy is born from repentance. Every phrase is a miniature descent and ascent—the Cross transcribed into tone. The sustained *ison*, the drone note beneath the melody, is theology itself: unchanging essence supporting infinite manifestation. The soloist's line may wander, but it never departs from that ground; as the Son proceeds from the Father without separation, so the melody proceeds from the drone without discord. Even the Coptic and Syriac melismas, winding endlessly like desert prayer, breathe the same truth: praise that transcends speech, a sonic icon of eternity.

The evolution of this musical tradition across East and West testifies to one divine pedagogy: the education of passion through beauty. In chant, passion is not extinguished but transfigured. Rhythm becomes order, intensity becomes offering, emotion becomes clarity. What philosophy calls the purification of the passions, music accomplishes through melody. Each sung word lifts the affections toward divine proportion; through sound, the believer's inner chaos finds rest. Music, at its summit, is moral formation in audible form.

Vesture performs the same conversion in visible texture. The priest's garments are not costume but theology draped upon humanity. The alb recalls baptismal innocence; the stole binds obedience to charity; the chasuble envelops the minister in mercy. Every thread rehearses salvation history: the nakedness of Eden clothed again in grace. The Church's vestments evolve as her understanding deepens, but the meaning remains—Christ clothing His ministers in His own priesthood. Even colour obeys the calendar of redemption: purple for repentance, white for light, red for love that bleeds, green for the steady hope between feasts. Time itself wears vesture.

Incense and light join this visual theology with their own dialect of fragrance and flame. The thurible's slow swing inscribes invisible icons in air, tracing the shape of prayer rising toward God. What ascends from the burning coal is not smoke but matter turned into praise. Each spark that dies in the censer preaches the destiny of creation: to be consumed without destruction, to pass into sweetness through fire. Candles, too, are sacraments of transfiguration. The flame devours wax to give light, teaching that charity's only logic is expenditure. The Paschal candle, towering beside the font, is not mere illumination but eschatological sign—the light that no darkness can master. To enter a church aglow with such light is to step into the first dawn of creation remade.

Even silence belongs to this liturgical harmony. The pause after the Word, the stillness following consecration, are not absences but fullness. They are the moments when the heart adjusts to the brightness it has seen. Silence is the frame without which beauty collapses into noise. Within the Church's temporal architecture, silence and sound alternate like inhalation and exhalation; together they form the breathing of the Mystical Body. In that respiration, human time synchronizes with divine eternity. The faithful who learn to keep silence in worship learn to hear the stillness of God within themselves. This is not passivity but contemplation—the liturgy of the heart echoing the liturgy of the Church.

The aesthetic unity of these elements—architecture, chant, vesture, fragrance, light, and silence—reveals that the liturgy is not a collage but an organism. Each part lives only in relation to the whole, as the senses do within one body. The Church's art is therefore integrative, not decorative. It reconciles the divided faculties of modern humanity: intellect and emotion, body and spirit, art and truth. In this reconciliation lies a moral as well as metaphysical beauty. The unity perceived by the eye and ear mirrors the unity grace restores within the soul. Beauty here becomes a school of integration—the gradual healing of fragmentation through harmony.

To worship in such beauty is to experience theology in its native mode. The dogmas of creation, incarnation, redemption, and resurrection are not abstractions hovering over ritual; they are its pulse. The dome's curve preaches creation's goodness; the apse's radiance proclaims the Incarnation's light; the altar's stone confesses the solidity of the Resurrection; the chant's ascent anticipates the Parousia. The entire church, filled with light and sound, is a visible creed—each sense perceiving a different article of faith. In this synthesis, the intellect kneels before the splendour of truth, and the body finds rest in the rhythm of eternity.

The purpose of such splendour is evangelization by beauty. When the Church builds, paints, sings, and blesses, she proclaims that the world is not accidental but beloved. Her art is not propaganda but testimony: proof that matter, when offered to God, becomes radiant. In every age this beauty has drawn souls to faith when argument could not. A single antiphon echoing in a dark nave, a single icon shining through candlelight, has converted hearts that reason left untouched. Beauty does not compel; it persuades by delight. It leads the senses to the threshold of mystery and, having led them, withdraws. It is the Church's first and last act of hospitality—the open door of divine joy.

Thus the aesthetic unity of Christian worship is no luxury of culture but the very shape of revelation in time. The liturgy's evolving splendour is the slow unfolding of the Incarnation's consequences: God dwelling among His people, not only in word and sacrament but in colour, sound, and form. Through centuries of artisans and monks, composers and architects, the Spirit has written the Gospel again and again upon matter. Each generation receives that task anew—to make visible what it believes, to let faith become form. The result is not art history but sanctified history: the world learning to praise through beauty.

The Church has never regarded beauty as a luxury; she has feared its absence more than its excess. For when beauty withdraws, faith grows opaque. Truth, separated from splendour, turns didactic and cold; goodness, stripped of radiance, feels severe. Only beauty reconciles them in joy. St Thomas Aquinas defined the beautiful as *id quod visum placet*—that which, when seen, gives delight. But the delight he meant was not aesthetic sentiment; it was the rest of the soul in the perception of harmony. Beauty is the splendour of truth and goodness united—the visibility of divine order. When the Church builds, paints, and sings, she is not embellishing dogma but giving it form.

St John Paul II, in his *Letter to Artists*, spoke of this vocation with prophetic tenderness: "Beauty is the key to the mystery and a call to transcendence." The artist, he said, becomes co-worker with the Creator, fashioning matter into signs of eternity. The Church, by her liturgy, exercises that same vocation corporately. Through ritual and art she shapes the world into icon. Each altar, mosaic, and hymn is a human answer to the divine act of creation. Beauty becomes the dialogue between Maker and made, echoing the rhythm of Genesis: *God saw that it was good… and man saw that it was beautiful.*

In *Ecclesia de Eucharistia*, the same pope drew this vision into Eucharistic focus: "Through her liturgy the Church makes Christ's beauty visible in the world." The Eucharist, he wrote, is not only the source of moral strength but the wellspring of aesthetic transfiguration. The form of bread and wine—so ordinary, so universal—becomes the form of glory. What is most common is revealed as most divine. Here the law of beauty reaches its paradoxical perfection: splendour arises from humility, magnificence from simplicity, divinity from the commonplace. The Church's art, when obedient to this law, evangelizes without speech. A single well-celebrated Mass becomes a homily of light.

Beauty evangelizes because it disarms. Argument can be resisted, command resented; but before beauty the soul falls silent. The heart that cannot yet assent can still admire, and admiration is the seed of faith. Augustine's conversion began not with syllogism but with song—"How sweet did it suddenly become to me to be without the sweetness of those vanities." The Church's task, then, is not to invent beauty but to reveal it: to let grace appear again in the familiar. When chant rises from stone and light trembles on gold, creation remembers itself. Evangelization by beauty is the world's anamnesis—the recall of what it was made to be.

Such beauty, however, is never mere prettiness. It contains within it the Cross. The loveliness of Christian art is the radiance of redeemed pain.

The Crucifix at the centre of every church prevents beauty from becoming narcotic; it keeps splendour honest. In the wounds of the Word made flesh, harmony and dissonance meet and reconcile. Without that scarred centre, aesthetic pleasure collapses into idolatry. The Church's beauty must therefore always be cruciform—light passing through suffering into glory. Only a pierced beauty can save.

Because beauty reveals divine order, it also demands moral order. The perception of harmony awakens the desire to live harmoniously. This is why the liturgy educates character as well as taste. The reverence with which a priest folds the corporal, the poise of the cantor's breath, the patience of silence between psalms—all these gestures train the soul in the virtues of heaven. Form becomes ethics. The decorum of worship is not aesthetic fussiness but moral pedagogy: it teaches that freedom without form decays into chaos, while form without freedom petrifies. Beauty alone unites them. In that unity the will learns to love what is fitting, and the passions, purified, become instruments of praise.

John Paul II saw this moral dimension clearly. In *Letter to Artists* he wrote that true beauty "awakens the yearning for the good." The longing stirred by beauty is not desire for possession but for participation. When the believer gazes on an icon or hears a motet by Palestrina, he does not wish to own it; he wishes to dwell in it. This shift from appetite to communion marks the transformation of eros into agape. Theosis begins precisely here—when desire ceases to consume and begins to contemplate. Beauty thus becomes a moral conversion of the senses: the eye no longer covets, the ear no longer flatters, the imagination no longer dominates. Each sense regains its innocence, learning again to receive rather than grasp.

The Christian theology of beauty therefore corrects both puritan suspicion and modern aestheticism. It refuses to despise the sensible, for the Word became flesh; yet it refuses to idolize sensation, for the flesh was crucified. Between those errors lies the sacramental way: matter transfigured but not deified, spirit embodied but not enslaved. Beauty mediates this balance. It rescues creation from utility and the soul from abstraction. It teaches that the world is not raw material but revelation awaiting interpretation. When art is faithful to that vocation, it becomes contemplative rather than commercial, a liturgy of the hands continuing the liturgy of the altar.

This is why the saints have always been artists of holiness. Their lives possess aesthetic coherence—rhythm, proportion, radiance. Francis of Assisi's poverty, Thérèse's simplicity, John Paul II's courage—each is a style, a form made luminous by charity. Sanctity is the divine artistry of grace shaping personality into icon. The beautiful life and the holy life are not two ideals but one. The saint, like the craftsman, obeys form so deeply that form becomes freedom. In this sense the Church's canonized are her masterpieces: living frescoes of God's beauty restored in human nature.

The theology of beauty culminates in eschatology. The world's destiny is aesthetic: "Behold, I make all things new." Heaven is not static radiance but the eternal unfolding of splendour. What we call glory is beauty without limit—truth and love endlessly manifesting each other. The liturgy's splendour is therefore rehearsal for vision. In the light of the Eucharistic chalice, the faithful glimpse the form of the world to come: creation transparent to Creator. Every colour in a window, every note in a Kyrie, anticipates that cosmic transfiguration when "the earth shall be filled with the knowledge of the Lord as the waters cover the sea." The arts of worship are not diversion but prophecy.

To participate in such beauty is already to be changed by it. The liturgy's forms enter memory and re-form perception. After long exposure to true splendour, the soul loses its appetite for the trivial. The senses, once trained by sacred proportion, begin to discern divine rhythm even in ordinary life. The sunset becomes a prelude to Vespers; a child's laughter sounds like an echo of the Sanctus. The world regains translucence. This is theosis in its aesthetic mode: the divinization of perception, the awakening of the soul to see the world as God sees it. Beauty is the exercise of redeemed sight.

When John Paul II called artists "custodians of beauty," he meant more than guardians of craft. He meant witnesses to the world's potential transfiguration. Every work of sacred art, every well-celebrated Mass, is a pledge of the final restoration of all things. The Church's beauty is thus eschatological memory: she remembers the future. In her splendour, time catches a foretaste of eternity. And so the artist, the liturgist, the believer who sings or carves or bows in prayer, participates in that creative remembering by which God renews creation. To make something beautiful in love is already to share the Creator's joy.

Therefore beauty, rightly understood, is the language of theosis. It is the manner in which divine life communicates itself to sense, draws the soul into wonder, and teaches it to love in proportion to glory. The Church's vocation is to let this beauty shine unshadowed: to show, in word and stone and melody, that creation is destined not for decay but for transfiguration. Every candle lit, every Kyrie sung, every fresco restored is the world rehearsing resurrection. Through such splendour, truth becomes luminous, goodness becomes radiant, and the creature begins to mirror the Creator.

Every created beauty is a trace of the uncreated Beauty who calls all things back to Himself. The cosmos is not a neutral theatre of divine action; it is the very material through which divinity communicates. When the Church speaks of "the beauty of holiness," she names not an aesthetic preference but an ontological destiny: the radiance that creation receives when it is fully itself in God. This is what the Fathers meant by *theosis*—not absorption into the divine essence, but participation in its energies, the creature made translucent to uncreated light. In this sense, beauty is the natural language of deification. To be beautiful is to exist according to grace: to mirror, in creaturely mode, the harmony of the Trinity.

Tradition is therefore not simply the continuity of rite but the continuity of radiance. It is the river by which divine beauty flows through time without dilution. The same Spirit who hovered over the waters at creation hovers still over the water of baptism, over the bread of Eucharist, over the hands that build and paint and chant. Through the centuries, this Spirit has taught matter to speak in a grammar of glory. The liturgy is that grammar's most perfect expression: the moment when creation, history, and grace converge into one articulate act of praise. In its continuity the

Church bears witness that God's self-giving beauty did not pass away with Christ's Ascension but continues to be embodied, century after century, in sacramental form.

The beauty of continuity, then, is the proof of theosis at work in history. Each generation of believers receives the divine pattern and re-enacts it in its own materials, as the soul receives grace and expresses it through its own temperament. The continuity of form is the continuity of transformation: the same fire burning through different wood. The liturgical tradition is not static perfection but living participation—the Church's ongoing entrance into the life of God. To guard tradition is therefore not to freeze time but to protect the conditions under which grace can act upon it. The true traditionalist is not a curator of ashes but a keeper of flame.

Within this flame, beauty functions as the bridge between grace and nature. It is grace made visible, the imprint of divine proportion upon created being. The Church's art, architecture, chant, and gesture are not *about* God in a didactic sense; they are modes of His self-communication. When light falls through stained glass or the Sanctus rings beneath a dome, matter is doing theology—proclaiming that it can bear divine life without annihilation. Every harmony, every symmetry, every fragrance rising in worship declares anew that the Incarnation was not an exception to nature but its fulfilment. The material world, by grace, becomes again what it was created to be: the place where God dwells.

Here beauty reveals its mystical logic: it is not a static attribute but a dynamic energy. To encounter beauty is to be drawn beyond oneself toward the source of all order and delight. In that movement, the soul participates in God's own self-diffusive love. Theosis is precisely this movement rendered permanent—the soul's faculties reordered until every act becomes participation in divine rhythm. The liturgy trains this movement into habit. Through repeated exposure to sacred proportion, the believer learns to live "from glory to glory." The eyes that contemplate icons, the ears that are disciplined by chant, the body that kneels and rises in unison with the Church—all are gradually configured to divine harmony. The senses, purified by beauty, become instruments of communion.

The Fathers often described this transformation as *spiritual perception*—the awakening of sight capable of recognizing the divine in the ordinary. St Gregory of Nyssa wrote that Moses, beholding the burning bush, was taught that the creature can burn with divine fire without being consumed. The liturgy extends that vision to every element of existence. The bread and wine, water and oil, vesture and architecture—all become burning bushes of grace. The faithful who behold them rightly begin to burn as well. The Church's continuity in beauty thus ensures the continuity of illumination: the same fire that shone from Sinai now glows through chalice and icon, through chant and marble. Deification is simply this light moving outward, conquering opacity with transparency.

This movement of divine light through matter mirrors the very structure of salvation. What God accomplishes in Christ—uniting divine and human natures without confusion—He continues in the Church's sacramental body. The liturgy is the hypostatic union extended through time: the divine life communicated without ceasing to be divine, the human received without ceasing to be human. Every Mass, every Vespers, every sanctified gesture is another union of heaven and earth. Through beauty, the Church lives the mystery of the Incarnation anew. As St Maximus the Confessor wrote, "The Word of God, who became man, wills always and in all things to accomplish the mystery of His Incarnation." The liturgy is the stage of that ongoing accomplishment, the visible theatre of invisible grace.

This is why the Church's continuity in beauty is not mere conservatism but metaphysical fidelity. The world's beauty fades because it is contingent; the Church's beauty endures because it shares in divine life. The form of her worship participates in the eternal form of the Son, "the image of the invisible God." To deform that form—to sever rite from revelation, or to treat art as self-expression rather than self-offering—is to interrupt the current of theosis running through time. But where the Church guards beauty in obedience, she guards her own deification. The Bride remains radiant because she remains conformed to her Bridegroom's image.

THE LITURGY: PARTICIPATION IN THE HEAVENLY WORSHIP

In this light, the continuity of the liturgy is itself sacramental. It is not only a sign of unity but a means of sanctification. Just as the Eucharist makes present the one sacrifice of Christ, so the continuity of rite makes present the one life of the Spirit animating all ages. When the faithful sing the Kyrie that their ancestors sang a thousand years ago, they are not recalling a past devotion but participating in the same divine act. The communion of saints is not only mystical but aesthetic: it has a sound, a colour, a rhythm. Tradition is the sensory form of communion. Through it, the faithful touch eternity in time.

Theosis, then, is not an esoteric ascent beyond the world but the world itself raised into doxology. The Christian does not flee matter; he offers it. In the sanctified arts of worship, wood, pigment, fabric, and voice are all assumed into praise. The liturgy thus becomes creation's own prayer. The stones of the church, the smoke of the censer, the wax of the candle—all fulfil their final cause when they glorify God. Man, as priest of creation, mediates this offering. By his hands, the mute materials of the world learn to speak again. The glory that once shone on the face of Christ now gleams on the chalice, echoes in the choir, and flickers in the candlelight. Beauty is the voice of creation confessing its redemption.

This cosmic dimension of theosis was never lost on the Fathers. St Maximus saw the liturgy as the microcosm of the universe, the place where heaven and earth, angel and man, intellect and sense converge. St Symeon the New Theologian spoke of the believer who, after Communion, sees all creation as light. For them, the Church's beauty is not an escape from the world's materiality but its sanctification. The Eucharist, as "pledge of future glory," is the seed of a new creation; and the splendor of the liturgy is its first blossoming. Every well-ordered liturgy is an eschatological event—the first day of the world to come breaking into the present age.

Yet this eschatological beauty does not distance the Church from suffering; it draws her more deeply into it. The same splendour that crowns the altar also illumines the Cross. Theosis does not abolish pain but renders it luminous. The incense that rises sweetly in the sanctuary recalls the smoke of martyrs' burning; the gold of the icons is the alchemy of tears transfigured. The continuity of beauty across centuries is not the triumph of comfort but of faithfulness. The Bride has remained beautiful because she has suffered in love. Her beauty is cruciform: radiant not despite the wounds but through them. Deification is not escape from the world's brokenness; it is the transmutation of that brokenness into glory.

This is why the Church's aesthetic tradition, though resplendent, is never self-satisfied. Every cathedral, every hymn, every vestment is provisional—a sketch toward the final vision. The most perfect liturgy on earth remains a rehearsal for the eternal liturgy where "night shall be no more." Yet precisely because it is incomplete, it is hopeful. Each act of beauty anticipates the world's consummation, each gesture of reverence is a prophecy. In that anticipation, the faithful are already deified in desire. Their longing becomes participation; their expectation becomes likeness. Hope itself is a mode of theosis.

In the end, the beauty of continuity is the visibility of divine patience. God has chosen to reveal His glory slowly, through centuries of prayer, through the craftsmanship of countless hands. Every restored fresco, every renewed chant, every careful rubric is a small act of cooperation with that patience. The Church does not hurry her beauty because she trusts eternity. Her history is a single icon painted in time: layer upon layer of human devotion receiving the touch of divine light. And when that icon is finally complete, it will not depict architecture or vesture or melody—it will depict the transfigured humanity of Christ shining in His saints.

To behold that glory even now, in the mirror of worship, is to begin already to share it. The faithful who step into the rhythm of the liturgy, who breathe its incense and kneel beneath its light, are not spectators but participants in divinization. The senses themselves are drawn into contemplation; the intellect, illuminated by beauty, begins to know as it is known. The body, disciplined by sacred gesture, becomes the dwelling of divine life. Thus the liturgy's continuity across centuries is not merely historical but ontological: the same divine life pulsing through every age, conforming all who enter to the likeness of the Son. Tradition is the history of humanity's slow glorification.

When the Church worships in beauty, she does not merely remember God—she becomes transparent to Him. Her continuity in form reveals her continuity in grace; her splendour is the manifestation of sanctifying glory at work in time. In her hymns, icons, and stones, creation itself has begun to shine with the light of the eighth day. The beauty of continuity is therefore nothing less than the first evidence of the world's transfiguration—the cosmos learning to adore. In that adoration theosis finds its consummation: the creature, radiant yet still creature, returning all things to the Father through the Son, in the unity of the Holy Spirit.

Through twenty centuries of unbroken praise, the Divine Liturgy has been the living heart of the Church's theosis. From the catacombs to cathedrals, from Basil's anaphora to the humble weekday Mass, heaven has bent low to feed earth with its own life. And still the same cry rises: 'Holy, Holy, Holy, Lord God of Hosts.' In that chant, humanity remembers its origin and glimpses its destiny — to become all flame."

Becoming Flame: The Lived Experience of Deification

The mystery has been announced and its way revealed. The first movement of this work showed *why* humanity exists—to bear the image of God and to grow into His likeness. The second traced *how* that likeness is restored—the descent of the Word, the sacramental river of grace, the disciplines that teach the soul to breathe eternity. The pattern is clear: God descends that man may ascend. The descent was the Incarnation; the ascent is theosis. Through flesh assumed, grace became tangible; through flesh sanctified, glory becomes visible.

We have followed this rhythm from creation's first echo to the altar's final amen. The Incarnation opened the way, the sacraments sustain the journey, prayer and fasting refine the traveller, and the liturgy discloses the destination. Every mystery along the path is the same mystery expressed in different keys: the divine life entering the human so that the human may live divinely. The baptized are not spectators of redemption but participants in it; their bodies and souls are being tuned to the harmony of the Trinity. Deification is not achieved by effort but received through participation—yet that participation must be lived.

Here the ascent ceases to be described and begins to be embodied. The doctrines that grounded Part II demand witnesses. The grace that courses through baptismal water and Eucharistic wine must at last appear in the countenance of those who have drunk deeply of it. The next part of this work turns from sacramental ontology to spiritual anthropology: from how God divinizes, to what divinized humanity looks like. The saints are this theology translated into flesh. In them, doctrine bursts into light. What we have examined as principle now speaks as presence.

If the first two parts have shown that man *can* become god by grace, Part III will show that he *has*. The saints stand as living icons of what every believer is called to be—proof that divine life can dwell in human limits without destroying them. They are the consummation of the sacraments and the continuation of the Incarnation, Christ extended through time in countless personal forms. Each bears the same fire, yet each burns with its own hue: the gentleness of Thérèse, the radiance of Seraphim, the consuming prayer of Symeon, the hidden flame of countless unknown souls. Their variety displays the inexhaustible creativity of grace; their unity discloses its source.

The movement from theology to life is not a change of subject but of depth. For the goal of knowledge is likeness. The mind that has contemplated divine truth must now consent to become what it knows. The next chapters therefore explore the psychology of transfiguration: the purification of the passions, the illumination of the heart, the transformation of suffering into communion. Here deification passes from liturgical participation to existential form—the Cross and Resurrection re-enacted within the individual soul.

The saints show that theosis is not reserved for mystics or monks but is the vocation of every baptized person. It is life conducted at the temperature of love. Their witness prevents doctrine from evaporating into abstraction; they prove that grace is historical, not hypothetical.

Through them the Church sees her own destiny: a humanity fully alive, breathing the breath of God.

Part III, then, begins where worship ends—in the lived fire of those who have become prayer itself. From here the narrative moves from altar to heart, from participation to possession, from beholding the flame to *being* the flame. The Word who once became flesh will now be seen becoming light in flesh renewed. The way of ascent has reached its summit; what remains is to dwell upon the mountain and see it burn.

III

Becoming Flame: The Lived Experience of Deification

PART III
The Saints: Testimonies of Transfigured Humanity
The Cross and Resurrection in the Life of the Believer
Union without Absorption: Theological Boundaries of Participation
You Shall Be All Fire: Living the Theotic Life in the World

9

The Saints: Testimonies of Transfigured Humanity

"Through His grace, God becomes visible in the saints, not as essence but as light, and they in turn become light by participation in His radiance."
— St Gregory Palamas, Triads I.3.23

The Saint as Living Theophany

The saint is not an ethical rarity but the revelation of what humanity was created to be. In them, the divine intention for man comes to fruition; the image has become likeness, the creature has become transparent to its Creator. They are theology incarnate—dogma translated *by participation* into light and gesture. In their existence, theosis ceases to be theory and becomes sight.

From the beginning, humanity was fashioned for participation. "Let us make man in our image, after our likeness" (Gen 1:26). The Fathers never read this as poetic flourish but as vocation. St Irenaeus taught that the image is given in creation and the likeness is achieved through the Spirit (Against Heresies IV.38.3); the saint is the *witness* that such likeness is not a metaphor but a destiny realised. In them, 2 Peter 1:4—"partakers of the divine nature"—is no longer promise but fact. Grace has reached its telos.

When St Athanasius declared, "The Word became man that we might become God" (On the Incarnation 54), he was describing not exalted rhetoric but anthropology restored. The Incarnation is not a divine exception; it is the template of redeemed humanity. What Christ united to Himself in His own flesh, He extends by grace to all who consent to be conformed to Him. "Those whom He foreknew He also predestined to be conformed to the image of His Son" (Rom 8:29). The saint is that conformity completed—the hypostatic mystery *reflected by participation, not repeated.*

The Church venerates such lives because they demonstrate that salvation is not a judicial pardon but a transfiguration. As the Catechism teaches, "The Word became flesh to make us 'partakers of the divine nature'" (§460). The saint embodies this participation in the most literal sense. Their faculties have become instruments through which uncreated grace resounds; their humanity, far from erased, has become translucent. St Gregory Palamas spoke of deification as "sharing in divine energy, not divine essence"—that is, sharing in uncreated grace, the divine life communicated without confusion (Triads III.1.23). The saint's will and God's will move in concert, not by coercion but by love's resonance.

Holiness, then, is ontology healed. It is not the abnormal state of spiritual athletes but the normal condition of a nature once sick and now made whole. St Maximus the Confessor called this "the natural activity of the soul moving according to its logos" (*Ambigua* 7). Sin fractured that movement; grace restores it. In the saint, the powers of the soul—mind, heart, desire—are again harmonised with the divine rhythm. They do not perform holiness; they breathe it. Their peace is not passivity but equilibrium: freedom restored to its original proportion, intellect illumined by divine wisdom, love purified of possessiveness.

Such transparency has an unmistakable atmosphere. Those who meet them often speak of clarity, as though the air itself has thinned. They convert without argument because truth in them has become visible. The moralist mistakes their simplicity for naïveté; the theologian recognises it as eschatology. For they are, in Augustine's phrase, *ordo amoris* made flesh—the right ordering of love manifest in a single life. When love regains its true order, every faculty becomes liturgy; thought becomes praise, and the body itself a Eucharist of thanksgiving.

The holiness of the saints is not dualistic. They do not escape matter; they transfigure it. Their bodies, marked by work and fatigue, become vessels of divine tenderness. The relic, the fragrance, the incorruption—all these are outward signs of a deeper truth: the flesh itself participates in redemption. The Incarnation leaves nothing untouched. St Symeon the New Theologian wrote that the deified person "is illumined entirely, soul and body together, with a great and divine light... seeing by the Holy Spirit God dwelling within him" (*Hymns of Divine Love*, I). In them, creation has begun to shine with the light for which it was made.

This transparency is not achieved by ascetic extremism but by the quiet death of self-will. Every discipline of fasting or vigilance serves one purpose—to polish the mirror. When the surface is clear, the light acts of itself. Hence the paradox of sanctity: effort gives way to ease. They obey because obedience has become joy. "My food is to do the will of Him who sent Me" (Jn 4:34). The saint eats that same food.

Their moral beauty is inseparable from humility. Because they no longer compete with God, they no longer compete with others. Their peace disarms. They carry within themselves what St Seraphim of Sarov called "the acquisition of the Holy Spirit." "Acquire the Spirit of peace," he said, "and thousands around you will be saved." Their holiness is thus generative; it multiplies by proximity. The deified person becomes a principle of communion, a human transparency through which divine life passes into the world.

The mystery at work in them is always Trinitarian. They are sons in the Son, animated by the Spirit, offering themselves to the Father. Their sanctity is nothing other than the inner life of the Trinity mirrored in human consciousness. The doctrine of deification finds its fullest commentary not in treatises but in their lives. What the Cappadocians taught, they embody: that "what is not assumed is not healed" (Gregory of Nazianzus, *Epistle* 101). They reveal that every dimension of humanity—

intellect, emotion, labor, even humor—can become vessel of divine light.

It is no wonder, then, that the saints are icons of joy. Joy is not a sentiment for them but an ontological signature, the echo of divine beatitude. They rejoice not because circumstances please them but because being itself has become sacramental. The fire that burned in the bush now burns in their heart without consuming it. To encounter such a person is to glimpse the end for which every creature exists: communion that does not erase distinction, love that does not annihilate the beloved.

The universal call to holiness proclaimed by *Lumen Gentium* is simply the universal call to theosis. "All in the Church… are called to holiness, whose pattern and source is God Himself" (*LG* 40). The saint is proof that this call is achievable. In them the Church beholds her own future—the Bride already radiant with the glory promised to her. What began at baptism and is nourished by the sacraments has reached completion: the created person living by uncreated life.

Such lives are not museum pieces but prophecy. They announce that the final transfiguration of the cosmos has already begun in miniature. "When Christ who is your life appears, you also will appear with Him in glory" (Col 3:4). The saints are that appearing anticipated. They stand in history as luminous breaches through which eternity shines. Their holiness does not remove them from the world; it renders the world more transparent.

Yet this light is not an end in itself; it is a movement. The holiness of the saints is centrifugal. It expands outward like ripples in a pond until the whole created order is drawn into its brightness. The uncreated energies that fill them do not rest within the individual but radiate through every bond of relationship—family, community, Church, cosmos. The deified person becomes a new principle of gravity in the world: the pull of divine charity embodied. Their life bends the space around them toward God. "You are the light of the world," Christ said (Mt 5:14), not as metaphor but as vocation. The light that burned on Tabor is entrusted to every heart that consents to bear it. The saint is simply the one in whom that consent has become total, the lamp without remainder. Through them the world begins, quietly, to glow with its forgotten purpose.

This radiance also reveals the Church's true identity. The saints are not ornaments to the Body of Christ; they are its organs most fully alive. Their existence shows what the Church herself is becoming—the communion of persons deified in one Spirit. In them the Church's sacraments find their consummation: baptism ripened into likeness, Eucharist into transformation, confirmation into witness. The "mystery hidden for ages" that Paul speaks of (Col 1:26) is unveiled not in abstract doctrine but in sanctified lives. Each saint is a kind of living liturgy: their whole being an offering, their actions a doxology, their silence a hymn. The holiness that once seemed confined to the altar now walks the streets, sits at tables, and heals by presence. Thus the Church's worship breaks its walls; the liturgy of heaven continues in human hearts.

But this light extends beyond ecclesial borders. Theosis has always carried a cosmic horizon. The saint stands at the intersection of heaven and earth as priest of creation, reconciling all things in Christ (Col 1:20). In them the groaning of the world finds a voice and its redemption a foretaste. The radiance that shines through their body is a promise for the body of the earth. St. Maximus saw this with unparalleled clarity: the deified person unites the divided realms of creation—intelligible and sensible, heaven and matter—until "God may be all in all." The sanctified human being is therefore the firstfruits of cosmic transfiguration, the miniature universe healed. When their hands bless bread, the whole harvest is blessed; when they pray for the dead, time itself begins to be redeemed. Their holiness is ecological before the term existed, for it restores the original harmony between creature and Creator. Around them even the simplest objects seem reconciled—the tree, the stone, the animal. They are signs that creation is not doomed to decay but destined for fire, the fire of divine presence that does not destroy but refines.

Finally, the saints teach us how to inhabit time. Their lives do not escape chronology; they sanctify it. The eternal enters their hours so completely that past, present, and future lose their hostility. In them memory becomes thanksgiving, anticipation becomes hope, and the moment becomes sacrament. They reveal that to be deified is not to abandon history but to let eternity suffuse it. The holiness of the saints is therefore the world's true calendar—the proof that history itself is capable of glory. When the Church celebrates their feast, she is not merely remembering; she is touching the edge of the consummation. Their names are written into the liturgy so that the faithful may recognise their own vocation mirrored there. For what the saints are, the Church is called to be; what the Church is, the world is invited to become. Through them the promise of Christ resounds anew: "Behold, I make all things new" (Rev 21:5).

To call them "living theophanies" is therefore to confess that God still reveals Himself through human flesh. The saints are His continuing self-disclosure, the ongoing Incarnation by participation. Each life adds a syllable to the Word spoken once for all in Christ. Their uniqueness of temperament and culture does not dilute the truth they bear; it displays the manifold artistry of grace. Athanasius, Augustine, Palamas, Thérèse—all speak the same sentence in different accents: humanity becomes radiant when united to God.

The holiness that shines through them is not moral success but metaphysical healing. Sin is opacity; grace is translucence. The saint is the healed lens through which the divine glory passes into visibility. "The glory of God," wrote Irenaeus, "is man fully alive; and the life of man consists in the vision of God" (*Against Heresies* IV.20.7). The saint is that vision embodied—life so alive that it becomes luminous.

Thus theosis, long treated as mystical aspiration, is revealed in them as the concrete outcome of grace. They show that salvation is not external deliverance but interior illumination, not merely freedom *from* sin but participation *in* divine life. In them, theology finds its proof: the fire of God dwelling within human clay without consuming it. They are what every liturgy anticipates, what every Eucharist initiates, what every human longing secretly desires.

The saint stands before us as the answer to the human question. What is man? A creature called to become flame. What is holiness? The transparency of love. What is salvation? Theosis—creation returning to communion. In their faces, the Church reads the end of the story already begun: God all in all, and man, finally, all light.

Comparative Lives: Seraphim of Sarov, Thérèse of Lisieux, and Symeon the New Theologian.

The communion of saints is not uniformity but polyphony. Grace is one fire; its colours differ according to the material it illumines, yet always the same uncreated grace. Each saint becomes a distinct tone in the same hymn of divinised humanity—the Spirit composing in human lives what the Logos first sang in the flesh. Their differences of temperament, language, and history reveal not contradiction but plenitude. As *Lumen Gentium 49* teaches, the communion of saints "joins the faithful with Christ and with one another." As St Paul writes, "There are varieties of gifts, but the same Spirit… and the manifestation of the Spirit is given for the common good" (1 Cor 12:4, 7). The lives of Seraphim of Sarov, Thérèse of Lisieux, and Symeon the New Theologian stand as three such manifestations—Eastern radiant joy, Western hidden love, and mystical illumination—each a different face of the one mystery of theosis.

Seraphim of Sarov, that gentle ascetic of the Russian forest, is remembered not for miracles of thunder but for the quiet miracle of joy. When pilgrims approached his hermitage, he greeted them with words that have entered the bloodstream of Eastern spirituality: "My joy, Christ is risen!" His theology was a smile. In his person the promise of resurrection became immediate experience. The radiance of his countenance, witnessed by Motovilov and recorded with trembling reverence, was not metaphor: his body itself became luminous by grace, not by nature, as though creation were returning to its primal transparency. Seraphim's famous conversation on the "acquisition of the Holy Spirit" is a catechism in lived theosis. "When the Spirit of God comes down to man," he said, "and overshadows him with the fullness of His presence, then the human soul overflows with an indescribable joy, for the Spirit fills all that He touches."

It was not ecstasy for its own sake but a deifying indwelling—the soul as living Temple, the human being irradiated from within. His face, shining with uncreated light—the same light of glory the West names as foretaste of the beatific vision—recalled the mountain of Tabor. Palamas would have recognised in Seraphim's countenance the visible energies of God. "We are transformed from glory to glory," wrote Paul (2 Cor 3:18), and in that transformation the saint's body becomes icon of the world's future: matter suffused by Spirit.

Yet the same fire that blazed outward in Seraphim burned hidden in Thérèse of Lisieux. Where the Russian monk embodied transfiguration in light, the Norman Carmelite embodied it in littleness. Her *petite voie*, the "Little Way," is the same mystery turned inward: not vision but surrender, not radiance but transparency through self-forgetful love. "To love is to give everything and to give oneself," she wrote in *Manuscript B*. In the cell of an obscure convent she rediscovered the secret of the Incarnation: that omnipotence hides itself in weakness. She wished to be "love in the heart of the Church." That line is pure theosis in miniature—the creature desiring to participate completely in divine charity. Her sanctity was not ascent but descent: kenosis lived daily in silence, patience, and hidden sacrifice. In this she embodies the doctrine that our merits are God's gifts, for "the charity of Christ is the source in us of all our merits" (CCC 2011). "If all weak and imperfect souls felt what the least of souls feels," she said near death, "no one would despair of reaching the summit of love." The summit she speaks of is not reward but union, the likeness achieved through trust. If Seraphim represents the Taboric light, Thérèse represents the Cross's interior illumination—radiance without visibility, the uncreated fire burning beneath ashes. Both witness that the same Spirit who dazzles can also conceal Himself, that theosis may manifest as childlike surrender no less than mystical light.

Long before either of them, in the tenth century, Symeon the New Theologian bore witness to that same transforming fire in the Byzantine monastic world. He was called "new" not because he invented, but because he reawakened—the perennial conviction that divine grace is not idea but experience, always within the communion of the Church's faith. In his *Hymns of Divine Love* he speaks in language incandescent with immediacy: "He who is God is seen within me in uncreated light... and I, a creature, share His splendor; I become light myself." In Symeon, theosis passes from doctrine to encounter. The "light of Tabor" becomes the interior illumination of the soul; the uncreated energies are felt as love's fire within the heart. His mysticism was no private reverie but ecclesial event: the baptismal grace brought to consciousness. He insisted that every believer, by repentance and tears, could know the same indwelling of the Spirit. His opponents accused him of excess, but the Church canonised him, recognising in his words the orthodox nerve of the Incarnation: that God truly communicates Himself, not metaphorically but substantially, through the Spirit, in full harmony with Chalcedonian faith. Symeon's vision is thus the theological bridge between Christ's historical glory and the saint's lived participation—the mystical interior of Chalcedon.

Across these three lives—Seraphim's luminous joy, Thérèse's hidden love, Symeon's interior fire—the same pattern recurs: divinity communicated, individuality preserved. Each reveals a different mode of participation in the one uncreated energy. Seraphim shows theosis as transfiguration of the senses, the body radiant with Spirit; Thérèse, as transformation of the will into pure charity; Symeon, as illumination of the *nous*, the intellect lit by divine knowledge. Body, will, and mind—three dimensions of the same anthropology healed by grace. In them, the total human person is sanctified; the whole image is restored. "May your whole spirit and soul and body be kept blameless at the coming of our Lord Jesus Christ" (1 Thess 5:23). What Paul prayed, they became. This unity of body and soul echoes the Catechism: "Spirit and matter, in man, form one nature" (CCC 364).

Their geographical and cultural divergence only underscores the universality of theosis. East and West are not two faiths but two articulations of the same mystery. Seraphim's radiant greeting, "Christ is risen, my joy," and Thérèse's dying words, "My God, I love You," are one proclamation spoken in different tongues. Both disclose the paschal nature of holiness—the victory of love over death. Symeon's vision of divine light echoes Athanasius's conviction that "He became what we are that He might make us what He is" (*On the Incarnation 54*). Thérèse's "Little Way" echoes Augustine's *humilitas Christi*—the descent of God teaching man how to rise. Seraphim's luminous peace embodies Palamas's doctrine of divine energies: that grace is not created help but the very presence of God, a truth the Latin tradition expresses when it speaks of sanctifying grace as a real participation in divine life (CCC 1999). Thus East and West converge in the saints as rivers meeting the same sea. Theosis becomes the shared grammar of sanctity, hidden or radiant, contemplative or active.

The communion that binds these saints does not remain their private correspondence across centuries; it extends to all who learn from them. Each of their lives becomes a pedagogy of participation. The pilgrim who learns joy from Seraphim, humility from Thérèse, or repentance from Symeon is already sharing their grace, for the holiness of the saints is communicative by nature. Their example is not external imitation but internal contagion. What they embody, they transmit. The Church does not study them as historical curiosities but communes with them as living instructors in the art of divinised existence. In this sense the saints continue the Incarnation; through their memory the Word keeps taking flesh in new hearts. Their stories become sacramental encounters in which grace leaps from page to soul, awakening the same fire in the reader that once burned in them. As the Catechism notes, "their intercession is their most exalted service to God's plan" (CCC 956).

They also mark a thread of continuity between the early patristic world and the spirituality of modern holiness. Seraphim and Symeon stand in direct lineage from the hesychast tradition of Palamas; Thérèse, formed in the Carmelite stream, draws unconsciously from the same well through John of the Cross and Augustine. The language differs, yet the substance converges: purification, illumination, union—the classic triad of deification recast in the vernacular of their age. Their convergence across a millennium demonstrates that theosis was never an isolated Eastern intuition but the beating heart of the Christian life. Even when the vocabulary faded in the West, the experience persisted. The saints preserved in their bodies what theologians debated in words, thus fulfilling the Church's conviction that the Holy Spirit continually renews His saints in every age (CCC 828). They are the living continuity of doctrine, the proof that the Spirit remembers what history forgets.

Each of them refracts a distinct facet of Christ's own mystery and, through Him, of the life of the Trinity. Seraphim mirrors the Transfigured Christ whose light blesses creation, the radiant generosity of the Father made visible. Thérèse mirrors the Crucified Christ whose littleness redeems from within, the humility of the Son made human. Symeon mirrors the Risen Christ whose interior glory fills the Church, the fire of the Spirit illuminating the heart. Together they reveal the whole Paschal movement—light through humility, death into life, flesh into Spirit. To contemplate them is to see Christ unfolded through time, His single life multiplied in countless forms, the Trinity's radiance expressed in human accents. The Church venerates them not for contrast but for consonance: three windows, one light; three notes, one harmony; three lives, one flame. St Gregory Nazianzen's words about the Incarnate Christ apply equally to them: "He remained what He was and assumed what He was not, that He might save the perishing by the grace of the union" (*Oration 29*). In them that union has borne its fruit; the Word's deifying work has reached completion in human history, and through their differing temperaments the same uncreated light shines forth—the Gospel translated into the music of diverse lives. Their growth confirms that "spiritual progress tends toward ever more intimate union with Christ" (CCC 2014; LG 41).

The fire in Seraphim's eyes, the hidden flame in Thérèse's heart, the uncreated light flooding Symeon's soul—all arise from the same source: the Spirit poured into human weakness until weakness itself becomes transparency. "The love of God has been poured into our hearts through the Holy Spirit" (Rom 5:5). That love, when allowed to mature, becomes light. The saints differ only in how the light shines—one dazzling, one veiled, one inward—but all disclose the same luminosity of being restored. Their lives are chapters in a single revelation: that God's glory is not reserved for heaven but already available to those who yield to it on earth.

To contemplate them together is to glimpse the catholicity of deification. Theosis is not an Eastern eccentricity nor a Western mystic's dream; it is the Church's universal anthropology, articulated in different accents of love. Seraphim shows that the transfigured body is the pledge of cosmic renewal; Thérèse, that the smallest act done in love participates in infinite charity; Symeon, that knowledge of God is experiential and interior. Each, in their own register, demonstrates that "grace builds upon nature" (Aquinas, *ST I.1.8 ad 2*), and as the Council of Trent affirms, grace truly heals and elevates nature (DS 1521).

The path they trace is not reserved for a few; it is the Church's ordinary road to extraordinary life. What they embody in distinct keys becomes our common music: baptism as new birth into participation (2 Pet 1:4), the Eucharist as daily transfiguration, confession as the patient polishing of the mirror, watchful prayer as the widening of the heart, works of mercy as love learning its own grammar. "All in the Church… are called to holiness, whose pattern and source is God Himself" (*Lumen Gentium* 40); "The Word became flesh to make us 'partakers of the divine nature'" (CCC 460). Thus every sacrament is a step in this same ascent toward likeness. To follow Seraphim is to let joy evangelize; to follow Thérèse is to let littleness become spacious with God; to follow Symeon is to let light rise within repentance until knowledge becomes love. None of this is moral heroism. It is the slow accord of our will with Christ's—"Have this mind among yourselves" (Phil 2:5)—until the sacraments we receive become the life we live. The saints are not ideals to admire from afar but intercessors who draw us into their flame; in their friendship, grace proves itself contagious, and the Church becomes what she beholds.

The radiant monk of Sarov, the hidden nun of Lisieux, the visionary of Constantinople—three witnesses, one fire. Their words and faces form a single doxology: *Gloria Dei vivens homo, vita hominis visio Dei*—"The glory of God is a living man, and the life of man is the vision of God" (Irenaeus, *Against Heresies IV.20.7*). To see them is to see humanity as it was meant to be: creation suffused with uncreated light, love made visible, theology become life. In their diversity the unity of theosis is revealed, and in their unity the diversity of grace is sanctified. Through them the Church beholds her own transfigured reflection—one body, many members, all fire.

Hallmarks of Deified Persons

The saints are not defined by uniform practices but by a shared atmosphere. One breath moves through all of them—the breath of the Spirit who divinises by indwelling through sanctifying grace, the created participation in His uncreated life (CCC 1999). Their virtues are not moral achievements to be measured but symptoms of communion. Joy, humility, compassion, interior light, and creative love are not virtues added to grace but the visible fragrance of a life in which grace has taken full possession. They are the recognisable hallmarks of the deified person, the fruit of participation in God's own energies.

Joy is the first note, the spontaneous sound of being reconciled with one's source. It is not the ecstasy of temperament but the serenity of ontological harmony—the soul no longer divided between longing and fear. "Rejoice in the Lord always," Paul commands (Phil 4:4), because joy is the native air of those who live in Christ. St Seraphim's greeting, "My joy, Christ is risen," was not affectation but theology compressed into a salutation. It was the recognition that the Resurrection has already invaded ordinary time. St Thérèse wrote in her final letter, "Everything is grace." The phrase is brief but metaphysical: she perceives that creation itself is Eucharistic, charged with gift. The deified person rejoices because reality has become transparent; even pain glimmers with purpose. Their joy passes through the Cross, for the Resurrection is the hidden form of every sorrow transfigured by grace (cf. Jn 16:20-22). Maximus the Confessor called this state "the well-being of the will," where desire is so purified that it delights spontaneously in the divine will (*Ambigua* 7). Joy, then, is the sound creation makes when theosis reaches the heart.

Not every bright feeling is joy, and not every silence is light. The Fathers insist on discernment (*diakrisis*) so that we do not mistake temperament or passing consolations for the fruit of the Spirit. As both John and the Fathers urge, discernment itself is a gift of the Spirit (1 Cor 12:10). Joy that is merely psychological withers when contradicted; the joy of deification endures as *eucharistia*—thanksgiving that persists even while it weeps (cf. Gal 5:22). Humility can masquerade as self-erasure; the real thing is fearless because it rests in being loved (Phil 2:5–11). Compassion can devolve into activism that forgets prayer; sanctified mercy flows from prayer and returns to prayer (Lk 6:36). "Test the spirits," says John (1 Jn 4:1): true joy widens freedom, true humility steadies hope, true compassion bears cost, true light deepens worship. The saint's radiance is recognized less by sensations than by stability—the slow, sturdy rejoicing of a will reconciled to God.

Humility is the second sign, and it may be the purest. Pride is the self-curvature of a being that has forgotten its relational nature; humility is the form of divine life within a creature. "Have this mind among yourselves, which was in Christ Jesus," Paul writes, who "emptied Himself" (Phil 2:5–7). The saint mirrors that kenosis. Humility is not the self's diminishment but its right proportion: a transparency that no longer blocks light. St Bernard of Clairvaux called it "the guardian of virtues, and the ornament of grace." In every authentic mystic, humility deepens with holiness; the closer they come to God, the more they perceive their dependence. Symeon the New Theologian, who saw uncreated light, wept at his own unworthiness even within the vision: "I see the light, and I am nothing but darkness—yet He loves me still." Such humility is not contradiction but participation in Christ's own descent—the virtue that most conforms man to the Incarnate Word (CCC 2546). In the deified, it becomes spontaneous reflex, as natural as breath.

These hallmarks ripen through synergy—grace and freedom working together, as the Council of Trent teaches: man cooperates freely with grace while never meriting it by nature alone (DS 1525). Maximus calls it the human powers "moving according to their *logos*" as grace heals and elevates them (*Ambigua* 7). The Catechism speaks of our real cooperation with God's action (cf. CCC 2008): baptism plants the seed of participation, the Eucharist feeds it with uncreated life, watchful prayer (*nēpsis*) clears the heart, fasting sobers desire, almsgiving trains love outward. None of this manufactures holiness; it removes impediments. As the mirror is polished, the light acts more freely. This is why the saints seem effortless: not because they skipped ascetic struggle, but because long consent has made obedience their appetite—"My food is to do the will of Him who sent me" (Jn 4:34).

Compassion is the third mark, and it is the most outward. The saint's love is not sentimental but kenotic—it suffers with the beloved because divine love itself is cruciform. "Be merciful, even as your Father is merciful" (Lk 6:36). St Isaac the Syrian defined mercy as "the heart burning for all creation, for men, for birds, for beasts… so that from its great compassion and strong pity it cannot bear to see any creature suffer." That is theosis in its affective dimension: God's universal sympathy reproduced in human feeling. The saints intercede, console, and bear pain not as moral duty but as ontological overflow. They participate in the priesthood of the Word made flesh, as every baptized person shares in Christ's priestly office (CCC 784), offering the world to the Father through tears. Thérèse's desire to spend her heaven "doing good upon earth" is the natural extension of this compassion: divine charity made boundless through communion. Love in them has become gravity—everything is drawn into its orbit.

Because these gifts are the Spirit's, they are ordered to the Body. "To each is given the manifestation of the Spirit for the common good" (1 Cor 12:7). Joy becomes mission, not display; humility becomes teachability within the Church; compassion becomes intercession that shoulders another's cross; interior light submits to the Church's wisdom so that vision does not outrun obedience; creative love builds communities, homes, and works of mercy. *Lumen Gentium* teaches that charisms "are to be received with thanksgiving" and discerned for the edification of all (LG 12). Holiness that isolates is suspect; holiness that knits persons together is authentic, for the discernment of gifts belongs to the pastors of the Church (LG 12).

The hallmark of the hallmarks is communion.

Interior light is the next hallmark, the luminous knowledge that accompanies love. It is not visionary spectacle but a new mode of perception. The purified *nous* begins to see with God's own simplicity—not as the blessed see in heaven, but as pilgrims sharing by grace in His radiance. "Blessed are the pure in heart, for they shall see God" (Mt 5:8). The Fathers never interpreted this as future reward but as present participation. Palamas described it as the intellect's union with the divine energies, the uncreated light of Tabor now shining in the heart (*Triads* III.1.23). This light is not self-generated; it is grace reflected. St Gregory of Nyssa said that Moses, entering the cloud, "was drawn ever upward into the light which is beyond all vision." The saint lives within that paradox—seeing by unseeing, knowing by love. This interior illumination does not abolish mystery; it deepens it. Their certainty is not conceptual but relational: they know God as one knows fire by warmth. Symeon's language—"He who is God is seen within me in uncreated light"—is less about experience than ontology: the human faculties themselves have become luminous through indwelling.

From this light proceeds creative love, the final and most dynamic mark of deification. Creation itself began as an overflow of divine generosity; the deified person shares in that same impulse. Their love is inventive, not static. It builds, heals, writes, paints, teaches, embraces. Holiness is not withdrawal but fertility—for sanctity, as Vatican II teaches, is missionary by its very nature (AG 2). In the saints, divine creativity becomes human vocation restored. "The Spirit of the Lord is upon me," Christ proclaimed, "because He has anointed me to bring good news" (Lk 4:18). The saint, filled with that same Spirit, cannot remain inert. Augustine's *caritas* is love that moves outward; Dionysius's *ecstasis* is love that leaves itself to find the other. Theosis flowers in both. In their art, counsel, hospitality, or endurance, the saints continue the creative act of God—order born from chaos, beauty rising from decay. The mark of deified love is that it never seeks its own reflection; it delights in the increase of others' glory. It is, as Aquinas wrote, "the friendship of man with God which overflows

THE SAINTS: TESTIMONIES OF TRANSFIGURED HUMANITY

to all" (ST II-II.23.1).

These five traits—joy, humility, compassion, light, and love—are not separate virtues but facets of one reality: the life of the Trinity communicated. Joy mirrors the Father's inexhaustible giving; humility expresses the Son's self-emptying; compassion and creative love are the Spirit's outgoing tenderness; interior light is their shared radiance dwelling in creation. In the saint, the triune pattern becomes personal rhythm. The human being, shaped by this circulation of divine life, becomes harmony incarnate.

Each hallmark finds embodiment in a thousand small gestures. Joy: the quiet laughter of Seraphim greeting a beggar with reverence. Humility: Thérèse sweeping the convent corridor as though it were an altar. Compassion: Francis embracing the leper and feeling the stench turn to sweetness. Interior light: Symeon praying in darkness until light rose within him. Creative love: Elizabeth of the Trinity writing her final prayer, "Make my soul Your heaven, Your beloved dwelling, and the place of Your rest." These are not anecdotes of piety but sacraments of ontology—moments when created freedom becomes transparent to uncreated grace.

If there is a single test of authentic holiness, it is this: the saint leaves others freer. They do not draw disciples into themselves but into God. Their presence liberates rather than binds because divine life is diffusive, never possessive. "Where the Spirit of the Lord is, there is freedom" (2 Cor 3:17), and as St John Paul II taught, freedom attains its full meaning only in the gift of self (RH 12). That freedom is the atmosphere of deification: the unforced harmony between the creature's will and God's. It is why even their suffering carries a fragrance of peace. They have learned that to lose oneself in love is to gain being itself.

The traits described here are not distant ideals but the natural end of the Christian mysteries already at work in every believer. Baptism plants the seed; the Eucharist nourishes it; repentance prunes it; the Spirit ripens it into fruit. The saints are simply those in whom the harvest has come early. Their lives demonstrate what the Church herself is becoming. The theosis visible in them will one day suffuse the entire Body of Christ, until, as Paul says, "God will be all in all" (1 Cor 15:28).

These signs prove themselves under pressure. Joy that is grace-born does not evaporate in affliction—it becomes quieter, deeper, more like bedrock than foam (2 Cor 4:7–10), a participation in the Cross that gives birth to resurrection (Col 1:24). Humility is most itself when misunderstood and serene. Compassion matures when it must forgive. Interior light clarifies in darkness, when God seems absent and yet the heart keeps praying. Creative love persists when there is nothing left to build but fidelity. St Isaac the Syrian wrote that the same fire of God that purifies the saints burns in all things; to the consenting heart it becomes sweetness. The hallmarks are cruciform: they are brightest when traced across a cross—anticipating the next chapter, where the Paschal pattern reveals why the flame that transfigures always passes through suffering.

The hallmarks of the deified life, then, are nothing other than the qualities of divine life rendered human. They are the grammar of glorified existence, the evidence that salvation is participation and that participation has begun. Joy is the sound of that participation; humility its posture; compassion its motion; interior light its knowledge; love its form. To see these qualities in another is to glimpse the end for which every heart was made—to behold, even if for a moment, a human being who has become all fire.

Spiritual Maternity and Paternity

The fire that transfigures a saint does not end in the saint. Love, by nature, overflows. The one who has been seized by divine life begins to beget that life in others. The deified person becomes parent, not by biological sequence but by spiritual fecundity — a human transparency through which God communicates and renews His grace in others. Every saint is, in this sense, maternal or paternal: the womb and the seed of divine life in history. "My little children, for whom I am again in travail until Christ be formed in you" (Gal 4:19). Paul's cry is the charter of all spiritual parenthood; the apostle labours with God's own creative pain, until the

Church's children bear the image of the Son.

Deification is therefore never solitary. The very energies that restore a person to likeness make them generative, because divine life is always self-diffusive. The Father's love begets the Son, the Son breathes forth the Spirit, and the Spirit reproduces that same rhythm within the saints. To share in the life of the Trinity is to share in its fecundity. Yet what the Father does by nature, the saint does only by grace and participation; divine fruitfulness never passes into human autonomy. Holiness that does not bear fruit would be a contradiction in terms, a closed flame. But the true fire of God spreads: it illuminates by igniting. This is why every authentic mystic becomes teacher, intercessor, or founder; why even the cloistered life radiates invisible maternity; why the aged hermit prays the world into being each morning. Grace reproduces itself in every soul that consents to be its vessel.

The Church herself is the great matrix of this fertility. She is not merely the assembly of the redeemed but the womb of redemption — "the Jerusalem above... our mother" (Gal 4:26). In her, divine life is not abstractly communicated but sacramentally conceived: her motherhood is historical, bodily, and ongoing. Baptism is conception, the Spirit overshadowing the waters as once He overshadowed Mary; the Eucharist is gestation, Christ feeding His own members with His life; confirmation, confession, anointing, and matrimony are all moments of this same maternal labour. The Church is the womb in which Christ is continually born until "Christ be formed in you." And within her, the saints act as midwives. They accompany new souls through the pangs of transformation, standing beside God as He brings forth new life.

This spiritual paternity and maternity has nothing of domination about it. The saint does not own his children, nor the spiritual mother rule her offspring. Their authority is that of fecundity, not control; they generate by love, not command. In them, fatherhood and motherhood are redeemed from possessiveness. The deified person's very presence awakens life: they call forth freedom in the other. "He must increase, and I must decrease" (Jn 3:30). That Johannine humility is the pattern of all spiritual parenthood. The true father is transparent to the Father; the true mother enlarges space for the Spirit to act. Their love makes room, as Mary made room.

Mary stands at the summit of this mystery. She is not only the Mother of God but the prototype of every soul that conceives the Word through faith. "Let it be done to me according to your word" (Lk 1:38): that fiat is the formula of deified maternity. In her, creaturely receptivity becomes creative; grace received becomes grace given. The saints follow her pattern. They receive the Word so deeply that it takes flesh again in their actions, counsel, and intercessions. Each one repeats the mystery of the Incarnation within their own sphere. Their sanctity is Marian not by sentiment but by structure: to receive, to bear, and to give Christ. When the desert elder gives a single word that heals despair, when the confessor absolves with tears, when the mother teaches her child to pray — these are extensions of that same maternal yes. The Church begets by listening as Mary listened, by giving space for the Word to become flesh anew.

The motherhood of Mary, mirrored in the saints, is not sentiment but structure. In her, receptivity becomes the highest activity: faith is fertile. Every "yes" to God conceives something eternal. This is why the Fathers called the believer's soul *Deipara kata charin*—"God-bearing by grace." When the Word finds rest in the heart, He does not remain there inert; He begins to take flesh again in works of mercy, counsel, and love. The saint's maternity is not confined to mystical experience but extends into the concrete: they generate culture, form consciences, and even shape epochs. The Mother of God continues her work through her children, each one becoming, in miniature, an annunciation renewed.

St Basil once said that the Spirit "makes saints, and through them sanctifies others" (*On the Holy Spirit* 9.23). The transmission of holiness is therefore pneumatic: the same breath that deified the saint now passes through them into the community. This is the secret of spiritual direction, of confession, of pastoral care — one flame lighting another until the whole Church burns with one fire. It is the mystery of apostolic succession at the level of grace itself: the life of God propagating through personal communion. No institution, however sacred, can replace that living chain. The saints are its living links; their holiness is the sacramental continuity of divine life in history.

This transmission of holiness is sacramental before it is instructional. Grace passes through gestures as well as words — through presence, silence, and endurance. A saint may teach without teaching, simply by the equilibrium of being in God. Their peace evangelises. "The Spirit breathes where He wills" (Jn 3:8), and through the sanctified person He breathes into others a deeper capacity for communion. The Fathers often spoke of this as "contagion of virtue," yet in truth it is the continuity of the Incarnation: the Word spreading through bodies and histories. The saint's very existence becomes an extension of Christ's touch — a new *laying on of hands* across time.

The generativity of the deified person is often hidden. Thérèse, who never left her convent, became patron of missions; Seraphim, who lived alone in the forest, became father to a nation; Symeon, a monk in obscurity, became teacher to centuries. Their fruitfulness defies geography. It arises not from effort but from indwelling. God reproduces Himself through them as light reflects itself in mirrors facing one another. Augustine spoke of the Church as "the mother who gives birth daily through the preaching of the Word" (*Sermon* 6). The saints extend that maternity into every human relationship: friendship, mentorship, art, even suffering. Wherever grace flows from one soul to another, the mystery of divine parenthood continues.

This spiritual fecundity also reveals the masculine and feminine faces of holiness within the economy of grace. Spiritual paternity protects, teaches, and begets through word and example; spiritual maternity nourishes, intercedes, and shelters life until it matures. Yet both are present in every saint, as both are present in God. The Father eternally generates; the Spirit maternally broods; the Son mediates both in His human love. In participation, man and woman each reflect the total fecundity of the divine. Holiness restores the lost harmony between masculine strength and feminine tenderness, between the authority that calls and the patience that waits. When sanctified, they cease to compete and begin to cooperate, imaging within time the generative rhythm of the Trinity.

Every generation rediscovers holiness through its own grammar of love. The desert's severity, the cloister's silence, the modern city's compassion — all are variations of the same generative rhythm. The Spirit adapts His maternity to the world's wounds. He speaks through fathers who correct and console, through mothers who endure and intercede, through artists, martyrs, and hidden friends of God who create unseen. This is why sanctity never repeats itself: each life translates divine fecundity into a dialect of its age. The history of the Church is not an archive of perfection but a genealogy of begettings — grace constantly inventing new forms of fidelity so that no century is left barren.

Thus the Church's holiness is not static perfection but continual birth. Every generation of saints carries within it the seed of the next. The Fathers become sons of their own disciples; the mothers are consoled by children holier than themselves. Grace circulates in this mutual begetting until all humanity becomes kin in God. The communion of saints is a single extended family, its genealogy traced not by blood but by fire. What began in Mary's womb and burst forth from the tomb continues through every soul that says yes to God's creative Spirit. "The Spirit and the Bride say, Come" (Rev 22:17): that final dialogue of desire is the song of the Church in labour until the new creation is born.

The saint's generativity is therefore eschatological. They do not merely transmit teaching; they generate the future of humanity. In them, divine life multiplies itself until history itself becomes pregnant with glory. Their prayer conceives mercy in the world; their suffering brings forth reconciliation; their presence makes others capable of God. This is the ultimate meaning of theosis lived communally — not only to see God, but to help others see Him; not only to be filled with fire, but to kindle the world. The deified person is the continuation of Pentecost: the Spirit descending through human consent, setting hearts ablaze until the whole earth becomes the Church's womb.

Spiritual paternity and maternity also anticipate the final reconciliation of all things. The saints are not simply individuals perfected in grace but bonds of relation made luminous. In them, history itself becomes parental — generations blessing generations until all creation becomes one family reconciled in love. Their fruitfulness crosses the boundaries of death: the intercession of the saints is not ghostly philanthropy but the continuation of their generative task beyond time. Their prayers are the arteries of the Mystical Body through which divine life circulates unceasingly. "For love is strong as death" (Song 8:6): their charity endures because it is the very vitality of God extending into eternity.

Through them, the circle of creation returns to its beginning. The Father's love, which spoke the world into being, now speaks again through sanctified voices; the Word that entered Mary's body now enters the Church's heart; the Spirit who hovered over the waters now hovers over the saints, bringing new creation from their surrender. Spiritual maternity and paternity are therefore not functions but the very shape of deified existence. Holiness is creative, endlessly. In the world transfigured, every soul will become both son and parent, every creature both receiver and giver of divine life. For the final state of redeemed humanity will be mutual generation — the endless exchange of glory in which God is all in all, and every heart, at last, becomes a womb of light.

Every saint bears the mark of the Cross, because the Cross is not a deviation from glory but its passage. The uncreated light does not bypass suffering; it transfigures it from within. The radiance of the saints, so often gentle and serene, is born of fire endured. Their peace is not the absence of wounds but the sanctification of them. They have learned that pain, offered in love, becomes the point of union between divine and human will — the place where grace accomplishes its deepest work. "Was it not necessary that the Christ should suffer these things and enter into His glory?" (Lk 24:26). What was necessary for the Head is also necessary for the members. Glory is the light that issues from a pierced side.

The same fire that illumines also burns, not to destroy nature but to heal it in its roots. Theosis is not an ascent to splendour detached from cost, but a slow cruciform illumination. Every saint has discovered that divine love is exacting, because it refuses to leave anything unhealed. When the light of God enters the soul, it exposes all that is still shadow, and healing feels like death before it feels like resurrection. The Fathers spoke of this as *purification unto illumination* — the path by which love consumes what cannot coexist with itself. St. Isaac the Syrian wrote that "the fire of God is the love of God that burns sinners as it burns the saints; but in the latter, it becomes sweetness." The difference is not in the fire but in the consent to be purified by it.

Thus, every sanctified life bears invisible stigmata. The joy of Seraphim shone from a body wracked by years of illness and assault; the sweetness of Thérèse was distilled through nights of spiritual darkness and physical torment; the mystical vision of Symeon was born from exile and rejection. In each, suffering became sacrament — the chalice through which divine life was poured. They demonstrate that grace does not protect from pain; it transfigures pain into communion. The saint's serenity is not insulation from the world's affliction but intimacy with its redemption.

The Cross is the archetype of that transfiguration. Upon it, Christ revealed not only what God does for man but what man becomes in God: love strong enough to suffer without hatred, to die without despair, to descend into hell and still sing mercy. To share that love is to enter its pattern. The deified person is therefore not a radiant exception to suffering humanity but its completion — pain having become prayer, vulnerability having become vessel. They bear the wounds of the world as Christ bears them, and their endurance becomes creative. Out of their cruciform hearts the world is born again.

This is the paradox that carries us forward. The same grace that glorifies also crucifies, because the divine likeness cannot be restored without passing through death to self. The saints prove that holiness is not escape from the human condition but its sanctification. Their light passes through suffering as sunlight through stained glass: it acquires colour, texture, and beauty in the process. The wounds do not vanish; they become luminous. "By His wounds we are healed" (Is 53:5), and by their wounds the saints heal others.

The journey of theosis therefore moves inevitably toward the Cross — not as a detour from deification but as its culmination. For the Cross is the moment where love reaches its fullest expression, and the Resurrection its eternal vindication. Every saint, knowingly or not, has followed this rhythm: crucifixion, burial, rising. It is the law of divine life now inscribed within human history. The light that shone at Tabor returns at Golgotha, hidden for a time in blood and tears, only to blaze forth again on the third day. In that Paschal fire all holiness is forged.

And so this chapter ends not in serenity but in invitation — to follow where the saints have gone, through the narrow gate that widens into glory. For the Cross is not the end of theosis; it is the door through which divine life enters the world. Every saint has walked through it, carrying the world's pain as their own, and in doing so becomes the Church's living continuation of Christ's Passion. The next chapter will linger there, before the mystery of suffering transfigured, where the divine flame passes through darkness and emerges brighter than before — the place where love, crucified, becomes light.

The Light that Passes through Wounds

Every saint carries the Cross. The splendor that crowns them is the same light that once poured from the wounds of Christ. The path of deification, traced in their lives, does not rise by escaping suffering but by consenting to let love pass through it. Holiness is not immunity from pain; it is pain transfigured into communion. In the saints, every scar becomes a window for grace, every loss an opening for the divine descent. The light of Tabor and the shadow of Golgotha are not opposites but a single fire seen from two directions: one dazzling, one consuming.

Their joy is cruciform. The more they burn with divine charity, the more deeply they share the world's anguish. Love cannot be deified and remain indifferent. The sanctified heart feels creation's groaning within its own ribs and answers not with despair but intercession. This is why the saints are never sentimental optimists; they are crucified realists. They do not deny darkness—they enter it bearing flame. In them, the Cross ceases to be a symbol of defeat and becomes the axis around which creation turns toward resurrection.

To carry the Cross is to allow divine love to heal the wound of existence from within. The uncreated fire purifies by participation: it does not bypass our mortality but inhabits it. The saint is one in whom that habitation has reached completion—suffering no longer isolates, it unites. Their peace does not come from escaping the world's pain but from discovering God already present in it. "Was it not necessary that the Christ should suffer these things and enter into His glory?" (Lk 24:26). The necessity remains: every glory still passes through a wound.

Thus the story of sanctity leads inevitably to the mystery of suffering transfigured. The light that the saints reflect is not untouched radiance but love refined in fire. To contemplate them is to glimpse the Cross already illumined from within, to see that the world's agony is not the negation of God's glory but its crucible. The next chapter turns there—to the place where love's flame meets its fullest resistance, where theosis becomes passion, and the light that saves the world burns through its own wounds.

10

The Cross and Resurrection in the Life of the Believer

"The Word of God, who willed always and in all things to accomplish the mystery of His love for man, united Himself to our suffering, that through suffering He might perfect the universe in Himself."
— St Maximus the Confessor, Ambigua 7

Paschal Theology and the Daily Ascent through Suffering

Creation begins with breath. "Then the Lord God formed man of dust from the ground, and breathed into his nostrils the breath of life" (Gen 2:7). Redemption begins with another breath—this time, exhaled. "He bowed his head and gave up his spirit" (Jn 19:30). What God breathed into Adam in the beginning He breathes out again upon the Cross, and the breath that once animated clay now sanctifies the world. When the risen Christ stands in the upper room and "breathes on them" saying, "Receive the Holy Spirit" (Jn 20:22), the circle closes. The same Spirit that shaped the first man now reshapes humanity from within. The whole Paschal mystery is divine respiration: the exhale of self-emptying love, the inhale of resurrected life. To live in Christ is to learn this rhythm—to die and rise with every breath until one's own breathing synchronises with God's.

This pattern is not a metaphor but the structure of Christian existence. In baptism the rhythm begins. The believer descends into the water as into the tomb and rises as a new creation. "You were buried with Him in baptism," wrote St Cyril of Jerusalem, "and in the same act you were raised with Him." What happens in the font is not symbolic drowning but ontological re-patterning: the old pulse of self-preservation gives way to the divine pulse of self-gift. From that moment onward the Christian life becomes a series of concentric baptisms—each act of repentance, each confession, each forgiveness another descent and ascent. Theosis matures as this baptismal rhythm deepens: dying to self, rising to love, again and again.

This dying and rising are not moral exercises but movements within God Himself. Grace is not external assistance but God's own life drawing the soul into its current. The Paschal pattern is the inner grammar of deification: what the Son lives by nature, the believer lives by participation. "For if we have been united with Him in a death like His, we shall certainly be united with Him in a resurrection like His" (Rom 6:5). The baptized no longer imitate Christ from without but are caught into His living rhythm, their very breath tuned to His divine respiration.

This daily rhythm becomes the pattern of conversion itself. Repentance is not a single act of remorse but a continual turning within the Paschal tide—falling into God, rising into joy. The saints speak of "compunction," not as despair but as the trembling point where death to sin and birth to grace coincide. Each confession is a miniature resurrection: what is surrendered in sorrow is returned transfigured in mercy. Thus even contrition is creative; it makes space for the Spirit's breath to begin again.

The pattern was first traced by Christ Himself. The hymn Paul quotes in Philippians 2 is the entire drama of theosis compressed into six lines: "Though He was in the form of God, He did not count equality with God a thing to be grasped, but emptied Himself." The descent (*kenosis*) is not loss of divinity but its perfect revelation; for God is love, and love reveals itself by giving itself away. The descent continues "to the point of death, even death on a cross." Yet this humility is not humiliation; it is the natural motion of divine charity entering creation's lowest place so that nothing may remain outside its reach. "Therefore God has highly exalted Him"—the ascent. Glory follows not as reward but as consequence. What God does by nature, the saint does by grace: descends in love to rise in light.

St Maximus the Confessor saw this rhythm everywhere—in the Incarnation, in history, in the soul. The Logos, he said, gathers the divided universe by descending into its fragmentation and uniting it from within. The Christian repeats this descent whenever he forgives, serves, or bears another's weakness. Each act of humility repairs a tear in the fabric of creation. The kenotic pattern is thus both cosmic and personal: God stoops to raise, and man rises by stooping. The believer's life becomes a series of small crucifixions that reopen the world to resurrection.

The saints knew that holiness does not leap from mountaintop to mountaintop; it walks through valleys. To die daily is to make space for God to live more freely within. These "small deaths" are woven through ordinary days—the quiet surrender of one's opinion, the refusal to retaliate, the decision to remain kind when misunderstood. Every relinquishment is a seed buried in faith. "Unless a grain of wheat falls into the earth and dies, it remains alone; but if it dies, it bears much fruit" (Jn 12:24). Christ's own parable is the logic of deification. The grain's breaking releases its life; the believer's surrender releases divine energy. The Eucharist makes this visible: bread is broken so that life may multiply. To receive that Bread is to consent to the same pattern—to become nourishment for others through one's own brokenness.

The Eucharist is therefore the Church's heartbeat. Every Mass is the Paschal pattern made audible: "We proclaim your Death, O Lord, and profess your Resurrection." Within that confession lies the very architecture of sanctity. The believer's participation in the liturgy is not attendance at a drama but entrance into the pattern itself. At the altar, descent and ascent meet; the broken Body becomes food, and the risen Body becomes communion. What Christ accomplishes universally, the Church relives sacramentally, and the soul relearns personally each time it kneels before that mystery.

The rhythm also lives within the Body as a whole. The Church suffers, prays, and rises as one organism. When her members endure persecution, division, or interior purification, she is not failing but following her Spouse into the tomb. Her wounds are bridal, her endurance sacramental. From the martyrs' blood to the quiet fidelity of hidden believers, the Church's history is one long Easter Vigil, waiting in darkness until the dawn breaks over all her altars. In this solidarity, every believer breathes with the same Spirit that raised Christ from the dead.

The rhythm of dying and rising is not confined to heroic virtue; it pulses in every act of love that costs something. A parent who stays awake with a sick child, a friend who bears another's sorrow, a monk who labours unseen—all breathe the Paschal air. Each renunciation is both crucifixion and resurrection. In relinquishing control, we receive peace; in forgiving, we are freed; in suffering, we discover compassion. The spiritual life is not a ladder upward but a heartbeat of descent and ascent: surrender and renewal, kenosis and glory.

Resurrection is therefore not postponed to the last day. It begins wherever surrender has opened a space for grace. "Behold, I make all things new" (Rev 21:5) is not merely eschatological; it describes what happens whenever the human will aligns with divine love. The moment the soul stops clinging, the Spirit breathes. Joy rises like air returning to the lungs. St Thérèse understood this when she said that holiness consists in "remaining little and rejoicing to be so." For her, resurrection began in the acceptance of limitation—light dawning in the crevice of weakness. St Gregory of Nyssa called the soul's journey an *epektasis*, an endless rising: each surrender leading to greater capacity for God. The Paschal mystery is infinite because love's expansion has no end.

This rhythm is inscribed not only in the soul but in the cosmos itself. Night yields to morning, winter to spring, silence to song. Even decay becomes fertility; what falls to the ground feeds what will grow. The Cross, far from foreign to creation, is its secret geometry. The universe breathes with the same cadence as its Creator: exhalation in death, inhalation in life.

"The whole creation has been groaning in travail" (Rom 8:22)—groaning not because it dies, but because it is giving birth. The Christian, reconciled to this rhythm, no longer fears it. He sees in every ending the outline of a beginning.

Even the stars obey this rhythm. Their burning is a kind of self-emptying—matter offering itself to light. Galaxies live and die in order that new worlds may form, an immense cosmic parable of resurrection. The created order bears the mark of the Cross in its very structure: transformation through surrender, increase through expenditure. When the Fathers said that the Cross is "planted in the heart of the world," they meant that this divine geometry shapes every atom of being. The cosmos itself keeps Good Friday and Easter in its pulse.

To live the Paschal pattern is to rediscover harmony with this cosmic breath. It is to let one's own will move in sympathy with God's respiration, so that even pain participates in praise. The ascetic disciplines of the Church—fasting, confession, silence—are simply exercises in breathing correctly. They teach the soul how to exhale pride, inhale mercy, and keep rhythm with divine life. The hesychasts called this *synkatabasis*—co-descension with Christ into the depths of one's own heart, there to rise renewed. Each prayer of the Jesus Prayer—"Lord Jesus Christ, Son of God, have mercy on me"—is an inhalation and exhalation of this rhythm, death and resurrection compressed into a single breath.

This pattern also renews how we see time. The unredeemed life moves in circles—birth, decay, loss. The Paschal life moves in spirals: each descent carrying hidden ascent, each sorrow containing seed of joy. This is why Christian hope is stubborn; it does not deny the grave but looks through it. The believer walks not toward darkness but through it, for the other side of every cross is light. Even sin, when repented, becomes raw material for resurrection—the place where grace proves stronger than failure. "Where sin increased, grace abounded all the more" (Rom 5:20): the law of Paschal gravity.

Thus the Paschal rhythm is the heartbeat of theosis itself. To be deified is to become rhythmic with God, to let one's own breathing echo His. It is the slow education of love learning its own law: that descent is ascent, that giving is receiving, that death is not the end but the necessary door of transformation. The Cross and Resurrection are not events behind us but energies within us, the continual tide by which divine life renews creation.

When the believer consents to this tide, the smallest acts become sacramental. Washing another's feet, bearing an insult, waiting in hope—all participate in the same mystery that turned a tomb into a womb. To live this way is to become transparent to the world's true rhythm: dying into joy, breathing out one's self so that God may breathe in the world.

To practice this rhythm is to become Eucharistic in soul. It means learning to die gently each day: to pride, resentment, and fear; to receive anew the breath of peace that Christ exhaled upon His disciples. This daily repetition forms what the ancients called *praxis of resurrection*—a habit of surrender that slowly becomes spontaneous. Over time, the Christian discovers that even ordinary frustrations can be altars, every act of patience a small Easter. The pattern ceases to feel foreign; it becomes the body's own memory of God.

To live this pattern faithfully is to enter mystery more than mastery. The rhythm does not yield its full logic to the intellect; it must be sung, not solved. Faith walks it step by step, trusting that each surrender will be met by a corresponding resurrection. The saints call this "the science of the Cross"—a wisdom that cannot be learned from books, only from love's endurance. In its school, every heart becomes both altar and flame.

The Paschal mystery, then, is not a drama to admire but a rhythm to inhabit. Christ's exhalation on Calvary continues in every act of mercy; His inhalation in the tomb continues wherever new life rises from loss. The Christian does not merely remember the events of Holy Week; he lives them. Each exhale of surrender draws the world a little closer to the moment when God will breathe again and all shall rise.

Martyria and the Kenotic Pattern of Union

In Gethsemane the world's story narrowed to a single prayer. Beneath the olive trees, the Word made flesh trembled, and sweat mingled with blood. The One through whom all things were made bent His human will beneath the weight of divine love. "Father, not my will, but yours be done" (Lk 22:42). In that moment the fault line between God and man closed, not by force but by consent. The Passion did not begin with nails but with surrender. It was there, in the winepress of Gethsemane, that the grapes of humanity were crushed into the chalice of God. The agony of Christ is not only to be observed but entered; for the same Spirit that sustained Him in His hour of surrender is poured into the hearts of the baptized. To suffer in Christ is to be drawn into that winepress—not as victims of fate, but as participants in redeeming love.

The Cross is not merely an event in history; it is the pulse of divine life entering time. "I have a baptism to be baptized with," Jesus said (Lk 12:50), and that baptism was the immersion of the divine into every depth of human pain. From that immersion flows the paradox of Christian existence: the closer one comes to God, the more one bears the world's wounds; yet the deeper the wound, the nearer the light. St. Paul's audacity—"I rejoice in my sufferings for your sake, and in my flesh I complete what is lacking in Christ's afflictions" (Col 1:24)—is not the arrogance of competition but the humility of cooperation. What is "lacking" is not efficacy but extension. The Cross lacks nothing in power; it lacks only our consent to let its power pass through us. When the believer unites his suffering to Christ's, grace flows outward again through human weakness, as new branches in the same vine.

Suffering in this sense is not punishment but participation. To share in the Passion is to share in the energy of divine love as it heals creation from within. "For as we share abundantly in Christ's sufferings," writes Paul, "so through Christ we share abundantly in comfort too" (2 Cor 1:5). The Fathers called this *martyria*, witness—not only the testimony of blood but the steady confession of faith in the furnace of trial. Martyrdom is not confined to the amphitheater; it occurs each time the will, wounded by self-love, yields again to grace. Every interior "yes" in darkness is a martyrdom of ego, and every endurance of pain without resentment is a participation in the Cross. The believer becomes co-redemptive not by adding to Calvary but by allowing Calvary to take form in his own flesh. Theosis passes through this co-suffering, for love that does not suffer remains unproven, and glory without sacrifice would be foreign to divine life itself.

Kenosis, the self-emptying of the Son, does not cease with the Ascension. It continues in His members, the Church. The mystical body carries the same rhythm: descent in love, ascent in glory. "If we suffer with Him, we shall also be glorified with Him" (Rom 8:17). Grace does not insulate the Christian from pain; it transforms the interior meaning of pain. The instinct of fallen nature is to resist suffering as chaos; faith discovers it as communion. The Cross is no longer merely what happens to us but what happens through us when divine love finds a dwelling place amid fragility. John Paul II, in *Salvifici Doloris*, wrote that in suffering "man discovers himself as one who has been particularly entrusted to himself." The wound becomes a site of responsibility: an altar where freedom meets love.

The baptized do not suffer alone. The Spirit who groans within creation (Rom 8:22–26) groans also in the believer. Every sigh of endurance is part of a larger symphony, the hidden solidarity of the mystical body. The sufferings of one are mysteriously fruitful for others, because all are members of one organism whose Head is crucified love. This is why saints who bore immense interior pain often radiated peace: they had entered the exchange of divine compassion. St. Catherine of Siena spoke of the Cross as 'a bridge stretching from earth to heaven, built from the wood of His body,' and she placed herself upon that bridge, offering her sufferings as planks for others to cross (*Dialogue*, chs. 60–63) . Such images are not pious exaggeration but theological fact: love in the Body of Christ is circulatory. To carry one's cross is to pump life through the veins of the Church.

The believer's suffering thus becomes priestly. It is not only endured but offered. In every Mass the faithful bring their wounds to the altar, not to discard them but to unite them with the Victim whose wounds have become fountains. "Present your bodies as a living sacrifice" (Rom 12:1)—this Pauline exhortation describes the ordinary vocation of every Christian. To live Eucharistically is to turn affliction into intercession, to let pain become prayer. The chalice raised by the priest contains not only wine but the invisible sorrows of the world; when the faithful reply, "May the Lord accept this sacrifice," they are consenting to let their own suffering be transfigured into that offering. In this exchange, weakness becomes priesthood.

St. Maximus the Confessor described creation as a vast symphony of ascending and descending movements that meet in the Cross. When man suffers in love, the cosmos resonates anew with its original harmony. Each act of patient endurance restores a note to the broken song. This is why the saints, even when crushed, often spoke of beauty. St. Ignatius of Antioch, on his way to martyrdom, wrote, "Let me be ground by the teeth of the beasts that I may become the pure bread of Christ." He saw not mutilation but transformation; the horror of the lions became an image of the Eucharist. To be ground is to be offered, and to be offered is to be joined to the creative act of God who brings life from destruction.

The Christian does not seek suffering for its own sake; to do so would be a distortion of love. Yet when suffering arrives, faith recognises it as a visitation from within the Trinity. The Son who descended into death remains the companion of every sorrow. "When you pass through the waters, I will be with you," promises Isaiah (43:2). The test of holiness is not the absence of pain but the presence of communion in pain. To say with Christ, "Into your hands I commend my spirit," is to discover that surrender itself is resurrection beginning. What breaks the heart opens the heart, and what opens the heart makes space for God.

The mystics understood this alchemy. St. John of the Cross spoke of "the dark night" not as punishment but as purification: the stripping away of every comfort that is not God, so that the soul may awaken to the divine presence even in apparent absence. In the night, all false lights go out so that the true light can be seen. The experience is agonizing precisely because divine fire burns deepest where attachment clings most. "The endurance of darkness," he wrote, "is the preparation for great light." Thérèse of Lisieux, echoing him in gentler tones, found joy not in relief but in offering: "I choose all." Her final months, spent in physical torment and spiritual dryness, became her hidden Pentecost. She prayed, "I feel that my mission is to make God loved." Her suffering, united to Christ's, became missionary; in her hidden passion the co-redemptive love of the Church was manifest (*cf. Salvifici Doloris* §26). Her suffering was thus apostolic; her bed a pulpit, her weakness a flame. In both mystics, pain becomes creative—the winepress producing new wine for the Church.

Beyond its apostolic fruitfulness, suffering bears a purgative grace. Because sin disfigures love's order, the soul must pass through fire to be healed. John of the Cross called this the *night of the senses and of the spirit*—a necessary stripping whereby every disordered attachment is burned away. It is not punishment but purification; love's heat consuming what cannot endure the divine. "He will sit as a refiner and purifier of silver" (Mal 3:3): this is the Scripture's own image of sanctifying pain. The Fathers called it *paideia*, the discipline of adoption, for through suffering the child of God is conformed to the Son's likeness (Rom 8:29).

The purifying dimension of suffering also continues what baptism begins and penance restores. It expiates temporal consequences of sin and detaches the heart from created dependencies. The Catechism teaches that every suffering "can take on a redemptive meaning when united with the Passion of Jesus" (CCC 1521) and that temporal punishment is healed through charity inflamed by grace (CCC 1472). Earthly suffering, freely accepted, is therefore the first draft of purgatory—the fire begun here so it need not be finished later.

The saints understood this mystery. Thérèse called suffering "a kiss from Jesus," not because it was sweet but because it was sanctifying. Catherine of Siena spoke of the soul as gold being refined until it could reflect God without distortion. This is why the saints rejoice in affliction: not in pain itself but in its result—purity of love. In this light, suffering becomes not divine absence but divine surgery, the mercy that removes what love cannot share.

This transformation depends on consent. Grace does not romanticize suffering; it divinizes it only when received in faith, through the indwelling of sanctifying grace that unites the soul to Christ's own life. Without love, pain is absurd; with love, it becomes revelation. The difference between despair and sanctity is not the degree of suffering but the direction of gaze. Christ did not escape His agony; He filled it with meaning. The believer, by grace, can do likewise. Every human sorrow can be opened toward communion; every loss can become an offering. "If we have died with Him, we shall also live with Him" (2 Tim 2:11). To accept the Cross is not to seek pain but to trust love's capacity to redeem it.

Suffering also teaches the soul to pray truthfully. When illusions of control are burned away, prayer becomes pure cry: "My God, my God." This cry, shared by Christ, is already a form of union. It is the Spirit Himself praying within us "with sighs too deep for words" (Rom 8:26). The very articulation of anguish becomes a participation in divine speech, the Logos uttering Himself anew through the believer's weakness. In this way, suffering purifies not only the heart but the language of faith. It returns prayer to its native simplicity, its primal honesty.

The world redeemed through suffering is not a world that glorifies pain but one that redeems meaning from pain's wreckage. The Resurrection does not erase Good Friday; it transfigures it. The risen Christ still bears His wounds, but they bleed light. Likewise, in the saints, the memory of pain remains but no longer festers. Forgiveness replaces resentment; peace replaces protest. The wounds become translucent—signs not of what was lost but of what was gained through love's endurance. St. Francis, bearing the stigmata, called his wounds "my sisters," because in them he recognized kinship with the Crucified.

In this transformation, creation itself finds healing. Paul's vision of "creation groaning in labor pains" (Rom 8:22) describes not despair but childbirth. The suffering of the world is labor toward new creation, and every Christian who suffers in union with Christ becomes midwife to that birth. Compassion, from the Latin *compati*, "to suffer with," is therefore participation in divine maternity. The saints' suffering is not sterile; it conceives mercy. Their intercession is born from pain transfigured into tenderness. Even hidden sufferings—illness, rejection, obscurity—become fruitful when united to the Crucified.

The Church, too, lives this collective motherhood. Her persecutions, her internal wounds, her seasons of apparent darkness all serve the same Paschal rhythm. John Paul II wrote that in her sufferings the Church "completes in a certain sense the sufferings of Christ." Not by adding to redemption, but by allowing the fruits of redemption to pass through time. Every generation of believers bears its share of the Cross, so that grace may touch every age and culture. The blood of martyrs, the tears of confessors, the fidelity of families—these are the ongoing rivers of baptismal water flowing through history. The Bride shares her Spouse's wounds, and through them the world receives life.

Yet suffering's purpose does not end in purification; it opens into glory. Every cross, when borne in faith, carries the seed of resurrection. "If we suffer with Him, we shall also be glorified with Him" (Rom 8:17). The believer's wounds will not be erased in heaven but transfigured—the scars of Christ shining as jewels of compassion. Benedict XVI wrote that purgation and glorification are "one and the same fire of love" (*Spe Salvi* §47). What burns now will one day blaze as beauty. In this hope, the Church prays that every tear become crystal, every loss light. The purpose of suffering, then, is not endurance but transformation—the turning of pain into praise until, at last, "death shall be no more" (Rev 21:4).

Even creation beyond humanity participates. The Cross planted in the earth sanctifies matter itself. The saints perceived that their own pain echoed the groaning of the elements: the drought of soul akin to a barren field, the tears of repentance watering the soil of renewal. Theosis extends to the natural order when man suffers redemptively, for in him the material world finds a voice of praise. Thus the Christian vocation is cosmic solidarity: to carry creation through the birth pangs into transfigured light.

At the center of this mystery stands Mary, whose presence beneath the Cross is the purest icon of suffering as participation. She does not intervene or protest; she consents. Her *stabat*—"she stood"—is the Church's posture amid every agony. In her, sorrow and faith are perfectly joined. She suffers not instead of Christ but with Him, and in that *compassio* her motherhood of the Church begins. Every disciple who suffers in love becomes Marian: bearing within his pain the seed of new life for others.

The pattern is therefore universal: suffering embraced in faith becomes the form of divine creativity in the world. It is the slow Paschal breathing of history—death and resurrection translated into every generation. The saints have shown that when love meets suffering, suffering changes name; it becomes gift. "If we share His sufferings, we shall also share His glory" (Rom 8:17). Glory is not postponed reward but present participation in divine endurance. The luminous peace seen on the faces of the suffering righteous is not denial but prophecy: they already bear the dawn.

To suffer in Christ is to stand within the winepress and discover that the pressure is love itself. What seems crushing is the compression of infinity into the finite, divinity pressing through mortality until every drop becomes sacrament. The pain that once isolated now unites; the weakness that humiliated now becomes Eucharist. This is why the saints could call the Cross their joy: they had tasted the vintage of God.

Suffering, then, is not an exception to theosis but its proving ground. Suffering, then, is not an exception to theosis but its proving ground. It is here that the action of sanctifying grace meets human resistance and transforms it into communion. Each tear absorbed into prayer becomes dew upon the garden of resurrection. The believer who consents to suffer with Christ finds himself drawn into the same circulation of love that moves between the Father and the Son. In the winepress of the Cross, the human heart is crushed only to be filled, emptied only to overflow.

This is the paradox that leads forward: the wound that opens becomes the door of union, the chalice of pain the vessel of glory. The next mystery unfolds here—the transfigured wound, where suffering no longer cries for release but for consummation, and the fire of love burns brighter because it has passed through the dark.

The Transfigured Wound: Wounds that Shine

"By His wounds we are healed" (Is 53:5). The phrase is both paradox and revelation: healing comes not from avoidance of pain but from its transfiguration. Christ's wounds are not erased in resurrection; they become the very proof of glory. The risen body still bears the nail-prints, but now they are radiant—wounds turned into windows through which uncreated light pours into creation. In them, love has completed its circuit: descent into death, return in glory, all held together in a single body that bleeds no more yet still shines with the memory of compassion. When Thomas places his hand into the side of Christ, he touches not only torn flesh but the heart of divine mercy. The wound that once gaped open in agony has become the gate of communion.

To gaze upon those wounds is to see what God has always desired: not a world without suffering, but a world in which suffering no longer separates. Pain has been folded into the life of God. The Cross, in that sense, is not merely the price of salvation—it is the revelation of who God is. The Almighty, having no lack, freely chose to bear lack; the impassible chose to suffer. As St Gregory of Nazianzus wrote, "He hungered, yet He fed thousands; He thirsted, yet He poured out the water of life; He was weary, yet He is our rest." In Christ's suffering, divine and human wills no longer collide but harmonize, each movement of agony turned into song. The Logos did not simply repair creation—He entered it, suffered it, filled it until even pain could become the vessel of glory.

The saints understood this: that the Cross is not a symbol of defeat but the grammar of divine love. The world speaks in the language of strength; God speaks in the language of wounds. It is here that theology bends toward mystery—what the Fathers called *theologia crucis*, the knowledge of God gained not through vision but through love crucified. The divine light, to mortal eyes, first appears as darkness because it shines through suffering. Thus the mystics say that one must pass through night before dawn. "The endurance of darkness," writes St John of the Cross, "is the preparation for great light." It is not that God hides His face, but that the soul's eyes must be purified to behold it. The dark night is therefore not God's absence but His unmediated presence, so luminous it blinds until love adjusts to its radiance.

Catherine of Siena called this paradox "the sweet wound of charity." She prayed that God would wound her heart with His own love, so that she might know what He feels for the world. Her mystical dialogues speak of Christ saying, "My wounds are flowers of love; in them I show you how much I love you." To be wounded with that love is both terrible and tender. It burns, yet heals; it empties, yet fills. In Catherine's language, the blood of Christ is not simply the price of redemption but the perfume of divine affection that draws all souls home. The Cross is no longer an instrument of torture; it is the bridal bed where divine and human natures consummate their union. She teaches us that the wounds of Christ are not to be pitied from afar but to be entered—each Christian invited to place their own pain within His pierced side, to let divine love flow through their suffering until it, too, becomes fruitful.

St John of the Cross deepens this same mystery. For him, suffering is not primarily moral trial but metaphysical purification. The "dark night" strips the soul of all sensory and spiritual consolations so that it may cling to God alone. It is an unlearning of attachment—the refiner's fire where love is purified of possessiveness. "To reach satisfaction in all," he writes, "desire satisfaction in nothing." The soul must become naked that it may be clothed in divine light. In this stripping, the human person experiences the pain of absence, yet paradoxically, it is in this absence that God's presence burns most intensely. The very desolation that seems like abandonment becomes the furnace of union. This is why John could say that "the flame of love is the Spirit Himself." The wounds of longing become the meeting place of the human and divine wills; the deeper the ache, the more capacious the heart becomes for God.

Thérèse of Lisieux, centuries later, reinterpreted the same cruciform mystery in miniature. Her "little way" was nothing other than the daily acceptance of powerlessness. Stripped of strength, she discovered divine tenderness. Her tuberculosis and spiritual darkness were not romanticized but received as invitation: to trust when every light goes out. "I will not be a saint by halves," she said; "I choose all." The "all" she chose included suffering, dryness, weakness—the very poverty through which Christ had redeemed the world. For Thérèse, to suffer was to love. Each act of endurance became prayer; each pain, a gift offered back to God. Her bedroom became a Calvary, her bed an altar. In her hidden agony, the Church's compassion expanded; she participated in the redemptive suffering of Christ not through grandeur but through surrender.

The pattern is Eucharistic: broken, blessed, given. Every act of love that costs something echoes the liturgy of Calvary. In the Mass, bread becomes Body only after it is broken; wine becomes Blood only after it is poured. Likewise, the human heart becomes Christlike only through its own offering. "Do this in memory of Me" is not merely liturgical instruction—it is ontological invitation. The believer's life, united to the Cross, becomes sacramental: outwardly ordinary, inwardly crucified and radiant. The Eucharist is the continual reminder that divine glory hides in fragility, that the infinite God continues to give Himself through wounds willingly received. When the priest elevates the host, the Church sees not merely transubstantiated bread but the world's pain redeemed and offered anew.

To the world, this logic remains madness. Yet it is the very logic of creation restored. The wound, when opened by love, ceases to be a prison; it becomes a door. St Francis of Assisi embodied this truth most literally. His stigmata were not decorations but participation—his own flesh bearing the marks of divine charity. The tradition tells us that the wounds shone with light, bleeding not blood but brilliance. Francis had become so conformed to Christ that even his pain was luminous. "I am crucified with Christ," Paul wrote, "yet I live; but not I, Christ lives in me" (Gal 2:20). In Francis, that verse became visible. His body became Gospel: vulnerability as victory, weakness as the vessel of divine fire.

The saints' wounds do not repel; they attract. People were drawn to Francis's broken hands as to relics of hope. In Thérèse's suffering, countless souls learned to trust; in John of the Cross's night, others found light for their own darkness. The sanctified wound always heals beyond itself. It is not exhibition but transmission: grace passing through the cracks of mortality into the world. Each saint becomes a conduit of the one wound of Christ extended through history. What was once the mark of shame becomes the seal of election—the human body joined to divine compassion so closely that even its pain becomes revelation.

The Cross, then, is not simply endured; it is inhabited. To enter its mystery is to discover that love, when absolute, must be vulnerable. The heart that refuses to be wounded also refuses to love. Theosis is thus not escape from suffering but its transfiguration. God does not eliminate pain; He changes its nature. Within divine life, suffering is not contradiction but communication—the way love manifests itself in a fallen world. The luminous Cross is both mirror and map: it reflects who God is and shows where humanity must go. To gaze upon it is to understand that the journey to deification passes not around but through the pierced side, where blood becomes light and the wound becomes womb, birthing new creation.

If the Cross is the mirror of divine love, the Eucharist is its heartbeat. Every Mass is the renewal of that transfigured wound—the moment when the Lamb once slain is made present not as corpse but as living sacrifice. Here suffering is not remembered with sorrow but embraced as communion. The believer kneels before the chalice and sees within it the whole history of human pain, now consecrated. Bread and wine—fruits of the earth and work of human hands—are crushed and pressed before they can become sacrament. Their transformation prefigures ours. We too are ground, pressed, and poured out, that divine life may be distributed through us.

The saints saw this connection clearly. St Catherine of Siena described the Eucharist as "a burning fire that draws the soul into itself and consumes every stain of self-love." The same fire that once blazed on Calvary now burns quietly on the altar, sanctifying all who approach it. Participation in that fire means allowing its heat to enter one's wounds until they glow instead of fester. The chalice we drink is not symbolic wine but the reality of divine self-offering. "Can you drink the cup that I drink?" Christ asked James and John (Mk 10:38). To say yes is to accept the invitation into redemptive participation—to become wine poured for the world.

St Francis of Assisi understood this not in concept but in body. The wounds he bore were not mystical embellishments but the outward imprint of an inward Eucharist. His stigmata, received on Mount La Verna, marked the culmination of a life lived entirely as offering. The seraphic vision he saw—Christ crucified, yet radiant—burned itself into his flesh, as though the divine fire could no longer remain merely spiritual. Francis's body became a living monstrance. When he preached, it was through the brokenness of those hands that light streamed. His suffering was not masochism but overflowing joy; he called his pain "my consolation," for it made him resemble the Beloved. What he carried visibly, every believer is called to carry invisibly: the shape of the Cross impressed upon the soul.

In this, the mystics converge. For John of the Cross, Thérèse, Francis, and Catherine, suffering is not simply endured—it is the matrix of love's creativity. God allows His children to suffer not because He delights in pain but because He desires intimacy. The wound is the meeting place of creature and Creator, where human limitation becomes the dwelling of infinite compassion. "Love is a wound that never heals," wrote St Bernard of Clairvaux, "for it is God Himself." When the soul allows that wound to open, grace enters like breath into lungs. In this way, suffering ceases to be a wall and becomes a threshold.

John Paul II captured this mystery with theological clarity in *Salvifici Doloris*. He wrote that human suffering "has been redeemed in its very essence" and that "in the Cross of Christ, not only is the Redemption accomplished through suffering, but also human suffering itself has been redeemed." To suffer in Christ is to enter that redemption from within. The believer does not stand beside Calvary as spectator but within it as participant. This participation is made possible through sanctifying grace, which infuses divine charity into the soul and transforms pain into cooperation. Grace does not anesthetize; it divinizes. It enables the believer to endure not stoically but fruitfully, so that each trial becomes a seed of resurrection.

The purpose of suffering, then, is not endurance for its own sake but transformation. Pain is the fire by which the dross of self-love burns away, revealing the image of God beneath. St John Chrysostom called suffering "the school of glory." When accepted in faith, it becomes the forge where love is refined into likeness. The human heart, once defensive and closed, learns through affliction to open itself to others. Compassion is born precisely where one has been pierced. This is why the saints are always gentle: their strength has been softened by pain. They have learned, as Christ did, that power without vulnerability cannot redeem.

At the deepest level, suffering reveals the difference between divine and human ways of love. The world loves what pleases; God loves what suffers. He does not withdraw from pain but fills it with His presence until it becomes radiant. "Where love is, there is pain," said Thérèse, "but pain itself is sweetness when it is shared with the Beloved." Such language is incomprehensible outside the Paschal mystery, yet it is the core of Christian sanctity. The saints do not romanticize agony; they recognize that the Cross is love's natural shape in a fallen world. To be united to Christ means to love as He loves, and to love as He loves means to suffer as He suffered—yet always with the hope that through this suffering, life will multiply.

At times this union becomes visible even in the body. The history of holiness is streaked with blood that shines. Think of St Pio of Pietrelcina, whose hands bled for fifty years yet emitted fragrance; or of Catherine of Genoa, whose body radiated warmth so intense it singed her veil. These are not embellishments for hagiographers but manifestations of what theosis looks like under pressure: divine life pressing through mortal flesh. Their wounds were not signs of excess devotion but of divine overflow—grace becoming visible through the fissures of fragility. Each of them bore witness to what Gregory Palamas taught: that the uncreated energies of God can permeate human nature without destroying it, just as light passes through glass and makes it luminous.

To contemplate such lives is to glimpse the eschatological destiny of all suffering. Every wound borne in love becomes translucent to glory. The nail-prints in Christ's hands are the archetype of this mystery: pain not obliterated but made radiant, individuality not dissolved but perfected in compassion. This is why the Church venerates relics—not from superstition, but because sanctified matter has absorbed divine fire. The bone of a martyr or the veil of a virgin is testimony that grace can penetrate even dust. The deified body is not free from scars; it carries them as trophies of communion. "The wounds of Christ," wrote Augustine, "are eternal love-marks of mercy." The same will be true of all who have suffered in Him.

The transfigured wound also restores meaning to human solidarity. In a culture that flees pain, the Christian stands as contradiction, not because he seeks suffering but because he refuses to let it be meaningless. Compassion (*compati*) means literally to suffer-with; and in that withness lies redemption. The saint's wound, far from isolating, becomes a bridge. Through it, divine empathy passes into the world. Thérèse's final agony made her patroness of missions; Francis's stigmata turned his body into a sermon; John Paul's own Parkinson's became a papal encyclical written in silence. Their pain communicated grace because it was no longer theirs—it had become God's language through them.

To live thus is to experience the Cross as interior light. The believer discovers that the flame which once burned painfully now illuminates. The dark night turns into dawn, not because the pain has ceased but because love has learned to breathe within it. The mystic Teresa of Avila said that "the soul in pain sees God more clearly than one in pleasure." Suffering clarifies vision because it purifies attachment. The heart, once cluttered with lesser loves, becomes single, and in its singleness, it reflects the simplicity of God. This is not stoicism but resurrection in motion—the soul already beginning to shine with the light it will one day fully bear.

Yet divine light does not remain confined to mystics and altars. The same fire that burned in Francis and Thérèse is meant to pass into every soul that consents to love. The Paschal pattern written in Christ's body becomes inscribed in ours through daily endurance. Some wounds appear dramatic; others are almost invisible: the slow attrition of caring for an aging parent, the long fidelity of prayer amid dryness, the interior pain of forgiving the unforgivable. These are not lesser crosses; they are the ordinary wood by which the world is redeemed. Sanctity lies not in the scale of suffering but in its orientation—toward communion, not self. When borne in faith, even the smallest ache becomes a particle of the Cross lifted for the life of the world.

The Fathers called this hidden participation *synchoresis*—a mutual indwelling, the human heart expanding to make room for divine compassion. Suffering enlarges capacity; it stretches love until it can hold more than itself. "The measure of love," wrote St Bernard, "is to love without measure." But such unbounded love cannot exist without wounding. Just as the heart's pulse depends on rhythmic contraction, so love's vitality depends on its willingness to be pierced. The Cross is that pulse—the contraction of infinite love into finite form so that life might flow again through the arteries of creation. Each believer who consents to suffer with Christ becomes a pulse in that circulation, carrying divine life to the furthest reaches of the human family.

The purgative function of suffering completes what baptism began. Sin distorts love's symmetry, curving the soul inward; suffering, accepted in grace, unbends it. "Whom the Lord loves, He disciplines" (Heb 12:6): not as penalty, but as refinement. Gold does not resent the furnace; it glories in its purity. St Catherine of Genoa wrote that purgatorial fire "is God Himself, whose burning love cleanses the soul as gold in the crucible." In this life, that fire already burns wherever love costs something. The Christian who bears trials with patience is already undergoing sanctification, already being shaped into Christ's likeness. Earthly suffering is the front porch of heaven's purification: the fire that begins here need not continue there.

This purifying aspect is often misunderstood as divine cruelty, but it is divine intimacy. God does not scourge to destroy; He touches to heal. The surgeon's scalpel is sharp, yet it saves. The difference between torment and purification is the presence of love. When pain is joined to love, it ceases to be punishment and becomes communion. "He will sit as a refiner and purifier of silver" (Mal 3:3): the prophet's image is one of delicate attention—the refiner never leaves the crucible, watching until the silver reflects his face. So God watches each soul in the furnace, waiting until His image appears, radiant in humility. In this way, suffering becomes revelation. The soul begins to understand that divine love is not sentiment but sanctifying fire, and that holiness is not exemption from pain but transparency to it.

The saints bore witness to this purification with startling serenity. Think of the joyful resignation of St Thérèse, who called suffering "a kiss from Jesus." The phrase was not naive piety but mystical realism: she recognized in each affliction an opportunity to resemble the Crucified more perfectly. Or of St John Paul II, who preached the dignity of suffering even as Parkinson's slowly erased his public strength. His trembling hands raised the Eucharist like a living homily: "In my weakness, He is strong." Through their wounds, the Church learned again what theology can only describe—that the divine life does not bypass fragility; it transfigures it.

Suffering's purgation is never purely personal. Because the Church is one Body, every purified soul becomes a source of cleansing for others. The Communion of Saints is not a sentimental metaphor but a circulation of grace. When one member offers pain in union with Christ, others receive consolation and strength. The early Christians spoke of *reparation*—not retribution but restoration, the mysterious economy by which love repairs what sin has shattered. In this exchange, human cooperation becomes the vessel of divine mercy. "I complete what is lacking," said Paul, meaning precisely this: that Christ wills His redemption to flow through His members, so that the Church herself becomes the prolongation of His compassion in time.

The Eucharist reveals this economy most clearly. On the altar, the Church gathers not only bread and wine but the world's suffering—the tears of children, the groans of the dying, the secret griefs of the faithful—and places them in the chalice. There they are mingled with Christ's own sacrifice and returned transfigured. "Through Him, with Him, in

Him"—the priest's doxology is the universe's sigh of relief. Nothing is wasted. Every pain that enters that chalice becomes communion. When the faithful receive the Body and Blood, they drink not only divine mercy but their own sorrows redeemed. The Eucharist thus teaches us to interpret pain not as absurdity but as liturgy: the slow consecration of creation through love.

Even nature seems to echo this pattern. The soil must be broken to receive the seed; the seed must die to yield fruit. Rivers carve valleys through erosion; mountains form through tectonic stress. In the natural world, beauty is the child of pressure. So too in the soul: grace chisels through resistance until the form of Christ emerges. "The world is charged with the grandeur of God," wrote Gerard Manley Hopkins, "It will flame out, like shining from shook foil." The shaking is necessary; without it, the light remains trapped.

Here the doctrine of theosis finds its most astonishing application. Deification is not mere moral improvement or mystical feeling; it is the penetration of divine life into every fibre of human existence—including suffering. The uncreated energies of God do not stop at the threshold of pain; they pass through it, transforming it into radiance. In the saints, we see what humanity is meant to become: flesh transparent to fire, wounds gleaming like jewels. Christ's glorified body is the prototype—His scars are not erased but exalted, shimmering like rubies beneath eternal light. In them the universe reads its destiny: matter filled with Spirit, sorrow translated into song.

St Francis, bearing the stigmata, is an icon of that destiny; but so too is every hidden sufferer who offers pain in love. The mother beside her child's hospital bed, the worker enduring monotony without bitterness, the elderly priest praying alone in the night—each participates in the same mystery. Their suffering, invisible to the world, is a Eucharist celebrated in silence. Grace expands through them like oxygen through a lung. The more they yield, the more the world breathes. Such lives remind us that sanctity is not spectacle but availability: a willingness to let God use one's weakness as conduit for His strength.

This hidden apostolate of pain is perhaps the Church's deepest ministry. Long before words convert, suffering prays. The saints who suffered silently have done more to heal the world than any preacher. They stand like candles before the altar—consumed, yet illuminating. Their wounds are not complaints but hymns; their endurance is doxology. In them, theology becomes flesh again: the doctrine of redemptive suffering no longer confined to paper but breathing, bleeding, and blessing in real time.

Through such witnesses the Church learns that the Cross is not an anomaly but the blueprint of sanctity. "If any man would come after Me, let him deny himself, take up his cross, and follow Me" (Mt 16:24). The call is not to morbid endurance but to creative participation. The Cross is not death's victory; it is love's invention—the means by which God turns destruction into communion. Every saint who has suffered in Christ becomes a continuation of that invention, an artisan of divine tenderness. Their wounds shape the world's redemption, just as the nails shaped salvation's door.

The transfiguration of suffering reaches its summit in Mary, who stands at the Cross as the silent priestess of consent. Her suffering is pure participation: nothing added, nothing withheld. She does not intervene to spare her Son, nor does she turn away; she simply remains—*stabat Mater*. In that stillness, humanity learns how to suffer rightly. Mary's pain is immaculate because it is unresistant; she suffers in perfect harmony with divine will. Her tears baptize the world's grief. "At the Cross her station keeping," the hymn says, and that station becomes the posture of the Church in every age: steadfast love standing beneath crucified love. In her, the compassion of God takes human form. The Fathers saw her as *co-redemptrix* not because she added to redemption, but because she mirrored it fully—her yes echoing Christ's yes, her heart pierced so that the Church might be born from it.

Beneath that Cross, suffering ceases to be solitary. The Beloved Disciple stands beside the Mother, and from their union a new family begins. "Behold your mother… behold your son" (Jn 19:26–27). Out of agony, communion; from rupture, relationship. The sword that pierces Mary's heart opens the space where the rest of humanity can dwell. This is the mystery of co-suffering: it unites rather than isolates. Every Christian who bears pain in love joins this Marian posture—suffering *with* Christ, not apart from Him, and thus becoming generative. The Church herself continues to "stand" at the foot of every cross in the world, holding vigil until resurrection dawns.

This Marian dimension extends to the whole cosmos. The earth, too, groans in labor, awaiting its own transfiguration (Rom 8:22). The suffering of creation is not a meaningless convulsion but the travail of birth. Every earthquake, every decay, every death is a shadow of the same Paschal rhythm. In the Incarnation, God united Himself not only to humanity but to matter itself. The Cross planted in the soil sanctified the dust; the Resurrection quickened it. When human beings suffer redemptively, the natural world is mysteriously drawn into that offering. The sigh of the forest felled, the cry of the animal hunted, the melting of glaciers—all these find voice when a saint prays through pain. The deified person becomes the conscience of creation, reconciling earth's anguish with heaven's promise. In their suffering, the material universe begins to heal.

Here the theology of theosis expands into a symphony of solidarity. Divine life, having entered flesh, radiates outward through every creature willing to be transparent. The saint's wound, luminous with grace, becomes a lamp for the cosmos. This is why icons often depict the saints surrounded by mandorlas of light: their suffering transfigured into radiance that blesses the world. "The creation waits with eager longing for the revealing of the sons of God" (Rom 8:19). That revealing is precisely this—human beings so filled with divine fire that even their wounds shine. In them, the purpose of suffering reaches fulfillment: not annihilation, but illumination; not resignation, but recreation.

John Paul II glimpsed this horizon when he wrote that "in the mystery of the Redemption, suffering has been taken up into the very heart of God" (*Salvifici Doloris* §18). If suffering has entered God's own life through the humanity of Christ, then nothing truly human is excluded from glory. The Cross, once a sign of degradation, now stands as the axis of the universe—the place where divine love and created pain meet, merge, and are transfigured. The saints' lives prove that this is no abstraction. Each of them, in a distinct register, shows how the same fire that burns also beautifies. Their wounds are not reminders of fragility but declarations of faith: God's strength made perfect in weakness.

To behold such holiness is to confront one's own vocation. The Christian is not called merely to endure suffering but to consecrate it—to let it become Eucharist, prayer, and light. "Present your bodies as a living sacrifice" (Rom 12:1): this is the Paschal grammar of every day. Every disappointment, every illness, every misunderstood act can be placed upon that altar. When offered in love, the mundane becomes magnificent, and what once seemed pointless becomes participation. Suffering ceases to be an argument against God; it becomes the alphabet through which He writes redemption anew.

The transfigured wound, then, is both revelation and promise. Revelation—because in it we glimpse the very nature of divine love: creative, cruciform, inexhaustible. Promise—because it foretells what awaits all creation. Every scar will shine, every tear will refract light, every broken thing will become the crystal through which glory passes. The mystics describe heaven not as escape from pain but as its completion, the moment when every fragment of endured love finds its echo in eternity. The Resurrection does not undo the Cross; it crowns it. In the final vision of Revelation, the Lamb still bears His wounds, and those wounds illumine the city. The light that fills the New Jerusalem is not separate from suffering—it is suffering fulfilled in love.

This is the paradox that carries us toward the next mystery: that the closer union with God becomes, the more deeply the Cross is inscribed, and yet the more serene the joy that follows. The saint is not absorbed into impersonal light but remains distinctly radiant, a human face forever marked by mercy. In them, the mystery of distinction and communion—the subject of what follows—is made visible. For the wounds that shine are not dissolved in glory; they are preserved as personal signs of love. And through them, the Church learns what the end of all suffering truly is: not oblivion, but beatitude—the heart of God beating in every transfigured scar.

Death as Gateway to Glory

Death is not a foreign intruder in the drama of grace. It remains the last enemy, yes (1 Cor 15:26), but an enemy Christ has already made to serve love's purpose. In Adam it was exile; in Christ it becomes exodus. The Word made flesh entered death, not as prisoner but as priest, carrying the whole of creation through its dark passage into the light of resurrection. Since that descent, death is no longer a wall but a door, no longer the extinguishing of being but the unveiling of glory. For those who die in Him, the grave is no longer a sealed chamber but a passage "from glory to glory" (2 Cor 3:18).

Every Christian life is a long apprenticeship in dying. The first lesson began at baptism, when water closed over the neophyte's head like a small death. "You were buried with Him in baptism, in which you were also raised with Him" (Col 2:12). Each sacrament since rehearses that same rhythm. In confession the self dies to pride; in Eucharist it learns to be broken and shared; in anointing, the senses themselves are consecrated for the final offering. Thus the whole Christian vocation is a preparation for the Paschal crossing. When the final hour comes, death does not introduce the soul to something new—it simply perfects the surrender long rehearsed.

The Catechism says that "death is the end of man's earthly pilgrimage, of the time of grace and mercy" (CCC 1013), yet in the same breath it calls it a "participation in Christ's obedience." To die well is therefore not passive collapse but active consent, the creature's final *fiat*. Theosis, begun as cooperation with grace, now becomes total yielding. The dying Christian becomes Eucharist: he offers the last thing still his—his being—to the Giver. "Into your hands I commend my spirit" (Lk 23:46) is the final word of deified humanity, the completion of baptism's promise.

Yet death does not divide the human person into alien parts. The

Christian does not believe in a soul escaping the body like smoke leaving an extinguished flame. The soul and body remain ordered to each other even when separated; their unity is only interrupted, never abolished. This distinction without divorce preserves the truth of personhood: man is not a spirit trapped in matter but a composite called to transfiguration. The moment of dying therefore holds a paradox—apparent dissolution that secretly guards integrity. What God once joined, He will rejoin. The soul's longing for reunion is itself a participation in the Resurrection already prepared in Christ's glorified flesh.

For this reason the saints have never spoken of death as annihilation. They call it *dies natalis*, the birthday of eternity. St Ambrose, preaching at his brother's funeral, said: "We have loved him in life; let us not be dismayed that we have lost him, for we have not lost but sent him ahead." St Ignatius of Antioch called his martyrdom "the birth pangs of God." The Church believes that in every faithful death, the grace of baptism flowers fully; the old man dies utterly so that the new may rise without hindrance. The breath that leaves the lungs is received by the same Spirit who first breathed into clay.

Yet the mystery of death is not only individual—it is ecclesial. The Church never lets her children die alone. The final anointing, viaticum, the commendation of the soul—all these rites express the solidarity of the Body accompanying one of its members to the threshold. The dying are never isolated units slipping into void; they are surrounded by prayer, folded into communion, carried by the living to the arms of the dead who await them. The Church's *Litany of the Departing* names the saints as escorts—Peter and Paul, Mary and all angels—as if heaven itself bends down to receive the traveller.

In this companionship, fear loses its tyranny. The devil's ancient boast—"You shall surely die"—is unmasked. The Christian still dies, but not alone, and not unchanged. Grace has entered even the molecular level of mortality. "If the Spirit of Him who raised Jesus from the dead dwells in you, He who raised Christ will give life to your mortal bodies" (Rom 8:11). That promise means the divine indwelling remains unbroken; even the disintegration of flesh cannot dissolve communion. The soul passes into God not as a spark returning to an impersonal fire but as a person recognized, loved, and awaited.

The saints' deaths bear witness to this serenity. St Francis sang the *Canticle of the Creatures* as he lay dying, blessing "Sister Death." St Bede the Venerable chanted the *Gloria Patri* with his last breath. Thérèse of Lisieux whispered, "I am not dying; I am entering into life." Such peace is not stoicism; it is participation. Their composure arose from union with the Crucified, who had already converted terror into trust. To die in Christ is to experience the interior climate of Calvary—anguish transfigured into obedience, darkness into faith's purest act.

The Fathers compared this passage to sleep. Paul wrote, "Those who have fallen asleep in Christ" (1 Thess 4:14), and the Church still prays, "Eternal rest grant unto them." The metaphor is not sentimental. Sleep suggests continuity; the sleeper is not gone but resting toward awakening. The Byzantine feast of the Dormition of the Theotokos unfolds this intuition in golden iconography: the apostles stand around Mary's bed, and Christ holds her soul as an infant wrapped in white. Death here is reversal of birth: the child returns to the arms of the Son. It is not defeat but homecoming. In her "falling asleep," Mary embodies the destiny of every deified life—body entrusted to the earth, soul cradled in glory, both awaiting reunion in resurrection.

This "falling asleep" does not erase the body's dignity. Christianity insists that salvation is incomplete without the resurrection of the flesh. The body is not a shell to be discarded but the very language through which the soul once spoke. At death that language pauses; it will speak again. Theosis requires that what was sanctified by sacraments—the hands that served, the eyes that wept—must also share in transfiguration. "We look for the resurrection of the dead," the Creed proclaims, because divine life is too generous to save the soul alone.

Between death and resurrection the Church teaches purification, not in punitive terms but as love's final refinement. The soul that has said "yes" but imperfectly must learn to bear full light. This is purgatory—the garden where unfinished love ripens. Benedict XVI called it "the fire of Christ's love itself" (*Spe Salvi* 47). It is the continuation of theosis by cleansing. Even there the soul is not exiled from Christ; rather, Christ's gaze purifies until no resistance remains. The flames are not God's wrath but His tenderness burning away shadows. Thus the believer's death is not completed until love is total.

The purifying fire is thus not external penalty but interior illumination. It is the unveiled gaze of Christ, whose love reveals and heals simultaneously. The saints have said that purgatory's greatest pain is the same as its greatest joy—the thirst for God. The closer the soul draws, the more it burns, and the burning itself becomes bliss. It is the pedagogy of glory, love teaching the creature how to breathe light without recoil. This stage of theosis is no waiting room; it is love's final lesson in receptivity. There, the creature's desire and God's desire converge until nothing remains but joy.

Beyond that threshold lies glory. The Resurrection of Christ is the template and pledge: "He will transform our lowly body to be like His glorious body" (Phil 3:21). What He possesses by nature, we receive by participation. The resurrected body, says Aquinas, will be "spiritual," not because it ceases to be matter but because matter becomes fully obedient to spirit. The East calls this *photismos*, illumination—flesh so permeated by divine energy that it shines. The saints in glory are the first fruits of this harvest. Their incorrupt relics, their fragrance, their radiance in icons—all hint that even dust can burn with divinity.

The Fathers loved to call this future state *pneumatic existence*—matter wholly suffused by breath. Gregory of Nyssa envisioned it as "mind made visible," the body so transparent that spirit shines through it unimpeded. Aquinas described its four properties—clarity, agility, subtlety, and impassibility—as notes in a single hymn of harmony, the hymn of a world made obedient to love. Nothing perishes; everything is perfected. What was once fragile becomes agile; what was once opaque becomes radiant. The resurrected senses will not abolish individuality but make it luminous—each saint a distinct hue refracting one uncreated light. Flesh itself will have learned contemplation; the body will pray simply by being.

In them we glimpse creation's destiny. "Behold, I make all things new" (Rev 21:5). The resurrection is not mere restoration but re-creation. The elements themselves—fire, air, water, earth—will share in the transfiguration of the children of God. The whole cosmos, says Paul, "waits with eager longing for the revealing of the sons of God" (Rom 8:19). That revealing is the final stage of theosis when matter itself becomes sacrament. The universe, once groaning, will sing. Every atom will echo the pattern of the Cross: dying into light.

The Church's liturgy already anticipates this dawn. In the funeral rites the Paschal candle burns beside the coffin, the same light that once stood at baptism. The body is sprinkled with water, recalling the first death in the font. Incense rises like breath restored. The words of the *Exsultet* are quietly present even in the requiem: "The night shall be as bright as day." In East and West alike, Christian burial is a miniature Easter Vigil. The lament psalms are answered by alleluias. Grief and glory intertwine like twilight and sunrise.

To believe this is to be freed from despair. Christianity does not glorify death; it glorifies the God who passed through death and emerged victorious. We do not call death good; we call it defeated. "O death, where is your sting?" (1 Cor 15:55). The sting remains for those who love, yet its venom is gone. The ache of separation is real, but beneath it runs a deeper assurance: communion is not broken, only hidden. Those who die in grace do not cease to belong to us; they enter us more deeply. The communion of saints is a single respiration—the living and the dead inhaling and exhaling the same Spirit.

From this communion arises intercession. The saints who now behold God face to face do not abandon the world; their love expands. Their perfected charity participates in Christ's mediation. The departed pray for the living as the living pray for the departed, and in this exchange the Church on earth and the Church in heaven form one continuous liturgy. The blood of martyrs, the prayers of the dying, the sighs of the living—all are drawn into one circulation of mercy. Death cannot disrupt that rhythm; it only removes the noise that once made it hard to hear.

To die in this communion is to die into joy. The soul, long accustomed to trust by faith, now sees. Vision does not abolish love; it completes it. The beatific vision is not static contemplation but eternal dynamism—love knowing itself as known. "We shall be like Him, for we shall see Him as He is" (1 Jn 3:2). In that seeing, theosis reaches its final form: creature fully transparent to Creator, yet unconfused. The saints shine because they are not swallowed; they are illuminated. Each retains his unique hue, and together they form the prism through which divine light becomes beauty.

The body too will participate. The resurrected flesh will be what it always longed to be: music made visible. Gregory Nazianzen said that in the resurrection, "Spirit shall embrace matter once more, and matter made divine shall cling to Spirit." The hands that once healed will shine with that memory; the feet that once walked in mercy will gleam like bronze. Every wound will have turned to jewel. The crucified body of Christ retains its scars; so shall ours, not as reminders of pain but as badges of praise. Wounds become windows—glory passing through what once was weakness.

This vision is not abstract comfort but the very architecture of Christian hope. It transforms ethics as well as eschatology. If the body is destined for glory, it must be reverenced now; if creation will be transfigured, it must be cherished now. The resurrection casts moral light backward into time: our gestures already shape the matter that will one day rise. Thus the Christian who buries the dead with honour, who tends the sick, who refuses despair—each already participates in the future kingdom. To live and to die with dignity is to anticipate the final festival of light.

As the final moment approaches, the Christian does not stare into emptiness but into a Face. Death, stripped of terror, reveals the personal dimension of eternity: *the meeting*. "When Christ who is your life appears, you also will appear with Him in glory" (Col 3:4). That appearance is both His and ours—the unveiling of mutual recognition. The saints call it the *hour of love's surprise*. Julian of Norwich heard Him say, "All shall be well," and in that assurance the fear of death dissolved. For when love is perfect, even judgment is joy: the soul sees itself at last as God has always seen it.

At the eschaton, this vision will expand until nothing remains outside it. The general resurrection will reveal the final harmony: every soul and every atom resonating with divine praise. "The righteous will shine like the sun" (Mt 13:43). The night of the world will end, and the universe will awaken as a single morning. The Cross, once a narrow instrument of death, will stand as the world-tree whose branches fill the cosmos. The new creation will not replace the old; it will be the old made transparent—history set ablaze from within.

Death, then, is not the cancellation of time but its fulfillment. Chronology flowers into kairos, the eternal present of divine life. The saint's "today" never ends. This is why the Church prays for a holy death, *mors sancta*, not simply painless but conscious—a final liturgical act. The dying Christian, even wordless, joins the liturgy of the universe: "Through Him, with Him, in Him." The last heartbeat becomes a doxology. The silence that follows is not emptiness but adoration too deep for sound.

To contemplate death in this way is to live differently now. Each small renunciation becomes a rehearsal of the final surrender; each act of forgiveness is a preview of the mercy that will greet us. Hope is not optimism about circumstances but confidence in the character of God. The believer carries this hope as an inner dawn. "Even though I walk through the valley of the shadow of death, I will fear no evil" (Ps 23:4). The shadow remains, but light has entered it.

When at last that light breaks fully, it will reveal what all our lesser dawns only hinted at. The body will rise, the cosmos will sing, and the human story will close not in silence but in symphony. The fire that once purified will become illumination; the wounds that once bled will shine; the love that once died will reign. God will be all in all (1 Cor 15:28), and His breath will fill creation once more. The Cross will open finally into dawn, and every creature will wake to its true name: beloved, transfigured, alive forever.

In that dawn, even the elements will rejoice. The stars that once guided shepherds will burn with conscious praise; the seas will mirror uncreated light; the earth, which bore both the Cross and the tomb, will tremble with gladness. The universe will not be discarded but delivered, lifted from corruption into sacrament. The ancient dream of the prophets—"the mountains and the hills shall break forth into singing" (Is 55:12)—will at last be literal. Matter itself will have learned to pray. Creation's final liturgy will be cosmic, every atom a syllable of thanksgiving, every galaxy a refrain of divine joy.

Fire Held without Fusion

Union with God, in its fullness, brings the mind to its highest wonder and its necessary question. If grace fills everything, what remains of the one who receives it? The saints, radiant as suns, are not dissolved into light; they shine with their own contours intact. The closer the soul draws to God, the more it becomes itself. The paradox of deification now stands at its threshold: when all distinction has been purified of opposition, what keeps communion from collapsing into sameness? The answer is not philosophical ingenuity but revelation's delicacy—the God who is "all in all" (1 Cor 15:28) is also the God who never ceases to call each by name.

The fire that fills does not consume the form it perfects. Moses saw the bush aflame yet unburned, and that vision remains the icon of all sanctity. Grace does not flatten the human into the divine; it transfigures the human according to its unique logos, its unrepeatable reason for being. In heaven, no one's light eclipses another's. Theosis is not fusion but resonance: many notes struck by one breath. Each person is a distinct syllable spoken by the Word, and deification is that syllable sung at last in perfect pitch. "The glory of God is a living man," said Irenaeus, "and the life of man is the vision of God." Vision does not abolish the seer; it makes him luminous.

St. Gregory Nazianzen spoke of this mystery with metaphysical precision and tenderness: "He remained what He was, and assumed what He was not" (Or. 29). The same pattern extends to the saints. They remain what they are and assume what they were not—divinity by participation. The human nature is neither overwhelmed nor replaced; it becomes radiant with the energies of God while keeping its hypostatic integrity. This is the grammar of glory: distinction without division, union without confusion. The Cappadocians, who defended the Trinity itself on these terms, teach that communion is perfected not by erasure but by reciprocity. To be filled with God is to become transparent, not indistinct.

St. Thomas Aquinas, gazing from the scholastic West toward the same horizon, affirmed that "grace does not destroy nature, but perfects it" (ST I.1.8 ad2). The light that transfigures is the same that defines. The more God inhabits the soul, the more capacious the soul becomes for love, for memory, for thought. In glory, individuality is not swallowed but completed—the seed's shell fallen away, its form preserved in fruit. Personality, cleansed of ego, becomes personhood in the truest sense: a face turned entirely toward the Other, finding its being in relation. Love does not erase difference; it makes difference eternal.

The saints themselves show this fire held within form. Francis burns with joy, Teresa with interior fire, Seraphim with radiant peace. The same light, endlessly refracted, yields infinite shades. Heaven is not monotone brightness but a symphony of hues. The Spirit, who "distributes to each as He wills" (1 Cor 12:11), does not revoke distinction in completion; He perfects it into harmony. Even the smallest soul will have its distinct timbre in the eternal music. The Kingdom's glory will not be a blinding white-out but the fullness of colour at noon.

The doctrine of participation safeguards this wonder. Participation means receiving being without becoming the source of it, sharing light without becoming the sun. The creature's union with God is analogical, not univocal: real, intimate, and transformative, yet always founded in difference. The divine energies communicate holiness, not divinity of essence. To be deified is to dwell in God as air in light—penetrated, surrounded, and enlivened, yet never identical with the light's substance. Gregory Palamas expressed it with exquisite clarity: "We share by grace what Christ possesses by nature." In that sentence rests the entire equilibrium of theosis.

This distinction is not a limitation of love but its condition. Only persons distinct can truly commune. If the self were lost, love would lose its object. The dance of deification requires two freedoms: the infinite generosity of God and the uncoerced receptivity of the creature. The saint's yes is eternally preserved, not overridden; it becomes rhythm within the divine music. The individuality God created is not an obstacle to union but its very possibility—the finite open wide to the Infinite. The clay vessel holds the fire precisely because it has shape.

The mystery, then, is not how the finite endures the Infinite, but how the Infinite desires the finite enough to preserve it forever. "I give them eternal life, and they shall never perish, and no one shall snatch them out of my hand" (Jn 10:28). That hand holds without crushing, burns without consuming. The resurrectional body is proof: it is not dissolved into spirit but made spiritual; not lost, but luminous. Love's triumph is not absorption but communion, where God is all in all yet all remain in Him.

We have reached the summit where vision must yield to understanding. Having followed the saints through fire and resurrection, the path now turns toward doctrine—to guard what contemplation has revealed. The next movement will slow, not to diminish wonder, but to preserve it from confusion. If in these pages we have seen creation aflame, the next will ask: what keeps the flame from devouring its form? Theology must now speak where experience has fallen silent. The fire is real; the fusion is not.

11

Union without Absorption: Theological Boundaries of Participation

"It is by participation that we become divine, not by nature; for the divine essence remains beyond all participation."
— St John of Damascus, *Exposition of the Orthodox Faith III.15*

Distinction of Natures in Theosis

The mystery of deification stands or falls with the mystery of the Incarnation. If Christ were not truly God and truly man, there could be no bridge between the Creator and the creature, no sharing of life across that infinite divide. All Christian talk of participation finds its grammar in one sentence written at Chalcedon in 451: the Lord Jesus Christ is "one and the same Son ... acknowledged in two natures, unconfusedly, unchangeably, indivisibly, inseparably." These four adverbs are the boundary stones of all Christian mysticism. They protect both the majesty of God and the dignity of man. They forbid confusion without enforcing distance, distinction without division. And what they preserve in Christ, they guarantee in us, for every true union with God must echo the logic of the Incarnation that made it possible.

Chalcedon did not arise in a vacuum. Nicaea confessed the Son as homoousios with the Father—the same substance, not a noble copy. Ephesus safeguarded the unity of the divine Person in Mary's title Theotokos—the Mother of God, not merely the mother of a human instrument. Chalcedon gathers these luminous threads and binds them into a single christological cord: one and the same Son, fully God and fully man. The four adverbs are the Church's way of saying how the Infinite crossed the finite without collapse, and how the finite received the Infinite without rupture. This is not abstract metaphysics; it is worship turned into grammar, doxology distilled into doctrine: the hymn of a God who unites without devouring and descends without diminishing.

The council fathers were not trading scholastic puzzles; they were naming salvation's mechanism. The hypostatic union—the Word assuming human nature without change or fusion—revealed that God could dwell in flesh without ceasing to be God, and that flesh could be deified without ceasing to be flesh. In Christ, the two natures meet without confusion (each retaining its properties), without change (neither becoming the other), without division (united in one Person), and without separation (never acting apart). These four boundaries describe not only the Incarnate Son but the law of every authentic participation in Him. The believer's communion with God must likewise be unconfused, unchangeable, indivisible, and inseparable—an echo of the Chalcedonian rhythm within the human soul.

This Chalcedonian logic undergirds the Catholic understanding of theosis. Union with God is real but analogical, participatory not hypostatic. No Christian becomes a parallel incarnation; every Christian is drawn into the one Incarnation. What Christ is by nature, we share by grace. Athanasius' daring formula—"God became man that man might become god"—finds its precise meaning here. We become god not by crossing the ontological boundary that separates creature from Creator, but by participation in the divine life poured out to us. In Christ alone subsists the hypostatic union; in us, the moral, sacramental, and mystical union wrought by grace. Our deification is derivative, dependent, and dynamic. It is communion, not composition.

The Eastern Fathers loved the image of iron in fire: the metal glows, radiates, and softens, yet remains iron. The fire does not destroy the iron; the iron does not dilute the fire; the two interpenetrate without fusion. So, too, with the human soul inflamed by God: suffused with light, yet not dissolved into divinity. The Western scholastics sang the same melody in another key. Aquinas teaches that grace is not the divine essence poured into us but a created participation in it: "a certain likeness of the divine nature infused into the soul." Created grace is the mode by which uncreated grace touches us without destroying us. It is God's life accommodated to creaturely measure. The human person becomes truly godlike while remaining irrevocably human. The fire does not consume; it transfigures.

Gregory Palamas later articulated the same safeguard with his distinction of essence and energies. God's essence remains inaccessible, forever beyond participation; His energies—His operations, presence, and light—are freely communicated. To share in the divine energies is not to possess God's essence, yet it is truly to share in God. Transcendence is preserved even as intimacy is given. Here Aquinas and Palamas meet across the centuries: both reject fusion, both affirm real participation, both insist upon the integrity of the creature. Grace communicates divine radiance, not divine self-subsistence. The current of uncreated light passes through created being without breaking either.

The same truth sounds in both lungs of the Church. The East speaks of participation in the energies; the West calls sanctifying grace a created participation in the divine nature. Both confess that deification is Trinitarian in shape: from the Father's generosity, through the Son's humanity, in the indwelling of the Holy Spirit—the "bond of love." Grace is not an impersonal force but the Spirit's own presence expanding creaturely capacity without erasing it. To be deified is to breathe with the Trinity: the creature remaining creature, yet living by uncreated life.

Because of this, Christian union is always personal. Theosis never occurs between anonymous substances; it occurs between persons. The believer is united not to an abstract divinity but to the living Christ, the divine Person who assumed our nature. The hypostatic union grounds the mystical union: we touch the Godhead through the humanity He assumed, as fire reaching us through the hearthstone. This is why the sacraments, which extend Christ's humanity through time, are the ordinary instruments of deification. Baptism grafts us onto the living Vine; the Eucharist unites body to Body; Chrismation seals the temple of the heart. Without the Incarnate mediation, mysticism would either collapse into pantheism or retreat into despair. With it, grace has a human shape, and the human is invited to a divine life.

Chalcedon clarifies sanctification's choreography. In Christ there is no confusion of natures; in us there must be no confusion of roles. Grace is God's action; yet it summons human cooperation. Divine and human wills interpenetrate without rivalry. Gethsemane reveals this harmony: "Not my will but yours be done." The consent that saves the world becomes the pattern that sanctifies the soul. Grace moves the will from within, yet the will remains free; love persuades, never coerces. Hence deification is neither self-divinisation nor passive absorption. It is synergy—the dance of omnipotence and freedom, the embrace in which God acts and the human person fully acts with Him.

The distinction of natures ensures that theosis is not self-obliteration. God does not wish to erase the creature but to make it fully itself. "The glory of God is man fully alive," says Irenaeus; and man is fully alive only when united to God. Sin fragments; grace integrates. Reason, desire, imagination—these are not annihilated by union but healed, clarified, and harmonised. In unconfused communion, man becomes more human, not less. To say "God lives in me" is not to dissolve into an oceanic totality but to awaken into relationship. Love requires otherness; only distinct beings can be one in charity. The saint does not lose his face; he becomes a face turned wholly toward the Face.

Chalcedon thus remains a permanent rule of discernment against two recurring errors. One is monophysite mysticism, imagining the human vanishing into the divine like a drop into the sea—beautiful and deadly. The other is Nestorian moralism, keeping God and man at such arm's length that grace becomes mere external favour—law without life. Catholic theosis avoids both by following Christ's own pattern: unconfused, unchangeable, indivisible, inseparable. The creature remains creature, yet participates truly in the divine life. The union is asymmetrical—God always the giver, man always the receiver—yet the gift is so total that the receiver glows with the giver's glory.

Beatitude confirms this asymmetry as splendour rather than lack. Heaven does not collapse the distinction between Creator and creation; it transfigures it into intimacy. The saints behold God "face to face," but that vision is given by the "light of glory," an infused capacity that elevates the intellect without changing what the intellect is. The blessed see God as He is, yet not as God sees Himself. They participate without possessing, comprehend without circumscribing. The distance that remains is not alienation but wonder—the everlasting humility of the creature before infinite beauty. The measure of our joy is precisely that God forever surpasses us.

Theology should take its posture from that humility. To speak rightly of deification is to bow before both poles of the mystery: divine prodigality and creaturely limitation. The mystic knows the fusion of love; the theologian guards the distinctions that keep love truthful. They serve one truth together. Where experience blurs, doctrine clarifies; where doctrine risks chilling, experience rekindles. Chalcedon keeps the flame from becoming a wildfire or a flicker: a bridge of four adverbs spanning the abyss of speculation. Like Christ's humanity, the soul is deified not by confusion but by communion.

Nature itself protests when we try to erase this order. The Fathers reached for metaphors because creation is already a commentary on the Creator. Light passes through air without destroying it; fire penetrates iron without changing its essence; the soul fills the body without mixing substances. Each image illustrates participation without fusion. The creature becomes luminous by proximity to the Source. Paradoxically, the more transparent it becomes, the more the distinction shines. Holiness is not the extinction of difference but its sanctification—the human reflecting God according to its own contour. The saint is a unique syllable in the one Word the Father speaks.

Individuality therefore endures even in total union. The person does not dissolve into the universal; he becomes the window through which universality shines. As Christ's humanity remains distinct yet perfectly expressive of divinity, so the believer's humanity remains distinct yet perfectly expressive of grace. The goal is not fusion but correspondence—the created echo answering the uncreated call. The Cappadocians loved the image: the human being becomes flame, yet the flame retains the form of the wick that bears it. Union shapes without erasing, fills without flattening, elevates without engulfing.

This is not a limit laid upon love but its very grammar. Were the creature absorbed into God, love would evaporate into sameness. True communion requires difference held in unity. The eternal life promised by the Gospel is not the loss of identity but its glorification. Heaven will be infinitely personal precisely because it is perfectly communal. The unconfused union of God and man in Christ is the archetype of that harmony—the law by which every saint lives and every world coheres. The Trinity itself, the everlasting feast of distinction-in-communion, is the source from which this law flows.

At the heart of this doctrine there is consolation. If the divine essence remains beyond participation, it remains inexhaustible. The soul will never cease to grow into God because God will never cease to exceed it. The Chalcedonian boundaries are not walls but horizons. They ensure that eternity will be dynamic—an endless approach, a perpetual deepening. The creature will always be creature, and thus always surprised by joy. The unconfused union guarantees that wonder is eternal.

The same logic safeguards the material world from contempt. If divinization concerned only the soul, creation would be left behind. But the Word became flesh, and the entire physical order is invited into glory. The Eucharistic transformation of bread and wine shows that matter can be the vessel of Presence without ceasing to be matter. Chalcedon's rhythm reverberates cosmically: unconfused, unchangeable, indivisible, inseparable. The earth will be renewed, not replaced. Deification thus affirms creation's goodness against every dualism. The Creator remains transcendent, yet His creation becomes the very field of His self-gift.

To contemplate this is to see why dogmatic precision is an act of charity. The clearer the boundaries, the safer the surrender. The believer who knows where the lines run can give himself without fear. The theologian who traces those lines is not limiting mystery but making wonder possible. Love needs truth as flame needs air: without clarity, it suffocates. The Chalcedonian adverbs are not fences around God but the open meadow where divine and human meet safely. Distinction does not cool love; it preserves it from counterfeit.

To dwell within these boundaries is to discover freedom inside mystery. One can adore only what is other, and unite only with what remains distinct. The adverbs of Chalcedon are thus not a cage for devotion but its horizon—an open space in which finite love may touch the Infinite without fear. Theology kneels here; reason yields not to muteness but to doxology. In that reverent clarity the soul learns what it was made for—communion that never collapses into sameness, wonder that never ends.

The Incarnation remains the perpetual scandal and consolation of this vision. God did not rescue from a distance; He stooped into the story. He assumed not an idea of humanity but the whole weight of our condition—time, hunger, weariness, suffering, death—so that our nature, joined to His Person, could be lifted beyond its wound. Because He took a concrete human nature, deification has a human texture; grace learns to move in a human gait. Every sacrament, every virtue, every prayer participates in this human-shaped traffic of grace. The path to union is not a vaporous ascent but a life lived in the footsteps of the God-man.

And so the Church insists not only on what Christ is but on how He is what He is for us. He is one and the same Son: what is visible in Him passes into the mysteries; what He did in His historical body, He continues in His mystical body. The Chalcedonian law is not dusty council-chatter; it is the living rail along which the current of grace runs. If the rail bends into confusion, the power escapes into fantasy; if the rail breaks into dualism, the current never reaches us. Held straight, it carries the fire of God into human clay.

If we press still further into the Chalcedonian adverbs, each one opens a facet of theosis. Unconfusedly names the refusal of fusion: the human does not melt into the divine like wax near a flame. In the spiritual life this means that divine consolations, illuminations, and gifts never override the creature's faculties as though grace were a trance. The saint's mind is bright and disciplined; the will is decisive and free; the affections are spacious and ordered. To be deified is not to be hypnotised by glory but to be clarified by it. The more God indwells, the more alert the faculties become, the more personal history is transfigured rather than erased. Ecstasy here is not oblivion; it is a heightening of attention, a simple and supple attunement to the Beloved.

Unchangeably guards the integrity of both natures: neither the divine becomes temporal and passible by essence, nor does the human cease to be a rational, bodily nature. Applied to the believer's union, this means grace elevates without mutating the kind of thing we are. The human remains human—bodily, historical, linguistic—yet the human is made radiant. Virtue, then, is not a superpower foreign to humanity; it is humanity healed and heightened. Chastity is not a strange angelic transplant; it is human love ordered to truth. Courage is not cold iron in the soul; it is love steady in danger. Hope is not daydreaming; it is human desire stretched upon the promises of God until it sings in tune.

Indivisibly names the unity of the one Person. What the Son does, the Son does as one Christ—no split agent, no divided subject. Extended to us, indivisible union means the spiritual life must not be a tug-of-war between two selves—a pious persona and a "real" self hidden in the wings. The graced person becomes integrated: work, prayer, friendship, suffering, laughter, silence all belong to one life offered to God. The duplicities of sin—mask versus face, performance versus heart—are healed. The saint does not have a religious compartment; he has a consecrated existence. His personality is not erased; it is gathered.

Inseparably names the permanence of union. In Christ the natures do not ever separate; in the graced there is no pendulum between divine presence and abandonment as if God came and went. There are seasons of felt consolation and desert, but grace abides unless expelled by mortal sin. The light remains even under cloud. In the dark night the soul learns a deeper adverb—faithfully. When God seems absent, one clings to the Chalcedonian promise that He is nearer than one's own breath. The union is not a mood but a covenant sealed in Christ's blood.

These adverbs stabilize the entire economy of salvation. Creation, covenant, Incarnation, Paschal mystery, Pentecost—each phase bears the same signature: God draws near in such a way that transcendence is displayed, not diluted. The burning bush blazes and does not burn up; Sinai trembles yet stands; the Virgin conceives without loss; the tomb is emptied, not violated; bread becomes Body while appearances remain. Everywhere: unconfused, unchangeable, indivisible, inseparable. The world is transfigured by this litany. The sacraments are not magic because they are personal; they are not merely personal because they are divine. God gives Himself in signs that do not deceive and in powers that do not overwhelm.

The pastoral fruit of this doctrine is immense. The person thirsting for holiness need not fear that God's nearness will erase the very self God commands to love Him. The person afraid of fanaticism need not flatten faith into mere ethics. Chalcedon protects against dissolution and against dilution. The mystic can burn without burning out; the thinker can reason without freezing. The parish priest can preach without turning the altar into a lecture, and the scholar can teach without turning the altar into a stage. Doctrine guards devotion so that devotion remains fire and not smoke.

The anthropology implicit in Chalcedon is equally bracing. Human nature is not a mistake waiting for correction; it is a wounded splendour awaiting healing. The senses are not enemies to be suffocated but doors to be sanctified. The body is not ballast; it is a temple. Language is not prison; it is sacrament. History is not rubble; it is the quarry from which living stones are carved. Grace does not levy war on any of these; it enters them, orders them, and makes them shine. The ascetical project therefore is not disdain for the human, but love for it under the surgeon's light. Fasting honours the body by refusing to let appetite be its master. Silence honours language by teaching it to mean what it says. Solitude honours community by freeing it from neediness. Everything is restored to order by a charity that cherishes the creature as the field of divine indwelling.

The theology of prayer stands on the same foundation. If union is personal and not impersonal, prayer is not technique. It is presence received and returned. One does not hack the divine; one consents to be held. The Jesus Prayer, lectio divina, the Divine Liturgy, silent adoration—each is a different way the human heart lets the Chalcedonian grace pass through it. Repetition is not incantation; it is fidelity. Silence is not emptiness; it is reverent space for the uncreated Word. Tears are not failure; they are the thawing of what grace warms.

Chalcedon also rescues theology from rivalry with contemplation. The intellect is not an intruder in holy ground; it is the lamp one brings into the sanctuary. Because the union is unconfused and unchangeable, thought can say true things about mystery without pretending to exhaust it. In an age tempted by either anti-intellectual piety or disenchanted rationalism, the Church's ancient grammar permits a third way: adoration with articulation. Theology bends the knee and then speaks; contemplation gazes and then sings.

Even suffering is transfigured by this pattern. In Christ, divinity does not mutate into weakness; humanity becomes the instrument of omnipotent love. The Cross is not divine failure dressed up; it is human flesh at full pitch of obedience, a free act made luminous by the Person who performs it. When suffering enters the graced life, it is not an interruption of theosis but an intensification. The wounds do not become our identity; they become the windows of it. The adverbs again: unconfused—pain is not good, but love within pain is divine; unchangeable—human fragility remains human; indivisible—the whole person suffers and offers; inseparable—God does not depart when the night deepens. Thus martyrdom, illness, injustice, and quiet daily crosses become the liturgy where union ripens.

The chalice of culture must be lifted to this altar as well. A Chalcedonian imagination refuses both secularism's exile of God from the world and sacralism's erasure of creaturely autonomy. The arts are not decorations but revelations of form; politics is not salvation but service; law is not the Kingdom but can be its guardian; scholarship is not the Temple but can be its porch. Christian culture at its best is a patient practice of unconfused fidelity—receiving what is human on its own terms while letting grace permeate it without crushing it. This is why the Church baptises languages, not abolishes them; heals customs, not homogenises them; elevates peoples, not erases them. Catholicity is Chalcedon writ large across history.

When the mind tires, the Liturgy finishes our sentences. There we see the adverbs enacted. The Priest invokes the Spirit "upon us and upon these gifts." The people, still themselves, become what they receive. The Bread, unchanged in appearance, is indivisibly Christ. The assembly, inseparably joined, sings with angels without confusion, for heaven and earth meet without collision. The faithful go forth still ordinary, yet charged with a splendour that will not fit inside their errands. The grammar of the altar becomes the grammar of life.

In the end, all language bows before the same joy: that the God who is "beyond all being" has made Himself near without ceasing to be beyond; that the creature who is dust has been lifted without ceasing to be dust; that love has devised a union that does not cancel difference but makes it fruitful. The four adverbs were coined for Christ; He lends them to His saints. They are the quiet music under every sacrament, every conversion, every answered prayer, every holy death.

Stand, then, within their horizon. Let them steady the steps of your desire. Let them keep your zeal from dissolving into blur, and your caution from calcifying into distance. Let them school your imagination until you can recognise true fire from mere flare. And when at last you see Him, when the Light of Glory lifts the lid from your vision, you will discover that the very distinction which now humbles you is the river of your joy.

For you will be yourself, and you will be in Him, and you will be in Him as yourself—unconfused, unchangeable, indivisible, inseparable—forever.

Grace and Personhood

If the distinction of natures shows how union is possible, grace shows how it becomes personal. Grace is not an impersonal substance poured into the soul, nor a moral assistance offered from afar. It is the personal self-gift of God—uncreated Love bending low, shaping a creature capable of friendship with Himself. Every word the Church has ever spoken about grace is an attempt to protect this paradox: what is divine becomes shareable without ceasing to be divine, and what is human receives divinity without ceasing to be human.

The Catechism calls sanctifying grace a "habitual gift," meaning not a passing sentiment but a stable principle of life, a new form given to the soul, making it "a partaker of the divine nature" (CCC 1999–2000). Habitual, because it abides; gift, because it originates wholly from God. The term "habit" does not mean routine, but rather a settled disposition—something woven into the fabric of the person until it becomes second nature. Grace, then, is the soul's new architecture. It is not an addition to our being; it is our being opened to God.

Thomas Aquinas, patient architect of theological clarity, names grace *a created participation in the divine nature* (ST I-II, q.110, a.2). Created, so that the gulf between Creator and creature is not confused; participatory, so that the gulf is bridged. Grace is the creature's way of receiving God without ceasing to be creature. It is not the divine essence transferred, but the divine life communicated analogically. It gives us not God's whatness, but His likeness. Aquinas explains that just as light modifies the air without making it luminous by essence, so grace makes the soul truly radiant, though the light it carries remains uncreated.

The East expressed this in the language of energies. Gregory Palamas distinguishes between the essence of God, which forever transcends every created intellect, and the energies of God—His operations, presence, and radiance—which truly deify. The soul does not become God's essence but becomes aflame with His activity, as iron placed in the forge glows with fire without losing its ironness. Palamas and Aquinas meet on this summit: God remains infinitely beyond and yet is intimately within. The participation is real, not metaphorical, yet ordered by distinction. The line between Creator and creature is not a wall but a horizon—the nearer one approaches, the more it recedes in wonder.

Grace, then, is the mode of divine indwelling. The Spirit does not hover abstractly above the soul but inhabits it as gift, transforming its powers from within. The intellect is illuminated, not supplanted; the will is strengthened, not coerced; the emotions are healed, not erased. "Grace does not destroy nature but perfects it," Aquinas writes (ST I, q.1, a.8 ad 2), meaning that divinization makes man more human, not less. God's action is not competitive with human freedom; it is its cause and fulfillment. When grace enters, nature is not discarded but tuned.

This tuning has moral consequence. Sin is disharmony—the faculties at war, the will bent inward, the intellect clouded. Grace restores consonance. It gives rhythm where chaos reigned. The human person begins to act according to its deepest structure, no longer as a fractured self but as a symphony directed toward the Good. To live in grace is not to perform under divine surveillance but to breathe with divine breath. When the Spirit dwells within, obedience ceases to be servitude and becomes resonance.

Grace thus personalizes. It does not reduce humanity to an anonymous vessel of divine influence; it reveals the irreducible uniqueness of each person. The goal of theosis is not the loss of individuality but its transfiguration. The divine fire finds a new hue in every soul it enters. "The glory of God is man fully alive," wrote Irenaeus, and man is fully alive only when he becomes transparent to the life of God. Every saint is a singular articulation of the same divine melody—one light, many colors, one fire, many flames.

This personal character of grace flows directly from its Trinitarian source. The Father gives, the Son mediates, and the Spirit indwells. The

Spirit, says Augustine, is the *vinculum caritatis*, the "bond of love" between Father and Son, and thus the bond by which the creature is drawn into that same communion. The Spirit is not a distant power but the nearness of God as love itself. To receive grace is therefore to be drawn into relationship, not merely to be elevated in essence. Theosis is not chemistry; it is communion.

The personal nature of grace also means that it requires freedom. Love cannot be infused by force. Grace precedes and enables human response, but it does not annihilate it. Divine and human wills move together, as dancer and music, each distinct yet inseparable. This is what the Fathers called *synergeia*: "Work out your own salvation with fear and trembling," says Paul, "for it is God who works in you, both to will and to work for his good pleasure" (Phil 2:12–13). The paradox holds: man acts because God acts within him, and God acts within him so that man may freely act. The cooperation of grace and freedom is not a compromise between two powers but the marriage of two freedoms—one uncreated, one created—meeting in the field of love.

In this synergy, personhood matures. The ego—fragmented, self-enclosed, anxious—yields to the person, which is self-gift in relation. The ego says "mine"; the person says "thine." The ego clings to control; the person consents to communion. Grace slowly dismantles self-possession, not to destroy selfhood but to liberate it into love. The more the soul yields to God, the more distinct it becomes, for the measure of distinctness is not isolation but depth of communion.

The image of a crystal clarifies the point. The crystal remains what it is, but when sunlight passes through, it ceases to be opaque. Its form becomes a medium of radiance. In the same way, the graced soul is not annihilated but illumined. The form of its being remains intact; what changes is its transparency. Personality is not consumed by the divine; it is completed by it. In heaven, individuality is not an obstacle to union but its instrument.

To say that grace perfects nature is therefore to say that grace preserves history. It redeems time rather than erasing it. Every wound endured, every capacity honed, every particular contour of one's life becomes part of the vessel through which divine light is refracted. The person God deifies is the same person who once sinned, wept, and hoped. Grace does not overwrite the story; it glorifies it. The scars remain, but they shine.

Such teaching guards against two perennial distortions. The first is a mechanical view of grace—as if God's action operated independently of human interiority, moving the soul like a puppet. The second is the opposite: a sentimental humanism that turns grace into moral uplift, reducing it to the psychology of improvement. The truth lies between and beyond both: grace is God acting *within* the creature as its new principle of life, elevating nature from the inside out. It is neither external pressure nor internal sentiment. It is presence—personal, active, transforming.

Grace therefore defines personhood not by autonomy but by communion. Modern culture imagines personhood as self-definition, the will inventing itself without reference to the Creator. Christianity reveals the opposite: personhood is received, not constructed. It is gift before it is project. The more a human being receives from God, the more truly personal he becomes. Grace does not flatten difference but deepens it; the more God dwells in a person, the more uniquely that person expresses God. Each saint becomes a word in the eternal dialogue between God and creation, an unrepeatable phrase in the one divine sentence of love.

To live in grace is thus to become articulate in God's language. Prayer, virtue, and contemplation are not rules imposed from outside but the gradual learning of divine grammar. As the Spirit shapes the soul, one begins to speak fluently in charity, to think with the mind of Christ, to desire with His heart. Grace makes theology autobiographical. Doctrine becomes experience. The truth once held in creed becomes the pulse of life itself.

This transformation, however, is not sentimental ease but cruciform discipline. Grace is costly because it is real. It reaches into the marrow of the will and reorders desire. To be deified is to be refined. Every selfish impulse, every false attachment, every illusion of control must pass through fire. Yet that fire is the same light by which God reveals

Himself. What burns is what cannot love; what remains is love itself. The soul that consents to this purification discovers that the command "Be perfect" is not a demand for flawlessness but an invitation to wholeness—the wholeness that comes from grace restoring nature to its proper orbit around God.

In this sense, grace and personhood are not parallel doctrines but two ways of describing the same mystery: God giving Himself so that man might become himself in God. The more grace penetrates, the more personhood flowers; the more personhood matures, the more grace becomes visible. Nature and grace are not two substances glued together but one life breathing in two registers—the divine and the human—unconfused, unchangeable, indivisible, inseparable.

The person deified by grace does not dissolve into a formless consciousness of the divine. The more one is filled with God, the more one becomes distinct. Love sharpens identity; only indifference blurs it. In Trinitarian life itself, the Persons are not masks of a single self but infinite relations of distinction-in-communion. The Father is not the Son; the Son is not the Spirit. Yet their otherness is precisely what allows their unity to be total. When human beings are drawn into that life, they do not lose their edges—they are refined into relation.

Here lies the difference between personality and personhood. Personality, in modern speech, means a bundle of temperaments and tastes; personhood, in Christian metaphysics, means hypostasis—an irreducible center of existence that can say "I" in answer to God's "Thou." Grace matures the "I" into dialogue. It rescues self-awareness from self-enclosure. To be sanctified is to stand unveiled before the Other, not dissolved in the Other. In the language of the Fathers, it is to become *prosopon*: a face turned toward the Face.

This is why deification can never be anonymous. The saints are not absorbed sparks disappearing into the flame; they are lamps that keep burning with their own steady colors. "The soul's growth in God is endless," writes Gregory of Nyssa, "for the one who ascends never ceases to go from beginning to beginning." The eternal life of heaven is not stasis but an unending expansion of personhood. To participate in infinite love is to be eternally individuated by it. Each encounter with God opens new depth in the self; each depth is a new way of saying "yes."

This endlessness of growth means that grace is not a single event but a perpetual motion. It is not a ladder climbed once and left behind, but a rhythm of ascent that continues even in glory. The distinction between Creator and creature guarantees that communion will never be exhausted. Beatitude is not the end of movement but its transfiguration into rest that is also journey. The will no longer fluctuates between choices, yet it perpetually expands in its capacity to love. The intellect no longer doubts, yet it forever discovers. Eternity will be dynamic because grace is inexhaustible.

Such vision corrects both spiritual complacency and fear. If grace is participation in the divine life, it can never be measured by moral accounting. We do not accumulate grace as coins; we deepen in it as a living current. Its measure is not quantity but transparency. The soul advances not by acquiring new favors but by shedding resistance. Holiness is not accumulation but simplification. The pure of heart are not those who have achieved much but those who no longer obstruct the light that is already given.

Yet this divine life remains creaturely. We are not transformed into self-sufficient gods, but into sons and daughters whose very glory is dependence. The logic of personhood in grace is filial. "You have received the Spirit of adoption, crying, Abba, Father" (Rom 8:15). Grace confers not autonomy but sonship—the freedom of those who know they are loved. This filial mode of being replaces the anxious self-definition of fallen humanity. The deified person no longer strives to justify his existence; he receives it perpetually from the Giver. Dependence becomes dignity. The creature's very contingency turns into praise.

This filial relation defines freedom itself. Modernity treats freedom as the power to choose; grace reveals it as the power to love. Choice without orientation is impotence; only love gives direction. Grace therefore interiorizes law. What was once external command becomes spontaneous delight. "Where the Spirit of the Lord is, there is freedom" (2 Cor 3:17)—freedom not from order, but within it; not from truth, but toward it. The soul liberated by grace obeys as a musician obeys melody.

In this transformation, reason too is healed. The intellect purified by grace ceases to treat God as an object of scrutiny and learns to know by participation. Faith becomes not merely assent to propositions but connaturality with divine things—a knowing born of love. Thomas Aquinas calls this the "light of glory" even in its beginning form: a new faculty, a higher sense, making the mind proportionate to what it contemplates. The mystics call it *seeing with the heart*. In both cases, knowledge and love converge until to know God is to love Him, and to love Him is to know.

The integration of intellect and will in grace is mirrored in the integration of body and soul. Theosis is not disembodied ascent. Grace seeks to divinize the whole human being. The body becomes temple, the senses instruments of contemplation. When the Eucharist enters the body, it sanctifies matter from within. Every heartbeat is invited into liturgy. As the soul is filled with divine life, even gesture and gaze become sacraments of presence. Holiness is not escape from the physical; it is its illumination.

This embodied grace grounds Christian ethics. Virtue is not self-generated heroism but grace translated into habit. The theological virtues—faith, hope, charity—are the interior architecture of the deified life. Through them the soul moves with divine rhythm: faith seeing the invisible, hope tasting the future, charity already living the divine now. To act virtuously is to cooperate with grace until it becomes second nature, so that spontaneity and sanctity coincide. The saint is not one who suppresses himself to obey God but one who has become so attuned that God's will feels like his own deepest pulse.

Because grace personalizes, it also differentiates. No two saints are the same because no two acts of divine love are redundant. In the communion of saints, individuality is not leveled but orchestrated. Heaven's unity is symphonic, not monotonous—"many mansions," as Christ promised (Jn 14:2), each echoing a unique timbre of divine beauty. The closer souls draw to God, the more distinct their harmonies become, for divine love multiplies rather than homogenizes. Every human face, purified of sin's distortion, will mirror one unrepeatable aspect of the Infinite. The God who is one creates difference as the space where unity can be love.

This theological anthropology rescues both freedom and intimacy from their counterfeits. Pantheism collapses distinction into undifferentiated being; individualism isolates it into loneliness. Grace holds the middle, or rather the summit: communion without confusion. To be saved is not to disappear into the Absolute, nor to guard a private self against God's encroachment, but to stand face to face, the finite enraptured yet intact before the Infinite. The intimacy of grace presupposes the distinction of persons, just as the unity of the Trinity presupposes the distinction of Father, Son, and Spirit.

Such vision also purifies mysticism. The Christian mystic does not lose consciousness in the One; he awakens within communion. The highest contemplation is not fusion but recognition: "I am my beloved's and my beloved is mine" (Song 6:3). Ecstasy—literally *standing outside oneself*—is not self-erasure but self-offering. In the experience of divine union, the soul discovers itself precisely as gift. The boundaries of the self become translucent, not destroyed; identity becomes relational, not dissolved. The measure of mystical depth is not absorption but the intensity of love's dialogue.

Grace therefore secures the permanence of personal history even in glory. The individuality forged in time is not sloughed off at death; it is consummated. The transfigured saints remain who they were—Peter, Paul, Mary, Thérèse—yet filled with light. Their earthly particularities become eternal symbols: the fisherman still casts nets, the mother still intercedes, the virgin still sings. The wounds of their stories are not erased but glorified. As Christ's risen body bore the scars of the nails, so every redeemed life will carry its story as the medium of its praise. Nothing truly human is discarded; everything is redeemed.

This permanence of personhood has cosmic consequence. If grace deifies without abolishing individuality, then the diversity of creation itself is destined not for dissolution but glorification. Every creature, according to its measure, will manifest divine beauty without losing its created nature. The stars will not cease to shine, nor the trees to root, but all will do so transfigured—matter radiant with spirit, spirit embodied in light. The pattern of grace in the soul mirrors the pattern of glory in the cosmos: communion that preserves form, unity that magnifies distinction.

Ultimately, grace reveals that the very being of God is relational. The doctrine of the Trinity is not an appendix to theosis; it is its foundation. To become divine by grace is to be drawn into that eternal exchange where each Person is gift to the other. Human deification is therefore not self-possession but self-donation. The more the soul participates in God, the more it becomes love in act—love that is always going out, always returning, always new. In this eternal motion of giving and receiving, personhood finds its rest.

Grace, then, is not an ornament of salvation but its substance. It is the divine life poured into created form, shaping intellect, will, and body into instruments of communion. It restores nature to its purpose and freedom to its truth. It reveals that individuality is not the enemy of unity but its condition. It assures that every "I" may endure forever in the gaze of the eternal "Thou." To speak of grace is to speak of God sharing His own mode of existence—personal, relational, inexhaustibly loving—with those who were nothing and are now called sons and daughters.

The soul that knows this begins to see the world differently. Every person encountered is potentially luminous; every life is capable of becoming fire. The smallest act of charity becomes a spark of divine energy working through human clay. And in those moments when grace is felt least—when prayer is dry and love costly—the truth remains unchanged: God's own life courses silently within, shaping the person into His likeness. What began in baptism as seed will end in glory as flame.

To stand in that fire without fear is the work of grace. To remain distinct within it is the mark of personhood fulfilled. The two together form the heart of Christian hope: that God's gift will make us radiant without erasure, eternal without uniformity, perfect without loss. The human person, purified of sin yet intact in freedom, will forever be the mirror through which the infinite Love beholds His own reflection. And in that reflection, the creature will finally know itself—not as rival to God, nor as shadow—but as His living image, alive with the light it receives.

Refuting Pantheism and Gnostic Misreadings

Every age that rediscovers the grandeur of theosis must also relearn its boundaries. To say that man is destined for divine life is daring language, and the Church has always known how easily it can be twisted into its opposite. When the Fathers proclaimed that "God became man so that man might become god," pagan ears often heard a familiar echo of their own cosmologies: the soul dissolving back into the Absolute, individuality swallowed by the universal. Against that timeless instinct for fusion, the Church drew a bright line in the sand: the Creator is not the creature, and the creature never ceases to be creature even when suffused with divine fire.

Pantheism begins as reverence and ends as confusion. It starts with the intuition that all things live from the One, but forgets that the One is not the sum of things. Scripture opens by smashing that illusion: "In the beginning God created the heavens and the earth." Creation is not born from divine substance but called from nothing by divine will. Athanasius pressed the point against the Neoplatonists of his day, writing that the world "was not made from the essence of God, but was established by His Word." The very fact that creation can fall, can turn from its Maker, is proof that it is other than He. If the world were divine, evil could not exist. The possibility of sin reveals the distance love must cross.

Augustine wrestled with this same temptation after his years among the Manichees and Platonists. "I found You above my soul," he confesses, "and I found that I was inferior to You because You made me." That final phrase—*because You made me*—is the hinge of all Christian metaphysics. It secures both reverence and intimacy: God is higher than the highest and nearer than the innermost. The Creator sustains all things by His presence, yet He is not identical with them. He is through all things, but not confused with any of them. In that paradox lies the grammar of deification: presence without identity, union without absorption.

Thomas Aquinas would later give this mystery its scholastic clarity. God is *ipsum esse subsistens*, the sheer act of being itself; creatures are participations in that act, dependent, finite, contingent. The world glows with divine radiance precisely because it is derivative. Were it identical with God, it would cease to shine, as light vanishes when there is no distinction between lamp and flame. Grace, too, follows this rhythm. It does not pour the divine essence into the soul but infuses a created participation in that essence—God's own life adapted to creaturely measure. What Christ is by nature, the soul becomes by grace, but always in a mode of reception.

Pantheism recoils from this humility. It wants immediacy without mediation, divinity without dependence. It speaks of merging into the divine, as if the highest good were to lose the capacity to say *Thou*. Yet love requires otherness. To adore is to face another, not to collapse into sameness. The Trinity itself teaches this: the Father is not the Son, nor the Son the Spirit, yet Their unity is perfect. Distinction is not the enemy of communion; it is its foundation. So too with Creator and creation: difference is the space where love becomes possible.

The Catechism summarizes this ancient line in a single, firm sentence: "God is infinitely greater than all His works" (§300). That infinitude does not drive Him away from the world; it makes His nearness possible. "In Him we live and move and have our being," says Paul, but that immanence is the immanence of the sustaining cause, not of shared substance. The world is a mirror, not a fragment, of God's being. Its beauty speaks of Him because it is not He.

The Church's rejection of pantheism, then, is not fear of mysticism but protection of mystery. It keeps wonder alive. If all things were God, wonder would die, for nothing would be other than the self. To kneel before the Creator requires the knowledge that He is not our reflection. The psalmist sings, "It is He that hath made us, and not we ourselves." The creature's dependence is not humiliation but glory—the freedom of being loved into existence.

This same logic underlies the sacramental vision of the world. Creation is holy not because it is divine, but because it is transparent to divinity. The heavens declare the glory of God precisely by not being God. Francis of Assisi called the sun "brother" and the moon "sister" because he recognized their difference as kinship, not identity. Each creature becomes sacrament, a visible sign of invisible grace. Pantheism destroys sacramentality by abolishing the distinction on which it depends; it leaves us with an undifferentiated godstuff incapable of revealing anything.

The Incarnation confirms once more that God enters His creation without confusion. "In Him the whole fullness of deity dwells bodily," writes Paul, yet Christ remains true man. The four adverbs of Chalcedon—unconfused, unchangeable, indivisible, inseparable—are the boundary stones of the cosmos. They describe not only the unity of the natures in Christ but the pattern by which all creation participates in God. Grace unites without mixing, perfects without replacing. The fire fills the iron, and the iron glows while remaining iron.

This image, beloved of Athanasius and later of Maximus the Confessor, captures the Catholic balance more vividly than any syllogism. The creature does not become divine essence; it becomes incandescent by contact. Maximus calls this the "interpenetration without confusion," the dance of Creator and creation in which each retains its nature while sharing its energies. His language of *perichoresis*—mutual indwelling became the Church's vocabulary for both Trinity and deification. Aquinas, using another idiom, says the same: "Grace does not destroy nature but perfects it." East and West breathe together here.

Pantheism, by contrast, refuses to breathe. It inhales unity and never exhales difference. Its peace is suffocation. It ends in the tragic irony of a spirituality without a subject—a devotion with no one left to pray. The Christian mystic, by contrast, stands upright before the burning bush: close enough to be aflame, distant enough to worship. The God who says "I AM" invites the creature to answer "I am Thine."

Thus, every authentic experience of theosis must carry within it the Chalcedonian refrain. To lose that rhythm is to slide into either absorption or alienation. The unconfused union of God and man in Christ is the pattern for the unconfused communion of Creator and creation. The iron glows; the fire delights; and love rejoices in the space between them.

If pantheism dissolves the boundary between God and creation, Gnosticism tears it apart. It is the opposite error, yet the twin of the first, for both recoil from the scandal of incarnation. The pantheist cannot accept distinction; the Gnostic cannot endure proximity. One abolishes difference, the other despises it. Against both, the Church holds up the crucified flesh of God as revelation's center: the Infinite made finite without ceasing to be Infinite, the divine life beating within mortal veins.

In the second century, St Irenaeus saw clearly that the Gnostic systems—those intricate genealogies of aeons and secret salvations—were not harmless speculations but assaults on the goodness of creation. "If the flesh is not saved," he wrote, "then the Lord has not redeemed us by His blood." Salvation for Irenaeus is never escape from the world but the world's transfiguration in Christ. Matter is not a prison to be shed but the theater of redemption. The same hand that formed Adam from dust now heals that dust by becoming it.

This conviction echoes through every age of Catholic theology. The human body is not a temporary costume but the permanent language of personhood. "The Word became flesh and dwelt among us" is not a metaphor for divine empathy; it is the metaphysics of grace. God has chosen matter as the medium of union. From the waters of baptism to the bread of the Eucharist, He communicates Himself through what He has made. The very sacraments that scandalize the Gnostic are the triumph of divine humility: touch, taste, and time become bearers of eternity.

Maximus the Confessor deepens this mystery by describing Christ as the cosmic mediator who unites all levels of creation—intelligible and sensible, angelic and material—within Himself. The Incarnation, he says, is the "recapitulation of all things in heaven and on earth." This is not an abstract reconciliation but a physical one. Every atom of creation finds its final form in the flesh of the Word. For Maximus, the deified world does not cease to be material; it becomes the hymn of God's glory.

Thomas Aquinas, centuries later, would articulate the same realism in a different idiom: "The sacraments are necessary for salvation because they apply the Incarnation to us." What Christ assumed, He sanctified; what He did not assume, He did not heal. Hence matter becomes the very instrument of grace. The Gnostic imagination, which despises matter, must also despise the sacraments, for they make salvation tangible. The Catholic imagination, by contrast, rejoices that the world is full of God's footprints.

The Second Vatican Council recovered this vision for the modern world. *Gaudium et Spes* declares that "the truth is that only in the mystery of the Incarnate Word does the mystery of man take on light." Human life, in all its corporeality and frailty, is the chosen arena of divine self-disclosure. The body is not an obstacle to grace but its dwelling. The resurrection of the dead will not undo the body; it will crown it.

Gnosticism, ancient or modern, cannot bear this. Its spirituality is always elitist—reserved for the few who possess hidden knowledge or self-generated enlightenment. It whispers that truth lies within, accessible through private awakening. But revelation, by its nature, is public. It is shouted from pulpits, inscribed in flesh, entrusted to the Church. The highest "knowledge" is not secret doctrine but love. "He who loves God," says Clement of Alexandria, "is the true Gnostic." Theosis is measured not by esoteric understanding but by participation in divine charity.

For that reason, Christianity will always scandalize the world that worships technique and self-creation. The Gospel's wisdom is not a map to escape the body but a path to transfigure it. To fast, to serve, to forgive, to receive the Eucharist—these are acts of the new creation. They reveal that matter itself can become transparent to Spirit. The Gnostic's ladder of ascent is replaced by a table of communion. The divine descent accomplishes what human climbing could never achieve.

The crucifixion stands as the final judgment on every attempt to spiritualize salvation. Here is God nailed to wood, His divinity not diminished but displayed in surrender. Here the body that seemed weakest becomes the world's axis of glory. The resurrection that follows is not escape but fulfillment—the body radiant with Spirit, history opened into eternity. In that luminous flesh, every created thing finds hope.

Thus, theosis cannot mean the flight of the soul into abstraction. It means the restoration of the whole person—body, soul, and spirit—in the embrace of the Trinity. It is not an ascent out of the world but the descent of God into the world, drawing it upward from within. The creature remains creature, yet becomes what it was meant to be: the living icon of the divine. Pantheism destroys this icon by erasing its lines; Gnosticism defaces it by despising its material. Only the Incarnation restores it to radiance.

In the end, the Church's defense against both errors is the same: the confession that "Jesus Christ has come in the flesh." That sentence, says John, is the test of every spirit. The God who became visible in a human body now makes Himself visible in the Church, in the saints, in the sacraments, and one day in the renewed creation. The divine fire does not consume the world but refines it until all things glow with the glory of God.

To be deified, then, is not to dissolve into the universe or to flee from it, but to love it with God's own love—to see creation as the chalice through which the Creator gives Himself. The iron remains iron, the fire remains fire, and together they shine.

The mystery of Christ does not end with His body; it radiates outward into the whole creation that shares that body's substance. "The Word became flesh," wrote John, and flesh means more than muscle and bone. It is the entire material order taken up into divine purpose. In Christ, the world itself becomes sacrament. The redemption He wrought in blood touches every element, every creature, every atom of dust that answered the Father's "let there be." The final horizon of theosis is therefore not merely personal union but cosmic transfiguration.

Paul glimpsed this when he wrote that "creation itself will be set free from its bondage to decay and obtain the glorious liberty of the children of God." The redemption of the sons entails the redemption of the cosmos, because the two belong to one another. Humanity is priest of creation, the voice through which matter offers praise. When man fell, the hymn faltered; when the Word became man, the music began again. The Incarnation is not an interruption in nature but its fulfillment. What had been mute begins to speak.

Maximus the Confessor calls this the *anakephalaiosis*—the recapitulation of all things in Christ. He sees in the Word made flesh the reunion of all the fragmented oppositions that define existence: heaven and earth, intelligible and sensible, eternal and temporal. In the theandric Christ, these divisions are not erased but harmonized. Each sphere finds its proper relation to the others. The Word does not dissolve creation into Himself; He binds it into symphony. The saints, transfigured in Him, become participants in that cosmic harmony, microcosms that echo the order of the whole.

Aquinas describes the same destiny in another key. In the *Summa contra Gentiles* he teaches that the end of creation is the return of all things to God, not by circular necessity but by love's attraction. Every creature is drawn toward its source according to its measure; rational beings return consciously, freely, as lovers responding to the Beloved. This final movement is the completion of participation: what began as gift ends as glory. The world does not vanish into the Creator but rests in His radiance.

Such vision guards against the subtle residue of both pantheism and Gnosticism. Against the first, it insists that the cosmos remains creature even in deification; its distinction endures eternally as praise. Against the second, it proclaims that matter will not be discarded but raised. The resurrection of the body is the eschatological sign that creation is good enough for eternity. Christ's risen flesh is not a temporary miracle but the permanent revelation of what matter is capable of when filled with God.

This cosmic dimension of theosis is already rehearsed in the Eucharist. There, the raw elements of earth—grain and grape, fruit of soil and toil—are taken up into thanksgiving, blessed, broken, and given back as divine nourishment. The transformation that occurs on the altar is not a magical exception but a prophecy of what God intends for all creation. Bread and wine become Body and Blood not by being annihilated, but by being perfected in purpose. They show that the created can bear the uncreated without confusion, that the finite can hold the Infinite through the humility of form.

The same pattern extends to the moral and aesthetic life of the believer. Every act of genuine creativity, every gesture of mercy, every truthful word participates in this eucharistic rhythm of offering and transformation. The artist who shapes beauty, the scientist who uncovers order, the parent who nurtures life—all perform priestly acts in the liturgy of the cosmos. Their work becomes prayer when it is offered back to the Giver. The Christian does not escape the world to find God; he finds God by learning to see the world rightly, as gift awaiting transfiguration.

This perspective explains why the Church guards dogmatic precision so jealously. The lines that separate Creator and creation are not barriers but contours of meaning. Without them, theology collapses into sentiment, and the world loses its sacramental depth. Chalcedon's four adverbs are not relics of metaphysical debate; they are the grammar of hope. They assure the believer that the same Word who unites without confusion in His own person will one day unite without confusion the whole of creation to Himself. The cosmos will remain cosmos, yet filled with the light of God.

Athanasius foresaw this final radiance when he wrote that "the Word became man that we, by partaking of His Spirit, might be deified and thus enter into incorruption." The corruption he names is not only death but disintegration—the scattering of creation from its center. The Incarnation reverses that entropy. The Word gathers the fragments into coherence around His own life. Each redeemed soul becomes a point of reunion where heaven and earth meet. Through the saints, the world learns its original melody again.

In this vision, knowledge itself is purified. The true *gnosis* of the Christian is not esoteric theory but contemplative gratitude. It is the knowledge born of participation—the mind enlightened because the heart has been inflamed. "He who loves knows God," writes John. The intellect transfigured by charity becomes luminous, not self-sufficient. The beatific vision, promised at the end of time, is the perfection of this same knowledge: the intellect raised by the light of glory to see God "face to face" while remaining finite, distinct, and forever surprised.

That surprise will never cease. The Chalcedonian distinction ensures that eternity will not be monotony but endless discovery. The creature will always have more to receive, more to adore, more to become. Gregory of Nyssa spoke of this as *epektasis*, the unending ascent into the inexhaustible beauty of God. Because the divine essence remains infinite, participation can never be completed. Heaven is not the rest of satiation but the rest of movement—joy without limit because the object of joy is limitless.

The cosmos, too, will share this dynamism. Revelation's final vision is not annihilation but renewal: "Behold, I make all things new." The New Jerusalem descends; heaven and earth are joined like bride and bridegroom. Matter and spirit, once estranged, are reconciled in a single liturgy. The river of life flows through streets of gold, symbols of nature and grace interwoven. What began as promise in the Eucharist becomes universal reality: creation itself becomes communion.

To contemplate this is to stand before mystery with confidence rather than fear. The Church's doctrinal boundaries do not imprison wonder; they make it possible. Pantheism and Gnosticism both destroy wonder—one by collapsing everything into God, the other by condemning everything as unworthy of Him. Orthodoxy preserves the space where awe can breathe. It teaches that we are not God, yet God has chosen to dwell in us; that the world is not divine, yet destined for divinity. This paradox is the pulse of Christian worship, the heartbeat of every sacrament, the rhythm of the cosmos itself.

As creation moves toward its consummation, the difference between Creator and creation will not fade; it will become music. Distinction will sound like harmony, otherness will shine like color. Each soul, transfigured yet unique, will add its note to the one eternal hymn. The universe will be a choir of distinction in communion, a flame of many tongues united in one fire. And at the center will stand the Lamb who was slain—the Word made flesh, the Mediator who remains forever both God and man. Through Him, all things will find their place; through Him, all things will become radiant with the light of His glory.

Person as Eternal Horizon of Glory

To speak of theosis without speaking of the person is to lose the very subject of glory. The mystery of salvation is not the diffusion of humanity into a divine mist but the transfiguration of each human face until it becomes what it was meant to be—a living icon of the Trinity. In the end, what God saves is not humanity in general but persons in particular. The Creator who numbers the hairs of the head does not dissolve the creature into a cosmic average; He calls each by name.

The Incarnation itself reveals this divine precision. When the eternal Word became flesh, He did not assume "humanity" as an abstraction; He assumed a concrete history—Jesus of Nazareth, born of Mary, circumcised on the eighth day, crucified under Pontius Pilate. Particularity is the vehicle of universality. In the mystery of Christ, the unique and the universal are reconciled: the salvation of all passes through the obedience of one. This concreteness guarantees that personhood is not an accident on the way to glory but its very form. "By His incarnation," teaches the Catechism, "He has united Himself in some way with every man" (§ 521). Each soul is reached through the singularity of a Person.

From the first pages of Scripture the mark of personhood is relation. "Let us make man in our image," says the Triune God, "male and female He created them." The image of God is stamped in communion. To be person is to be *toward*: toward the other, toward God, toward the world. Sin fractures this orientation; grace restores it. Redemption therefore does not erase the self but re-centers it. The person becomes capable again of the word "Thou." In that capacity lies eternal life.

Boethius defined person as "an individual substance of a rational nature," a formula Aquinas accepted but suffused with charity. Substance protects continuity; rational nature grounds freedom; but grace adds relation. For the Christian, personhood reaches its perfection not in autonomy but in gift. The self finds itself only in surrender—what John Paul II would later call "the law of the gift." Heaven is the completion of that law: selfhood wholly given, wholly received, never lost.

Gregory Nazianzen glimpsed this when he wrote, "I am a creature of God, yet I am called to become God by grace." The transformation does not abolish what he is; it reveals it. Grace intensifies identity. The more the soul is filled with God, the more distinct it becomes. The fire does not melt the iron into anonymity; it brings out its luster. So, too, the saints in glory are not interchangeable flames but a constellation of names.

This permanence of personhood explains the Gospel's insistence on memory. The risen Christ calls Mary Magdalene by name; He invites Thomas to touch His wounds; He breaks bread in Emmaus exactly as He did before. Nothing personal is lost in resurrection. The body is glorified but remains itself; the voice that once spoke still speaks, now luminous. "It is I," says the Lord, not "It is all." Eternity begins with recognition.

Augustine's vision in the *City of God* echoes this realism. The saints, he writes, will know one another not by new symbols but by purified sight. Their loves will be ordered, not erased; their differences, harmonized, not flattened. Heaven is social because God is Trinity. The unity of the blessed mirrors the divine communion: one life of love shared among irreducible selves. Were individuality lost, love would have nothing to bind. Unity would revert to uniformity, and worship would collapse into monologue. The persistence of "I" and "Thou" is the guarantee that heaven is not silence but song.

This teaching rescues Christian hope from the vaporous consolations of monistic spirituality. The end of the soul is not absorption into the divine but conversation with Him. "Now we see in a mirror dimly, but then face to face." The promise is not diffusion into light but encounter with Light. What passes away is not distinction but distance. The creature remains other, yet the otherness becomes joy.

Even the resurrection body, says Aquinas, will preserve its individuality: each soul reunited with its own form, each body transfigured according to its measure of glory. The blessed will differ in brightness as stars differ, yet all will share one sky. This diversity is not hierarchy of worth but harmony of grace—the reflection of a God who delights in variation. Creation began as multiplicity within order; it ends the same way, gathered but not erased.

The vision of the Transfiguration already reveals the pattern. On Tabor, Christ's face shines "like the sun," yet Peter, James, and John remain themselves. Moses and Elijah appear, not as nameless symbols but as the men they were, now alive in God. Light fills distinction without destroying it. Glory personalizes. That moment on the mountain is prophecy of heaven: individuality rendered translucent, relation radiant, communion unconfused.

If this permanence of personhood is true, then eternity is the triumph of freedom. The saints do not lose choice; they lose the possibility of choosing against love. The will rests because it is wholly ordered to its end, yet it remains itself—the delight of perfect consent. Grace here reaches its ultimate purpose: not to override the human act but to make it effortlessly divine. The person becomes the place where divine and human freedom coincide without rivalry.

Every saint therefore becomes an unrepeatable word in the one eternal sentence God is speaking. The Incarnation is the capital letter, the Spirit the breath between phrases, and the Father the meaning that gathers them all. To be saved is to find one's syllable in that speech, to resonate forever without fading. The communion of saints is not a sea of sameness but a choir of distinct notes forming one chord—the music of difference redeemed.

To say that the person endures forever is already to say that it will never stop moving. The human person is not a closed crystal fixed in perfection; it is a living flame drawn upward by the very Beauty it beholds. Eternity, for the saints, is not immobility but participation in the inexhaustible life of the Trinity. Gregory of Nyssa gave this mystery a name that has never been surpassed: *epektasis*—the soul's ceaseless progress into God.

In his *Life of Moses*, Gregory writes that "this truly is the vision of God: never to be satisfied in the desire to see Him." For him, satisfaction that ends desire would be the end of love itself. God, being infinite, can never be comprehended; therefore the soul that loves Him is always advancing, always tasting and thirsting at once. "Every desire fulfilled," he says, "becomes the starting-point of a new desire." Heaven is not rest from longing but the transfiguration of longing into joy. Desire there is no longer pain; it is participation in the endless generosity of the divine life.

Maximus the Confessor took Gregory's insight and gave it metaphysical precision. In the *Ambigua* he writes, "The end of motion is union with God, and union itself is without end." All created movement—intellectual, moral, or physical—tends toward repose in the Absolute Good; yet when that repose is reached, the soul finds motion again, for the Good it has attained is infinite. In another text he warns, "The one who ceases to progress ceases to share in God." For Maximus, immobility is the only death left possible to the redeemed. To live in God is to move eternally within Him, "ever-moving rest," as he calls it—the paradox of peace that dances.

Aquinas, writing eight centuries later in a very different idiom, reaches the same conclusion. The blessed see God not by nature but "by a light created in them," a *lumen gloriae* that raises their intellect to a divine mode of knowing (*Summa Theologiae* I q.12 a.5). Yet even with that gift, the intellect remains finite: "Comprehension is proper to the infinite alone; what is finite may see the divine essence truly but never totally" (*ST* I q.12 a.7). The blessed, therefore, are never bored with God because there is always more of Him to see. Their joy is the perpetual increase of vision: *intueri et tendere*—to see and to reach. "In every delight," Aquinas adds, "there is movement, for delight increases with possession" (*ST* I-II q.31 a.1). Heaven's peace is not the stillness of exhaustion but the rhythm of intensifying joy.

These three masters—Gregory, Maximus, and Aquinas—together form the Church's doctrine of endless becoming. Gregory preserves the biblical sense of pilgrimage: "They go from strength to strength; the God of gods will be seen in Zion." Maximus gives it its Christological heart: motion finds its measure in the motion of the Word made flesh. Aquinas grounds it in metaphysics: the finite can rest only in an infinite act that forever exceeds it. Each perspective reveals a single truth—that the creature's perfection lies in participation, and participation can never be completed.

This unending growth does not imply change in God, who is "the same yesterday, today, and forever," but transformation in us. The divine essence is still, while the soul expands. The Fathers loved the image of a vessel cast into the sea: the sea remains what it is, but the vessel fills according to its capacity, and as it dilates, it takes in more. In heaven, that dilation never stops. The saint enlarges without limit because love has no limit. The expansion is not repair from imperfection but the vitality of perfection itself. A love that did not grow would already be fading.

The whole Trinity is the source of this eternal movement. The Father is the Fountain of life, the Son the stream of Wisdom, the Spirit the living current that carries the soul ever onward. The procession of the Spirit within the Godhead becomes participation of the Spirit within the creature. To be deified is to be drawn into that divine circulation where giving and receiving are simultaneous. The soul moves because the Spirit moves it; the Spirit moves because He is Love in motion.

Such teaching rescues eternity from monotony. The popular imagination fears heaven as an endless afternoon of sameness; Gregory and Aquinas alike assure us that it will be the opposite. Infinity means inexhaustible novelty. Each act of sight opens another vista, each embrace discloses new depth. There is no repetition, only deepening. "Eye has not seen, nor ear heard, nor has it entered into the heart of man, what God has prepared for those who love Him." The bliss of the blessed is not the cessation of adventure but its transfiguration. Wonder becomes their element; discovery, their rest.

Because the blessed behold God "face to face," they know all things in Him. Yet even that knowledge grows. As they perceive more of His goodness, they love more; as they love more, they are enlarged to perceive more still. The circular movement of love and knowledge is endless, each feeding the other. The soul's ascent is not competition with others but communion with all; every increase of one becomes enrichment for all, for the vision of God is shared light.

This doctrine carries immense pastoral consolation. It means that heaven will never be dull, that our capacity for joy will never reach its limit. It means also that no finite good we love on earth—truth, beauty, friendship—will be discarded; it will be taken up and purified to become the medium of divine praise. The scholar will still delight in truth, the artist in beauty, the friend in love, but all in God, and therefore all in one another. The individuality of each will be the prism through which new colors of the same light appear. "In Your light," sings the psalmist, "we shall see light." That seeing never ends.

Gregory calls this unending movement the "stretching of the soul." It is the athletic image of the spirit eternally in training, never weary. The finish line is always the next step because God's goodness is always more. Aquinas translates the same into scholastic calm: "The act of the will resting in God is itself endless progress, because God's goodness is boundless." The two voices, mystical and metaphysical, harmonize perfectly. The dynamism of heaven is not frantic motion but the pulse of the divine heart. Love beats, and the cosmos keeps time.

Seen in this light, epektasis becomes not an eccentric flourish of Greek speculation but the mature expression of Chalcedonian faith. The natures remain distinct, yet the communion is real; grace does not obliterate the creature but makes it ever more itself. The saints' eternal progress is the last echo of those four adverbs—unconfused, unchangeable, indivisible, inseparable—translated into joy. The creature remains creature, yet participates truly in the divine life, and therefore can never cease becoming. Heaven will be the endless astonishment of finitude alive with infinity.

Heaven is not an undifferentiated blaze but a harmony of distinct radiances. Every saint remains uniquely himself or herself; individuality is not an obstacle to divine communion but its very instrument. The glory of the blessed is not equality of sameness but equality of love. "In my Father's house are many mansions" (John 14:2): not compartments of isolation but chambers resonating with the same music. Each soul receives the whole God, yet no two receive Him in quite the same way, for the reception itself is personal. The difference becomes the measure of praise.

Athanasius once said that the saints are "mirrors that catch the light of the Sun of Righteousness in diverse ways, according to their purity and capacity." The image fits the whole communion of heaven. One glory, many refractions; one light, infinite hues. Grace does not abolish the natural variety of human temperaments, gifts, and histories; it consecrates them. Each becomes a facet through which the divine splendor passes. The individuality that seemed a limitation on earth becomes, in glory, the means of endless manifestation. If God is infinite, then only an infinity of distinct creatures can begin to express His beauty.

Thomas Aquinas, meditating on the degrees of beatitude, puts it this way: "The vision of the blessed is more or less perfect according to the measure of their participation in the light of glory" (*Summa Theologiae* I q.12 a.6). The light is one, but the vessels differ. Yet he adds at once: "Nevertheless, all are perfectly happy, because each attains the fullness proper to his capacity." The very diversity of glory is the completion of justice, for love gives to each what is his own. Heaven's order, far from envy, is mutual delight. The lesser shares in the joy of the greater, the greater rejoices in the beauty of the lesser, and both exult that God is magnified in both.

This symphony of distinct perfections is prefigured already in creation. The universe sings because it is plural. "The heavens declare the glory of God," says the psalm, "day unto day pours forth speech." Stars differ from stars in glory, yet all form one sky. The natural order, with its species and varieties, is an icon of the supernatural order where each redeemed soul becomes a new species of praise. The Creator's delight in multiplicity is not whimsy but wisdom: His essence, being infinitely simple, can be mirrored only through the manifold. The one Word, uttered in eternity, echoes in time as a million distinct melodies.

Gregory Nazianzen perceived this when he likened the saints to "rays proceeding from one sun." Each ray retains its direction and brightness, yet none is apart from the source. The Father's light shines through the Son by the Spirit, and the saints become the atmosphere through which that radiance dances. What appears as diversity is simply the plenitude of love refracted through freedom. The more the soul becomes transparent, the more its particular contour shines.

In this way, individuality itself becomes eschatological. Our differences—of mind, culture, charism—are not temporary accidents of history but prophetic hints of the future. The communion of saints is the final transfiguration of all human variety into a unity that does not erase. Just as the Trinity is unity without confusion, so heaven is unity without uniformity. Distinction and communion no longer struggle; they coincide. The multiplicity of saints is the visible sign that divine love can be both one and infinite.

Maximus the Confessor saw this clearly. In the *Mystagogy* he describes the Church as "a living icon of the world to come," in which "the unity of faith joins the distinctions of persons as harmony joins different notes in one song." The liturgy, for him, is a rehearsal of heaven's music: many voices, one word; many bodies, one Body. The Eucharist enacts that future reality even now. Around the altar, differences of language, temperament, and culture are not suppressed but drawn into consonance. Each communicant receives the same Christ whole and entire, yet the effect of that reception is irreducibly personal. What is now a foretaste will be consummation: individuality transfigured into polyphony.

Aquinas articulates this same mystery with scholastic clarity: "In the multitude of the blessed there will be order, which belongs to the beauty of the universe" (*ST* I q.47 a.2). For him, beauty requires proportion and distinction; harmony presupposes parts. Thus heaven's diversity is not an afterthought but the very form of its loveliness. The Creator's intention was never to gather identical spirits but to assemble a choir where each voice heightens the others. "God is glorified not by one creature but by all," he says, "for from the variety of beings arises the perfection of the whole."

To contemplate this is to glimpse why charity, not uniformity, is the bond of perfection. Charity is the virtue that rejoices in another's good as its own. In the eternal kingdom, every saint will be pure charity, and therefore each will rejoice infinitely in the holiness of all the others. The joy of one becomes the joy of all, the praise of one becomes the praise of all, and so the blessed share in one another's beatitude without jealousy or loss. The body of Christ does not divide His life; it multiplies His glory. The communion of saints is the triumph of difference reconciled in love.

The poets have intuited this more vividly than the philosophers. Dante, standing before the heavenly rose, sees each soul as a petal "radiant with its own hue, yet all kindled by the same light." His vision translates theology into vision: hierarchy turned into harmony, degrees into color. The saints are not ranked but arranged—each in the place where it can reflect divine love most fully. What appears as order is simply love finding its proper shape.

Scripture's images confirm the same truth. The Apocalypse speaks of "a multitude that no man could number, of every nation, tribe, people, and tongue." The eschatological city is built of precious stones, each with its own color and brilliance. Jasper, sapphire, emerald, topaz—the catalogue of Revelation is not decorative but symbolic: the redeemed creation scintillating with innumerable differences, all illumined by "the glory of God that gives it light." The New Jerusalem is not glass but gem. The diversity that now divides the human family will then be its beauty. No color is lost, no language silenced, no memory wasted; all will be gathered into the prism of divine light.

Such vision rescues the very idea of eternity from monotone abstraction. Heaven is not the fusion of personalities into a collective divinity; it is the unending discovery of God through the uniqueness of each other. The blessed will see God in God and God in one another, for "God will be all in all" (1 Cor 15:28)—not by displacement but by indwelling. Every saint will be a distinct window through which the one light shines. The vision of one enriches the vision of all; the delight of one magnifies the delight of all. There will be no spectators, only participants in the great exchange of seeing and being seen.

Gregory of Nyssa describes the final state of the just as "a choir of human nature in concert with the angelic ranks, each order praising in its own tongue yet all tuned to one harmony." That phrase—*each in its own tongue*—captures the essence of glory. The saints do not cease to speak their native language; they speak it perfectly. The stammering of history becomes eloquence; the accents of culture become cadences of praise. The symphony of redeemed creation will sound like Pentecost perfected: many tongues, one Spirit.

This symphonic vision also reveals why the communion of saints extends beyond the merely human. The whole cosmos, says Paul, will "obtain the glorious liberty of the children of God." The redemption of persons is inseparable from the renewal of creation. The stars and stones, the rivers and birds, will join the choir—not as rational singers but as resonant instruments. The universe will be the cathedral of persons, every element vibrating with their glory. The sound of the new creation will be silence that sings, light that speaks, matter that prays.

In such a vision, individuality is not selfish isolation but transparent relation. Each self becomes a window through which God's infinity shines in a distinct colour. To lose oneself would be to lose that colour; to be oneself in God is to become translucent. Heaven is the place where transparency replaces competition, where all distinctions remain but none divide. "As the body is one and has many members," writes Paul, "so it is with Christ." The unity of the body is not the loss of the members; it is their orchestration. The Head is not alone; He reigns surrounded by countless faces reflecting His own.

The saints, says Augustine, will be "a city where each rejoices in the joy of all." The very structure of eternity is reciprocity. What began in the Trinity—love between persons without confusion—becomes the pattern of the redeemed cosmos. The distinction of persons is eternal; communion is the mode of oneness. Heaven's unity is symphonic, not uniform. The everlasting "one song, many voices" will be the very sound of divine life shared.

The mystery of eternal personhood is not a doctrine to be admired from afar; it reshapes every moral choice and every vocation. If the destiny of the human being is an unending communion of distinct persons in God, then all of Christian ethics becomes rehearsal for that communion. To love, to forgive, to create, to serve—each is a training in the way eternity loves. The moral life is the pedagogy of glory.

Thomas Aquinas says that grace "perfects the person according to his nature." Nature's end is relation; therefore the perfection of a person is charity. In this world, charity is apprenticeship in the triune life: learning to love the other not as rival but as revelation. The eyes of faith begin even now to see every person as an icon of divine possibility. "The saints," wrote Catherine of Siena, "see themselves in the mirror of God, and see God in the mirror of themselves." That mutual reflection is the seed of heaven planted in history. It obliges reverence. Every face we meet is destined for transfiguration; every stranger is a future glory.

Such vision exposes the gravity of sin. Sin is not merely disobedience to a command but refusal of communion. It is the turning inward that anticipates hell's solitude. In the light of theosis, moral evil appears as self-exile from the music of heaven. To hate is to silence one's voice in the choir. Yet even this silence can be healed. Every act of repentance is a step back into the harmony; every confession, a return to one's note. The moral law, then, is not constraint but the architecture of participation—it shapes the soul so that it can resonate again.

This is why the Church insists on the dignity of the person as the cornerstone of social teaching. The truth that each human being is an image of God, called to eternal communion, forbids every utilitarian calculus that treats lives as expendable. "Man," said Gaudium et Spes, "is the only creature on earth that God has willed for its own sake." To harm another is to wound the future glory of the world; to serve another is to polish a facet of the coming city. The ethics of the Gospel are not temporary rules but eschatological training. To practice justice, mercy, and fidelity is to begin sounding the harmonies of the kingdom.

Athanasius saw this link between deification and ethics when he wrote that "the Word became man that men might become gods, and the life of the gods is the life of virtue." Grace does not bypass moral formation; it fulfills it. The habits of virtue are the muscles of participation. The ascetic struggle, the works of mercy, the patience of love—all are anticipations of the eternal movement into God. As the iron must be purified before it can glow, the soul must be purified before it can shine. The saints' final radiance begins in the forge of daily fidelity.

Gregory of Nazianzen adds another dimension. In one of his orations he exhorts the faithful: "Become God's so that you may be with God." The phrase *become God's* carries a double meaning: belong to Him, and become like Him. To belong to God here and now—through prayer, service, and sacrament—is already to enter the pattern of belonging that will never end. Every surrender to grace enlarges the soul's capacity for eternal communion. This is the moral logic of theosis: what you practice in time becomes your posture in eternity. The self bent toward love here will find itself naturally upright in glory.

Such vision also transfigures mission. Evangelization is not recruitment to an institution but invitation into participation. The Christian does not bring strangers into a club; he awakens persons to their own destiny. The Gospel announces that humanity is called not to mere survival but to divinization—to become "partakers of the divine nature." When the believer lives this truth, his presence itself becomes proclamation. The deified life is persuasive because it shines. The saint does not argue the world into belief; he reveals what the world was made to be.

This missionary character of theosis is visible in the saints themselves. The more united they are to God, the more open they become to creation. Their individuality does not contract; it expands. "My love is my weight," said Augustine; "by it I am borne wherever I am carried." The soul heavy with divine charity gravitates toward others. The saint cannot remain enclosed in contemplation; his contemplation spills into compassion. Heaven begins wherever divine charity overflows through human hands.

The same logic applies to beauty and creativity. If personhood is eternal, then every genuine act of making participates in the divine artistry. The painter who catches light on canvas, the poet who shapes words into wonder, the scientist who uncovers order—all prefigure the redeemed intellect beholding the cosmos in God. Creation was entrusted to persons so that it might be offered back transfigured. In that offering the world is already being renewed. "Behold," says Christ, "I make all things new." The newness begins wherever the creature cooperates with the Creator.

This transformation of action and vision culminates in the Eucharist, where the destiny of personhood is rehearsed most completely. Each communicant receives the same Christ whole and entire, yet in a manner proper to himself. Communion thus both unites and personalizes. The Body of Christ does not erase faces; it illuminates them. The Eucharistic life—the continual offering of self to the Father through the Son in the Spirit—is the pattern by which all creation will one day be transfigured. The altar is the world's future condensed into bread and wine.

The Church, therefore, is not merely the community of those who believe; she is the anticipation of the communion of saints. Her task is to cultivate persons capable of eternal relation. Her sacraments train the senses for glory; her disciplines prepare freedom for love. Even her dogmas, those careful delineations of mystery, are not intellectual fences but invitations into deeper participation. To confess the faith is to enter the rhythm of the eternal Word, to begin speaking the language of the world to come.

Seen this way, moral effort and mystical contemplation converge. The one who prays well will act rightly; the one who acts in love will enter contemplation. Both movements are movements toward communion. The difference between them is only emphasis: action as love expressed, contemplation as love received. In the life of the deified, the two become one. The eternal person will be wholly active and wholly receptive—mirroring the divine life itself, which is pure act and pure gift.

This eschatological dignity of personhood also defines Christian hope for the world. The final renewal of creation is not the replacement of the earth but its liberation through human sanctity. The saints, transfigured, will be the priests of the new cosmos. Their glorified bodies will mediate divine light to matter; their praise will sustain the rhythm of the renewed world. "Creation waits with eager longing for the revealing of the sons of God," writes Paul, because creation's own destiny depends on theirs. The cosmos will be restored through the persons who have learned to love.

Such vision clarifies the Church's mission in history. Holiness is not flight from the world but fire within it. The deified person becomes transparent agency—God acting through human freedom without violation. The more one becomes God's, the more the world around begins to shine. "You are the light of the world," said Christ. The light He meant was not moral superiority but the radiance of participation. The Christian's vocation is not to dominate history but to illumine it. When the saints live, they become what the universe is waiting for.

From this perspective, even suffering and death acquire new dignity. The person who endures pain in union with Christ is not diminished; he is being shaped for eternal capacity. The wounds that grace transfigures will remain as marks of glory, as in the risen Lord. The individuality of love is not erased by death; it is sealed. Martyrdom, patience, fidelity—these are the chisels that carve the face that will endure forever.

When all this is gathered up at the end of time, the redeemed creation will not be an anonymous radiance but a communion of faces, each shining with its own hue of divinity. The eternal city will be a living icon of the Trinity: distinction without division, unity without confusion. Each "I" will look upon the "Thou" of God and of neighbor in the same gaze. The more distinct, the more united; the more united, the more distinct. The saints will be perfectly personal because they are perfectly one.

This is the horizon that now opens toward the world. The person clarified becomes mission; the soul set ablaze becomes leaven. The world will not be converted by systems or slogans but by persons who have begun to shine with the light they will bear forever. "You shall be all flame," said Abba Joseph, and that flame will spread not by conquest but by communion. The eternal horizon of the person is the same as the horizon of the cosmos: the love of God diffused through every created heart until all things sing together, "To Him be glory forever and ever."

Leaven for the World

Theology, when true, always ends in motion. Contemplation does not terminate in private ecstasy; it ripens into mission. The person who has seen God cannot remain still, for divine light is by nature diffusive. The transfigured soul becomes leaven—quiet, invisible, yet transforming the whole. What was inward illumination becomes outward transparency. Grace, having perfected nature, now perfects history through persons.

The soul that has passed through the purifying fire of theosis no longer asks, "What must I do?" but "What is God doing through me?" In this new mode of being, agency itself is transfigured. The self remains fully itself, yet its activity has become translucent to the divine will. The human faculties are no longer instruments of self-expression but conduits of divine compassion. "It is no longer I who live," says Paul, "but Christ who lives in me." The Apostle's paradox names the final stage of participation: distinction preserved, possession transformed. The deified person becomes a living window for the uncreated light.

Thomas Aquinas describes this synergy with scholastic precision. "God moves every creature according to its mode," he writes, "so that in acting it fulfills both divine providence and its own freedom." Grace does not override the will; it heals it into harmony. The more perfectly a person is united with God, the more freely he acts. Divine action and human decision coincide without confusion. This is the paradox of the saints: they appear most themselves when they are most possessed by Another. The fire that fills them does not consume personality but illuminates it from within.

Gregory Palamas captured the same reality in more luminous imagery: the deified soul "becomes light, not by nature but by participation, as iron glowing with fire." The iron is still iron, yet its radiance no longer belongs to itself. So too the sanctified person: still bounded, still human, yet blazing with the energy of divine love. What the scholastics expressed through the logic of grace, the mystics expressed through the poetry of light. Both mean the same thing—that vocation itself is made possible by distinction. Because the human remains human, it can be the vessel of the divine.

This truth dismantles both activism and quietism. The saint is neither restless reformer nor passive contemplative, but the place where love becomes deed. The active and the contemplative, long seen as opposites, converge in the theotic life. Action is suffused with prayer; prayer becomes the soul of action. "Mary has chosen the better part," said Jesus, yet it was Martha's hands that prepared His table. In the deified person, the two sisters live as one heart. Love listens and serves in a single motion.

The world encounters God not through abstractions but through persons in whom divine life has become visible. The Church's mission is therefore personal before it is institutional. Every saint is a microcosm of evangelization. Francis of Assisi preached most eloquently when he walked silently through the fields; Thérèse of Lisieux converted multitudes from a cloistered cell; Seraphim of Sarov said, "Acquire the Spirit of peace, and thousands around you will be saved." These are not romantic anecdotes but revelations of theology in practice. The clarified self becomes transparent agency—God acting through human freedom, God visible in human gentleness.

Here the meaning of vocation reaches its height. To be called by God is not merely to receive a task but to participate in His own self-giving. Each calling—teacher, parent, priest, artisan, nurse—is a unique mode by which the divine Word continues His Incarnation in the world. The deified person does not escape history; he redeems its texture by inhabiting it with love. The carpenter's bench, the scholar's desk, the sickroom, the marketplace—all become altars when the heart that labors there is united with Christ's. "Whatever you do, do all to the glory of God." To act thus is to sanctify the ordinary until it gleams with sacramentality.

The saints are the true interpreters of the Creed, because they embody what they profess. Doctrine in them becomes flesh again. The truths of Chalcedon, Nicaea, and Constantinople are not relics of dogmatic archaeology but living powers. The unconfused, unchangeable, indivisible, inseparable union that defined Christ's person is translated into their lives:

divinity and humanity meeting without violence. In them, theology walks the streets. They become living commentaries on the Word—exegesis in action.

This is why the Church's final word on theosis is not speculation but sanctity. The dogma guards the flame; the saint carries it into the world. Doctrine without holiness is abstraction; holiness without doctrine is sentiment. In the theotic life, both are one: truth burning, love made intelligible. The saint is the meeting point of Logos and flesh, where thought becomes song. "You are the light of the world," Christ said, not because the disciples would manufacture brilliance, but because they would one day reflect His own. Transparency becomes transmission; the glass window catches the morning sun.

The spiritual writers often spoke of this state as *cooperation* or *synergy*—the human freely consenting to be the organ of divine purpose. Synergy is not equality of partners but consonance of wills. God remains God, the creature remains creature, yet between them passes one pulse of love. The will that once resisted now vibrates to the same rhythm. "The Spirit Himself intercedes for us with sighs too deep for words." Those sighs become our breath. The sanctified life is simply the life in which that breath is unhindered.

When this happens, even silence becomes apostolic. The saint may never speak to crowds or write a line of theology, yet his very existence becomes wordless witness. Holiness, said Newman, "is never out of date; it is the most persuasive of all preaching." The world will not be saved by argument but by radiance—the quiet contagion of souls who burn with God. Their transparency is their eloquence. The Church calls them "light of the world" not metaphorically but metaphysically; through them, the uncreated light continues to enter time.

Thus the long contemplation of personhood resolves itself in mission. The more clearly the soul knows that it is not God, the more freely it can be filled with God. Distinction makes vocation possible; identity within communion makes charity unstoppable. The universe, waiting for its renewal, leans toward the saints who are already aflame. In them, the final future begins.

From here the path leads naturally outward. The next chapter will speak of this diffusion of divine life—how the sanctified soul becomes leaven for the world, how ordinary existence becomes Eucharist, and how love expands until it touches the edges of creation. "You shall be all flame," said the desert elder. That fire, born of contemplation, now leaps into mission. The window that once caught the morning light has become itself a source of dawn.

12

You Shall Be All Fire: Living the Theotic Life in the World

"He who is united to God becomes fire; and wherever this fire goes, it sets ablaze everything around it."
— St Symeon the New Theologian

Ongoing Conversion and Unceasing Prayer

The baptized life is not a single crossing but a river that keeps flowing back toward its source. In Baptism, we entered the waters once; but those waters continue to enter us, carving channels through the heart, returning the soul again and again to its first astonishment—that God desires to dwell within His creature. The Christian life, therefore, is less a completed initiation than an ever-deepening consent. The Spirit who hovered over the Jordan now hovers over every moment of human time, waiting for another "Fiat," another yes. Conversion is the shape that this yes takes inside history. It is not the memory of a moral turning-point but the perpetual reorientation of existence toward the fire that first kindled it.

To repent, in the language of the Fathers, is not merely to feel remorse for sin but to change direction—*metanoia*, a turning of the mind itself toward the light. It is the act by which the soul ceases to orbit itself and begins again to revolve around God. The sinner turns back from darkness; the saint keeps turning toward brightness that has no edge. Gregory of Nyssa described this movement with his unending verb *epektasis*—the soul's eternal stretching toward beauty. "The one who rises never stops rising," he wrote, "for each ascent reveals a higher summit." Sin is finite, but goodness is infinite, and thus the soul's ascent cannot end. The perfection of the Christian is not completion but growth. Even in the beatific vision, says Nyssa, there will be motion: the blessed will move forever deeper into God, because infinity cannot be exhausted. Theosis, in this sense, is sanctified restlessness—the soul's eternal rest in motion.

The first fruits of conversion are contrition and obedience; the later fruits are joy and freedom. The penitent who weeps learns soon enough that grace desires not only cleansing but expansion. John Chrysostom said that "the proof of true repentance is not tears but joy." To be forgiven is to awaken to hunger; to taste holiness is to crave the infinite. The one who repents truly begins to discover that holiness is not a separate sphere but a new way of seeing. Grace is not a new substance poured into the soul but a new light in which the soul begins to perceive reality rightly. Ongoing conversion means allowing that light to reach places still unlit—the motives half-pure, the virtues tinged with pride, the habits of self-protection that masquerade as prudence. Every deeper surrender reveals a deeper grace waiting behind it.

The rhythm of this continual return becomes prayer's heartbeat. When Paul commands the Thessalonians to "pray without ceasing," he is not asking for continuous speech but for continuous awareness. Prayer, in its mature form, is the transformation of consciousness—the soul's remembrance of God as naturally as the lungs remember air. The Desert Fathers called this *mnēmē Theou*, the remembrance of God. To remember God in all things is to restore creation to its first vocation: to be praise. For the one who remembers, every act becomes doxology—the craftsman shaping wood, the scholar tracing words, the mother tending her child. Each becomes a priest of the ordinary, consecrating the hour with attention. "If you are a carpenter," said Abba Lucius, "make each stroke of your adze an act of praise." In this way, life itself becomes the temple of unceasing liturgy.

Among the many paths toward this remembrance, the Jesus Prayer has stood as the surest school.

"Lord Jesus Christ, Son of God, have mercy on me."

The sentence is as short as breath and as vast as eternity. In those few words the entire Gospel is compressed: His divinity confessed, His incarnation remembered, His mercy invoked. The repetition of His Name is not incantation but communion. "Let the remembrance of Jesus be united to your breath," wrote St John Climacus, "and you will know the meaning of silence." When the prayer descends from the lips to the heart, it becomes the pulse of existence itself. The Name enters the rhythm of inhalation and exhalation, descent and ascent: mercy breathed in, thanksgiving breathed out. The very physiology of man is baptized into adoration. Breath becomes theology; the body becomes doxology. In that rhythm the creature learns to live as it was created to live—in ceaseless dialogue with its Maker.

The West knew the same mystery in a different idiom. Benedict called it *stabilitas*, the constancy that makes every hour an hour of prayer. Teresa of Ávila called it *recollection*—the soul gathered into "a little heaven within." Aquinas and Palamas, though separated by centuries and vocabulary, would have understood each other perfectly here. Both knew that grace does not bypass the faculties but fulfills them: it does not destroy reason or affection or body but lifts them into their proper harmony. The one who prays always is the one whose whole being—thought, emotion, breath, and gesture—has been integrated by love. The will no longer jerks between impulses; it moves with single purpose. "Where the Spirit of the Lord is," wrote Paul, "there is freedom." Freedom, in the end, is nothing other than simplicity—the heart's capacity to love without interruption.

The daily disciplines of prayer—fasting, vigils, confession, the cycle of psalms—exist to train that simplicity. They are not mechanical duties but the choreography of desire. The body, when rightly schooled, remembers what the soul believes. To fast is to proclaim dependence; to keep vigil is to declare that time itself has become liturgical. To confess is to unmask the illusions that divide. Each practice shapes the faculties into instruments of praise. Paul calls the body "the temple of the Holy Spirit," and temples are not prisons but resonant chambers. The human being is designed to resound when the divine Word is spoken. The disciplines of ascetic life merely keep that chamber clean so that the echo may be clear.

Fatigue and failure, far from interrupting this rhythm, become part of it. The one who falls and rises again discovers that holiness is not flawlessness but perseverance of desire. The canon of saints is full of such perseverance. Peter denied, Augustine wrestled, Mary of Egypt wandered, yet in each the Spirit transformed defeat into intimacy. "It is not enough," said Origen, "to leave Egypt; we must also cross the desert." Ongoing conversion is this desert crossing—the long apprenticeship of trust. Each thirst becomes the sign that grace is near. The very incompleteness of the journey becomes its sanctity. God does not demand perfection of achievement, only fidelity of direction. The pilgrim who keeps turning toward the light is already walking in it.

When prayer ripens, the distinction between contemplation and action fades. The two become aspects of one energy, like flame and light. Gregory the Great defined contemplation as "rest in God," yet he also warned that its fruit is always charity. The monk who prays rightly becomes the world's hidden benefactor. His solitude is not flight but service: through him, unseen, the peace of God enters history. The hesychast in his cell and the mother at her child's bedside share the same vocation: one guards the flame, the other carries it. Both participate in the same fire.

At this point, the world itself begins to change aspect. The heart purified by remembrance perceives reality no longer as material to be used but as mystery to be received. Maximus the Confessor called this the discovery of the *logoi*—the divine intentions shimmering within things. The deified mind reads creation as Scripture: the wind as whisper, the bread as presence, the neighbour as sacrament. To those who see thus, every encounter becomes an epiphany. "I see Him," wrote Symeon the New Theologian, "in the trees, in the grass, in the air; the whole creation speaks

His name." Such vision is not escape from the world but entrance into its depth—the rediscovery of the divine Word still echoing in matter.

The remembrance of God cannot remain a matter of thought alone. It must descend into the body, for the body is not an obstacle to prayer but its necessary form. The Scriptures never portray the soul praying in abstraction: Moses lifts his arms, Daniel kneels, Christ falls upon His face in Gethsemane. Gesture is theology in motion; posture becomes confession. The body teaches the soul what it means to believe. When the Christian stands, he remembers resurrection; when he kneels, he remembers humility; when he raises his hands, he remembers offering. The body is the first catechism of the Church. It carries memory before the mind can articulate it.

To forget this is to reduce prayer to psychology. Modern piety, tempted to see the soul as a disembodied awareness, risks losing its sacramental grammar. Yet the Incarnation forbids such dualism. The Word took flesh, not as symbol but as reality, and that flesh remains the medium of union. The Christian's body is therefore the field where grace displays its victory. To fast, to bow, to trace the sign of the Cross upon one's skin—these are not superstitions but participations in the mystery of the Word made visible. The flesh that once carried rebellion now becomes the carrier of praise. "Present your bodies as a living sacrifice," says Paul; this is not metaphor but instruction. To live eucharistically is to discover that the body itself has become altar, and breath itself incense.

This bodily dimension extends to the rhythm of time. The hours, sanctified by prayer, become the architecture of remembrance. The Church, in her ancient wisdom, divided the day not to constrain but to consecrate it: dawn, noon, evening, and night—each hour a facet of the cosmic doxology. Matins greets creation renewed; Vespers blesses its setting; Compline entrusts the darkness to mercy. When the believer learns to inhabit this rhythm, time ceases to oppress; it becomes transparent. The passing of hours no longer signals decay but invitation. Every moment, however trivial, can carry the weight of eternity. The merchant at his stall, the student over her books, the nurse in the ward—

all can mark the hour with inward thanksgiving. "In every work of your hands," says Basil the Great, "remember the Creator, and your work itself will become prayer."

This sanctification of time is the foundation of peace. Anxiety feeds upon division—between what is and what might be, between the present and the imagined. Unceasing prayer reconciles these divisions by returning attention to the present grace. "Give us this day our daily bread" is more than a petition for sustenance; it is the training of desire to trust the moment. When the heart learns to receive the present as gift, fear loses its vocabulary. The believer becomes poor in the evangelical sense—possessing nothing, yet lacking nothing. Poverty of spirit is not deprivation but participation in divine sufficiency. In this simplicity, prayer matures from request into communion.

The watchfulness of the heart—what the hesychasts called *phylakē kardias*—guards this simplicity. It is the discipline of attention, the refusal to let thought wander into fantasy or resentment. The watchful heart stands before God with the single eye praised by Christ: "If your eye is sound, your whole body will be full of light." Such vigilance is not tension but readiness, not nervous self-monitoring but alert love. It is the stance of a servant awaiting the master's return, candle lit, heart awake. The desert elders taught their disciples to keep a short prayer upon their lips precisely to hold this wakefulness. "Guard your mind," said Abba Poemen, "and you will see the angels with you." The one who guards the heart begins to discern the movements of grace and temptation as distinctly as shifts of weather. The spiritual life ceases to be confusion; it becomes navigation by light.

Stillness, the fruit of watchfulness, is not passivity but receptivity. The Greek word *hesychia* implies not silence alone but tranquility of soul—a harmony between the inner faculties and the divine presence. "Be still, and know that I am God." The knowing is not conceptual; it is experiential. To know God in stillness is to permit His being to resonate within ours. The mind ceases to grasp and instead gazes. Isaac the Syrian described this state as "the Sabbath of the heart." In such stillness, time thickens; each second expands into eternity. The Spirit, finding no resistance, breathes freely; and the believer tastes the peace that surpasses understanding—not absence of disturbance but the still center that can contain disturbance without breaking.

Yet this interior peace is not isolation from the world's pain. The deeper the stillness, the wider its embrace. The one who lives in continual prayer becomes the world's intercessor. Every sigh becomes petition, every joy thanksgiving. The soul begins to carry others in its silence. "When you are at peace," said Seraphim of Sarov, "thousands around you will be saved." The heart burning with love for God cannot but radiate love for His creatures. Compassion ceases to be sentiment and becomes ontology; the one who prays truly participates in divine mercy itself. His glance absolves; his patience instructs; his mere presence consoles. Theosis does not draw the saint away from others but makes him transparent to them. Through him, others glimpse the kindness of God.

Such transparency extends to speech. The mouth trained by silence learns reverence for words. "Let your words be few," says Ecclesiastes—not as austerity but as homage to meaning. In a culture where language is spent like small coin, the person of prayer recovers its weight. Each word becomes a seed. The hesychasts said that a true monk speaks only when his words are better than silence. Even then, his speech carries the rhythm of prayer. Conversation becomes communion; listening becomes a mode of adoration. The saint listens as God listens—without haste, without judgment, attending to the heart's unspoken need. To listen thus is to become mirror of divine patience.

Through this continual dialogue—silent or spoken—the soul is purified of self-concern. Pride, which is the gravitational pull of the self inward, loses its magnetism. The heart begins to expand, to take delight in the holiness of others. This is humility in its true sense: not self-disparagement but spaciousness. "The humble man," said Macarius, "is he who rejoices in another's virtue as in his own." In humility, freedom is born. The person who no longer defends himself cannot be enslaved by insult or praise. His peace does not depend on circumstance; it rests upon the immovability of God. "Christ is the same yesterday, today, and forever." Anchored in that sameness, the soul becomes steady flame—its motion constant, its light unquenchable.

This constancy is the summit of ongoing conversion: the transformation of volatility into endurance. It is not stoicism but participation in divine stability. To love always, to forgive readily, to hope despite delay—these are the marks of the soul that has ceased oscillating between enthusiasm and despair. The Spirit has tempered it like metal in fire. It glows without consuming itself. The Fathers compared such steadfastness to the burning bush—ablaze yet unburned, radiant yet rooted. The Christian who lives in this state no longer seeks extraordinary experiences. His wonder is endurance itself: that grace continues, that prayer endures, that God remains.

When the heart thus steadies, it begins to perceive suffering differently. Pain no longer negates meaning; it becomes its proof. The believer learns, in the pattern of Christ, that obedience and joy are not opposites. The prayer "Not my will but Yours" becomes the axis of life. Each sorrow endured in faith opens a new capacity for compassion. Suffering ceases to isolate; it binds the sufferer to the Crucified and through Him to all creation. "The Son of God suffered unto death," said Augustine, "not that men might not suffer, but that their suffering might be like His." The deified soul suffers with God, and therefore with all who bear His image. Intercession becomes empathy; empathy becomes participation; participation becomes redemption.

In this continual conversion of heart, prayer itself changes character. What began as petition becomes praise; what began as effort becomes rest. The person who once struggled to find words now finds silence articulate. Prayer becomes less something done and more something *undergone*. The Spirit prays within, as Paul says, "with sighs too deep for words." The soul becomes the instrument of another's music. "I live, yet not I," wrote Paul; "Christ lives in me." This is the end of the path: when the creature, without ceasing to be itself, becomes transparent to the divine will—when the human breath carries the cadence of the eternal Word.

When prayer ripens into this transparency, the world itself is seen anew. The old distinction between sacred and secular dissolves, not by confusion but by illumination. What was once ordinary becomes charged with significance. Washing a dish, writing a letter, greeting a stranger—all are transfigured when done in grace. "Whether you eat or drink, or whatever you do, do all to the glory of God" (1 Cor 10:31). Paul's words are not moral exhortation but metaphysical revelation: to live in Christ is to live sacramentally. Every act can become liturgy when performed in the Spirit's awareness. The believer begins to sense that the boundaries of the temple stretch as wide as the world. The workshop, the marketplace, the kitchen—all can become altars. The true miracle of the Incarnation is not that God entered one human life but that He entered all human life.

The Christian who abides in unceasing prayer becomes, as the Fathers loved to say, a living altar. His heart is the sanctuary where heaven and earth meet. The fire that once fell upon the apostles now burns in the hidden chamber of his soul. The smoke of his offering is not confined to the hour of worship; it rises continually through his actions, his choices, his patience. Even sleep becomes a form of prayer, for in the night the heart keeps its quiet rhythm of remembrance. "I sleep, but my heart wakes," says the Song of Songs. The one who has entered this state no longer distinguishes between moments of devotion and moments of labor. Every breath becomes a repetition of the Name; every heartbeat an Amen.

The sanctification of daily life reveals what the tradition calls the "liturgy of the heart." In this interior temple, the Eucharist never ends. Each reception of the sacrament extends outward through memory into the smallest gestures of the day. The bread received at the altar becomes the generosity that feeds the hungry; the cup shared becomes the patience that bears with the difficult. The Mass, celebrated inwardly, transforms every moment into communion. "Be a living Eucharist," urged St. John Chrysostom, "so that wherever you go, the altar goes with you." The deified life does not escape the world; it consecrates it. Theosis is not an abstraction hovering above experience but the baptism of experience itself in divine love.

In this light, the virtues appear not as moral accomplishments but as the lineaments of divine likeness. They are the colors of charity refracted through human temperament. Faith, hope, and love are not three virtues among others; they are the modes by which participation in divine life is lived. Faith opens the eyes to perceive God's action in all things. Hope stretches desire beyond what is visible, refusing to limit reality to what is measurable. Love completes them both, because it unites the knower and the known in one motion. Aquinas called the virtues "the form of the soul's beauty," for they reveal how grace has taken shape within freedom. Patience is the endurance of divine long-suffering within time; humility is the transparency of the creature before glory; chastity is the harmony of eros and agape—desire purified by gift. Virtue is grace made visible.

Such virtue is learned not in exemption from struggle but through struggle itself. Temptation becomes the forge in which freedom is purified. The Christian who endures trial with trust discovers that the battle itself is prayer, for every resistance to sin is an act of love. The Spirit's grace does not bypass effort; it sanctifies it. Cooperation—*synergeia*—is the ongoing exchange between divine initiative and human consent. God knocks, man opens; God fills, man yields; God commands, man obeys; and in this rhythm the creature grows luminous. To pray without ceasing is therefore to live in continual cooperation—each thought, each impulse, each act offered back to the Giver who inspires it. The soul becomes instrument, yet not passive: the musician and the lyre both alive, both sounding one harmony.

This cooperation is nowhere more tested than in suffering. Pain, which the world calls meaningless, becomes under grace the school of compassion. The believer who has learned unceasing prayer does not ask to be spared suffering but to suffer redemptively. "If we suffer with Him," Paul writes, "we shall also be glorified with Him." The difference between despair and sanctity lies not in the quantity of pain but in its orientation. The cross borne with resentment isolates; the cross borne with love unites. The person who prays within suffering becomes co-redemptive—not in the sense of adding to Christ's work, but of allowing that work to pass through him into the world. His wounds become channels of intercession. "The Son of God suffered unto death," said Augustine, "that we might learn to suffer unto life."

When this pattern becomes habitual, even the smallest inconveniences—the delay, the misunderstanding, the fatigue—become altars of participation. The soul ceases to divide life into sacred and profane; everything is folded into Eucharist. This is the hidden heroism of saints who never leave their homes or cloisters, whose lives appear uneventful but whose patience holds the world together. Their prayer does not shake nations, yet it keeps them from collapsing. "A single soul in the state of grace," said Catherine of Siena, "is of more value than the whole universe." Such is the dignity of the deified life: through one heart turned fully toward God, creation is sustained.

This sanctification of the ordinary does not annul human weakness; it redeems it. Even distraction can serve grace when recognized as longing. The mind may wander, but the soul knows where to return. Sin itself becomes less a catastrophe than a homesickness. To fall and rise again is the rhythm of sanctity. Each failure becomes the place of deeper humility, and humility is the soil where love grows quickest. Julian of Norwich, with serene boldness, called sin "behovely"—needful—because through it the soul learns both its poverty and God's gentleness. "He did not say you shall not fall," she wrote, "but that you shall not be overcome." Ongoing conversion means precisely this: that every wound becomes a place of meeting. The Cross is not an interruption in the divine plan; it is the plan made visible.

The fruit of this continual turning is joy—quiet, steady, indestructible. Joy is not the denial of sorrow but its transfiguration. It is the echo of resurrection within the tombs of daily life. The Christian who lives in unceasing prayer carries Easter in his heart even on Good Friday. His peace is not the absence of struggle but the presence of meaning. "Rejoice always," Paul commands, and he writes from prison. Joy, for him, is not optimism but participation in divine constancy. The soul anchored in God does not rise and fall with circumstance; it floats upon a deeper tide.

Such joy is the true hallmark of sanctity, for it reveals that the human heart, though finite, has become capacious enough for the Infinite.

At this point, prayer ceases to be something done and becomes something *undergone*. The Spirit prays within with groanings too deep for words. The human voice becomes the echo of another Voice speaking eternally. The intellect rests, the will consents, the heart adores. This is the "prayer of quiet" spoken of by Teresa of Ávila, the *Sabbath of the heart* described by Isaac the Syrian. It is not achievement but arrival—arrival into the rhythm of God Himself. The soul no longer struggles to reach heaven; heaven breathes within it. Every motion, every thought, every affection becomes participation. The creature lives the life of the Creator without ceasing to be creature. The distinction remains, but it has become music: difference held in perfect harmony.

Such is the state toward which all prayer tends: not the extinction of desire but its perfect orientation. The heart has become altar, the breath incense, the world sanctuary. What began in contrition ends in adoration, and adoration is perpetual renewal. Ongoing conversion is nothing other than the soul learning to live from that renewal. The saint does not think of God occasionally; he thinks with God continually. His mind is Christ's mind; his love Christ's love. The Spirit has made his life liturgy, his presence benediction. He moves through the world like light through glass—unchanged in essence, yet everywhere transformed. In such a life, prayer is not an act of will but the atmosphere of being.

And from that atmosphere the next mystery arises. The fire that has purified the interior now seeks to spread. The heart that has become altar must now become mission. For divine love, once kindled, cannot remain contained. The one who prays without ceasing becomes the channel through which the world itself is offered back to God. Theosis is not the end of action but its transfiguration. From the stillness of the heart begins the movement of renewal. The soul that has learned to burn quietly is now ready to set the world ablaze.

Theosis as Mission: Evangelization and Ecclesial Witness

The flame that has purified the interior cannot remain enclosed. Love, as Dionysius the Areopagite insists, is *ecstatic*—it goes out from itself toward union with the beloved. To share the divine life is therefore to share its movement. Within the Trinity, love is procession: the Father gives Himself to the Son, the Son returns all to the Father, and the Spirit is that gift made fire. Whoever participates in this life must move outward with it. Theosis is not static elevation but participation in divine motion. At Pentecost the same Spirit who descended upon the Son in the Jordan descended again upon His Body, the Church, turning contemplation into proclamation. Fire became language. As Gregory Nazianzen said, "The Spirit comes like fire, not to burn but to illumine; not to consume, but to make radiant." That radiance is the beginning of mission.

Christ's Incarnation did not end with the Ascension. It continues sacramentally through His Body. "As the Father has sent Me, so I send you" (Jn 20:21). The Church is this sending extended through centuries. *Lumen Gentium* opens with the astounding claim that "the Church, in Christ, is in the nature of a sacrament—sign and instrument of intimate union with God and of the unity of the whole human race" (§1). She is not an institution that owns a mission; she *is* mission embodied, "the continuation of the Incarnation," as Pius XII called her in *Mystici Corporis*. Augustine named her *Christus totus*, the Whole Christ—Head and members sharing one life. The believer's deification is thus ecclesial: to be joined to Christ is to become part of His self-giving extension into the world. The saint is the frontier where the Incarnation advances.

From the beginning the Gospel spread not by force of argument but by the contagion of sanctity. "See how they love one another," marveled the pagans of Rome, as Tertullian records (*Apology* 39). Their astonishment was theological: divine charity had become visible. The Church's earliest homily was not treatise but conduct. Irenaeus, writing against the Gnostics, observed that "the glory of God is man fully alive, and the life of man is the vision of God" (*Adversus Haereses* 4.20.7). The fully alive human being—one who lives from God—is irresistible. Evangelization begins when grace makes humanity beautiful again. "Beauty," said Basil the Great, "awakens the soul to longing." The world is converted not by slogans but by wonder.

Truth persuades when it becomes luminous, and it becomes luminous in the saint. Aquinas, commenting on John 1, calls Christ "the light that enlightens every man" (ST I q. 12 a. 11 ad 3), and adds that through grace that light is refracted in the faithful as participation. The saint is theology in translation, doctrine transposed into flesh. His mercy interprets dogma; his patience explains providence; his joy defends the Creed. "The Church," wrote Paul VI in *Evangelii Nuntiandi* (§41), "will evangelize the world above all by her holiness." Evangelization, then, is not persuasion but presence: holiness made visible, the Word once more "becoming flesh and dwelling among us."

The Spirit performs this double work—divinization and mission—simultaneously. He is the stillness that unites and the wind that sends. The same breath that formed Adam now animates apostles. Luke's account of Pentecost echoes Genesis: creation renewed by respiration. The Spirit who overshadowed Mary now overshadows the Church, conceiving Christ anew in every believer. "The Spirit is God's love," writes Augustine (*De Trinitate* 15.17), "by which we are made lovers of God." When that love fills the soul, it cannot remain private; love desires diffusion. Hence the logic of mission: the indwelling Spirit becomes outgoing charity. "You shall receive power when the Holy Spirit has come upon you, and you shall be My witnesses" (Acts 1:8). The Greek *martys*—witness—already anticipates the cross. To testify is to be consumed by what one proclaims. The Spirit makes missionaries by making martyrs.

Holiness, then, is the true apostolate. Grace that does not overflow has not yet matured. Gregory the Great warned that "no one truly possesses charity unless he strives to share it" (*Homilies on the Gospels* 30). The saint's interior flame becomes expansive by nature; it communicates itself as light communicates brightness. "Out of his heart shall flow rivers of living water" (Jn 7:38). The deified person becomes fountain, not reservoir. His very presence begins to heal: words are unnecessary because being itself has become eloquent. Newman observed that "the world believes the saints as it believes the sun, by seeing them shine." Theosis reaches its proof when it turns to generosity.

Mission is therefore the natural metabolism of grace. When the soul ceases to share, it stagnates. The Church breathes outward as necessarily as the lungs breathe air. "Every Christian is a missionary," wrote John Paul II in *Redemptoris Missio* (§71), "to the extent that he or she has encountered the love of God in Christ Jesus." Encounter is the spark; mission is its flame. To evangelize is simply to let that love move through one's own converted humanity. There is no division between mystic and apostle: contemplation without communication suffocates, and action without contemplation burns out. Bernard of Clairvaux called these the two streams of the Spirit—contemplation filling the soul, compassion overflowing from it.

This flow takes Eucharistic shape. The pattern enacted at every altar—take, bless, break, give—is the grammar of Christian existence. The believer receives the world as gift, blesses it through thanksgiving, allows it to break his heart in compassion, and gives it back transfigured. "The Eucharist," taught Benedict XVI in *Sacramentum Caritatis* (§70), "carries within itself a dynamic of mission." To receive the Body of Christ is to become His body for others. The dismissal—*Ite, missa est*—does not conclude worship; it commissions it. The faithful depart not from the liturgy but as the liturgy extended into streets and workplaces. Theosis is the inner dimension of this same sending: the believer who has become fire becomes also light.

Where this pattern is lived, evangelization ceases to be program and becomes presence. The holiness of the ordinary transfigures culture from within. Francis of Assisi's poverty, Dominic's preaching, Thérèse's hidden charity—all are expressions of one truth: sanctity is social energy. It reshapes institutions by transfiguring persons. "The Church does not grow by proselytism but by attraction," Benedict XVI reminded the faithful at Aparecida. Attraction is the radiation of divine beauty through the transparency of grace. When people meet a life that is serene in suffering, humble in authority, joyful in restraint, they glimpse the architecture of heaven inside human flesh. That glimpse is the first form of faith.

Thus the interior fire of deification becomes the outward light of evangelization. The Spirit who unites the soul to God unites the Church to the world without confusion, as Christ's two natures were united without division. The same Chalcedonian logic holds: unconfused, unchangeable, indivisible, inseparable. The divine does not replace the human in mission; it perfects it. Grace does not override culture; it consecrates it. The Church's task is not to escape the world but to reveal it as potential sacrament. Every baptized person, filled with that Spirit, becomes the meeting point of heaven and earth—a lamp set not under a basket but upon a hill, until the whole city is lit.

The holiness that radiates outward through mission is never abstract idealism; it is the concrete transfiguration of human vocation. The Spirit does not make us angels but restores us as human beings capable of divine transparency. "Grace," says Thomas Aquinas, "perfects nature without destroying it" (*ST I–II, q. 109 a. 7*). Therefore, the sanctification of the world proceeds not by abandoning the secular but by consecrating it. The field, the factory, the family table—each can become an altar where the priesthood of the baptized is exercised. Leo the Great already proclaimed in the fifth century, "All who are reborn in Christ receive a share in His royal priesthood" (*Sermon 4.1*). To be baptized is to be anointed for participation: the laity are not spectators but living stones in the temple of God (1 Pet 2:5).

In every age the Church must rediscover this lay theotic vocation. John Paul II called it the "spirituality of ordinary life," insisting that "the call to holiness is addressed to everyone" (*Novo Millennio Ineunte*, §30). The world is not the enemy of theosis but its material. Just as the Word entered time without defilement, so the Christian enters culture without compromise, bearing the seed of transformation. "Do not flee the world," wrote Francis de Sales, "but sanctify it; devotion does not destroy business, it purifies it." The more deeply the believer unites with Christ, the more capable he becomes of renewing what he touches. The doctor's compassion, the artist's truthfulness, the worker's integrity—all are small revelations of the divine energies. In them, the infinite bends down and takes local habitation.

This truth rescues mission from clerical reduction. The priest stands at the altar so that the world might become one, but the world is represented there by the lay faithful whose labor fills the offertory. "Upon the altar are placed all the works of the faithful," writes Benedict XVI in *Sacramentum Caritatis* (§47). Every legitimate human endeavor—science, politics, education, craftsmanship—can become oblation when offered in charity. The Christian does not escape the city to find God; he learns to discern God already hidden in its streets. "There is no place," said the Cappadocian fathers, "where the sun of righteousness does not wish to rise."

To live this way is to perceive work itself as a sacrament of cooperation. The Greek Fathers used the word *synergeia* to describe salvation: divine grace and human freedom laboring together. That same word can describe the Church's mission in history. God does not act without us. The sanctified intellect, illumined by faith, extends the divine Logos into culture; the sanctified will, strengthened by love, extends divine charity into social structures. The craftsman who shapes wood well, the legislator who serves justice without pride, the mother who forgives daily—they are all theologians in action. Maximus the Confessor foresaw this when he said that "the one who loves God truly also loves every creature, for in each he sees the Creator's presence" (*Centuries on Love* I.13). The Christian who lives in such vision becomes a hinge between heaven and earth.

This vision reaches into the heart of social life. Justice and mercy are not projects added to faith; they are its natural radiation. "Faith without works is dead" (Jas 2:26) not because works purchase grace, but because grace without overflow ceases to be itself. The divine energies, entering human faculties, seek embodiment in concrete compassion. Basil the Great thundered to the rich of Cappadocia: "The bread you keep belongs to the hungry; the cloak you store belongs to the naked." His rebuke was not political but sacramental: withholding mercy is withholding Eucharist. The same logic reappears in John Paul II's *Sollicitudo Rei Socialis*: "Solidarity is not a feeling of vague compassion but a firm determination to commit oneself to the common good." When mercy and justice are understood as participations in God's own activity, they become forms of worship. Every act of reconciliation renews the Incarnation in miniature.

The Spirit's fire thus burns in social conscience as well as in private prayer. The world's healing does not proceed from ideology but from sanctity. The saints are the true reformers because they reorder society from within. Their influence is quiet yet seismic: Francis rebuilding a ruined Church by poverty, Elizabeth of Hungary transforming governance by charity, John Bosco re-creating education through fatherhood. None set out to revolutionize structures; they allowed holiness to become contagious. "It is the saints," wrote Benedict XVI, "who have truly changed the world—only the saints" (*Deus Caritas Est* §42). Their lives prove that theosis is not withdrawal from history but the divine life penetrating it through the pores of grace.

Evangelization therefore includes the renewal of culture. Truth must become flesh not only in persons but in civilizations. The arts, sciences, and institutions that shape human perception must be re-illumined from within by the Logos. This does not mean confessional imposition but transfiguration: reason purified by faith, creativity disciplined by charity, freedom fulfilled in truth. "The glory of God," wrote Irenaeus, "is the living man," and a living culture is one in which man's full stature is visible. Whenever the Gospel re-enters art or politics, it restores proportion—the harmony of the human image that modern fragmentation has lost. Christian mission in society is not moral policing; it is artistic healing: revealing again the beauty of the human form shaped by love.

Such vision can never forget the poor. Christ identified Himself with them absolutely: "Whatever you did to one of the least of these, you did to Me" (Mt 25:40). The saint who recognizes God in contemplation must recognize Him also in deprivation. "Do you wish to honor Christ's body?" asked Chrysostom. "Do not neglect Him when you see Him naked." In this theosis becomes ethics: divine compassion made flesh through human hands. Mercy is the practical face of deification. When the deified soul bends to wash feet, it is the Trinity stooping through clay. To serve the poor is not humanitarianism; it is liturgy extended beyond the sanctuary.

The same truth appears in suffering freely endured. The believer who unites pain with love becomes missionary in its purest form. "In my flesh I complete what is lacking in Christ's afflictions," writes Paul (Col 1:24). That lack is not deficiency in redemption but participation in its unfolding. Every cross embraced with faith becomes a point where divine compassion touches the world anew. John Paul II, in *Salvifici Doloris*, called suffering "a particular call to manifest the power of salvation." The martyr embodies this revelation: his blood becomes seed, his silence proclamation. "Martyrdom," said Ignatius of Antioch, "is to be God's wheat, ground by the teeth of beasts that I may be found pure bread." The martyrs are not merely witnesses to truth; they are continuations of the Eucharist. The Word is broken again in their bodies so that the world might taste life.

Here the Eucharistic rhythm of mission reaches its full intensity. The liturgy does not end when the candles are extinguished; it expands when the faithful step into the street. *Ite, missa est*—Go, you are sent—echoes the very sending of the Son. Mission is the "Mass of the world," as Teilhard de Chardin once intuited: the entire cosmos drawn into offering through human cooperation. The believer who forgives in the office, who blesses the persecutor, who speaks truth gently, continues the consecration begun at the altar. Bread becomes Body; the body becomes offering; the city becomes sanctuary. Evangelization is simply Eucharist prolonged.

The Church's history confirms this pattern again and again. The same Spirit who inspired the hermit in his desert inspired the missionary on his ship. Anthony's stillness and Patrick's zeal are one energy expressed in two forms. Both reveal what Gregory Nazianzen confessed of himself: "I am not my own; I am consumed in the good of others." Love, when divine, always moves outward without losing interior depth. Contemplation and proclamation are therefore not two vocations but one flame seen from different angles. The saints live this synthesis effortlessly: Catherine of Siena dictating letters to popes between ecstasies, Teresa of Calcutta holding the dying with the same hands that once folded in adoration.

Their genius is unity of posture—the same kneeling before the Host and before the poor. Mission is simply adoration continued in motion.

Thus the Church's outreach is nothing less than the divine life expanding. The Spirit who once overshadowed Mary now overshadows the world through the baptized. In them, God continues to say *Fiat*: "Let there be light." Each act of faithfulness—each unnoticed kindness, each word of truth, each endurance of sorrow—adds another flame to the growing dawn. Evangelization is not conquest but irradiation: the world slowly catching fire from hearts already burning. When believers live this rhythm, the old world begins to smell again of Pentecost. The breath that once filled the Upper Room moves through the streets, and the city becomes a sanctuary in which the Word is again made flesh.

The flame that becomes charity in the city also becomes light upon creation. The mission of the deified person does not end with human society; it extends to the whole cosmos. When man fell, all nature groaned; when man is transfigured, the universe begins to heal. Paul saw this clearly: "The creation itself will be set free from its bondage to decay and obtain the glorious liberty of the children of God" (Rom 8:21). The liberation of the world depends on the sanctification of man, for humanity is creation's priest. Maximus the Confessor called man the *microcosmos*, the creature who unites the intelligible and the sensible, the spiritual and the material. In him the whole universe finds voice. The deified human being becomes the mouth of the cosmos, offering it back to its Creator in thanksgiving. "Man," wrote Maximus, "is a workshop of union," for in him "what is divided is brought into harmony." To fulfill this vocation is to complete the Incarnation's purpose: God dwelling in all through the mediation of the human heart.

When the sanctified soul prays, the world prays within it. The saint who loves the earth with the compassion of Christ becomes a steward of transfiguration. The great ascetics of the East understood this: their fasting was not rejection of matter but its sanctification. Isaac the Syrian taught that "a merciful heart burns for the whole creation—man, bird, beast, even demons." The soul aflame with divine compassion becomes an atmosphere in which creation breathes freely again. In that mercy, ecology becomes theology: stewardship is not sentimentality but sacramental realism. Francis of Assisi, whose wounds reflected the Cross, called the sun brother and the moon sister because he saw their transparency to the divine. Theosis restores this vision—every creature seen as word spoken by the Word. The Christian who lives in this awareness begins to undo the cosmic alienation wrought by sin. His thanksgiving becomes antidote to exploitation; his reverence becomes healing to the earth.

The Eucharist embodies this vocation perfectly. The elements placed upon the altar—grain and grape, fruit of soil and work—symbolize the entire material order drawn into praise. "The world, discovered as gift," wrote John Paul II in *Ecclesia de Eucharistia* (§8), "is redeemed by being returned to the Giver." The Eucharist is creation in miniature transfigured. Bread and wine, products of labour and nature, become Body and Blood: matter permeated by Spirit. What happens upon the altar reveals what God intends for the universe. Theosis is cosmic Eucharist—the world becoming transparency of divine life without ceasing to be itself. Benedict XVI captured this vision in *Sacramentum Caritatis*: "The Eucharist draws creation into itself and directs it toward divinization." Mission, therefore, is nothing less than extending this Eucharistic transformation into every corner of existence. The Christian who lives eucharistically teaches the world to give thanks, and gratitude is the first form of healing.

The cosmic horizon of mission rescues evangelization from anthropocentrism. It reminds the Church that her task is not to annex but to illuminate. The Gospel does not colonize; it consecrates. Wherever the Spirit breathes, there life becomes liturgical. The Christian artist who reveals form, the scientist who rejoices in order, the peacemaker who reconciles enemies—all are collaborators in God's re-creation of the world. "Behold, I make all things new" (Rev 21:5) is not only promise but ongoing process. The renewal begins wherever love triumphs over fear, wherever truth heals confusion, wherever mercy interrupts vengeance. These are the frontiers of the new creation, and the deified man is its pioneer.

Even suffering participates in this cosmic renewal. When endured in love, pain becomes sacrificial energy. The martyrs are the archetype of this mystery: their deaths are not defeat but participation in divine fecundity. "The blood of martyrs is seed," Tertullian wrote, because every drop becomes a grain in the soil of resurrection. In their offering the earth itself is baptized anew. The Church calls this *martyria*—witness—but the Greek word also implies revelation: the martyr unveils what creation was made for, self-gift. The final word of human history will not be destruction but offering. The world's destiny is Eucharistic, and the saints are already living that liturgy.

John Paul II called this dynamic the "law of the gift." "Man cannot fully find himself," he said, "except through a sincere gift of himself" (*Gaudium et Spes* §24). Theosis as mission means precisely this: the creature discovering its joy in participation, not possession. The saint's generosity is not moral virtue but ontological truth; to give is to live according to the image of the Giver. Within the Trinity each Person is total self-donation; the redeemed humanity, drawn into that life, begins to share the same rhythm. The Father gives, the Son returns, the Spirit circulates—the whole economy of salvation is a single act of mutual bestowal. Mission is that eternal motion continued in time.

For this reason the Church's evangelizing activity cannot be reduced to propaganda or moral reform. It is the visible form of Trinitarian life expanding through history. "The Church evangelizes," taught Paul VI, "because she is sent; she exists in order to evangelize" (*Evangelii Nuntiandi* §14). Every act of witness, every gesture of mercy, every word of truth participates in that ongoing procession of divine love. The Christian is not merely God's employee but His extension—God acting through human freedom. When the Spirit moves the will, it does not coerce; it invites. Mission is freedom at its highest pitch: humanity cooperating with omnipotence. Gregory of Nazianzus likened the missionary to a lyre vibrating under the divine touch; the music is God's, but the tone is human. Each saint becomes a distinct timbre in the symphony of salvation.

This symphony resounds across time and beyond death. The communion of saints is not merely fellowship of memory but continuation of mission. Those who have entered glory continue to intercede; their charity does not expire. In their contemplation they still work. "The saints," wrote Thérèse of Lisieux, "love us more now than when they lived among us." Their glorified freedom amplifies grace on earth; their intercession is participation in Christ's eternal priesthood. The Church militant, suffering, and triumphant form one organism of mission—earth and heaven collaborating in the Spirit. When the faithful invoke their intercession, it is not sentiment but synergy: the same charity circulating through multiple realms. Theosis breaks down the walls between states of being until creation itself becomes one choir.

That choir sings with cosmic breadth in the vision of Revelation. The New Jerusalem descends, not we ascending; heaven embraces earth. The Lamb stands at the center, "and His servants shall serve Him, and they shall see His face" (Rev 22:3–4). Service and vision are one: to behold is to act, to adore is to renew. The kings bring their treasures into the city—human culture redeemed, art and science purified, politics transfigured. All that is true, good, and beautiful finds fulfillment there, not annihilation. The theotic mission begun in time culminates in this liturgy of eternity, where creation finally becomes communion without confusion. Gregory of Nyssa's epektasis continues even in glory: the saints ever growing, the cosmos ever deepening into light.

The missionary Church lives by anticipation of that day. Her labour is eschatological rehearsal: building communities that already reflect the mutual indwelling of divine Persons. When she baptizes a child, reconciles enemies, or sings the psalms at dusk, she is performing prophecy—the world as it shall be. Mission is therefore not merely expansion of membership but revelation of destiny. The Christian who lives in theosis carries the future into the present; he becomes a walking preview of resurrection. "The Spirit and the Bride say, 'Come,'" and every act of witness is an echo of that final invitation.

The vision of mission as deified action also reveals why despair is the gravest sin against hope. To lose faith in the world's transformability is to deny the Resurrection's reach. Evil is formidable but not ultimate. The Church's confidence rests not on human optimism but on Paschal realism: the tomb is empty, therefore history is open. The world may reject Christ, yet it cannot undo His victory; its resistance only highlights the endurance of grace. The saints return to the world not as dreamers but as those who have seen light stronger than death. Their courage is the purest apologetic, their endurance the most eloquent argument.

In the end, theosis as mission converges in one image: fire spreading from altar to city, from heart to cosmos. The Spirit who set aflame the disciples in the Upper Room has never withdrawn that flame; He merely seeks new fuel. Every believer who consents to love becomes another candle in the wind of Pentecost. "I came to cast fire on the earth," said Christ, "and how I wish it were already kindled" (Lk 12:49). That fire burns still—in the Eucharist, in the saints, in the hidden faithfulness of the poor. Its heat is holiness; its light is mission. The world's night is wide, but even a small flame can show the way. The Christian's task is not to outshout the darkness but to burn within it until it becomes dawn.

And when the dawn finally comes, it will not extinguish the stars but gather them. Every life lived in charity, every act of truth, every prayer whispered in secret will shine as part of the one fire that is God's glory reflected in creation. The Church's mission will then be complete, because creation itself will have become sacrament. The cosmos will sing, and its song will be the same that burned in the hearts of the apostles: *Glory to God in the highest, and peace on earth to men who are beloved of Him.*

The Restoration of the Cosmos through the Deified Man

The redemption that began in a garden does not end in a soul; it ends in a universe transfigured. Salvation is never a private corridor to heaven but the renewal of creation itself through the sanctification of its priest. Humanity was placed at the centre of the world not to exploit but to offer. "The heavens are the Lord's," sings the Psalmist, "but the earth He has given to the sons of men." The gift implies vocation. In the beginning

Adam was set amid the garden "to till and to keep" — verbs of worship as much as labour. The Fall was therefore not merely moral disobedience but liturgical failure: the refusal to celebrate the world as thanksgiving. When man closed his hands on the fruit, he broke the Eucharistic gesture of open palms. In Christ the gesture is reversed. Upon the cross, the Second Adam stretches His arms again in offering; in Him the lost thanksgiving is restored, and creation begins to breathe praise once more. The hand that closed in grasping is opened again in offering; this is the whole Gospel's shape, the sacrament's grammar, the world's cure.

Maximus the Confessor called this cosmic reconciliation *anakephalaiosis*, the recapitulation of all things in the Word (Eph 1:10). For him the Incarnation is not an episode within history but its centre of gravity, the moment in which the divine and the created are bound without confusion. "The Word," he writes, "made Himself the uniting principle of all the divided elements of creation." Heaven and earth, intelligible and sensible, angel and animal — all are reconciled in the flesh of the God-Man. Through His body the universe discovers its coherence. The chalice of the world, long cracked by sin, is re-fused in His blood. Every Eucharist prolongs that healing: the altar becomes axis mundi, the turning point where matter is again transparent to glory. When the priest whispers *hoc est enim corpus meum*, the entire cosmos leans in to listen, for in those words its destiny is declared. And the union it declares remains unconfused, unchangeable, indivisible, inseparable.

Aquinas, speaking in the cooler diction of scholastic metaphysics, says precisely the same. "The end of the whole creation," he writes in the *Summa contra Gentiles* (III 25), "is that the divine goodness, which in itself is perfect, might be represented by created things in many ways." The multiplicity of creatures is therefore not divine excess but divine pedagogy: each thing, by its order and proportion, reflects some facet of the infinite. Sin fractures this harmony; grace restores it by perfecting the rational creature, through whom the rest of creation is ordered. "The entire universe," he continues, "returns to God through the rational creature who knows and loves Him." In the saint this return becomes visible. The deified man is the hinge of the world, the intellect and heart of matter. When he loves rightly, stones and stars rejoice.

Creation thus awaits the liberty of the children of God (Rom 8:19). The groaning of the cosmos is not metaphor but sympathy: the world longs for its own transfiguration, which depends on ours. When the image is healed, the mirror clears. The Fathers were fearless in speaking of this solidarity between man and matter. Irenaeus declared that "the glory of God is man fully alive, and the life of man is the vision of God." The vision he speaks of is not detached contemplation but communion; as man beholds God, he mediates light to creation. The mountains and the seas, the beasts of field and forest, live beneath that benediction. The curse that fell upon the ground because of Adam is lifted when another Adam walks the earth with pierced feet and blesses it by His tread. Every saint who carries that blessing forward becomes a continuation of the Incarnation: the earth feels lighter beneath their steps.

The transfiguration of matter was foreshadowed upon Tabor. When Christ's garments shone with uncreated light, He was not performing spectacle but revealing potential. The same light destined for His humanity is promised to ours. The Eastern Fathers insist that this radiance was not borrowed brilliance but the manifestation of what grace does when it fully inhabits flesh. "He showed the glory of the future," says John Damascene, "that we might know to what we are called." Tabor is anthropology revealed as eschatology: the human being made transparent, and through the human, the material world itself. The apostles who witnessed it were blinded because their eyes were not yet trained for glory. The Church's task is to train such sight—to teach the world to look at itself eucharistically until even the dust becomes luminous.

This cosmic perspective rescues spirituality from sentimental minimalism. To love God is not to despise creation but to see it rightly. The temptation of every age has been to divide: spirit against matter, heaven against earth, grace against nature. Yet the Creed confesses one God, maker of heaven and earth. The Incarnation vindicates both realms. "Through Him all things were made," says John, and through Him all things are redeemed. The same Logos who spoke the galaxies into being now breathes within bread and wine. The entire sacramental economy is the divine refusal to abandon matter to meaninglessness. When the Christian blesses water, oil, or flesh, he is declaring that nothing is too humble for divinity to dwell in. Holiness is realism carried to its limit: the recognition that God loves the world more than we ever could.

This vision carries moral consequence. Ecological concern, often treated as secular fashion, is in truth a corollary of the Creed. To pollute creation is to blaspheme the Artist; to cherish it is to participate in His tenderness. Pope Francis, echoing Basil and Bonaventure, writes in *Laudato Si'* that "the world is more than a problem to be solved; it is a joyful mystery to be contemplated with gladness and praise." The environmental crisis is, at its root, a crisis of adoration: forgetfulness that the earth is gift. The remedy is not activism alone but doxology. When man again gives thanks, the earth begins to heal. The saint, even when tilling soil or mending tools, does more for creation than a thousand programs, because his heart has recovered gratitude. Thanksgiving is the ecology of heaven.

Yet this gratitude is not passive; it drives the Church's mission outward. The believer who perceives the world as sacrament becomes incapable of indifference. The hungry are no longer statistics but living icons; the wounded planet is no longer scenery but sibling. The *theanthropic* compassion of Christ presses outward through His members. "Christ continues His Incarnation in us," wrote Elizabeth of the Trinity, "for we are His humanity on earth." This continuation extends beyond moral imitation; it is ontological participation. The Spirit who formed Christ's body in Mary now forms His Body in history. The same overshadowing that made the Virgin fruitful makes the Church fecund. Her task is not only to baptize souls but to baptize reality—to immerse every sphere of culture, labor, and matter in the Trinitarian tide.

In this sense mission is cosmic priesthood. The deified man stands before creation as mediator, receiving and returning. When he offers praise, he gathers the silent hymns of beasts and stones and sets them to music. When he sins, the harmony falters; when he loves, it resumes.

The liturgy dramatizes this truth. The priest lifts up the elements not as symbols but as ambassadors of the entire world. "Lift up your hearts," he cries, and heaven answers through earth's substance. Bread and wine become what they signify: the universe redeemed. The communicant who receives them worthily becomes what he eats—the Body through which God continues to sanctify the material order. In this reciprocity of offering and indwelling, matter is no longer opaque but translucent, and history itself becomes a slow epiclesis: the Spirit hovering until everything burns with divine clarity.

The resurrection of Christ is the hinge upon which this cosmic liturgy turns. If the Cross is the altar of redemption, the resurrection is its consecration. In rising bodily, the Word did not merely prove divinity; He revealed the destiny of matter. The tomb's emptiness is not escape but transfiguration. Paul insists that "He is the firstfruits of those who have fallen asleep" (1 Cor 15:20): the pattern of what creation shall become. The risen body is not a phantom but continuity transfigured—flesh freed from corruption, still bearing the wounds but now radiant with life. It is the definitive refutation of Gnosticism's contempt for matter. The same hands that once gathered dust to make Adam now gather the dust of death to make it shine.

In that glorified flesh all creation is represented. Christ carries atoms as well as angels into communion. "The whole creation," says Irenaeus, "receives the Word of God as its King" (*Adv. Haer.* V.18.3). The resurrection is therefore the world's coronation, the first dawn of the new heaven and the new earth. When the women grasped His feet, they touched the future of the cosmos. The Christian faith stands or falls on this scandal: that matter can be filled with God without ceasing to be matter. Every sacrament, every saint, every star exists because of that affirmation. Without the resurrection, religion collapses into ethics; with it, existence becomes epiphany.

The Fathers perceived this as the heart of the Good News. Athanasius wrote that "in Christ's resurrection, creation began to be renewed again." Maximus went further: the resurrection inaugurates the cosmic Sabbath, when God "rests" in His perfected creation, not by withdrawal but by indwelling. The universe, once groaning, now begins to breathe the peace of the eighth day. The Church's liturgy preserves this rhythm: every Sunday a miniature resurrection, every Mass an irruption of eternity into time. "See," cries Chrysostom in his Easter homily, "the table is full; enjoy ye all the feast of faith!" The table of faith is also the table of the world. Through the consecrated elements, the cosmos receives its own blessing.

This Paschal horizon transforms how we inhabit creation. The Christian does not await a disembodied afterlife but the resurrection of the body and renewal of the earth. As Aquinas taught (*ST Suppl.* q. 92), the glorified body will retain its materiality while participating in spiritual qualities—impassibility, brightness, agility, subtlety. These are not ornamental but teleological: they reveal what matter is for when fully obedient to spirit. The cosmos itself shall share this glorification in proportion to its nature. "The creature," wrote Augustine (*City of God* XXII.29), "shall be freed from vanity and enjoy a peace most wonderful." Heaven will not abolish space and time but transfigure their experience: no longer succession but simultaneity, no longer decay but dynamism without loss. The glorified creation will be history healed into harmony.

In the saints this future breaks in early. Their bodies, even before death, become pledges of resurrection. The incorruptibility of relics, the fragrance of sanctity, the miracles wrought through touch—these are not curiosities but previews. "The body of a just man," wrote John Damascene, "has been sanctified by the indwelling of God; it may even work miracles." The saint's very bones are theology embodied. Grace has penetrated the fibres of mortality, making them instruments of charity. When Francis of Assisi kissed the leper, the contagion of corruption became communion; when Thérèse of Lisieux smiled through suffering, pain itself became perfume. Each gesture of love advances the resurrection by an inch. The world's healing does not begin in laboratories but in hearts that burn.

This transformation is not postponed to the end of time; it unfolds wherever love sanctifies matter. The Christian who blesses his meal, who lights a candle before an icon, who buries the dead with tenderness, participates already in the renewal of the world. The material order becomes the theatre of grace, not its obstacle. Benedict XVI described this as "the Eucharistic form of existence": every action offered, every object received as gift. The believer who learns this rhythm becomes incapable of contempt. He cannot look upon a river without thanksgiving or upon a face without reverence. In him the world regains its sacramental transparency. "Bless the Lord, all you works of the Lord," sings the Canticle of Daniel—an invitation to universal liturgy.

Even technology, when purified by this vision, becomes collaboration rather than domination. Human creativity is an echo of the Logos' fecundity. "Culture," wrote John Paul II in *Laborem Exercens*, "is that by which man becomes more man." The craftsman and scientist, when acting in charity, continue the divine artistry. Theosis is not retreat from progress but its baptism. Innovation ordered to communion becomes sacrament; technology without reverence becomes Babel. The criterion is always Eucharistic: does this invention give thanks or grasp? The saint invents as he prays—open-handedly, with wonder, as co-creator rather than conqueror.

Such wonder is the beginning of eschatology. The world's renewal will not abolish its beauty but unveil it. The patristic imagination saw the final kingdom not as blank radiance but as infinite variety redeemed. "The splendour of the sun will not overcome the stars," wrote Gregory of Nazianzus, "but each will shine in its own order." Individuality, purified, becomes contribution to cosmic harmony. The redeemed creation will be symphonic: mountain and molecule singing one melody in countless tones. Even now, hints of that harmony can be heard in music, mathematics, and mercy—fragments of the future scattered through time.

For the mystics, contemplation of creation was already participation in that future. Symeon the New Theologian described how, in prayer, "the light of God shone in my heart, and I saw creation filled with the divine fire." He was not indulging metaphor but glimpsing ontology: everything exists by being held in God's love, and when that love is perceived without distortion, all things blaze. The Christian mystic does not leave the world behind; he beholds it as it shall be. This vision, far from disengagement, fuels the Church's mission. For when one has seen the world aflame with glory, one cannot rest until others see it too.

The cosmic dimension of theosis thus returns mission to its proper horizon: not proselytism but participation. Evangelization, at its core, is an invitation to perceive reality in this Eucharistic light. "The Church," said Paul VI in *Evangelii Nuntiandi* (§14), "exists to evangelize," yet evangelization is not addition but revelation. The world is already sustained by grace; the Church's task is to awaken recognition. When she teaches, she names what creation silently sings. When she celebrates, she consummates that song in Christ. The Great Commission is therefore the extension of the Great Thanksgiving. Go, teach, baptize—transmit the fire until everything becomes altar.

Such is the mission of the deified man: to stand at the meeting point of time and eternity and let grace pass through unhindered. His holiness is centrifugal, never hoarded. Like the chalice lifted high, he catches light to pour it out. The world's future depends on such vessels—ordinary believers who have learned the art of gratitude. Their fidelity is the quiet architecture of the kingdom. Empires rise and vanish, but a single act of pure love reorders galaxies, for it participates in the eternal exchange of the Trinity. "Love," wrote Dante, "that moves the sun and the other stars," is the engine of the universe; the saint merely consents to move with it.

The restoration of creation does not advance by spectacle but by communion. The same Spirit who hovered over the waters in Genesis now hovers over the Church, knitting together what sin had torn apart. The cosmos is not saved by force but by consent—by countless acts of free cooperation echoing Mary's *Fiat*. In her yes, the universe found its first answer to the Word's summons; in every believer's yes, that answer continues. The Mother of God remains the prototype of redeemed creation: her flesh became the dwelling of the Infinite, and through her, matter was crowned. "In her," writes John Paul II in *Redemptoris Mater*, "creation has reached the apex of its dignity." The saintly life is nothing other than this Marian posture universalized—matter made transparent to Spirit, creation made receptive to the Creator.

The Church is the womb where this transformation matures. She is not parallel to creation but its sacramental form: the visible body through which invisible grace restores the world. When the baptized assemble, water and word reunite heaven and earth. In every sacrament the material is entrusted with divine agency—stone holds chrism, hands bear absolution, bread becomes God. The sevenfold economy is thus the architecture of the new creation. "The sacraments," wrote Augustine, "are the visible words of God." Through them the cosmos learns again how to speak. Their elements—water, oil, touch, light—are not discarded instruments but participants in redemption. In their humble materiality, the scandal of the Incarnation continues. The Church, said Henri de Lubac, "is the world in the process of transfiguration." The saint is simply the world already aglow.

This vision refines our sense of providence. Creation is not a neutral stage on which salvation happens; it is the very fabric being rewoven by divine hands. Every circumstance, every relationship, every sorrow becomes raw material for sanctity. "All things work together for good for those who love God" (Rom 8:28) is not pious consolation but metaphysical law. The universe is tilted toward deification. Even chaos, when surrendered, becomes compost for glory. The artist's failure, the farmer's toil, the martyr's silence—all are threads in the tapestry of providence. The deified soul begins to perceive this pattern and lives without despair because it trusts that no stitch is wasted. "In His will is our peace," wrote Dante, for he had seen that divine governance is artistry rather than automation. The Spirit is the composer who turns dissonance into harmony.

In this harmony the communion of saints has cosmic resonance. Holiness is never solitary; grace is contagious. The prayers of one sustain the lives of many, and the intercession of the glorified radiates through creation like sunlight through glass. "If one member is honoured, all rejoice together" (1 Cor 12:26). The Body of Christ is not an institution but an organism whose circulation is charity. The saints in heaven are not spectators but collaborators; their contemplation energizes the Church's mission. Catherine of Siena saw this clearly: "The service of the saints in glory is to pray for us, that we may grow in the fire they possess." Their love bridges mortality's gap. Even the souls in purgatory participate, purified by longing, drawing near to that same flame. All creation is being caught up in this vast exchange of prayer, a circulation of love that reaches from seraph to sparrow.

Here, the cosmos becomes choir. Each creature, each redeemed life, contributes its note to the symphony of reconciliation. The Father is the composer, the Son the melody, the Spirit the rhythm. Human freedom, healed and tuned, adds harmony. This is why freedom matters: without it, the music would be mechanical. The gift of liberty, even when misused, is the condition for love's glory. The restoration of the cosmos therefore requires not domination but persuasion—God winning back His creation by melody rather than mandate. The Incarnation itself was such persuasion: omnipotence made persuasive by beauty. The Cross, far from contradiction, is the song's climax, the dissonance resolving into resurrection's major key.

Every sacrament rehearses this music. Baptism initiates the rhythm of death and life; Confirmation breathes melody into courage; the Eucharist sustains the harmony of communion. Marriage becomes counterpoint—two distinct voices united without confusion; Holy Orders expands the theme into ministry; Reconciliation restores notes gone flat; Anointing modulates suffering into praise. Through this sevenfold symphony the Spirit re-scores the world. In it, even mortality learns to sing. The dying Christian who whispers "Into Your hands" joins Christ's own cadence, completing the measure of his life in a perfect rest.

The saints, being consummate musicians of this grace, teach the world its forgotten harmony. Seraphim of Sarov greeted every visitor with "My joy, Christ is risen!" not as pious formula but as metaphysical proclamation: resurrection is the structure of reality. Thérèse of Lisieux, enclosed in a convent, offered her "little way" as a cosmic instrument: every small act, done in love, changes the temperature of the universe.

Such lives demonstrate that sanctity is the world's true creativity. Where sin disintegrates, holiness integrates; where selfishness isolates, love harmonizes. The deified person becomes *catholic* in the deepest sense—his heart spacious enough to hold all being.

This universality finds expression in the Church's worship. When the liturgy begins, the boundaries of geography and time dissolve. Angels join the procession, the departed take their places, and the elements themselves participate. "Let all creation bless the Lord," chant the psalms, and at that moment the air is filled with obedience. The bread upon the paten is the harvest of continents; the wine in the chalice the joy of centuries. Every Mass is the world returning to its Maker. The priest's hands tremble not from fear but from recognition that the entire cosmos rests between his fingers. The faithful who respond *Amen* are consenting to their own divinization. Heaven and earth meet not as opposites but as lovers reunited. Liturgy is love made audible.

From this altar, mission resumes. The believer who receives the Body of Christ becomes the body of Christ extended. He leaves the church as emissary of glory, carrying the fragrance of the eternal into offices, marketplaces, and fields. In him the sacraments overflow into gestures—the sign of the cross over a sleeping child, the patience that absorbs insult, the beauty that ennobles work. Every baptized soul is meant to become a living tabernacle, a place where the divine fire rests and radiates. The cosmos is transformed not by programs but by presence. The saint's existence is the most persuasive sermon; his joy is theology incarnate. "Let your light shine before men," said the Lord—not as advertisement but as revelation of what the world is becoming.

Thus the Church's universality is not imperial ambition but cosmic vocation. She exists to gather all things into one, to reveal creation's latent communion. When she blesses water, she blesses oceans; when she reconciles sinners, she reconciles nations. Her holiness is centrifugal—the love of the Trinity made visible in motion. In her, the prayer of Christ continues: "That they may be one, as We are one." This unity does not erase distinction but perfects it. The stars remain separate, yet their light

THEOSIS

joins to form one sky. So it shall be with the redeemed creation—countless, particular, luminous, one.

All things tend toward consummation, but the Christian knows that the end is not cessation. *Telos* in the scriptural sense means fulfillment, the flower of what was always hidden in the seed. Creation's story is not a tragedy of entropy but a pilgrimage toward radiance. The same fire that blazed in the burning bush, in Sinai's thunder, in the eyes of the Transfigured One, will one day ignite the whole universe. "Behold, I make all things new," says the enthroned Lamb (Rev 21:5). Not *some* things, nor only souls, but *all* things—the total fabric of being. The new creation is not ex nihilo but ex vetere: renewal from within. The divine Artist does not discard His canvas; He illumines it until even its shadows shine.

Patristic writers never separated eschatology from creation. They saw history as a vast liturgy moving toward doxology. Origen spoke of the *apokatastasis*, the restoration of all things in Christ—not a universalist erasure of freedom, but a vision of love's victory as the final word over chaos. "God will be all in all" (1 Cor 15:28): not by annihilating distinction, but by indwelling it perfectly. Gregory of Nyssa interpreted this as the endless expansion of delight, *epektasis*, the soul and cosmos alike stretching infinitely toward infinite beauty. Eternity, in this view, is not static perfection but motion without fatigue, participation without end. Heaven will not be a frozen tableau but a dance—creation's liturgy unceasing, every moment discovery, every breath praise.

Aquinas, interpreting Paul through the metaphysics of participation, calls this final union the *visio beatifica*, the vision of God that perfects every created faculty. The blessed, he says, "will see the divine essence itself," not as grasped object but as horizon that gives joy without limit (*ST* I.12.7). The intellect will be elevated by the light of glory, the will inflamed by love that never wanes. Yet even here the distinction between Creator and creature remains, for "the finite cannot comprehend the infinite." The cosmos does not dissolve into divinity; it becomes transparent to it. The divine radiance will shine through everything that was ever made, as sunlight through crystal, each refracting its particular hue. "The saints shall differ in glory," he writes (*ST Suppl.* q.93 a.2), "for charity is the measure of their brightness." The universe will be a cathedral of difference illumined by one fire.

In that fire, time itself will be transfigured. The succession of moments will yield to simultaneity—the "eternal now" of divine life—yet without erasing memory or story. The wounds of history will remain, not as scars of shame but as windows of light. In the risen Christ, the nails have not vanished; they have become jewels. So it shall be for the world: what was torn shall be translucent. Suffering, integrated into the divine economy, becomes the grammar of compassion. "The Lamb stands as slain" (Rev 5:6) forever, because redemption is not undone but glorified. The saints who bore crosses will shine all the brighter for their burdens; their endurance will be melody in the eternal hymn.

This vision discloses the cosmic dimension of justice. The renewal of creation is also the rectification of wrong. Evil will not merely cease; it will be unmasked and converted into meaning. Every innocent tear will find its reply in joy, every mutilated hope in resurrection. Julian of Norwich's mystical certainty—"All shall be well, and all shall be well, and all manner of thing shall be well"—is not optimism but prophecy. For if God truly became flesh, then there is no wound too deep for divinity to fill. The last judgment is not a tribunal of vengeance but the revelation of coherence: truth brought to light, love vindicated, beauty unveiled as the final law of being. The stars themselves will bear witness that mercy has triumphed.

The final act of creation's drama is worship. John's apocalypse ends not with individuals escaping to heaven but with a city descending: "The holy city, new Jerusalem, coming down out of heaven from God" (Rev 21:2). Heaven embraces earth; the divine life saturates matter. The New Jerusalem gleams not because it is alien, but because the old stones have been purified. Its gates are always open, its streets gold like glass—the symbols of transparency fulfilled. There is no temple, "for its temple is the Lord God Almighty and the Lamb" (Rev 21:22). The world itself becomes sanctuary, and the light that illumines it needs no sun, for "the glory of

God is its light, and its lamp is the Lamb." What began as garden ends as city: nature and culture reconciled, history flowering into eternity. The labour of the saints, the wisdom of scientists, the beauty of artists—all find their consummation there, distinct yet harmonized in the chorus of praise.

This consummation does not abolish the Church; it reveals her ultimate shape. The Bride and the City are one. Every sacrament, every act of witness, every hidden act of mercy is a stone in her walls. "Come, I will show you the Bride," says the angel to John, and he shows him the City: the community of the redeemed shining with Trinitarian glory. The communion of saints thus expands to cosmic proportion. The martyrs are its foundations, the virgins its windows, the confessors its towers, the poor its gates. Even the redeemed creation—trees of life bearing fruit in every season—sings from its roots. The entire universe has become ecclesial: visible form of invisible charity.

In this final harmony, Christ remains centre and circumference. The Alpha has become Omega, not by consuming creation but by embracing it. His pierced heart is the sun around which the galaxies of redeemed being revolve. Every motion, every joy, every relation finds its coherence in that love. "In Him all things hold together" (Col 1:17); what was once figure becomes fact. The Incarnation proves eternal, for the Word remains flesh forever. The God-Man is not an episode in divine history but its everlasting condition: the bridge never withdrawn, the union never dissolved. The hypostatic union becomes the metaphysical principle of the universe—God and creation bound in perpetual communion.

And so the cosmos, finally healed, does what it was made to do: it sings. The rivers clap their hands, the trees of the field applaud, the morning stars shout together for joy. The symphony begun before time is completed in the key of praise. Each redeemed creature becomes a note in the Triune harmony, its sound unique, its participation total. "There are many mansions in My Father's house," says Christ; the infinite diversity of being has become the architecture of bliss. The saint will look upon every leaf, every soul, every atom, and see the same fire. Nothing common, nothing lost—each thing radiant with the memory of having been loved into glory.

What began as doctrine in Part I, moved through sacrament and struggle in Part II, and ripened as witness in Part III now reveals its full radius: the same grace that restored the image in man restores the garden around him; the same Chalcedonian clarity that kept love from confusion keeps creation from collapse; the same Eucharist that fed the heart becomes the pattern by which the world is taken, blessed, broken, and given back as praise.

This is the goal toward which every Eucharist gestures, every prayer ascends, every tear of repentance falls. The restoration of the cosmos is not a distant hope but a current within history, drawing all things homeward. Each act of faith, each forgiveness, each moment of beauty accelerates the dawn. The believer who lives eucharistically is already citizen of that city; his life is a rehearsal of the end. To live in grace is to stand where heaven and earth meet and keep the door open. The saint becomes gatekeeper of glory, ushering creation into its own fulfilment.

When that day arrives, time will not be abolished but fulfilled, and love will be all in all. The fire that once burned secretly in hearts will blaze across galaxies; the Name once whispered in prayer will resound from every creature. The last word of theology will not be definition but doxology, not system but song. The universe will have become what the Eucharist always was: God giving Himself through matter, matter returning itself through praise. The circle of love will be complete, yet forever expanding. And the voice that once said "Let there be light" will speak again, softly, tenderly, eternally: "Behold, it is very good."

Come then, let us live as kindling. Let the Name be our breath, the Eucharist our heart, the poor our treasure, the Cross our melody. Let our homes become little altars and our work a patient liturgy, until kitchens smell of Pentecost and streets remember Eden. You were made for fire. Be all flame—until the world is bright enough to see His Fac

APPENDIX A - Key Catechism Passages on Participation in the Divine Nature

Key Catechism Passages on Participation in the Divine Nature

Quick Reference Map – The Five Core Paragraphs

CCC 460 — Incarnation and Deification
"The Son of God became man so that we might become God."
→ Shows the heart of theosis: participation through the Incarnate Word.
(See Ch. 2 *Hypostatic Union* ; Ch. 11 *Deified Person*.)

CCC 1996-2000 — Grace as Participation
Grace is "a participation in the life of God."
→ Defines sanctifying grace as habitual divinizing life.
(See Ch. 4 *Grace and Personhood*.)

CCC 260 — Trinitarian Destiny
"The ultimate end of the whole divine economy is the entry of God's creatures into the perfect unity of the Blessed Trinity."
→ States the goal of all creation.
(See Ch. 1 *Imago Dei* ; Ch. 12 *Restoration of the Cosmos*.)

CCC 221 — God's Inner Life of Love
"God Himself is an eternal exchange of love... He has destined us to share in that exchange."
→ Grounds participation in the divine communion of love.

(See Ch. 6 *Interior Life*.)

CCC 2781 — Prayer and Participation

"When we pray the Our Father, we are drawn into the mystery of the Son and of the Father in the Holy Spirit."

→ Prayer as entry into Trinitarian life.

(See Ch. 10 *Prayer and Stillness*.)

1. Creation and Image

CCC 355–357 — Man created in the image of God; capacity for communion.

CCC 358 — Man willed for his own sake; dignity rooted in vocation.

CCC 1711 — Freedom ordered to beatitude and likeness.

(See Ch. 1 *Imago Dei*.)

2. Grace and Deification

CCC 1996–2000 — Grace as participation and filial adoption.

CCC 1265–1267 — Baptism makes us "partakers of the divine nature."

(See Ch. 4 and Ch. 5.)

3. Sacraments and Eucharistic Life

CCC 1129 — Sacraments necessary as mediations of grace.

CCC 1324–1327 — Eucharist as "source and summit."

CCC 1391–1396 — Communion increases union with Christ.

(See Ch. 5 and Ch. 8.)

4. Prayer and Ascesis

CCC 2558 — Prayer as covenant relationship.

CCC 2565 — Prayer as "living relationship" of children with the Father.

CCC 2708–2712 — Contemplation as gaze of faith.

CCC 2015 — Perfection through the Cross.

(See Ch. 7 and Ch. 10.)

5. Eschatology and Glory
   CCC 1023–1024 — Beatific vision as consummated theosis.
   CCC 1042–1048 — Renewal of heaven and earth.
   CCC 1050 — Creation re-established in Christ.
   CCC 1720–1722 — Beatitude as participation in divine happiness.
   (See Ch. 11 and Ch. 12.)

Usage note: This appendix provides a quick-reference chain of the Catechism's teaching that grace is participation, participation is communion, and communion is deification.

APPENDIX B - Select Patristic Texts on Theosis (Greek and Latin)

I. Apostolic & Ante-Nicene (2nd–early 3rd c.)

St. Irenaeus of Lyons (c. 202)
   [Against the Gnostics; creation–incarnation–divinization arc.]
   "The Word of God, our Lord Jesus Christ, through His boundless love became what we are, that He might bring us to be even what He is." (AH V, Pref.)
   "God became man and the Son of God became the Son of Man so that man, by entering into communion with the Word and receiving adoption, might become a son of God." (AH III.19.1)
   → Deification as filial adoption and participation in the Word (adoptio filiorum; *participatio Verbi*).

St. Justin Martyr (c. 165)
   [Apologist; Baptism as new birth and illumination.]
   "We call this washing illumination… Those who learn these things are enlightened in their understanding." (1 Apology 61)
   → Regeneration as real share in Christ's life, ordered to likeness (εἰκὼν Χριστοῦ; *illuminatio*).

St. Theophilus of Antioch (late 2nd c.)
   [Creation and moral ascent.]

"If he should incline to the things of immortality, keeping the commandment of God, he shall receive immortality and become God." (To Autolycus II.27)

→ "Become God" by grace and obedience, not by nature (θεὸς γενήσεται—by gift).

Origen of Alexandria (c. 253)

[Participation theology; sonship in the Son.]

"The first-born of all creation becomes, as it were, the teacher of deification for those who are made gods by Him." (Comm. in Ioan. II.2)

"We become gods by participation in God." (Fragm. in Ps. 82(81):6)

→ Participation and pedagogy of the Logos (θεοποιοῦν; κατὰ μεθέξιν).

St. Hippolytus of Rome (235)

[Paschal homily; baptismal mystagogy.]

"He bestows His own Spirit and makes men gods by grace." (In sanctum Pascha, fragm.)

→ Grace divinizes as gift (θεοὺς ποιεῖ κατὰ χάριν).

II. Nicene & Fourth-Century Fathers (4th–early 5th c.)

St. Athanasius of Alexandria (373)

[Against Arians; Incarnation's purpose.]

"The Son of God became man so that we might become god." (De Incarnatione 54.3)

"For He was made man that we might be made divine." (Ad Adelphium 4)

→ Classic formula of theosis (by participation, not essence: ἵνα ἡμεῖς θεοποιηθῶμεν).

St. Gregory Nazianzen (390)

[Theological orations; baptismal preaching.]

"Let us become as Christ, since Christ became as we are... let us become gods for His sake." (Or. 1.5; Or. 40.43–45)

→ Exchange: assumption and elevation (ἀντίδοσις; θεοὶ γενώμεθα—by grace).

St. Basil the Great (379)

[On the Spirit; sanctification and adoption.]

"The Spirit makes us like God; through Him we attain to God." (De Spiritu Sancto 9.23)

→ Likeness and access as the Spirit's proper work (ὁμοίωσις; πρόςβασις).

St. Gregory of Nyssa (c. 395)

[Life of Moses; endless ascent.]

"The true vision of God consists in never being sated in the desire to see Him." (Vita Moysis II.239)

→ Epektasis: unending growth into divine likeness (ἐπέκτασις).

St. Cyril of Jerusalem (386)

[Mystagogical Catecheses; baptismal adoption.]

"Having become partakers of Christ, you are rightly called Christs; and of God, sons and gods by grace." (Cat. Myst. III.1)

→ Sacramental participation yields filial deification (χάριτι; μέτοχοι Χριστοῦ).

St. Ambrose of Milan (397)

[On the mysteries; Eucharistic transformation.]

"As often as we receive, we proclaim the Lord's death... that what we receive may make us divine." (De Mysteriis 9.58)

→ Eucharist oriented to divinizing union (*ut divini efficiamur*).

St. Augustine of Hippo (430)

[Sermons on Christmas/Easter; adoption through the Word.]

"God became man that man might become God." (Sermon 13A; cf. Tract. in Ioan. 2.9)

"Let us rejoice and give thanks: not only have we become Christians, but Christ." (In Io. Ev. tr. 21.8)

→ Adoptive deification in the Totus Christus (*deus per participationem*).

St. Cyril of Alexandria (444)

[On John; union by the Spirit.]

"By receiving the Spirit we are made partakers of the divine nature." (Comm. in Ioan. 1.12)

→ Spirit-wrought sonship (θείας κοινωνοὶ φύσεως).

St. Hilary of Poitiers (367)

[De Trinitate; adoptive filiation.]

"Through the sacrament of regeneration we are made partakers of the divine nature." (De Trin. II.26)

→ Baptismal participation (Latin echo: *participes divinae naturae*).

St. Leo the Great (461)

[Nativity homilies; dignity renewed.]

"Christian, recognize your dignity… you have been made a sharer in the divine nature." (Serm. 21.3)

→ Moral and mystical consequence of deification (*consors divinae naturae*).

III. Post-Chalcedon / Byzantine (5th–8th c.)

St. Maximus the Confessor (662)

[Cosmic mediation; deification as final cause.]

"The Word of God… wishes always and in all things to work the mystery of His Incarnation." (Ambigua 7)

"Deification is becoming all that God is, except for identity of essence." (Quaest. ad Thal. 22)

→ Personal participation without confusion (θέωσις... χωρὶς τῆς κατ' οὐσίαν ταυτίσεως).

St. John of Damascus (c. 749)

[Orthodox Faith; participation vs. nature.]

"We become gods by participation, not by nature; for the divine essence is incommunicable." (De Fide Orth. III.15)

→ Clear boundary of participation (μετουσία, not οὐσία).

St. Symeon the New Theologian (1022)

[Mystical Hymns; experiential theosis.]

"God Himself is united to me... I am illuminated and become god by grace." (Hymns of Divine Love)

→ Lived experience of deifying indwelling (θεὸς κατὰ χάριν).

IV. Medieval Latin (12th–13th c.)

St. Anselm of Canterbury (1109)

[Cur Deus Homo; fittingness of the Incarnation.]

"Man was created to be happy in God; only God-man could restore him." (CDH II.1–4)

→ Restored capacity for beatifying participation (*beatitudo in Deo*).

St. Bernard of Clairvaux (1153)

[Sermons on the Song; nuptial participation.]

"Let the soul cleave to God and be made one spirit with Him." (Serm. in Cant. 83.4; cf. 1 Cor 6:17)

→ Nuptial union as mode of deification (*una spiritus*).

St. Thomas Aquinas (1274)

[Grace as created participation; vision as consummation.]

"Grace is nothing other than a certain participation in the divine nature." (ST I-II, q.110, a.2)

"In the beatific vision, the created intellect is elevated by the light of glory to see God as He is." (ST I, q.12, a.5–7)

→ *Gratia creata* divinizes now; *lumen gloriae* consummates (Latin: *participatio divinae naturae*).

St. Bonaventure (1274)

[Itinerarium; ascent into God.]

"Passing over into God through the Crucified, we are led into that excess where peace dwells." (Itinerarium VII)

→ Seraphic path: conformity to Christ as deification (*transitus in Deum*).

APPENDIX C — Magisterial & Conciliar Witness

Catechism of the Catholic Church (CCC)

- §260 → "The ultimate end… that we may become partakers of the divine nature" (2 Pet 1:4) → *Ch.3 What is Theosis; Ch.11 Distinction.*
- §221 → God is love in Himself; creation is invited into this Trinitarian communion → *Ch.1 Image; Ch.12 §1 Prayer.*
- §460 → "The Son of God became man so that we might become God" (Fathers quoted) → *Ch.3 Patristic Witness; Ch.4 Incarnation.*
- §1996–2000 → Grace as God's free initiative; sanctifying grace makes us participants in divine life; habitual/actual grace → *Ch.2 Union not Transaction; Ch.11 Grace & Personhood.*
- §521 → Christ's mysteries are "ours" (we live them in Him); personal participation in His life → *Ch.5 Sacraments; Ch.10 Paschal Pattern.*
- §774–776 → The Church as sacrament (sign/instrument) of communion with God and unity of humanity → *Ch.12 §2 Mission & Ecclesial Witness.*
- §950, §1323, §1324 → Eucharist builds the Church; source and summit → *Ch.5 Eucharist; Ch.12 §2 Mission (Eucharistic form).*
- §1391–1396 → Eucharist divinizes by uniting us to Christ and to one another → *Ch.5; Ch.12 §2 Mission as communion.*
- §1257–1261, §1265–1270 → Baptism as necessary and as new birth: divine filiation, indwelling, incorporation → *Ch.5 Baptism; Ch.9 Saints as Theophany.*

- §2012–2016 → Universal call to holiness; perfection is charity; growth by grace and the Cross → *Ch. 7 Asceticism; Ch. 10 Cross & Resurrection; Ch. 12 §1 Ongoing Conversion.*
- §2558–2565 → Prayer as covenant/communion: God thirsts for man; man for God → *Ch. 6 Interior Life; Ch. 12 §1 Unceasing Prayer.*
- §294 → God creates to "make us share in his blessed life" (glory as man fully alive) → *Ch. 1 Purpose; Ch. 3 Theotic Goal.*
- §1042–1050 → New heavens/new earth; cosmic renewal in Christ → *Ch. 12 §3 Cosmic Restoration; Ch. 11 Distinction of natures safeguarded in glory.*

Vatican II — Dogmatic & Pastoral Constitution

Lumen Gentium (LG)

- §2–3 → Father's plan: humanity called into communion in Christ; Church as sacrament of unity → *Ch. 2 Union not Transaction; Ch. 12 §2 Mission.*
- §11 → Sacraments, especially Eucharist, communicate divine life and build the People of God → *Ch. 5 Sacraments; Ch. 12 §2.*
- §39–42 → Universal call to holiness: perfection of charity for all states of life → *Ch. 9 Hallmarks; Ch. 12 §2 Lay vocation.*
- §48 → Eschatological nature of the Church: journey toward consummation in glory → *Ch. 10 Paschal; Ch. 12 §3 Cosmic horizon.*

Dei Verbum (DV)

- §2, §4 → Revelation is God's self-communication culminating in Christ; we share in divine life by receiving the Word → *Ch. 3; Ch. 4 Incarnation.*
- §21 → Scripture "gives the strength of the Church's life"; nourishes participation in salvation → *Ch. 6 Prayer & Lectio; Appendix C Prayer Rule.*

Unitatis Redintegratio (UR)

- §2–4 → Unity is willed by Christ; holiness and continual renewal serve credible witness → *Ch.12 §2 Mission as luminous unity.*

Orientalium Ecclesiarum (OE)

- §1, §6 → Eastern traditions are equal in dignity; their spiritual heritage (incl. divinization) belongs to the whole Church → *Ch.3 History; Ch.6 Hesychastic thread.*
- §23 → Encourage the Eastern spiritual disciplines and liturgy (theosis-shaped praxis) → *Ch.6 Prayer; Ch.8 Liturgy.*

Papal Magisterium — John Paul II, Benedict XVI, Francis

St. John Paul II

- **Redemptor Hominis §8–10** → Christ reveals man to himself; divine life offered in Him → *Ch.1–3 Anthro & Theosis; Ch.12 §1 Conversion.*
- **Novo Millennio Ineunte §30–31** → Program for the Church: holiness and contemplation of Christ's face → *Ch.6 Prayer; Ch.12 §1 Unceasing Prayer.*
- **Ecclesia de Eucharistia §1, §34–36** → Eucharist builds the Church and divinizes believers → *Ch.5 Eucharist; Ch.12 §2 Mission from altar.*
- **General Audience (Nov 14, 1979)** → "Man becomes God's image in communion" (communio personalism) → *Ch.1 Image & Likeness; Ch.11 Personhood.*

Benedict XVI

- **Deus Caritas Est §1–2** → Christianity is encounter with the Person of Love; participation in Trinitarian charity → *Ch. 2 Union; Ch. 12 §2 Witness of love.*
- **Sacramentum Caritatis §70–92** → Eucharistic form of Christian life; mission flows from adoration → *Ch. 5; Ch. 12 §2 Eucharistic mission.*
- **Spe Salvi §10, §38** → Hope as shared participation in God's life; purification ordered to glory → *Ch. 10 Suffering; Ch. 12 §1 Perseverance.*
- **Catecheses on the Fathers (Athanasius, Maximus, Symeon)** → Patristic witness to deification normalized within Catholic doctrine → *Ch. 3; Appendix B.*

Pope Francis

- **Evangelii Gaudium §3, §264** → Mission springs from personal encounter; contemplatives in action → *Ch. 12 §2 Fire to city; §1 Prayer → Mission.*
- **Laudato Si' §83, §236** → Cosmic Christology; sacraments as "ways of the Spirit" to divinize creation's matter → *Ch. 8 Liturgy; Ch. 12 §3 Cosmic restoration.*
- **Gaudete et Exsultate §7, §19–24** → Universal call to holiness lived in daily life; grace perfects ordinary → *Ch. 9 Saints; Ch. 12 §1 Daily rule.*

APPENDIX D - Glossary

Abstinence — A limited, periodic renunciation of good things (food, media, comforts) to train desire and free love for God and neighbor. See also *Fasting, Ascesis*.

Acedia (ἀκηδία) — "No-care," spiritual listlessness or resistive sadness that drains prayer and charity; classically countered by stability, psalmody, and manual work. See *Sloth*.

Adoption, Divine (Filiatio adoptiva) — God's making us sons and daughters in the Son; not legal fiction but real participation in Christ's filial life. See *Deification, Grace*.

Adoration (Latreía/λατρεία) — Worship owed to God alone; distinguished from veneration (*proskýnēsis*) given to saints and icons. See *Veneration*.

Agápē (ἀγάπη) — Self-giving divine love poured into us by the Spirit; source and form of all Christian virtue. See *Caritas*.

Almsgiving (Eleēmosýnē/ἐλεημοσύνη) — Mercy to the poor as Eucharistic overflow and renunciation of possessiveness; a pillar of ascetical life.

Anáfora (ἀναφορά) — The Eucharistic prayer of offering and thanksgiving, culminating in epiclesis and consecration. See *Epíclesis, Anámnēsis*.

Anámnēsis (ἀνάμνησις) — Liturgical "remembrance" that makes the Paschal Mystery present and effective, not mere recollection.

Anaphora—St. John Chrysostom/St. Basil — Principal Byzantine Eucharistic prayers; catechetical lenses for sacrifice, thanksgiving, and deification.

Anaphora of Addai and Mari — Ancient East-Syriac Eucharistic prayer; witness to the Church's earliest sacramental language.

Anaphora vs. Canon — "Anaphora" (East), "Canon" (Latin West) for the central Eucharistic prayer; both indicate one priestly action of Christ.

Anakephalaiōsis (ἀνακεφαλαίωσις) — "Recapitulation": Christ sums up human history to heal and transfigure it (Irenaeus). See *Recapitulation*.

Apátheia (ἀπάθεια) — Patristic "freedom from the passions"—rightly ordered desire enabling contemplation; not emotional numbness.

Apokatástasis (ἀποκατάστασις) — "Restoration." A debated patristic term; in orthodox usage, restoration of creation in Christ, not a doctrine of guaranteed universal salvation.

Apophatic Theology (Via negativa) — Speaking of God by negation and transcendence, safeguarding mystery alongside positive affirmations (*cataphatic*).

Apotaxis (ἀπόταξις) — Monastic renunciation (of the devil, the world, self-will) at baptismal/monastic vows; pattern of daily spiritual warfare.

Ascesis/Askēsis (ἄσκησις) — "Training" of body and soul through prayer, fasting, vigil, and mercy; synergy with grace that purifies love.

Attention (Prosoche/προσοχή) — Watchful care of the heart; practical guard on thoughts, senses, and speech. See *Nepsis, Logismoí*.

Atonement — Christ's reconciling work. In this book: juridical, sacrificial, and participatory (deifying) dimensions held together.

Avodah/ʿĀbad (עבד) — "To serve"/"cultivate": priestly service language for Eden and Temple; humanity's primordial vocation. See *Šāmar*.

Beatific Vision (Visio beatifica) — The consummated sight of God that transforms the blessed without dissolving creaturely identity; harmonized here with theosis.

Beatitudes (Makarioi/Μακάριοι) — Christ's charter of the Kingdom; portraits of deified life now and in glory.

Berith (ברית) — Covenant: God's binding gift-and-response relationship forming a people and shaping liturgy and ethics.

Bishop (Epískopos/ἐπίσκοπος) — Overseer; high-priestly ministry of unity, teaching, and sanctification in apostolic succession.

Body (Sōma/σῶμα) — Not a shell but the person in visible mode; temple for the Spirit and destined for glory. See *Resurrection*.

Canon (Kanon/κανών) — Rule/measure; also a fixed liturgical order (e.g., "Canon of St. Andrew") or the biblical canon.

Capax Dei — "Capable of God." Human nature is fashioned to receive and bear divine life.

Caritas — Latin for divine love (agápē) in us; theological virtue ordering all action to God.

Catechesis (Κατήχησις) — Echoing the faith: systematic formation into the mystery, especially via mystagogy.

Catharsis/Kátharsis (κάθαρσις) — Purification: healing of disordered passions and sins as first movement toward illumination.

Catholic — "According to the whole": fullness of faith in space (universal) and time (apostolic), not mere largeness.

Charis (χάρις) — Grace as unmerited gift and effective divine life; not a "thing" but God's self-communication.

Charisms — Gifts of the Spirit for building up the Body; ordered to love and liturgical communion.

Christification — Becoming Christlike by participation in His life; practical term for theosis in moral/spiritual keys.

Christology — Doctrine of Christ's person and work: Incarnation, hypostatic union, two natures/wills, deifying economy.

Communicatio idiomatum — "Communication of properties": what is predicated of Christ's humanity can be predicated of His person (and vice versa), underpinning sacramental realism.

Communion (Koinōnía/κοινωνία) — Participation/communion: our share in Trinitarian life; ecclesial, sacramental, and ethical.

Compunction (Pénthos/πένθος) — Grace-filled sorrow for sin that opens the heart to joy; allied to tears and hope.

Concupiscence — Disordered inclination left by sin; healed by grace and virtue, not destroyed by nature's abolition.

Contemplation (Theōría/θεωρία) — Loving awareness of God given by the Spirit; fruit of purification and silence.

Conversion (Metánoia/μετάνοια) — "Mind-change": reorientation of desire, thought, and habit toward God.

Cosmic Liturgy — Creation's praise; the world as temple offered through human priesthood and Christ the High Priest.

Covenant Sacrifice — Sacrificial signs that seal God's promises and form a people in worship and ethics; fulfilled in the Eucharist.

Creatio ex nihilo — Creation "from nothing": God's love, not necessity, grounds all being; basis for gift and gratitude.

Deification (Theōsis/θέωσις) — Participation in God's life by grace: healing, elevating, glorifying; never confusion of essences. See *Energies, Grace*.

Demeanor of Prayer (ἦθος προσευχῆς) — The interior "ethos" of reverence, attention, and filial boldness befitting sons/daughters.

Demuth (דְּמוּת) — "Likeness": dynamic movement toward divine resemblance; paired with *Tselem* (image).

Deposit of Faith — Scripture and Tradition as one sacred deposit entrusted to the Church's living Magisterium.

Desire (Eros/ἔρως) — "Ascent" of desire transfigured into agápē by grace; not suppressed but healed and elevated.

Detachment (Apathéia rightly understood) — Release from possessiveness and self-curvature for freedom in love.

Dianoia (διάνοια) — Discursive reason; ordered to, not opposed to, the *nous* (spiritual intellect).

Dignity of the Human Person — Inviolable worth grounded in the imago Dei and destiny for communion.

Dikaiosýnē (δικαιοσύνη) — "Righteousness/justice": covenant fidelity; in Paul, God's saving right-making in Christ.

Divine Economy (Oikonomía/οἰκονομία) — God's plan of salvation unfolding in history and sacrament.

Divine Energies — God's real, uncreated operations/presence by which we truly participate in His life; distinct from essence.

Divine Filiation — See *Adoption, Divine*.

Divine Hiddenness — God's seeming absence that tests desire and purifies faith; addressed liturgically in anamnesis.

Divine Names — Biblical names (Good, Light, Shepherd, etc.) as participable perfections; apophatic reserve remains.

Dogma — Spirit-guarded teaching binding the faithful because it safeguards communion and life, not mere propositions.

Doxology — Praise (Glory to the Father...): language of theosis; theology becomes worship.

Dyothelitism — Orthodoxy that Christ has two wills (divine and human) in one person; basis for synergy and salvation.

Eden — Primordial sanctuary where humanity served (ʿābad) and guarded (šāmar) in priestly sonship.

Epektasis (ἐπέκτασις) — Eternal "stretching forward" into God (Gregory of Nyssa)—endless growth in the Infinite.

Epíclesis (ἐπίκλησις) — Invocation of the Holy Spirit to consecrate the gifts and the people; seal of sacramental realism.

Eremitic/Cenobitic — Solitary vs communal monastic life; two rhythms of the same baptismal radicalism.

Eschaton (ἔσχατον) — The "last things" made present now in sacrament and virtue; the Kingdom arriving hiddenly.

Essence (Ousía/οὐσία) — God's inaccessible being; distinguished from energies (communicable presence).

Evangelization (Kérygma/κῆρυγμα) — Proclamation that births faith and leads into mystagogy.

Ex opere operato / operantis — By the work worked (Christ's action) / by the worker's disposition; both matter for fruitful sacramental participation.

Fasting (Nēsteía/νηστεία) — Voluntary hunger to reorder love, sharpen prayer, and free resources for mercy.

Fear of the Lord — Awe before holiness; beginning of wisdom and antidote to self-sufficiency.

Filioque — "And the Son." Western addition to the Creed; addressed ecumenically with care to maintain the Father as source.

Fire (Divine) — Biblical image of God's purifying, illuminating presence; central to your "becoming flame" motif.

Freedom (Eleuthería/ἐλευθερία) — Capacity for the good fulfilled in grace; not mere license but love's maturity.

Glory (Dóxa/δοξα; Kabôd/כבוד) — Radiance of divine presence; weight of God's beauty shared with the saints.

Gnosis (γνῶσις) — Knowledge as communion; distinct from mere information (*epistēmē*).

Grace (Gratia, Cháris) — Unmerited, effective participation in God's life; heals, elevates, and divinizes nature.

Habitus — Stable disposition enabling acts (virtues); grace establishes theological habits (faith, hope, love).

Hagiasmos (ἁγιασμός) — Sanctification/holiness as set-apartness for God and participation in His life.

Hamartía (ἁμαρτία) — Sin as "missing the mark": disordered love; healed through metanoia and sacrament.

Hardened Heart — Biblical image for resistant will/affections; softened by compunction and mercy.

Heart (Kardía/καρδία) — Scriptural center of the person where God is known; focus of hesychast prayer.

Hesed (חסד) — Covenant steadfast love; divine mercy as reliable fidelity.

Hesychía (ἡσυχία) — Stillness; interior silence where the *nous* descends into the heart for unceasing prayer.

Henōsis (ἕνωσις) — Union with God; goal of the ascetical-mystical path. See *Theōsis*.

Holiness — God's own life shared; not moralism but radiance of love.

Homoousios (ὁμοούσιος) — "Of one essence" with the Father; Nicene confession safeguarding worship of Christ.

Homoíōsis (ὁμοίωσις) — "Likeness/assimilation" to God through virtue and grace.

Hope (Elpís/ἐλπίς) — Theological virtue holding us in the promises amid darkness.

Humility (Tapeínōsis/ταπείνωσις) — Truthful self-reception from God; gateway of all virtue and knowledge.

Hypostasis (ὑπόστασις) — Concrete personal existence; in Trinity, three hypostases in one essence; in Christ, one divine hypostasis assuming humanity.

Hypostatic Union — Union of divine and human natures in the one person of the Word; foundation of sacrament and theosis.

Icon (Eikōn/εἰκών) — Image; humans as living icons, and sacred images as windows of presence, not idols.

Iconostasis — Screen of icons marking sanctuary; catechesis in color; theology of presence and mystery.

Illumination (Photismós/φωτισμός) — Enlightenment of the heart by grace; baptismal term and ongoing reality.

Imago Dei — "Image of God": gift and call; universal dignity and priestly vocation.

Incarnation — The Word became flesh; the hinge of theosis and sacrament.

Indwelling (Enoíkēsis/ἐνοίκησις) — The Spirit's presence within believers, making them temples.

Infallibility — Spirit's protection of the Church from error in definitive teachings; service to communion of truth.

Intellect (Nous/νοῦς) — Spiritual intellect that knows God by communion; healed through prayer and virtue.

Jesus Prayer — "Lord Jesus Christ, Son of God, have mercy on me": hesychast path of unceasing prayer.

Justice (Tzedek/צֶדֶק; Dikaiosýnē/δικαιοσύνη) — Right-ordering of relationships grounded in covenant love.

Kabôd (כבוד) — "Glory/weight": biblical presence of God; see *Dóxa*.

Kairós (καιρός) — Charged moment of grace; liturgy as God's time invading ours.

Kenōsis (κένωσις) — "Self-emptying" of the Son; pattern of humble love we share in by grace.

Kérygma (κῆρυγμα) — The apostolic proclamation that births faith and initiates discipleship.

Kingdom (Basileía/βασιλεία) — God's saving reign; already and not yet; manifested in sacrament and sanctity.

Koinōnía (κοινωνία) — See *Communion*.

Kontakion/Troparion — Byzantine hymn forms that condense doctrine into prayer.

Ladder (Klimax/Κλίμαξ) — Spiritual ascent imagery (e.g., St John Climacus); purification → illumination → union.

Lectio Divina — Prayerful reading: lectio, meditatio, oratio, contemplatio; bridge from word to union.

Leitourgía (λειτουργία) — Public service; in Church, Christ's priestly work made present in worship.

Lex orandi, lex credendi — "Law of prayer is the law of belief": liturgy forms and expresses doctrine.

Likeness (Demuth/Homoíōsis) — See *Homoíōsis*, *Demuth*.

Light (Uncreated) — Taboric radiance of the divine; experienced by the saints through purification.

Logismoi (λογισμοι) — Thought-patterns tempting or consoling; discerned and sorted in prayer.

Logos (Λόγος) — The divine Word; meaning, ratio, and Person through whom all is made.

Logoi (λόγοι) — The "inner principles" of creatures in the Logos (Maximus); basis for contemplative ecology.

Love (Agápē/Caritas) — The very life of God shared; form of all the virtues.

Lumen gloriae — "Light of glory": grace elevating the intellect to see God in the beatific vision.

Magisterium — Church's teaching office serving Scripture and Tradition; safeguards the path of life.

Martyrdom — Witness unto blood or daily fidelity; supreme conformity to Christ.

Meditation (Meletē/μελέτη) — Reflective prayer that feeds contemplation; not opposed to silence.

Mercy (Eleos/ἔλεος; Hesed/ח) — God's faithful compassion; Christians become rivers of it.

Metánoia (μετάνοια) — See *Conversion*.

Methexis (μεθεξις) — Participation/sharing; philosophical term for real communion.

Microcosm — Humanity as "little cosmos," bridging material and spiritual realms; priest of creation.

Mysterion (Μυστήριον) — "Mystery/sacrament": effective sign that communicates the reality it signifies.

Mystagogy — Post-baptismal catechesis unveiling sacramental depths; lifelong pedagogy of the mysteries.

Nepsis (Νῆψις) — Watchfulness/sobriety of heart; foundation of spiritual discernment.

Nestorianism — Heresy dividing Christ's person; rejected in favor of hypostatic unity.

Nous (νοῦς) — See *Intellect*.

Obedience (Hypakoē/ὑπακοη) — "Listening under": trusting consent to God that births freedom.

Oikonomía (οἰκονομιά) — See *Divine Economy*; also pastoral application of discipline for salvation.

Orthodoxy/Orthopraxy — Right glory/belief and right practice; inseparable in theosis.

Ousia (οὐσία) — See *Essence*.

Palamism — The orthodox articulation of essence–energies distinction and uncreated light (Gregory Palamas).

Palingenesia (παλιγγενεσιά) — "New birth/renewal": baptismal re-creation.

Panagia (Παναγιά) — "All-holy": title of the Theotokos; icon of deified humanity.

Passions (Pathē/πάθη) — Disordered movements of soul/body; healed and re-ordered by grace.

Participation (Methexis/μεθεξις) — Sharing in divine life; grammar of theosis.

Penance (Poenitentia/ἐξομολόγησις) — Sacrament and habit of conversion; medicinal, personal, ecclesial.

Penthos (πένθος) — See *Compunction*.

Perichōrēsis (περιχώρησις) — Mutual indwelling of divine Persons;

analogously, Christ's two natures and the Church in Christ.

Philautia (φιλαυτία) — Disordered self-love; root of vices; healed by humility and charity.

Philokalia — Anthology of ascetical/mystical texts shaping hesychast spirituality.

Philonikia (φιλονεικία) — Love of strife; the ascetic weeds it out by meekness.

Phronēma (φρόνημα) — Mindset/disposition of the Church; ecclesial way of thinking and living.

Photismós (φωτισμός) — See *Illumination*.

Pneumatology — Theology of the Holy Spirit and His gifts, indwelling, and missions.

Prayer of the Heart — Interior invocation of the Name of Jesus; union of mind and heart.

Praxis (πρᾶξις) — Practice: embodied life of virtue and worship; theology in action.

Presence (Shekinah/הניכש) — Indwelling divine presence; Old Testament term echoed in Christian liturgy.

Priesthood (Common/Ministerial) — Baptized share in Christ's priesthood and the ordained service for sanctifying the Body.

Prosopon (πρόσωπον) — "Face/persona": language for personhood; in Trinity and Christ, refined to avoid modalism or division.

Providence (Pronoia/πρόνοια) — God's wise governance ordering all toward salvation.

Purification (Katharsis) — See *Catharsis*.

Qorban (ןב‎ — "Offering/that which draws near": sacrificial heart of worship; fulfilled in Christ.

Recapitulation — See *Anakephalaiōsis*.

Redemption (Lýtrōsis/λύτρωσις) — Liberation by the price of Christ's blood; entry into filial life.

Repentance — See *Conversion*.

Resurrection (Anástasis/ἀνάστασις) — Bodily rising of Christ and the faithful; cornerstone of Christian hope.

Ritual — Enacted symbol shaping desire and identity; in the Church, vehicle of grace.

Ruach (רוּחַ) — Spirit/breath/wind; Old Testament matrix for Christian pneumatology.

Rule of Life — Pattern of prayer, fasting, mercy that stabilizes freedom and growth.

Sacrament (Mysterion) — See *Mysterion*.

Sacramental Worldview — Creation as sign and instrument of grace; the world is charged with God.

Sacrifice — Self-gift to God culminating in Christ; Eucharist as sacramental participation in the one sacrifice.

Sanctification (Hagiasmos) — Ongoing growth into holiness; fruit of indwelling Spirit.

Sanctifying Grace (Gratia gratum faciens) — Habitual gift making us participants in divine nature.

Satisfaction — Aspect of atonement: Christ offers perfect obedience and love, repairing the breach of sin.

Scripture and Tradition — One source in two modes; interpreted within the Church's worship and life.

Seeing God — Biblical hope realized as deifying vision, safeguarded by apophatic humility.

Sheol/Hades — Realm of the dead; harrowed by Christ to free captives.

Silence (Sigē/σιγη) — Reverent stillness in which God speaks and the heart rests.

Similitude (Similitudo) — Latin for "likeness"; see *Homoiōsis*.

Sloth (Acedia) — See *Acedia*.

Sobriety (Nēpsis) — See *Nepsis*.

Soteriology — Theology of salvation; here, participation/deification at the core.

Sophia (Σοφία) — Wisdom; divine attribute and gift; Mary sometimes titled "Seat of Wisdom."

Spirit, Holy (Pneûma Hagion/Πνεῦμα Ἅγιον) — Personal Love proceeding from the Father (and, in Western expression, through the Son);

giver of deification.

Stability (Monastic) — Vow binding a monk to a place and people as school of love; lay analogue is fidelity to one's rule/state in life.

Synergy (Synergía/συνεργία) — Cooperation of divine grace and human freedom; neither Pelagian nor quietist.

Synaxis (Σύναξις) — Gathering of the faithful for the Eucharist; also a liturgical commemoration.

Taboric Light — Uncreated light manifested at the Transfiguration; sign of theosis.

Teleology/Telos (τελος) — End/goal: likeness to God; gives meaning to ascetic struggle and joy.

Temptation (Peirasmos/πειρασμός) — Trial/testing; resisted by watchfulness, Scripture, and the Name of Jesus.

Theandric (θεανδρικός) — "God-manly": actions of Christ's one person through both natures; in saints by participation.

Theologia (θεολογία) — Theology in the strict sense of God's inner life; also the fruit of prayerful knowing.

Theophany (Θεοφάνεια) — Manifestation of God (e.g., Jordan/Baptism); sacramental and scriptural moments of unveiling.

Theōria (θεωρία) — See *Contemplation*.

Theōsis (θέωσις) — See *Deification*.

Therapeia (θεραπεία) — Healing/cure; ascetical tradition as therapy for the passions.

Theotokos (Θεοτόκος) — "God-Bearer": title of Mary safeguarding Christ's unity of person.

Tradition (Parádosis/παράδοσις) — Living transmission of the Gospel in the Church's worship, teaching, and life.

Trinity (Triás/Τριάς) — One God in three Persons—Father, Son, Holy Spirit—coequal, coeternal, consubstantial.

Typology — Reading Scripture as patterns fulfilled in Christ and the Church.

Uncreated Grace — The Spirit's own presence as grace; distinguished from created habits in the soul.

APPENDIX D - GLOSSARY

Union (Henōsis) — See *Henōsis*; consummation of purification/illumination.

Unction (Anointing) — Sacramental oil signifying and effecting healing, strength, and consecration.

Veneration (Proskýnēsis/προσκύνησις) — Honor to saints, relics, icons; distinct from adoration (*latreía*) owed to God.

Virtue (Aretē/ἀρετη) — Stable excellence of soul; theological (faith, hope, love) and cardinal (prudence, justice, fortitude, temperance).

Vision of God — See *Beatific Vision*; in this life, glimpsed by faith and contemplation.

Vocation — Call to holiness lived concretely in state of life and daily charity.

Watchfulness (Nepsis) — See *Nepsis*.

Will (Thelēma/θελημα) — Natural (what a nature is ordered toward) and gnomic (personal deliberation); Christ has no gnomic conflict.

Wisdom (Sophia) — See *Sophia*.

Word (Logos) — See *Logos*.

Worship (Latreía) — See *Adoration*.

Zōē (ζωη) — Divine "life" (as opposed to mere biological *bios*); gift of the Spirit.

Šāmar (שׁמר) — "To guard/keep": Edenic/temple vocation alongside *ʿābad*; grounds Christian watchfulness.

Tselem (צ) — "Image": given dignity and priestly vocation of every human person.

APPENDIX E - Sources and References by Chapter

CH. 1 — Why You Exist: The Divine Image and Likeness

- John Paul II. *General Audience,* 14 November 1979.
- *The Holy Bible: Revised Standard Version—Catholic Edition (RSV-CE).* (Gen 1:26–28; 2:7; 5:1–3; 9:6; Wis 2:23; Sir 17:3–4; Luke 3:38; Rev 22:4–5; Rom 8:14–17, etc.).
- *Targum Onkelos to Genesis 1:26.*
- Basil the Great. *On the Holy Spirit.* Translated by Stephen M. Hildebrand. Yonkers, NY: St Vladimir's Seminary Press, 2011.
- Gregory of Nazianzus. *On God and Christ: The Five Theological Orations and Two Letters to Cledonius.* Translated by Frederick Williams and Lionel Wickham. Crestwood, NY: St Vladimir's Seminary Press, 2002.

APPENDIX E - SOURCES AND REFERENCES BY CHAPTER

CH. 2 — More Than Forgiven: Deification as the True Goal of Redemption

- The Holy Bible, Revised Standard Version, Catholic Edition. San Francisco: Ignatius Press, 2006. (2 Pet 1:4; Ps 103:3; Isa 1:18; John 3:3; John 17:21–23; Rom 6:3–5; 2 Cor 5:17, etc.)
- Anselm of Canterbury. "*Cur Deus Homo.*" In *Anselm of Canterbury: The Major Works*, translated by Brian Davies and G. R. Evans, 260–356. Oxford: Oxford University Press, 1998.
- Gregory of Nazianzus. "Epistle 101" and "Oration 45 (On Holy Pascha)." In *On God and Christ: The Five Theological Orations and Two Letters to Cledonius*, translated by Frederick Williams and Lionel Wickham. Crestwood, NY: St Vladimir's Seminary Press, 2002.
- Irenaeus of Lyons. *Against Heresies.* In *The Ante-Nicene Fathers*, vol. 1, edited by Alexander Roberts and James Donaldson, 315–567. Peabody, MA: Hendrickson, 1994.
- Thomas Aquinas. *Summa Theologiae*, III, q.48. Translated by the Fathers of the English Dominican Province. New York: Benziger, 1911–1925.
- Council of Trent. *Decree on Justification (Session VI).* In *The Canons and Decrees of the Council of Trent*, translated by H. J. Schroeder, O.P. Rockford, IL: TAN Books, 1978.
- Second Vatican Council. *Gaudium et Spes (Pastoral Constitution on the Church in the Modern World).* In *Vatican Council II: The Basic Sixteen Documents*, edited by Austin Flannery, O.P., 903–1014. Northport, NY: Costello Publishing, 1996.
- Catholic Church. *Catechism of the Catholic Church.* 2nd ed. Vatican City: Libreria Editrice Vaticana, 1997. (For §§460, 655, 1997 cited in this part.)
- Basil the Great. (Death destroyed by death—patristic doctrine summarized.) See *On the Holy Spirit* (SVS Press, 2011) as a representative edition.

Scripture cited

RSV-CE: 2 Pet 1:4; Ps 103:3; Isa 1:18; John 3:3; John 17:21–23; Rom 6:3–5; 2 Cor 5:17, etc.

CH. 3 — What Is Theosis? A Historical and Dogmatic Overview

- Athanasius of Alexandria. *On the Incarnation.* Translated and edited by John Behr. Yonkers, NY: St Vladimir's Seminary Press, 2011. (For §§44, 54.)
- John Paul II. *Orientale Lumen.* Vatican City: Libreria Editrice Vaticana, 1995.
- Second Vatican Council. *Gaudium et Spes.* In Flannery, *Vatican Council II*, 903–1014. Northport, NY: Costello, 1996.
- Catholic Church. *Catechism of the Catholic Church.* 2nd ed. Vatican City: Libreria Editrice Vaticana, 1997. (For §§460, 521, 655.)
- Hilary of Poitiers. *On the Trinity.* Translated by Stephen McKenna. Washington, DC: Catholic University of America Press, 1954.
- Ambrose of Milan. *On the Mysteries and the Treatise on the Sacraments.* Translated by T. Thompson. London: SPCK, 1919.
- Leo the Great. *Sermons.* Translated by Jane Freeland and Agnes Conway. Washington, DC: Catholic University of America Press, 1996.

Scripture cited

RSV-CE: 2 Pet 1:4; Rom 6:9; Phil 3:21; Rom 6:3–4; 1 Cor 10:17; Gal 2:20, etc.

CH. 4 — Grace and Personhood (nature, grace, person; Western witnesses)

- Augustine of Hippo. *Sermons.* Translated by Edmund Hill, O.P. Brooklyn, NY: New City Press, 1990–1998. (For Serm. 192; Serm. 95.7; Serm. 23.2.)
- Augustine of Hippo. *Tractates on the Gospel of John.* Translated by John W. Rettig. Washington, DC: Catholic University of America Press, 1988–1993. (For *In Iohannis Evangelium Tractatus* 12.13.)
- Augustine of Hippo. *The City of God.* Translated by Henry Bettenson. London: Penguin, 1972. (For *De Civitate Dei* XXII.30.)
- Augustine of Hippo. *The Trinity.* Translated by Edmund Hill, O.P. Hyde Park, NY: New City Press, 1991. (For *De Trinitate* XV.27.)
- Leo the Great. *Sermons.* Translated by Jane Freeland and Agnes Conway. Washington, DC: Catholic University of America Press, 1996.
- Hilary of Poitiers. *On the Trinity.* Translated by Stephen McKenna. Washington, DC: Catholic University of America Press, 1954.
- Ambrose of Milan. *On the Mysteries and the Treatise on the Sacraments.* Translated by T. Thompson. London: SPCK, 1919.
- Thomas Aquinas. *Summa Theologiae.* Translated by the Fathers of the English Dominican Province. New York: Benziger, 1911–1925. (I–II, qq.112–113; III, q.1, a.2.)

Scripture cited
RSV-CE: Rom 5:5 (charity poured forth).

CH. 5 — The Sacraments: Real Participation in the Divine Life

- Second Vatican Council. *Sacrosanctum Concilium (Constitution on the Sacred Liturgy)*. In *Vatican Council II: The Basic Sixteen Documents*, edited by Austin Flannery, O.P., 1–39. Northport, NY: Costello Publishing, 1996.
- Catholic Church. *Catechism of the Catholic Church*. 2nd ed. Vatican City: Libreria Editrice Vaticana, 1997. (Baptism and Eucharist sections echoed in the chapter.)
- Ambrose of Milan. *On the Mysteries and the Treatise on the Sacraments*. Translated by T. Thompson. London: SPCK, 1919. (Patristic sacramental voice presupposed.)
- Hilary of Poitiers. *On the Trinity*. Translated by Stephen McKenna. Washington, DC: Catholic University of America Press, 1954. (Patristic sacramental voice presupposed.)

Scripture cited in the chapter summary of the sacraments
RSV-CE: Rom 6:4–5 (Baptismal death and rising); John 6:53–58 (Eucharist); 1 Cor 10:16–17 (Eucharistic communion); 2 Pet 1:4 (participation in the divine nature).

Chapter 6 — The Interior Life: Prayer, Stillness, and the Illumined Heart

- Ambrose of Milan. *On the Mysteries and the Treatise on the Sacraments*. Translated by T. Thompson. London: SPCK, 1919.
- Augustine of Hippo. *The Trinity*. Translated by Edmund Hill, O.P. Hyde Park, NY: New City Press, 1991.
- Catherine of Siena. *The Dialogue*. Translated by Suzanne Noffke, O.P. Mahwah, NJ: Paulist Press, 1980.
- Catholic Church. *Catechism of the Catholic Church*. 2nd ed. Vatican

City: Libreria Editrice Vaticana, 1997.
- Evagrius Ponticus. *The Praktikos & Chapters on Prayer*. Translated by John Eudes Bamberger, OCSO. Spencer, MA: Cistercian Publications, 1972.
- Gregory of Nyssa. *The Life of Moses*. Translated by Abraham J. Malherbe and Everett Ferguson. Mahwah, NJ: Paulist Press, 1978.
- Gregory Palamas. *The Triads*. Edited by John Meyendorff. Translated by Nicholas Gendle. Mahwah, NJ: Paulist Press, 1983.
- John Chrysostom. *Homilies on the Gospel of Matthew*. Translated by John N. Hogg. Grand Rapids, MI: Eerdmans, 1957.
- John of the Cross. *The Dark Night*. Translated by Kieran Kavanaugh, O.C.D., and Otilio Rodriguez, O.C.D. Washington, DC: ICS Publications, 1991.
- Palmer, G. E. H., Philip Sherrard, and Kallistos Ware, eds. *The Philokalia*. 4 vols. London: Faber and Faber, 1979–1995.
- Schillebeeckx, Edward. *Christ the Sacrament of the Encounter with God*. Translated by Paul Barrett. Lanham, MD: Rowman & Littlefield, 1963.
- Symeon the New Theologian. *Hymns of Divine Love*. Translated by George A. Maloney, S.J. Mahwah, NJ: Paulist Press, 1995.
- *The Divine Liturgy of Our Father among the Saints John Chrysostom; The Divine Liturgy of Saint Basil the Great*. South Canaan, PA: St Tikhon's Seminary Press, 1986.
- *The Holy Bible, Revised Standard Version, Catholic Edition*. San Francisco: Ignatius Press, 2006.
- Thérèse of Lisieux. *Story of a Soul: A New Translation*. Translated by John Clarke, O.C.D. Washington, DC: ICS Publications, 1996.

Chapter 7 — Asceticism: Purification unto Illumination

- Athanasius of Alexandria. *On the Incarnation*. Translated and edited by John Behr. Yonkers, NY: St Vladimir's Seminary Press, 2011.
- Basil the Great. *On the Holy Spirit*. Translated by Stephen M. Hildebrand. Yonkers, NY: St Vladimir's Seminary Press, 2011.
- Evagrius Ponticus. *The Praktikos & Chapters on Prayer*. Translated by John Eudes Bamberger, OCSO. Spencer, MA: Cistercian Publications, 1972.
- Gregory Palamas. *The Triads*. Edited by John Meyendorff. Translated by Nicholas Gendle. Mahwah, NJ: Paulist Press, 1983.
- John Chrysostom. *Homilies on the Gospel of Matthew*. Translated by John N. Hogg. Grand Rapids, MI: Eerdmans, 1957.
- John Climacus. *The Ladder of Divine Ascent*. Translated by Norman Russell. Mahwah, NJ: Paulist Press, 1982.
- John of Damascus. *On the Divine Images: Three Apologies Against Those Who Attack the Divine Images*. Translated by David Anderson. Yonkers, NY: St Vladimir's Seminary Press, 1980.
- John Paul II. *Redemptoris Missio*. Vatican City: Libreria Editrice Vaticana, 1990.
- Pseudo-Dionysius. *The Complete Works*. Translated by Colm Luibheid and Paul Rorem. Mahwah, NJ: Paulist Press, 1987.
- Second Vatican Council. *Lumen Gentium* (Dogmatic Constitution on the Church). In *Vatican Council II: The Basic Sixteen Documents*, edited by Austin Flannery, O.P., 1–95. Northport, NY: Costello Publishing, 1996.
- *The Holy Bible, Revised Standard Version, Catholic Edition*. San Francisco: Ignatius Press, 2006.

Chapter 8 — The Liturgy: Participation in the Heavenly Worship

- Ambrose of Milan. *On the Mysteries and the Treatise on the Sacraments.* Translated by T. Thompson. London: SPCK, 1919.
- Augustine of Hippo. *The Trinity.* Translated by Edmund Hill, O.P. Hyde Park, NY: New City Press, 1991.
- Basil the Great. *On the Holy Spirit.* Translated by Stephen M. Hildebrand. Yonkers, NY: St Vladimir's Seminary Press, 2011.
- Catholic Church. *Catechism of the Catholic Church.* 2nd ed. Vatican City: Libreria Editrice Vaticana, 1997.
- Gregory of Nazianzus. *On God and Christ: The Five Theological Orations and Two Letters to Cledonius.* Translated by Frederick Williams and Lionel Wickham. Crestwood, NY: St Vladimir's Seminary Press, 2002.
- Hilary of Poitiers. *On the Trinity.* Translated by Stephen McKenna. Washington, DC: Catholic University of America Press, 1954.
- Hippolytus. *On the Apostolic Tradition.* Translated by Alistair Stewart. Yonkers, NY: St Vladimir's Seminary Press, 2015.
- John Chrysostom. *Homilies on the Gospel of Matthew.* Translated by John N. Hogg. Grand Rapids, MI: Eerdmans, 1957.
- Paul VI (see implicit magisterial background in liturgical theology—if a specific text is cited elsewhere in your draft, we can add it explicitly).
- Pius XII. *Mystici Corporis Christi.* Vatican City: Typis Polyglottis Vaticanis, 1943.
- Second Vatican Council. *Sacrosanctum Concilium* (Constitution on the Sacred Liturgy). In *Vatican Council II: The Basic Sixteen Documents*, edited by Austin Flannery, O.P., 1–39. Northport, NY: Costello Publishing, 1996.
- Second Vatican Council. *Dei Verbum* (Dogmatic Constitution on Divine Revelation). In *Vatican Council II: The Basic Sixteen Documents*, edited by Austin Flannery, O.P., 750–786. Northport, NY: Costello

Publishing, 1996.
- *The Divine Liturgy of Our Father among the Saints John Chrysostom; The Divine Liturgy of Saint Basil the Great*. South Canaan, PA: St Tikhon's Seminary Press, 1986.
- *The Holy Bible, Revised Standard Version, Catholic Edition*. San Francisco: Ignatius Press, 2006.
- The Anaphora of Addai and Mari. In *The Eucharistic Prayers of the Ancient Church*, edited by R. C. D. Jasper and G. J. Cuming. London: SPCK, 1963.
- Thomas Aquinas (if quoted in your text—e.g., *Summa Theologiae* I–II on grace—add the specific question/article; otherwise omit).

Chapter 9 — The Saints: Testimonies of Transfigured Humanity

- Athanasius of Alexandria. *On the Incarnation*. Translated and edited by John Behr. Yonkers, NY: St Vladimir's Seminary Press, 2011.
- Augustine of Hippo. *The Trinity*. Translated by Edmund Hill, O.P. Hyde Park, NY: New City Press, 1991.
- Catherine of Siena. *The Dialogue*. Translated by Suzanne Noffke, O.P. Mahwah, NJ: Paulist Press, 1980.
- Catholic Church. *Catechism of the Catholic Church*. 2nd ed. Vatican City: Libreria Editrice Vaticana, 1997.
- Gregory of Nyssa. *The Life of Moses*. Translated by Abraham J. Malherbe and Everett Ferguson. Mahwah, NJ: Paulist Press, 1978.
- Gregory of Nazianzus. *On God and Christ*. Translated by Frederick Williams and Lionel Wickham. Crestwood, NY: St Vladimir's Seminary Press, 2002.
- Irenaeus of Lyons. *Against Heresies*. In *The Ante-Nicene Fathers*, vol. 1, edited by Alexander Roberts and James Donaldson, 315–567. Peabody, MA: Hendrickson, 1994.
- John Chrysostom. *Homilies on the Gospel of Matthew*. Translated by

John N. Hogg. Grand Rapids, MI: Eerdmans, 1957.
- John Climacus. *The Ladder of Divine Ascent*. Translated by Norman Russell. Mahwah, NJ: Paulist Press, 1982.
- John of Damascus. *On the Divine Images*. Translated by David Anderson. Yonkers, NY: St Vladimir's Seminary Press, 1980.
- Leo the Great. *Sermons*. Translated by Jane Freeland and Agnes Conway. Washington, DC: Catholic University of America Press, 1996.
- Maximus the Confessor. *On the Cosmic Mystery of Jesus Christ: Selected Writings from St Maximus the Confessor*. Translated by Paul M. Blowers and Robert Louis Wilken. Yonkers, NY: St Vladimir's Seminary Press, 2003.
- Pseudo-Dionysius. *The Complete Works*. Translated by Colm Luibheid and Paul Rorem. Mahwah, NJ: Paulist Press, 1987.
- Second Vatican Council. *Lumen Gentium*. In Flannery, *Vatican Council II*, 1–95. Northport, NY: Costello, 1996.
- *The Holy Bible, Revised Standard Version, Catholic Edition*. San Francisco: Ignatius Press, 2006.
- Thérèse of Lisieux. *Story of a Soul*. Translated by John Clarke, O.C.D. Washington, DC: ICS Publications, 1996.

Chapter 10 — The Cross and Resurrection in the Life of the Believer

- Athanasius of Alexandria. *On the Incarnation*. Translated and edited by John Behr. Yonkers, NY: St Vladimir's Seminary Press, 2011.
- Augustine of Hippo. *The Trinity*. Translated by Edmund Hill, O.P. Hyde Park, NY: New City Press, 1991.
- Basil the Great. *On the Holy Spirit*. Translated by Stephen M. Hildebrand. Yonkers, NY: St Vladimir's Seminary Press, 2011.
- Catholic Church. *Catechism of the Catholic Church*. 2nd ed. Vatican City: Libreria Editrice Vaticana, 1997.
- Gregory of Nazianzus. *On God and Christ*. Translated by Freder-

- ick Williams and Lionel Wickham. Crestwood, NY: St Vladimir's Seminary Press, 2002.
- Gregory of Nyssa. *The Life of Moses*. Translated by Abraham J. Malherbe and Everett Ferguson. Mahwah, NJ: Paulist Press, 1978.
- Hilary of Poitiers. *On the Trinity*. Translated by Stephen McKenna. Washington, DC: Catholic University of America Press, 1954.
- Irenaeus of Lyons. *Against Heresies*. In *The Ante-Nicene Fathers*, vol. 1. Peabody, MA: Hendrickson, 1994.
- John Chrysostom. *Homilies on the Gospel of Matthew*. Translated by John N. Hogg. Grand Rapids, MI: Eerdmans, 1957.
- John of the Cross. *The Dark Night*. Translated by Kieran Kavanaugh, O.C.D., and Otilio Rodriguez, O.C.D. Washington, DC: ICS Publications, 1991.
- Leo the Great. *Sermons*. Translated by Jane Freeland and Agnes Conway. Washington, DC: Catholic University of America Press, 1996.
- Maximus the Confessor. *On the Cosmic Mystery of Jesus Christ*. Translated by Paul M. Blowers and Robert Louis Wilken. Yonkers, NY: St Vladimir's Seminary Press, 2003.
- Pius XII. *Mystici Corporis Christi*. Vatican City: Typis Polyglottis Vaticanis, 1943.
- Second Vatican Council. *Gaudium et Spes*. In Flannery, *Vatican Council II*, 903–1014. Northport, NY: Costello, 1996.
- *The Holy Bible, Revised Standard Version, Catholic Edition*. San Francisco: Ignatius Press, 2006.
- Thérèse of Lisieux. *Story of a Soul*. Translated by John Clarke, O.C.D. Washington, DC: ICS Publications, 1996.

Chapter 11 — Union without Absorption: The Theological Boundaries of Participation

- Athanasius of Alexandria. *On the Incarnation*. Translated and edited by John Behr. Yonkers, NY: St Vladimir's Seminary Press, 2011.
- Augustine of Hippo. *The Trinity*. Translated by Edmund Hill, O.P. Hyde Park, NY: New City Press, 1991.
- Basil the Great. *On the Holy Spirit*. Translated by Stephen M. Hildebrand. Yonkers, NY: St Vladimir's Seminary Press, 2011.
- Catholic Church. *Catechism of the Catholic Church*. 2nd ed. Vatican City: Libreria Editrice Vaticana, 1997.
- Gregory Palamas. *The Triads*. Edited by John Meyendorff. Translated by Nicholas Gendle. Mahwah, NJ: Paulist Press, 1983.
- Gregory of Nazianzus. *On God and Christ*. Translated by Frederick Williams and Lionel Wickham. Crestwood, NY: St Vladimir's Seminary Press, 2002.
- Hilary of Poitiers. *On the Trinity*. Translated by Stephen McKenna. Washington, DC: Catholic University of America Press, 1954.
- John Chrysostom. *Homilies on the Gospel of Matthew*. Translated by John N. Hogg. Grand Rapids, MI: Eerdmans, 1957.
- John Paul II. *Orientale Lumen*. Vatican City: Libreria Editrice Vaticana, 1995.
- Pseudo-Dionysius. *The Complete Works*. Translated by Colm Luibheid and Paul Rorem. Mahwah, NJ: Paulist Press, 1987.
- Second Vatican Council. Unitatis Redintegratio. In Flannery, Vatican Council II, 451–468. Northport, NY: Costello, 1996.Second Vatican Council. Orientalium Ecclesiarum. In Flannery, Vatican Council II, 271–281. Northport, NY: Costello, 1996.

Chapter 12 — You Shall Be All Fire: Living the Theotic Life in the World

- Ambrose of Milan. *On the Mysteries and the Treatise on the Sacraments*. Translated by T. Thompson. London: SPCK, 1919.
- Augustine of Hippo. *The Trinity*. Translated by Edmund Hill, O.P. Hyde Park, NY: New City Press, 1991.
- Basil the Great. *On the Holy Spirit*. Translated by Stephen M. Hildebrand. Yonkers, NY: St Vladimir's Seminary Press, 2011.
- Benedict XVI. *Sacramentum Caritatis*. Vatican City: Libreria Editrice Vaticana, 2007.
- Benedict XVI. *Spe Salvi*. Vatican City: Libreria Editrice Vaticana, 2007.
- Catherine of Siena. *The Dialogue*. Translated by Suzanne Noffke, O.P. Mahwah, NJ: Paulist Press, 1980.
- Catholic Church. *Catechism of the Catholic Church*. 2nd ed. Vatican City: Libreria Editrice Vaticana, 1997.
- Francis. *Lumen Fidei*. Vatican City: Libreria Editrice Vaticana, 2013.
- Gregory Palamas. *The Triads*. Edited by John Meyendorff. Translated by Nicholas Gendle. Mahwah, NJ: Paulist Press, 1983.
- Gregory of Nazianzus. *On God and Christ*. Translated by Frederick Williams and Lionel Wickham. Crestwood, NY: St Vladimir's Seminary Press, 2002.
- Gregory of Nyssa. *The Life of Moses*. Translated by Abraham J. Malherbe and Everett Ferguson. Mahwah, NJ: Paulist Press, 1978.
- Irenaeus of Lyons. *Against Heresies*. In *The Ante-Nicene Fathers*, vol. 1, edited by Alexander Roberts and James Donaldson, 315–567. Peabody, MA: Hendrickson, 1994.
- John Chrysostom. *Homilies on the Gospel of Matthew*. Translated by John N. Hogg. Grand Rapids, MI: Eerdmans, 1957.
- John Climacus. *The Ladder of Divine Ascent*. Translated by Norman Russell. Mahwah, NJ: Paulist Press, 1982.
- John of Damascus. *On the Divine Images*. Translated by David Anderson. Yonkers, NY: St Vladimir's Seminary Press, 1980.

- John Paul II. *Redemptoris Missio*. Vatican City: Libreria Editrice Vaticana, 1990.
- Leo the Great. *Sermons*. Translated by Jane Freeland and Agnes Conway. Washington, DC: Catholic University of America Press, 1996.
- Maximus the Confessor. *On the Cosmic Mystery of Jesus Christ: Selected Writings from St Maximus the Confessor*. Translated by Paul M. Blowers and Robert Louis Wilken. Yonkers, NY: St Vladimir's Seminary Press, 2003.
- Pius XII. *Mystici Corporis Christi*. Vatican City: Typis Polyglottis Vaticanis, 1943.
- Pseudo-Dionysius. *The Complete Works*. Translated by Colm Luibheid and Paul Rorem. Mahwah, NJ: Paulist Press, 1987.
- Second Vatican Council. *Gaudium et Spes*. In Flannery, *Vatican Council II*, 903–1014. Northport, NY: Costello, 1996.
- Second Vatican Council. *Lumen Gentium*. In Flannery, *Vatican Council II*, 1–95. Northport, NY: Costello, 1996.
- Symeon the New Theologian. *Hymns of Divine Love*. Translated by George A. Maloney, S.J. Mahwah, NJ: Paulist Press, 1995.
- *The Holy Bible, Revised Standard Version, Catholic Edition*. San Francisco: Ignatius Press, 2006.

About the Author

About the Author

Matthew Sardon is a Catholic writer based in Melbourne, Australia, formed by the depth and breadth of the Church's spiritual heritage. His path has taken him through years of study, prayer, and immersion in both the Roman and Byzantine traditions, giving him a single, integrated Catholic vision rooted in Scripture, nourished by the Fathers, and shaped by the Church's unbroken life of worship.

His work centres on biblical theology and exegesis — exploring how the ancient Word speaks with living power — but it also engages the pressing questions of the modern world. In an age marked by confusion and restless searching, he writes to help readers find clarity, refuge, and strength in the Church's tradition: the wisdom that has shaped saints, sustained families, and offered meaning to every generation.

Alongside his theological works, Matthew creates children's stories that open young hearts to faith and wonder through simple narrative and timeless imagery. Whether speaking to adults or children, he writes with the same purpose: to reveal how grace transforms the human heart and how the truths of the faith illuminate every corner of ordinary life.

When not writing, he serves in his local Catholic community, continues his theological studies and formation for ministry, and spends time with his family — seeking to live the beauty he teaches, one act of love at a time.

You can connect with me on:

🌐 https://matthewsardon.com

www.ingramcontent.com/pod-product-compliance
Lightning Source LLC
Chambersburg PA
CBHW060107230426
43661CB00033B/1422/J